Business Communication

Process and Practice

The Scott, Foresman Series in Business Communication
Norman B. Sigband, Consulting Editor

Business Communication
Process and Practice

Arthur H. Bell
University of Southern California

Scott, Foresman and Company
Glenview, Illinois   London, England

To my son and good friend, Arthur James

Acknowledgments for photographs appear in a section at the back of the book on page 591, an extension of the copyright page.

Library of Congress Cataloging-in-Publication Data

Bell, Arthur H. (Arthur Henry), 1946–
  Business communication.

  Includes index.
  1. Communication in management.   I. Title.
HF5718.B455   1987   808′.066651   86-24844
ISBN 0-673-18326-2

Foreword to the Instructor

Every book represents an enormous amount of work on the part of its author. This book is no exception; it has been conceived, written, and revised over a period of five years. We are very pleased to be able to publish *Business Communication: Process and Practice*.

But in addition to this book, Professor Bell—together with his colleagues—has assembled an exceptional resource package to assist you. The following resource materials have been put together with the same dedication, hard work, and care that went into the textbook:

- Instructor's Resource Guide and Casebook
- Student Study Guide
- Testbank
- Computerized Testbank with Classroom Management Software
- Computer Tutorial
- Computer Diagnostic
- Videotape Program
- Color Transparencies

We commend the efforts of the author and his colleagues, Judith Leder, Joanne Jasin, and Patricia Thomas, for developing this exemplary ancillary program. You can use these resource materials with confidence.

We published our first textbook in business communication almost twenty years ago. Since then, we have published many other successful communication texts. This book and its supplements are yet another sign of our continuing commitment to you and to being your complete source for materials in business communication. We look forward to being your partners in education for another twenty years.

Scott, Foresman and Company

Preface

This book offers guidance on how to win with words in business. Students will find new communication perspectives and techniques that should help them build important skills for college and career.

Process and Practice, the subtitle, has special significance. The word *process* names an increasingly popular approach to teaching writing that typically includes three stages: generating ideas, or invention; forming, or shaping, those ideas into a logical piece of communication; and then revising, or polishing, those ideas into a finished product. But in a more general sense, *process* means simply gradual change leading toward a particular result. Both meanings inform this book. Though this text does not confine itself to a process approach to writing, it does adopt and adapt from the best that this approach to teaching writing offers to business communicators.

Practice, the other half of the subtitle, is also intended in at least two senses: the practicality of the lessons and the need to practice. The text has certainly been written with an eye toward *what works* in actual business practice—that is, the communication needs and habits of real business men and women. Its abundant examples and models reflect the working papers and presentations of the business community. But the book is also about *practice* in the sense of exercise. Writers and speakers learn by doing. This book provides many, many opportunities to write and speak in a wide variety of business contexts.

One of the many ways in which this book imitates actual business practice is in its use of cases. Few students know from their own experience what a manager thinks or feels. But almost all students can successfully view communication dilemmas "through someone else's eyes," especially when stimulated by brainstorming, role plays, and class discussion. The case method allows real business situations to rise to life and urgency. By learning to extend interests and insights beyond the self, a student meets a larger goal of communication instruction: finding the common ground of understanding among interpersonal differences.

Business Communication: Process and Practice has been written to serve instructors as a thorough, reliable, and engaging text. The unparalled ancillary program should help both instructor and student use the text creatively and profitably.

Dozens of my colleagues have helped to shape and refine this book. To all of them I offer sincere thanks. In a marathon of stylistic fine-tuning, most sentences were turned every which way but loose during years of field testing and revision. In particular, I will always feel gratitude to these colleagues: Professors J. Douglas Andrews, Dayle Altendorf, Keith Berwick, Paul C. Feingold, John Gould, Tom Housel, Shirley Orechwa, Carol Shuherk, Eric Skopec, Jim Stevenson, and Pat Thomas, all colleagues at USC's School of Business Administration; Professor Grant T. Savage, Texas Technical University; Professor Thomas Kloskey, Glassboro State University; Professor Carolyn Beth Camp, Oregon State University; Dr. Thomas R. Swanson, Wayne Willette, Robert A. Bell, Sharon R. Anderson, Sharon Lindsay, and Roger Wyse. I am especially grateful to my colleague and friend, Professor Norman B. Sigband, for leading the way in so many areas of business communication.

At Scott, Foresman and Company, the following people have worked skillfully and tirelessly on behalf of this project: Jim Sitlington, John Nolan, Jane Steinmann, Jeanne Schwaba, Ellen Pettengell, and many others. My thanks to all of them.

Finally, I have dedicated this book to my son, Arthur James, in the hope that this text will prove useful to a new generation of communicators, with new problems demanding new solutions.

Arthur H. Bell
University of Southern California

Overview

Contents

8   Developing Effective Visual Aids   187

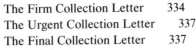

PART FOUR **Successful Business Speaking and Listening** 343

PART FIVE **Communicating About Employment**   403

PART SIX Other Applications of Business Communication 449

Supplemental Cases   537

Fundamentals of Successful Business Communication

PART ONE

Communications satellite being launched

Kathryn Malory and Gene Segerstrom, both in their mid-twenties, work in the communications division of a major auto manufacturer. As communication specialists, they try to make sure that messages pass efficiently back and forth between managers and workers.

Kathryn Malory: My first year on the job was a real learning experience. College had prepared me to work with pen, paper, and typewriter, but not word processors, electronic mail, and "smart" telephones. I've had to adjust to a new standard of speed in the production and distribution of messages.

Gene Segerstrom: That speed causes some problems for us, Kathryn. Good news and especially bad news seem to fly around the corporation at amazing speed, often without all the information needed for proper interpretation. I think we have much less control over communication within the company than we used to. I'm not sure whether that's good or bad.

It's a fact that you and I have more and more communication devices at our fingertips. What challenges and problems do those new communication opportunities pose? Are you ready, for example, for a telephone in your car? Do you want to be able to work from your home as well as from the office?

The Communication

Revolution 1

LEARNING OBJECTIVES

To understand the importance of changing communication technologies

To recognize ways in which writing, speaking, and listening habits are changing to meet the challenges of new technologies

To grasp the crucial differences for communicators between word processors and previous print technologies such as the typewriter

To adjust to new speaking and listening requirements posed by audio and visual teleconferences

To prepare for change not as a temporary occurrence but as a recurring aspect of your future business career

Revolution? You may not hear any noise; in fact, the campus may seem relatively calm this year. But listen closely. That simulated voice announcing the time of day by telephone is a silicon wafer—a computer chip. The frantic buzz coming from campus offices is the sound of high-speed printers typing words at up to 200 characters per second fed from a computer disk. The gentle hum from the library is the new laser printer. In the Physics Department, four faculty members participate in a teleconference by communication satellite with colleagues in Europe. Your roommate sits at a word processor, making last minute revisions on an assignment that can be sent to the prof by modem, literally at the speed of light.

These are the sounds of profound revolution. The machines bearing chips were at first novelties, but now they are accepted as appliances and seem like essential furniture in our lives.

We feel at home with the modern telephone, computer, word processor, communication satellite, and the rest because they *extend a part of us*. In earlier revolutions, men and women extended their voices by systems of writing, their legs by transportation advances, and their fists by gunpowder and nuclear arms. In the communication revolution, we have extended our minds. Where we used to send our bodies—scurrying across campus, for example, to deliver a paper—we now send electrons bearing messages that speak our minds.

As with all true revolutions, we need not worry whether or not we are individually included in the sweeping changes around us. We are—even if we have never touched a microcomputer or sent a message by satellite. The communication revolution, like the breaking of a dam, draws us all into one flood moving toward the future.

You are now studying to participate meaningfully in that future. You want to equip yourself with tools to help you achieve personal and social goals. But choosing tools for the future can be unnerving. In a time of rapid change, will your educational experience offer you more than the tools your professors needed when they were in college? In short, are you preparing for the future or the past?

WRITING, SPEAKING, AND LISTENING IN THE COMMUNICATION REVOLUTION

Writing, speaking, and listening—these three extensions of our minds have been called social glue. They bind us one to another. Without the ability to communicate verbally and nonverbally, our perceptual worlds would end at the epidermis. We would feel our stomachs growl, notice an occasional headache, and dream dreams. We wouldn't know one another.

Learning to write, speak, and listen for the future, therefore, is not a matter of "brushing up" on career skills. Instead, it is preparing ourselves to keep in contact with one another and the world around us. Our abilities to write, speak, and listen let us escape isolation and influence our own life paths and those of others. If those abilities become outmoded, we can find ourselves as disoriented in modern life and business as a New Guinea tribesman suddenly dropped on a New York street corner.

Writing for the Future

Writing has always been easy to define for any age: "proper words in proper places," as Jonathan Swift proposed. But what will be proper—appropriate, timely, necessary—in business messages of your career?

Consider tone, for example. Your grandfather struck a formal tone in business correspondence—"I beg your leave to inform you"—that now strikes us as excessive and somewhat humorous. What tone will suit business readers in your future? Will the proliferation of electronic communication devices cause our messages to be more blunt and sterile ("Send bolts. Payment upon receipt.")? Or will we try to replace the lost warmth of flowing penmanship with an equal measure of personal pizzazz ("Hi, Frank—great speech last Friday!")? How can you choose words for your business documents until you have a "feel" for an appropriate, useful tone?

Then consider diction. Will business readers with plush offices and expensive computers expect you to "ameliorate," "preclude," and "adhere"? Should you spend your last semesters in college acquiring a sesquipedalian vocabulary (getting big words) for later use? Or will business readers be happier with the common touch—short, crisp words that say what they mean?

And what of length? When your future supervisor asks for a report on your business trip, will he or she expect a paragraph, a page, or a portfolio? How much or how little should you say? What should be put first (good news or bad news?) and what should be put last (your suggestions or expense record)?

These questions are all intended to make a point: you must prepare now to deal successfully with a language environment that is changing. You must locate writing tools that will serve you well for the future.

And, yes, the questions do have answers—but not simple, checklist answers ("Be brief! Be simple!"). Like a traveler preparing for a trip around the world, you should equip yourself not with a list of rigid behaviors but instead with the knowledge and creativity to *meet communication needs* as they arise. In each communication encounter, you will consider the needs of your audience, search out your own ideas and intentions, and then choose language and formats to suit your purpose. No single checklist can prepare you to meet these changing circumstances.

But you can get ready to communicate by

- knowing what communication is and how it works.
- understanding how your audience affects what you choose to say or write.
- developing a variety of voices, tones, and choices of diction for changing circumstances.
- judging length, placement, and format of your messages.

Then, whether you are dashing off a message for electronic mail or finishing a formal report for publication to stockholders, you will be equipped with the writing tools needed to accomplish your goals. This text will help you master those tools.

Communication skills are powerful allies in your efforts to move up the ladder in the company. Don Karcher, president of the large chain of Carl's Restaurants, remembers:

In my own career, real advancement didn't begin until I had developed a facility for written and oral expression, and that facility becomes more important as my responsibilities increase.

Speaking for the Future

Have you noticed that powerful, effective speakers all have mastered the *medium* of their communication? Famous actors and actresses know precisely how to manage camera angles and effects to their advantage. Presidents (actors in their own way) reach office only after demonstrating "media presence" on television and radio.

What communication medium will you have to master to be an effective speaker in business? More and more business conferences will be held by teleconference (in which participants from across the country or around the world interact on a video screen). As a part of your training in business speaking, surely you will want to speak effectively in a teleconference (discussed at length in Chapter 19).

The telephone is a more obvious example of a medium the speaker needs to master. In many businesses, the majority of sales, negotiations, and contacts are accomplished by phone. Do you use this common medium effectively? We all know people who do not. Perhaps they sound brusque and unfriendly, or they may talk on and on, not recognizing that the phone imposes different length limits on speakers than does face-to-face conversation. You don't want to make their mistakes, yet you may never have learned how to use the telephone with skill (see Chapter 15).

To be an effective business speaker requires knowledge of the primary mediums of spoken communication. Not all of these mediums are electronic, of course. Much spoken communication occurs in interviews, meetings, presentations to groups, and casual one-on-one contacts. But even in these areas, the old rules for effective communication need careful scrutiny and revision. Should you "get to the point" at all times and in all places? No. Many business encounters necessitate a certain amount of small talk—"getting-to-know-you talk"—prior to the discussion of business terms. At other times, such preliminaries will be entirely out of place.

Again, knowing how to speak effectively, like knowing how to write, is more than memorization of rules ("Stand up straight! Gesture freely!"). To become a skilled communicator, you must equip yourself with a full range of speaking techniques and develop the judgment to choose among them to achieve your ends.

Listening for the Future

We spend most of our college time doing something for which we have had little or no training—listening. No wonder, then, that we often move on to business careers ill-equipped to listen effectively. To prepare to listen your way to success, recognize that

- listening is more than mere hearing. Listening is literally thinking along with the speaker, but in a receptive way that allows you to take in messages and at the same time mull over what you've heard.
- listening seeks out the whole message. Speakers communicate by their pauses, nonverbal gestures, dress, and expressions of feeling, in addition to the words they choose for their message. An effective listener is attentive to the whole message being communicated.
- listening always must overcome barriers to communication. These barriers can include the fact that you don't like the speaker, that you're bothered by the hum of the air conditioning or heating, that you're not interested in the topic, that you think you know what's going to be said, and other impediments to understanding.

As more and more of our listening in business is directed toward electronic sources—telephones, video equipment, voice chips, and so forth—we will have to adapt old listening skills in new and flexible ways. For example, we may find it harder to hear the "whole message" when listening to a slick, commercial video presentation of a new product or service. We may have to learn new skills to listen for what's not said or what is overstated in such communication forms. Just as we have all had to develop what Hemingway called a "b.s. detector" when listening to advertisements, so we must build shrewd listening skills for the dominant media of the future. For that reason, we have devoted Chapter 14 to listening.

Writing, speaking, and listening are changing more rapidly today than at any time in the last several hundred years. We can meet this challenge by incorporating previously learned rules and guidelines into a larger and on-going evaluation of what it means to communicate with purpose and persuasiveness.

THE MACHINES OF THE COMMUNICATION REVOLUTION

Instruction in communication has always emphasized the importance of communication technologies, some of them quite simple. In the Middle Ages, monks no doubt instructed students to scribe their letters carefully, to leave meaningful spaces in manuscripts, and to illuminate key passages to good effect. These strictures were efforts to use the simple technologies of pen and paper with skill. Sloppy letters and crammed manuscripts were unreadable and, hence, failed as communication.

The technologies of pen and paper have been supplemented, but not replaced, by some familiar and some not-so-familiar writing tools. If we ignore these technologies, we are apt to use them poorly and fall increasingly silent as modern communicators. In the spirit of the medieval monk who wanted to use paper and pen to best advantage, let's ask the technological question of our age: What are the communication machines of the late twentieth century and why do they matter?

Electronic Typewriters

Traditional, clack-clack typewriters have disadvantages well-known to every student: errors are hard to correct, passages are difficult to rearrange, and no words, once typed, can be automatically recalled for future use (as, for example, in a term paper for another class).

Electronic typewriters, by contrast, provide the typist with a small screen on which letters, as they are keyed in, appear before being committed to paper. If errors occur, the typist can make corrections—or even rearrange whole passages—before pressing a key to print out the document. In addition, electronic typewriters store business documents for later use. A general sales letter can be held in the electronic memory of the typewriter and used again and again, with personalized addresses, for a variety of purposes.

Typists (who today can range from secretaries to managers) report faster typing speeds, easier production of documents, and less frustration using electronic typewriters.

These machines matter to the communicator, therefore, because they help to remove the bottleneck of mechanical difficulty that inhibits the free flow of thoughts onto paper. This text, for example, would not have been written if only pen and paper technology existed. The author simply would not and could not have penned and recopied all of the pages for a wide audience. In the same way, the electronic typewriter frees writers from the drudgery of white-out and correction tape as well as the frustration of having to "cut and paste" all major rearrangements of text. In addition, standard passages can be used again without retyping, thanks to the typewriter's memory.

This feature, of course, raises a spectre for the writer: will the ease of recall discourage the writer from the hard work of crafting a new communication for a new situation? Will messages tend to become more stereotyped as the supply of stock letters increases? Let us hope not. Better, let's recognize that such stock responses will inevitably fail as communications because they often will not meet the precise, timely needs of our audience.

Word Processors

Like the electronic typewriter, the word processor displays words on a screen (a larger one) before printing, stores documents (usually on a disk), and enables the user to make a wide variety of corrections and rearrangements. To that extent, a word processing system can be thought of as "more of the same" when compared to an electronic typewriter.

Word processors exceed the capabilities of electronic typewriters, however, in their abilities to print documents in a wide range of fonts (type faces), their storage and communication features, and—most of all—their graphics and statistics capacities.

Just as pages from a carbon ribbon typewriter looked "fancy" and prestigious when compared to old ink ribbon type, so the new fonts of word processors set a new standard for prestige in business documents. "Prestige" here is not meant in a precious sense. Some business documents, for sound reasons, need to impress the reader in every way, including the style of type font used. If the document looks typeset in an attractive font, that feature may distinguish it from communications from competitors. You can review some of the fonts available to business writers in Figure 1–1. Ask yourself how each might be used to advantage in the range of business documents you'll be writing in your career.

Word processors generally store many more documents than an electronic typewriter. Such storage is accomplished by a "floppy" or "hard" magnetic disk. A single floppy disk commonly holds as many as 500 typed pages, with a hard disk storing many times that number. Word processors can retrieve a directory of all documents on each disk, allowing easy access to any particular paragraph or page within any desired document.

When linked by modem (a communication device connecting a computer with a communication channel such as a telephone line) to other word processing stations, the word processor can send and receive documents with incredible speed. A long report, for example, can be transferred from one word processor in New York to another in California in a matter of seconds. Once arrived, it can be edited, printed out, or sent on to other stations. We'll consider this communication aspect of the word processor more fully in our later discussion of electronic mail.

But the newest and perhaps most exciting feature of modern word processors is their ability to use graphics and statistics software (in effect, com-

FIGURE 1-1

Word Processor Fonts

Courier
Courier Italic
Courier Bold
Courier Bold Italic

Times
Times Italic
Times Bold
Times Bold Italic

Helvetica
Helvetica Oblique
Helvetica Bold
Helvetica Bold Oblique

puter programs) to enhance business documents with illustrations, charts, graphs, renderings, and even photographs. Several word processing systems now allow the user to enter statistical information (sales figures, for example, for 1980–86) and then to choose what kind of chart or graph the user would like to include in a business document. For example, the user could select a pie chart (see the discussion of graphics in Chapter 8) for use on page 3 of his or her report, and a bar graph on page 8. The computer will automatically generate the desired graphics, sized to fit whatever space the user allots to them, and in a range of striking colors. Or the writer may choose to include a schematic or actual drawing of a product. As illustrated in Figure 1-2, all those enhancements are easily accomplished by modern word processing technology.

What does this new capability mean to the writer? First, new standards are being set by new technologies. Reports containing meaningful graphics will simply be more powerful than comparable reports written without graphics. "A picture," in the old saying, "is worth a thousand words"—and many modern business documents will achieve desired brevity by the use of well-placed graphics.

We are not suggesting that all business writers be trained as graphic artists to compete in the future. But neither should writers ignore the obvious and powerful effects of graphics as communication devices. Whether produced by the writer using word processing software or added by a professional artist, such graphics are *a part of* the message being communicated, not a frill for decoration.

Electronic Mail

Business people wryly comment about traditional mail: "The check's in the mail," "Bills are always delivered on time," and "Only important letters get lost." In most cases, these quips are criticisms not of the U.S. Postal Service but of the nature of traditional mail delivery itself. Writers put paper in envelopes addressed to readers, often far away. Mail employees pick up those envelopes, sort them, pack them onto trains, planes, and buses, unpack them, re-sort them, then attempt to deliver them by hand to the reader's address. No wonder a first-class letter from New York to California can take four or five days for delivery. (And no wonder, in addition, that "express" services have proven so immensely popular, promising delivery within twenty-four hours.)

Electronic mail proposes to by-pass almost all the middlemen in the transfer of written messages. Once joined together by an electronic network (such as GTE's TeleNet or CompuServe), users can type messages onto their computer screen, then send them directly to their reader's computer terminal or to a storage computer for later access by the reader. The message, of course, can be printed out and saved in computer memory by the reader.

Such transfers of messages take a matter of seconds and, especially when former mail preparation time is considered, often cost less than traditional letters. The ease of using electronic mail, in fact, has given rise to unexpected

FIGURE 1-2

Computer Graphic

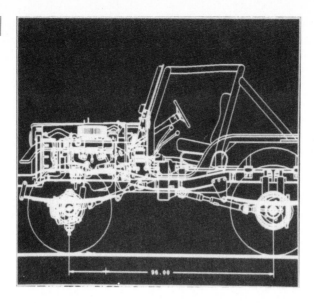

problems. A message can be sent to all users, for example, by simply pressing a key. Imagine the comparable difficulty in sending hundreds and even thousands of letters. Yet that ease of use has tempted many writers to clutter the electronic mail network with unnecessary messages, often sent to uninvolved readers. The paper glut that electronic mail was intended to relieve has, in many offices, turned into the electronic glut. Messages from network users back up so that simply sorting through the morning's electronic mail is a major task for many employees.

Learning to write (and *not* write) for electronic mail should be an important part of every business communicator's preparation. With time, that technology seems certain to replace the physical posting and delivery of mail for most messages. Like other communication technologies, electronic mail can be used to business advantage by trained writers or can be abused so that messages are ignored, lost, or read with displeasure. Chapter 19 focuses on specific skills you can use to write effectively for electronic mail.

Data Storage and Retrieval

Often the most far-reaching changes are least visible. At the microscopic level, circuitry within microcomputer chips no bigger than a fingernail can now hold hundreds of pages of information. On the horizon are super-chips capable of holding virtual libraries. Without exaggeration, the day may not be far off when you can hold your entire college library in a set of chips the size of a playing card.

Being able to access information quickly already proves to be both a benefit and a challenge to business communicators. On one hand, they enjoy sending several search words to one of hundreds of available data base retrieval services, then to have a literature search complete with titles and abstracts ready for use within minutes. On the other hand, the availability of information imposes a challenge and responsibility on business communicators. They can no longer allow themselves "writer's license" to generalize about unresearched facts. Previously, such license was often defended because exhaustive research meant time and money spent in travel to business libraries. Now research assistance is only seconds away by computer modem, adding a new sense of opportunity and obligation for the writer.

Data bases, as Peter Drucker has pointed out, can accidentally blur the distinction between data (information) and communication. Many business writers have made the mistake of throwing any and all relevant research material into a bundle and calling it a report. Communication, by contrast, is the arrangement of facts and arguments in order to persuade or inform. The use of data bases in business research and writing is treated in Chapter 6.

Audio and Visual Teleconferences

Estimating the amount of money spent by American corporations on business travel is difficult if not impossible. Ballpark guesses range from $20 billion in 1985 to as high as $60 billion. What, after all, is to be included? Airfare, hotel, and meals, of course, but what of "downtime" spent in travel and hotels, employee turnover due to excessive travel, and support expenses in scheduling and accounting for travel?

Enter the audio and visual teleconferences. While not a replacement for in-person business meetings, these communication links do suffice for a large portion of the contacts previously made only by business travel. Business people in Miami, for example, can gather in their own teleconference facility (or in a rental facility at one of the larger hotels) to meet electronically with associates in Seattle. As each participant speaks, the large conference screen fills with his or her face and upper body. Facial expressions, hand gestures, and body signals are readily apparent to viewers. On a split screen, visuals such as graphs and charts can be placed for continuous viewing. In more expensive systems, a full range of motion and color comparable to network broadcasts is available.

Teleconferencing is not inexpensive, with transmission costs coast-to-coast often exceeding $2000 per hour. But that expense must be weighed against the larger amount that would have been spent flying business bodies where only business minds needed to go.

Audio teleconferences, of course, are much less expensive and, perhaps for that reason, much more common. Using conference speaker systems and telephone connections, participants in various locations can talk naturally to one another, much as they would if they were physically present.

These new meeting technologies require training for effective use. Just as writing for electronic mail differs from writing for traditional letters, so participating in a teleconference can feel quite different from interacting in a traditional meeting. Practical ways to adjust to these crucial differences are treated in Chapter 19.

The New Telephone

You probably have noticed from telephone company literature and advertising that the traditional telephone is undergoing drastic changes. Phones can put a caller into a "camp 'on" queue instead of giving a busy signal. They can report the number of the party calling you (useful for screening or accounting purposes). They can be your computer's link to data bases, voice-to-print stations, and a wide variety of other useful business services. Their range and mobility have increased so that you can now not only reach a Yak by phone, but indeed by car phone—his or hers as well as yours.

Have you evaluated your telephone communication skills? This text spends time on such an evaluation because, for most business people, the telephone will continue to be the primary communication channel for day-to-day business. Can you make your point on the phone? Can you avoid lecturing? Do you know how to solicit response and listen to what's being said? Can you gauge the appropriate length of your phone conversations? Are your voice and telephone manner conducive to your business purpose? These are the kinds of concerns a business communicator should raise in a self-evaluation of the use of the new telephone (see Chapter 19).

PREPARING FOR CHANGE

Past communication revolutions meant stepping from an old technology to a new one—from pen and paper, let's say, to set type and typewriters. Once the new technology had been mastered, communicators could relax for generations at a time.

Not so in the electronic communication revolution. Just when we have mastered the keyboard word processor, the voice-driven word processor already in development will come on-line. Just when we've perfected our technique for the visual teleconference, holograms will allow us to see three dimensional figures. And just when we've gotten used to turning to data bases as steady sources of information, up will pop computers with artificial intelligence—computers that will offer an opinion as to what we should know and say when preparing a business document.

In short, this communication revolution promises perpetual and almost unimaginable change in our deepest habits as communicators. What business documents will be in common use in twenty years (perhaps the height of your career)? We can only guess. Certainly many traditional forms will be vastly changed or entirely extinct.

How do we prepare for such unceasing change?

First, we can identify those aspects of communication that do not change. We can reexamine the purpose of a business document, and how that purpose can be found and presented. We can refine our sense of audience. To whom are we speaking? What do they need? What do they want us to say? What do they expect us to say? What will they do with what we say? We can reevaluate the importance of style and format in business writing and speaking. How is the effect of our communication influenced by the handling of the *medium*, whether paper, screen, or sound? We can study techniques for writing and speaking not as final answers to future needs but as alternatives—arrows in our quiver—as communication targets emerge.

Second, we can resolve to be lifelong learners, always preparing to prepare. We can keep an eye on the dizzying spectacle of new chip advances to discover, as Dr. Johnson said in a different age, "what can be put to use."

Finally, we can keep the larger picture of communication in view—the picture which embraces but extends far beyond business communication. In that picture, human beings carry on the stuff of life by the words they say and write, the words they hear and read, the nonverbal impressions they give and receive. As channels of communication improve, we become more aware of important problems and more able to do something about them. Heading toward the year 2000, business communicators stand in the vanguard of those who want to know what communication is, how it can be used, and how it is changing.

Summary

1. New communication advances extend our influence over one another and the environment.
2. Writing habits will change as writing technologies change.
3. Like writing, our speaking will have to adapt to the possibilities and limitations of new communication links such as the teleconference and modern telephone.
4. Listening is far more than mere hearing. Listening seeks out the whole message by paying attention to both verbal and nonverbal cues. Listening actively overcomes barriers to achieve full understanding.
5. Electronic typewriters and word processors influence writing habits by making revision, printing, and saving of documents easier.
6. Electronic mail has reduced the number of letters and paper memos in corporations. This new technology creates its own forms and rules for writing.
7. Audio and visual teleconferences break some of the ordinary conventions of person-to-person conversation. We must learn new ways to speak and listen to use these technologies successfully.

Questions for Discussion

1. What is revolutionary about the communication revolution?
2. Why do we refer to writing, speaking and listening as "social glue"? What would life be like without social glue?
3. Why is it important to consider tone, diction, and length when composing business communications?
4. Is it necessary to master the medium of your communication? What common mediums do business communicators regularly encounter?
5. How would you define effective listening skills?
6. How do electronic sources affect listening skills?

7. Is it possible to rely on standard checklists to determine "good" or "bad" communication? Explain your response.
8. List the five premiere communication machines of the twentieth century.
9. How might the easy recall of electronic typewriters affect your writing style?
10. Identify a new exciting feature of the word processor. How can this feature enhance business documents?
11. What are the shortcomings of traditional mail delivery?
12. What unexpected problems might users of electronic mail be faced with?
13. In what ways does quick access to information both benefit and challenge business communicators?
14. Is the high cost of coast-to-coast audio and visual teleconference transmissions justifiable?
15. How might business communicators prepare for the use of voice-driven processors, holograms and pop computers with artificial intelligence?

Exercises

1. Imagine what a world without words would be like. Describe how people would communicate.
2. Go about the routine of your day, but when speaking to people, try to maintain a poker face. Show no emotion. Keep the muscles of your face relaxed, and try not to respond to their words with facial expressions. How do your listeners react to you? Record your findings.
3. Monitor your "b.s. detector". List the kinds of information you shut out in the following situations: watching television, listening to a friend or family member describe his or her day, and listening to an instructor's lecture. In each case, what kind of input startles you into paying attention again? What characteristic of that information—the method of presentation or the subject matter itself—overcomes the effects of your b.s. detector?
4. Compose a business letter of your choice using a typewriter. Then compose a letter using a word processor. Compare the two experiences.
5. Photocopy a graphic aid (a chart or graph) from one of your textbooks and bring it to class. Without providing its accompanying written interpretation, trade graphic aids with a partner. Now try to write text reflecting the information contained in the graphic aid. Is this "picture worth a thousand words"?
6. Now photocopy text summarizing information contained in a graphic aid. As you did in the exercise above, trade samples with a partner, and try to generate a graphic aid reflecting the information contained in the text. Compare your graphic aid with the text. Which is most useful?
7. What implications do computer phones and teleconferences have for business communicators? Envision yourself in an environment where your picture can be transmitted along with your voice over the telephone lines. What new considerations will you have to make each time you reach for a ringing phone?

Leonard Blasman is chief executive officer of Blasman Plastic Technologies, Inc. Throughout the growth of his company, he has tried to manage by open communication.

Communication—I used to think that I understood what the word meant. When one of my employees threatened to quit, for example, I used to calm things down by discussing the communication *problem we seemed to be having. When sales dipped, I urged all departments to work on better* communication *with clients. When employee morale was low, I campaigned for better worker-to-worker* communication.

I've used the word so often as a fix-all patch that I'm not sure what it means. How do you tell someone else what communication is? How do you teach others to communicate more effectively?

The answers to these questions are the main business of this chapter specifically and the entire text generally. Knowing what communication is and is not can help us use it skillfully in business practice.

Principles

of Communication

2

LEARNING OBJECTIVES

To define communication in ways useful to business applications

To understand how words can limit the boundaries of our perceptions

To recognize that the same words can have different meanings for different people

To grasp the nature of the whole communication act, including feedback

To understand the importance of censors and filters in communication

To distinguish, where possible, between the medium and the message in communication

To recognize communication patterns within organizations

Understanding basic theories of communication has never been more important than now when both the medium and manner of communicating is rapidly changing. What is "communication"? For that matter, what is "theory"? Both of these key words have revealing histories. *Communication* springs from the Latin verb *communicare*, which means "to make common." Notice that the primary meaning of *communication* is *not* to recite, deliver, speak, write, or sermonize. All of these activities fall short of "making common" the flow of ideas and feeling. Mere speaking is a one-way activity, while communication involves *common* ("communal") interests shared by all parties involved in the communication.

True communicators participate in the give and take of ideas and feelings. Even when they do most of the actual speaking, communicators receive responses from their audiences. A man smiles in the front row. An older woman leans forward to hear from the back row. Two teenagers yawn and squirm. All of these responses demonstrate the active participation of others to create the event called "communication." The speaker alone can only utter; the audience alone can only wait for a stimulus of some sort. Together, they can communicate in the mutual activity of making thoughts and feelings common to the group.

Theory comes from the Greek word for *spectator*, *theoros*. We may tend to think of a theory as a formula ($E = mc^2$) scribbled on a blackboard or placed in a box in a textbook. To the ancient Greeks, a theory was literally "something for the spectator"—something you stand back and look over. (The word *theater*, for example, is a cousin to *theory*.)

And what do we see when we step back, as it were, and look at a group of objects or events from a distance? Let's say that we are looking over events (or "theorizing") in the area of communication. We've mentally stepped back so that we no longer take note of isolated and individual characteristics. We've put ourselves in the position of *theoros*, spectator, to watch the panorama of events involved in communication. We're looking for general patterns and truths, not individual idiosyncracies.

Stop for a moment to consider your own conclusions. What is your theory, your spectator's view of what goes on in the act of communicating?

If that question gives you pause, you're not alone. Some of the twentieth century's brightest minds—Dewey, Chomsky, Korzybski, Sapir, Whorf—have devoted themselves to one of the great remaining mysteries of philosophy and science: how is it that we think, shape thoughts into words, and use those words to awaken similar thoughts in others and to elicit responses?

THE IMPORTANCE OF THEORY

"What does it matter?" the student in the back row asks. "Do I have to know theories of communication to order a burger or talk to Zelda?"

Frankly, no. We can communicate rather well without any conscious theories the same way that we can drive a car without an engineer's knowledge of auto mechanics.

But what if we want to build the car? Then the "natural" approach fails us. Theories, methods, and applications—the hard thinking behind the smooth lines—become indispensable to our creative efforts.

In your professional life, you will build communication patterns. You'll help to shape the kind of communication that takes place between you and your employers, your employees, and your clients. The decisions you make and the example you set as a communicator will construct channels by which you exchange and create meaning with others.

Some insight into communication theory will help you build those channels by design, not serendipity. Represented graphically, communication theory is the hub of all the writing and speaking we do.

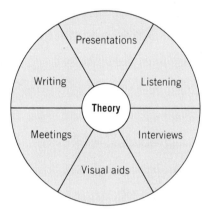

Notice that when theory changes—when the hub is renamed—all the applications of the theory, the spokes of the wheel, undergo drastic changes.

Here's a quick example. Suppose we theorize that oral communication is nothing more than words placed correctly into sentences and pronounced clearly and loudly for an audience. Here's the "application wheel" that extends from such a theory (or "hub").

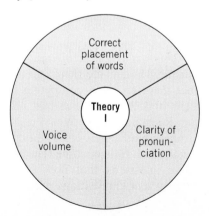

Now let's change our theory and rename the hub. We can theorize that oral communication involves not only giving but also receiving on the part of the speaker. Audience members give as much as they take in the mutual act of communication.

Notice now the differences in our application spokes. New topics, previously unimportant, are now crucial. There are more spokes, more kinds of applications to be considered.

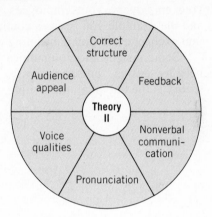

Then why does communication theory matter? Simply because it helps to determine which applications deserve your energy. As a spectator or *theoros* of communication events, you're able to see the big picture, not just the local skirmishes.

AN APPROACH TO COMMUNICATION THEORY

What does the "big picture" of communication theory look like in the last decades of this century? Rather like an expanding mushroom cloud. Old theories and models swirl one into another while new directions for investigations billow out almost daily. Linguists, psychologists, sociologists, philosophers, rhetoricians, computer scientists, and a host of other specialists study aspects of communication as seen from the perspective of their own disciplines.

This explosion of interest makes it meaningless to suggest in a textbook that there is a single theory of communication today. Nor are there a few distinct theories, each competing for dominance (somewhat like Fords, Chevrolets and Hondas). For that reason, we won't distort the work of pioneers like Ruesch, Berlo, Weaver, Shannon, Wiener, Lasswell, and others by "summing up" their contributions in a paragraph or two.

Instead, let's become theorists ourselves and ask eight of the most provocative questions that now occupy some of the world's best minds. Our answers and applications need not be original; inevitably, we will draw upon the insights of many communication theorists, including the pioneers listed above.

But most of all, these questions can help us feel the challenge and exhilaration of theoretical inquiry into communication skills we often take for granted. To add a bit of life to the process, we'll place the eight questions below into the mouth of Socrates. He enjoyed the process of searching for truth—the act of theorizing—much more than memorizing someone else's simplifications. In addition, we owe him this latter-day tribute as one who asked profound questions about the nature of thinking and communication.

1. WORDS AND REALITY: *Words Create Their Own Reality*

Socrates: *I have a problem. Perhaps you can enlighten me. I see, taste, hear, touch and feel the world around me—and I call that "reality." But often I have difficulty finding words to tell others about that reality. Why don't we have words for everything, instead of just some things?*

Have you ever felt Socrates' frustration? Particularly at the heights or depths of emotion, you may say that "words can't describe how I feel." Consider the important issue here. If much of what we experience as "life" or "reality" lies outside the boundary of words, how can we talk—or even think—about those ideas and feelings?

Let's say, for example, that one dollar bills were distinguished from ten dollar bills only by color: the one dollar bills were a lighter shade of green than the ten dollar bills. What would we do if we had only one word to express greenness—the word "green"? Perhaps we would demand payment by saying, "Give me a green bill." We would then look at it to see if it were light green or dark green—and keep it or hand it back accordingly. Or perhaps we would hold up the color green we wanted, with the instruction "Match it."

You may have already thought of a far more likely solution. When people feel strong needs—for ten dollar bills, let's say, rather than one dollar bills—they change their language to express those needs. "Give me the umphabratic green bill, not the flegilistic one," we would soon find ourselves saying. The new words "umphabratic" and "flegilistic" would help us match our language more adequately to our reality.

Socrates: *Oh, I congratulate you on your insight. You have been most helpful. But I still have a problem. After I learn your new words for the two shades of greenness, I may cease to see all the other shades of green. I will only let myself think about those aspects of reality that I have words for. Language would be a prison that keeps me from knowing reality in a deep way.*

Benjamin Whorf considered this problem for years. Too easily, he concluded, language becomes a set of blinders that keep us from seeing or thinking about what we have not named. Tourists visiting Eskimo villages look out and see "only miles of ice"—while Eskimos looking at the same terrain see much, much more. Their language provides dozens of words to name different colors, ages, densities, and configurations of ice. They see more because they can name more. By the same token, Eskimos looking at an urban street might well see much less than we do. Our language provides us with a wealth of words for stores, shops, delicatessens, stands, markets, booths, boutiques, and so forth.

A Business Application. Let's apply our thinking about the necessity of words and the limitations of words to a business dilemma at Melrose Insurance. Franklin De Grange, operations manager, took on the job of writing a brochure for filing clerks at the company. Previously, trainers had led clerks through the large filing room, pointing out banks of files. "Premium receipts go over there, but expiration notices belong in these files," the trainers would say. *De Grange faced the task of giving each of the files an identifiable reality by assigning a name to each one.* Then, and only then, could new clerks be expected to find the right file without a personal guide.

De Grange's brochure backfired in an unexpected way. It described the main tasks of clerks clearly, but failed to suggest the many and varied other activities that they were supposed to perform during the business day. The new clerks clung to the *language reality* of their job described in the brochure. They considered the imposition of other tasks to be "outside my job classification." De Grange bemoaned the fact that "we used to tell them too little about their jobs, and they did whatever they were asked. Now we tell them too much!"

The point: you will encounter important aspects of your business practice that need the clarification and definition provided by words. Be prepared to find ways to say necessary things. On the other hand, language can become a mental straitjacket for creative thinking and perceiving. Remain open to the realities of business beyond the buzzwords and catch phrases.

2. THE PERCEPTION OF WORDS: *Words Have Unexpected Meanings*

Socrates: *I notice a dimple on your chin. You do not smile. I am so sorry that my dimple is not your dimple.*

Early dictionary writers often prefaced their works with the expressed hope that uniform definitions of words would lead to less confusion and misunderstanding in the world. "Dimple," for example, is defined in most dictionaries as "a small, natural hollow on the surface of the body." How is it that Socrates' student—let's call her Fran—could be offended by having a dimple noticed on her chin? Hadn't Fran read the dictionary? Did she have a different definition of "dimple" from the one intended by Socrates?

Yes and no—and more "yes," for our purposes. She and Socrates shared the *denotative* meaning of "dimple"; Fran knew that Socrates was not talking about a kumquat. But they departed radically in the *connotative* meaning they assigned to the word. Here's what Socrates meant: "Well, I had in mind a cute little bulge on the chin like my adorable niece had when she was about five years old. 'Dimple' to me means innocence, health, freshness—everything good and childlike."

But how different is Fran's understanding: "Dimple! I've spent my life on dreary, painful diets. My grade-school friends made me feel awful for being overweight. I would do anything to get rid of my dimples."

This misunderstanding bears great significance for business communicators. Are words virtually identical to things? When you conjure up a thought or object in mind and find a word to name it, does the saying or writing of that word automatically bring the same thought or object into the mind of your audience?

No, Roger Brown reminds us in his books *Words and Things* and *Psycholinguistics*. Words may be the stimulus to thought, like a knock at the door, but they are by no means the guest that comes to call. Consider the analogy. A knock at your door may tell you with some certainty who's there. Your father, for example, may characteristically knock three times, then pause, then knock once more. Words, too, provide rather certain clues to some kinds of meaning. "Here's your notebook," for example, tells you that a notebook is being returned right now. But can you see the face—the expression, the intent, the underlying messages—of these words as they knock at your perceptual door? No. The words could be said sarcastically after the notebook proved to be of little help in studying for an exam: "Here's your notebook (dummy)." Or the words could be said in an apologetic mode, the notebook soaked with rain: "Here's your notebook (and I'm so, so embarrassed)."

In recognizing that words are not things, we leave behind a bit of immaturity and egotism. It takes patience and wisdom, after all, to deal with the fact that your strongest feelings and favorite thoughts (and the words you attach to them) are not necessarily present in other human beings. "I don't get no *respect*," moans Rodney Dangerfield—and his audiences laugh at the comedian's vast faith in the power of that word to provide meanings and explanations.

A Business Application. At Academy Mortgage you have to draft a report to major stockholders on the company's new plans for Southbay Park, a forested tract being developed by Academy for use by employees. Your own feelings are clear to you: you think the park is a great idea, and you look forward to hiking, rowing, and generally relaxing in the healthful environment. As you draft the report, you notice the prevalence of certain key words: "recreation," "leisure," "peaceful," "relaxing," "calm," and "refreshing." These are all "plus" words for you—words that would persuade you to support the development of the park. But you begin to mentally "reread" your draft from the perspective of Stockholder Mortimer Creed, a millionaire who hasn't taken a day off in twenty years. You wonder, with foreboding, what Creed understands the word "leisure" to mean (laziness?). You call to mind Stockholder Jill Benforth, the child genius. She graduated from Yale at 17 and made her fortune by 25. She wants the company "to push employees on toward excellence—push, push, push!" What will "peaceful" and "calm" mean to her?

The point: words are not miniature dump trucks that deliver preformed packages of meaning from our heads into our audience's heads. The same words can be expected to produce somewhat different meanings in each of your readers or listeners. As a communicator, learn to plan for those differences.

3. THE EFFECTS OF WORDS: *Hearing Is Not Understanding*

Socrates: *Help me with yet another problem of mine. When I teach, I send out my words as sound waves through the air or light waves from ink on paper. These signals strike all of my students at about the same time. Some students say, "Aha! I see!" but many don't seem to understand. Why don't the same signals produce consistent and universal results?*

In 1949, Claude Shannon and Warren Weaver published what they called the "mathematical" theory of communication. Its key terms will sound familiar to anyone with a radio or television. The message begins at an information source, proceeds as a signal through a transmitter to be borne to its destination along a channel of some sort. In rough paraphrase, we think (information source); we speak or write (transmit) a stream of words (signal) in some form, such as a speech or report (the channel); we send the words toward an audience (destination or receiver).

This formulation, for all its deceptive simplicity, helped to isolate the parts of the communication act. Even when theorists drastically revised or embellished parts of the model, they knew they were contributing to the understanding of a generally shared pattern. The mathematical theory has been called the heart of a growing snowball which, though modified by Berlo, Osgood, Schramm, and others, still is a recognized and influential model for communication, including computer communication, today.

The problem Socrates describes relates directly to the major concerns of the mathematical theory. Why do the signals we send in our written and spoken words often seem to bounce off our listeners—or, just as bad, produce radically different results among listeners? For Shannon and Weaver, "noise" could be the culprit. "Noise" is broadly defined as a signal interference—everything from literal noise, which keeps our audience from hearing us, to mental noise such as preoccupation or prejudice on the part of our hearers.

Just as interference can be reduced or eliminated in electronic transmissions, so "noise" in written and spoken communication can be identified and removed. In written documents, the generous use of white space can reduce the visual "noise" produced by all-print pages. In speeches, a pace-changing story or visual aid can restore "signal reception" distorted by lagging attention spans. Such "noise," of course, can be present in differing degrees for different individuals in an audience.

Different age groups are prone to different forms of noise. Young people may receive your signals through a haze of "semantic noise"—the interference of assigning different connotations to your words. Older audience members may experience "noise" if you talk too quickly or too softly. In written documents, poor formatting as well as grammatical/mechanical slips can produce signal-distorting "noise."

Part of the answer, therefore, to the problem Socrates describes lies in an analysis of the noise factor. What is my audience hearing or seeing along with (or instead of) the signal I'm sending?

But we must also consider the limitations of the "signal" analogy. A signal from the boss to the secretary—"Let's keep this area a bit neater"—may be heard as a distinctly different message when compared with the same signal sent by the janitor. Theorists like C. E. Osgood and Wilbur Schramm emphasized the role of social context in the signals we send. We clearly do not impart "new thoughts" by means of the words we send; rather, Schramm and Osgood argued, we use words to jog and massage patterns of meaning already in process within the minds of our hearers.

In answer to Socrates, then, the process of communication can be hindered by "noise" and by the presence or absence of conducive social contexts and bases of shared knowledge. The signals we send do not "flip switches" in our listeners; that analogy works only for machines and, less successfully, for pets ("Sit, Fido!"). Human communication is more akin to the process of comparing notes. We send out a configuration of thoughts for purposes of stimulation and comparison with similar thoughts already brewing in the minds of our audience. What we mean by "understanding" is not the reception of new signals and resultant new thoughts, but instead the sensation of "likeness" as we find our internal thoughts in harmony with the pattern of thoughts suggested by the signals coming to us. In casual language we indicate this harmony by such phrases as "I'm with you" and "I understand" (literally in its Old English root, I "stand among" your ideas).

A Business Application. If you've told them once, you've told them ten times—and you're getting angry. As Manager at Efton Shipping, you insist on one-hour lunch breaks for your employees. You've posted a general memo, in fact, demanding "compliance with company procedures regarding punctuality." Some workers have gotten the message, but others, particularly the bunch down on the loading platform, don't seem to understand you.

Notice in this example how "noise" (the "semantic noise" of difficult vocabulary and the "channel noise" of the posted memo) may be interfering with the signal carrying your message. At the same time, consider the mindset of your workers. How would you redesign your message if you considered it not as a "new thought" but as a partner to meanings already present in their minds? Perhaps you could make more sense talking about how all workers in the company depend on one another—hence the importance of getting back from lunch on time. The message can still be strong in tone, but its method of development will no doubt change when you follow the theory of "comparing notes" rather than "flipping switches."

The point: oral and written signals do not produce automatic responses in human receivers. The process of making meaning is not comparable to flipping switches within an electronic receiver or physically importing new thoughts.

Socrates: *Here's a riddle for you, my students. I quit talking each afternoon at 4 P.M. but I quit communicating at 4:15 P.M. Explain how this can be.*

Only a few months after Shannon and Weaver announced their mathematical theory of communication in 1949, Norbert Wiener published *The Human Use of Human Beings*, with its important concept of "feedback." The act of communication, Wiener argued, should not be perceived as a one-way delivery of goods from speaker to hearer. Instead, true communication takes the form of a "loop." The speaker delivers a message to the hearer, who in turn interprets the message and, by word or expression, sends feedback to the speaker. If the communication continues, the speaker uses the feedback received to adapt any new messages. The feedback, for example, may have communicated "I think you're being unnecessarily pretentious"—in which case the speaker can choose to be more direct and common.

Feedback does not wait for obvious breaks in a speech or written document. An audience flashes signs of understanding, approval, disapproval, curiosity, frustration, pleasure, and so forth on a second-by-second basis. Wiener calls this form of feedback "immediate," and credits good communicators with the ability to respond to it in an almost unconscious way. A presenter at a business meeting, for example, watches the eyes, faces, and physical gestures of his or her audience. Feedback in the form of sleepy eyes and drumming fingers can tell the speaker to speak more forcefully, or perhaps to pull an interesting story or visual aid into play.

In this regard, eye contact with an audience is crucial. Of course such attention makes the audience feel that you are talking to them, not at them. But just as important, eye contact keeps open the feedback channel. The audience can tell you in subtle and not-so-subtle ways whether they are enjoying your speech or dying on the vine. Key feedback indicators are physical posture (watch for the "deadman's slump"), active hands (scratching, drumming, flexing), averted eyes, and of course yawns and physical stretching. Experienced communicators do not interpret such signs as negative criticism; rather, they are efforts by the audience to participate in creating a communication event. Members of the audience are signaling you to take action that will make communication more successful. By adjusting your content and delivery to such cues, you will give your audience the pleasure of being coproducers with you of the communication that takes place.

In many communication situations, feedback arrives too late to make on-the-spot adjustments. In the case of a business letter, for example, you may not know for days or weeks—or perhaps will never know—whether the letter found or missed its mark. For Wiener, this often overlooked form of feedback is called "delayed feedback." We ignore it, unfortunately, because we feel that communication has ceased when our voices cease or the letter or report has been drawn up and delivered.

To ignore delayed feedback is to miss an opportunity to learn and improve as communicators. Some writers and speakers take a proactive approach to delayed feedback by concluding documents and presentations with a sincere invitation for comments and questions from the audience. In the case of a report, the writer can phone readers to hear suggestions and comments. Some writers attach a brief ''opinion check'' or questionnaire to important proposals and reports. Readers like to feel that their opinions matter, and that they have a channel by which to make their opinions felt. Speakers, similarly, can offer to stay for a few minutes of informal conversation after an address. These gestures remind the audience that true communication involves work on everyone's part—no one sits back as an uncommitted spectator.

Socrates' riddle, therefore, has a simple solution. Even though his lecture ceased at 4 P.M., important messages were still being sent until the last student departed. Because the historical Socrates was such a superb questioner, we have reason to believe that he had equally developed listening skills. In this friendly game of cat-and-mouse, the speaker pays close attention to the attitudes and ''moves'' of the audience. Such feedback lets the speaker build on successes and avoid failures.

A Business Application. Gwendolyn Pontelli continued to lead an important fashion design house at the age of 72. Once a month she met with her eighteen unit managers; the meeting usually began with Gwendolyn's 20- to 30-minute overview of agenda items.

Gwendolyn over the past several months felt her notorious blood pressure rising over these presentations. Certainly her employees were polite during the speech. ''Just beef on the rack,'' Gwendolyn complained to her secretary. ''They all sit there letting me do all the work.''

Gwendolyn tried a bold experiment. In the middle of her next overview presentation, without changing her tone of voice, she repeated the same sentence again and again:

- Button prices, of course, seem to rise each summer.
- Button prices, of course, seem to rise each summer.
- Button prices, of course, seem to rise each summer.
- Button prices, of course, seem to rise each summer.
- Button prices, of course, seem to rise each summer.

No one in the group looked up or gave a glance of special interest after the second repetition of the sentence. After the third and fourth repetitions, some of the brightest managers looked at her quizzically—but well over half absent-mindedly went on with their doodling and daydreaming. Not until the fifth repetition of the sentence did she have every eye solidly, though curiously, on her.

''Now,'' she said, ''let's reach an understanding. At 72 I'm up here working hard to communicate with you. By the way you sit, the way you nod, the way you look at me, I want you to work hard, too. Make decisions about what I'm saying. Send me your reactions in your faces and eyes. If you don't communicate with me, I'll go my own way. If you do communicate while I'm up here speaking, there's a good chance I'll go *our* way.''

The point: feedback completes the communication act by letting the message sender know if the message got through and how it was received. That information lets the message sender plan for the next stage of communication.

---

5. RHETORIC: *Knowing What to Say Depends on Knowing How to Say It*

Socrates: *Each year I see a new group of students. I never know exactly how to move them. But I always know approximately how to move them.*

Rhetoricians like Kenneth Burke (*A Rhetoric of Motives*) and James McCroskey (*An Introduction to Rhetorical Communication*) have helped a generation of communicators to make educated guesses about how to structure the message they send to receivers. True, the composition and content of that message may change drastically in the course of communication, as feedback lets the speaker or writer make judgments about the relative success or failure of his or her efforts. But every act of sending a message involves some pre-design—what Coleridge called ''initiative''—on the part of the communicator.

Rhetoricians are interested in the relation between the structure of the message and the response of the audience. If the words ''our country,'' for example, always made an audience applaud, politicians could plan for successful speeches simply by using those words often. While our response to words is far more complicated than this example suggests, at heart we share a tendency to respond to certain words and ideas in similar ways.

Why? Many rhetoricians point to our similar needs. In *Toward a Psychology of Being*, Abraham Maslow suggests that, first and foremost, we share a need for physical comfort (including food, drink, sleep, health, and so forth). After these needs are satisfied, we share common needs for safety, for love, for self-esteem, and for the fulfillment of our potential. Writers and speakers can design messages to address these and other needs. In doing so, they are employing a ''rhetoric,'' a conscious method of expression calculated to produce an intended response.

In the quotation above, Socrates claims to know the *approximate* means to move virtually any group of people. In actual fact, Greek schools of rhetoric drilled students in hundreds of specific ways to produce emotional and rational responses within their hearers. In our century, we do not train writers and speakers in such precise rhetorical modes (although some texts, like E. M. Corbett's *A Classical Rhetoric for Modern Students,* make the attempt). Instead, we discuss general persuasional strategies (such as the use of the buffer in some ''no'' messages) in the hope that students can develop a personal rhetoric that is at once effective and sincere.

There is the danger, after all, that a knowledge of rhetorical tricks—let's say 500 or so, as in the case of Greek orators—could reduce business writing and speaking to manipulation. Perhaps as heirs to the Romantic age, we cling to the value of sincerity in communications as an effective commodity even when less manicured than some traditional rhetorical techniques.

A Business Application. You direct credit services for a large furniture company. For the past year you've argued that the company's collection letters are sadly out of step with the times. Finally the company president has given you the go-ahead to draft better letters for review by top management. As you plan the letters, you find yourself thinking less and less about what you want to say (''pay up!'') and more and more about what your overdue accounts are thinking and feeling.

Most of your debtors, you conclude, expect a bitter or angry letter from you. They've let you down. But what do they need to hear? How can that need be used to your advantage? Gradually the letters take shape. Top management reviews them, and congratulates you on your shrewd psychological insight and your persuasive rhetoric. You shrug off the compliment: ''Really I didn't write the letters—they did.'' Some of the managers understand what you mean. Only a few need your explanation that the needs of your overdue accounts dictated the words in the letters. You focussed on the ''you'' in communication rather than the ''I.''

Six months later you are able to show management a 36 percent increase in collections due to the new series of letters.

The point: speakers and writers can count on the presence of certain basic needs in any audience. Messages can be structured to fulfill those needs—the art of rhetoric—and in so doing win the support and approval of the audience.

6. CENSORS AND FILTERS: *Many Barriers Can Prevent Mutual Understanding*

Socrates: *When I speak and write I hear myself from the inside. I have always wondered what I sound like from the outside. I hear you from the outside. I also wonder what you were trying to say on the inside.*

In 1979 an important communication study appeared entitled *Communication Theory* by Werner Severin and James Tankard. The authors suggest that messages have trouble ''getting through,'' due to a series of conscious and subconscious filters. At the same time, messages often have trouble ''getting out'' of the speaker in intended form due to a series of censors explored most notably by Freud, Erikson, and Jung.

Socrates complains first that the message that finally comes out of his mouth or pen sometimes differs in important ways from the message he intended to express. We've all felt this dilemma. Look back at an old term paper or creative writing assignment. Many of us cringe at the thought. The ''self'' that comes through in such writing often seems stilted, awkward, defensive, and posing. One common explanation students give for hating to write, in fact, involves just this perception of self: ''I feel so stupid when I read what I've written. It just doesn't sound like me.''

What are the forces that take a message in its free-formed internal state and censor it (often, from our perspective, ruining it) for public consumption? Freud (and many transactional theorists) suggest that we each carry around parent-like judges inside. When we begin to make an assertion, these voices leap up (just at the edges of our consciousness, it often seems) to cry, "Wait! Is that a safe move? Have you accidentally revealed how dumb you really are? Have you opened the door to questions you can't answer?" These questions cause us to mull over our assertion again and again before giving it "life" in actual words. We try it this way and that. Ironically, we sometimes have to create crisis moments (like the night before the term paper deadline) to quiet the internal censors enough to get a few thoughts onto paper.

No wonder we often feel awkward about the words that we write and speak. The solution is easy to recommend but harder to live out in a consistent way. If you don't sound like Dan Rather when you speak, that's probably because you are not Dan Rather. Neither was Socrates. If internal censors are going to make you uncomfortable so long as you fall short of some mythical standard of excellence, they will make you uncomfortable forever.

At some point—college is a good time—every speaker and writer should give himself or herself permission to simply *be*. The pretending and posing of high school years can be put aside as a necessary rite of passage, and the real "you" can speak out for better or for the worse. Almost without exception, the experience proves for the better, not for the worse. We all respond to someone's straight-forward, open effort to communicate. We are far less critical of slips and hesitancies than most speakers imagine. What counts most is a communicator's best effort to touch us with his or her thoughts and, in turn, to be influenced by ours.

On the part of the reader or listener, filters can distort our message. Severin and Tankard point to the exposure filter, which causes a message receiver to ignore all aspects of a message except those he or she wants to hear. Managers, for example, have been known to "bury their heads in the sand" by reading only those reports and evaluations supportive of their efforts. Other, more negative documents are dismissed.

The perceptive filter, similarly, picks and chooses—but this time from material the eye or ear has actually seen or heard. In business introductions, for example, some people pick up some insignificant detail about a person's life (a smudge on his or her jacket, perhaps, from changing a flat tire) while hardly perceiving information that could be much more important, such as the person's name and company affiliation.

Finally, a message receiver can filter out aspects of a message by means of the retention filter. Does the message feel good? Remember it. Does it hurt? Forget it.

To Severin and Tankard's list can be added other filters: the experience filter (have I experienced what the message is talking about?), the personal filter (is the message about me in some direct way?), the age/sex/race/religion filter (do I credit a message from "that" sort of person?), and so forth. But no matter what the list, the point for the communicator is clear: powerful psychological forces operate to distort the message we intend to send. Knowing what these filters are can be a first step in planning our messages so they can't be filtered beyond recognition.

A Business Application. Dean Harrison Edwards at Midwestern University thought he had a happy faculty. The three or four cronies he ate with regularly seemed supportive of his efforts. In fact, the faculty was on the verge of mutiny over a number of issues including delayed salary increases, class cancellations, and tenure denials. Faculty "filters," therefore, were especially active as professors read the following memo from Dean Edwards:

> *In my position as Dean of this university, it gives me deep pleasure to announce the Visiting Scholars Lecture Series. Four established and respected experts will present lecture/discussion sessions in the fields of computer science, literature, history, and art. Representatives from our faculty will serve as university hosts for these scholars.*

The Dean was dumbfounded to learn that his faculty had decided to boycott the lecture series, calling his memo "insulting."

Let's examine what the aroused faculty filters picked out of this memo for emphasis:

1. "*In my position as Dean . . . it gives me great pleasure . . .*" He's patting himself on the back again. Who cares what gives him pleasure?
2. ". . . *established and respected experts.*" He's as much as saying that none of us are established and respected!
3. ". . . *in the fields of computer science, literature, history, and art.*" How expected that the Dean should choose the fields of his cronies!
4. ". . . *faculty representatives will serve . . .*" Notice that he doesn't ask us—he tells us what we'll do. The guests are called "scholars" while we're just "representatives."

If we wish to place blame for this communication disaster, the faculty certainly could be more charitable in its interpretation of the memo. But the primary responsibility probably falls upon the Dean—a leader who failed to consider the presence and activity of powerful filters that distorted the message he meant to send.

The point: it is not enough to mean well in sending a message. We must design messages well to counter the effects of powerful and often subconscious filters active in our readers and hearers.

7. MEDIUM AND MESSAGE: *"The Medium Is the Message"*

Socrates: *You have no doubt seen a conveyor belt carrying packages. Let me pose a question. If the packages are words, what is the conveyor belt? And, more important, what is the message?*

For the first half of this century, and certainly for earlier centuries, messages were thought to consist of words exclusively. If you wished to become a better "messager" in those days, you would probably be told to study words—how they are spelled and how they join together into sentences (hence the emphasis on traditional grammar in past years).

Translating Socrates' analogy above, earlier generations thought that messages were delivered by various means, such as letters, reports, and speeches (the conveyor belt), but were essentially composed of words. Put another way, what the receiver finally grasped as the message was due to the words, not the means of conveyance.

With a famous rallying cry—"the medium *is* the message"—Marshall McLuhan led a group of theorists who changed our ideas about the perception of messages. For McLuhan, the means by which the words are conveyed (the "medium") participates in the creation of meaning along with the words for the recipient. For example, McLuhan points to the vast difference in a message created by a printout as compared to one that has been typeset. Judge the differences for yourself:

```
Barclay Jewelers proudly announces the opening
of its Western Hills branch.  This new addition
to the Barclay family will specialize in diamond,
sapphire, and emerald creations for both men and
women.
```

Barclay Jewelers proudly announces the opening of its Western Hills branch. This new addition to the Barclay family will specialize in diamond, sapphire, and emerald creations for both men and women.

At first glance, we're tempted to say "both sets of words communicate the same message." But do they? Which set of words would you send out to customers if you were president of Barclay Jewelers? Probably the typeset version. Those words communicate all that you mean by "proudly" and "diamond" and "creations." In the printout version shown above, the medium (the printout type font) actually detracts from such words, as if to say the sender is not proud enough to put these words in an attractive medium. McLuhan's point is that words "mean" differently when they appear in different media—and that words together with their medium create the eventual message communicated.

In your business career, and already in your academic life, you have many media to choose from. For letters and reports, you must choose a paper stock—crisp, bond paper or thin "ditto" paper. You choose a type ribbon—carbon or fabric. You set margins. You decide how much white space to place on the page, and how to distribute it effectively. In the case of speeches, you determine a suitable length. You incorporate visual aids. You decide how to dress, where to stand, how to move, and when to pause. In all these ways, you surround your words with a medium of one kind or another. The message you send is a blend of words and medium. Your readers and hearers usually are not aware that the meaning they are perceiving is created by far more than your words. But you, as a communicator, must be aware of this fact. It puts you in control of all the tools at your disposal to communicate ideas effectively.

A Business Application. Sharon Montoya directs the Dealer Sales Team for a major automobile manufacturer. Each month Sharon publishes the "Dealer Update," a bulletin/newsletter informing dealers of special policies and programs authorized by the manufacturer. This month Sharon has special news for her dealers: they will receive free automatic transmissions on all cars ordered from the factory during the month of December. The factory has authorized this special program as a Christmas bonus to dealers to help stimulate Christmas buying.

Sharon writes copy for the "Dealer Update", but isn't happy with the impact the words make. She adds a few exclamation marks and boxes the whole story with a bold line. Still the words seem rather pale, considering the special nature of the factory offer. In this case, Sharon's words alone cannot create the whole message she wants to send to dealers. She must change the medium. Then the words, together with the new medium, may have a better chance of scoring a sales success.

Sharon contacts a local printer and has 1000 formal announcements printed—the sort that are sent out for weddings and formal parties. Sharon sends one to each dealer, and is thrilled to hear soon that orders are pouring in. Words that could easily have been overlooked in the medium of the monthly newsletter created a powerful message when set in the medium of a special announcement.

The point: words alone do not create messages. Words always appear in the context of a medium of some sort, and together with that medium make up messages. By choosing both your words and your medium with care and insight, you can communicate the whole message you intended to send.

---

8. LANGUAGE AND MACHINES: *Machines Move Toward Artificial Intelligence in Using Language*

Socrates: *Yesterday I received an odd phone call. I answered the phone, and a computer spoke to me—a marketing survey, I believe. The computer (a female voice chip) introduced its business, then asked me a question, with the instruction to answer "Yes" or "No" in a clear, loud voice. I was fascinated with the idea of talking to a machine. When it came time for me to answer its question, I asked the computer if it would rather discuss the meaning of life. Why didn't it respond?*

One of the perpetual technological flirtations of the twentieth century has been the talking machine. Thomas Edison began the love affair with the radio and phonograph. Later came the television, tape recorder, and video cassette recorder. It was almost as if another human being were inside the box talking to us—almost, that is, because we could not interact with the voices and images coming from the first talking machines. Jackie Gleason and the Honeymooners would not answer back when we spoke to them.

With the advent of the computer, we seemed to take a giant step backward. At first, the computers did not speak to us or show us pictures of people; they merely displayed words and numbers on a screen or on a printout. But at least they had one advantage over the radio and television: we could enter our own directions and comments into the computer and be "heard." The machine would change its course of action based on our input.

The voice chip, an electronic circuit that can generate the sounds of the human voice, was on the market by the late 1970s. Now the computer could begin to speak to us, much as a radio did, but with a great difference. No human being had ever prerecorded the sounds coming from the voice chip. They were generated afresh from the building blocks of language itself—ideas, words, grammar, sentences.

By the mid-1980s, the "fifth generation" computers developed in large part by the Japanese were providing ways for us to speak to the computer by voice instead of by fingers on a keyboard. We were coming closer to the dream spawned by Edison—a machine that talked as we talked, and responded to our speaking.

It is one thing, of course, to say to the computer "recite the alphabet," and have the computer run a voice-chip program of the ABCs. It is quite another thing to say to the computer, "What is your opinion of the senatorial race?" and have the computer, in a reasoned way, begin to express its "thoughts."

That latter possibility, so long the province of science fiction writers (recall HAL in *2001* and *2010*), is now coming close to reality. Computer scientists and linguists working in the field generally known as "artificial intelligence" are perfecting incredibly complex programs that allow computers to "process"—in effect, deal with in a reasonable way—the language as it is commonly spoken (hence the term "natural language processing"). The development of artificial intelligence has gone hand-in-hand with dramatic improvements in the computer's memory capacity. For effective processing of language, the computer must have almost immediate access to a staggering amount of information: the words of English, including the various shades of meaning created by different contexts. (For example, consider the different meanings of "hold" in these sentences: "Hold my hand" vs. "Hold my order.")

At the same time, the computer must contain information on how words join together in English to form sentences and paragraphs—a system called the "grammar" of the language. This systematic description of English (in effect, a recipe book) is an enormous undertaking, and now occupies the day-to-day efforts of thousands of computer theoreticians, designers, programmers, and linguists around the world. At this time, no complete machine-version of English grammar has been completed. But in the near future, computers will begin to sound human. They will process information in a way close to what we mean by "thinking".

We have taken time in this chapter to discuss the matter of machine communication because, of all developments in contemporary communication theory, it now occupies the greatest amount of scholarly attention and seems to offer promise of substantial advances in theory and application. In addition, the prospect of not just a talking machine but also a thinking machine must give every business communicator a chill half of excitement and half of foreboding. Words have from the dawn of human civilization been the primary bond between people. Soon—have you checked today's mail?—we will receive letters generated entirely by machine. Not long after we will communicate orally, by phone or in person, with machines programmed to handle routine matters of business. You may have already heard the use of voice-chip computers in the telephone company's "Information" service. And after that who knows? Will we be interviewed by computers for employment positions? Will we find ourselves doing final polish work on reports and proposals generated by computers? Will we cease to "believe" in language altogether when so much of what we receive comes from an unfeeling machine? Or will they feel?

These questions are no longer the stuff of science fiction. Visit your local computer store or read a current computer magazine to see how fast the world of tomorrow's communicating machines is coming toward us all.

A Business Application. The year is 1997. Bud Jenkins has received a request from an important client for information on his company's "Utility Economiser" device, a machine that monitors utility use in large buildings for maximum efficiency.

Jenkins speaks to the computer occupying a small cabinet in his office. "We need to explain to Nathan Financial Associates how the Economiser can save them money. I've entered the information they've sent about their headquarters building. Generate a report, with action steps for their approval. Explain on a nontechnical level the major components of the Economiser system. Let's keep it to within eight pages. Try to hit about a tenth grade reading level, with illustrations where you think they're appropriate. I want to pick up my copy from the laser printer in ten minutes. If it looks OK, you can send a copy to the Nathan people immediately by electronic mail."

The ability to carry out this command may be years in the future for business computers—but not as many years as we might guess. At the University of California Irvine, the Navy is developing a computer system to "understand" and summarize reports received from nuclear submarines. Programs like SpellStar and Grammatik demonstrate ways in which the computer can quickly check our writing for correctness in some areas of spelling and grammar.

The point: the future of business communication is intimately bound up with technological change. We can expect an ever more rapid increase in chip-driven changes to the ways we communicate. Such changes will require all business communicators to adapt old skills to new uses and new devices.

In some time/motion studies, employees wear chalk-laden booties so that their habitual "trails" in the workplace can be traced. Words that pass within a company cannot be "chalked," but patterns are nonetheless noticeable in any business environment. We will explore the most common of these patterns, with the goal that you, as a decision-maker, can learn to recognize the communication patterns within your organization, and use them to your advantage.

Communication patterns are either structured or unstructured. Examples of structured communication include the company newsletter, the weekly meeting for mid-level managers, and the annual stockholders' meeting. Unstructured communication includes the "grapevine" by which rumors spread through the work force, the after-hour chat between employees, and the water-cooler conversations.

Structured Communication

You can learn to recognize and assess structured forms of communication within a company by certain clues. Structured communication is usually

1. recorded or documented in some form. This may include printed copies of a newsletter, the written minutes of a meeting, and the printed agenda for a conference.

2. less subject to change than unstructured communication. The existence of a newsletter, for example, is usually fixed in a way that a chat over coffee is not.

3. more widely known and more easily accessed. Structured communications like quarterly financial reports are visible to a broad public and open to scrutiny. Private conversations, on the other hand, are generally unknown and unremarked on by other employees—and certainly cannot be accessed without eavesdropping.

Unstructured Communication

Though less fixed as to time and place, unstructured communication is no less important than structured communication to the effective functioning of a business. Notice these three characteristics about unstructured communication.

1. It is dependent upon personal emotional factors. John and Frank both receive a structured communication like a company memo whether they like one another or not; but their conversation over a cup of coffee depends almost entirely on their attitudes toward one another

2. It is more flexible and open-ended than structured communication. Conversations tend to raise questions and express attitudes and feelings more than to propound arguments and answers.

> Channels of communication are sometimes the chess board on which organizational games are played. These kinds of exercises undermine the effectiveness of the manager. But it does pay to be sensitive to the needs of various people within the organization. . . who should get copies of a particular memo, or when it's the right time to place an important phone call.
>
> The Effective Manager DELTAK, Inc., 1979

3. It is more personalized than structured communication. Most memos, newsletters, reports, and speeches for a general audience are necessarily couched in general terms. Unstructured communication, however, can change the message to suit individual interests and attitudes. The rumor of an impending layoff based on seniority, for example, can be told in very different ways to Jan Fernandez, a long-term company vice-president, and to Bill Victors, an employee hired just last month.

Of all the forms of unstructured communication within a company, one of the most useful—and potentially most destructive—is the company grapevine. Somehow, good news never gets better, but bad news always gets worse when it travels along the grapevine. Inevitably, each hearer adds his or her own prejudices or anxieties to the rumor before passing it along. Motives are attributed, often without cause, to the decision-maker involved in the news.

Learn to involve yourself in the company grapevine for positive ends. The grapevine exists, after all, because people without knowledge in a company are people without power. You can use this perfectly understandable need to know to build team spirit and mutual trust rather than crippling suspicion and jealousy. Here are three concrete suggestions for nurturing a fruitful grapevine:

1. Make sure, in your own involvement with the grapevine, that you make contact in several different places. If you are a mid-level manager, for example, don't restrict your casual knowledge of what others say to the bits and pieces you hear from other mid-level managers. Find interesting associates at other levels in the company.

2. Make time, don't wait for a convenient time, to tune in to the grapevine. In the same way that you block out time for reading important structured communications like reports and letters, set aside time for regular contact with key people in the company grapevine. These contacts need not, and probably should not, be scheduled as formal meetings of any sort. Instead, mark your calendar with likely times to find your key people at coffee or relaxing after work.

3. Participate in the grapevine in a natural way. Don't lecture or "spy." The grapevine grows by trust and mutual need. It will not include you if you openly stand on a soap box or "take notes" on others' opinions. Take your

lead from others in the grapevine and be yourself. Both the information you get and the influence you exert will be richer for your effort.

Communication Patterns

The following diagrams primarily apply to structured communication patterns within business, though several also can be found in unstructured communication settings.

The Barbell

In this pattern, both partners to the communication depend on the other's confidence. Typically, neither wants to stand alone as an isolate, and so relies heavily on the communication partner. When involved in a "barbell" pattern of communication, recognize the importance of discretion, confidence, and trust.

The Triangle

Three people or work units joined in a triangle pattern face the challenge of dealing with different points of view without making any one party to the triangle feel like "odd man out." Communication triangles work well in an atmosphere of mutual trust. You can recognize the breakdown of communication triangles when they begin to take this shape:

In this case, two of the parties have severed communication. With time, they may also sever connection with the one party they have in common. Usually it is difficult to remain the one trusted associate of two enemies.

The Pyramid

In pyramidal communications, one party usually assumes the "apex" or leadership role. In some cases, this party generates much of the information received by the group. In other cases, the leader acts as a clearinghouse and distribution point for information to be shared with members.

The Series

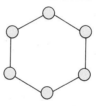

A chain of linked parties presents the challenge familiar from the old party game called "Rumor, rumor." In the game, one person whispers a sentence or two to the next person, who then passes it on down the chain. By the time it gets to the last person in line, the message has usually changed—often with hilarious result.

If linked chains of communication are necessary in your business structure, keep them as short as possible. One way to shorten the "chain of command" is to have direct contact with parties farther down the line. Many executives, for example, make it a regular practice to hold "open office hours" on Friday afternoons, a time when anyone can stop by for a business-related chat.

The Circle

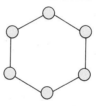

This pattern also helps to avoid the distortions possible from communication chains. The message is sent around the circle, but eventually finds its way back to the initiator. He or she can then alter the message, if necessary, or start a new one on its way around the circle.

Hub and Spokes

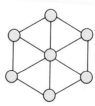

This pattern combines aspects of the pyramid—the hub resembles the apex of the pyramid—and the circle. The leader initiates a message that is then disseminated throughout the business group. At any point, however, individual parties can respond directly to the leader (feedback) or to one another.

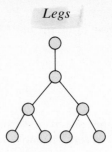

In this organizational communication pattern, messages are communicated through levels of responsibility to more and more workers. The legs pattern has distinct advantages. It frees the time of the central decision-maker: he or she need only explain the message once, instead of many times to many parties. The pattern also puts mid-level managers in a position of authority over the workers entrusted to them. These managers have important knowledge to dispense, and are therefore seen as important figures by the workers they supervise. The legs pattern also promotes credibility in company messages so long as the employees consider the immediate supervisor a credible figure. ''I wouldn't have believed it,'' a worker may say, ''but I heard it from my own supervisor.''

The legs pattern, when misused, can isolate company leaders from important feedback from lower levels within the company. Especially if the first or second tier of control is populated by ''yes'' men and women, executives at the top may find themselves disastrously out of step with the work force.

The Crossfire

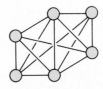

Freedom is the key word for this pattern. Members can speak freely to anyone in the group. The pattern works especially well for a brainstorming session, in which the goal of the meeting is to get a broad range of ideas out on the table. The pattern has the danger, of course, of leading to communication chaos. In business environments where an agenda and leadership responsibility are crucial, use the crossfire pattern only for brief periods.

UPWARD, DOWNWARD, AND LATERAL COMMUNICATION

Each of the patterns above, when translated into actual business contexts, could be described in terms of direction. Were lower level employees talking to upper level employees? Were employees on the same level talking to each other? The direction of communication becomes important insofar as it reminds us of possibilities and pitfalls.

Upward Communication

Possibilities

1. It allows upper level managers to keep informed of concrete progress and problems regarding company projects.
2. It gives lower level employees the opportunity to participate in the decision-making process in the company.

Pitfalls

1. It can cut heavily to a chief executive's time, especially when many parties demand " qual time" to express a variety of viewpoints.
2. It can involve upper level managers in petty decisions which should be handled at a lower level of decision-making.

Downward Communication

Possibilities

1. It comes naturally because communication to less empowered individuals in the company is nonthreatening to those in control.
2. It builds a sense of team spirit and mutual dependence through shared knowledge.

Pitfalls

1. It may lead to a sense of expectation on the part of lower level employees to be informed of all company matters, however sensitive.
2. It can devolve into a "command" structure in which bosses send down orders to lower employees. At this point, communication may cease as these employees grow increasingly resentful of their powerless positions.

Lateral Communication

Possibilities

1. It helps to create social bonds between employees—a powerful force in preventing turnover and disruptive behavior.
2. It builds credibility for company messages, since they are heard from an employee's equal rather than from an upper level manager, who might be seen as having ulterior motives.

Pitfalls

1. It sets the stage for mutinous grouping of workers.
2. It may be used to isolate certain individuals or classes of workers, who are purposefully excluded from lateral communication by their peers.

You don't have to wait for the first day of your business career to observe the fascinating workings of upward, downward, and lateral communication. Watch for these communication directions in your campus organizations, classes, and social life. Do people put on different personalities as they speak upward, downward, or in a lateral direction? Does their use of language change? Do they choose different media for communicating in different directions? Pursue these questions in your own observations and speculations. The answers you discover will help you use upward, downward, and lateral communication to your business advantage.

TEN BARRIERS TO COMMUNICATION

Finally, let's consider the obstacles to communicating in business. Volumes could be written on each of the obstacles treated briefly below. For our purposes, it will be enough to recognize that the obstacles exist, and to suggest a few ways to overcome them.

1. PHYSICAL BARRIERS

After we have given a substantial amount of work to a speech or business document, we have the inevitable tendency to feel that the world "owes" us polite attention. Not so. The members of our audience are under bombardment by several physical forces that can ruin our effort to communicate.

Time, for example, puts pressure on each individual with whom we wish to communicate. Let's say, for example, that we have prepared a twenty-page report. Have we considered whether our audience has time to read so many pages? In the case of a speech, do they have time to hear us out?

Environmental conditions such as heat, cold, noise, and drafts can subvert communication. Environmental engineers working for major television studios find that they can control the mood of a studio audience by manipulating the thermostat. A chilly room will often lead to a hostile group; a warm room produces a lethargic, unresponsive audience.

In written documents, physical barriers include the amount of print bunched together on a page. Must the reader's eye find its way through a page-long paragraph? Fuzzy or irregular type can cast an unprofessional look over a document, posing yet another physical barrier to conveying your message.

2. CULTURAL BARRIERS

An entire chapter in this text is devoted to the barriers that can exist between cultures. Recognize, however, that communication can also break down between subcultures and the dominant culture. The Old Money Club, for example, may list among its members the industrial magnates of a particular region. How will they receive a financial presentation from a non-member, perhaps a young upstart just out of business school? Learn to assess the cultural barriers that you must overcome to communicate with a social group to which you do not belong.

3. EXPERIENTIAL BARRIERS

Whenever we present new information to a group, we're tempted to simply spill out the new information with the unspoken advice, "Trust me—I've been there." Unfortunately, the members of our audience are seldom so willing or gullible. They have trouble believing what they have not seen for themselves. Therefore, whenever you plan to take people on a mental journey beyond the limits of their own experience, relate your new material to something the audience has experienced. The astrophysicist Carl Sagan, for example, regularly wins over nontechnical audiences by such descriptions as the "fried-egg" shape of our solar system. We've seen a fried egg, and can now relate to Sagan's communication.

4. PERCEPTUAL BARRIERS

Be aware that your audience may be filtering out major portions of your communication, as discussed earlier in this chapter. At the same time, recognize that individual audience members may be seeing other meanings than you intend. What, for example, do you see in the following figure? Might another viewer just as certainly see something different in the same figure? (Hint: if you saw a young woman, try to see an old crone—or vice-versa.)

In the same way, your audience may draw conclusions that you did not intend. Whenever possible, let another person preview a communication you want to send on its way to a larger group. Your reviewer can help you spot areas where unintended conclusions can be drawn by your eventual audience.

5. MOTIVATIONAL BARRIERS

Your audience may simply not want to be set into motion by your communication. Once they do begin to move with your thoughts, they may need help to keep going. This mental inertia is increasingly common among hassled business men and women. "Just give me some peace and quiet!" they seem to plead by their postures and facial expressions. You can use many of the motivational devices suggested in this text (in the various writing and speaking chapters) to wake up and motivate a stolid audience.

6. EMOTIONAL BARRIERS

Business situations rarely are able to entirely avoid the personal element. People's feelings get hurt. Or, more positively, people develop strong emotional attachments. When you send messages to people with strong negative or positive emotions, you cannot expect the message to sail undisturbed through the heavy emotional weather. Often your best alternative will be to face up to the presence of strong feelings early in the message—and then to proceed with communication. For example, a letter to a disgruntled client might well deal first with his or her anger:

> *You have expressed your disappointment with this company. I'm writing in an effort to mend fences with a client we respect and want to serve.*

7. ORGANIZATIONAL BARRIERS

In Renaissance England it was popular to talk about the Great Chain of Being, which represented a proper time and place for everything. That chain, while sadly worn in our time, still applies in certain ways to business practice. Projects, for example, are scheduled in distinct stages. Construction projects happen according to a carefully organized scenario of trades.

Be forewarned that your communication, no matter how well constructed, can fall flat if it is not synchronized with the organizational schedule in the minds of the audience. A typical example is an impassioned speech at a business meeting—a speech that earns only the reply, "That's well and good, George, but we're past that point."

You can test the organizational timeliness of a communication with the *Need Test.* Simply ask yourself, "Does my intended audience know they need the message I intend to bring them?" If the answer is "no," you must first convince them that they need your message. If the answer is "yes," design your message to address as closely as possible the need they perceive.

8. LINGUISTIC BARRIERS

This is no compliment: "I didn't understand much of what he said, but it was an excellent speech." Communicators who use vocabulary and sentence structures beyond the limits of their audiences are not communicators at all. They are merely speakers, different from stereo speakers only in the fact that they lack a tweeter. Language is neither a hammer with which to beat your audience nor a mirror in which to admire your own intelligence. Use words to create mental windows through which you and your audience can see your message clearly.

9. NONVERBAL BARRIERS

As discussed in the text's chapters on speaking skills, your nonverbal gestures can create serious barriers to be overcome by your words. Sagging posture can undo the effect of the most enthusiastic words, telling the audience "I don't really feel or believe what I'm saying." Lack of eye contact communicates embarrassment or insecurity over the words you are saying. In some cultures, seemingly innocent acts like showing the soles of one's shoes or making the "V" sign with one's fingers are insulting barriers to communication. These and other nonverbal signals will be discussed in detail in other chapters.

10. COMPETITION BARRIERS

Your audience seldom is "captive" to you alone. Members can choose other activities, some more exciting, perhaps, or less work than the communication activity you propose. Your long business letter, for example, may arrive in someone's daily mail along with the monthly issue of a favorite magazine, a pressing bill, and several short business letters. No matter how persuasive your words, your letter may not even be opened for several days—because of competition for the reader's attention. Remember, your words have to fight for attention. Use attractive, readable formats and energetic, eye-catching beginnings to place your communication ahead of the competition.

Summary

Definitions can be revealing. *Communication* means "making common" your thoughts and feelings and, in turn, receiving the response of your audience. *Theory* stems from the Greek word for *spectator,* and suggests looking over a set of events from a distance. Communication theory is important because it helps us explain and design effective communication patterns.

Theoretical interest in communication has centered on eight primary questions.

1. Do words limit our perception of reality?
2. Does a word mean the same thing to two different people?
3. Do words create meaning or awaken meaning?
4. What makes up the complete communication transaction?
5. Can the effects of words be predicted in a general way?
6. What censors and filters influence communication?
7. How do words combine with their medium to create a message?
8. What are the implications of machines that talk and even seem to think?

Within organizations we can observe both structured and unstructured forms of communication. Patterns to be noticed include the barbell, triangle, pyramid, series, circle, hub and spokes, legs, and crossfire. Each offers advantages and potential disadvantages. In such patterns, communication can flow upward, downward, or in a lateral fashion—all, again, with unique possibilities and pitfalls. Finally, we can observe at least ten common barriers to effective communication: physical, cultural, experiential, perceptual, motivational, emotional, organizational, linguistic, nonverbal, and competition barriers. They can each often be surmounted if identified by communicators and counteracted.

Questions for Discussion

1. Define "communication." What qualities do true communicators possess?
2. How might knowing a theory of communication help you to be an effective communicator?
3. Discuss the prison-house of language. Is language always adequate for our needs, or are there times when words simply can't express our thoughts?
4. What is the difference between denotative and connotative meanings?
5. How would you describe the "mathematical" theory of communication?
6. What are some effective ways to overcome "noise" in business communication?
7. What role does "feedback" play in determining your strategies as a communicator?
8. Is it necessary to maintain eye contact with your audience?
9. What are the dangers of depending too heavily on precise rhetorical modes?
10. Why do speakers and writers feel compelled to censor themselves? What is the best way to overcome excessive self-censoring?
11. In what ways do listeners and readers "filter" messages? How can understanding filters help you to construct effective messages?

12. Do you agree with Marshall McLuhan that "the medium *is* the message"? How do the means by which words are conveyed participate in the creation of meaning?
13. What are the various features of structured and unstructured communications?
14. How can you nurture a fruitful company grapevine?
15. Make a list of communication patterns, dividing the list into two columns; the efficient patterns versus the inefficient patterns. Is there any pattern which might be correctly listed in both the "efficient" and "inefficient" columns? What pitfalls might users of this pattern encounter, and how can these pitfalls be overcome?

Exercises

1. Before a writing or speaking occasion, listen carefully to internal censors telling you what *not* to say or write. Where did those censors come from? Are they a help, a hindrance, or both? Write responses to these questions, illustrating your points with details and examples.
2. Visually represent the grapevine among your school acquaintances or fellow workers. Discuss in writing the speed, accuracy, and motives of the grapevine.
3. List the various forms of feedback you receive during a typical day. Which are most influential upon your actions? Why?
4. Think about a familiar person or object—perhaps someone or something in your home or workplace. Describe the person or object verbally to a friend. Now do the same thing in a letter to your friend. Compare the two descriptions. How did your strategies change? Which description was more effective, and why?
5. "The medium *is* the message." Compare two advertisements for the same product—perhaps a billboard and a television or radio commercial. In what ways have the marketers of this product adapted their message to each medium?
6. Find a communique you consider to be poorly structured, and restructure it. Compare the two versions and consider the revision process you underwent. Why is the new version superior?
7. Enact the rumor game. See if it's true that a message changes substance drastically when carried by word of mouth. Choose a somewhat complex piece of information and involve as many "rumor-mongers" in the game as possible. Record your findings.
8. "What unique qualities do you possess which you feel distinguish you from your peers?" Many universities will ask you this difficult question as you seek admittance or financial aid. Businesses, too, will want to know how you view yourself in relation to others. Practice for these situations by writing a personal biography. Do you feel compelled to censor yourself? How can you overcome self-censorship and yet present yourself in the best possible light?

Meaghan Walker supervises a unit of eleven technical writers at an East Coast computer company. She's proud of the high quality work her people produce. She's also aware of a pressing and expensive problem.

Running through our office floor is a central wall—the "Hundred Thousand Dollar Wall," I call it. You see, my employees spend about that much money in wasted time just staring at the wall. "Writer's block," they call it, or "Monday blahs." Whatever you call it, those wasted hours are a major obstacle to productivity.

I wish I could train my writers to actively pursue ideas instead of waiting for inspiration. Actually they don't like staring at the wall either. It's frustrating. There has to be a better way to begin writing projects.

Have you ever experienced the kind of frustration Meaghan Walker describes? How do you get started when beginning a major writing assignment? What blocks occur along the way?

Guidelines for
Business Writing
3

LEARNING OBJECTIVES

To analyze your audience so that words are chosen and arranged to achieve your intended goals

To break writer's block by trusting your audience to hear you out

To identify and limit the purpose of your communication

To generate ideas using both the idea circle and the classic questions

To organize ideas in a logical, persuasive way

To support your points with details and examples

To write your first draft with confidence

To revise your drafts with care

In many occupations, the planning process takes top priority for important projects. Contractors and architects develop elaborate site plans, renderings, and blueprints before a single nail is pounded on a new office building. Pilots file a detailed flight plan before takeoff. Computer analysts work out thorough problem-solving algorithms before a line of actual computer code is written.

Writers, too, depend on planning as the first key step to successful documents. When such planning does not take place, the result is too often "Writer's Block." Even experienced writers can find themselves grasping for words when they should begin by grasping a plan.

The cure for Writer's Block begins before a single word is written. The writer develops—and usually writes down—a mental flight plan: to whom am I speaking? what do I want to say? how do I wish to say it? Since this plan lays out the course for the writing journey ahead, we should examine its parts in detail.

AUDIENCE: TO WHOM AM I WRITING?

The ability to write naturally and easily depends not on our audience itself, but on how we *think* of our audience. If, for example, we believe that our audience likes and supports our ideas, we have no difficulty expressing ourselves. Ideas flow quickly and gracefully into sentences. We've all written this way at least once, perhaps in a letter to a good friend.

Your View of Your Audience

Not all people, of course, are members of our fan club. Business writers must often write to a hostile audience that, frankly, wants to find as much fault as possible. In an adjustment letter, for instance, you may face the responsibility of saying "no" to Raymond K. Beasley (who, for your information, is outraged over the loud engine noise produced by your product, the Grasswizard). You may have to draft a termination letter for Grace Cotton, who is livid with anger over a negative quarterly evaluation.

At these times, words are hard to find. Writing begins, then stops, then starts again only to reach a dead end. We all stall on these occasions because our minds drift away from what we want to say toward how our audience will react to our words.

A writer cannot simultaneously be pitcher and catcher in the same ballgame. When writing to hostile or negative readers, take a moment to think through their feelings. This process may be described as "taking aim." Next, turn your energies toward your purpose as a writer: to send a message as effectively as possible. No writer should sidetrack the act of composition by endless second-guessing about each frown, grimace, sneer, and guffaw on the part of a negative audience.

The majority of audiences, of course, are not composed solely of friends or of enemies. Most readers are simply neutral toward you: interested if you interest them, bored if you bore them. But like a hostile audience, neutral readers can prove trying for writers prone to frequent blocks and blank-outs. How do you write for faceless, emotionless, and utterly unpredictable readers?

Recall the facility with which you wrote to friends. On those occasions, you could almost see their smiles as they approved the news and warmth your letter contained. Besides, you could assure yourself, they're friends. I can say what I want.

That very freedom to write resides in your own head and heart, and lies entirely within your control. You have the power to give the blank faces of a neutral audience whatever faces you would prefer to see—and why not the faces of friends? When you choose to impose a friendship upon your audience, you relax. In every way, the language that springs from you in that mood is more natural, more vivid, and more persuasive than writing born of hesitation, fear, and doubt.

Observe in the following two letters the drastic change in tone, all because the writer chose to be friends with a neutral audience.

(The circumstances: Frank Wirten prepares to open a tire store in a new community. Unsure of how to express himself to people he has never met, he writes a stiff and nervous promotional letter to the community.)

Our market analysis demonstrated that the northern suburbs of Seattle lacked a full-service tire store. We have decided to open such a store at 41120 N.E. 88th St. We are prepared to handle general tire problems as well as specialized needs such as alignment, spin balancing, and chassis adjustment.

Note the lack of feeling in Frank's choice of language. He hesitates to "warm up" to his audience because he doesn't know how they feel about him. He is controlled *by* his audience. In part to shield himself against their disapproval, he chooses cerebral language—"analysis" and "demonstrated"—and defensive arguments. He risks no enthusiasm toward his new store or his prospective customers.

Notice the crucial change in the letter when Frank takes a new attitude toward those blank, threatening faces. He decides to take control of his feelings toward his audience. He decides to look upon his readers as friends.

The northern suburbs of Seattle have deserved a full-time tire store for years. Friends, we've arrived! Visit us at 41120 N.E. 88th St. just to say "hello" and to look us over. We'll take pride in providing you with the best tire at the best price. Alignment, balancing, and chassis work? Right up our alley. We look forward to meeting you. At Wirten Tire, we're new neighbors, but good neighbors.

You may find this revision a bit schmaltzy, perhaps. For Frank, however, this friendly version of his promotional letter came as a vast relief after his efforts to write a stiff, formal, and frightened letter.

To sum up, your perception of your audience (whether hostile, neutral, or friendly) does influence your ability to write with ease. *You* control those perceptions. No audience holds you captive to an unproductive set of mental images. Simply decide to outwit threatening audiences, real or imagined, by substituting the faces of friends.

In this way, you can answer the question, "To whom am I speaking?"

I'm speaking to people who, in a friendly way, are willing to hear me out. For them, I can write in a relaxed, straightforward way. I don't need the false armor of inflated language, pretentious phrases, and impenetrable circumlocutions. My audience expects me to be myself. Frankly, that's my favorite role.

Analyzing Your Audience

Of course you will consider other aspects of your audience after making this initial and crucial attitude adjustment. Most of your considerations will stem from common sense and not a memorized list in this text or another. Maturity in writing, in fact, depends upon your growing confidence that the "rules" of good business writing are deeply reasonable and need not be committed to memory like multiplication tables. The following list, for example, probably just rehearses audience considerations that you already make by habit:

- Evaluate the experience of your audience. Do they know background information necessary to understand your words? If not, what information should you provide?
- Evalute the intellectual level of your audience. Have you chosen words, examples, and arguments they will grasp?
- Evaluate the time commitments and attention span of your audience. How much can they be expected to read with ease?
- Evaluate the predominant tastes and beliefs of your audience. Will your point of view have to swim upstream against the heavy current of those beliefs? Can you make use of their beliefs to support your arguments?

Business majors recognize these kinds of evaluative questions from another field: market analysis. In a real sense, writers too must assess the "marketability" of their words and ideas. This act of evaluation sets the stage for "product design"—the topic of the letter or report—and "distribution strategies"—the way the writer handles the topic.

How long does a writer spend assessing his or her audience? We asked two experienced writers, and summarize their responses here:

Shirley Housholder is an Account Executive for a large midwestern stock brokerage. She had just completed a prospect letter to be mailed to 5,000 potential clients.

To tell the truth, I prepared to write by sitting down and paging through my present accounts. I asked myself, "What kind of people are these? What do they want for themselves? What do they want from me?" I suppose I thought along those lines for ten or fifteen minutes. Looking back, those were probably the most valuable minutes I spent on the whole letter. The writing got easier when I convinced myself that I was writing to real people.

Roman Chavez is a loan officer at a Dallas savings and loan. Roman had the responsibility of writing a quarterly report for the Board of Directors on an uncomfortable subject: bad or shaky loans made by the bank.

Our loan record was generally good—but, yes, there were some rotten apples. I had never met any of the members of the Board of Directors for the bank, though I had seen them in the bank from time to time. At first I kept starting the report, then tearing it up, starting over again and again. I couldn't forget that old saying, ''They kill the messenger who brings the bad news.'' It came to a crisis one night about midnight. I had papers strewn all over the kitchen table at home, and was nearly berserk over my inability to write a decent report. I knew how, but the words just wouldn't come out.

My wife helped me. She said, ''Look, these people on the Board aren't ogres. They're probably just like me—willing to understand. Write the report to me, Roman, and see what happens.''

I did just that. The writing came quickly because I didn't have to con anyone. I just told both sides of the story—our many loan successes and the few failures. I did my best to show how we could avoid the failures in the future.

The report went over big. I got a phone call from the Chairman of the Board thanking me. She asked me to handle a couple other writing tasks. I think it's a good sign.

PURPOSE: WHAT AM I TRYING TO COMMUNICATE?

Moving targets are hard to hit with arrows or words, and nonexistent targets can't be hit at all. Be sure, therefore, to decide upon your target or purpose *before* taking aim with your words, sentences, and paragraphs.

This notion may seem little more than common sense—but, as Will Rogers liked to point out, ''common sense just isn't very common.'' Call to mind speeches, lectures, or sermons you've endured, all the while asking yourself, ''What is the speaker driving at?'' Like crazed archers, too many speakers and writers shoot their expressive arrows in all directions at once. We don't listen, we duck.

In general terms, your purpose will probably fall within one of the ''Purpose Circles.'' You'll notice that the circles overlap, suggesting that you can certainly have more than one purpose in a document or speech (page 54).

Decide at the outset of any communication task which of these purposes you wish to fulfill. You're the president, let's say, of a midsized manufacturing firm experiencing a mild downturn in third quarter revenues. You have to address your Board of Directors with some kind of explanation for the bad news. But where to begin?

Try, first, to establish a firm purpose (or a series of different purposes for

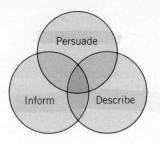

a longer speech or document). You may, for example, want to *inform* your directors of the facts: sales have been off across the industry, supply costs are up 18 percent, and the new union contract has cut heavily into profits. You may then want to *persuade* them not to lose confidence in your leadership. In your conclusion, you may want to *describe* better days ahead for the company, giving details of your plans for financial recovery.

INVENTION: WHAT IDEAS SHOULD I CONSIDER?

Finding Ideas

Once you have settled upon a purpose, your business document begins to take shape based on ideas. For most writers, gathering ideas involves an expedition of sorts. Unfortunately, ideas rarely present themselves in a top-down, A, B, C order. Instead, they arrive like cards in gin rummy—a possibility here, a combination there, a reject here, but all in flux awaiting some final sorting and ordering.

Resist the temptation to impose that final order upon your ideas too early. Let a wide variety of ideas come to you—mixed up, sideways, upside down, in any form. The relatively simple task of arranging ideas can be done later. For now, open yourself to the possibilities.

The art of possibility thinking again enjoys immense popularity, thanks to the exciting speculations of science fiction authors and cinematists, futurists, and poets. These creatures of a brave new world share a common ability to hold open what William Blake called the "doors of perception"— eyes, ears, thoughts, feelings, and all the rest. They resist the common tendency to let the senses shut, traplike, when a usable idea ventures into the mind.

Business writers particularly must guard against the temptation to "lock-in" on ideas in a premature way. The competitive nature of business life exerts extreme pressure on business writers to sound *definite* in all pronouncements—no "waffling" or "shilly-shallying." Too often, business writers respond to such pressure by putting aside valuable competing ideas so that their writing can sound simple and certain. They half succeed; they do sound simple.

Consider what single-minded obsession produces in business writing. This memo, in two versions, comes from the pen of a laboratory supervisor in a large chemical corporation.

This laboratory pursues pure research, not applications of known results. Our work has been hindered in the past year by demands for applications by other divisions within the company.

The supervisor wrote this memo in the grip of a single obsessive idea: his lab is for pure research only. It happened, however, that he "slept on" the content of the memo before sending it to his superiors. Two competing ideas came to mind:

1. He had to admit that those "demands" made by other divisions gave two of his less productive workers something to do.
2. One of the "demands", though irksome at the time, led to a new and exciting route of inquiry among his "pure" researchers.

The supervisor, aware of the danger of single-idea thinking and writing, revised his memo.

This laboratory's mission and primary contribution lie in pure research. As time and personnel allocations permit, we welcome inquiries and requests for assistance from other divisions within the company.

Good business communicators distinguish themselves by their ability, from the very beginning of a writing project, to escape the tempting mind-traps of single ideas.

Idea Circle

Probably we writers are fortunate that ideas do not come in strict 1, 2, 3 order. Once an acceptable pattern lies formed before us, we may fail to see a much better order waiting in the wings. Let's say, for example, that you and I must conjure up ideas to market a new brand of vinylized paint. Ideas come to us in this order:

1. Fade resistant
2. Durable, washable
3. Easy clean-up with water
4. Application by roller
5. Full range of bright colors
6. Safe for children (no lead)

If, at this point, we begin to develop a marketing approach or an advertisement, we may be seriously handicapped by the order of the topics on the page. We have trouble playing mental gymnastics with the topics, moving them around in one order after another. The list seems to enshrine that particular order of ideas, or one close to it.

We could, of course, jot each topic on an index card. But given the difficulty of finding index cards when you want them (top drawer? briefcase?), we may find an "Idea Circle" most useful.

Here's how this idea generator works. Whenever you seek a variety of ideas on a topic, simply write the topic on a sheet of paper accompanied by an "idea circle." The number of slices you draw in is entirely up to you.

Idea Circle

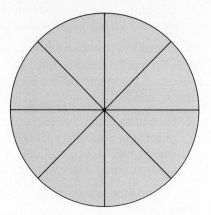

As ideas occur, fill in the slices of the pie. Our innate love of completeness (they called it ''horror vacui'' in the Renaissance) urges us to fill in all the slices even when we've wracked our brains in vain for more ideas. Why? Because a blank slice still sits waiting on the ''idea circle'' before us.

Notice that the circular arrangement of the slices allows each idea to exert equal weight as we mull over which pattern makes the best sense.

Figure 3-1 represents an idea circle for marketing vinylized paint; it illustrates how the mind can freely mix the topics in various orders in search of the best marketing approach. In the advertisement that actually grew out of this set of ideas, notice how the copywriter saw her central theme in the idea circle in a way that was hidden when the ideas were listed in 1, 2, 3 order down the page:

> *Brighten up the kids' room this Saturday with the rainbow colors of Vinyl-Brite. This one-coat, lead free, all purpose interior paint lasts for years. Handprints wipe off with a sponge. Worried about that painting mess? No problem—Vinyl-Brite rolls on, and cleans up with water. Hurry! It's on sale now for $9.99 a gallon!*

The Classic Questions

There are times, alas, when ideas do not spring full-blown from the brow of Zeus. The idea circle sits empty on the page before you. On such occasions, practice the technique perfected by Greek orators—the Classic Questions—presented here in adapted and modernized form.

Mentally fill in the blank in each question with your topic. Say the question aloud if possible. The odds are high that most of the questions will produce usable ideas for your business writing.

1. Why do I/others even care about _____?
2. If I had to divide _____ into parts or stages, what would they be?
3. What forces/circumstances led to _____?
4. What kind of person is interested in _____?

FIGURE 3-1

**Marketing Vinyl-Brite
Paint**

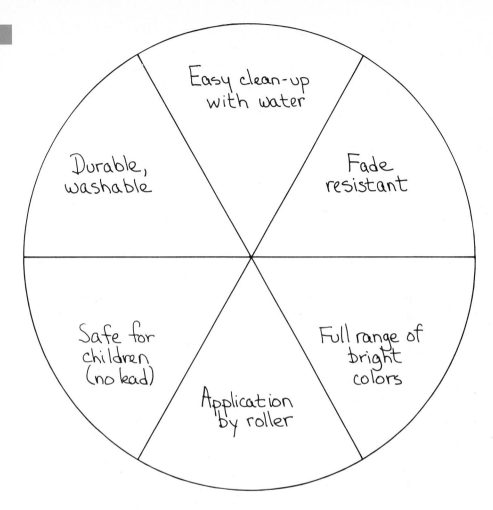

5. If _____ did not exist, how would things be different?
6. What aspect of _____ do I like best? Least?
7. What larger movement, field, or situation provides background for _____?
8. What are the principal benefits of _____?
9. If _____ fails or is ignored, what barriers were to blame?
10. How could _____ be explained to a 10-year-old child?

These questions are not to be considered short-essay exam questions. In the press of a business day, no writer has time to laboriously work out prose answers. Rather, use the questions as mental prods to get the mind moving.

As ideas come to you, jot them down within an idea circle. The entire process may take no more than four or five minutes. Certainly that investment of time is preferable to staring at a blank sheet of paper waiting for inspiration. The Classic Questions claim to deliver inspiration by the installment plan.

FIGURE 3-2

**Profit-Sharing Plan
Idea Circle**

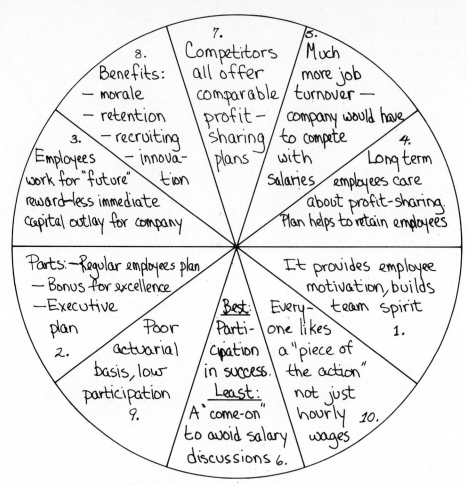

Consider the above idea circle on the topic, Profit-Sharing Plans (Figure 3-2). For convenient reference, the number of each Classic Question appears next to each idea.

Notice that some questions didn't pan out at all. That should not discourage you. The Classic Questions are intended to suggest possibilities. At times several questions will not apply directly to a given topic.

PATTERNS AND OUTLINES: HOW CAN I BEST ARRANGE MY IDEAS?

Organizing Ideas

In the last decades of the eighteenth century, business men and women served their culture as inventors of technological devices—all the buzzing, whirring, pumping, ticking machines that made up the Industrial Revolution.

In the last decades of this century, business people will increasingly play the role of "meaning-makers" in business organizations.

Data banks and high speed information retrieval techniques already make it possible for a schoolchild to call up most of the human race's knowledge on a particular topic, such as "goldfish." In business, information access through such massive data banks as Dialogue and ERIC gets less expensive in time and money each year. Such developments bring problems and challenges for communicators: surrounded by stacks of computer printouts, someone has to make *meaning* out of the welter of data. In the language of this chapter, someone has to formulate and organize ideas.

In his day, Aristotle performed the role of meaning-maker. He created elegant meaning-structures, or ways of thinking for such diffuse topics as animal life, physics, rhetoric, music, art, and poetry. We won't pay ourselves the extravagant compliment of claiming to be small Aristotles for our age. But in kind if not in degree, we business communicators face the same challenge Aristotle faced. Our culture gives us chaos—usually on fan-fold computer paper—and asks us to develop an idea, a silver thread that runs through the chaos, binding it together in an orderly, understandable way.

At Remson Office Supply Wholesale, for example, Personnel Manager Ron Chavallo was given chaos in a basket by a corporate vice-president. "Ron, we've had an unusual run of resignations in the past six months— twelve in production, six in accounting, and three among supervisory staff. Here are all the exit interview records. Work up a report for the Board on the 'whys,' O.K.?"

Ron Chavallo jotted down a "flight plan" or organizational agenda for himself—

My Goal: to explain the unusual frequency of resignations.

1. Needs: what data do I want?
2. Resources: is the data available? Where?
3. Input: read all available data
4. Evaluation: locate common factors and themes among resignations
5. Organization: order my points with appropriate evidence
6. Presentation: write the report in an effective way

For now, let's look specifically at Ron's handling of points 4 and 5 on his agenda, Evaluation and Organization. As Ron read the exit interviews, he organized reasons for resignation according to a pattern.

The Most Common Reason	Cost of living in this region is too high in relation to salary
Significant Minority Reason	Poor chance for advancement
Isolated Reasons	Return to school, spouse's relocation, illness

We already know where Ron got his evidence—from the exit interview records. But where did he get his organizing pattern?

That crucial pattern came from Ron's own thinking, not from the data. He imposed his orderly pattern upon the data. He felt that his pattern "fit" the data, or did justice to its complexity.

A large part of the art of good business writing lies in finding (or inventing) the right pattern to make sense out of the data at hand. Like Ron Chavallo's, these patterns can be simple common-sense frameworks for thinking. While these patterns may seem natural and obvious, we certainly complain when they are absent: "This report rambles" or "This letter just doesn't go anywhere."

For many of you on the threshold of a business career, the day will arrive too soon when a supervisor hands you chaos in a basket. No colleague or writing instructor will be present in the wings to whisper, "Psst! Here's an organizing pattern to use. . . ." Acquaint yourself with the twenty-two common organizational patterns or "skeletons of thought." Used with judgment, they can provide useful frameworks for shaping the meaningful structure of a memo, letter or report. In each case below, the accompanying example illustrates a use to which each pattern can be put.

The Time Pattern	***Example (from an annual report)***
In the past	In the past we supplied local retailers with prescription
At present	pharmaceutical articles. At present, we have expanded
In the future	our line to include toiletries. In the future, we want to
	break into the over-the-counter pharmaceutical sales.

The Space Pattern	***Example (from a sales letter)***
Far away (at a	For busy brokers in Trent, time means money,
considerable	especially in choosing an escrow company. Twenty
distance)	miles north in Atlanta are the old-name escrow firms.
Close at hand	Closer at hand, but still twenty minutes by freeway,
Right here	are their satellite branches offering limited services.
	But beginning Jan. 1, Jenson Escrow is pleased to open
	a full service escrow office right here in Trent.

Cause	***Example (from a claims letter)***
Situation A	Misdirections in the instruction manual to accompany
caused event B	my Starflite Moped caused an expensive mishap.
Event B can be	Because you neglected to specify that oil had to be
described as	mixed in with gasoline for the moped, I had to pay
Event B can be	$182 to have a frozen engine repaired. Please send me
undone/	reimbursement in that amount. May I also suggest that
repeated/	you issue an amended copy of the Starflite instruction
furthered by	manual.

Emotion	***Example (from a resignation letter)***
Once I felt	As a new engineer here at CLT in the 1970s, I felt that
Things changed	my work would earn me respect and financial rewards.
Now I feel	But twice now in the last three years I have been

passed over for raises. Therefore, I resign effective Dec. 20.

Logic	***Example (from a memo)***
All A situations have B characteristics	All new accounts feel hesitancy as new hands take over the books. Our latest new account, Winston Lumber, is no different. We can be sensitive to Mr. Winston's reticence at first to reveal all his financial dealings in a forthright way.
C is an A situation	
Therefore C has B	
Relative Significance	***Example (from a letter of recommendation)***
What matters most	Above all else, Janice Jobren can *sell*, as demonstrated by her stellar track record in wholesale hardware since 1979. She has also distinguished herself as an accurate record-keeper and field supervisor. The fact that she has little formal education interferes in no way with her productivity.
What must also be considered	
What we can safely ignore	
Hidden Significance	***Example (from an internal personnel memo)***
A has obvious characteristics	Certainly Mr. Lance Nash presents himself in an assured, groomed, and socially comfortable way. I noted, however, his passing remark that his college grades were always "right up there." His transcripts reveal only a "C" average. This slip, I think, cuts deep into my favorable impression of Mr. Neal as a candidate for Head Teller at the bank.
A also has a seemingly insignificant characteristic	
Why this seemingly insignificant characteristic is important	
Absolute Significance	***Example (from a charity promotion letter)***
A matters because B matters	Almost everything has a clear purpose. We invest our money, for example, to spend it later; we spend it later to gain pleasure. We gain pleasure and then what? Give. Give only to give.
B matters because C matters	
D matters independently	
Perspectives	***Example (from a proposal)***
One way to look at the topic	We all agree that L&M Auto needs more exposure. The sales staff recommends a freeway sign. Our advertising consultant favors a flyer tucked in with the daily newspaper. The approach outlined here takes a new tack: a huge hot air balloon tethered to the roof of our dealership.
A second way to view it	
Finally, a third revealing view	

Doubt
Others say that A
 will happen
We doubt that A
 will happen
Here's why

Example (from a real estate sales letter)
They're singing the old lament again: housing prices
are bound to fall, so wait to buy. At Merton Realty we
just don't believe it. We point out that land, materials,
and labor costs continue to rise at 13 percent or more
per year. A better buy next year? Don't bet your
money on it.

Contrast
A is not like B
A has _____,
 but B has

_____
Only A has _____

Example (from a relocation report)
Seattle differs from L.A. in several ways. In Seattle,
commercial office space rents for 35 cents per square
foot; in L.A., comparable property rents for 60 cents
per square foot. Only Seattle offers clean air,
reasonable housing costs, and all the rain you'll ever
wish for.

Comparison
Both A and B
 have _____
Neither A nor B
 has _____
Only A has _____

Example (from the same relocation report)
Both Seattle and Spokane have a variety of
commercial banks. Neither has a regional stock
exchange. Seattle, however, does offer an international
airport and harbor.

Reputation
A is reputed to
 have _____
In actuality, A
 does (does not)
 have _____
A's reputation is
 deserved/ must
 be adjusted

Example (from a consumer report)
A new pain reliever, Loado, claims to provide four
potent pain killers in addition to common aspirin. Our
laboratory analysis reveals only the presence of inert
dyes in addition to aspirin. Loado offers more hype
than common aspirin, but not more pharmaceutic
power.

Convenience
We seek the
 easiest way
 because
A is easier than B
A is easier than C
We seek A

Example (from a memo from the Board of Directors)
We are willing to pay the present tax bill, though our
accounting staff says it is unwarranted. We do not wish
to undergo a complete IRS audit. Paying the tax bill is
preferable to the greater expense of hiring tax
attorneys and extra accountants. Paying the tax bill is
also preferable to tarnishing the company's public
image in tax court. We direct you to pay the tax.

Variety
Item A comes in
 these sizes/
 shapes/aspects
 1., 2., 3.

Example (from a health club promotional letter)
Beauty comes in different forms: first, the irrepressible
natural glow of the teen; next, the warmth and fire of
young adulthood; and finally, the cultured radiance of
maturity.

Opinions	*Example (from a sales report)*
Some people say	Some of my clients feel it is a mistake to restock
Others claim	inventory during the next quarter. Others claim that
But most will	prices will fall still lower in the coming months. But
admit	most will admit that all retailers will have to make
	major purchases before the traditional fall surge.

Preference	*Example (from a Grants Committee report)*
We see the merits	We admire the fine work done by Dr. Merrick's team
of A	at Mayo Clinic. We also have the highest respect for
We also recognize	M.I.T.'s computer simulation of genetically passed
the merits of B	diseases. We chose, however, to award the 1983
But we prefer C	Research Grant to Boston Hospital's heart team for its
(because)	advanced work in cardiology.

Chain of Authority	*Example (from a memo recording interview data)*
A told B to act	Jane Clayton, my supervisor, told me to quiz the
Here's how B	interviewee closely on his technical skills. I proceeded
acted	to ask detailed and difficult questions. As a result, the
Here's the result	job candidate left in a huff, protesting that he didn't
of B's action	come to be grilled. Jane Clayton, hearing of his
Here's how A	departure, sent me a stern note blaming the course of
responded	events on my lack of interviewing skills.

Reduction	*Example (from a report to the Vice-President of Advanced Design)*
A dislikes point 1	The Human Factors team objected that the rear seat was
Point 1 is one among	uncomfortable for people weighing over 250 lbs. May we
one thousand	point out that only 1 percent of the population reaches
points	that weight. Certainly you will not choose to redesign the
A's complaint is of	rear compartment for this narrow segment of the
$\frac{1}{1000}$ degree of	population.
importance	

Likelihood	*Example (from a reply to an order)*
A is possible	While truck express may be able to deliver your parts by
B is likely	April 4, a somewhat later date is more likely. Certainly
But C is certain	air express could guarantee delivery in time for your
	assembly deadline.

Faith	*Example (from an annual report)*
We believe in A	At Genoweld, we have staked our reputation and fortune
We have no firm	on the future of genetic engineering. To date, we have
evidence for A	not marketed our products commercially. We remain
We find it	confident, though, that this emerging technology will
valuable to	eventually produce substantial gains.
continue	
believing in A	

Value	Example (from a private aerospace memo)
We want A	We need an open door to military decision-makers.
B provides A	Former Rear Admiral Benerly promises, as a consultant,
We value B	to open channels of communication in a direct way. I recommend that we retain Admiral Benerly for his requested fee of $500 per day.

These brief patterns help to create order out of chaos. They serve as reminders, too, that every well-written document has a basic and easily stated chain of argument or "pattern" at its heart.

To sum up: when you have successfully filled an idea circle with ideas, find or invent a pattern to organize the ideas in a straightforward way. Write down your pattern of ideas as a rough working outline.

Outlining

Patterns of organization provide the essential backbone for a business document. By themselves, however, they prove too slight a framework to guide the business writer's efforts paragraph by paragraph. An outline, a list of orderly thoughts, must flesh out the framework.

Almost all professional business writers use an outline of some sort during the writing process. True, not all of these working frameworks reflect that strict "I, II, III" order taught in grade school and high school. Writers often work out personal systems for outlining. The following system may prove useful to you.

How to Outline.

Decide upon a "master pattern" of thought, perhaps drawing on one of the patterns already treated in this chapter. Write down that pattern along the left margin of your page, leaving plenty of blank space for outline additions.

Jot down major points, using a common set of symbols like I, II, III, or A, B, C. Place these major thoughts, as illustrated in the example that follows, along the same margin to remind you that they are logically linked together. You need not work with fully developed sentences at this point. Simply find phrases that will remind you of your central points.

Now begin to fill in supporting points beneath each of the major points. Again, use a common set of symbols (perhaps 1, 2, 3) and a common margin for these points. When necessary, you may want to break out subpoints under these points, using a, b, c notation.

Master Pattern
  Topic: Changes in How We Communicate

Past
I. Fastest forms of communication survived slower forms
  A. The natural world
    1. Carrier pigeons vs. human runner
    2. Visual signals (smoke, etc.) vs. voice

B. The technological world
   1. Telegraph over Pony Express
   2. Telephone over telegraph

Present

II. New fast modes now compete with familiar slower modes
  A. What we send and receive
    1. Word-processing vs. typing
    2. Computer modem vs. traditional mail
  B. What we store and retrieve
    1. Computer memory vs. file drawers
    2. Data base vs. directories

Future

III. More speed lies ahead, with inevitable changes in how we communicate
  A. How messages are generated
    1. Artificial intelligence devices that help us find appropriate words
    2. Model documents stored in computer for our use
  B. How messages are transmitted
    1. Satellite networks for world-wide communication
    2. Speech-driven computers to free us from the keyboard

This sample outline may not reflect your precise outlining habits. You may find it helpful to put down more or less words. The point is this: find a personal outline method and *use it* to guarantee orderly, logical thought development in your speeches and written documents.

DETAILS AND EXAMPLES: HOW DO I SUPPORT MY POINT?

Once your outline states your major and supporting points clearly, begin to develop the "hidden persuaders" in business speaking and writing—the actual details, examples, and stories that give life and substance to your claims.

Details and examples play three important roles in business writing.

1. *To inform.* A trip report to a major client's office includes precise details of who visited whom, when, where, and what was said. These details and examples are provided in the memo or report to supply data for future planning. The goal of the writer is to give an instant snapshot of sorts, recording as many of the key details of the meeting as possible for later review and assessment.

2. *To prove the truth of an assertion.* Abstract propositions such as "hard work pays off" must rely upon evidence for their truth value. True, we do not always require the writer to supply actual proof. As a general rule, in fact, we require less proof from those we like and trust than from those we dislike and distrust. Often, however, business writing must substantiate its assertions by demonstrating, through detail and example, the concrete reality

supporting the abstract assertion. Let's prove our former assertion that at Jackson Engineering "hard work pays off." In order to decide which examples to provide as proof, we must resolve two questions:

- What do we mean by "hard work"?
- What do we mean by "pays off"?

For purposes of argument, let's say that "hard work" means working at least 20 hours overtime per month for the last year. Let's say that "pays off" means receiving a 14 percent pay raise.

Now we are prepared to develop an appropriate example to prove our assertion.

> *At Jackson Engineering, hard work pays off. (example) Thirty-one of our ninety engineers worked at least twenty hours overtime per month for the last year. All thirty-one men and women received a 14 percent pay raise in recognition of their commitment to the company and its goals.*

Notice that we have not proven that "hard work pays off," but merely that hard work (by our definition) pays off at Jackson Engineering. Note also that we've fudged a bit: we have actually demonstrated that hard work has paid off (in the past) at Jackson Engineering. But our original assertion—"At Jackson Engineering, hard work pays off "—not so subtly suggests that present and future hard work will meet with the same reward as that received by the thirty-one engineers.

We must distinguish, then, between true proof and what may be called "overclaim." Can you spot the logical "overclaim" in each of these advertisements.

> *If Brighto can clean this brat's clothes, it can certainly get your wash spring fresh and super clean.*

> *Over 100 dentists of those surveyed found Stiki-sweet perfectly safe for children's teeth. (Note: 4532 dentists were surveyed.)*

> *You're in good hands with All-Fate. Our local agent, Mark Teirs, saved the town of Missoula, Montana, with his bare hands during a recent tornado.*

While business writing cannot pause to formally prove each and every one of its assertions, it cannot afford blatant overclaim. No reader likes being led down the path of half-truths and hype. When you feel your details and examples may be misunderstood as overclaim, insert a qualifying remark (underlined here):

> *Morgan Trust protects your money.* <u>While our money market accounts are uninsured,</u> *our passbook savings accounts are backed by FSLIC insurance for up to $100,000.*

Your qualification prevents people from making the easy assumption that all accounts at your bank are insured to $100,000. A qualification maintains your integrity and credibility by pointing out that your example is not to be taken as universal proof.

3. *To illustrate a principle or assertion.* Often business writers want to show that abstract thoughts and propositions actually work on common, day-to-day materials. Consider the following principle followed by an illustration:

> *Relatively small towns usually can supply a wide variety of talented personnel [illustration]. When our drilling project began in Marysville last year, we were able to hire all of our secretarial help, half of our laborers, and more than one third of our white-collar staff from among the towns-people.*

Notice that the Marysville example does not prove the writer's point about the labor supply extant in small towns. At best, the example merely illustrates or supports the assertion. Without deceit, business writers often use illustration in this way to create the *impression* of proof without undertaking the laborious process of actual proof. Consider how many examples would be necessary to formally prove the truth of the writer's assertion. Many small towns in the nation would have to be reviewed in an effort to statistically measure their ability to provide a talented labor pool—clearly a prohibitive task.

The writer has chosen to trade on *trust*, not *fact*, with the reader. We are willing to accept illustration in place of formal proof whenever the writer has established credibility by his or her credentials and/or common sense. If we doubt the writer's integrity or acumen, we often refuse to allow illustration to stand in place of proof. Consider the following bit of bluster:

> *The employees in this company have no sense of loyalty. Last week Jack Friedkin quit without giving even a week's notice.*

We find ourselves protesting that one employee's quick departure has no relation to general employee loyalty. We have refused to take illustration as proof.

Just as they love pictures in a book, so readers appreciate frequent details and examples. Even an elegant chain of abstract assertion gets hard to follow without the frequent admixture of concrete examples from the physical world. Whether we are Chairman of the Board or stockboy, we understand and trust the physical world of flower pots, crying babies, bicycle tires, and burnt toast. That's where we live. If a business writer wants to ''sell us'' on the reality of his or her arguments, these propositions have to seem real in the way a flat tire is real.

In at least four ways, good business writers manage to persuade us that their details and examples have the ring of real life.

1. Good details and examples are *specific*. Don't write ''an important account'' when you mean ''the Sudbury account.'' Notice how each vague detail in the following example gains strength when transformed to a specific detail.

Vague: Some classic automobiles have risen steeply in price in recent
    years.
Specific: Such auto classics as the gull-winged Mercedes, the MGTD, and
    the Porsche Speedster have risen 400 percent in real dollar value
    since 1965.

Part of our pleasure in reading specific details lies in the mental images
they produce. "Gull-winged" and "Speedster" certainly evoke more powerful images in our minds than flatter words like "automobiles."

2. Good details and examples are *lucid.* Your readers want to hold onto
the expected and familiar. The secret for good business writers lies in always
allowing readers to hold onto the old world as they reach for the new. Lucid
examples reveal new thoughts by referring in part to old, familiar images and
experience.

Consider an astrophysicist's description of our galaxy:

Difficult, Unfamiliar Our galaxy, a protracted spheroid mass of stellar
    bodies and vaporous amalgams arranged primarily along a single
    plane, revolves in space.
Lucid The Milky Way, its countless stars drawn together into a shape not
    unlike an immense fried egg, revolves in space.

Strive to keep your business details and examples in touch with the common
things of daily existence.

3. Good details and examples are *condensed.* In business writing, an example should never take wing as a short story. Writers purposely condense
examples in order to fulfill the larger purpose of their writing task. In her report on employee theft at Krayco Department Store, for example, Security
Officer Jean Torson condenses the following scenario to a crisp, telling example.

*The Long Version: Since her promotion to night shift Manager Level 4,
employee 20114, Barbara Conway, has had the responsibility to lock up
the south loading ramp door adjoining the Women's Wear department.
Inventory control checks ordered by Sarah Martin, Corporate Vice-
President of Krayco, revealed the loss of the following items over a
period of nine months in Women's Wear:*

32 dresses (average $34 each)
16 pairs of jeans (average $28 each)
42 blouses (average $22 each)
12 belts (average $9 each)
18 pairs of socks (average $3 each)
* 2 cloth coats (average $105 each)*
* 1 ski jacket ($79)*

*Investigation was initiated with approval of Henry Martinson, Krayco
store manager. On Oct. 4, Oct. 7, Oct. 12, and Oct. 16, I established a*

surveillance point in Women's Wear. On each date I observed Barbara Conway setting aside unpurchased merchandise in plastic garbage bags identical to those used for department trash. At closing time she set all bags, both trash and merchandise, alongside the south loading ramp, ostensibly for trash pickup. She herself was observed picking up the bags containing clothing on two of the four nights in question. She was apprehended and now awaits the decision of management regarding prosecution.

The Condensed Version: *The night manager in Women's Wear, Barbara Conway, was arrested in mid-October for stealing clothing. She stashed dresses, jeans, and blouses worth more than $2000 in trash bags behind the store. After closing, she picked up the "trash" bags. Prosecution is pending.*

If a security report contained many such cases, and if the writer expected the report to be read by management, the examples would have to appear in condensed form. That shortened version should still contain vivid detail ("trash bags," "dresses, jeans, and blouses"). It may omit, however, all information that is marginal to the basic purpose of the report.

4. Good details and examples are *directed*. Business writers probably overestimate the care and attention their work receives. Studies of attention spans and eye-to-print reading patterns show how often readers pause, lose track, retrace, and even skip large passages of writing. Therefore, good business writers go out of their way to direct the reader toward their intended meaning. Notice how the first example lacks such guidance.

Undirected Example

Few coal miners participated in the Grants-for-Education program. "I worked until six o'clock every night. Saturdays we drove to my parents' house. Sundays I watched football. I didn't have time, that's all."

Directed Example

Few coal miners participated in the Grants-for-Education program. Bret Jolleson, 28, explains why he turned down a $2500 grant: "I worked until six o'clock every night. Saturdays we drove to my parents' house. Sundays I watched football. I didn't have time, that's all."

The crucial directed transition between the major point and the example itself can be called the "shoehorn." The directed transition slips the reader painlessly into the heart of the example. It tells the reader in advance what the example contains and why it is important. Notice the transitional "shoehorn" (underlined) in each of the following examples.

Since 1976, Burton Plastics has doubled its work force every three years, as the following chart demonstrates:

Year	Number of Employees
1976	46
1979	102
1982	199
1985	405

Since assuming the president's chair at Western Development, I have had steady trust and cooperation from the Board of Directors. <u>Let me single out but one example of their support.</u> *During our infamous cash flow problem in May 1979, the Directors accepted my radical rescue plan largely on faith. The plan, I'm glad to say, worked well—mainly because they gave me a free hand to act quickly in the crisis.*

Use such directed statements to make the intended meaning of your examples unmistakably clear to the reader.

WRITING THE FIRST DRAFT

Because you have taken the time to develop a working outline and a set of well-developed supporting details and examples, the writing of the first draft may come with surprising ease. You know approximately what you want to say, and somewhere in the back of your mind the actual words have already begun to form during the outlining process.

The trick to writing the first draft is letting go. Of course you will make mistakes. Of course you will use unnecessary words. Of course you will wander at times. But decide, bravely, to let the words flow. You will discover what almost all professional writers assert: quite a bit of the very first draft is usable material. The sentences may have to be trimmed and patched, but the essential message is intact.

You may have to turn off internal editors and censors to write an effective first draft. There's the voice, perhaps, of a former English teacher somewhere inside whispering "Stop! Have you spelled correctly? Stop! Have you punctuated correctly?" There may be the voice of a parent or sibling: "That sounds awkward. Shouldn't you sound more intelligent?"

To all such voices, the effective writer says "Wait." Recognize that there is a time and place to edit and polish. But that time is *not* during the writing of the first draft.

Two techniques professional writers use may help you to generate successful early drafts. First, set your pen or pencil to the paper and do not lift it until you have finished a paragraph. Try to keep your pen or pencil moving across the page, even if you have to draw a line to mark places where a particular word or phrase should occur but doesn't. At the end of each paragraph, lift your pen or pencil, stretch and relax, then tackle the next paragraph.

A second technique employs your considerable powers of conversation to motivate effective writing. Talk out a sentence or two before trying to write it. Once you have a bit of writing on the page, read it aloud and try to continue the thought in your speaking voice (you may want to imagine yourself talking to a friend about your idea). After you speak out what you have to say, write it down (not necessarily in the same words you used in speech).

More than a few famous writers (Wordsworth and Tolstoy included) were thought by the townsfolk to be "touched" for their habit of talking out loud during the writing process. Take the risk. Your success in effective first drafts will answer the occasional raised eyebrows of those watching you work.

Revising

By general consensus among professional writers, the revision process (while still challenging) is much more enjoyable than the process of "giving birth" to the first draft. The rough diamond lies before you, ready to sparkle as you cut, trim, and polish.

Like your personal approach to writing the first draft, the actual steps you take to revise your work may differ in order or substance from the steps listed below. If you have no systematic method for revision, however, you may want to practice the following steps until they become a habit.

Step 1. Eliminate Unnecessary Words. As you read your rough draft, you will find "fat" words that contribute little or nothing to your message. Cut them out. Watch, in particular, for these common forms of unnecessary words:

Repetitious language: "We trusted the unfounded misrepresentations." (Notice that the underlined word repeats the substance of a following word.)

Meaningless language: "It was the manager who decided which plan to accept."

Wandering language: "My uncle's company (founded in 1937 by my uncle together with Al Bennett, an insurance salesman) earned $.98 per share last quarter." (Note that the underlined words draw us away from the central point.)

Step 2. Check for Logical Connections. In the heat of argument, written or spoken, we are all prone to make logical errors. These can prove fatal to our effect if they appear in the final draft of a speech or document. Three logical errors in particular often surface in business communication:

Either/or thinking: "Either this company buys new equipment or it faces a long and inevitable decline." (Are there really no other solutions? Should you confine your argument to a black/white, either/or presentation?)

Circular reasoning: "The sales manager's poor social skills prevented him from working successfully with people." (Think about the logical circle here: the second half of the sentence repeats the meaning of the first half.)

False cause: "Johnson joined this company in 1983, and we've had nothing but problems since then." (It may be true that Johnson joined the company in 1983, and it may even be true that there have been nothing but problems since then. Does it necessarily follow that Johnson *caused* the problems? Of course not.)

> *If I'd had more time, I'd have written a shorter book. —Mark Twain*

Step 3. Check for Appropriate Transitions. Readers or listeners should not feel a mental lurch as you move from one sentence or paragraph to the next. When your thoughts take a significant step forward, provide a "bridge" by using transitional words and phrases. Notice how an appropriate transition ties these two separate sentences together.

> *Videotape rentals increased 80 percent last year. Revenues at movie theaters dropped by 15 percent.*

> *Videotape rentals increased 80 percent last year. At the same time, revenues at movie theaters dropped by 15 percent.*

The transitional phrase "at the same time" shows that the two thoughts are related.

Here are transitional words that you may use to tie your thoughts together.

but	still	in short	inevitably
yet	because	in sum	consequently
however	although	in brief	gradually
furthermore	thus	first, second	increasingly
therefore	hence	by contrast	more and more
similarly	nevertheless	of course	for example
in addition	for instance	probably	in effect

Such words serve as traffic signs to your reader or listener, providing early warning of the direction in which your thought is heading. Like traffic signs on a highway, however, too many of these words can create more confusion than they resolve. Read over your transition words, listening to both the rhythm of your sentences and the flow of ideas. Be on the lookout for too many and too few transitions.

Step 4. Test Your Diction for Power and Propriety. Diction, of course, is the choice of words. Some words may be too weak to use. The word "nice," for example, pales in comparison to more descriptive words:

"The corporate headquarters were nice" —"The corporate headquarters were luxurious."

When reviewing your choice of words, consider both the *denotative* meaning (dictionary meaning) and *connotative* meaning (emotional shading) of the language you use. Would you, for example, want to refer to the unmarried female president of your firm as a "spinster"? That word, no matter what its narrow dictionary definition, reeks with negative connotations. Exercise similar care in the words you choose.

Step 5. Check for Grammatical and Mechanical Errors. Slips in grammar and mechanics lead readers to feel that the author either did not know or did not care about rules that the rest of the English-speaking and -writing world abides by. Often, these slips lead to mistrust. Readers, for example, may be justly suspicious of someone's claim to expertise as an ''acountant'' (notice the missing ''c'') or as a ''bookeeper'' (notice the missing ''k'').

Here is a checklist of grammatical and mechanical categories. Each is treated in Appendix A.

Spelling	Semicolon uses
Sentence Structure	Colon uses
(fragments, run-ons,	Apostrophe uses
comma splices)	Quotation marks
Dangling sentence parts	Italics
Subject-verb agreement	Dashes
Correct parts of verbs	Parentheses
Pronoun agreement	Hyphens
Pronoun form	Capitalization
Comma uses	

Step 6. Make Stylistic Improvements.   The next chapter concerns business style and its improvement. When you understand each of the stylistic suggestions in Chapter 4, you may find the following checklist a useful summary.

Use the active voice	Avoid unnecessary questions
Vary sentence types	Choose words carefully
Emphasize important words	Avoid awkward constructions
through placement	and repetitions
Be specific	
Eliminate wordiness	
Create parallels	
Choose pronouns carefully	
Control paragraph length	
Avoid trite and slang	
expressions	
Avoid a posed, rhetorical style	
Avoid unacceptable contractions	
and abbreviations	
Use parentheses correctly	

By applying these six steps in your own way, you can shape a polished document out of the roughest of first drafts. At times you may have to be brutal in excising long strings of words that have no place in the final draft. At other times you may have to be willing to give up a particularly interesting phrase or idea for the sake of general logic and clarity. The fruit of such revision, however, is a clear and stylish piece of writing. To borrow Jack LaLanne's exercise motto, ''No pain no gain.''

Summary

1. What you write depends in part on your audience. Analyze that audience with care.
2. Write naturally and with confidence by trusting your audience.
3. Every communication has a purpose. Knowing that purpose before you begin to write helps you to shape your words and ideas in accordance with your purpose.
4. Ideas do not usually come by simple inspiration. The techniques of the idea circle and the classic questions can help to generate ideas under the pressure of time.
5. Ideas must be arranged in a logical, persuasive pattern in order to communicate effectively.
6. Ideas can be made more persuasive and memorable by supporting them with details and examples.
7. Writing the first draft should be a free, no-holds-barred attempt to get your major thoughts down on paper.
8. Revising involves a careful look at each word, phrase, sentence, and paragraph for conciseness, clarity, and other revision goals listed in the chapter.

Questions for Discussion

1. Why is it important to answer the question, "To whom am I speaking?" before writing a letter or memo?
2. What characteristics of your intended audience should you evaluate?
3. List the "Purpose Circles." Might there be times when you will want to fulfill more than one of these purposes?
4. What are the dangers of "locking-in" on ideas prematurely?
5. How can using an "Idea Circle" and the Classic Questions benefit the business communicator?
6. Is it possible to organize business documents effectively without first outlining your message? Defend your response.
7. What are the "hidden persuaders" in business speaking and writing?
8. What are the dangers of "overclaim," and how can they be avoided?
9. When are readers likely to accept an illustrated assertion in place of formal proof?
10. List four ways in which business writers manage to persuade us that their details and examples have the ring of real life.
11. What is the "shoehorn" in business writing? How does it help business writers to communicate clearly?
12. What advice would you give to a friend who has trouble starting the first draft of an assignment because he is afraid to misspell words and make grammatical mistakes?
13. What techniques do professional writers use to generate successful early drafts?

14. Which process do you find most enjoyable, generating the first draft or revising it? Explain your response.
15. List some steps in the revision process. Which of these steps in particular might help you to create a clear and stylish piece of business writing?

Exercises

1. Things have been a little tight lately, and you need some money to get you through to the end of the school term. Ask for a loan of $500, 1) in a letter to a friend, 2) in a letter to a parent, and 3) in a letter to a bank loan officer. How do your approaches to these audiences differ in tone, style, and content?
2. Describe a product or service with which you're familiar in three paragraphs. In the first, merely describe its physical characteristics; in the second, inform people about it; in the third, persuade people to buy it. Which is the more difficult paragraph to write, and why?
3. Of the paragraphs written for exercise two, which required the most "outlining" (whether mental or written)? Why was this paragraph more difficult to organize and present than the others? Explain.
4. Find a merchandise catalog from any major department store or merchandise outlet. Are there any items which you would hesitate to buy because they are not described in great enough detail? What information would you like to have seen included in the catalog description?
5. Choose an object with which you and your intended reader are familiar. Write a very general description of the object for your intended reader. Have the reader try to name the object. How often are you asked to clarify your directions? To what degree are the reader's feelings toward you affected by his or her reaction to your text?
6. Now describe the object you treated in exercise five in great detail for a reader who is not familiar with it. Repeat the procedure followed above. Compare the two experiences. Which communication encounter was more pleasant, and why?
7. Choose an article, letter, or document which you feel lacks sufficient formal proof to back up the author's assertions. On a separate sheet of paper or marginally, point to passages where the author's assertion clearly needs further proof. What has the author substituted in place of the needed proof? Be specific.
8. Select an article, letter, or document which you feel lacks sufficient transitions between ideas. Edit the document. What "shoehorns" would you insert, and where would you insert them?

Ted Erickson took a job with the Environmental Protection Agency after two years in the private

sector. In his new position, he's responsible for writing a broad range of pamphlets, articles, and

television messages on environmental issues.

I like my government job more than I thought I would. But I still haven't warmed up to "Governmentese"—that stiff, awkward, obtuse language that seems to crop up so often in government publications.

I face a real problem in my job. If I write in a natural, straightforward style, I'm afraid my supervisor will think I'm "unprofessional" or uneducated. On the other hand, I can't bring myself to use ten big words when three small ones will do. If it were up to me, I'd call a meeting of the entire office to discuss just one thing: style *in written documents.*

How would you describe your own writing style? Do you have more than one style? Where did you learn your present styles of writing? How can you go about learning new styles?

Business

Style 4

LEARNING OBJECTIVES

To choose a "voice" appropriate to your purpose in business writing

To make stylistic choices to increase the effectiveness of your words

To organize your paragraphs for clarity, logic, and persuasive impact

To link paragraphs into a complete document by using transitional words, related key terms, and other techniques discussed in the chapter

The word *style*, sadly, has fallen on hard times. At best it suggests an upscale quality tinged with more than a little snobbery: "She certainly has style." At worst it conjures up past and present affectations, "the style of the times."

In our use, style will mean nothing more or less than what it meant for Jonathan Swift: "proper words in proper places." To write with style is not to write with pomp or dramatic devices. If anything, those qualities are the opposite of what such writers as Swift, E. B. White, and Ernest Hemingway meant by style.

To write with style means to fit your words to the situation and audience. Business style is less descriptive and imaginative than literary style precisely because the business world is concerned with practical and immediate situations.

Don't misunderstand: business style is not a watered-down or corrupted version of literary style. Rather, business style selects what it needs from the stylistic techniques used in other forms of writing. In general, business style emphasizes clarity because money and jobs depend on clear meaning. Business style emphasizes brevity because time is money. Business style, especially in the last decades of this century, emphasizes the discreet inclusion of personality because solid business relationships often depend upon human warmth and trust.

But how can style be learned? As a start, let's turn to the matter of "voice"—that speaking personality that comes through your writing and mine.

SETTLING UPON A VOICE

Every business writer has a variety of "voices" for use in memos, letters, and reports. Perhaps you recognize one or more of these common "voices" from your own writing experiences:

The Encyclopedia Voice

Characteristics: stiff, unemotional

Example: It is possible to define the term "headquarters" as the central location or primary residence of a corporation. In general, such a definition may be said to include geographically propinquitous peripheral satellites of the central base, as in the case of Kodak, whose headquarters is in Rochester, N.Y.

The Emotional Voice

Characteristics: blunt, childlike, repetitive, often slangy

Example: I can't believe that I wasn't promoted. Look, my sales were up this year. I didn't miss a day of work. I worked overtime. I came in early. What else can a guy do? It's just unbelieveable to me that I wasn't promoted.

The Business Voice

Characteristics: direct, controlled, reasonable, clear, personal but not self-centered.

Example: For six months we have sought a new headquarters for Dynavision without asking one basic question: do we all share the same meaning for the word "headquarters"? Do we mean several floors in an urban high-rise? A single building of our own? A cluster of buildings in a town?

If we wish to use the categories of transactional psychology, we could say that the *encyclopedia voice* comes from the "parent" within: authoritarian, rigid, hyperconscious of propriety and status. Business writers have little use for this voice. It burdens the writer with the unnecessary difficulty of finding awkward, stiff ways to say simple things. The reader, too, is burdened by this voice (Figure 4-l). He or she must untangle meaning from a jumble of big words. No business writer should use the word "propinquitous," for example, if "near" will do.

The *emotional voice*, in transactional terms, rises from the "child" within: selfish, whining, insistent (though also playful, excited, and daring). Every business writer uses this voice, but with discretion. Like all emotional statements, sentences written by the "child" within burn deep into the reader's memory, for good or for bad. An executive with a major airline recalls a memo in which his "child" surfaced—with near disastrous results.

Before I took over scheduling, we had been falling slowly but steadily from our leadership position among nationwide carriers. My first act as a new supervisor was to dash off a red-hot memo to ticket counter personnel. Here's part of it:

". . . I've personally witnessed your extended coffee breaks and lackadaisical attitudes. As your supervisor, I want to see hustle on the job. I mean it. We're falling behind the competition. I'm sick and tired of popping in on our counters and finding them half-staffed and half-witted. Give this company an honest day's work, for heaven's sake. I mean it."

Well, I was new at the job and I thought I was being tough and assertive. The president of the company had other words for it when he found out. I didn't lose my job, but I learned to control my language and temper, especially in written form.

Not all expressions of the emotional voice are improper. Indications of irritation and disappointment as well as excitement and elation do have a place in business writing, particularly in memos and letters. Business writers do well to remember that emotion easily can be overdone. When you suspect that your emotional voice has overplayed its role, let a trusted colleague read your business communication before sending it on. Listen to his or her response to the tone of your writing, and revise accordingly.

The *business voice*, like a comfortable pair of sneakers, should be the mode of writing you slip into by habit. In this voice, you speak directly to the

FIGURE 4-1

Encyclopedia Voice

EXCERPTS FROM THE EQUAL PAY ACT OF 1963

Sec. 3 (d) (1) No employer having employees subject to any provisions of this section shall discriminate within any establishment in which such employees are employed, between employees on the basis of sex by paying wages to employees in such establishment at a rate less than the rate at which he pays wages to employees of the opposite sex in such establishment for equal work on jobs the performance of which requires equal skill, effort, and responsibility, and which are performed under similar working conditions, except where such payment is made pursuant to (i) a seniority system; (ii) a merit system; (iii) a system which measures earnings by quantity or quality of production; or (iv) a differential based on any other factor other than sex: *Provided,* That an employer who is paying a wage rate differential in violation of this subsection shall not, in order to comply with the provisions of this subsection, reduce the wage rate of any employee.

(2) No labor organization, or its agents, representing employees of an employer having employees subject to any provision of this section shall cause or attempt to cause such an employer to discriminate against an employee in violation of paragraph (1) of this subsection.

(3) For purposes of administration and enforcement, any amounts owing to any employee which have been withheld in violation of this subsection shall be deemed to be unpaid minimum wages or unpaid overtime compensation under this Act.

(4) As used in this subsection, the term "labor organization" means any organization of any kind, or any agency or employee representation committee or plan, in which employees participate and which exists for the purpose, in whole or in part, of dealing with employers concerning grievances, labor disputes, wages, rates of pay, hours of employment, or conditions of work.

issue and respectfully to your audience. In psychological terms, you let the "adult" within do the writing. This adult personality is aware of the parent's rules and the child's strong feelings. But the adult chooses to master those forces, and selects those which are most productive. The parent is held captive by rules, the child by feelings. The adult—the business voice— escapes such captivity by making reasonable choices and setting conscious goals.

One way to call up the business voice, particularly in moments of pressure and emotion, is to remember that you control your language. No one can force words from you, or provoke you to say or write something contrary to your wishes.

Employers appreciate such control on the part of their business communicators. As Brent C. Ernst, of the accounting firm Ernst and Abersmith, points out,

> *My managers each speak and write in a personal, unique voice. At the same time, they all speak with one voice—the voice of Ernst and Abersmith. Particularly when they are involved in stressful, high stakes situations, I remind them that each word in their communications to clients comes from the company.*

The business voice supports the company's image. Like the business voice, a company wants to appear reasonable, forthright, reliable, and wise.

WORDS WITHIN THE SENTENCE

To this point, you have learned to overcome "writer's block" by assessing your audience, finding ideas, developing a plan, arranging examples, and settling upon a voice.

Now what comes out on the page?

Words. One at a time, these small building blocks line up to create larger and larger language structures. By looking closely at words within the sentence, you can assure yourself that the basic building blocks of business writing are sound and true to form.

Making Language Specific and Concrete

Readers have only one motive in reading your writing. What's here, they ask, that can be put to use? When you use specific and concrete words, you give your reader useful tools instead of airy approximations. The following memo announces a staff meeting first in a vague way and then in a specific way. Observe the important differences.

> A client wants a brief overview after lunch tomorrow. Bring along anything we can use to show off our company.

Consider the vague, abstract language:

Vague: "a client"—Which client?
Specific: Allyson Royce, Operations Manager for Norton Hotels.

Vague: "brief"—20 minutes? Two hours?
Specific: 45 minutes

Vague: "overview"—A lecture? A slide-show?
Specific: A presentation of our services

Vague: "after lunch"—1 P.M.? 3 P.M.?
Specific: 2:30 P.M.

Vague: "anything"—Drapery? Pictures of the kids?
Specific: Letters of appreciation, files from open accounts, and photos of current buildings we manage.

Vague: "company"—The building? The logo?
Specific: our maintenance and rental services

Revised in a specific form, the memo makes its point clearly.

Ms. Allyson Royce, Operations Manager for Norton Hotels, can meet with us for 45 minutes tomorrow at 2:30 in my office. Please bring letters of appreciation, files from open accounts, photos of the buildings we now manage, and any other items that demonstrate the quality of our maintenance and rental services.

The specific memo will produce a better attended and more productive meeting.

One way to test for unnecessary abstractions in your writing is to watch for -tion, -sion, -ance, -ence, and -ness words. While no writer avoids all such words, their overabundance can cast an abstract haze over your writing. In the following example, abstract words undergo a transformation into more direct, specific words.

> *Vague:* The *definition* of leasing here at Boylston Leasing is the investment of a small amount of money to gain the use of large dollar amounts of equipment.
> *Specific:* Boylston Leasing *means* large value for small dollars.

> *Vague:* The *expansion* of Tri-City Freight has progressed at a pace in step with the *expansion* of the West.
> *Specific:* Tri-City Freight *grows* with the West.

> *Vague:* Mr. Yong deserves your *reliance* in his role as your account manager.
> *Specific:* *Trust* Mr. Yong to handle your account.

> *Vague:* It was her *experience* that friends were easy to make among her clients.
> *Specific:* She makes friends easily among her clients.

Such abstract language is called "Latinate" because so many vague words stem from Latin roots. No business writer avoids all Latinate words. At best, we can become aware each time we use a -tion, -sion, -ance, -ence, -ness abstraction and be more specific at the next opportunity.

The vague word "very" and its speech twin "really" weaken business writing. A business writer uses "very" in a feeble effort to turn up the volume on another word: very nervous, very upset, very hungry, very good. Business writers who know the power of specific words prefer to amplify the *content* of the word at hand, not its volume. Instead of "very nervous," they write "frantic"; instead of "very upset," "furious"; instead of "very hungry," "ravenous"; and instead of "very good," "outstanding." Specific words help the business writer say more with fewer words.

Using the Active Voice

A verb, as the underlined word in the following sentence illustrates, communicates action: "The manager dropped the vase." In general, English sentences work best when they pulse with action. Readers appreciate the sense of energy in the sentence, and its easy readability. "Who" did "what" to "whom" stands out loud and clear in action sentences. In addition, readers notice that action sentences usually take fewer words (hence, less work for the reader) than nonaction sentences. Compare the length of these two sentences:

Action: The manager delegates tasks well.

Non-Action: One of the manager's skills is her ability in the delegation of tasks.

Readers seldom feel much energy or motivation from sentences containing only an "is," "are," "was," or "were" at their heart. Writers, too, grow weary of such pedestrian ways of expressing their thoughts. As a business writer, you want to recommend, develop, suggest, argue, refute, substantiate, summarize, begin, continue, grasp, reveal, glimpse, fulfill, and all the other activities that make up business life. Notice, by the way, that not once have you leaped out of bed on a gorgeous spring morning, eager to "is."

One variety of the "is" construction requires a special note. Passive verb forms ("The cash register is/was fixed by Henderson") dilute the sense of action in business writing. Instead of telling "who" did "what" to "whom," passive sentences awkwardly unfold "whom" got done "what" by "who," if you pardon the grammar. The *victim* or object, in other words, appears first in the sentence: "The crown was crushed by the beauty queen." Not until the final word of the sentence does the reader discover the *actor,* in this case the beauty queen. While we can tolerate this reversal occasionally for variety, we prefer the native English pattern of *actor→action→object.*

Another difficulty with the passive form lies in its most irritating habit of dissolving key figures in the sentence. An active sentence tells us that "Betty embezzled the money." But when that news appears in a passive sentence, notice who's missing: "The money was embezzled." Betty, if she wishes to hide behind the grammar of the passive sentence, can disappear entirely (perhaps to Costa Rica).

Observe in the following sentence how the central *actors* have misused the passive form to conveniently step out of a negative personnel evaluation.

Ms. Bradford is generally disliked here. Her work habits are frequently criticized. Prior to beginning work as supervisor, she was rated poorly as a leader.

Wait a minute, Ms. Bradford has a right to insist. Who dislikes (active) me? Who criticizes (active) me? Who rates (active) me poorly? Rewrite my evaluation in active form, not passive, so I can confront my accusers.

Business writers will never completely eliminate passive and is/are constructions from their writing, nor should they. For occasional emphasis and variety, the passive form serves well. We can, however, learn to look upon every is/are/was/were and passive verb as a taunt: "change me if you can."

Strong business writers pack their prose with lively, action verbs. The Internal Revenue Service, by contrast, loads its manuals with is/are/was/were and passive constructions. Pick your company.

Choosing Positive Language

Business writers and speakers recognize that happy, optimistic people are more open to new ideas and change than are discouraged, cynical people. Therefore, such communicators lose no opportunity to "accentuate the positive," in the words of an old song.

Notice in the following pairs how a dreary, guilt-ridden message is recast into a brighter form by the choice of positive language:

> Your complaint is being dealt with by Mr. Flores.
> Your inquiry will be answered promptly by Mr. Flores.
> Ten percent of the sales force failed to attend the conference.
> The conference attracted ninety percent of the sales force.

No one needs a list of the negative words in the English language. They are among the most memorable words from our upbringing: "no, don't, can't, won't, shouldn't, failed, forgot, omitted, destroyed, complained, ruined," and so forth. These words, while sometimes quite accurate for the situation at hand, rarely have the power to *change* the situation for the better. Business writers wisely choose positive language whenever possible to motivate an audience to new courses of thinking and action.

Avoiding Noun Clusters

A noun, as you know, names a person, place, thing, or quality. "Computer" is a noun and so is "difficulty" and "pebble." Readers of English expect most nouns either to do something ("the computer beeps") or to have something done to them ("Spot swallowed the pebble.").

Business writers sometimes short-circuit this expectation by surrounding nouns not with action but with other *nouns*.

> *Be sure to attend the business opportunities youth guidance session.*

The what? If we do attend, we undoubtedly will receive a copy of the "Business Opportunities Youth Guidance Session Report." Back at our office, we may have to discuss the report with colleagues. Let's not call our meeting a business opportunities youth guidance session report evaluation.

The simple solution to the problem of noun clusters lies in using adjectives and verbs.

Noun Cluster	*Revision with Adjectives and Verbs*
the franchises investment opportunity	the opportunity to invest in franchises
the candidate interview patience measurement	the measurement of a candidate's patience in interviews

Closely related to noun clusters are prepositional strings (*to* the park *by* the lake *with* four ducks *under* the bridge). As a general rule, never string together more than two prepositional phrases in a row.

Not: the receipt *of* the package *of* tools *by* the supervisor *at* Benson Mechanics Center.

Instead: the supervisor at Benson Mechanics Center received the tools.

Replacing Vague Pronouns

Business writers would never send out a memo, letter, or report pockmarked with penny-sized holes in the typed page. Yet vague pronouns (this, it, that, these, those) can leave gaps of meaning comparable to actual holes in the page. Consider the gap in meaning left by the vague use of "this":

At its last meeting, the Employee Safety Committee's discussion focused on instruction manuals for new production line tools, improved air conditioning in the welding units, and the buddy system for particularly hazardous duty. This met with opposition from management representatives.

This what? The possibilities are many:

- this discussion met with opposition
- this agenda met with opposition
- this system met with opposition
- this duty met with opposition

The page has a gap of meaning just as big as the word "this."

To spare readers an annoying guessing game, we could place an identifying word or phrase immediately after "this," and revise the sentence to specify that "this safeguard met with opposition from management representatives."

The problem of the vague "it" can be solved even more easily. Rephrase the sentence to remove the meaningless "it" entirely.

Not: Johnson's perpetual questions make *it* impossible to concentrate.

Instead: Johnson's perpetual questions make concentration impossible.

Controlling Emphasis

In a business conversation, have you stopped to listen to the first sound out of someone's mouth when he or she begins to speak? Quite often no word is said at all. Rather, a short cough, a clearing of the throat, or the taking of an audible quick breath signals a person's intention to speak. If the speaker actually says a word, it often turns out to be a non-word—a verbal cough—like "well" or "uh."

Business writing, like speaking, has its rituals of introduction. Like "well" and "uh," these sentence openers have little or no meaning. They exist merely to get things underway. Good business writers learn, though, that business prose gets underway quite well, thank you, without such inane devices. Notice that we lose no meaning but gain considerable sentence strength by eliminating the meaningless openers, "it is" and "there is/are":

Not: There is an oak beam supporting the roof.
Instead: An oak beam supports the roof. (Actor→Action→Object)

Not: It is possible that Williams will apply for Section Leader.
Instead: Williams may apply for Section Leader.

Of course, such revision has the virtue of making the sentence shorter for the reader. But more important, by removing meaningless words from the beginning of the sentence, the opening slot—the *strong slot*—is free to contain significant words.

Readers are understandably eager for the first word or two in each sentence. There, after all, lies the first clue to understanding the meaning of the entire sentence. The *strong slot* words are like a compass arrow providing orientation for the reader. Hence, words placed there receive special attention and emphasis from readers. For that reason alone, waste-words like "it is" and "there is/are" should be removed entirely, or at least placed later in the sentence.

Such removal is painless. In almost all cases, meaningless phrases can simply be snipped out of the sentence.

Not: There are meaningless words that should be removed.
Instead: Meaningless words should be removed.
Or: Remove meaningless words.

Using Words Correctly

English presents the business writer with several pairs of problematic twins. Be careful to choose the word you mean rather than its look-alike or sound-alike double.

disperse-disburse	"Disperse" means to scatter; "disburse" means to pay out
site-cite	"site" is a location; "to cite" is to point out
lead-led	"lead" is a heavy gray metal; "led" is past tense of the verb, "to lead"
lose-loose	"to lose" means to be without; "loose" means unconnected
bear-bare	"to bear" means to carry a burden; "to bare" means to expose
principle-principal	"principle" is a truth; "principal" is a school official or amount of money excluding interest

Eliminating Wordiness

Wordiness has little to do with the length of a document. Some reports, after all, are long simply because they have a great deal to say. Even a one-paragraph memo can be guilty of "excessive reliance upon the use of somewhat redundant terms" (in short, wordiness).

Watch for wordiness in these three disguises:

1. Unnecessary doubling. Notice how the following sentence states, then restates, its point by doubling each key word.

   Not: If and when we can establish and define our goals and objectives, each and every member will be ready and willing to give aid and assistance.
   Instead: When we define our goals, each member will be ready to help.

2. Unnecessary modifiers. Are the *italicized* modifiers really necessary in the following sentence?

   Not: In this world of today, official governmental red tape is *seriously* destroying the *motivation* for *financial* incentive among *relatively* small businesses.
   Instead: Governmental red tape is destroying incentive for small businesses.

3. Deadwood that interferes with natural phrasing. In the following sentence, notice how the verb "is" forces all of the action in the sentence into nouns (like "intention"), and makes the sentence unnecessarily wordy:

   Not: It is our intention to hire a new supervisor.
   Instead: We will hire a new supervisor. (or) We intend to hire a new supervisor.

Avoiding wordiness is especially important in a era when most decision-makers find themselves with too much to read. Each document must compete for its share of attention—and unnecessarily wordy documents lose out.

Avoiding Sexist Language

There was a day not long ago in this country when these sentences seemed perfectly proper:

A lawyer must choose *his* clients carefully.
Every surgeon washes *his* hands before operating.

Some grammar handbooks still allow "his" to stand generically for mankind instead of simply males. Other handbooks (and the author of this text) recommend that you avoid even the appearance of sexist assumptions by conscientiously providing "his or her" in place of "his" or "her" by itself, when the sex of the person is not known.

A lawyer must choose his or her (or, her or his) clients carefully.
Every surgeon washes his or her hands before operating.

Admittedly, the phrase "his or her" can become stylistically awkward when repeated several times in a paragraph. In that case, consider making your subject plural:

> Lawyers must choose their clients carefully.
> Surgeons wash their hands before operating.

Notice that the plural form manages to avoid the sex issue altogether.

SENTENCES WITHIN THE PARAGRAPH

To return briefly to our earlier analogy, words are the building blocks of communication. Sentences, then, are the rows of blocks, well laid out and properly planned. Before reviewing several plans for laying out sentences in your business writing, we should take a stand on a sensitive issue: sentence fragments.

As you may remember from English instruction, a sentence fragment lacks either a subject (Actor) or verb (Action).

> *Fragment:* Fixed mortgages lasting thirty years.
> *Sentence:* Fixed mortgages lasting thirty years have disappeared.

> *Fragment:* Being thoroughly reviewed.
> *Sentence:* His loan application is being thoroughly reviewed.

You may also remember from English instruction that sentence fragments are often treated as the almighty no-no in formal writing. That attitude makes the issue sensitive. On one hand, sentence fragments can be glaring errors; on the other hand, sentence fragments can be powerful expressive devices. Automobile advertisements, for example, use sentence fragments freely:

- The luxury you've earned.
- Plush bucket seats.
- An incredible powerplant.
- Lines to lure da Vinci.
- Yours at last. Enjoy.

Without disputing the appropriateness of sentence fragments in such ads, business writers usually choose to avoid fragments in memos, letters, and reports. In these contexts, sentence fragments can sound either wrong, glib, affected, or churlish. Consider the effect of the underlined fragment in this short paragraph from a report:

> *When the security officer pointed out to the manager that his actions were against store policy, he simply laughed. Showing his degree of respect for the company.*

Especially because most readers of English do not expect sentence fragments in business writing (and so count them as mistakes), writers do well to avoid fragments entirely.

One other sentence construction causes the "reject" light to flash on in readers' minds: the comma splice. This error occurs when two perfectly content English sentences are unceremoniously married or "spliced" together by a comma.

Not: Profits were down in 1982, the Board blamed the recession.
Instead: Profits were down in 1982. The Board blamed the recession.

Comma splices ring such wrong bells that they are rarely if ever found in even the most casual advertising copy.

Business writers who cherish the *strong slot* at the beginning of each sentence have a special reason to dislike the comma splice. The construction takes two strong slots and reduces them to only one.

Stock options seemed risky to Jack.   *Real estate* looked safer.
(strong slot)   (strong slot)

Comma Splice: Stock options seemed risky to Jack, real estate seemed safer.
(strong slot)

Like sentence fragments, comma splices should not appear in your business writing.

Let's turn from such linguistic disasters to positive, practical techniques for developing strong sentences in business writing.

Life would be simple (but boring) if all sentences followed the Actor Action pattern:

The whistle blew. We dressed. The coalcart came. We rode, It stopped. We worked. We stopped. We ate. We talked. We worked. We stopped. The coalcart came. We rode. It stopped. We showered. Then, man, did we break loose at Rosy's Bar and Grill.

Except for the last sentence, these short sentences have little to fault them. They are direct, clear, and orderly, but they are *boring* in the repetition of the Actor Action pattern.

Business writers achieve interesting variety in their writing by mixing sentence patterns. Without involving elaborate grammatical descriptions in our discussion, we can describe five useful sentence patterns.

1. The Actor→Action→Object sentence

Example: The balance sheet showed a significant loss.

2. The -ing or -ed opening with a comma

Example: Rifling through his papers, the salesman found the missing receipt.

3. The -ing beginning without a comma

Example: Joining Ralph meant everything to Sarah.

4. The middle break

   Examples: If she takes vacation in July, I'll have to schedule mine in August.
   Few employees noticed Ms. Adams, but her genius showed as the yacht neared completion.
   Traffic snarled in front of the plant; Mr. Todd had been playing policeman again.

5. The guide word beginning

   Examples: Consequently, Burton took his invention to an engineer.
   Reluctantly, the manager ordered the plant closed.
   By contrast, the two youth groups in Salem won civic awards.

From a long list of such guide words, here are some:

for example	on the other hand
for instance	frequently
by comparison	moreover
in addition	notably
increasingly	hence
often	therefore
however	recently
nevertheless	inevitably
on one hand	unfortunately

These initial words provide guidance to the reader; they function much like traffic signs, telling of conditions that lie ahead in the sentence.

Developing Effective Sentences

Effective sentences begin strong. Readers are eager to know at the beginning of each sentence, "Who did what?" Writers satisfy that interest by providing the subject or a key transition word as soon as possible.

Notice what happens in the following sentence when the subject (underlined) is delayed:

Of course, without knowing the full circumstances or complete terms of agreement between the two parties, my client *cannot. . .*

We as readers feel a growing edginess as the writer piles more and more words up before giving us the subject. How much more satisfying to find the subject early in the sentence:

My client, *of course, cannot act without knowing the full circumstances.*

Transition words can also appear early in the sentence with powerful effect.

Nevertheless, Morton kept his goal solidly before him.
On the contrary, Maxine spoke highly of her.

The advice to "begin strong" must be tempered by stylistic considerations. Sentences that *all* begin with subjects would soon make the writing sound like "Dick and Jane" fare. For occasional variety, begin with an -ed phrase ("rated first among colleges, Harvard . . .") or an -ing phrase ("Bracing for a hard winter, the village . . .")

Strong sentence beginnings should be followed by the central verb in the sentence as quickly as possible. When the verb is delayed, readers begin to squirm. Consider:

> *The vacation so well-deserved by Ms. Kaye but postponed by her Supervisor, Ms. Virginia Ward, for petty reasons finally took place.*

We have an almost insurmountable need as readers to know "Who did what?" Once that information has been given (in other words, once we are oriented to the meaning of the sentence), we will be content with long stretches of related information:

> *Virginia Ward denied Ms. Kaye her well-deserved vacation for petty reasons.*

Finally, effective sentences vary in length. As readers, we like variety in sentence "pulse" or rhythm as well as in content. By mixing short, medium, and long sentences, a skilled business writer keeps us from falling into a humdrum stagnation. By "long sentence," of course, we do not mean a multi-lined monster of the type Victorian essayists wrote. In modern usage, a "long" sentence can extend to three typed lines, but rarely beyond. Short sentences, by contrast, can be as short as one or two words. Sometimes the most potent sentence in a paragraph contains the fewest words. Brevity counts.

Effective Paragraph Development

Too many business writers create paragraphs the way they bake cookies: "Well, that should be long enough." A paragraph is not a measurement of length; paragraphs can properly be as short as a single sentence or, under some conditions, longer than a page. Like the word "stomach," the word "paragraph" names an *internal organization of parts*.

Business writers find three traditional patterns particularly useful. Although the following examples provide only one sentence to illustrate each part within the paragraph, that part can and often should include more than a single sentence.

Exposition Pattern. Sentence 1: sets forth the *topic* or *main idea* of the paragraph. Sentence 2: expands the meaning of the major terms in the topic sentence. Sentence 3: provides an example or illustration of the topic sentence. Sentence 4: answers the question, "So what? So what if the rest of the paragraph is true? What can be said in conclusion?"

The *exposition* plan serves as the standard paragraph model in reports and proposals. Observe how each sentence plays its part in this paragraph from a marketing proposal for a new kitchen utensil.

All nutcrackers now on the market in the U.S., Canada, and Europe require extraordinary grip strength from the user. Traditional nutcrackers, as tested by Underwriters' Laboratory, can demand up to 110 lbs. of hand pressure to crack an average walnut. In testing the West German "Nut Jaws," for example, the laboratory staff cracked 100 walnuts and 100 pecans with an average grip pressure of 105 lbs. per nut. One staff member dislocated a thumb in the effort. Since such grip requirements far surpass the average grip strengths in the general population, the market may be ripe for a gear-ratioed device.

Enumeration Pattern. Often in the course of a memo, letter or report, you may wish to list items, events or circumstances. The following pattern of sentences offers a model.

Sentence 1: presents topic sentence announcing the nature of the list.
Sentence 2: expands or qualifies the key terms occuring in the topic sentence.
Sentences 3-5: First . . . _____
Second . . . _____
Finally . . . _____.
Sentence 6: concludes by answering the question, "so what?"

The Sixth U.S. Circuit Court of Appeals has ruled that a loan agreement violated the Truth in Lending Act because of its "indecipherable" language. The offending sentence:

A deferment charge may be made for deferred payments equal to the portion of the regular finance charge applicable by the sum of the digits method to the installment period immediately following the due date of the first deferred installment times the number of months of deferment.
Detroit Legal News, Nov. 9, 1981

Like the exposition plan, the *enumeration* plan can be useful throughout the broad range of business writing. Observe the role of each enumerative sentence in the following paragraph from a job description.

The position of sales manager requires academic preparation and practical work experience in general retail sales. While a college degree is not mandatory, at least one year of successful sales experience in each of three capacities will be required. First, the candidate must evidence a knowledge of cash and register management. Second, the candidate must have demonstrated in past work experience superior leadership and supervisory abilities. Finally, the candidate must present a record of reliabililty and diligence. After interviews have been concluded, the company will make hiring decisions within seven days.

Inquiry Pattern. A substantial portion of business writing asks rather than answers questions. The *inquiry* plan organizes the sometimes difficult task of asking questions in an orderly and tactful way.

Sentence 1: Here's why I need to ask a question. Sentence 2: Here's my question. Sentence 3: Here are specific aspects of my question. Sentence 4 (so what?): Here's what I can do when you give me your answer.

Observe how the inquiry paragraph develops in this example from a commercial property manager's letter to a client.

(1) We're unable to rent Unit 4 in the Ashbury Warehouse until we determine the status of the previous lease. (2) Did you formally release a Mr. Robert Duncan from his three-year lease on the unit? (3) Specifically, we need to know if you possess written proof of that release, or if Mr. Duncan has signed a forfeiture of any kind. (4) When we receive your response, we can act quickly to either lease the unit again or locate Mr. Duncan for a resolution to the current problem.

Business writers find that clients prefer to know both the reason (sentence 1) and the use (sentence 4) for most inquiries. These crucial sentences have the additional rhetorical value of imposing a sense of urgency on the inquiry: "I need your answer."

At the risk of overworking our building block analogy, we can observe that in paragraphs, as in masonry, connectives and adhesives (mortar, as it were) hold the parts together in a unified way. The most powerful of these adhesives is the force of connected, logical ideas, as developed in the sentence patterns above. Certainly you will develop variations on these basic patterns and invent new frameworks of your own. The key to tight, smooth connections between sentences lies in starting the thought of one sentence where the thought of the previous sentence left off. At no point within a paragraph should the reader be startled by a new and unexpected point of beginning.

The advice to start one sentence where the previous sentence left off cannot be applied to the actual words you use. Under no circumstances should the last word of one sentence be used as the first word of the following sentence.

Not: We received notice that Boston was sending down a *Geiger counter. The Geiger counter* was supposed to help us evaluate the waste dump in the East Yard.

Instead: We received notice that Boston was sending down a *Geiger counter. The device* was supposed to help us evaluate the waste dump in the East Yard.

Be careful not to use the same word over and over within a paragraph. If you have used the word "Geiger counter," for example, switch to "this instrument" or another variant in the next reference to the device.

Questions   Use questions in your business writing with discretion. Readers can be made to feel "set up" at best and foolish at worst when the writer stages what could be called "manikin questions." These have the look of real questions, but are in fact dummies arranged by the writer for purposes of show and effect. Observe the unnecessary and mildly insulting effect of such "manikin questions" in this paragraph from an industrial report.

> *Our purchase of the 904 sheetmetal press has increased output of duct-work and connectors.* But did we know what we were doing? Did we think the matter through? Did we take our time? *No. We will have to run the press for thirty years at full speed to recoup our expenditure for the new equipment.*

The writer of this passage knows the answers to each of these questions before he or she asks it. The reason, then, for casting the matter in question form is manipulative: the writer wants to raise eyebrows and perhaps tempers in an artificial way.

Readers don't enjoy such prods and charades. The technique reminds them too much of children's bedtime stories: "And what did the giant do next? Well, I'll tell you." Faced with unnecessary questions, readers may well mutter, "If you know the answer, just tell me."

Sincere questions, of course, are most appropriate. Notice how the "manikin questions" from the previous example can be rewritten as a sincere question.

> *Our purchase of the 904 sheetmetal press has increased output of duct-work and connectors. In the past three weeks, though, we have tried to answer an important question: Has our investment been justified by increased profits due to the new machine? We have determined that, in present market conditions, we will have to run the press at full speed for thirty years to recoup our investment.*

Sincere questions are distinguished from "manikin questions" in one essential way: writers ask sincere questions also of themselves; they ask "manikin questions" only of their readers.

Checking for Paragraph Unity and Coherence

As we have seen in the foregoing examples, the primary ingredient holding a paragraph together is the glue of logical development. Certain stylistic techniques, however, can assist that process of bonding ideas together.

First, use transitional words generously. If one idea grows out of a preceding idea, tell the reader by using "therefore." If an idea contrasts with an earlier idea, signal the difference with "however," "but," or "by contrast." In similar ways, you can "signpost" the flow of meaning within your paragraphs with words like "nevertheless," "of course," "in short," "consequently," and others listed earlier in this chapter.

Second, trace the relation among key words in your paragraph. Some writers go so far as to underline every subject in a paragraph and then to ask, "how do these subjects lead from one to another?" Notice in the following paragraph how the underlined key words, including several subjects, form a meaningful progression:

> *Funeral homes in America have endured a decade of criticism since the early 1970s. Their elaborate decoration of death, some say, is grotesque and unethical. Critics point to smooth-talking morticians who present their sales pitch (often involving thousands of dollars) just at the time when bereaved relatives are least able to make wise financial choices.*

Third, examine each paragraph to make sure it treats one central idea, not two or three. After announcing a central point, a paragraph may, of course, go on to examine two or three aspects of the matter. But no paragraph should include two distinct, separable ideas. When such combinations appear in your writing, devote a separate paragraph to each.

Summary

Business writers choose voices appropriate to their audience. In general, the proper voice for business documents is the business voice, since the encyclopedia voice is too stiff and the emotional voice is nonrational. Having settled upon a voice, the writer looks to individual words within the document, striving to make them

- specific and concrete.
- active, not passive.
- positive, not negative.
- distinct, not clustered.
- clear, not vague.
- emphatic.
- correct.
- lean.
- unbiased.

Such words create effective sentences which, in turn, find their place in paragraphs ordered by the exposition, enumeration, inquiry, or other pattern. Paragraphs achieve coherence and unity through transitional words, linked key terms, and organization around central ideas.

Questions for Discussion

1. What does business style generally emphasize, and why?
2. What three "voices" are available to you as a business communicator?
3. How do these three voices relate to each other in psychological terms? Which one is the voice you want to strive for?
4. Should Latinate terms be avoided in your text?
5. Is it more important to amplify the content of a word or its volume? Why?
6. How do readers respond to active verbs?
7. In passive constructions, where does the object appear in the sentence? What is the preferable native English pattern?
8. Might dissolving key figures in a sentence cast in the passive voice irritate readers?
9. What is a noun cluster? How can you avoid it?
10. How can you solve the problems created by vague pronoun references?
11. Where are the strong slots of sentences located? How can you make use of them to create impressive business prose?
12. What are the three disguises of wordiness?
13. How can sexist language be avoided?
14. Are sentence fragments or comma splices ever acceptable in business writing? In what cases?
15. What effect do "manikin questions" have on the reader?

Exercises

1. Find a writing sample containing either the encyclopedic or the emotional voice and rewrite it using the business voice.
2. Rewrite the following vague sentences, providing specific information: a) He was tall for his age. b) The company took a big loss last year. c) Henderson quit because he needed more money.
3. Transform the following passive sentences into active voice: a) It was decided by the committee that parking fees should be raised. b) The job was performed well by them. c) The library was staffed by only two librarians this weekend.
4. Substitute positive words for negative ones in the following sentences: a) I absolutely deny any involvement with union activists. b) She refused to work overtime, claiming that she wanted to spend the weekend with her family. c) Don't make the mistake of coming to work without the proper attire again, please.
5. Change vague pronouns to strong slot words in the following sentences: a) This is the most productive time of year for us. b) It must seem like you've gone through a time warp when you visit Williamsburg, Va. c) That she would agree to go out with him on Friday night was all he wanted.

6. Write a paragraph about your preparation for a business communication course, following the exposition patter.
7. Write a paragraph listing your best qualities as a communicator, following the enumeration pattern.
8. Write a paragraph requesting information about a class lecture which you missed, following the inquiry pattern.

Communicating Inside the Company: Memos, Proposals, and Reports

PART TWO

Walter Soville heads up the Telemarketing division of a major insurance company. He supervises

nineteen employees in three locations. Because frequent group meetings are both expensive and imprac-

tical, Walter communicates with his employees primarily by memo.

I send out a weekly memo updating my people on everything they have to know to achieve company goals. Typically my memos contain new client information, suggestions for effective telephone selling, charts of current achievement levels, and so forth. To keep things interesting, I usually throw in the bowling scores from the company teams and notes about developments in the company and industry.

Either my employees can't read or they're lying to me. On several occasions an employee has said to my face, "You didn't tell me that." When I point to my words in the weekly memo, he or she claims not to have received the memo. I've checked my distribution. All employees do receive my memos each week. Can't they read?

Why aren't Walter's memos succeeding as communication devices? What should—and shouldn't—a memo try to do? How can Walter change his memo-writing habits to achieve his management goals?

Writing

Memos 5

LEARNING OBJECTIVES

To recognize the importance of even the simplest in-house documents for effective communication

To exercise judgment in choosing what to commit to written form

To use positive language to produce positive results

To write several memo forms with skill

To use well-organized memos to solve business problems

To incorporate statistical information and key facts into the structure of your memos

Most of you will find, in your business careers, that the great majority of your written and spoken words will be addressed to people inside the company—employees under your supervision, your peers, and your supervisors in upper management.

Late in 1984, four mid-level managers from the communications, insurance, aerospace, and real estate industries agreed to keep a two-month log of the various forms of written communication they personally produced. The study proved surprising.

First, written communications took a much wider variety of forms than any of these managers would have guessed. Here is a partial list from the compiled logs:

Letters of recommendation
Trip reports
Work orders
Congratulatory notes
Sympathy notes
Quarterly reports
Memo reminders
Announcement memos
Staff memos
Invitation notes
Replies to orders and inquiries
Summaries of meetings
Information sheets
Résumés
Proposals for changes in procedures
Task analysis memo
Cover letters
Job position descriptions
Job applications
Mailgrams, telegrams, cablegrams
Letters of authorization for
    subcontracts

Sales and promotional letters
Rough draft of contract prior to
    revision by legal staff
Adjustment and claims letters
Personnel evaluations
Statement of objectives, goals,
    targets
Press releases
Written suggestions for budget
    planning

Besides their surprise at the sheer variety of writing tasks they performed, these managers expressed surprise that at least 80 percent of the written words they produced in the two-month period were for an audience inside the company. The manager of a regional telephone headquarters put it this way:

The communication seminars and classes I've attended prepared me to write business letters to clients. But now I discover that most of my writing is to fellow employees and my bosses here within the telephone company. Are there special techniques for this kind of writing? I have a feeling my career may be influenced by my skills, or lack of them, in this area.

There are techniques for effective in-house communication—but they are universal writing principles, not special tricks.

IN-HOUSE COMMUNICATION PRINCIPLES

Give In-House Writing Your Best Effort

No business writer should allow sloppy writing to leave his or her desk with the excuse that it's just for in-house consumption. An immensely successful executive with an East Coast computer firm privately calls his in-house memos his "promotion tickets":

> *I've had corporate officers look up when my name is mentioned at a business meeting. They know me not by my face, but by my memos. I've tried over the years to write good memos, emphasizing the progress we're making as a company. The executives I mentioned appreciate hearing from me; they use the good news I send in their own conversations and planning.*

Every word leaving your pen helps to create your business identity within the company. If your prose is abrupt, haphazard, inaccurate, or verbose, your associates can't help but call your professional abilities into question. On the other hand, your conscientious effort to write stimulating, persuasive, and skillful memos, letters, proposals, and reports reflects positively upon your capabilities. While each of your memos may not literally prove to be a "promotion ticket," the sum total of your written work can drastically hurry or halt career advancement. Dr. William F. Bauhaus, chief executive officer at Beckman Instruments, has seen it happen again and again :

> *Executives must be able to convince not only their superiors but also their colleagues and subordinates that their programs make sense and are understandable. It takes precise communication to convince. It takes convincing to get proper action. Pure ability without the capacity to communicate and to convince is oftentimes wasted ability.*

Exercise Judgment in In-House Communications

When committing personal opinion and sensitive records to words, use discretion and tact. The ability to use words, like the ability to balance on flagpoles, can bring disaster as well as fame and fortune. As a business communicator, you may want to join the thousands of business leaders who practice the "next week rule." Every memo, letter, proposal, and report is evaluated against a wise criterion: will I want to see these words above my signature next week—after the waves of anger, excitement, rush, and personal feeling have passed?

Here are specific occasions when the "next week" rule spared unnecessary hard feelings and contributed to effective leadership.

Situation	Initial Reaction	Next Week Rule
Tracy Clete, a new programmer, stretches her lunch hour each day. Her supervisor has mentioned the problem to her, without result.	You feel like writing a direct, no-nonsense memo to Tracy, with a copy to her personnel file. You want to tell her to obey the rules or face firing.	You decide to send a general reminder to all staff in Tracy's unit regarding the lunch hour regulations. On Tracy's copy you handwrite, "Please see me if there are circumstances I should know about."
Bret Thomas, a real card, continues to tell offensive jokes about minorities at work.	You feel like writing a scorching memo to Thomas regarding his insensitivity and prejudice.	You send a copy of the company's Affirmative Action and Professional Dignity manual to Thomas. You ask him to read the manual, then speak to you privately.

The "next week" rule does not force you to play Mort or Mildred Milquetoast. Instead, your discretion and judgment in the use of words marks you as a responsible, farsighted leader. You recognize that not every business situation needs to be or should be recorded in words. Managers who use language with abandon, without regard for the pain and "waves" a simple memo can create, run the risk of the boy who cried "Wolf!" once too often.

You will make your own judgments regarding what matters and opinions should be committed to writing. In preparation, decide how you would handle each of these sensitive issues:

- Seven reams of paper have simply disappeared from the office supply room (to which six employees have regular access).
- One of your key supervisors, Nancy Lincoln, has talked to you about her continuing mental health problem. She is under a psychiatrist's care, but her duties must be lightened without angering the other supervisors.
- As City Building Inspector, you come in contact with many developers, a few quite unscrupulous. Developer Davon Trebley took you aside at his Seagate Resort project to hint at—not actually offer—a bribe: "One of these condos could be yours. I'm not talking about money changing hands. What could change, of course, is the City's insistence on copper plumbing here at Seagate."

As you consider your options in each of these sensitive situations, you recognize the potential power of words. At times, words can say too much; at other times, words must be set down, if only for the file, to protect yourself from later accusations.

Use Positive Language to Produce Positive Results

The meaning of your written words depends upon more than their dictionary meanings (or "denotations"). Words also carry feelings or "connotations" to your reader. The art of business writing in large part consists of orchestrating both denotative and connotative meanings to suit your purpose.

Unintended connotations can often subvert the intended meaning of your message. Notice how negative connotations distort the following message.

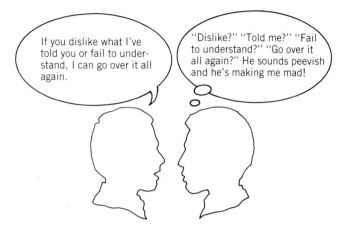

If you dislike what I've told you or fail to understand, I can go over it all again.

"Dislike?" "Told me?" "Fail to understand?" "Go over it all again?" He sounds peevish and he's making me mad!

Unfortunate connotations occur in two principal ways. First, the writer's tone can be unnecessarily pushy, abrupt, or inappropriately personal.

Abrupt: Don't reorder item #2076.
Too Personal: You probably oppose my plan because of your son's unfortunate experience.

Second, the negative slant of individual words can give a negative cast to an entire document. Notice the crucial difference between these negative and positive statements:

Negative		*Positive*	
	You failed to notice		May I point out that
	You neglected to mention		We also can consider
	You overlooked the fact		One additional fact is
	You missed the point		From another perspective
	If you persist in		If you choose to
	I see no alternative but		Our clear plan of action

Negative language usually addresses what the reader did wrong (failed, neglected, overlooked, or missed). Positive language emphasizes what the reader can do right or what you and the reader together can do. Certainly, no one likes to be reminded of failure or threatened with negative consequences. Your readers are motivated and persuaded by encouragement, not accusation and discouragement.

Identify Standard Procedures for In-House Writing in Your Business

Each company develops over time a set of standard operating procedures for most in-house communication. Take the case of the memo.

Stationery and Envelopes. Many companies prefer their employees to use company memo stationery. Typically, this office stock is labeled *Memo* or

Memorandum in large letters at the top of the sheet. The cues To:, From:, Date:, and Subject: usually appear along the left margin. Quite often other cues and warnings may be found at the top or bottom of the page: "For your eyes only," "Keep it brief," and "File a copy."

Memo paper itself usually costs the company substantially less than the fancy rag bond paper used for business letters. New employees should think twice, therefore, before passing over poorer quality memo paper for rag bond in an effort to make a first memo look impressive. The result is too often an unexpected backfire: a company executive may hold the fancy bond memo at arm's length, muttering "who's spending the company's money putting out memos on our good stationery?" Are we suggesting that upper level managers care about such trivial matters as the company's stationery bill? You bet your career they do.

Most memo stationery is white. Some companies, however, have adopted a useful color code for in-house messaging: a blue memo, for example, has to do with accounts payable; a red for accounts receivable; a yellow for inventory; and white for all other matters (personnel, policy, and so forth). While such a scheme may seem troublesome at first, it can provide "at-a-glance" readability for the busy manager.

If your company has an established system for routing memos (such as reusable mailers), follow the system. New employees, in a well-intentioned effort to make their business communications distinctive, may send the memo in an expensive company envelope. This practice backfires not only because it strikes the executive as wasted expense, but also because it leads to a moment of anticlimax. The executive may receive high level information (promotions, policy shifts, new product decisions) in such envelopes. When your less crucial memo arrives in the same medium, the disappointed executive thinks, "Oh, it's just . . ." This mood can color his or her reaction to your message itself.

Routing. Use judgment in routing memos throughout the chain of command. Often just the right memo for your fellow employees may prove to be just the wrong memo if circulated to other groups within the company.

Consider the following fiasco that grew out of a new employee's good intentions.

Barbara Smathers felt proud that her first real assignment at Welcom Insurance had turned out so well. Ms. Olney, her supervisor in Underwriting, had asked Barbara to review claims arising out of the use of mopeds by the company's insured. Specifically, Ms. Olney needed a reading, "on how well my idea of free moped insurance with any auto policy has worked out."

After two weeks of investigation and statistical analysis, Barbara wrote a fine memo report showing conclusively that moped liability cut drastically into company profits from auto policies. She routed her report to Roleen Travis, Vice-President of Internal Operations, Harlan McCoy,

Director of Legal Services, Burton Tschev, Director of Auto Insurance Division, Priscilla Troy, Head of Underwriting, and Olivia Olney, Supervisor of Automobile Underwriting.

The memo report was sent out in the company mail on Friday afternoon. Barbara expected to arrive at work Monday morning to backslaps of praise from company executives. She was dumbfounded on Monday morning to confront a furious Ms. Olney. "Look, Barbara," her supervisor seethed, "never embarrass me before my bosses like that again."

Barbara learned in a painful way that communication can make and break careers. Ms. Olney, after all, was the person who had recommended free moped insurance along with auto policies. To learn that her idea had cost the company money was one thing; but to have her mistake broadcast up and down the executive ranks was quite another matter. "I wanted to handle this smoothly for my own sake and that of the Auto Division," Ms. Olney explained later.

While it is true that solid writing skills can get you noticed in business, use judgment in routing communication beyond your immediate supervisor. Before distributing your work to a broad audience in the company, take the time and the courtesy to seek your supervisor's advice.

Filing Considerations. Recognize that your business communication will probably become part of a file, a long-term reservoir of business matters (and a lasting record of your abilities). Avoid, therefore heat-of-the-moment surliness and satiric comments in your communications. While a sarcastic jibe— "Jack Wilford amazed us all by making a sale"—might cause office titters, the remark will seem increasingly inappropriate with time. A file full of such indiscretions can work against your career.

It is also wise to provide a brief framework of background knowledge necessary to place the memo or report in some context at a later date. A memo dated Feb. 3, 1983, to the effect that "we have Air Force approval" can have little meaning months later when an auditor tries to establish which of twenty-seven Air Force contracts you signed on that date. Take time to spell out the essential details necessary to make sense out of the central message.

Initialing. It is customary to sign your name or initials alongside your typed name on a memo. This notation signifies that you have read over and approved the typed copy of your communication. In this way, you are waiving any right to claim later, "but that's not what I said."

Presentation Considerations. While memos routinely are sent through company mail or hand carried to appropriate offices, you may want to evaluate alternate presentation strategies when delivering longer, more substantial communications. Consider the comments of Frank Francisca, vice-president of planning at Martel Development, regarding two reports he received.

Before a meeting at the bank, I had five minutes free to shuffle through two or three days' worth of company mail in my in-basket. There, among the usual clutter, was Ed Beal's report on utility costs at our Twin Lakes subdivision. I had been waiting for that report for days. Why didn't he let me know he was sending it?

Kathy Blake made a brief appointment for 10:30 A.M. She was right on time, handed me her report on condo conversions, and told me where she would be if I had questions. As it turned out, we chatted about her findings, and she was able to give me a good understanding of the report before I began reading. Ms. Blake left me with a good impression of herself and her work.

Whenever possible, treat important work you have done with special presentation strategies.

SEND THE WHOLE MESSAGE

Business communications, like many layer cakes, have at least four levels:

Past meaning—what has happened?
Present meaning—what is happening?
Future meaning—what will happen?
Emotion—how do I feel?

When business communication focuses too narrowly on any one aspect of the total message, the writer's intent can go astray.

Notice, in the following example, how a series of incomplete messages proves ineffective, and how, at last, a complete message brings productive action.

The Situation: Operations Manager Rita Collins has to deal with a breakdown of discipline in Unit 6. Employees there have regularly been leaving work well before quitting time. She writes a memo to Unit 6 supervisor, Terry Carston.

Aug. 1 Ms. Collins to Supervisor Carston

```
I just received a summary of your unit's time cards for the
past six months.  Your people regularly left work fifteen to
twenty minutes early.
```

Supervisor Carston's reaction to this memo was light-hearted. He quipped to his workers, "Well, our time cards didn't win us any awards for the past six months, gang."

Notice that Ms. Collins concentrates solely on *past* events, which are easily dismissed by her readers as ancient history.

Aug. 8 Ms. Collins to Supervisor Carston

```
I stood by the door today from 4 P.M. to 5 P.M. More than
half of your employees left work early.
```

Carston again treated the matter casually when he spoke to his employees: "Some of you kind of blew it on August 8."

Notice that Ms. Collins concentrates solely upon *present* events. Her readers can discount the importance of the message because it seems to deal with only a one-time, local occurrence.

Aug. 15 Ms. Collins to Supervisor Carston

```
We're going to have to develop some new procedures for
strict enforcement of working hours.
```

Supervisor Carston interprets this message to his workers in a facetious way: "Ms. Collins is thinking about developing some new rules. Isn't that swell?"

Notice that Ms. Collins emphasizes only *future* implications in her message. Like all projections, these can be put out of mind by readers as one more "I'll-believe-it-when-I-see-it" experience.

Aug. 20 Ms. Collins to Supervisor Carston

```
I'm extremely upset at you and your entire crew.  What makes
you think you can flout the rules around here?
```

Carston is dumbfounded. He confides in his workers that "for some reason, Ms. Collins is really on our case. I don't know why."

Notice that Ms. Collins focuses solely on the *emotional* content of her message. Such an outburst can cause readers to wince, but not to respond in productive, directed ways.

Aug. 29 Ms. Collins to Supervisor Carston

Past
Present

Future
Emotion

```
Since January, more than half of your employees have been
leaving work early. I noticed in spot checks this week that
the problem continues. From now on, I insist that your
people follow personnel procedures to the letter regarding
quitting time. This on-going problem deeply concerns me;
let's end it now.
```

In this statement, Ms. Collins finally achieves her whole message. She leaves her readers no loopholes. Whole communication need not, of course,

Brevity matters more and more in business documents. Paul Dillingham, vice-president of Coca-Cola, comments:

I can recall a chief executive officer who expected that any memo to him be no more than two pages and preferably one. In unusual situations where longer memos and reports are essential, I find it useful to prepare a one-page Executive Summary and attach it to the longer report, which may be referred to if the reader's time and interest permit.

always contain elements of past, present, future, and emotion. These divisions serve only to remind us to search for the full content of our messages before we commit them to writing.

One way to check the completeness of your message is to step into your reader's shoes for a moment. Ask these questions of your message:

- What can be misinterpreted?
- What options does the message allow me?
- What response does the message seem to ask for? Has the writer asked for that response in a specific way?

Whole communication reduces the "ifs, ands, and buts" on the part of the reader. As a business writer, you want to leave no room for procrastination; you're interested in action.

Emotion in business communication as in life generally has an important role in motivating action. Your deep feelings about an idea or project can be contagious, as in this closing sentence from a real estate sales letter: "We are proud to offer houses that simply require *you* in order to become homes."

On the other hand, your irritation and even outright anger, used appropriately, can stir up a stagnant situation: "We placed our order four months ago. We waited patiently, and now are waiting impatiently. Ship the order today, or consider it canceled."

Even your emotional ambivalence can be used to awaken caution in your readers: "Certainly the planners are right that historic old Henderson pier has the visibility and accessibility necessary for a restaurant site. I have my misgivings, though, about the public's response to this alteration of the old landmark. I recommend further study."

A frank statement of your emotions—never a gush or a whine—announces your priorities loud and clear. Business writers who indicate their emotional commitments rarely hear a reader respond, "I didn't know it meant that much to you." Readers may choose not to follow your emotional lead, but they cannot claim you failed to take a stand.

To summarize briefly, five writing principles can stand you in good stead for the challenges posed by in-house writing tasks.

- Give your best effort
- Exercise judgment
- Use positive language
- Identify standard procedures
- Send whole messages

We can now turn to specific forms of in-house writing and to the techniques that build success in these forms.

THE MEMORANDUM

In its original business use in the eighteenth century, a memo was little more than a stray slip of paper bearing a name, fact, or figure. An eighteenth century businessman's pockets might be filled, in fact, with old hat checks, coins, and memos.

With time, this class of jottings took on more importance in business practice. Short in-house messages of any kind came to be referred to as *memos*. Some contained quite significant information: matters of company policy, communications regarding personnel, summaries of transactions, announcements of meetings, and so forth.

Today the memo, from its humble beginnings, enjoys distinction as the most popular and most used form of in-house business writing. Its humble reputation, ironically, has contributed to its popularity and usefulness. Many business writers find a memo easy to write because the form itself is not difficult or threatening; the writer's fear of failure is not aroused. (The organization and writing of a report, by contrast, threatens many writers. The report seems to require so much more attention to form and conventions.) But the memo seems (and even sounds) friendly—a handy bag ready and willing to hold anything the writer chooses.

The Short Memo

Once the business writer has filled out the heading of the memo—To, From, Date, Subject—he or she has only to state a message clearly. The message need not be centered on the page. It may be single- or double-spaced. What business writer could help but like such a tractable form?

But alas, the angel Freedom casts the shadow License. Many business writers manage to ruin memos through casual, unthinking mistakes. Their errors fall into four categories. Make sure you avoid each in your own writing.

The Teletype Writer. Writers who otherwise function smoothly in ordinary speaking sometimes exhibit an odd communication disorder when they write memos. Perhaps in an effort to sound professional, they leave out major portions of sentences—often the subject itself:

```
To: Sandra Phillips

From: Natalie Forbes

Date: April 22, 198_____

Subject: National Association of Realtors convention

Attended the seminar on exchanges.  Discussed ways to trade
our New Haven building for an industrial site.  Met Jerry
Hausing of Dynaflite Corp. Mentioned being interested in
such a trade.  Eager to talk more about this.
```

Consider what this teletyped form of writing does and does not communicate. Who attended? Who discussed? Most crucially, who showed interest in the trade—Hausing or Forbes? Who is eager to talk more? Business life may be hurried, but using teletype language in memos only complicates and therefore slows the progress of the business day.

The Scrawler. Because memos are often branded with the word "just"—it's "just a memo"—some writers relax into grievous spelling, grammar, style mistakes, and even illegible handwriting.

```
To: Harvey
From:
Date: Wednes-
Subject:
        Prelim. designs will be ready
        for next yrs. modles by
        next Tues. or so.
                        GO
```

Such informal language may be easy to write, but it destroys the credibility of the message and the writer. Readers assume that glaring little mistakes (desines for designs, modles for models) portend underlying big mistakes in judgment and, possibly, limited intelligence.

Because such handwritten scrawls too often prove illegible, because they often cannot be photocopied clearly, and because they are difficult to file, handwritten memos are less and less common in modern business practice.

The Windbag. We use the abbreviated term *memo* instead of the full word *memorandum* because time matters in business. Let the short form of the word remind you that the message, too, needs to be brief and to the point.

Consider this first paragraph from an eight-paragraph memo written by a confirmed windbag:

> I'm writing this memo upon my return from St. Louis
> where, as you know, I represented the company in my role as
> Midwest sales supervisor at a trade show aptly named "Farm
> Expo '86." I saw many new techniques and products
> demonstrated at the trade show, all of which I plan to
> summarize at an upcoming seminar which I will conduct for
> interested parties within the company.

At Ford Aerospace, Vice-President Louis Heilig gives this advice to his people:

Write down on one sheet the objectives and criteria for the project you wish to carry forward. Make it so straightforward that it is essentially impossible to misunderstand.

Now the business of this memo was supposed to be simple. The writer needed to communicate promptly the message that the printed brochures gleaned from the trade fair were available in his office. Instead, he uses the memo to bore his readers and stall business by too many words.

The Tease. Some memo writers consciously or unconsciously irritate their readers by hinting at information they should reveal in full:

> Regarding that matter at lunch, I want to give you the green light, provided you clear it with the appropriate people.

Writers who hint at unstated but necessary information in this way are trying to sound intimate with their readers. They have the mistaken notion that the sensation of shared secrets makes memos work.

Memos are not treasure maps. Never try to build a sense of suspense or intimacy at the expense of your message. First, let the message be clear. Then add whatever social or personal remarks you wish to add warmth and intimacy. Figure 5-1 is an example of an effectively written short memo.

The Longer Memo

In the last ten years, managers who hate to write (about 90 percent, according to surveys) have grudgingly preferred to write a four-page long memo instead of a four-page short report. Not surprisingly, they relax when they think of the thousand-word document as just a memo. The memo form brings back none of the school traumas and writer's blocks associated with reports. As a result, companies find it twice as cost effective to require memos instead of reports from their managers.

In form, the long memo resembles the standard short memo with few exceptions. The *Subject* statement may be somewhat longer, to encompass the extended range of material treated. The *To* statement may contain a routing list of several names, if the long memo has extensive circulation within the company. Because the long memo must burden the reader with many more words and ideas than the short memo, the longer form relies upon four techniques to create clarity and conciseness.

Provide Early Orientation. The first sentences of the first paragraph of the longer memo should provide orientation for the reader: what is the subject of the memo? What does the writer propose to do with the subject?

Unfortunately, the first paragraph of extended business documents has traditionally been called the *introduction*. Writers have never been quite sure what to do in an introduction—to introduce, of course, but what does that mean?

Because of this uncertainty, some writers now prefer to think of their first paragraphs as an *overview* rather than an introduction. In an overview, the writer takes a broad look at the past and present status of the topic at hand. Then he or she suggests where the memo is headed, what work it proposes to do—in short, its statement of purpose:

FIGURE 5-1

Short Memo

Memo

To: Brad Taylor
    Design Specialist

From: Katherine Fremont KF
         Vice-President

Date: March 1, 198_

Subject: City approval of solar panels on Burke project

I received a letter dated Feb. 26, 198_, from City Planner Richard
Ortiz. He wants us to present exterior elevations showing all
proposed solar panels on the Burke project.

Let's meet in my office at 2 P.M., Wednesday, March 3, to prepare
this aspect of our presentation to the City.

Background

Purpose

Since 1978, Cosmos Fabric Mills has sought a reliable supply
of long—staple cotton at mid—market prices for its
operation. Five times since then, our purported suppliers
have failed to meet their contracted obligations, often at
the height of our production season. This analysis of the
problem will address two key issues: How can we find a
reliable supplier for the near term? How can we acquire a
wholly owned subsidiary producing long—staple cotton for the
long term?

Notice that an overview includes only the background necessary to give
context to the statement of purpose. In a more extended overview, the writer
may also choose to describe how he or she plans to handle the material under
discussion. Each of the following statements describes methods (the *how*) of
explanation and analysis:

By reviewing the root causes of supplier failures, I will point out . . .
Through computer analysis of the wholesale market suppliers of long-
staple cotton, I can demonstrate . . .
We will examine the relationships our three most successful competitors
maintain with their long-staple cotton suppliers. From these relationships,
we can learn . . .

Maintain a Plan of Development. Once you have oriented your reader in the
overview, set forth the first step of a developmental plan from which you do
not wander.

Topic Headings   One of the best ways to ensure that your reader sees your intended plan of development is to mark it clearly through the use of topic headings. These short statements of purpose appear in capitalized or underlined form along the left-hand margin or centered in mid-page throughout the long memo.

By convention, a first degree heading—marking the largest block of content material within the memo—usually appears centered in capital letters;

BACKGROUND: COTTON SUPPLIERS

Within that large block of content, subcategories can be marked by second and third degree headings, placed respectively in underlined form along the left-hand margin and in centered position.

<u>Arizona Long-Staple Gins</u> (second degree heading)

<u>Southwestern Arizona Gins</u> (third degree heading)

Fourth degree headings are also underlined, but are placed five spaces (standard indentation) from the left margin.

<u>Yuma County</u>   Three gins process most of the cotton . . .

Topic headings, taken together, form a clear outline for both writer and reader. Consider the first, second, third, and fourth degree headings in our longer memo (Figure 5-2).

You have probably noticed what careful headings produce: a clear outline of your material. Earlier, outlining was discussed as a useful pre-writing technique. When converted to headings, the outline becomes useful also as an aid to readers.

Readers love topic headings because these labels do so much of the task of meaning-making in a long memo. Like names on a map, topic headings tell readers precisely where they have been and where they are headed.

College business writers particularly need to be coaxed and coached to use topic headings freely in business writing. Perhaps because headings are not common in English essays, college writers find these convenient shortcuts a bit awkward at first. The reason for their hesitance may also lie, of course, in the very nature of the topic heading: it forces the writer to decide what subjects in what order will fill the memo. If the topic headings eventually prove valuable to the reader, that value is earned by the writer's hard thinking and planning.

Patterns of Thought   Long memos can develop by any of the patterns treated in Chapters 3 and 5. Without unnecessarily repeating those patterns here, we can generalize that most long memos say (in effect):

1. Here's the problem or the issue (the current situation).
2. Here's what we've tried to do about it (the past situation).
3. Here's what we should do about it (the future situation).

FIGURE 5-2

Headings in the Longer Memo

BACKGROUND: COTTON SUPPLIERS

Arizona Long-staple Gins

Phoenix Cotton Cooperative

History
Scale of Operation
Recent Accounts

Yuma Agricultural Associates

History
Scale of Operation
Recent Accounts

OUR NEEDS

Price

Allowable Fluctuations

High Season
Low Season

Quality

Minimum Standards

Tensile Strength
Fiber Length

Volume

Supply Requirements

High Season
Low Season

FUTURE PROJECTIONS

Short Term

Reliable Suppliers

Utah Cotton Growers Association

Long Term

Proposed Acquisition: Phoenix Cotton Cooperative

While not universally applicable to all topics, this pattern often provides a useful model when time is short and complications are many. In topic headings, the pattern could be represented in this way:

DEFINITION OF THE PROBLEM
PAST EFFORTS TO RESOLVE THE PROBLEM
RECOMMENDED FUTURE ACTION

As business writers, we should remember that our readers need all the help they can get to understand our messages. That help, however, comes from a clear plan of development in the memo, not from boring repetition.

Set Off Statistical Information and Key Facts. Like a Las Vegas casino paywindow, writers throw different denominations of information—names, ideas, dates, and figures—into the reader's lap, hoping that the jumble can be quickly sorted into meaning. But as we have all experienced, sometimes the jumble remains a jumble. Writers can prevent this confusion by providing something akin to a cash register drawer along with the flow of words and figures (Figure 5-3). In other words, writers can physically arrange the page (in the way a cash drawer is physically divided) so that categories and sub-categories are visually pre-set, ready to be filled with meanings by the reader. Visually, the writer has created a place—a distinct division—in which the reader can store like items.

Statistics are most often placed along a deep left-hand margin, triple spaced from surrounding words. Use a third or fourth degree heading, or a caption, to identify the intent or subject matter of a chart, graph, or statistical breakout. This identifying label can prove vital to understanding. Nothing perplexes the reader so thoroughly as an array of statistics apparently unrelated to the prose of the memo.

Provide Clear Transitions To make sure that the intent of your statistical example is clear, include a transitional sentence (exemplified in Figure 5-4) to smoothly take your reader out of word meanings and into chart- and figure-meanings.

Similarly, key facts and questions can be set along a deep margin, again prefaced by a transitional explanatory statement. Each key item can be marked by a dash, asterisk, number, or letter.

Use White Space Effectively Notice how the deep margination creates impact for these key assertions. Visually, such margination and spacing suggest to the reader that we are "getting to the heart" of the matter. Make a conscious effort to use the "heart" of your page as a target zone, planting crucial information there to catch the reader's attention in a powerful way.

Conclude with a Please Act on Timely Specifics (PATS) Statement. In a clear way, spell out precisely what you want done and when you want it done. The word "Please" in the formula reminds you to maintain a polite tone.

FIGURE 5-3

**Long Memo Page
Arrangement**

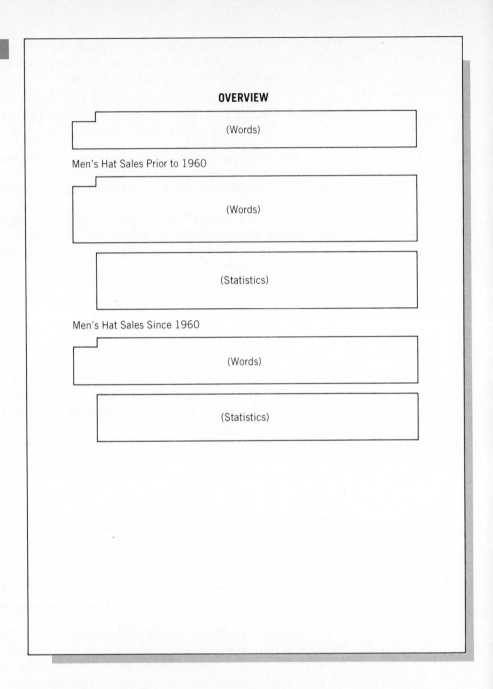

OVERVIEW

(Words)

Men's Hat Sales Prior to 1960

(Words)

(Statistics)

Men's Hat Sales Since 1960

(Words)

(Statistics)

Not: I assume we'll be seeing you at the meeting.

Instead, PATS: Please call me on extension 2705 between 9 and 11 A.M., Friday, Sept. 25, to reserve your place at this important meeting.

Some beginning business writers shy away from such forthright PATS statements for fear of sounding pushy. Readers, however, want writers to take a

FIGURE 5-4

**Transitional Sentence
in the Long Memo.**

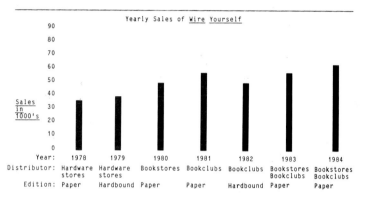

Memorandum

To: David Thompson
From: Nancy Ortiz NO
Date: Nov. 13, 198_
Subject: Kamtron Home Improvement Manuals

At the Board meeting of Oct. 5, 198_, you asked me to
examine this company's success in our line of home
improvement manuals.

BACKGROUND
In 1971, Kamtron Communications Group published Wire
Yourself, a 90-page booklet ($1.95 retail) that sold 95,000
copies in its first two years of publication.

Factors for Success
We can learn from the publication and sales of that initial
effort. Notice in the following chart that sales rose
according to distributor, not according to amounts spent on
revised and enhanced editions of the booklet.

Yearly Sales of Wire Yourself

Year:	1978	1979	1980	1981	1982	1983	1984
Distributor:	Hardware stores	Hardware stores	Bookstores	Bookclubs	Bookclubs	Bookstores Bookclubs	Bookstores Bookclubs
Edition:	Paper	Hardbound	Paper	Paper	Hardbound	Paper	Paper

Sales in 1000's

The charts contained in Appendix A lead to inescapable
conclusions:

-Kamtron's expensive efforts to produce a better looking
 book have not produced a better selling book.

-Sales of Wire Yourself have done worst where Kamtron
 has spent the most advertising dollars (retail hardware
 stores) and have done best where Kamtron has spent
 virtually no advertising money (bookstores and book clubs).

stand, to pose clear choices, to point out paths. Readers may not always
choose your path, but often they will if the path is made clear to them.

Specialized Forms of the Memo

The Letter Memo. Many in-house business situations call for a document with
all the business clarity of a memo, yet also with some of the style, grace, and

FIGURE 5-5

Letter Memo

To: Sheila Graham, Unit #4 Ass't. Controller

From: Ralph Crane, Supervisor

Date: May 9, 198_

Subject: Your Community Involvement

Dear Ms. Graham,

Though we have not met personally since you joined the company last year, I feel I've come to know you from your outstanding reputation as a community leader.

I refer specifically to the Handicrafts by the Handicapped fair you so successfully brought into existence last month, with some financial assistance from the company. Of course, Georgia Utilities is pleased to see its name attached to such a worthwhile endeavor. But beyond company interests, let me personally commend you on the practical way you have chosen to care about others. I received news clippings about the fair from your local newspaper. Your community apparently shares my enthusiasm for your work.

Count on my support when you renew your grant application with the company for next year's fair.

As you may have heard, I'll visit your unit on May 22 for a performance review, and I hope you can arrange to meet for lunch on that day. If so, please drop a note to me or call (296-3121) prior to my departure on May 20.

I look forward to hearing more about your worthwhile work.

Cordially,

Ralph Crane

Ralph Crane

FIGURE 5-6

Memo to File

Memo to File

From: Ralph Torson
        Personnel Director

Date: May 12, 198_

Subject: Selection Committee meeting, May 12, 198_

On the above date, the Selection Committee met to recommend
a replacement for Lillian Todd, recently retired Supervisor
of Word Processing.

Elizabeth Garcia, a Selection Committee member, asked and
received the permission of the committee not to participate
in the recommendation process. She explained that her
brother, Frank Garcia, was an applicant under consideration.

The Committee, after thorough consideration of all
applicants, unanimously recommended Frank Garcia for the
position. This memo will serve to record the fact that Mr.
Garcia was reviewed solely on his own merits, and that
Elizabeth Garcia in no way influenced or attempted to
influence the committee in his favor.

personal warmth of a business letter. Here the letter memo is invaluable, as more business writers discover each year.

Consider the case of Georgia Utilities supervisor Ralph Crane. In all, he supervises 167 employees located in 28 offices throughout the state. One of his people, Sheila Graham, distinguished herself and the company by sponsoring a local Handicrafts by the Handicapped fair.

Supervisor Crane considers his options. Usually he sends regular memos for in-house communication. But this communication will be mailed halfway across the state to an employee he has not personally met. Though a memo seems inappropriate, he hesitates to simply send her a business letter—it may make her feel like an outsider, no matter how friendly the tone.

Crane chooses the *letter memo* (Figure 5-5). Notice that this form allows him to create a document with all the "feel" of an in-house communication, yet with the additional warmth and style created by a salutation ("Dear Ms. Graham"), complimentary close ("With all best wishes"), and personal signature (instead of initials).

The Memo to File. Sometimes the most awkward memo to write—and the greatest temptation to slipshod writing—is the simple memo to file (Figure 5-6). Addressed to no one specific and yet to everyone in general who happens upon the file, the memo to file matters as much as any other business communication. Its audience may range from an auditor to the chairman of the board. Therefore, choose your words with care. Be specific about names, places, dates, events, order numbers, and so forth.

Since the file cannot shoot back questions—"What do you mean here? Was the convention in Chicago or Detroit?"—be thorough, even to the point of stating what seems obvious at the moment of composition.

Figure 5-6 presents one standard memo-to-file form used throughout the business world. Note that it cues the writer to record necessary information.

Summary

1. Most business writing is in-house writing.
2. Not everything that can be said *should* be said in written form.
3. Positive language can achieve positive results in written communications.
4. It is important to learn standard procedures for in-house communications within your company.
5. Effective in-house communications convey the whole message, not a partial message.
6. Style and form are as important in brief in-house communications as they are in longer documents sent out of the company.
7. Early orientation to your message and the use of topic heads are particularly important in longer memos.
8. The letter memo combines the directness of the memo form with the formality of a letter.
9. The memo to file serves the function of creating a written record of business events.

Questions for Discussion

1. To what kind of audience are the majority of business documents addressed?
2. What would you say to a colleague who writes sloppy memos because they're "just for in-house consumption"?
3. What is the "next week rule" and how can it help you to exercise discretion and tact when writing memos?
4. Discuss the importance of using positive language to produce positive results.
5. Why is it important to exercise judgment in routing communications within your company?
6. What are some points to keep in mind when writing memos which will become part of a permanent file?
7. If you feel you have written a strong business document, should you bother with special presentation strategies for delivering it, or should you simply let the quality of the writing speak for itself?
8. Will anticipating your reader's reaction to your message help you to create a complete message? Explain.
9. Define "memo." Why do business writers in general find the memo the easiest business document to write?
10. Discuss the shortcomings of "the teletype writer." What effect is this writer trying to achieve? What kind of impression does he or she make?

11. What erroneous assumptions about memo writing does "the Scrawler" make? How does the reader react to "the Scrawler"?
12. Who is "the Windbag"? What opportunity does memo writing present to this type of writer?
13. What fundamental tenet of good business writing does "the Tease" violate?
14. In what ways does the long memo differ from the short memo? What techniques for creating clarity and conciseness become especially relevant for writers of long memos? Why?
15. When might you choose to write a letter-memo rather than a regular memo for an in-house communication? Will audience considerations influence your choice?

Exercises

1. At some time each of us has been angered by a faulty product or service. Write a letter of complaint and say exactly what you wanted to say to that greasy mechanic who overcharged you for installing that faulty radiator, for instance. Be sure to ask for a specific remedy to the bad situation. Remember, you're mad as hell, and you're not going to take it anymore!
2. Now write the letter you composed for exercise one, applying the "next week rule." Compare the two versions. Which version do you think would be most effective in getting the remedy you want, and why?
3. Write a letter turning down an invitation to speak at a Young Achievers luncheon, but try your best to transform what should be a neutral message into a negative one. Use the appropriate negative words to refuse (there's a good example of a negative word!) the invitation and to make your reader regret that you were even asked in the first place.
4. Now write the letter you composed for exercise three, but make it a positive "no." What are the advantages of creating a positive attitude?
5. Wait, don't throw that junk mail away. Cull through the typical batch of wasted paper that you find stuffed in your mailbox each week, and rank three to five samples in order from least to most effective. You might consider an effective letter as one whose physical appearance catches your eye and at least invites you to read before discarding. A less effective letter might really look like junk—thin paper, poor printing, etc. Record your reactions to these various letters.
6. Find an example of "teletype writing" or, if you can't, transform a lucid piece of prose into teletype form. What features are especially prominent in the example you chose?
7. Find a piece of writing that exemplifies the best qualities of "the Windbag." (Extremely heavy textbooks are a good possible source.) Transform a passage of windbag prose into clear, concise English.
8. Find an example of writing by "the Tease." Revise the passage to improve communication. What kinds of changes were necessary? Did you have to revise the style, the content, or both?

Samantha Bowman worked for six years for a Big Eight accounting firm before starting her own

management consulting firm, Bowman Associates. She now employs twelve management specialists.

I've found that my business is most profitable when I take a direct hand in most of our major accounts. To that end, I'd like to ask each of my employees to sum up information and recommendations for me in reports. But often I can't. At least half of my staff thinks of a report as the work of several days. I certainly can't afford hundreds of dollars in staff time every time I need a report.

How can I convince my employees that reports can be concise, complete, and well-written and won't take up too much of their valuable time? It's almost as if they're afraid of reports—or of writing itself.

Samantha Bowman faces a common management problem: she needs information in the form of reports from her employees, but they can't generate those reports efficiently. Where does the problem lie? Are the employees simply lazy? Are Samantha's expectations too high? Or does the problem involve the skill of report-writing itself?

Writing
Short Proposals
and Reports

6

LEARNING OBJECTIVES

To overcome inhibitions and anxieties often associated with the writing of proposals and reports

To analyze your audience in order to achieve effective written communication

To understand the roles logical and psychological order play in the structure of proposals and reports

To place "good news" and "bad news" strategically within your written communications

To revise your proposals and reports

To develop successful presentation methods for your written communications

What emerges when we write for the boss—and his or her bosses—can be compared to a faint squeak stuck halfway in the throat. Psychologists call this influence *audience inhibition,* and the rest of us call it running scared.

THE IMPORTANCE OF RELAXATION

So long as we devote our imaginative energies to the soap opera called "Big Them and Little Me," we cannot do our best writing or thinking. In the face of fear, three things happen to our business prose. First, we begin using sesquipedalian verbiage—big words—in an effort to impress others. Next, we express ourselves in stilted sentence rhythms; the naturalness goes out of our writing:

Stilted

> *For your consideration when you find the time to, and knowing the importance you place on communication networks within the company, it is my purpose to act upon your appreciated suggestion.*

Finally, we lose hold of that precious silver thread called clear thinking. When the mind flits compulsively to endless "what ifs" and images of the boss's frowning face, we cannot simultaneously think, write, or speak in a lucid and logical way.

For all these reasons, the most important principle to master when writing for upper management has nothing to do with form, stationery, phrases, or margins.

Simply *relax.*

That prescription may sound silly to beginning business writers. "Relax? Do you realize that my future depends upon the report I'm writing for the vice-president? It's almost 3 P.M., and I've got to get something to the typing pool by 4:30. If I could only settle down and think!"

Relax—not because the writing task is trivial, but because it is important. You will need all of your word skills to do your best work. That state of readiness comes about only when you let yourself relax.

Especially in the middle of a hectic business day, business writers may find it hard to let go, to relax, to let language flow. Therefore, many successful communicators have personal relaxation routines for use before important writing occasions. A construction executive in New York takes five minutes for a brisk walk around his office building. He breathes deeply, swinging his arms freely. An administrator of a large Chicago hospital uses what she calls "gravity meditation." She consciously tries to imagine each major muscle group in her body growing heavier and heavier, drawn down by an irresistible gravitational force. Within two or three minutes, she reports feeling peaceful, clear-headed, and ready to write.

Whether you relax by walking, rubbing a pet rock, or simply drinking a cold glass of water, try to develop dependable ways to bring about a state of calm before beginning to write.

CONSIDER YOUR AUDIENCE

When writing for upper management, take a moment to size up your audience. In the case of your boss, what are his or her primary interests and responsibilities in the company? What will he or she be looking for in your work? Just as tailors do their best work when fitting actual clients, so business writers succeed most often when they "tailor" their words to specific needs and specific personalities.

The partriarch of a Miami food chain is frank with his seven midmanagers. "I'm an old man, and I've stayed a happy man. How? By hearing good news—lots of it—as often as possible. In reports from my managers, I want to read about many successes in the stores, and then maybe a problem or two." For this boss, managers design their quarterly reports to emphasize progress and profits.

By contrast, the crusty chief executive officer of a downtown Philadelphia loan office regularly tells her managers to get to the heart of business problems without any "hype" or buffer. "Save the 'sell' for the customer," she says. "Give me the straight scoop on the problems we face."

Business writers get to know the style and preferences of upper management in various ways:

- by asking others in the company.
- through business conversations and contacts with upper management.
- by studying the boss's own writing in letters, speeches, and reports.

Such clues give business writers marked advantages in their efforts to reach an executive audience in a persuasive way.

THE PROPOSAL

Contracts do not simply arrive on a company's doorstep, or—despite certain advertising—come marching out of the Yellow Pages. Contracts are usually earned through words, most often cast in the form of a business proposal.

What does a business proposal do? It describes ideas in such a way that they appear to fulfill the client's needs. Sometimes clients don't have a clear idea of their needs. In that case, the proposal must provide not only solutions but a description of the problem as well. An old maxim is often quoted in this regard: "Give them the answer, but first make sure they know the question."

The power of your proposed ideas, that is, stands in direct relation to the powerful need perceived by the client. Even a proposal for a miracle drug can bring yawns and shrugs to an audience unconcerned about health problems.

How long is a business proposal? This crucial business document can range in length from a single typed page to several bound volumes (as in the case of a proposal to the military from an aerospace contractor). Abraham Lincoln liked to remark that a man's legs should be long enough to reach the ground. Similarly, a proposal must be long enough to do the work it sets for itself—no more and no less.

What are the parts of a proposal? While proposals differ according to use and length, most are made up of an Overview, Problem Analysis, Proposal Specifics, Budget, and Conclusion. These five parts are treated in detail later in this chapter.

How is a proposal arranged? No arrangement of parts in any business document can be defended solely on the grounds of convention—"that's the way it's done." Parts find their place according to one criterion: the role they play in the overall purpose of the document. In the case of the business proposal, the central purpose is to persuade an audience to act. All parts of the proposal, then, must be arranged to serve this purpose.

But how do we go about persuading others to act? Consider three powerful forces.

Logical Order

The parts of a proposal must be arranged in such a way as to appeal to the reader's sense of reason. Readers who can follow an argument point-by-point feel confident that the writer has thought through the material with care. Such readers are much more likely to say "yes" to the ideas proposed in the document.

The chain of logic in a proposal can be viewed as a row of dominoes. Each acts upon the next in an onward movement toward the conclusion of the proposal. Only a missing link—a logical flaw—can halt the onward movement of the reader's mind.

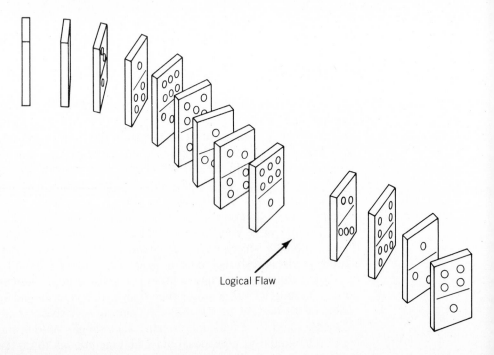

Logical Flaw

By carefully reviewing the logical order of ideas within a proposal, the writer makes sure that the reader's thoughtful consideration of the document is not interrupted or frustrated by logical errors.

Consider, for example, the sequence of logical steps at the heart of a proposal to install brighter street lights in a residential neighborhood.

Point 1: Residents care most of all about safety and property values.

Point 2: Brighter street lights discourage crime (thereby making the neighborhood more safe).

Point 3: Brighter street lights increase property values (because safer areas have higher property values).

Point 4: Residents can be expected to support the proposal (because it gives them what they want—safety and higher property values).

This logical design is not complex, but it serves to illustrate the "domino effect" of solid logical argumentation. One point leads to the next, which in turn leads to a related point. Taken all together, the points lead to a conclusion that appeals to common sense.

Logical Flaws

Too many proposals, however, fail for lack of a cogent logical design. Be on guard for the "Ten Most Unwanteds" in logical ordering of ideas.

1. Circular Reasoning. What was supposed to be an explanation turns out to be a mere restatement.
   All employees are encouraged to participate in after-hours company recreation programs because such programs are especially for the use of employees after the workday has ended.

2. Hasty Generalization. The conclusion reached is based on too little evidence.
   Democrats can't win the election because of their stand on animal rights.

3. Non Sequitur. A conclusion is reached that does not follow from the evidence presented.
   Johnson owns two homes, a boat, and a sports car. I trust his investment advice.

4. Bias. Personal opinions and viewpoints become the standard for evaluating objective arguments.
   Ms. Wilmington has every right to apply for the new position. But she won't get it. I just don't want to work with a woman.

5. Either/Or Thinking. Two alternatives are presented as the only alternatives.
   Either he apologizes or I quit.

6. False Cause. An earlier occurrence is incorrectly presented as the cause of a later event.

We switched to leased cars instead of company-owned cars in 1984. No wonder we have so many auto repair bills each month!

7. Straw Man. A false target is set up for the main thrust of an argument. Knocking over the straw man creates the illusion that the argument has succeeded.
This company's problems can be blamed on poor benefits. How can anyone expect workers to concentrate on their jobs when they have doubts about their medical and dental coverage?

8. Faulty Syllogism. A pattern of thought leads to an unjustifiable conclusion.
All managers wear moustaches. I wear a moustache. Therefore, I must be a manager.

9. Stacking the Argument. Presenting evidence on behalf of one side of the argument while ignoring evidence on the other side.
Undersea mining operations are dangerous, expensive, time-consuming, and unreliable. We should not consider undersea mining in deciding how and where to mine for gold.

10. False Elimination. From an array of possible alternatives, one by one is eliminated until only one alternative remains. The illusion is thereby created that the final alternative is the best.
In reviewing cities for our company move, we've seen why Toledo, Miami, Dallas, Chicago, and Milwaukee won't meet our needs. That leaves Phoenix as our new company home.

Such logical flaws can collapse the credibility of a proposal. Eliminate them from your own proposal writing.

Psychological Order

Skilled proposal writers try to influence feelings as well as intellectual evaluation. They want readers to *want* to agree with the ideas of the proposal.

One technique used by such proposal writers is the careful placement and timing of *good news* and *bad news* in proposals.

The Placement of Bad News. Bad news can be defined as a message that threatens our welfare, stability, or reputation. A manager may hear the bad news that his or her division is being reduced in size and influence. A company may hear the bad news that it faces a major lawsuit.

Proposal writers don't shy away from bad news. Instead, they recognize bad news as the stage—the necessary precondition—for good news. Bad news forms the question, in a sense, that good news (the proposed idea) attempts to answer.

Consider, for example, a major proposal for road improvements on a mountain pass highway. The bad news is that several accidents have occurred because of poor road conditions, particularly during bad weather. The proposal writer explains the causes of the accidents in detail, all in preparation for the proposed solution of re-paving, better signs, and speed limitations.

The Placement of Good News. Good news may be welcomed by every reader, but that does not mean it will be believed by every reader. Good news must be presented in such a way as to seem not only *possible* but *probable*. This entails careful analysis of what the reader may resist in the good news being presented.

In the case of a proposal for land development, for example, the proposal writer might point to three items of potential good news for those interested in investing in the venture:

- Housing prices are higher than ever before
- The exclusive area in question has only a few remaining tracts for development
- The architect has worked up some very creative initial renderings of the kind of homes that can be built

Each of these items of good news falls flat, however, if the proposal writer does not take into account the *resistance* that may be felt by readers. If housing prices are higher than ever before, will there be a market for the finished homes? If the exclusive area has only a few undeveloped tracts, have they remained undeveloped for a reason, such as permit problems, drainage, and so forth? Finally, will the architect's creative plans prove economically feasible?

Delivering good news, then, requires timing and sensitivity to surrounding issues. Bright, desirable ideas must face and overcome whatever obstacles are present in the reader's mind before they become influential ideas.

Solid Evidence

Readers are swayed to accept ideas by the skilled use of evidence in the form of examples, illustrations, statistics, and details. Such evidence can be *general* or *specific* in nature.

General evidence is made up of a great number of specific examples gathered together (or "generalized"). "The air in metropolitan areas is 16 percent cleaner this year because of federal pollution legislation" is general evidence.

By contrast, specific evidence treats precise details of a single case. "Air quality measurements during the month of July in Los Angeles show a 16 percent improvement in over-all air quality." Specific evidence, especially when supported by reputable and knowledgeable sources, helps to convince the reader that the proposal writer's major ideas are sound.

Successful proposal writers mix both general and specific evidence to create a case for their ideas. Too much general evidence will make the proposal sound vague and unfocused. Too much specific evidence can make the proposal sound narrow, local, and parochial in its concerns. Used with balance, however, general and specific evidence can earn the reader's acceptance of ideas within the proposal.

Proposal-Writing Strategies: A "How-To" Guide

You will probably write proposals often in your business career to attract contracts, obtain research money, change in-house procedures, fund new facilities, or argue for product or policy revisions. Use this step-by-step guide to construct practical, successful proposals.

1. DETERMINE REQUIREMENTS FOR YOUR PROPOSAL.

Specific guidelines may already exist for developing your proposal. Many government agencies, for example, have strict requirements for the way topics are described, the order in which they are treated, the length of the proposal, and so forth. Some of these requirements may strike you as unnecessary and even inane. Never, however, should you purposely break the assigned guidelines issued by a granting agency or client without written permission. You may wish to attach such written permission, once obtained, to the proposal itself as a convenient way to remind reviewers why your proposal has not followed the prescribed form.

2. DETERMINE WHO WILL EVALUATE YOUR PROPOSAL.

Once you know whether your work will be read by content specialists or by a more general audience, you can choose language designed to communicate clearly.

3. CREATE AN OUTLINE FOR YOUR PROPOSAL.

Specific Plans

Jot down ideas, examples, and details for possible use as you work your way through each section of the outline.

While you should develop an outline specially suited to your own topic, you may want to consider parts of a common model used by many professional proposal writers.

I. Overview. Provide the background information your reader will need to grasp the significance of your proposed idea. You probably will want to explain briefly why the proposal is needed; who needs the proposal; why the proposal should be accepted, and when. Once you have made the reader aware of the need for your proposal, you can go on to define your approach. What are your objectives? How does your approach differ from past approaches?

II. Problem Analysis. If you wish your proposed idea to strike the reader as necessary and timely—an action item—set the stage by analyzing the problem with care. What caused the problem? Who suffers from its effects? What

> Like mastering the fundamentals of tennis, golf, or sailing, learning to communicate involves taking one step at a time. Learn a technique, then practice; learn another technique, then practice. Along the way, surprising things can happen.
>
> We find ourselves enjoying what we previously resisted. Erasmus knew it in 1508:
>
> *The desire to write grows with writing.*

measures have failed in an effort to deal with it? What is the current scale of the problem? What will be its future scale? These questions are intended to suggest the kind of analysis to pursue in this section of the proposal. Use both general and specific evidence to let bad news weigh upon your reader.

III. Proposal Specifics. Describe in detail your proposed plan of attack. Are your methods proven? If so, by whom? What personnel will be involved? What is their training? What time schedule have you established for your work? What are major checkpoints in that schedule?

Also discuss your plan of evaluation. What significant indications of progress will you look for? When? How will you measure success? Will your research results be observable? Preservable? Repeatable?

Conclude this section with a *summary estimation*—a convincing statement of the likelihood that your plans will produce the results desired. Often, proposal writers describe their ultimate goals as a series of achievement plateaus, any one of which justifies the work proposed. In this way, writers allow funding agencies to feel that even if the highest predictions of their proposals bear no fruit, important results can nonetheless be accomplished at plateaus along the way.

The summary estimation is the writer's last chance to persuade the audience before introducing the boogey-man in so many proposals.

IV. The Budget. Outline the costs of your proposed work, including the following items:

- Equipment acquisition
- Facility rental
- Salary and wages, with benefit allowances if applicable
- Supplies
- Travel expenses
- Research expenses
- Contingency funds

In less frugal times, proposal writers somewhat roguishly padded their budgets ("pudgets," they were called when properly fattened) as a hedge against inevitable slashes during the approval process. The "Two for One" rule applied: determine what is really needed, ask for twice as much, and hope to end up with what was needed in the first place.

That game is played less and less in the 1980s. In part, because of Senator Proxmire's famous Golden Fleece award to overbudgeted, under-thought programs, a dramatically padded budget simply doesn't slip by the shrewd evaluators now reviewing important proposals in business, science, and government.

Nor is there merit in purposely under budgeting your proposal (with the false hope of presenting a real bargain to evaluators). An underbudgeted proposal makes promises it cannot keep, and no evaluator chooses to approve something that will be an exercise in frustration.

Perhaps the best advice is Will Rogers's: "Well, there's always the truth." State to the best of your ability what you will need to spend if your proposal is approved. Manipulative efforts to distort budget truths are fraught with peril on every side.

V. Conclusion. A proposal should never begin or end with a dollar sign. Conclude your proposal by expressing your willingness to answer questions and to provide further information; to meet with or speak by phone to the evaluators, referees, or others; perhaps to consider reshaping your proposal as necessary to meet the needs of the client or agency.

Appearance Counts

Because proposals are often judged competitively, they must win attention and respect by how they *look* as well as what they *say*. Wandering margins, bleary type, and smudged graphics all say "amateurish" and "unreliable" to an evaluator trying to get value for money invested. Here are five ways to give your proposals a crisp, professional appearance:

1. Use carbon ribbon rather than fabric ribbon in your typewriter. Your stationer can demonstrate the drastic difference in effect.
2. Use heavy bond white paper. Beware of pastel shades, especially if you plan to photocopy the work.
3. Abide by strict margins (see Appendix B for formatting standards) on all sides of the page. Word-processing systems now make right-justified margins possible without typesetting.
4. Decide if your proposal will have a more powerful effect in bound form, with a vinyl or heavy paper cover (usually in a conservative color). Proposals of just a page or two, of course, are not bound. Most photocopy and fast-print businesses can bind your work inexpensively.
5. Make sure that photocopied versions of your proposal are comparable to your original in clarity and crispness. Some writers feel that photocopies can be gray and blurred, just so long as they are readable. The excuse goes: "They wanted a copy—and you know how bad those copy machines can be." Copy machines in most photocopy businesses produce quite clean copies, at times almost indistinguishable from the original. Don't compromise for gray, wet copies out of a corner drugstore copy machine.

FIGURE 6-1

Using Topic Headings and Insert Material for Effect

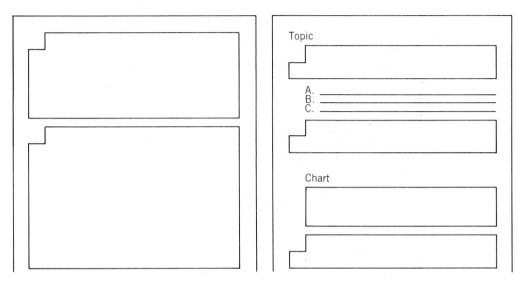

A Final Word of Advice

We have discussed how to make proposals logical, orderly, persuasive, accurate, and attractive. Finally, consider using a few final touches to help you create winning proposals.

1. *Use topic headings and inset material freely.* Look at Figure 6-1 and judge for yourself the difference in effect.

2. *Never bury crucial information in appendixes or footnotes.* If the reader needs to know a fact to make sense out of your proposal, include that fact in the text itself. If necessary, state the fact briefly in the text, elaborating elsewhere in a footnote or appendix. Never, however, should the reader simply be told "See footnote 34" for important information.

3. *Be direct and specific, not vague and general.*

Vague, General: Production has been hampered by the physical separation of related work units (from a proposal to remodel the floorplan of a factory).

Direct, Specific: The company loses $400 per day in lost time as employees from the Graphic unit and the Word-processing unit walk the 70-yard path between their two related work areas.

Vague, General: In the past, our company has had success marketing floral fragrances (from a proposal to market a new perfume).

Direct, Specific: Since 1982, our company has marketed "Orchid Memories," "Gardenias in May," and "Roses are Red." Each of these flower fragrances produced a profit margin of well over 56 percent in the first nine months of sales.

Proposals are the primary means by which business asks for work to do, for money to earn. The proposal requires the writer's sharpest writing skills whether it be long, or as shown in Figure 6-2, short. Business writers who demonstrate the ability to write winning proposals reap substantial professional and financial rewards. These writers quickly make themselves indispensable in businesses small and large.

THE SHORT REPORT

"Frank, we'll need a report for the Board by Friday." Report! The word still sends dread into the hearts of many managers. Let's follow an actual office scene, with the names changed to protect the guilty.

Monday

9 A.M. Vice-president to Frank Farley, head of employee training: "The Board needs that report on the costs of our training program for the past few years. Have it ready by noon on Friday, O.K.?"

9:10 A.M. Farley to his secretary: "Drop everything. Dig out all the files on whom we've trained, how much it has cost, whether they're still with the company, our equipment expense, salaries—everything! Put it all on my desk and set up the tape recorder with a long-playing blank tape."

11:00 A.M. Farley to himself, buried in files: (unprintable).

3:00 P.M. Farley to Sharon Levison, secretary: "Say, Sharon . . . I've paper clipped the most important pages in these files on my desk. Type up a rough draft—you know, something like a report— on the cost of our program for the last few years. Let me know if you have any questions."

5:00 P.M. Levison to Farley: "Mr. Farley, just what did you want me to type up? There are hundreds and hundreds of pages in these files. Did you say you had a report for me to type up?"

5:01 P.M. Farley to Levison: "It's after five o'clock. Let's start fresh tomorrow."

Thursday

Frank Farley is approaching panic. Sharon Levison has called in sick, for fear of having the writing of the report foisted on her. Farley calls the vice-president's office for an extension of time but is told: "I'm sorry, Mr. Farley, but he's out of town until tomorrow. He did leave a message for you, though. He says that he absolutely has to have your report no

FIGURE 6-2

A Sample Short Proposal

```
A Shuttle Service for State University



proposed to
The Board of Trustees
State University



by



Student Body Association



May 16, 198_
```

FIGURE 6-2

A Sample Short Proposal (continued)

EXECUTIVE SUMMARY

The Student Body Association urges the Board of
Trustees to approve the expenditure of $36,000 for a one-
semester pilot test of a student/faculty shuttle bus at
State University. The shuttle would alleviate parking
problems, increase safety, reduce air pollution, and save
money both for the university and for its members. The
Student Body Association offers its human and financial
resources in support of the pilot project.

ii

FIGURE 6-2

A Sample Short Proposal (continued)

I. OVERVIEW

Each year university administrators, faculty, staff, and students share a common complaint: too little parking on campus. Because most student living quarters and faculty homes do not lie within comfortable walking distance, particularly during the winter, most members of the university community drive a car to campus. A Student Body Association survey during fall semester, 198_, showed 2945 automobiles being driven to campus each weekday. Sixty-eight percent of those automobiles traveled less than two miles to campus from home. The great majority (82 percent) contained only one person. Arriving on campus, these drivers found limited and expensive ($138 per semester) parking.

The Student Body Association proposes a shuttle bus service from student and faculty living areas within a two-mile radius of the campus.

II. ASPECTS OF THE PARKING PROBLEM AT STATE UNIVERSITY

Bounded as it is by residential properties, State University has little chance to open auxiliary parking areas in the coming years. Nor can a significant portion of campus land be converted to parking because of building plans already approved in the university's master plan.

FIGURE 6-2

A Sample Short Proposal (continued)

Therefore, we must consider the university's 2475 student/faculty/staff parking places relatively fixed for the coming years.

<u>Too Many Cars for Too Few Spaces</u>

These 2475 spaces cannot accommodate the estimated 3000 cars per day driven to campus, even though 96 percent of this number have purchased on-campus parking permits. The overflow of approximately 350 cars per day (allowing for half-day parking use of spaces) must currently find parking in residential neighborhoods. This necessity has led to sixteen written complaints by university neighbors to City Hall in the past six months. Clearly, the neighborhoods surrounding State University do not wish to become auxiliary parking lots for students, faculty, and staff.

<u>Walking Is Impractical for Most Students</u>

At recent public hearings on the parking problem, university administrators have cited the Student Body Association survey showing that 68 percent of university commuters drive less than two miles to campus. Could not a substantial portion of these commuters, administrators asked, simply walk to school?

On April 7, 198_, the Student Body Association completed a poll of 500 such university members, selected randomly. Only 9 percent indicated a willingness to walk

2

FIGURE 6-2

A Sample Short Proposal (continued)

to campus and, of that number, 76 percent said they would
walk only occasionally. Reasons cited by 91 percent who
said they would not consider walking include
* difficulty in transporting books and school
    materials.
* discomfort in bad weather.
* use of an on-campus car for storing books,
    calculators, gym clothing, and so forth.
* time constraints (leaving campus for a job, etc.).
    The parking problem, we can safely conclude, will not
be resolved by a sudden willingness of State University
students, faculty, and staff to walk to campus.

III. A PROPOSAL TO RELIEVE THE PARKING PROBLEM
    The Student Body Association urges the Board of
Trustees, at their next regular meeting, to approve the
expenditure of $36,000 for a one-semester pilot test of a
shuttle service. As detailed below, the shuttle bus would
serve students, faculty, and staff within a two mile radius
of the campus.
    Transportation consultants donating their services to
the Student Body Association estimate that such a shuttle
service, operating from 7 A.M. to 7 P.M. weekdays, could
provide transportation for approximately 400 students per

3

FIGURE 6-2

A Sample Short Proposal (continued)

day. That number exceeds the overflow now using
neighborhoods around the university for parking.

A student, faculty, and staff survey completed April
30, 198_, by the Student Body Association showed that 86
percent of a random sample of 500 participants indicated a
strong willingness to use shuttle transportation to the
university if the cost per ride were 50 cents or less.

We project with some confidence, therefore, that a
shuttle pilot program would be accepted by members of the
university and would relieve the current parking problem.
If the pilot program proves successful, the concept can be
replicated for several shuttle busses, each earning its own
way from rider revenues.

IV. BUDGETARY CONSIDERATIONS

An expenditure of $36,000 will allow the Student Body
Association to take the following steps:

1. Rent a state-approved 35 passenger
    shuttle bus for six months . . . .$6,000.

2. Pay two drivers' wages and benefits for
    six months . . . . $24,000.

3. Pay for garage expenses, upkeep, and
    contingencies . . . . $6,000.

                                        ========

                    Total Expenditure $36,000

4

FIGURE 6-2

A Sample Short Proposal (continued)

We project that at a conservative rate of 400 paying rides per weekday at 50 cents per ride, the bus will produce gross revenues of $1000 per week, netting approximately $400 after gas and oil expenses. It is the intention of the Student Body Association to apply this net profit to the repayment of the $36,000 pilot fund. Over the course of six months (26 weeks), this repayment can amount to as much as $10,400 (26 weeks x $400 net profit per week). If the shuttle bus becomes more popular than we have estimated, the repayment figure will be even higher.

The Student Body Association agrees to repay the $36,000 expenditure in full from profits arising out of a shuttle service growing out of a pilot program before any profits are distributed to the Association itself.

V. CONCLUSION

Because it offers the best alternative for alleviating the severe parking problem faced by members of the university, the Shuttle Pilot Program deserves the serious consideration of the Board of Trustees.

The officers of the Student Body Association will be happy to elaborate upon aspects of this proposal and to answer questions of the Board. We look forward to working with you in serving the needs of our mutual constituency.

5

> Winston Churchill gave the idea immortal expression in our era:
>
> *Writing is an adventure. To begin with, it is a toy and an amusement. Then it becomes a mistress, then it becomes a master, then it becomes a tyrant. The last phase is that just as you are about to be reconciled to your servitude, you kill the monster and fling him to the public.*

later than noon tomorrow. Apparently the president has been asking about it.''

Let's leave Frank in the middle of his dilemma for a moment while we examine ten steps specifically designed to produce good short reports, even when the pressure is on and time is short. Since pressure and time seem to be major factors in real business experience, these ten steps can be considered a general guide, not an emergency escape.

Ten Steps to Good Short Reports

Step 1: Think About the W-O-R-M. W-ho will read the report? What is the O-bject of the report? What's the R-ange of the report? What's the M-ethod of presentation in the report?

Thinking about the W-O-R-M not only calls to mind important aspects of the report. It also helps to relieve the tensions that accompany the often painful first steps in report writing.

W-ho will read the report? Think carefully about your immediate and long-term audiences. What are their interests? Their needs? Their biases? The answers to these questions can help you determine what to discuss and how to shape your material to best effect.

What's the O-bject of the report? Learn as much as possible about the object and intended use of your report before beginning to write. Don't be misled by the tentative title you or someone else has given to your report. Titles don't always reveal the true object of the report. A report on creative financing, for example, still requires the writer to decide upon an object or purpose. Should the writer show creative financing from the bank's point of view? The realtor's? The home buyer's? The seller's? Many experienced report writers jot down their object on an index card, which they keep before them while writing. The card serves as a constant reminder that every aspect of the report must serve the ends of the object. Other writing, no matter how eloquent, is wasted effort.

What is the R-ange of the report? How wide a net do you expect to cast over your topic? Do you want to summarize facts? To interpret facts? To predict future patterns of growth?

Determine the range of your report before beginning to write. At times, you may hesitate to limit the range of your work for fear of leaving out important information. Recognize, however, that there will always be important topics beyond the scope of any given report you write. Like stones thrown into a pond, almost all business writing topics ripple out implications and suggest further areas of study. A business writer cannot always follow the topic where it leads; the report would become unmanageably long and disjointed. Control the range of your report by deciding what belongs and what does not belong within your area of investigation.

What's the M-ethod of presentation? Words do not find their places automatically on the sheet of typing paper. Good business writers exercise extreme care in placing words well on the page.

Remember, for example, the importance of first impressions. Use topic headings, graphics, tables, and white space wherever they will aid the at-a-glance readability of your report. Write for the reader who will merely peruse your report as well as the reader who will read it with care.

Your consideration of the W-O-R-M—Who, Object, Range, and Method—can take less than twenty minutes—twenty crucial minutes that will contribute significantly to the success of the report.

Listed below are ten steps to good short report writing. After you have taken the first step, you will be ready to tackle the meat of your report by working your way through the other nine.

1. Think About the W-O-R-M.
2. Know Your Topic.
3. Brainstorm About Your Topic.
4. Research Your Topic.
5. Arrange Major Points.
   Review logical, persuasive order
   Plan for topic headings
   Arrange research under appropriate headings
6. Write the Rough Draft.
7. Revise the Rough Draft.
   Ten revision tools
8. Review the Draft.
   Eye appeal
   At-a-glance messaging
   Use of evidence
9. Prepare the Final Copy.
10. Present the Report Advantageously.

Step 2: Know Your Topic. In actual business practice, writers too often finish a report only to be told by upper management, "You missed the point." When such writers hear what the report was supposed to treat, they usually respond, "Why didn't you say so?"

On the other hand, why didn't the writer ask? The report writer bears primary responsibility for knowing the topic. Upper management can be notoriously brief and cryptic in setting forth the topic for a report.

Thus, report writers have to learn to decode the short prescriptions of upper management. Usually this decoding process involves limiting broad, unmanageable topics. In the passages below, notice how what was said gets translated by the report writer into a limited, manageable topic.

Executive Requests Report	*Report Writer Limits Topic*
On the minority hiring situation here at Plantron	Affirmative Action Hiring at Plantron Since 1976.
On automated tellers for the bank	Four Highly-Rated Automated Tellers Suitable for Installation at Salton Bank.

This limiting process usually happens naturally and quickly in day-to-day business conversation. When the report writer formulates a limited version of an assigned topic, he or she checks it out with upper management—usually by means of a brief memo, conference, or phone call. These important few minutes help the writer avoid wasted days of effort on misunderstood or misdirected topics.

In addition to limiting broad topics, report writers must often convert topics to specific problems. If a vice-president of a large air-conditioning manufacturer orders "a study of sick leave at Dynatemp," he or she may in fact want a report on the *problem* of rising numbers of sick days taken by workers at the company. Pity the fate of a report writer who fails to convert the topic to a problem, and merely summarizes the sick leave policies of the company.

Consider how each of the following topics has been converted into a specific problem for purposes of the report:

Topic	*Specific problem*
How well we get our product to our retail outlets	Four bottlenecks in Amax shipping procedures and routes
Plant security	Points of security vulnerability at the Southgate plant

Not all topics need to be converted into problems, of course. In Frank Farley's case, for example, simply limiting the topic produced a manageable report title: "The Costs of Employee Training since 1982 at Benson Engineering."

Step 3: Brainstorm About Your Topic. Consider Frank Farley's use of a helpful brainstorming technique, the Classic Questions (see Chapter 3).

The Classic Questions

1. Why does the company care about the costs of employee training?
   Costs have been rising dramatically in the last two years.

2. If I had to divide the costs of employee training into parts, what would they be?
   New employee orientation
   On-the-job training programs
   Re-training veteran employees

3. What forces/circumstances led to the rising costs of employee training?
   Efforts to refurbish training facilities
   Acquisition of new electronic teaching aids

4. What kind of person is interested in the rising cost of employee training?
   Executives in the company who want to see results for dollars spent are interested.

5. If rising costs due to new equipment did not exist, how would things be different?
   The training program would be labor-intensive, relying on repeated lectures and workshops by company instructors. This method would be 30 percent more expensive than the present program.

6. What aspect of the employee training program do I like best? Least?
   The CAI lab has been worth the investment.
   Filmstrips and film loops have become outdated too quickly.

7. What larger situation provides background for an investigation of the costs of training?
   The new president of the company has embarked on a systems analysis and projection of company needs in the next three years. He wants to make sure that the rising costs in training are a one-time occurrence, not a fixed feature.

8. What are the principal benefits of employee training?
   Faster transition to new jobs
   Increased safety
   Employee retention

9. If employee training is curtailed, what barriers are to blame?
   Shortsighted view of immediate profits
   Lack of understanding regarding the value of training

10. How could the rising costs of training be explained to a 10-year-old child?
    Our teaching tools were old fashioned and worn out. We needed to buy new ones.

Forty-five minutes spent with the Classic Questions can start your mind working in productive directions. You can better understand your manager's interest in the topic.

In order to select major ideas from among the many approaches conjured up by the Classic Questions, Frank Farley begins filling in an idea circle (see Chapter 3). As Figure 6-3 demonstrates, when arranged in circular fashion, the wedges of the idea circle impose no premature, 1-2-3 order on your thoughts. You can mentally rearrange them as necessary when the time comes to outline.

Step 4: Research the Topic. Piles of records and files may be heaped on your desk. But now you know what to look for. Frank Farley, for example, looks up the total amount spent on the acquisition of new teaching equipment in

1985 and in 1984, and his secretary quickly locates a file containing final remodeling costs in 1984 for a training facility. You will find that research is no longer a needle-in-a-haystack experience. A firm grasp of what you are looking for provides a powerful magnet to draw appropriate data together.

Use research cards to record helpful information turned up in your investigation. Many researchers fill out both sides of 3 x 5 or 5 x 7 cards. If you follow this practice, on one side of the card provide full bibliographic data on the source of your information. (This sample shown is for a book.)

Research Card

> Blake, Karen. _Effective Employee Training Programs._ (New York: Windsor Press, 1983).

On the other side of the card, jot down the content information you may want to use. You may, of course, jot notes and reminders to yourself on the research card. It is wise, however, to clearly box off such commentary so that your words do not become entangled with those of your source.

Key Point

Page Reference

> Training costs save money for the company
> "By hiring relatively unskilled workers and investing in their training, business and industry avoid the more costly alternative of attracting skilled workers at significantly higher wages." (p. 94)

Inevitably, beginning report writers gather much more information than they can use in the report at hand. As writing skills increase, writers develop better "research radar," allowing them to locate and copy down

FIGURE 6-3

Frank Farley's Idea
Circle

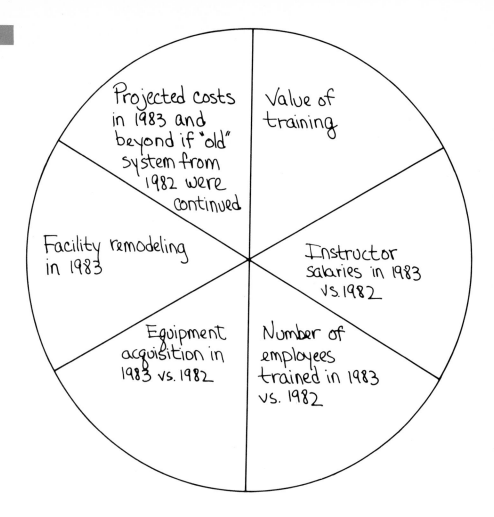

precisely the information needed. The "wasted" cards of unused information get fewer and fewer with practice.

For most of the twentieth century, business research took place in company files or in company, school, or public libraries. While those traditional
sources are still valuable, the last decade has seen the development of new
and powerful research tools. For example, many business and university libraries now use the computer to research topics.

For a computer search, the researcher provides a number of key words
to the librarian who uses these words as a guide while conducting the
search. Several data-bases might be tapped. The huge ERIC data-base maintained by the Department of Health, Education, and Welfare, for example,
contains hundreds of thousands of individual documents, representing millions of pages dealing with aspects of education and training.

Only minutes after the computer search begins, the titles of books and articles come spilling out of a high speed printer. If you wish, the search can provide abstracts for the books and articles as well. For a few dollars, you can obtain hundreds of individual citations that it would ordinarily take days to ferret out.

Step 5: Arrange the Major Points. There are many patterns of thought by which you can organize your work (twenty patterns are included in Chapter 3). Frank Farley, in the case above, decided to use his own common sense to forge a straight-forward thought pattern for the outline. We can "listen in" on his thinking as he developed this pattern:

> I want my readers to know—and realize that I know—*the issue we're dealing with: why has training cost so much lately? Is it worthwhile? Those questions should appear early in the report.*
>
> *But I also want to remind them what training does. If they don't understand why we have a training program, none of the facts and figures will make much sense to them. That information must appear early in the report, too.*
>
> *Then I can give background from 1982—what we spent, how we taught, and how many students we had. I'll compare that year with the major, expensive changes we made in 1983.*
>
> *I can then point out that the 1983 program, even with its high equipment expense, cost the company less than the alternative of continuing the labor-intensive program of 1982.*
>
> *Finally, I think I'll show them a bit of the future. I'll demonstrate that the cost of training will be less and less in years ahead as we automate the training process.*

Think not only about what you want to say, but also about placing each aspect of your argument in its appropriate location. When Frank had thought through the logical, persuasive appeal of his pattern of thought, he wrote down a working outline.

Logical Persuasive Order

I. Overview
   The purposes of the training program
   The key question: is the company getting its money's worth?
II. Past Methods of Training
   What we used to do
   Why we did it that way
   How much it cost
III. Present Methods of Training
   What we do now
   Why we do it
   How much it costs
IV. Evaluation
   Old methods vs. new methods
   Old costs vs. new costs

V. Conclusions

New costs are due to one-time equipment acquisition
New methods are worth this expenditure
Training per employee will cost less and less in the future

Once your outline has been completed, sort your research cards into groups appropriate to each outline heading. Where evidence is weak or missing, return to the files for additional research.

Overview Use an *overview* rather than an *introduction* for the first section of your report. For one thing, introductions have traditionally been the sorriest sections of business reports: writers have not been sure quite what belongs in an introduction.

Overview, by contrast, tells both writer and reader what to do with that section of the report. Both look to the overview for a point of perspective, a view of the purpose of the report, a suggestion of the approach it will take. Readers particularly like the word "overview" with its implicit promise of orientation.

Be certain to distinguish between an evaluation section (how to think about the topic) and the conclusion (what you decide about the topic). The evaluation unfolds the *process* by which ideas are compared, contrasted, weighed, and balanced. The conclusion reveals the *products* of your thinking.

Step 6: Write the Rough Draft. Time may indeed be running short, but you should feel no discouragement. At least you have put panic behind you; your outline sits ready before you. Your research cards are organized to support each major point in the outline.

Now you begin writing the rough draft. From time to time, remind yourself that your purpose is to communicate, not to impress. If you begin to experience writer's block, study the outline. It will indicate where you are in the total argument of the report, and specify what comes next. Your research cards fall naturally into place throughout the report.

Step 7: Revise the Rough Draft. Your completed rough draft—with cross-outs, erasures, asterisks and arrows— is lying on the table before you. Now to the all important task of revision. Like a diamond in the rough, the report must be polished before its worth appears to the reader. The following checklist should prove useful as you rework each line of the rough draft.

Eight Revision Techniques

1. Replace most weak verbs (is, are, was, were, has, have, seems to be) with strong, vivid verbs (reveal, grasp, demonstrate, fall, strike, seize).
2. Use the strong slot (the crucial space filled by the first two or three words in each sentence) for meaningful words and phrases (not "it is," "there is/are," or "and").
3. Repair the vague, detached "this" ("*This* proves that we can begin to . . .") by placing an identifying word after "this" ("This *discovery* proves that we can begin to . . .").

4. Repair awkward repetitions of words and phrases by substituting synonyms (words of similar meaning).
5. Vary sentence beginnings, mixing the most common subject-beginning with such alternatives as the -ing or -ed, beginning ("Reach*ing* his desk, Morton smiled sheepishly" or "Rat*ed* first in her class, Allyson thrived on challenges"). Try using complex sentence openers ("*Although we worked overtime,* our paychecks showed no bonus") and guide word beginnings ("*By contrast,* Galaxy Mills earned 42 cents per share last quarter").
6. Vary sentence length, using an occasional short sentence (three to six words) for emphasis.
7. Review diction (your choice of words), substituting specific, vivid words for general, abstract words ("Her sales career *developed* → Her sales career *blossomed*").
8. Check *all* matters of spelling, grammar, and mechanics (Appendix A will provide guidance).

Step 8: Review the Rough Draft. Recognize that your report must please the eye if it is to please the mind. Arrange your paragraphs and visuals for at-a-glance appeal. Use topic headings, varied margins, white space, underlines, and where appropriate, helpful graphics to create a document that readers will *want* to read.

Pay particular attention to your use of quotations, tables, and charts. Do you provide helpful transitions into and out of such supportive materials? The following sentence, for example, provides a transition to a chart:

> *In the following chart, note the sudden decline after 1979 in the price of imported wines.*

Step 9: Prepare the Final Copy. Prepare a crisp, clean typescript of the report, with photocopies. If done at a word processor, be sure to make a backup of your file for future reference and revision. You may want to experiment with different type styles or printer fonts to give your report an attractive edge.

Pay careful attention to footnote rules, pagination, and all the other conventions of report writing exemplified in Figure 6-4. If appropriate, you may want to consider binding your report. Several inexpensive bindings are now available through print and photocopy shops.

Step 10: Present the Report Advantageously. You now hold several copies of the finished report in your hand. You're rightfully proud of your work. But the production cycle of report writing has not yet ended. You have yet to consider the presentation of your efforts.

Instead of sending the stack of reports to your manager by office courier, for example, you may opt to deliver the copies in person. You reason that if your manager has comments or questions, you'll be on the spot to deal with them.

FIGURE 6-4

Sample Short Report

EEW, Inc.

Executive Offices ● 903 Yates Road, Oshkosh, Wisconsin ● 59783

January 6, 198_

Ms. Gloria Demers
Chair, Executive Board
EEW, Inc.
903 Yates Road
Oshkosh, WI 59783

Dear Ms. Demers:

We are pleased to enclose "Policies on Pregnancy at EEW,
Inc.," the brief report requested by the Board for
consideration at its mid-January meeting.

The report sums up our review of over 800 personnel cases
involving pregnancies at EEW in the past two decades. On
the basis of that evidence, we recommend that the Board
consider a more liberal maternity leave policy, as detailed
in the report.

We invite the Board's comments and questions regarding our
findings. If you wish, we will be happy to attend the
Board meeting to answer any immediate inquiries.

Thank you for this opportunity to investigate a problematic
area of company personnel policy.

Sincerely,

Margery Vickers
Margery Vickers

Sheldon Ramirez

Sheldon Ramirez
Co-directors, Personnel Department

MIV,STR/epv
Enclosure: "Policies on Pregnancy at EEW, Inc."

FIGURE 6-4

Sample Short Report (continued)

EEW, Inc.

Executive Offices • 903 Yates Road, Oshkosh, Wisconsin • 59783

September 4, 198_

Ms. Margery Vickers
Mr. Sheldon Ramirez
Co-directors, Personnel Department
EEW, Inc.
44 Layton Street
Milwaukee, WI 48953

Dear Ms. Vickers and Mr. Ramirez:

You both know of my interest over the years in improving
our policies regarding maternity leave. The Executive
Board now shares my interest in that matter.

The Board directs you to prepare a short report summarizing
past and present policies on maternity leave at EEW. We
are particularly interested in the real dollar costs of
losing trained employees due to pregnancy. We will welcome
any recommendations growing out of your review of the
evidence.

We wish to review your report at our mid-January sessions.
Therefore, I ask that you have your work to me by the first
week in January.

Thank you for your help in this matter. Certainly feel
free to call me if questions arise as your research
proceeds.

Sincerely,

Gloria Demers

Gloria Demers
Chair, Executive Board
EEW, Inc.

GLD/wbe

FIGURE 6-4

Sample Short Report (continued)

Policies on Pregnancy at EEW, Inc.

Submitted to
The Executive Board

by

Margery Vickers
Sheldon Ramirez
Co-directors, Personnel Department

January 6, 198_

FIGURE 6-4

Sample Short Report (continued)

TABLE OF CONTENTS

ii

FIGURE 6-4

Sample Short Report (continued)

ABSTRACT

From 1963 to 1968, EEW, Inc. granted no maternity leaves for pregnant workers. As a result, more than 50 pregnant workers per year quit their jobs. Less than 10 percent returned after delivery. Late in 1968 the company began granting selective maternity leaves, without pay, based on an employee's record of accomplishment. Because few employees applied for such payless leaves and fewer received them, resignations due to pregnancy still totaled forty to forty-five workers per year in the time period 1968-72. Since that time, company policy has been liberalized to permit pregnant workers to take maternity leave, still without pay, but with no loss of position in seniority if they return to work within six months. While this policy has helped to stem the steady flow of resignations due to pregnancy, the company should consider a policy of maternity leave with half-pay as an effective way to retain trained employees and, in the long term, to save money.

iii

FIGURE 6-4

Sample Short Report (continued)

I. <u>Overview</u>

   Motivated by Federal and State legislation, union demands, and its own interests, EEW has assigned the Personnel Department the task of reporting on past, present, and future company policies regarding pregnancy among company workers. This report details past practices, summarizes present policies, and evaluates the factors that will guide future policy.

   The report concludes that EEW should provide up to four months maternity leave, with half-pay. These measures, while not yet common among our competitors, are justified in the report on the basis of employee retention and long-term savings to the company.

II. <u>Past Policies on Pregnancy at EEW</u>

   At the time of the company's founding in 1963, it had no written policy for pregnancy among the staff. Workers routinely quit their jobs when they discovered their pregnancy or were dismissed when the pregnancy became obvious to their supervisors. Company personnel files show that a few workers requested leaves of absence without pay for the period of their pregnancy and the months after. Without exception, these requests were turned down by the company.[1] In the words of an infamous internal memo from the now-deceased former president of the company,

FIGURE 6-4

Sample Short Report (continued)

"Absolutely no. If she has one child, she'll probably have
more. There is no end to that kind of thing."

Under pressure from union negotiators and women's
groups, the company in 1968 began to grant leaves without
pay to workers who had demonstrated a record of achievement
and promise. While no statistics can be gathered to make
the point in a concrete way, many pregnant workers still
were dismissed in the late 1960s on the grounds that their
records weren't "promising enough." Despite repeated
efforts by the company's personnel director during those
years, management resisted all efforts to set forth clear
work standards by which "enough" could be measured.
Pregnant employees well into the early 1970s, therefore,
found themselves dependent upon the whim of a supervisor
for a leave of absence, of course without pay.

In 1972, a watershed event changed the company's
policies overnight. Interestingly, this event came not
from legislation or external pressure. A talented vice-
president of the company proudly announced her pregnancy to
a somewhat shocked Board meeting on June 2, 1972. She went
on to speak of her commitment to the company and her
earnest desire to take up her duties again as soon as
possible after giving birth.

A discussion ensued, pitting the traditionalists in the
company against those interested in finding new and more

2

FIGURE 6-4

Sample Short Report (continued)

flexible policies. Traditionalists argued that profits, not parenthood, were the sole concern of the company. Pregnant employees, they said, could not be retained, nor could their positions be held open for them. More liberal minds argued that companies had far-reaching obligations to their employees and could not simply turn them out for choosing to bear children.

The pregnant vice-president brought both groups up short in a brief statement still recorded in the minutes of that meeting: "Let me put it this way, gentlemen. I led the successful company effort to attract over $4 million in contracts and grants last year. I have an offer to do that kind of work for your main competitor during my pregnancy and after. I spoke of my commitment to this company. Now you must decide if I'm worth your commitment. In the long term, will I make you enough money to compensate for my pregnancy leave?"[2] At that point she smiled and left the meeting.

As a result of that meeting, she was offered a leave of absence without pay for the last three months of her pregnancy and the first three months of motherhood. (Incidentally, she left the company to accept an identical offer <u>with</u> pay from the competitor.) Leaves without pay were available from that time on throughout the 1970s to other pregnant workers. Relatively few workers took such

3

FIGURE 6-4

Sample Short Report (continued)

leaves, however, because they could not afford to live for that period without an income. They opted instead for unemployment compensation or other work that allowed them to earn right up to the week of delivery.

III. <u>Present Polices</u>

Since 1980, the Personnel Department sponsored a successful drive in the company to allow pregnant workers to stay at their occupations with the company as long as their personal physician would allow. Barring company-wide layoffs, these workers could return to their jobs within six months after giving birth, without loss of seniority or pay level.[3]

That policy continues to the present. No salary is paid during leaves of absence due to pregnancy. Benefits may be paid, depending upon the fringe package selected by the employee.

At present, the work force of EEW totals 1152 workers, of which 802 are women. While the Personnel Department does not claim to know of every pregnancy among the workers, we estimate that each year fifty to sixty workers become pregnant with the intention of bearing a child. Of this number, no more than 10 percent apply for a leave without pay for the period of pregnancy and delivery.[4]

4

FIGURE 6-4

Sample Short Report (continued)

IV. <u>Evaluation</u>

   Those pregnant workers who do not request a leave of absence simply quit. Few return to the company in later months or years. As illustrated in Figure 1, these resignations result in a substantial loss to the company each year. Note in the chart that an employee usually requires at least five months to reach the production level of our average experienced employee:

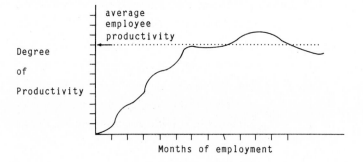

Figure 1 Productivity During First Year of Employment

   During this period of learning, the company is paying out an average salary of $2000 per month, only a percentage of which is earned by employee production during the learning process. Thus, the company invests on average $5000 in the training of each employee, as demonstrated in the table below.

5

FIGURE 6-4

Sample Short Report (continued)

Month	Salary	Production %	Training Cost
1	$2000	10%	$1800
2	$2000	30%	$1400
3	$2000	50%	$1000
4	$2000	70%	$ 600
5	$2000	90%	$ 200
		Total	$5000

In addition to this $5000 spent in training, the Personnel Department spends on average $1240 in advertising, interviewing, and processing costs for each new employee hired.[5]

Therefore, if fifty workers quit during a year due to pregnancy, the cost to the company in wasted training, advertising, interviewing, and processing is $312,000 (50 x $5000 + $1240).

For prudent policy decisions regarding pregnancy, that substantial sum must be weighed against the cost of simply providing half-pay for pregnant workers during the last month of pregnancy and the first three months of motherhood. Assuming that all fifty workers accepted such an arrangement, the company would pay 50 x $1000 (half-pay) x 4 months = $200,000.

The resultant saving to the company under such a plan would be $112,000. More difficult to measure but equally

6

FIGURE 6-4

Sample Short Report (continued)

important are such advantages to the company as improved employee morale, enhanced company image for job-seekers, and fewer trainees in the work force.

V. Conclusion

Over the two decades of the company's existence, policies on pregnancy leave have been steadily liberalized in favor of the worker. Based on the training and replacement costs set forth in this report, the trend toward partial salary during pregnancy leave is in the financial interest of the company. EEW will spend one-third less to retain pregnant employees through half-pay leaves than to lose them and pay for advertising, interviewing, processing, and training for replacements.

7

FIGURE 6-4

Sample Short Report (continued)

APPENDIX: FIVE CASE STUDIES

All aspects of the following five cases are factually true. Names have been changed to protect privacy.

1964-Ruth

After six years with the company as an accountant, Ruth asked her supervisor for leave without pay during her pregnancy and first few months of motherhood. The request was routinely denied. Ruth resigned her position at EEW, had her baby, then found employment with EEW's main competitor, Technoelectric Designs. Today Ruth heads the accounting division at that company. Recently she was honored by the National Accounting Association for innovative and money-saving approaches to economic forecasting at Technoelectric.

1967-Jan

Fearing that she would be fired, Jan hid her pregnancy as best she could into the sixth month. Her supervisor recommended her dismissal at that time in spite of Jan's excellent work record at EEW. Jan's husband, a senior engineer at EEW, expressed outrage at the handling of the situation. Both found employment elsewhere.

8

FIGURE 6-4

Sample Short Report (continued)

1969-Francine

An assembly-line worker, Francine requested a leave of absence without pay. Her request was turned down because her work record, in the words of the rejection memo, "did not merit such concessions by the company." Acting through her union, Francine took the matter before the National Labor Relations Board and won a judgment against the company. After receiving back pay and a settlement, Francine voluntarily found employment at Micro-circuitry, Inc. She now supervises an assembly unit there.

1973-Barbara

Barbara applied for and received a maternity leave without pay. She left EEW in the fifth month of her pregnancy. Faced with rising financial obligations, however, she found temporary work at Technoelectric Designs during the latter months of her pregnancy. A few weeks after delivery, she returned to the work force--but not at EEW. She manages the sales support team at Technoelectric Design today.

1981-Cathy

Cathy in early 1981 came to the Personnel Department for counseling. She and her husband planned to start a family, she said, but could do so only if she could be

9

FIGURE 6-4

Sample Short Report (continued)

assured of returning to her job a few weeks after
delivery. The personnel officer explained that she could
return to her job up to six months after delivery. Cathy
kept her job at EEW, returning two months after her baby
was born. She resigned a few months later, explaining in
her exit interview that she and her husband were making
plans for another child. She wanted to find employment
with a company that offered some kind of financial support
during pregnancy leave.

10

FIGURE 6-4

Sample Short Report (continued)

```
                             NOTES
1.  Annual Personnel Summary, 1966, Vol. IV, p. 68.

2.  Corporate Minutes, Oct. 1972, p. 137.

3.  For a full description of this policy, see Personnel
Policies and Procedures, 1980, pp. 387-98.

4.  This figure is based upon leave applications formally
filed with the Personnel Department during the 1983 fiscal
year.

5.  For a detailed explanation of this estimated average,
see Internal Economic Report No. 7, Jan., 1983, p. 204.




                               11
```

The reward for your hard work comes in many forms: self-satisfaction with a task accomplished; your manager's compliments; your own career mobility; your company's success.

Summary

1. Relaxation and self-confidence are necessary to achieve a natural style for proposal and report writing.
2. Effective written communication depends upon a careful analysis of the audience.
3. Proposals are the primary documents by which businesses gain work.
4. Both logical and psychological order are crucial in the development of winning proposals.
5. General and specific evidence can be used to support your points in proposals and reports.
6. The final appearance of your document matters as much as what it says.
7. The W-O-R-M pattern (W-ho, O-bject, R-ange, M-ethod) can guide your early development efforts in a short report.
8. You can often get to the heart of the issue at hand in a report by distinguishing between the topic and the problem implicit in the topic.
9. Eight revision techniques can help to clarify your points and professionalize your style.

Questions for Discussion

1. Discuss the importance of relaxation for business writers. What kind of prose can an author who is intimidated by his or her intended audience expect to produce?
2. What does a business proposal do?
3. Why is logical reasoning a crucial part of any business proposal?
4. What are the psychological effects of bad news and good news?
5. Where should proposal writers place bad news and good news to achieve positive psychological effects?
6. How can steering a middle course between the strengths and weaknesses of general and specific evidence help to create a persuasive proposal?
7. If specific guidelines already exist for developing your proposal, must you always follow them?
8. "Since the proposal writer's main job is to sell the proposal, he or she should feel free to slightly distort budget truths, without actually lying, in order to gain a persuasive edge." Attack or defend this assertion.
9. Why is it important for proposals to be visually attractive?
10. How can thinking about the W-O-R-M help anxious report writers?
11. If upper management has assigned you to report on a broad, unmanageable topic, should you resist the temptation to limit the topic to a manageable size? Defend your decision.

12. How can converting a topic to a specific problem help business writers to organize reports effectively?
13. Why is an overview preferable to an introduction?
14. What distinguishes an evaluation section from a conclusion?
15. How important is at-a-glance appeal in reports? What techniques create at-a-glance appeal?

Exercises

1. The next time you are faced with an intimidating writing task (writing a timed essay or an important business document, for example), try this very simple procedure for achieving relaxation: before taking the exam or beginning the memo or letter, take three minutes for a physical exercise of some kind: stretching, a short, brisk stroll, and so forth. Describe in writing your experience with exercise as an aid to natural, effective composition.
2. List as many methods as you can think of that you have found to be useful tools for relaxation or for relieving the fears of public writing or speaking. Share these with your classmates; in turn, copy down any of their suggestions that you think might be useful.
3. Write a "bad news" letter, perhaps one in which you decline an invitation of some kind. Be positive and stress the you-viewpoint as you customarily would. But in this letter, rather than leading up to the bad news and breaking it gently, start off the strong slot of your opening sentence with it. Revise the letter, placing the bad news in a more strategic location. Show both letters to friends or family members. Record their reactions to the two different examples.
4. Generate a list of broad topics you would like to get more information on—job possibilities in the local community or the effect of climate on the clothing industry, for instance. Trade lists with a partner. Limit the broad topics you receive to more manageable ones. The first topic, for example, might become "job openings in the local aerospace industry," or better still, "engineering opportunities in the local aerospace industry." Get together with your partner and trade notes, justifying the limitations.
5. Now trade back the lists of manageable topics that you produced for exercise four. Convert each topic into a specific problem to be solved. For instance, you might want to determine how to cultivate the right personal contacts for gaining an entry level engineering position in the local aerospace industry.
6. Take a previous essay you've written for another class—in short, a "tell-them-what-you're-going-to-tell-them, tell-them, tell-them-what-you-told-them" essay—and rewrite it in the form of a long memo. What differences in the two forms do you perceive? How does your old introduction differ from your new overview? How does your old conclusion differ from your new evaluation section?

7. Find a letter or document which you think lacks at-a-glance appeal. Rewrite it, providing the missing appeal.
8. Rewrite a letter or document which has at-a-glance appeal, transforming it into a dull, rambling collection of words on the page. Show one version to one group of friends, and the other version to another. Ask each group to summarize the message and react to it. Although the content of the message has not changed from the first, visually appealing version to the second, visually unappealing version, do you note a difference in your readers' ability to comprehend the message? Which seemed to be most effective?

In 1978, Raphael and David Torres started a small business specializing in hydraulic hoses and fittings for the aerospace industry. Today they list Lockheed, Ford Aerospace, and McDonnell Douglas among their customers. With the growth of their company have come problems, some of them quite unexpected. Rapheal Torres discusses one of their most pressing and expensive concerns:

Whenever we bid a new contract, we have to submit a formal proposal to the client. If we receive the contract, we're obligated to supply formal progress reports—often as long as one hundred pages—at certain stages of the work.

Our basic problem is that no one in the organization, including David and myself, feels competent to generate these long documents. We know what needs to be said, of course, but we've never been trained to write a professional report or proposal. So we've had to bring in consultants to do the writing for us. They are expensive, often as much as $1000 per day, and usually need quite a bit of technical coaching before they can communicate our exact intent in a report or proposal. The process is costly and slow. We've missed important deadlines at times because we couldn't get documents out quickly enough.

Analyze the communication problem at Torres Hydraulics, Inc. Are long reports and proposals as difficult to write as Raphael seems to think they are?

Writing Longer Documents: Reports, Proposals, and Instructional Materials 7

LEARNING OBJECTIVES

To structure long reports and proposals in professional ways

To write accompanying documents such as letters of transmittal

To develop helpful footnotes and bibliographies

To write a variety of informational and instructional documents

Some business occasions call for reports longer than a dozen or more pages. A long report, however, is not simply a fat short report. Instead, the term suggests the addition of "machinery" to the text of the report.

Machinery refers to the various pages prefacing and appending the body of the report. In most cases, the purpose of these pages—abstract, table of contents, bibliography, index, and so forth—is to make the long body of the report easier to grasp.

PAGES AND PAGINATION IN THE LONG REPORT OR PROPOSAL

Listed below, page by page, first to last, are all the pages of a typical long report. Pay particular attention to pagination. Notice that some pages are numbered in Roman numerals (iii, iv, v) and some are numbered in Arabic (1, 2, 3). Following the chart of pages is an item-by-item description of each element in the machinery of the long report.

Cover Don't count and don't place a number.
Flysheet Don't count and don't place a number.
Title Page Count, but don't place a number.
Letter of Transmittal Count, but don't place a number.
Letter of Authorization Count, but don't place a number.
Table of Contents Count and place a Roman numeral (small, e.g., iv).
Table of Tables Count and place a Roman numeral.
Abstract Count and place a Roman numeral.
First Page of Body Count as Arabic number 1, but don't place number.
All Succeeding Report Pages Count and place Arabic number.
Placement of Page Numbers Numbers are placed in either the top margin of the page or the bottom margin, centered vertically and horizontally. Once you have chosen either the top or the bottom of the page for page numbers, be consistent throughout the proposal or report.

ELEMENTS OF THE LONG REPORT OR PROPOSAL

The Cover

Long reports may be bound in typical book fashion. Less expensive binding (of the sort done at photocopy shops) uses vinyl or heavy paper covers, many with windows so that the title of the report appears through the cover. The cover has no page number.

The Flysheet

A single sheet of blank paper separates the cover from the title page. This sheet has no page number and bears no marks of any kind. In more formal documents, the flysheet is often parchment- or translucent-quality paper.

The Title Page

On this important page, center the title of your report, your name, title, professional affiliation, and the date. The title page is counted as page one of the report, but has no number printed on it.

The Letter of Transmittal

Just as your résumé will be sent in the company of a cover letter, so a long report is introduced to your intended reader by means of a letter of transmittal. While this business letter can cover a wide number of topics, three areas of focus are virtually mandatory and a fourth is desirable.

1. *To whom are you sending the report?* Address the letter of transmittal to that person or organization.
2. *What are you sending?* Name the report by title in the letter of transmittal, then go on to comment briefly on the highlights that might be especially interesting to your audience. You may wish to mention your authorization to write the report.
3. *What do you wish your readers to do after reading your report?* Spell out in specific detail any action you expect from them (for example, "Please notify Ms. Jill Clayton, Director of Advanced Design, when you have read this report and are prepared to meet with the Engineering panel.")
4. *What are you willing to do for your readers?* If you wish, offer your assistance.

The Letter of Authorization

You will probably *receive* this document more often than *write* it. Usually (and unfortunately) written in the contorted jargon of militarese and legalese, the letter of authorization answers three key questions:

1. *Who authorizes work to be done?* Government agencies and large corporations will commonly refer to not only an authorizing individual, naming his or her position but also to an authorizing or "enabling" document such as a work order, legislative measure, or appropriations bill.
2. *What work is authorized?* The letter briefly describes the work to be undertaken, referring in most cases to a more thorough description of the work contained in a Request for Proposal (RFP) or other documents.
3. *By whom will the work be done?* The letter names specific people and groups who will complete the work as described. Because the letter often serves as a binding contract, it is usually signed and dated by the authorizing official. The inclusion of the letter in a long report bears indisputable testimony that the writer has the backing of the authorizing agency.

The Abstract

Usually restricted to one page, the abstract condenses or summarizes the matter of the report into one or more paragraphs. An abstract typically answers five questions (though the answers appear, of course, in paragraph form).

1. What is the subject of the report?
2. What is the purpose of the report?
3. How is the report argued?
4. What kind of evidence is employed?
5. What conclusions and recommendations are reached?

An abstract should never be used to create suspense (omitting, for example, a statement of conclusions). Rather, an abstract should leave the reader with an accurate estimate of what your report contains. The abstract is numbered in Roman numerals.

The Table of Contents

This familiar directory simply lists topic headings with appropriate page numbers. Do not confuse this table with the Index, which lists page references for terms, names, places, and so forth for the long report.

The Table of Tables

Though the redundancy of the name can prompt smiles, this table can prove useful when the reader is trying to locate charts, graphs, and statistical breakouts throughout the text of a long report. The table also helps to demonstrate the statistical wealth of the report. This page receives Roman numerals.

The Body

Beginning with the first page of text, numbers change from Roman to Arabic, and start over again at 1. The first page of the text is counted as number 1, but no number is actually printed on the page. Arabic numbering starts with a 2 on the second page of the text, and continues through the end of the report.

Notes or Endnotes

This page differs from footnotes in that the notes contained here appear at the end of the report rather than at the foot of each page. The report writer may choose to use either footnotes or notes. Certainly grouping notes at the end of the report makes the typing task easier, though this practice may be somewhat more cumbersome for readers.

Bibliography

Aside from slightly different punctuation and ordering, the references listed on this page differ in three ways from similar references contained in notes:

1. A bibliography lists all materials the author found useful in preparing the report, not merely the works quoted directly.
2. The bibliographic list of works appears in alphabetical order, not in the order of citation in the text.
3. Bibliographic citations usually do not include authorial comments from the report writer.

There are, of course, several styles you can follow to prepare footnotes and bibliographies. Some of these styles, such as the APA (American Psychological Association) style, require that brief notes be placed in the text itself. These notes refer by number to sources listed in a more thorough way at the end of the document. When trying to determine which style to use, check the predominant practice within your company. Also check on the reader's preferences or requirements. Once you have settled upon a single convention for notes, stick with it in close detail. Don't mix styles.

TYPES OF INFORMATIONAL AND INSTRUCTIONAL WRITING

As a skilled business writer, you often will be called upon to write an in-house information sheet or set of instructions. Sometimes these will be cast in the form of a memo (see Chapter Five). More often, however, your company will want to reproduce your work in sheet or booklet form for distribution and posting.

Consider some of the types of informational and instructional writing you may be called upon to do in your career.

Good writing skills are learned, not inherited. Even the most skilled writers can recall the painful process of learning their art. Henry Anderson, dean of the Business School at Florida State University and noted author of accounting texts, recalls that

. . . during my undergraduate years, writing was always a chore. I struggled through paper after paper. It was not until the completion of my Master's thesis that I realized that I could write, and write well. Today I am the author of several books and professional articles. My point is that I was not "born" with the talent to write; that talent was developed through many years of perseverance.

Procedural Writing

The office staff needs to learn an entirely new procedure for checking ad copy before sending it in for publication. You're chosen to write a step-by-step guide to new ad procedures for the eighteen-member office staff.

Policy Writing

The Company decides policy in verbal form at Board meetings and sends word to you by means of brief and often cryptic executive memos. Based on these slim documents, you are asked to write out policy statements to be distributed to employees, and included in the company handbook.

Instructions

Production workers have their doubts about the Master-Mill Automation unit installed last month. The directions that came with the machine were obviously written for engineers, not assembly line workers. You are asked to write up a clear set of instructions for workers trying to adapt to the new machine.

Public Relations and Employee Relations Writing

The Corporation wants a who-what-where-when information bulletin about recent company meetings, promotions, and products. You volunteer to write the monthly newsletter.

Promotional Literature

Each spring the Company mails a recruitment letter to area college graduates. You are asked to write a page titled "The Wide World of Opportunity at Cole Corporation."

We haven't listed, of course, the most obvious forms of informational and instructional writing: user manuals, catalogs, and direction sheets for new products. Strictly speaking, these major tasks fall to technical writers, not general business writers. It is beyond our purpose in this text to review the broad and exacting field of technical writing. If you find yourself pressed into service on a writing project requiring a close knowledge of graphics, type fonts, layouts, military specifications, and so forth, seek help in one of the excellent technical writing books available. Instead of presenting that information here, we will concentrate on those principles and tricks-of-the-trade most useful to informational and instructional writing in nontechnical areas.

INFORMATIONAL WRITING

Finding Ideas

To begin work on an information sheet, first examine the range of ideas available to you. To describe your city for potential new hirees, for example, begin by setting down in an idea circle the many possible areas of interest.

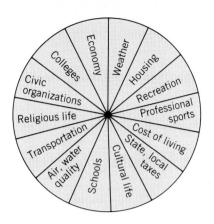

Limiting Ideas

Unless you plan to write a tome instead of a page or two of information, you now will have to limit your range of ideas. From the ideas jotted in the idea circle, we may choose to discuss Housing, Cost of Living, Weather, Transportation, and Schools as the key concerns to our audience of new hirees.

Arranging Ideas

Next, arrange your topics according to a plan. We can plan, for example, to "hook" our readers on our undeniably splendid Weather and Schools and to put off the bad news about the Cost of Living and Housing for later in the information sheet.

Providing Specific Details

After you have imposed some order on your ideas, provide specific details for each. We accomplish little by describing the climate as *moderate,* the housing prices as *high*, and the schools as *good*. Instead, specify that the daily temperature highs in winter average 54 degrees and in summer, 78 degrees. Specify that a 3-bedroom, 2-bath house within ten miles of the office starts at $110,000. Specify that test scores for the local schools show students scoring well above the national norms.

Being Clear

Finally, follow your outline and specfic details to write a clear draft of your information sheet. Remember that your purpose is to inform, not to impress. Choose common, colorful words.

Consider the example of an information sheet in Figure 7-1. Note the effective use of topic headings and white space.

FIGURE 7-1

Information Sheet

HOW TO OBTAIN DESK SUPPLIES AT OAKBROOK

Oakbrook Insurance maintains a supply room, currently staffed by Jerry Knulton. The Company requests that all office supplies be obtained from or requisitioned through Jerry.

Hours
The supply hours are 8-10 A.M., Monday through Friday. Please don't ask Jerry to open at other times without signed authorization from the Supervisor's office.

Supplies
Jerry stocks a full range of desk supplies:

*stationery
*envelopes
*pens
*pencils
*rulers
*paper clips
*filing supplies

More expensive items such as staplers, calendars, and file baskets can be obtained through sign-out procedures described below.

Supply Limitation
To keep our use of office supplies within budget, Jerry will distribute supplies according to a fixed schedule (posted in front of the supply room). If you require quantities of supplies in excess of those allowed on the schedule, submit a written request to Jerry with a brief statement justifying your needs. Within the limits of the budget, Jerry will try to distribute our resources equitably.

Checkout Procedures
Jerry will keep track of supplies given to you by means of a Supply Card, which you will be asked to initial whenever you check out major items or large quantities of supplies. More expensive items such as file cabinets and electric pencil sharpeners must be returned when you terminate employment.

Questions and Comments
Contact Jerry at extension 2986. We appreciate your adherence to these guidelines. With your cooperation, we can all avoid the costly inconveniences of sudden supply shortages.

Unlike informational writing, instructional writing provides explicit, step-by-step guidance for such business activities as operating a new machine, mastering a new business technique, and understanding new office routines. Just as informational writing can be investigated in numerous technical writing texts, so the field of instructional writing occupies a virtual library of books and articles. While business writers cannot be expected to digest such a mass of material, they can abide by five commonsense Don'ts and Do's.

1. *Don't* fragment instructions into an unmanageable number of little steps. Like parents assembling a complex toy on Christmas Eve, learners can feel overwhelmed by too many instructional cues. Imagine, for example, how you would feel if, at this moment, you were considering *fifty* discrete rules for instructional writing instead of five.

   Do find umbrella headings under which smaller steps and topics can find a place. Instead of a list of twenty small instructional steps for using a new word-processing system, seek out a few umbrella headings, with subtopics grouped beneath each umbrella. Consider this instructional outline:

   ```
     I. How to submit work for word-processing
        Where
        When
        In what form
        With what accompanying information
    II. How to get back a yellow draft for editing
        Approximate return time
        Proper form for corrections
   III. How to get final copy and future copies
        When to claim final copy
        How to alter master copy
        How to order future copies
        How to look up storage file names
   ```

2. *Don't* clutter straightforward directions with marginal asides, comments, and qualifications. In instructing employees on wiring procedures, for example, it can only slow learning to insert "Up until 1975, we used 6 gauge wire for this operation. When OSHA passed new regulations, we changed to 8 gauge wire." History may fascinate you, but exercise caution that history does not interfere with learning.

   Do put each sentence of instructional writing to the "So What?" test. If your readers can do without an item of information, leave it out.

3. *Don't* talk down to your audience. When one person has knowledge that another person needs, there is the unfortunate tendency to sound superior. Consider the unappealing effect of such

> In his role as dean of a business school, Dr. Anderson confronts many students who complain that they hate to write. He responds:
>
> *People don't hate to write; they are embarrassed to write because they have poor writing skills. Once those skills are mastered, it is a real kick to be able to communicate through writing.*

instruction: "I realize that most of you know absolutely nothing about this subject, so we'll take it v-e-r-y slowly for you."

Do follow the Golden Rule of Instruction: Teach as you would like to be taught.

4. *Don't* booby-trap instructions with unnecessary cross-references. Learners are put off by instructions pockmarked with parenthetical insertions as shown below.

```
Prior to proofreading yellow copy (see step 6) remember to
verify the document code (for definition and location, see
subsection b in step #4) and when needed date (which can be
altered by following procedures detailed in steps 1, 2,
and 3).
```

The human mind, especially the business mind, does its best work when it stays on one track at a time. Unnecessary insertions maddeningly force the mind off its chosen path of concentration.

Do practice "Instructional Geometry": get from one point to the next by as straight a line as possible.

5. *Don't* create a word jungle of long, dense paragraphs. Even the best-intentioned learners feel frustration in trying to follow your sentences deeper and deeper into the heart of darkness (Figure 7-2).

Do use white space in margins and spacing to provide an attractive, structured page for easy reading.

```
An Ideal Location
     Certox Industries' modern headquarters occupies seven
acres of rolling hillside less than twenty minutes north of
San Francisco.  Employees enjoy the peace of the countryside
and the excitement of the city.  Consider the advantages of
          * rapid transit directly to your office.
          * membership in the Certox recreational park.
          * company-owned apartments at affordable rates.
```

Notice in this example how an umbrella topic visually stands over and embraces its subjects. Even the margins tend to make meaning: sentences moved over to the left margin are perceived to be general in nature, while sentences along an interior margin are perceived as subpoints.

FIGURE 7-2

Long, Dense Paragraph

Our region offers many opportunities for advanced education. Six community colleges serve more than 28,000 students and the State University with an enrollment of 31,000, now grants degrees in forty-five subject areas. Students graduating from these institutions of higher learning have found employment opportunities in the area that have offered competitive salaries and the opportunitytoadvancetohighlevelmanagementposi

Rapid advances in many business and scientific fields, especially in hi-tech industries, have necessitated crystal-clear instruction manuals. Unfortunately, the production of lucid manuals has not kept pace with technological advances. The most notorious cases of foggy instruction probably stem from the experiences of the computer industry, where mega-buck computers often sit useless for weeks and months while their owners pore over confusing and inaccurate instruction manuals (often called "documentation"). One wag suggests that computer designers master one more language in addition to BASIC, FORTRAN, and PASCAL: the language called "English."

While your business career may not carry you into the relatively specialized field of instructional writing, you will no doubt be called upon to review and approve the instructional writing of others within your company. Use the Do's and Don'ts suggested in this chapter to guide your evaluation. Figure 7-3 illustrates an effective use of the Do's of instructional writing.

Summary

1. Long proposals and reports contain "machinery" not found in shorter documents.
2. Writing clear informational and instructional documents depends upon finding, limiting, arranging, and supporting your ideas.
3. Instructions should not be fragmented into too many individual steps.
4. The tone of instructional writing should be direct and sincere.
5. Unnecessary cross-references should be eliminated from instructional and procedural writing.
6. Considerations such as white space and topic heads are as important in instructional and procedural writing as in other business documents.

Questions for Discussion

1 . What purpose does the addition of "machinery" serve in the presentation of long reports?
2. What important features should you include in the letter of transmittal introducing your long report?

FIGURE 7-3

Instruction Sheet

```
                 HOW TO PUT PAPER IN THE COPY MACHINE

        Please note that the company has no employee assigned to
    the care and feeding of the photocopy machine.  We all do
    our part.
        When the copier runs low on paper, follow these six easy
    steps to keep the copies coming.

    1.  Turn off the machine when the red "Paper" light
        flashes.  The "On-Off" switch is located on the back of
        the copy machine.  Reach over the Copy Control dial.
        The toggle switch you feel there is the "On-Off" switch.

    2.  Pull out the paper tray on the left-hand side of the
        machine.

    3.  With one hand, push down the paper loading spring
        (colored pink) on the paper tray.  With the other hand,
        neatly stack about one inch of paper onto the tray.

    4.  Release the paper loading spring, then push the paper
        tray back into the machine.

    5.  Turn the machine to "On," using the "On-Off" switch
        mentioned in step no. 1.

    6.  Wait 30 seconds for the copier to warm up, then begin
        copying.

        If any of the lights continue to flash red on the
    machine after you have filled it with paper, call United
    Photocopy Servicing, 894-5938.
```

3. What purpose does the letter of authorization serve?
4. Why is the abstract an important addition to the long report?
5. Do you favor the use of footnotes or end notes in lengthy reports? Respond first as a reader, and then as a writer. Did your responses differ?
6. What types of informational and instructional writing may you be called upon to do in your career?
7. What feature distinguishes instructional writing from informative writing?
8. What effect can you expect to produce on your audience if you fragment instructions into an unmanageable number of little steps?
9. Why should instructional writers avoid marginal asides and comments?
10. What is the Golden Rule of Instruction, and why is it important?
11. What is Instructional Geometry?
12. Do dense paragraphs relate instructions effectively? Discuss.
13. What is an "umbrella topic"? How can umbrella topics help to organize sub-points clearly?

Exercises

1. After completing a long report for a class assignment, have a friend read it, but do not include an abstract. Later, have the friend reread the report with the abstract. Tell your reader that you've significantly revised the report. Record your friend's response to the "revised" version.
2. Find two reports or informative texts of about equal length and complexity, one of which places notes at the bottom of each page where a citation occurs, and the other of which places all notes at the end of the document. Read each report, timing yourself. Which report took longer to read? Which seemed the better organized? Did the procedure for notations followed in each text make a difference to your reaction? How?
3. Examine an instruction sheet accompanying a product (unassembled toys and furniture are good sources). Respond to the instructions. Do they seem clear and easy to follow? Bring the instruction sheet to class and compare it with examples provided by your colleagues. Judge the most inviting set of instructions. Account for your choice.
4. Write up two sets of instructions for the same process. In the first version, give a clear overview of the general steps to follow, providing enough information for your reader to do the job. In the second version, break these clear instructions into as many fragmented little steps as you can. Have friends follow these different sets of instructions, and record their psychological reactions.
5. Describe three ways that instructional and informational writing can be kept interesting. Provide a brief example of your own creation to illustrate each way.
6. Write instructions for some aspect of college life. Your audience is a foreign exchange student unfamiliar with American universities.
7. Write instructions for some aspect of daily life—cooking, transportation, dating, and so forth. Show your instructions to someone very familiar with your topic. Make revisions based on feedback from this person.

E verett McMeane leads a group of six students determined to put to work some of the valuable les-

sons they've learned in the Entrepreneur Program of a major East Coast university. Some weeks ago,

Everett's group submitted a lengthy, detailed proposal to the university's business manager. The group wanted to contract with the university to supply t-shirts, sweatshirts, and other dress items to the university bookstore. The group received word on their proposal today. Everett McMeane is angry:

To say that we're disappointed is an understatement. We worked for weeks on that proposal. The numbers made sense for everyone. The bookstore would have made more money, the university would have been represented by a better product, and our group would have profited handsomely.

We learned that we lost out to Hanson Academic Sportswear, a private company specializing in university-related clothing. The business manager showed us their proposal. I didn't think it had the real "meat" ours did. In fact, it was only half as long as our document. I'll admit, however, that their proposal was slick, worked out with flow-charts, diagrams, graphs, charts, and even photographs of the products they will supply. We didn't do any of that in our document because we didn't think it was necessary.

All things being equal, why did McMeane's group fail to win the proposal competition? Was the business manager at fault for "not really reading" the students' proposal? What strategy lay behind the Hanson proposal?

Developing
Effective Visual Aids   8

LEARNING OBJECTIVES

To use a variety of graphics with discretion and skill

To understand the relation between graphics and words

To grasp the importance of placement of graphics in documents

To be aware of computer graphics software for business use

To understand common errors in the construction of graphics

Many otherwise skilled business writers and presenters feel uncomfortable when it comes to visual aids. On the one hand, these communicators know how important graphs, charts, illustrations, photographs, and other visual aids can be in making a point. But many writers and speakers wilt at the time-consuming, somewhat creative task of preparing visual aids.

"I'm afraid," confesses a financial counsellor in Dallas, "that my artistic efforts will look amateurish. Yet I don't have the time or the patience to work with a professional artist."

NEW TOOLS FOR NON-ARTISTS

Advances in word processing and computer graphics technology have put the artist's pen in every business communicator's hand. Tables, line graphs, bar charts, wedged pie charts, flow charts, maps, and many other visual aids are now easier to produce than ever before. Such popular IBM-compatible programs as ChartMaster and SignMaster make it possible to prepare professional visual aids in a matter of moments.

What has not changed, however, is the necessity to *think* about whether you want or need visual aids; to decide where they should be placed; to decide what kind you need; and to determine how your words and visual aids together can form a mutually supportive package of meaning.

REASONS FOR USING VISUAL AIDS

While it is true that visual aids provide attraction for the reader and momentary relief for the print-tired eye, those reasons are among the less important for using visual aids. Consider five key reasons for using visual aids in your business documents and presentations.

1. *To clarify your point*. A visual aid can show a process, procedure, relationship, cross-section, or quantitative view of topics.
2. *To emphasize your point*. Visual aids, much larger and more vivid than words, call attention to key ideas.
3. *To simplify your point*. Relationships among ideas, facts, and statistics can be rendered simply in graphic form.
4. *To unify your points*. Several ideas can be brought together in one visual aid.
5. *To impress your reader*. Readers are swayed by your imaginative approach to the communication of ideas.

WHERE TO BEGIN

Which graphics you use, if any, depends entirely upon your audience's *need* for such visual supports to meaning. Begin, therefore, by asking yourself

- What are the key points of my talk? Which of these should be under-scored by visuals? Will they achieve my objectives?
- Will my visuals clarify my ideas? Or will they merely support them? If they only support them, should I consider them?
- Are my visuals appropriate and concrete? Are they informative?
- What visuals should I plan to use? Transparencies to be used with the over-the-shoulder projector? Slides? Filmstrips? Motion pictures? Opaque materials? Flannel board materials? Models? Drawings? Di-agrams?
- Have I considered the cost, time, and thought any of these visuals will take? Does the particular presentation of my topic justify these? Can I manage just as well without them, or without some of them?
- Is each visual I plan to use consistent with my objectives? Do they add up to a consistent basic structure and unity? Are they free from compli-cating type faces, art techniques, and symbols?
- Can my audience easily grasp what they see, or is an added explanation necessary? Are my visuals direct and to the point?
- Should my visuals be representational, pictorial, or symbolic? Which treatment is best for my topic? Which treatment is best from the stand-point of the audience?
- Is the sequence with which I plan to use the visuals logical? Are they so organized that they add strength and cogent relevance to one another and to my overall topic? Is my purpose sequential disclosure, or build-up?
- Are my visuals as effective as they can be made? Did I put enough thought and effort into the planning of the visuals? Did I consider all the ways in which the topic could be reinforced and clarified by the visuals?
- Are my visuals believable in terms of the overall topic? Will my audience appreciate and understand them? Will they be completely readable and will my audience have an unobstructed view of them?

Source: Eugene Raudsepp. "When It's Your Turn To Speak at the Podium." Excerpted from *Administrative Management*, Copyright 1982, by permission of Dalton Communications, Inc., New York.

what passages in your document or presentation should be enlivened and clarified for the sake of your audience. This requires reading your work as if for the first time, watching and listening objectively for those portions that will seem difficult, vague, or unnecessarily complicated for your audience. Look also for *emphasis* opportunities—places in your communication where a visual aid would make a key point in a memorable way.

Having found these possible locations for visual aids, you're ready to choose which graphics belong where. The discussion of the many visual aids depicted in this chapter can help you make an informed choice. But before turning to those visual aids, it is worth noting that graphics by themselves can hurt a business communication as easily as help it. A chart or table that appears out of context can perplex readers, drawing their attention away from your text and undercutting your credibility.

To avoid misusing visual aids, follow five commonsense Do's and Don'ts:

1. Do point out the conclusions you wish your reader to draw from a visual aid. Don't expect a reader to automatically see your point in a chart, graph, or illustration.
2. Do locate your visual aids next to the text that explains them. Don't expect your reader to hunt for the text that explains a visual aid or vice versa.
3. Do simplify your visual aids so that they make their primary point within a second or two of the reader's attention. Don't cram visual aids so full of information that they cannot be interpreted by the reader.
4. Do provide keys, legends, captions, and titles as required by your visual aids. Don't assume that the reader will understand the intent and symbols of your visual aids.
5. Do scale your graphic aids and place them on the page in such a way as to make for easy viewing and interpretation. Don't frustrate the reader with postage-stamp sized graphs and charts.

DISTORTION AND DECEPTION IN VISUAL AIDS

Like words, visual aids can be used to lie or, put more politely, to "shade the truth." It is not the purpose of this text to investigate in detail such misapplied use of visual aids. But three deceptive practices appear so frequently as to deserve notice:

Disproportion: The visual representation of statistic data is disproportionate to the data itself.

Example: a pie chart showing a large wedge identified as "welfare cheaters" when the proper wedge should have been no more than 6 percent of the circle.

Misalignment: The measurement scales along the axes of graphs and charts have been misaligned, often by moving or omitting the zero point, to create more dramatic graphic effects than the data deserves.

Example: Profits at an automobile company grew only by 2 percent. By changing the measurement numbers along the vertical (y) axis, the upward curve of profits seems much more substantial than a mere 2 percent rise.

Omission: Visual aids are simplified representations of data. As such, they are especially vulnerable to distortion by omission of neutral or unfavorable data items.

FIGURE 8-1

Photograph

Example: A software company has had several rocky months but, because of tax write-offs, is able to show somewhat steady growth at the end of each fiscal quarter. The roller-coaster nature of the company can be masked entirely by a bar chart showing only quarterly results.

VISUAL AIDS FOR BUSINESS DOCUMENTS AND PRESENTATIONS

The following gallery of visual aids treats those graphics most common to business documents and presentations. At the end of the sampler appear several visual aids exclusively used in oral presentations.

The Photograph

While certainly a powerful visual communicator, the photograph can sometimes be difficult and expensive to reproduce by ordinary photocopying. Depending upon the distribution you intend for your work, you may need to obtain written releases from all human subjects pictured in the photo.

Photographs can prove invaluable in communicating product descriptions, geographical information, and personalities. For that reason, they stand as the most common graphic technique used in annual reports (Figure 8-1).

FIGURE 8-2

Line Drawing

Effective marketing managers define their job as creating and delivering the proper market impact to well-defined market targets. This is a rifle approach that aims at a specific market target. This marketing manager does not waste resources and effort on the nontarget area of the market.

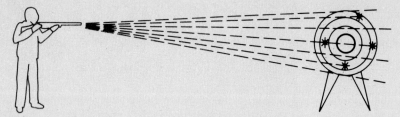

Ineffective marketing managers define their job as selling products. They do not aim at well-defined market targets. This is a shotgun approach. Although some "hits" are made, a lot of effort and resources are wasted on nontarget areas.

Line Drawing

Because of the advanced state of fashion- and cartoon-art today, public standards for line drawings are quite high. If your abilities with a pen don't measure up, find the help of a professional artist to create line drawings. These can add emphasis and attraction to your documents and presentations (Figure 8-2).

Line Graph

This, the simplest of all comparative visual aids, shows trends at a glance (Figure 8-3). Note that only the dots (the data points) represent accurate measurement. The line between the dots does not portray, point for point, an accurate measurement of data.

Multi-Line Graph

By differentiating lines by color, size, or texture, the multi-line graph portrays simultaneous trends for purposes of comparison (Figure 8-4). Care must be taken not to include too many different lines (three are usually the maximum advisable) or to portray lines that intersect one another too often for easy visual interpretation.

Visual Aids Enhanced by Color and Dimension

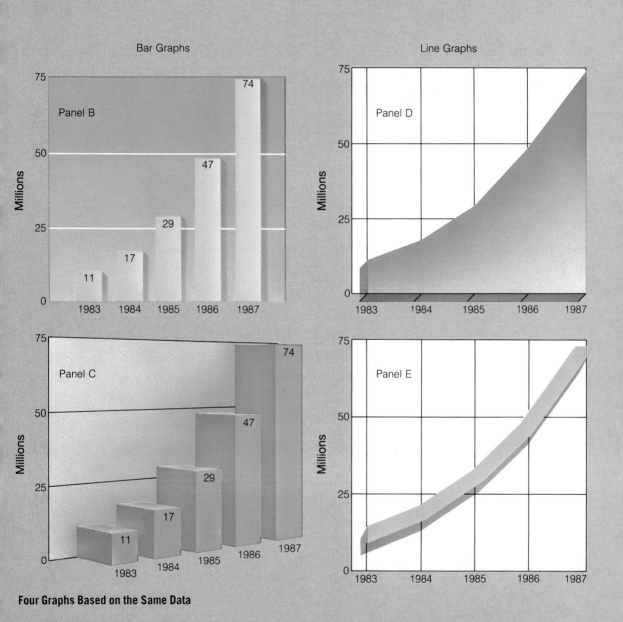

Bar Graphs

Line Graphs

Panel B

Panel D

Panel C

Panel E

Four Graphs Based on the Same Data

Flowchart

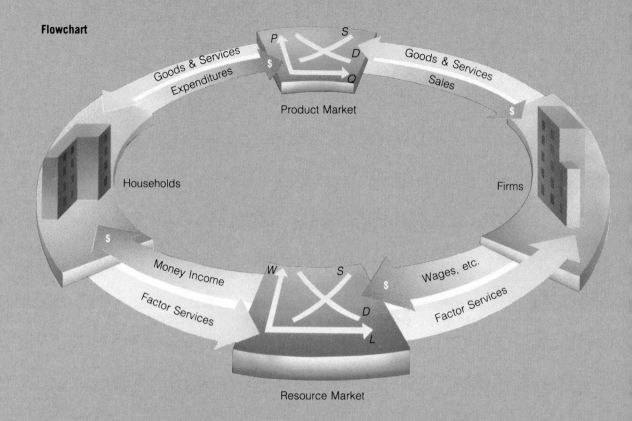

Grouped Bar Graph

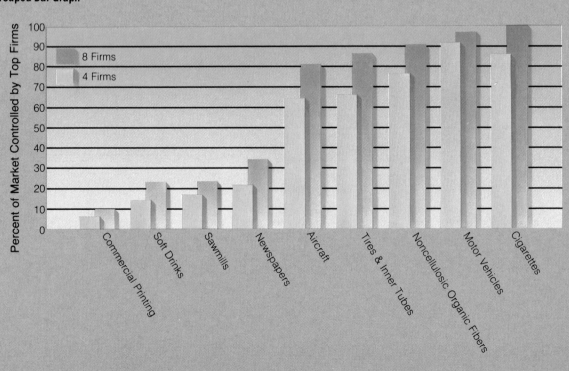

Map

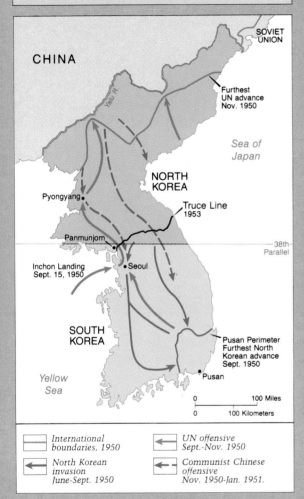

The Korean War, 1950–1953

After a year of rapid movement up and down the Korean peninsula, the fighting stalled just north of the 38th parallel. The resulting truce line has divided North and South Korea ever since the July 1953 armistice.

SOVIET UNION

CHINA

Furthest UN advance Nov. 1950

Yalu R.

Sea of Japan

NORTH KOREA

Pyongyang

Truce Line 1953

Panmunjom

38th Parallel

Inchon Landing Sept. 15, 1950

Seoul

SOUTH KOREA

Yellow Sea

Pusan Perimeter Furthest North Korean advance Sept. 1950

Pusan

0   100 Miles
0   100 Kilometers

International boundaries, 1950

UN offensive Sept.-Nov. 1950

North Korean invasion June-Sept. 1950

Communist Chinese offensive Nov. 1950-Jan. 1951.

Multi-Line Graph

DRINKING LESS COFFEE—BUT MORE DECAFFEINATED

Cups per person per day

3.0
2.5
2.0
1.5
1.0
0.5
0

All coffee

Decaffeinated

1962 '73   '75   '77   '79   '81 '83

Bar Graph

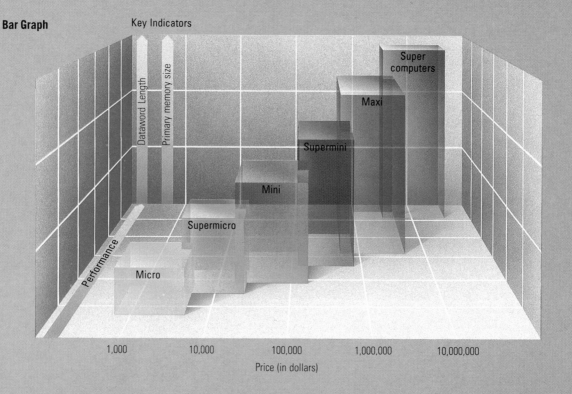

Key Indicators

Dataword Length

Primary memory size

Super computers

Maxi

Supermini

Mini

Supermicro

Performance

Micro

1,000   10,000   100,000   1,000,000   10,000,000

Price (in dollars)

Organizational Chart

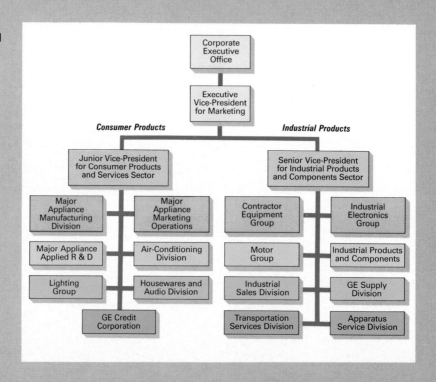

Corporate Executive Office

Executive Vice-President for Marketing

Consumer Products

Industrial Products

Junior Vice-President for Consumer Products and Services Sector

Senior Vice-President for Industrial Products and Components Sector

Major Appliance Manufacturing Division

Major Appliance Marketing Operations

Contractor Equipment Group

Industrial Electronics Group

Major Appliance Applied R & D

Air-Conditioning Division

Motor Group

Industrial Products and Components

Lighting Group

Housewares and Audio Division

Industrial Sales Division

GE Supply Division

GE Credit Corporation

Transportation Services Division

Apparatus Service Division

Time Chart

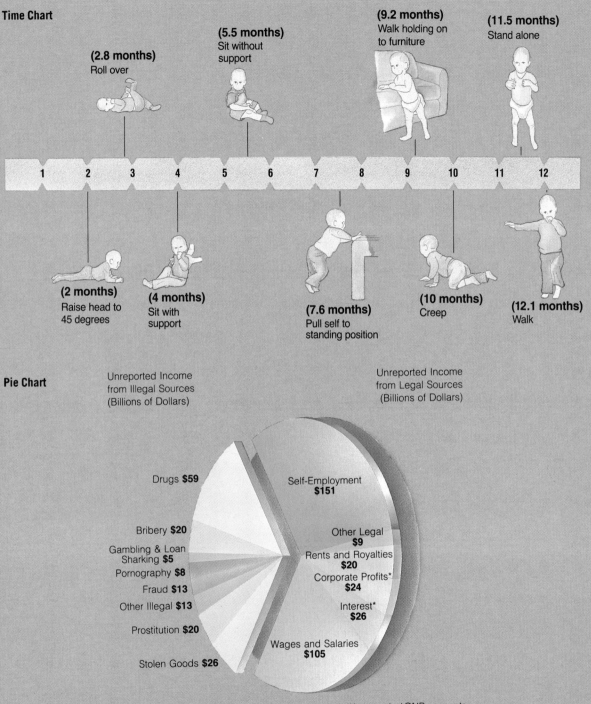

(2.8 months)
Roll over

(5.5 months)
Sit without
support

(9.2 months)
Walk holding on
to furniture

(11.5 months)
Stand alone

1 2 3 4 5 6 7 8 9 10 11 12

(2 months)
Raise head to
45 degrees

(4 months)
Sit with
support

(7.6 months)
Pull self to
standing position

(10 months)
Creep

(12.1 months)
Walk

Pie Chart

Unreported Income
from Illegal Sources
(Billions of Dollars)

Unreported Income
from Legal Sources
(Billions of Dollars)

Drugs **$59**

Bribery **$20**

Gambling & Loan
Sharking **$5**

Pornography **$8**

Fraud **$13**

Other Illegal **$13**

Prostitution **$20**

Stolen Goods **$26**

Self-Employment
$151

Other Legal
$9

Rents and Royalties
$20

Corporate Profits*
$24

Interest*
$26

Wages and Salaries
$105

*Partly included in recorded GNP accounts

Total Illegal **$163** billion   Total Legal **$332** billion

Total Legal and Illegal **$495** billion

Computer Generated
Visual Aids

Line Drawing

Cutaway

Map

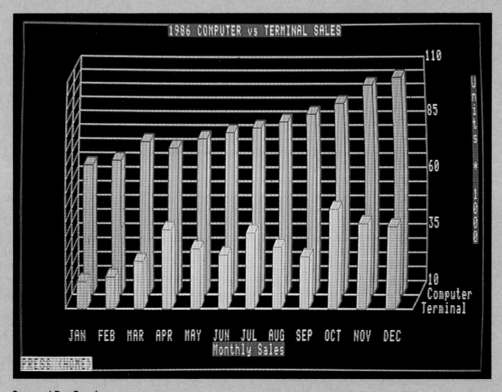

Grouped Bar Graph

Computer Generating a Pie Chart

FIGURE 8-3

Line Graph

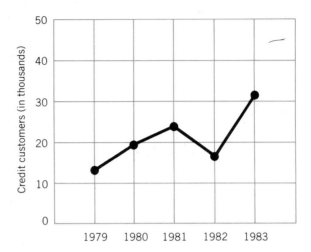

FIGURE 8-4

Multi-Line Graph

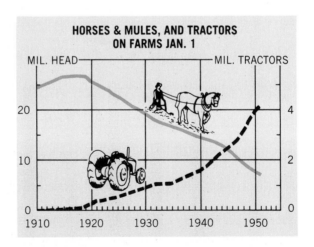

FIGURE 8-5

Bar Graph

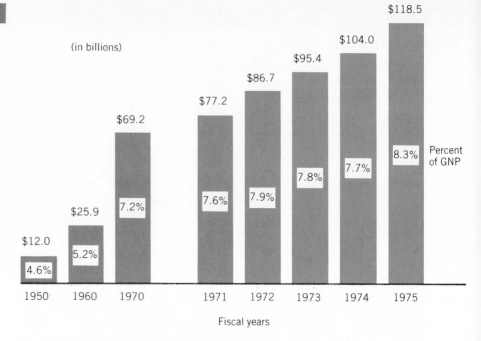

FIGURE 8-6

Grouped Bar Graph

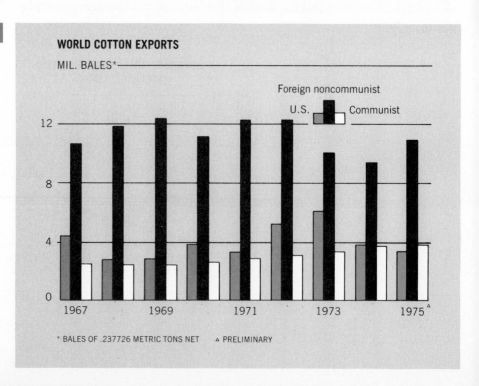

FIGURE 8-7

Segmented Bar Graph

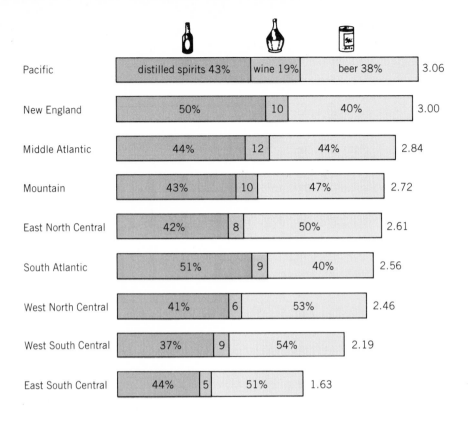

Pacific	distilled spirits 43%	wine 19%	beer 38%	3.06
New England	50%	10	40%	3.00
Middle Atlantic	44%	12	44%	2.84
Mountain	43%	10	47%	2.72
East North Central	42%	8	50%	2.61
South Atlantic	51%	9	40%	2.56
West North Central	41%	6	53%	2.46
West South Central	37%	9	54%	2.19
East South Central	44%	5	51%	1.63

Bar Graph

In thermometer fashion, the bar graph creates strong visual statements for comparative measurement (Figure 8-5). Trends can still be gauged, but without the sloping (and often inaccurate) lines of a line graph. The simple bar chart compares two or more values and can be drawn either horizontally or vertically. Exact quantities represented by each bar are often written within or at the top of each bar.

Grouped Bar Graph

A grouped bar graph is, in effect, a series of simple bar charts, each measuring two or more values at specified intervals (Figure 8-6).

Segmented Bar Graph

The segmented bar graph distinguishes different parts of the whole by color or texture (Figure 8-7). Each bar is segmented into parts corresponding to amounts represented.

FIGURE 8-8

Line-Bar Graph

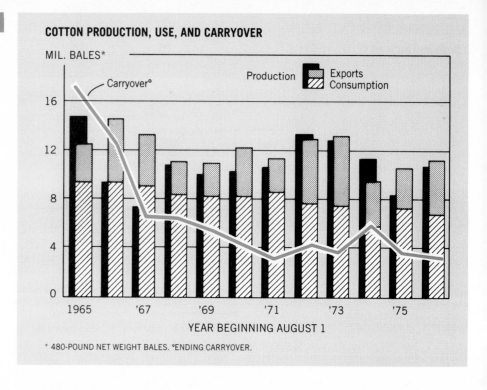

COTTON PRODUCTION, USE, AND CARRYOVER

FIGURE 8-9

Pie Chart

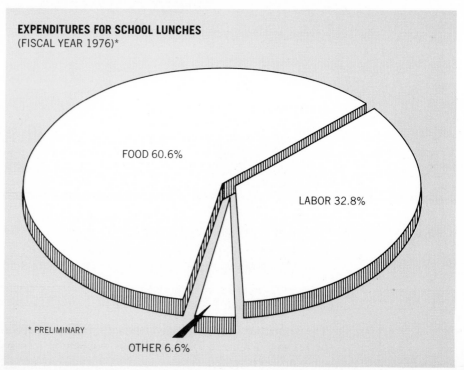

EXPENDITURES FOR SCHOOL LUNCHES
(FISCAL YEAR 1976)*

Line-Bar Graph

The line-bar graph simultaneously emphasizes individual measurements and trends (Figure 8-8).

Pie Chart

In a pie or circle chart, each portion represents part of the total amount of value depicted in the full circle (Figure 8-9). Portions represented must be proportionate in size to the value they represent. To prepare the pie chart, compute percentages of the total for each portion and then multiply each percentage by 360 degrees. Using a protractor, mark the degrees for each part starting with the largest portion at the top of the circle. Proceed clockwise to smaller and smaller divisions. In general, the pie chart should not contain more than eight parts to avoid clutter and confusion. Names for segments can be placed inside or outside the chart itself. Names, however, should always appear horizontally on the page.

Pictograms

Pictograms usually combine graphic devices from line, bar, and pie charts to make a point in an attractive, eye-catching way (Figure 8-10). In using a pictogram, a communicator attempts to influence emotions and attitudes. In no case should the creativity involved in a pictogram become an end in itself, distorting or hiding the central point of the statistics represented.

FIGURE 8-10

Pictogram

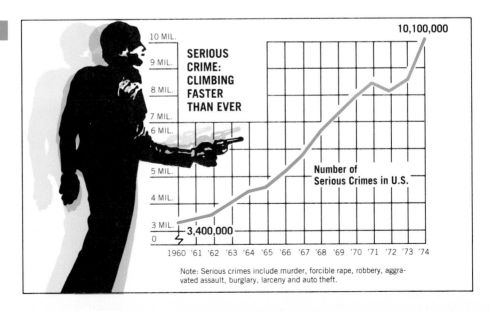

SERIOUS CRIME: CLIMBING FASTER THAN EVER

10,100,000

Number of Serious Crimes in U.S.

3,400,000

1960 '61 '62 '63 '64 '65 '66 '67 '68 '69 '70 '71 '72 '73 '74

Note: Serious crimes include murder, forcible rape, robbery, aggravated assault, burglary, larceny and auto theft.

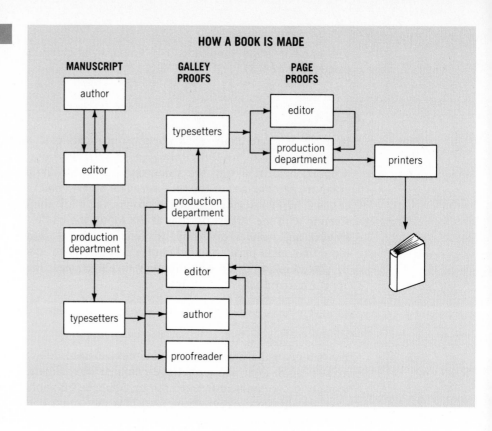

FIGURE 8-11

Flowchart

HOW A BOOK IS MADE

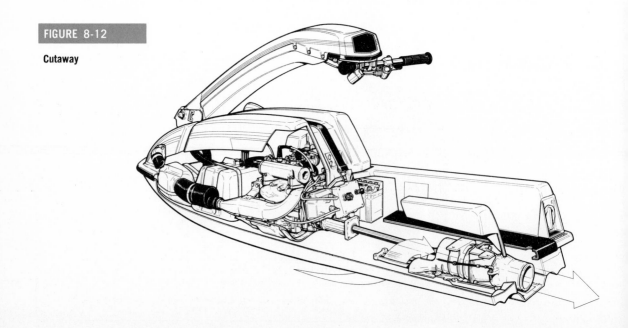

FIGURE 8-12

Cutaway

FIGURE 8-13

Time Chart

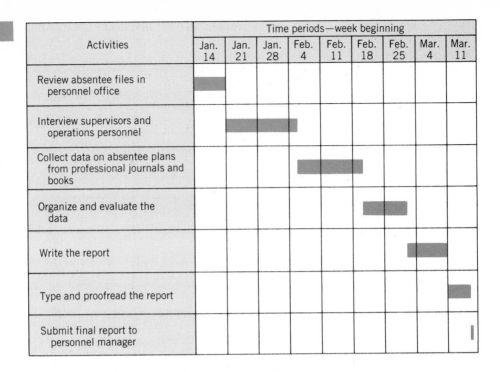

Activities	Time periods—week beginning								
	Jan. 14	Jan. 21	Jan. 28	Feb. 4	Feb. 11	Feb. 18	Feb. 25	Mar. 4	Mar. 11
Review absentee files in personnel office	▇								
Interview supervisors and operations personnel		▇	▇						
Collect data on absentee plans from professional journals and books				▇	▇				
Organize and evaluate the data						▇			
Write the report								▇	
Type and proofread the report									▇
Submit final report to personnel manager									❙

Flowcharts

Flowcharts present a process or procedure (Figure 8-11). Examples include the steps involved in applying to college or the stages of a chemical process. Steps should be labeled clearly and may be differentiated by shape to suggest different functions.

Cutaway or Exploded Drawing

The cutaway or exploded drawing lets us see within a structure to perceive the relation among its parts (Figure 8-12). Such representations are often used in product descriptions and technical discussions.

Time Charts

Time charts use bars or lines against a work/time matrix to show when jobs or other activities will begin and end (Figure 8-13). Used often in reports and proposals, the time chart serves as a work progress schedule for projects.

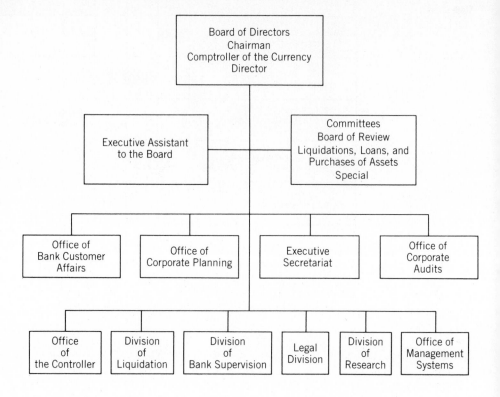

FIGURE 8-14

FEDERAL DEPOSIT INSURANCE CORPORATION

Organizational Chart

Organizational Charts

Organizational charts are similar to flow charts, but represent structures rather than processes or procedures (Figure 8-14). An organizational chart, for example, could show related functions or departments within a corporation.

Maps

Maps present geographical representation of data (Figure 8-15). Family incomes, for example, could be represented on a state-by-state or region-by-region basis using a United States map. Shading, coloring, or texturing can distinguish different regions on the map.

Tables

Tables, while not a visual aid by strict definition, represent statistical data in columns and rows (Figure 8-16). As labeled below, tables are commonly formatted with row headings, row identifiers, column headings, data, and row totals. General purpose tables present nonspecific data (as in a computer

FIGURE 8-15

Maps

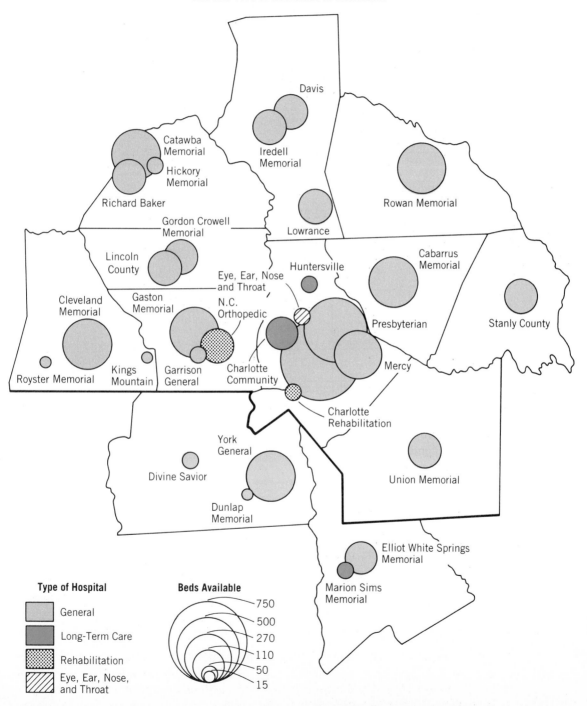

SIZE AND TYPE OF HOSPITALS IN METROLINA

Davis

Catawba Memorial

Hickory Memorial

Iredell Memorial

Richard Baker

Rowan Memorial

Gordon Crowell Memorial

Lowrance

Lincoln County

Cabarrus Memorial

Huntersville

Eye, Ear, Nose and Throat

Cleveland Memorial

Gaston Memorial

N.C. Orthopedic

Presbyterian

Stanly County

Royster Memorial

Kings Mountain

Garrison General

Charlotte Community

Mercy

Charlotte Rehabilitation

York General

Divine Savior

Union Memorial

Dunlap Memorial

Elliot White Springs Memorial

Marion Sims Memorial

Type of Hospital

General

Long-Term Care

Rehabilitation

Eye, Ear, Nose, and Throat

Beds Available

750
500
270
110
50
15

FIGURE 8-16

SALES OF UNITS 201, 404, AND 605, JUNE 5-10.

Tables

Example 1

Station No.	Total Sales
1	350
2	820
3	870
4	440
5	375
6	950
7	475
8	675
9	550
10	525
11	1150
12	1050

(Reflects specific data, though not effectively presented)

Example 2

Station No.	5 ft. Display Case	2 ft Display Case (Blinker)
1	350	
2		820
3		870
4	440	
5	375	
6		950
7	475	
8		675
9	550	
10	525	
11		1150
12		1050

(Reflects specific data)

Example 3

Station No.	5 ft Display Case	2 ft Display Case (Blinker)
1	350	
4	440	
5	375	
7	475	
9	550	
10	525	
2		820
3		870
6		950
8		675
11		1150
12		1050

(Reflects specific data; distinguishes types)

Example 4

Station No.	5 ft Display Case	Station No	2 ft Display Case (Blinker)
1	350	2	820
4	440	3	870
5	375	6	950
7	475	8	675
9	550	11	1150
10	525	12	1050

(Reflects specific data; well organized)

printout) that may serve the reader as a reference. Special purpose tables are designed, highlighted, and placed in such a way as to support a point made in the text.

Tables are used primarily to represent quantitative data where exact amounts, not trends, are most important.

VISUAL AIDS FOR ORAL PRESENTATIONS

Visual aids exclusively for speakers include handouts, slides, acetate transparencies, films, videotapes, storyboards, flipcharts, and physical objects.

Handouts

Handouts can provide additional information, agendas, and feedback devices to an audience (Figure 8-17). Take care to distribute handouts so they add to, not interrupt, the concentration of your audience on what you have to say.

FIGURE 8-17

Handout

PROOFREADING PROCEDURES

A. <u>Editorial Styling References</u>. In preparing copy for the
typesetter, College Division editors should use the following
authorities:

   1. For spelling and capitalization, <u>Webster's Seventh New
      Collegiate Dictionary</u>, backed up by <u>Webster's Third
      New International Dictionary</u>. Specific problems in
      spelling and capitalization are also covered in the
      points under Item C of this entry (Scott, Foresman
      House Style).

   2. For other points of editorial styling, the Scott,
      Foresman's house style indicated in Item C and <u>The
      Scott, Foresman Author's Manual</u>. For editorial
      problems not solved by the references listed above,
      editors are referred to <u>A Manual of Style</u>, 12th. ed.,
      University of Chicago Press.

(See also *EDITORIAL STYLE SHEETS and AUTHOR'S MANUAL: LETTER
TO ACCOMPANY.)

B. <u>Proofroom Procedures</u>. Proofreading of materials set in
type is the primary concern of the Scott, Foresman Proofroom.
In some instances, however, College titles are proofread by
free-lancers or by a combination of author and manuscript
editor. Free-lancers, authors, and editors are expected to
follow essentially the same procedures as the Proofroom. For
some books, the author will read proofs against the
manuscript; for others, the manuscript editor will retain the
manuscript and have the author read the raw galleys.

   1. <u>Galleys</u> are read against the final manuscript and are
      read for:

      a) typographical errors
      b) word breaks at ends of lines
      c) consistency of style
      d) all possible errors
      e) accuracy of facts (if schedule permits and
         information is available in Proofroom)

   2. <u>Revised galleys</u> are checked against original galleys
      and are checked <u>only</u> for:

      a) correctness of revisions
      b) omission or addition of lines (line check)

FIGURE 8-18

Slides

FIGURE 8-19

Acetate Transparency

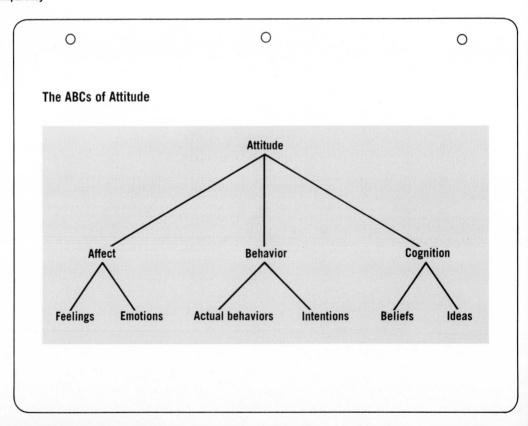

FIGURE 8-20

Film

Slides

Slides, though somewhat time-consuming to prepare, are quite popular for formal presentations. Both "word" slides and pictures can be intermixed in the presentation (Figure 8-18). Do not create slides that simply repeat what you have to say, and never read directly from a slide to your audience. It is now possible to create graphics on your computer screen, then photograph them for use as slides. Before using slides for a presentation, practice the mechanics of using the slide projector. Nothing interrupts presentations so frequently as stuck, upside-down, or misordered slides.

Acetate Transparencies

Acetate transparencies can be prepared in color using a 3M Thermofax machine or other transparency-capable photocopy machine (Figure 8-19). Transparencies, like slides, should not merely repeat the words of your presentation. Use words and graphics on transparencies to emphasize key points, unify your argument, and demonstrate principles in visual ways. Practice using transparencies until you are sure to avoid standing in the path of the projection or laying transparencies crooked or upside-down on the projector.

Films

Films and videotapes, as set pieces within your presentation, can provide visual and auditory relief for the audience (Figure 8-20). Because these are

FIGURE 8-21

Storyboard

high interest items, be sure they are coordinated well with the central concerns of your presentation. Too often audiences leave presentations mumbling about "a great movie but a poor presentation." Neither films nor videotapes need to be played nonstop from start to finish. Often a presenter can stop a film or videotape to discuss a point before returning to the media portion of the presentation.

Storyboards

Storyboards, either on cloth or more recently on computer screen, allow the presenter to prepare in advance a series of words, shapes, and pictures that literally "tell the story" of the presentation as it unfolds (Figures 8-21a and b). On a cloth background, these words, shapes, and pictures can be put up, rearranged, or removed as the speaker makes his or her point. On the computer screen, the pre-prepared "screens" can be called up at the press of a key. IBM now markets a popular presentation software package called, appropriately enough, *Storyboard*.

FIGURE 8-22

Flipchart

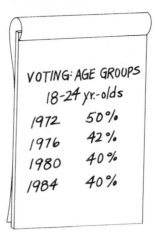

Flipcharts

Flipcharts are pads of large-sized paper mounted on a display stand (Figure 8-22). Pages can be prepared in advance, then "flipped" as the speaker goes on from point to point. Or the speaker can choose to create visual interpretations on the spot, using bold-stroke pens in a variety of colors.

Physical Objects

Finally, physical objects that can be held up and perhaps passed among the audience serve presenters well in making ideas, descriptions, and functions concrete (Figure 8-23).

FIGURE 8-23

Physical Object

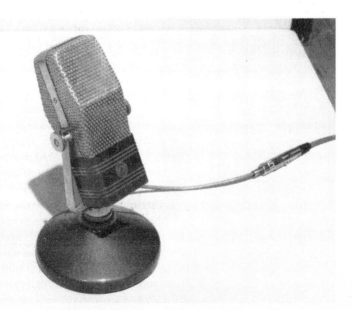

Taken together, visual aids are an important ally in the writer's or speaker's efforts to inform and persuade an audience. Attractive visual aids clarify, simplify, and make vivid the main points of a communication.

Summary

1. Computer graphics software now allows non-artists to create professional visual aids.
2. Visual aids can clarify, emphasize, simplify, and unify your points as well as impress your audience.
3. Visual aids must be specifically introduced and identified in nearby text.
4. Writers and presenters must take care not to distort statistics and deceive audience members by disproportionate, misaligned, or incomplete visual aids.
5. Common visual aids used in written communications are the photograph, line drawing, line graph, bar graph, pie chart, pictogram, flow chart, organizational chart, time chart, maps, cutaway drawings, and tables.
6. Common visual aids used by oral presenters are handouts, slides, acetate transparencies, films, videotapes, storyboards, flipcharts, and physical objects.

Questions for Discussion

1. Discuss the relation between words and graphics in business documents. How do they support one another?
2. Why do readers like graphic enhancements in the form of photos, charts, graphs, pictograms, maps, and so forth? Explain in detail.
3. On what basis would you decide to use a bar chart instead of a line graph? Give an example.
4. Discuss common errors in constructing the following graphics:

   Pie chart
   Table
   Bar Chart
   Line Graph
   Pictogram
   Map

5. Discuss the impact of computer software packages for generating graphics. How have such packages influenced the "look" of typical business documents?
6. Are graphics always appropriate? If not, discuss a situation where words are more appropriate than graphics.
7. Discuss the placement of graphics on an 8 1/2 by 11" page. What guidelines can you suggest? Explain the reasons for each guideline you mention.
8. How can even a low-budget office operation make use of graphics in its documents? Discuss.

9. In what ways can particular parts of a graphic be made to catch the reader's eye?
10. Discuss the impact of color in graphics. In what ways can color add emphasis and effect to graphics?

Exercises

1. Choose a short document (perhaps a letter or brochure) that has no visual aids. Create a visual aid and, by retyping or cutting-and-pasting the original document, place the graphic into the document with any additional words you require. Write a paragraph in which you justify your selection and handling of the visual aid you chose.
2. Visit a local computer store and learn about graphics packages for business use. Write a brief report of your findings, appending any literature you receive from the store.
3. Create a portfolio of at least eight different kinds of visual aids used in a business context. You may find such graphics in magazines such as *Fortune, Forbes, U.S. News and World Report, Business Week, Nation's Business,* and others. Write one paragraph evaluating each item in your portfolio. Assess the success or failure of the graphic at hand.
4. Select or take a photograph, then include it in a business document at least one page in length. Take particular care to identify and introduce the photograph using the words that surround it on the page.
5. Assume that you want to graphically represent the income levels of various neighborhoods, areas, or towns in your region. (Unless your instructor specifies otherwise, you may make up statistics for the purpose of this exercise.) Show at least six different income groups by number, annual income, and any other distinguishing characteristics you wish to include. Choose three different visual aids by which to represent your statistics, and create each visual aid with pen and paper or a computer software package.
6. Photocopy a map of the United States. Use it to create a statistical map in which you point out regional differences in a category of your choosing. (You may, for example, show population differences for states or regions; education differences; age differences; and so forth.)
7. Create a flow chart showing, step-by-step, the progress of a process or procedure of your choice. Your chart should have at least eight distinct stages.
8. Create two transparencies for use in an in-class presentation. Write one or two paragraphs in which you explain what you are attempting to achieve in the transparencies. Deal particularly with your choice of words, shapes, and pictures, including their placement.
9. Investigate computer storyboard software such as Framework and Storyboard. Write a brief report in which you discuss the uses of these programs for business presenters. Attach any literature you are able to acquire on the programs.

Communicating
Outside the Company

PART THREE

Optical character reader for processing mail

Barbara Kennedy directs mass marketing for a major wholesaler of sports equipment.

We send dozens of letters out of my office each day to clients around the world. I thought I had an efficient system worked out: my staff and I dictated letters without attention to paragraphing or form on the page. We just spilled out the messages. The secretaries in the typing pool would then give the letters some shape, as they thought best, and send them back up for review, signatures, and mailing.

In other words, I divided the writing task. Some wrote words, and others placed those words on the page.

Well, to summarize a year of problems, my plan hasn't worked out well. When my staff members see their letters in typed form, they often complain, "that's not what I meant" even though the typist hadn't missed a word from the dictation tape. Frankly, I'm not happy with the way my own correspondence looks when it goes out the door.

What, in your opinion, has gone wrong in Barbara's operation? What could she do to correct it? Should she hire new typists? Should she dissolve the typing pool?

Style and Format

of Business Letters 9

LEARNING OBJECTIVES

To recognize the strong impressions made by the form of a business letter

To understand and achieve the *you* emphasis in business correspondence

To know the uses and limits of letter recipes and guide letters

To recognize and produce four common letter formats and envelope conventions

To place the parts of a business letter correctly and advantageously on the page

To name and write examples of the major internal parts of the business letter

To appreciate the importance of a personal, sincere tone in business writing

Company names can bring sights, sounds, and feelings to mind: Sears, Mutual of Omaha, Saks, John Deere, Allstate, Coca-Cola, Ford, Apple Computer, Bank of America, Sheraton. These familiar corporate names conjure up associations that we call "the company image." For the hundreds of millions of dollars American businesses spend each year on advertising, these companies want instant identification on the part of the buying public. Some companies want their names to conjure up a mood (carefree luxury) or a visual image (a reassuring pair of cupped hands) or a slogan ("the customer is always right").

Company images depend upon the words a company uses about itself and the words others use about the company. As a business writer, you cannot be completely responsible for the words your customers choose to use about the company: "marvelous," "reliable," "sharp," or "disorganized." But you *can* take charge of the words your company uses about itself which do affect the impressions of the public. Those words, especially as they are found in business letters, should occupy a major share of your attention during each business day.

This chapter discusses the written messages in the form of business letters that pass from your company to people outside. Taken together, these letters represent your company in a literal way: they re-present or re-create the company image to each letter recipient. From letters alone, customers can form opinions on whether the company is friendly or aloof, fast or slow, modern or antiquated, fair or arbitrary, organized or chaotic. To judge just how quickly such judgments are formed, decide what you think about the company that allowed the letter in Figure 9-1 to be mailed.

When customers form negative judgments, businesses soon notice an undesirable change. Orders dry up. Sales people find doors closed to them. Profits begin to fall.

Your words, in short, *matter* for the company.

They also matter for your personal success. While your business relationships with clients may sometimes receive a boost from a round of golf or a pleasant lunch, the most significant and lasting impression of your professional competence appears in the permanent records you send to people outside the company—business letters. Here are words for your customers and others to mull over, to show to associates, to re-read. Your business letters create your image before the public as a reliable, educated, sensible, and personable professional.

MESSAGE AND MASSAGE: ACHIEVING CLARITY AND EMPATHY

Your most important task as a business writer is to communicate your message clearly. In the following pages we will discuss several specific organizational patterns designed to produce clear, easy-to-read letters. You may also wish to review the techniques covered in Chapters 1 and 2.

But a clear message alone will not bring all the rewards asked of your business writing. Skillful business writers combine a clear message with words and expressions that convey concern for the reader—empathy, in

FIGURE 9-1

Response Letter for Evaluation

Haeber Hardware Supply

1121 Main St.　　Duncan, Virginia 55634

Jn. 4th, 198_

Mister Bob Thomas
Western Village Hardware
342 oak lane
Duncan, Virg.

Dear. M. Thomas;

    We got your complaint about the missing items. We must
have been low or out on stock. Look at the bill of lading-
are the items listed? If not, you were'nt billed. Our
copy of the bill of lading has been already filed, but we
can probably dig it out if you need to check. What do want
us to do if we get more in?

                          Sincerly,

                          Burton Coy, manager

An Evaluation Scoresheet
I judge this company

__efficient	__likely to succeed	__slow-witted
__helpful	__disorganized	__unreliable
__intelligent	__uncooperative	__doomed to failure
__reliable		

short, a *you* emphasis. Marshall McLuhan called such empathy the "massage" that accompanies the message. By whatever name, this persuasive emotional aspect of business writing can be crucial to a successful letter. Can you spot the *you* emphasis in the following messages?

> *Message Alone:* Jack Millens will meet with you on Feb. 6 at a location of your choice.
> *Message plus Massage:* Your regional representative, Jack Millens, is eager to meet you when he visits Portland on Feb. 6. If you are free, he invites you to lunch on that day as his guest.

> The very act of writing and rewriting helps us to clarify our ideas, to understand better what we want to say, to find the best way to organize our material, to speak to the real interests and needs of our readers.
> Joseph M. Williams, *Style*, 2nd ed., Scott, Foresman and Company, 1985.

Massage in business writing includes all those techniques that win the reader over to your point of view and path of action. In the following chapters you will learn the upbeat attitudes, gracious approaches, and marks of sincerity that distinguish effective business letters from ineffective messages.

The single most powerful form of *massage* in business communication remains the *you* emphasis. In every letter you write, set aside self-interest (*I* fascination) to concentrate on the client's interest, the *you* perspective. When people show interest in us, we warm up to them. We find it easy to accept their ideas and suggestions. Notice how *I* fascination gives way to *you* emphasis in two versions of an announcement.

The "I" version

        I'm Diamond Jim Bradley, and I'm thrilled to open my
    thirteenth stereo discount store this weekend at the corner
    of Fourth and Main. I'll be there in person to cut the
    ribbon to my newest store.

The "You" Version

        Your own Diamond Stereo Discount Store opens this
    Saturday at 9 A.M. on the corner of Fourth and Main. You'll
    find incredible bargains in stereo equipment, all priced to
    say "Pleased to meet you, neighbor." Come cut the ribbon to
    stereo savings at Diamond's, this Saturday at 9 A.M.

The *you* emphasis can be one of your best tools in creating attractive, persuasive business letters.

LETTERS AS A LEGAL RECORD

Businesses large and small now often require that letters leaving the office first be reviewed by an authorized manager. At the Newport Beach office of Cushman and Wakefield, a commercial real estate brokerage, the office manager each day faces the substantial task of reading, and often rewriting, each and every business letter directed to a client.

The manager's interest, of course, is to preserve and enhance the company's image by catching misspellings, poor grammar, improper punctuation, and so forth. But even more important, the manager weighs the legal implications of each business letter. Do the writer's assertions to the client constitute a binding promise—a contract, in effect? Do the words in the letter fairly reflect the truth of the situation at hand, or do they leave the door open for later legal challenge? Are the words clear, or can they be misinterpreted?

After a few months of such editorial activity, managers develop a built-in "danger-detector" that sounds off when company business writers stray into legally hazardous territory. In the letter in Figure 9-2, note the changes penned in by one manager before it, in retyped form, could be sent to the client. guideline for Fig. 9-2

Helen's manager has wisely revised those claims that may leave the salesperson or the company open to charges of misinformation. Helen, in her understandable enthusiasm for the sale, has forgotten that letters stand as signed, permanent legal records of assertions, claims, and representations. Imagine the potential problems Helen faces if the unedited version of her letter had been sent to the client. If the roof had leaked disastrously, Helen could be called to account for misrepresenting the property ("the roof is in fine shape"). If the neighborhood turned out to be unbearably noisy, the new owners or their attorney would have every right to question Helen's assurance that "the neighborhood is as quiet as the country."

Words on company stationery, signed by you, *matter*. They create lasting impressions of the company and of you. They stand as permanent legal records of representations you have made. Chapter 20, Business Communication and the Law, discusses the legal pitfalls business writers must avoid in such areas as personnel matters, credit and collection communications, and product representations.

EVALUATING THE RECIPE APPROACH TO LETTERS

Earlier eras of business communication had a straightforward way of guarding against misstatements in business writing: just follow the standard recipe line-for-line, word-for-word. Next to the dictionary on many writers' desks used to stand a guidebook to business letters. One simply looked in the index and turned to the proper model to emulate.

Figure 9-3, for example, shows a guide letter from the 1950s regarding an overdue account. Writers had only to fill in the blanks.

FIGURE 9-2

Letter Edited by a Manager

MARTINDALE REALTY, INC.

4422 Trendville Lane
Benchton, Iowa 77342
(222) 768-3698

May 2, 198_

Mr. and Mrs. Ralph Crown
532 Lincoln Boulevard
Benchton, Iowa 77342

Dear Mr. and Mrs. Crown:

Together, we have searched for the "right" family home for you. As you remarked last week, 1942 Ridgecrest Drive seems to be just what we've been looking for.

I checked into the two matters that concerned you.

1. The roof is ~~in fine shape~~ _only ten years old_. It was replaced in 1981 by Standard Roofing of Everlyville.
2. ~~The neighborhood is as quiet as the country.~~ _Neighbors on both sides of your chosen home told me they enjoyed the quiet, country-like neighborhood._

Let's plan to see the house once more this Thursday morning. I'll stop by at 10:30 A.M. Please phone if you would like to arrange an alternate time.

Sincerely,

Helen

Helen Townsend
Realtor

FIGURE 9-3

Guide Letter

```
Dear

     We beg to inform you that your account, no.          ,
now stands in arrears.  Calculated to         , the amount
owing is

     In the event that we do not receive your remittance in
a timely way, the matter will be referred promptly to
counsel.

                              Sincerely,
```

We recognize such stuffy prose as outdated. Business correspondence in the 1980s and, we can project, in the 1990s, attempts to strike a tone that says, in effect, "I care about my reader." We call this tone the *you* emphasis or empathetic element in business writing.

You can practice three techniques to warm up business communication that tends to be cold or uncaring in tone.

1. Emphasize the *you* approach. Keep your emphasis in business letters steadily on your *reader's* needs, not your own.

> *Not: I* emphasis   I am sending information on peripheral devices suited to the computer I sold you.
> *Instead: You* emphasis   You'll receive complete instructions with details on capabilities and prices of optional add-ons suited to your new computer.

The difference in these two statements may at first seem slight—both do get the message across. Yet the recurring use of *I* in a complete business letter causes your reader to lose interest in the letter and lose connection with you as well. Show genuine reader concern by emphasizing *you* and downplaying *I* as much as possible.

2. Concentrate on *people* in addition to things. In the following passage, a manager tries to compliment an employee on a good report. Notice how the emphasis of the message falls on the document rather than the person and hence ends up sounding hollow and cold.

Version 1: "Alternatives in Pension Planning" presents four popular pension plans, each with advantages and disadvantages. The report evaluates the plans in relation to specific company needs. The report is clear and orderly.

Version 2: Thank you, Mary, for your good work in "Alternatives in Pension Planning." You've analyzed the four competing plans in a clear, orderly way—just what we need to help us choose the best plan for our company.

When you concentrate upon objects, any praise you give falls upon the object. Readers can hardly be expected to care when an object receives praise. When you relocate your emphasis to people, however, you create human warmth and solicit positive responses.

3. Show your feelings in an appropriate way. Perhaps because business life involves so many complex mental activities—analyzing, organizing, evaluating—business writers may tend to fill their letters with correspondingly complex constructions:

Trace elements no. 5 and no. 7 appeared in 14% of the Westbury samples, as summarized in Report no. 22, dated May 2, 198_, of the Soils Chemistry Laboratory.

Only when our readers yawn or shrug are we reminded that business is a people-centered world. As the sales success of *People* magazine has demonstrated, men and women are deeply interested in what others do, think, and feel. In reminding a client about a 3 P.M. meeting, for example, don't hesitate to reveal your feelings about the occasion:

Not: We will meet at 3 P.M.
Instead: I will enjoy talking with you at our 3 P.M. meeting.

Feelings are certainly not out of place in the midst of the hard realities of business. Together with expressions of intellectual analysis and evaluation, our feelings reveal the determination of our *will*. Analysis describes what has happened or what may happen, but our feelings foreshadow what we will *make* happen. When you show your feelings, you reveal what you want.

Readers understand the force and importance of feelings in business letters and accurately translate feelings into a significant part of the business message:

The Manager Writes: The Sundance Peak project shows some promise.

The Reader Interprets: The project sounds tentative, iffy.

The Manager Writes: You'll probably share my excitement about the potential of the Sundance Peak project.

The Reader Interprets: Excited? There's something worth looking into here.

Writers, of course, can overdo the inclusion of personal feeling. A sane guide seems to be the familiar knock-at-the-door analogy: be as personable in business writing as you would be face-to-face in a personal business encounter. While our business associates and customers may never know us as well as our best friends do, we nevertheless can show many of our feelings in our business writing—and, just as important, we can be sensitive to the feelings of our readers.

AUDIENCE-BASED LETTER WRITING

When you send a business letter, you send an extension of yourself to visit the client. This simple observation has some important implications. The organization and presentation of your business letter follows the pattern of actions and attitudes of a visitor at the door.

The business letter, as it arrives in its envelope, is a knock at the client's door. Envelopes that remind the client of junk mail may fail to knock loudly enough to be opened.

In unfolding your business letter, the client opens the door to you. In effect, the client asks, "Who's there?"

Your letterhead should answer that question in an attractive way.

Kabel Wholesale Lighting

111 Murphy St.   Salt Lake City, Utah 45388   (312) 845-6744

The client next wants to ask, "What do you want?" (Figure 9-4). In the case of a negative message, you may want to provide a sentence or two establishing goodwill before getting right to the point. Such goodwill passages are called *buffers* and often help to allay feelings of anger and disappointment.

Notice the social transaction that has taken place in your letter. Just as if you were a stranger at the door, you begin by orienting and reassuring your reader—"Here's who I am and here's my purpose." You provide full information on all actions and events that will affect your reader. You interpret the meaning of those actions and events as they apply to the reader. Only then do you make specific requests—"Here's what you can do."

Writers who ignore the ordinary paths of human interaction often produce unexpected responses from their readers:

The Client's Response: "I don't like being told what to do."

Dear Ms. Owens:

Call me right away at 1-800-423-3456 to reserve a date for our visit.

The Client's Response: "What visit?"

Dear Ms. Owens:

We have scheduled our visit for Friday, Aug. 22.

FIGURE 9-4

Audience Based Business Letter

Kabel Wholesale Lighting

111 Murphy St.   Salt Lake City, Utah 45388   (312) 845-6744

August 4, 198_

Ms. Millicent Owens
4533 Sanborn Lane
Salt Lake City, Utah 45338

Dear Ms. Owens:

The Client Asks: "What do you want?"

At 9 A.M., Friday, August 22, our analysis team will drop by your home to evaluate your use of electricity, as you requested. Their work will be neat, quick, and thorough. You need not move furniture or carpets.

The Client Wonders: "How do I profit?"

By Monday, August 25, you will receive a computer-developed assessment of your electrical usage patterns. The report contains recommendations for achieving savings without sacrificing comfort or convenience.

The Client Feels Special: "All this for me?"

You are a valued customer, and we are eager to help you get the most out of your utility dollars.

Finally, the Client Asks: "What should I do?"

Mail in the enclosed registration card to confirm the date and time of your electrical analysis. Or, if you prefer, phone in your reservation to Kabel by calling 1-800-423-3456.

Sincerely yours,

Graham Trevor

Graham Trevor
Operations Manager

GT/pm
Enclosure: Registration card

The Letter

Let's take an overview of the major business-letter formats (Figures 9-5, 9-6 and 9-7). Although the various letter parts named here will not be discussed until later in the chapter, most are probably quite familiar to you already.

Notice the distinguishing features of each of the major format styles.

Block Style (Figure 9-5). All parts of the business letter are placed against the left margin. Paragraphs have no indentation and are separated from one another by one or two extra spaces on the typewriter or printer. In this popular business style, open punctuation—that is, the omission of punctuation after the salutation and complimentary closing—is sometimes used.

Indented Style (Figure 9-6). Three elements of the indented style are moved to the right margin: the return address (if letterhead stationery is not being used), the date, and the signature block, including the complimentary close. Paragraphs are indented, usually five spaces. This style, somewhat more traditional and literary in appearance than the block style, is still in common use. It requires more care and effort on the part of the typist, however, and partly for that reason is less popular in business today than the block style. The open style of omitted punctuation is rarely if ever seen in this more conservative format.

Modified Block Style (Figure 9-7). In this format, elements of both the block style and indented style appear. The return address (when not using letterhead), the date, and the signature block are moved to the right margin. All other letter parts are placed along the left margin. Paragraphs are not indented. Omission of punctuation is commonly practiced. The modified block style is less common than block style and indented style, but can be useful when the writer is trying to strike a modern look that still appears balanced on the page.

When the letterhead supplies the address of the sender, that information need not be repeated in a return address. When using blank paper, supply any addresses or division/unit/group/office numbers that your reader may require to reply to your letter. The date appears above the inside address, usually separated by double-spacing.

Block, indented, and modified block are all used frequently in contemporary business. The block style is most popular. It is easy to type (and easy to instruct new typists to use) since all lines are placed flush to the left margin. For some writers and readers, this style has a bold, urgent appearance.

Others still prefer the softer, more balanced patterns in the indented and modified block formats. These writers and readers like the way the reader's name and address take full prominence (the *you* emphasis) without visual interference from the date and, in some cases, the return address. They like the placement of the complimentary close, feeling that it has more impact when set on a margin of its own together with the date and return address. Some advocates point to the symmetrical balance of these formats.

Other experimental formats appear from time to time. However attracted writers may be to such innovative forms, they must consider the risk that

FIGURE 9-5

Block Style

Letterhead

Date

Inside Address

Subject Line

Salutation

No Indentation

Body

All Letter Parts Along
Left Margin

Complimentary Close

Signature

Reference Initials
Enclosure

Postscript

WILLIAMS ELECTRONIC SUPPLY, INC.

3892 Breston Place   Ft. Collins, CO 69483   (489) 389-9540

January 7, 198_

Mr. Frank Devlin, Manager
Devlin Industrial Wiring, Inc.
55 Leavitt Street
Denver, CO 89483

SUBJECT: Upcoming Industrial Arts Fair, May 15-17, 198_

Dear Mr. Devlin:

Your booth at last year's Industrial Arts Fair certainly
made a hit. No doubt your creative staff is already
planning surprises for us at this year's fair.

Williams Electronic Supply wants to team up with Devlin
Industrial Wiring for this year's fair. Together we can
put on a fascinating demonstration of recent advances in
domestic and industrial uses of electricity. You and I
spoke briefly of this possibility at last year's fair, Mr.
Devlin. We agreed then that our mutual efforts would be
great for the fair and, of course, good advertising for our
companies.

I'm planning to visit Denver on January 18, 198_. Can we
meet to discuss our common interests? You can reach me
weekdays at the number above. If we haven't made
connection by January 15, I'll give you a call before my
trip to Denver.

Until then, best wishes from all of us at Williams
Electronic.

Sincerely,

Cindy Galloway

Cindy Galloway
Advertising Director

CG/woi
Enclosure: "Planning for the 198_ Industrial Arts Fair"

P.S. We have reserved the booth space next to yours in
hopes that we can expand both booths into one large display
area.

FIGURE 9-6

Indented Style

WILLIAMS ELECTRONIC SUPPLY, INC.

3892 Breston Place   Ft. Collins, CO 69483   (489) 389-9540

January 7, 198_

Mr. Frank Devlin, Manager
Devlin Industrial Wiring, Inc.
55 Leavitt Street
Denver, CO 89483

SUBJECT: Upcoming Industrial Arts Fair, May 15-17, 198_

Dear Mr. Devlin:

     Your booth at last year's Industrial Arts Fair
certainly made a hit. No doubt your creative staff is
already planning surprises for us at this year's fair.

     Williams Electronic Supply wants to team up with Devlin
Industrial Wiring for this year's fair. Together we can
put on a fascinating demonstration of recent advances in
domestic and industrial uses of electricity. You and I
spoke briefly of this possibility at last year's fair, Mr.
Devlin. We agreed then that our mutual efforts would be
great for the fair and, of course, good advertising for our
companies.

     I'm planning to visit Denver on January 18, 198_. Can
we meet to discuss our common interests? You can reach me
weekdays at the number above. If we haven't made
connection by January 15, I'll give you a call before my
trip to Denver.

     Until then, best wishes from all of us at Williams
Electronic.

                              Sincerely,

                              Cindy Galloway

                              Cindy Galloway
                              Advertising Director

CG/woi
Enclosure: "Planning for the 198_ Industrial Arts Fair"

P.S. We have reserved the booth space next to yours in
hopes that we can expand both booths into one large display
area.

FIGURE 9-7

Modified Block Style

WILLIAMS ELECTRONIC SUPPLY, INC.

3892 Breston Place   Ft. Collins, CO 69483   (489) 389-9540

January 7, 198_

Mr. Frank Devlin, Manager
Devlin Industrial Wiring, Inc.
55 Leavitt Street
Denver, CO 89483

SUBJECT: Upcoming Industrial Arts Fair, May 15-17, 198_

Dear Mr. Devlin:

Your booth at last year's Industrial Arts Fair certainly
made a hit. No doubt your creative staff is already
planning surprises for us at this year's fair.

Williams Electronic Supply wants to team up with Devlin
Industrial Wiring for this year's fair. Together we can
put on a fascinating demonstration of recent advances in
domestic and industrial uses of electricity. You and I
spoke briefly of this possibility at last year's fair, Mr.
Devlin. We agreed then that our mutual efforts would be
great for the fair and, of course, good advertising for our
companies.

I'm planning to visit Denver on January 18, 198_. Can we
meet to discuss our common interests? You can reach me
weekdays at the number above. If we haven't made
connection by January 15, I'll give you a call before my
trip to Denver.

Until then, best wishes from all of us at Williams
Electronic.

Sincerely,

Cindy Galloway

Cindy Galloway
Advertising Director

CG/woi
Enclosure: "Planning for the 198_ Industrial Arts Fair"

P.S. We have reserved the booth space next to yours in
hopes that we can expand both booths into one large display
area.

No Indentation

Date and Signature
Block on Right

FIGURE 9-8

Envelope Conventions

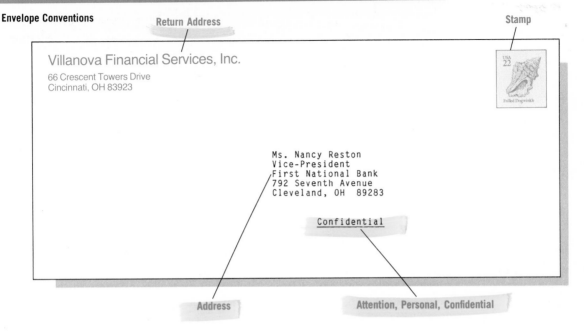

some readers may expect traditional business formats as a sign of traditional business practices. Such readers may react negatively to experimental formats.

Envelopes

Business letters should be mailed in standard letter-sized (4" x 9 1/2") envelopes, usually the same color as your letter stationery. Note the elements and placement of parts on a business envelope, as shown in Figure 9-8.

Folding

Fold full-sized letters as follows:

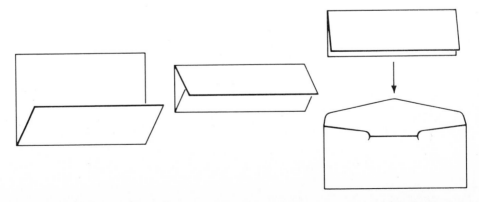

Note that the tab at the bottom of the folded letter allows the reader to open the letter easily.

Place the letter in the envelope so that the reader lifts the letter out and opens the first fold to see his or her name and the beginning of your message. The reader should never have to turn the letter right side up to begin reading.

Careful folding matters. Typical junk mail we receive has been folded quickly and stuffed into envelopes, either by hand or machine. We have come to recognize junk mail, in fact, by its off-center folds and cheap paper. Business letters can go a long way toward distinguishing themselves from junk mail merely by paying attention to absolutely accurate folds, with the side edge of the paper lining up without overlap as the fold is made. A little practice with blank sheets can make this slight but important skill a matter of business habit.

Type and Print

Business letters have always had ways to impress the reader. For the last several decades, significant business correspondence has distinguished itself from junk mail by individual typing. Among the individually typed letters, the pecking order descended from flawless, carbon-ribbon letters at the top (the look of book type) to fabric-ribbon letters at the bottom, often with "white-out" lines and erasures.

The appearance of your business letters is determined in large part by the quality of the type and inking medium used to produce them. Review the common forms of type and print in Figure 9-9. Judge which would create the most professional appearance.

The advent of word processing and high speed letter-quality printers has brought a new standard of attractiveness to business letters. With the new standard has come a new challenge. Now virtually every business letter you receive can be uniformly impressive in the way it is printed on the page. Junk mail and a letter from your lawyer both can be delivered economically to you via carbon-ribbon letter-quality printers. If the sender wishes, the words in each line of the letter may be spaced evenly across the page from margin to margin (right justification) so that the letter appears like the page of this text.

The challenge to us as business writers is obvious. We can no longer rely on "attractive typing" to suggest quality or importance to the reader. In an era when junk mail is as effectively designed as personal business correspondence, writers must look to new techniques by which important letters can stand apart from the crowd.

Placement by Difficulty

Writers of business letters can get a step up on word processed junk mail by designing the business letter for at-a-glance appeal. An old formula for creating a pleasing design still makes good sense: each written work should have a perceivable beginning, middle, and end.

FIGURE 9-9

Samples of Type and Print

Fabric-ribbon manual typewriter.

The writer's selection of font, ribbon, and machine can influence the readers' attitudes.

Carbon-ribbon electric typewriter.

The writer's selection of font, ribbon, and machine can influence the readers' attitudes.

Fabric-ribbon dot matrix printer.

The writer's selection of font, ribbon, and machine can influence readers' attitudes.

Carbon-ribbon letter-quality printer.

The writer's selection of font, ribbon, and machine can influence readers' attitudes.

Ink-jet laser printer.

The writer's selection of font, ribbon, and machine can influence readers' attitudes.

Applying this formula to a business letter, we can envision a shape some-what like the one shown in Figure 9-10. The boxes, of course, are only roughly suggestive of what a letter with a distinct beginning, middle, and end might look like. The importance of the pattern lies primarily in its effect upon readers. They perceive at a glance that the beginning of the letter will be easy: it requires the reading of only a sentence or two. Similarly, in peripheral vision they notice that the ending, too, is easy—again, requiring that only a sentence or two be read and understood.

The larger middle paragraph, they deduce, must contain the *heart* of your message. Though some work will probably be required there, they trust that the brief introductory paragraph and brief concluding paragraph will guide their efforts to make sense out of the middle paragraph.

Readers resist having to form meaning structures that the writer could and should have formed for them. They express their displeasure by also

FIGURE 9-10

Visual Appearance of a Business Letter

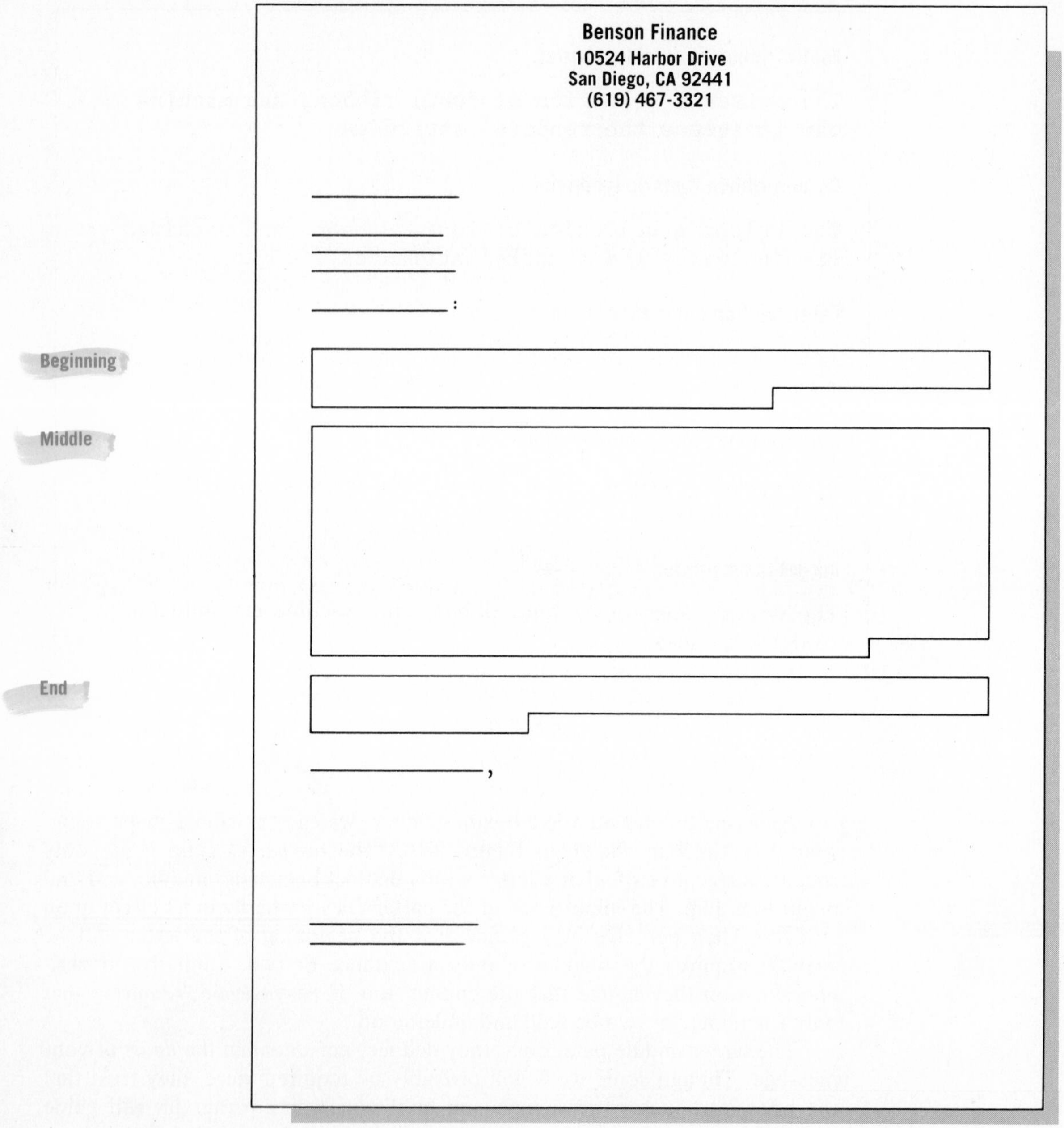

Benson Finance
10524 Harbor Drive
San Diego, CA 92441
(619) 467-3321

Beginning

Middle

End

resisting the force of the writer's argument. Form, therefore, becomes important to the business writer not for the sake of arbitrary rules or attractiveness, but for the most important reason of all: form helps persuade the reader.

Not all letters, of course, will have only three paragraphs. But even longer business letters can indicate a distinct beginning and end, letting the rest of the letter serve as a middle. The pattern, as shown in Figure 9-11, still creates at-a-glance appeal on the page.

Readers approach this kind of letter without hesitation, believing that they can make sense out of your points without undue mental labor. By using logical format, white space, and indented lists, you break up the unbroken string of words that at first glance looks so complicated and dense. When readers can move almost effortlessly through your prose, they are apt to be comfortable and confident. They trust not only your ability to express yourself but also your ideas and proposals. Letters without visual appeal and effective design, however, can cause the reader frustration—which eventually is vented upon the writer, the message, and even the firm.

THE PARTS OF THE BUSINESS LETTER

The Letterhead

This form of business stationery always identifies the company, either by name, company logo, or both. The letterhead usually includes the address, city, state, and zip code of the company, as well as one or more telephone numbers and a cable/telex address code. In some contemporary letterheads, the company name stands at the top of the letter, with all other information arranged at the bottom of the page. Figure 9-12 illustrates three kinds of letterheads.

Sometimes even the most artful letterheads leave out information the recipient needs in order to write back: the street address, the full company name, or the zip code. In such cases, be sure to include the missing information in a return address. This block of information about the sender appears first in the order of business letter parts, as illustrated in Figure 9-12. Note that the writer's name and title do not appear in the return address. They are reserved for an identifying line after the signature at the end of the letter. Return addresses and letterheads always append a zip code after the city and state.

The Date

Type the date of the letter below the return address, double-spaced above the inside address. (If several days pass between the time you write the letter and mail it, you may want to type the date the letter is to be mailed, not written.) Do not mix letters and numbers in the date (not Feb. 2nd). Nor should you make a practice of reducing months to numbers (8-4-83). Modern business

FIGURE 9-11

Parts of a Longer Letter Arranged for Easy Reading

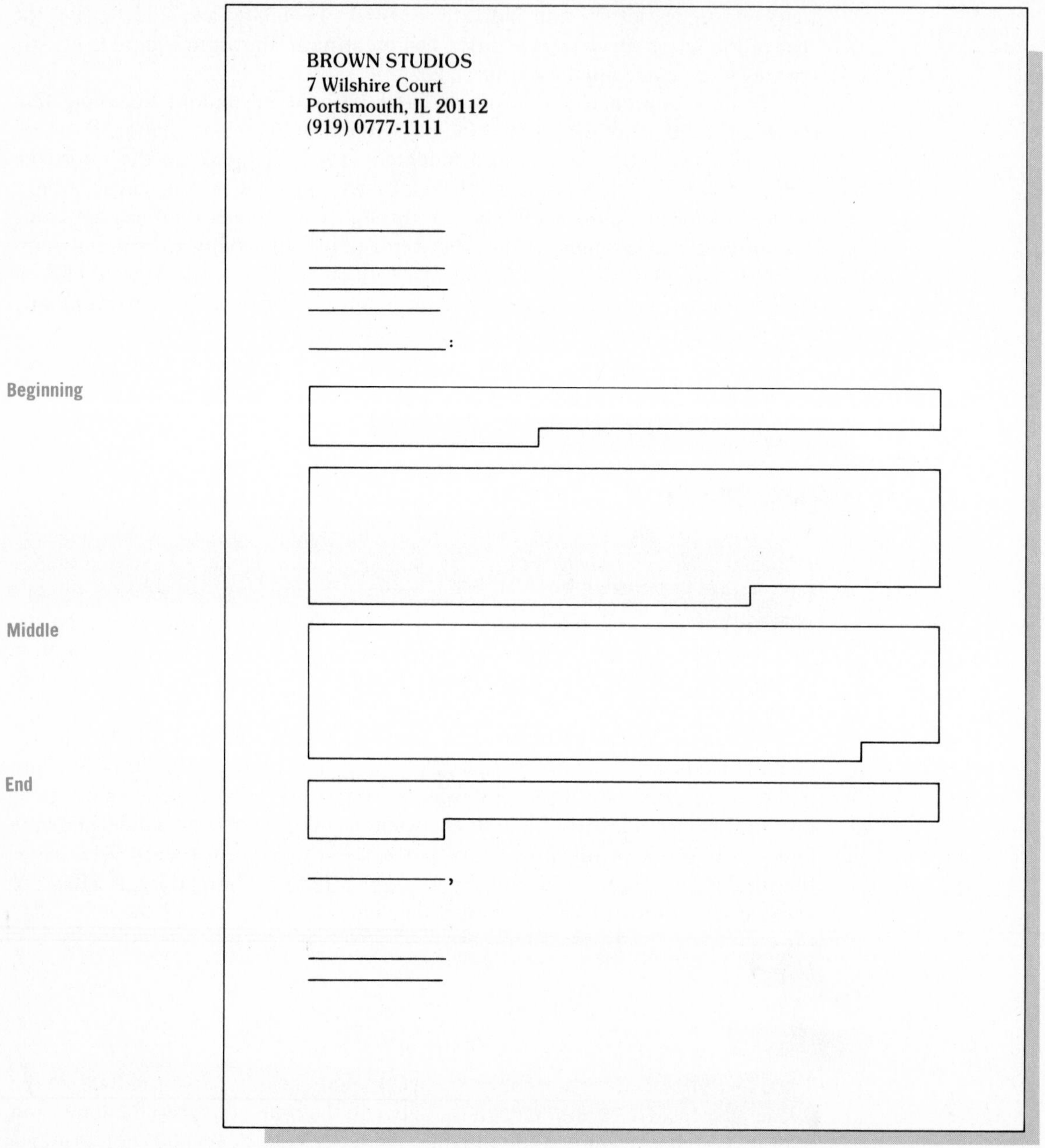

BROWN STUDIOS
7 Wilshire Court
Portsmouth, IL 20112
(919) 0777-1111

Beginning

Middle

End

FIGURE 9-12

Samples of Letterheads

Leland Office Supply
241 Main Street
Trenton, NJ 01152
1-800-726-5100

Seahorse Marine

Bay Drive, Suite 47   Marina del Rey, CA 92411
(714) 662-4301

Sordelli's

271 Olive Avenue   Baltimore, MD 61615   (717) 696-2101

communication certainly has enough codes, identifications, and serial numbers without reducing the date, too, to numbers. There is no agreed-upon business practice for deciding whether to spell out or abbreviate the month. If you do abbreviate, be sure to do so according to standard practice.

The Inside Address

Address your reader by his or her full professional name in the inside address, even if you plan to use a more informal name in the salutation.

```
Ms. Margaret Finch
Vice-President
Bennington Savings and Loan
381 Fifth Ave.
Princeton, NJ 30283

Dear Margaret,
     (or)
Dear Ms. Finch:
```

When the reader's name is unknown, use the job title both in the inside address and salutation:

```
Director of Marketing
Victory Products, Inc.
300 Buena Vista St.
Ft. Worth, TX 46839

Dear Director:
```

If the person to whom you are writing has no professional title, simply type the name and then the company affiliation:

```
Mr. Ralph Nelson
Sunrise Auto Sales
498 Parkway Drive
Minneapolis, MN 79382

Dear Mr. Nelson:
```

The abbreviation *Ms.* is the feminine equivalent of *Mr.* and should be used when addressing women. Do not use *Miss* or *Mrs.* unless your reader has expressed a preference for these abbreviations. It is also accepted business practice to address both men and women without the prefacing abbreviation of *Mr.* or *Ms.*

```
          Barbara Fischer
          Sales Manager
          Pets International
          17 Westmoreland Ave.
          Tampa, FL 59030
```

Notice that titles (Sales Manager) usually appear on the line beneath the reader's name. It is also permissible to attach a short title, following a comma, after the name and on the same line.

```
          Walter Fredericks, Supervisor
          Office of Social Welfare
          400 State of Iowa Building
          Dubuque, IA 40230
```

In such cases, the writer's goal is to produce an inside address that looks somewhat balanced, with lines of approximately the same length. When the job title requires more than one word, place the entire title on the line following the recipient's name.

Next, type the department or division (if any) within the company where the reader is employed. Then comes the company name on a separate line, followed on the next line by the street address. On the next line comes the city, state, and zip code. If you abbreviate the state, use capital letters for the entire abbreviation and do not add a period after the abbreviation:

```
          CA  MA  AZ  OR  MN  FL
```

```
          Mr. Harold Robley
          Head of Engineering
          Division of Mechanics
          Raycon Scientific, Inc.
          4 Brenton Place
          Bellevue, WA 92683
```

The SUBJECT Statement

A SUBJECT statement may be placed between the inside address and the salutation, separated by double-spacing, as shown in Figure 9-13, or between the salutation and first paragraph of the body of the letter, again separated by double-spacing. The abbreviation *Re:* for the Latin phrase *in re* means *in regard to*. It has now given way to the more direct word, SUBJECT, usually capitalized for emphasis. A colon follows the SUBJECT notation. The key words you use to describe the subject of your letter need not make a sentence. Try to say precisely what your letter is about in as few words as possible.

```
SUBJECT: Flood insurance
SUBJECT: Tax considerations of the proposed merger
```

At times, you will see the SUBJECT statement set after the salutation, separated from surrounding text by double-spacing. This practice is a carryover from older forms of business writing and seems to be fading from use.

SUBJECT announcements have the advantage of setting forth in a bold, clear way the topic of your letter. They can be particularly useful, therefore, in business dealings when it is necessary to catch and hold the reader's attention in a direct if somewhat blunt way. Because SUBJECT headings announce content of a letter in headline fashion, they can prove useful for quick filing of business letters.

SUBJECT headings often have the disadvantage of sounding too urgent and impatient, especially in a relatively friendly business letter where personal warmth plays a key role. In addition, SUBJECT headings can rob the crucial first sentence of your letter of its content and hence its importance. After you have announced the SUBJECT, you can hardly restate the same idea in the first sentence of the letter. Use a longer SUBJECT line, therefore, or an entire sentence only when your meaning requires it.

Probably the best policy is the adage so often applied to punctuation marks: "When in doubt, leave it out."

The Attention Line

When you address your letter directly to the company, use the attention line to name a person, position, or department whose attention you are calling to the message. The word *Attention* is often capitalized for emphasis. The use of a colon after the word *Attention* is optional. Place the attention line after the inside address:

```
Bondaroy Paving Contractors, Inc.
173 Highway 95
Tucson, AZ 60023

ATTENTION: Personnel Director
            (or)
ATTENTION: Personnel Office
```

The Salutation

This traditional greeting (Dear Mr. Bevins:) appears beneath the inside address and occurs in all major business letter formats (except the little-used AMS style, where it is omitted). By convention, we continue to address business correspondents as *Dear*, even when our feelings are far from fond. This adjective has been so established by use, however, that no one attaches emotional meaning to it any longer. Therefore, feel free to address even stern collection letters to "Dear" without fear that you are softening your message.

FIGURE 9-13

Letter with Subject Line

Morgantown Insurance Brokers

25 Weston Road
Morgantown, PA 49293
(638) 783-2984

July 17, 198_

Ms. Kona Shors
113 Marilyn Place
Morgantown, PA 49293

SUBJECT: Flood Insurance

Dear Ms. Shors:

You may be interested in the enclosed brochure describing this agency's four plans for insuring your property against flood damage.

Because your home at 13 Marilyn Place lies within flood District #7, as defined by the Morgantown Emergency Plan, we recommend that you consider Plan C (p. 7) in the brochure to meet your needs. This plan provides $250,000 in coverage, but includes a $1000 deductible per year, making possible the economical premium described on p. 9.

Please count on us, Ms. Shors, to provide any further information you require for this insurance decision or others in the future. You can begin coverage today by calling us at (638) 783-2984.

Sincerely,

Sheldon Matthews

Sheldon Matthews
Agent

SM:cos
Enclosure: Brochure

Alternatives include the use of *Gentlemen* when writing to an all-male audience, in which case *Sir:* and *Dear Sir:* may also be used. These latter phrases are used less and less today. When addressing a general audience of both men and women, you may want to consider such salutations as *Dear Friends,* or *Dear Colleagues:.* You may also address a group by job or organization affiliation as *Dear Members of the Police Academy:* or *Dear Editors:.*

When writing to a recipient whose sex is not known, try whenever possible to use a job title in the salutation: *Dear Supervisor McCoy.* Or use the recipient's full name: *Dear Chris Morton.* Often a telephone call can clear up any potentially embarrassing misstatement in the salutation.

The phrase *Ladies and Gentlemen* is of little use because of its dated Victorian overtone and its inevitable association with public speeches, airport announcements, and circus acts.

Use careful judgment in deciding whether to use the first name of your correspondent in the salutation. Certainly business prospers when all parties share a friendly relationship, often marked by the use of first names. But a strong taboo still exists in most regions of the country against the premature use of a first name. If, for example, Allyson Florence, Director of Florence Medical Supply, requests information about your company, your communication may be more successful if it begins Dear Ms. Florence rather than Dear Allyson. After one or more conversations with her, you may find it natural to move to the more friendly first name in the salutation. One sure sign that the first name may be used appears when your correspondent signs a letter to you with his or her first name. Consider that mark of friendliness an invitation to use only your first name in signing future correspondence.

You may use either a comma or no punctuation at all after a first name in a salutation. Most writers do not use a colon, though no hard and fast rule applies here. The colon is a formal mark and defeats the tone you are trying to achieve in using the first name. After formal versions of a name—Mr. Franklin, Ms. Florence—use a colon.

The Body

The body—the text of the business letter—is the heart of your business communication. Your care in making a good impression and setting out a professional format in the earlier parts of the letter can be undone by a letter body that strikes the reader as illogical, unattractive, and therefore unreadable. Put in a positive way, you have the opportunity in the letter body to sustain the professionalism with which you began the letter. Your design and placement of the date, inside address, salutation, and optional Subject or Attention lines have already said to the reader, in effect, "This is a professional letter, not an amateurish effort." The body of the letter can prove that impression to be correct.

The next four chapters discuss specific ways to structure the body portion of more than thirty different types of business letters. Without repeating that information here, we can give an overview of what to look for in the letter body by means of the Six C's checklist:

Complete Coherent Concise Concrete Convincing Considerate

Complete

1. Is the body of your letter *complete*? Have you included all the facts, arguments, examples, and details you need to make your point?

Coherent

2. Are your points *coherent*? Do they link together in an organized, logical way? Have you provided necessary transitions between different thoughts? (Check your use of transition words like *therefore*, *however*, *but*, and *in addition*.)

Concise

3. Is the body of your letter *concise*? Have you pared your language down to the essential words you need to express your ideas?

Concrete

4. Is your language *concrete*? Have you gone straight to the point in understandable words? Do many of your verbs convey action (*grasp*, *lead*, *direct*, and so forth rather than *is*, *are*, *was*, and *were*)?

Convincing

5. Is the body of the letter *convincing*? Have you ordered your points to produce both understanding and acceptance on the reader's part?

Considerate

6. Is your message *considerate*? Have you looked at your ideas from the reader's point of view? Have you emphasized the *you* perspective in the expression of your thoughts? Have you maintained a tone that is sensitive to the reader's feelings?

The *Six C's* suggest goals for the writer as well as areas for evaluation after the body of the letter has been written. These guidelines, however, do not sum up everything a writer looks for in an effective letter body. Also check for

Shape	Does the body of your letter have at-a-glance appeal? Does it look balanced, attractive, and organized on the page?
Type	Have you chosen type that looks professional? Have you avoided smudges, half-printed characters, uneven spacing, and the worn-ribbon look?
Accuracy	Are all words spelled correctly? Are all punctuation marks placed correctly? Is your grammar correct in all cases?

Beginning business writers may use these guidelines to revise the rough draft of a business letter. With experience, these standards can become almost second nature to the writer—good habits that make the task of letter writing fast, effective, and satisfying.

The Complimentary Close

This brief word or phrase (*Sincerely, With best wishes*,) is a final expression of feeling or regard. It stands at the top of the signature block in all modern letter formats (except AMS style, where it is optional or omitted). From the days of the nineteenth century complimentary close—

```
        I am, believe me, dear Sir, your devoted servant,
              With deepest regards for your well-being.
                   Most Sincerely,
```

—we have settled for virtually one word to close most business communications:

```
                   Sincerely,
```

When business people find they like their customers, they feel an urge to express personal regard. While this extension of friendliness permeates the tone of the entire letter, the complimentary close offers an opportunity to show genuine feeling. In place of *Sincerely*, for example, you may want to type *Cordially*, to an acquaintance on the way to becoming a business friend. Alternately, you could offer *Best wishes*, or *Warm regards*, to a client or customer. Complimentary closings like *Cheers*! or *Greetings to all* also have their place, though you must judge their appropriateness in each particular message.

How do you know when to use a warmer complimentary closing than *Sincerely* in a business letter? To a large degree, your own feelings will guide you correctly. In weighing those feelings, keep in mind these common business practices:

1. A first letter to a new client or unknown reader usually closes with a conservative ending such as *Sincerely*. Warm personal regards in such an initial letter can be seen as insincere because the reader has no basis yet for judging your feelings.
2. Business letters that begin with a first name—Dear Jenny—can close with a warmer ending than *Sincerely*.

Sincerely may make the reader feel the you have chosen a rather traditional, noncommittal closing for what may have been a warm and somewhat personal letter.

The Signature

Because your typed full name and professional title (optional) appear beneath your signature, you need not take pains to make sure that each letter in your signature is a model of penmanship. Most business signatures have a bit of personal flair—a hint regarding the personality of the signer. Nor is it always necessary to sign your name exactly as it is typed on the business letter. In a particularly friendly letter, you may wish to sign with just your first name—

```
Best wishes,

Frank
Franklin J. Clinton
Director of Sales
```

In a more formal letter, you may sign your entire name.

Best wishes,

Franklin J. Clinton (signature)

Franklin J. Clinton
Director of Sales

Signatures are the only non-machine mark on a typed letter. As such, those few strokes of the pen provide valuable clues to the reader about your temperament, vitality, and even your reliability. No, you don't have to accept an elaborate theory of handwriting analysis to grant the importance of signatures. Simply notice your own responses to this signature:

Franklin J. Clinton (signature)

In short, business writers should take a moment to evaluate their professional signatures in the same way they appraise the rest of their messages. Beginning writers often find they try too hard when signing an immaculately typed letter. You may want to practice your signature several times on scratch paper. Achieve a signature that pleases you, then use that natural signature confidently on your business letters.

Final Notations

A series of notations often appears at the bottom of business letters, always below the signature and along the left hand margin.

Copy notation. The *cc* notation, followed by a colon, stands for *carbon copy*, though now that messy stuff has generally been replaced by photocopies. The letter *c* indicates *copy* and *pc* or *xc* indicates *photocopy* or *Xerox copy*. Writers place these notations at the bottom of letters to tell their readers to whom copies of the letter have been sent. It is also appropriate, especially for emphasis, to note *copy* instead of using a letter. If you wish to send a copy of a letter to a third party *without* the knowledge of the original reader, you may note *bc* for *blind copy* on the copy you send to the third party as well as on your own copy. Do not, of course, also include the *bc* notation on the original letter.

Enclosure simply records on the business letter the list of additional items you have included with the letter. In the letter in Figure 9-14, this brief notation tells the reader what Mr. Clinton sent along with the letter. If a secretary prepares Mr. Clinton's letter for mailing, the enclosure notation serves as a

FIGURE 9-14

Letter with Final Notations

MORTAN BUILDING SUPPLY

253 Lansdon Street   Cheyenne, WY 59823   (834) 374-2839

September 12, 198_

Ms. Barbara Wilkins
Manager, Supply Group
Lakston Wholesale Supply
2493 Peterson Blvd.
Santa Fe, NM 59832

Dear Ms. Wilkins:

For the past four years, we've been a steady customer of
yours for R-19 insulation. But in the future, we'll be
using R-24 insulation.

Wyoming has just changed its building code requirements
regarding insulation in residential properties. From now
on, only R-24 or better insulation meets state and local
codes.

That leaves us with a problem: we have 117 units of R-19
now in stock. May we return them for credit?

Please let me know if you plan to stock R-24 insulation,
and what our volume price will be.

My thanks.

Sincerely,

Franklin J. Clinton

Franklin J. Clinton
Director of Sales

cc: C.Busrin, D. Henderson

FJC/dc
Enclosure: "198_ Insulation Requirements"

P.S. We received your Christmas calendar. Thanks very
much.

reminder to also enclose the materials specified. When the reader files the letter, the enclosure note stands as a record of pertinent related materials. In short, the note serves the reader. When he or she comes across the letter in a file some time later, the enclosure notation will guide the reader to the 1986 Insulation Requirements long after than document has been separated from the letter. For this reason, list enclosures by title whenever possible.

Reference initials identify both the author of the letter—Franklin J. Clinton—and the typist (*dc* for David Collins). The writer's initials can be separated from the typist's by a colon or slash. An identifying code number for word processing may also be included with, or take the place of, the reference initials.

When mailing copies of a letter to others, attach a brief note to the copy or clearly label it COPY. Photocopy machines have made copies look so much like originals that many business readers can't tell at a glance whether they are reading the typed version or a copy. They become disconcerted to read half-way through a letter (often in confusion) only to realize, "Oh, this letter isn't for me. It's just a copy." You can prevent this misunderstanding by attaching a note of guidance: "For your information" or "For your files." You may also simply circle the *cc* line to make clear that the letter is a copy.

The Postscript

Located below all other matter on the letter, a postscript indentifies a message that you wish to add to the letter—often a thought or request that deserves special attention by the reader. The postscript is marked by the letters *P.S.*

```
P.S.   If you act now, we'll include a free Map Atlas
       with your set of encyclopedias.
```

Historically, postscripts were used to set down afterthoughts. In modern business practice, if you discover that you have omitted an important sentence or two from your letter, retype it to include the message in the body of the text. Reserve postscripts for occasional use to highlight an idea or action step you wish to emphasize. Used with discretion, postscripts can serve the writer as a highlighting technique. Used too often, they make business correspondence seem hasty and disorganized.

Summary

1. Both company images and career advances can depend upon business letters.
2. Good writers combine a clear message with effective persuasional techniques (massage) in their writing.
3. Business letters have important legal implications for the writer and the company.
4. Effective business writers emphasize the *you* perspective in letters.

5. Feelings, appropriately expressed, have an important place in business letters.
6. No set of fixed recipes can be given for business correspondence.
7. Business letters usually appear in block, indented, or modified block style. The AMS style is rarely used.
8. Conventions of folding letters and the placement of address information on envelopes are important to the success of business letters.
9. Business letters should be arranged on the page to allow easy reading.
10. The major parts of the business letter are the letterhead, date, inside address, subject line (optional), attention line (optional), salutation, body, complimentary close, and signature.
11. Minor parts of the business letter include final notations such as reference initials, enclosure, copy information, postscript, and others.

Questions for Discussion

1. Do the expectations of your readers influence the format you choose in business letters? How? Why?
2. How do the three major letter styles differ?
3. How does the less popular AMS style differ from the three major styles?
4. Can the salutation and complimentary close emphasize feelings of friendship? How?
5. Name and discuss six basic considerations to bear in mind when composing the body of a business letter.
6. How should a business letter be folded? Does care really matter?
7. How would you define the following abbreviations and describe their placement on the business letter: cc, pc, bc, enc, AHB/sra, AHB:sra, WP30465, P.S.?
8. What is a letterhead? What is its importance on the business letter?
9. What is the importance of an appropriate business signature?
10. Can business correspondence always be written according to fixed recipes? Explain your answer.
11. How would you define the *you* perspective in business correspondence? Give an example of this perspective.
12. What are some of the legal implications of letters sent from your company?
13. Consider "junk letters" you receive. In what ways do they abide by and/or ignore the principles discussed in this chapter.
14. List at least six common complimentary closes. Which do you prefer? Why?
15. What should a company consider when developing a letterhead for all stationery?

Exercises

1. Collect at least three letters that, in your opinion, reflect negatively upon the writer or the company. On a separate sheet or in marginal notations, show why. Then rewrite the letters to repair the problems.

2. Find a business letter that you think is well done. With a red pen or pencil, locate (by underlining) aspects of persuasional language (massage) in the letter.
3. Write a short business letter announcing the opening of a new student clothing store. Address your letter to area residents. In the first version of the letter, express your message from the *I* point of view. Then rewrite the letter to emphasize the *you* perspective. Compare the two letters. Write a short statement explaining which, in your opinion, is most successful.
4. Find a business letter written in block form. Rewrite the letter in indented or modified block style. Compare the results in a written statement.
5. Fold the letter in exercise 4 or 5 (or a blank sheet of paper) and place it correctly in an envelope. Address the envelope.
6. Find a business letter that, to you, looks unattractive on the page. Rewrite it for a more pleasing effect.
7. Write a business letter on a subject of your choice, using any of the three major styles. Use all major letter parts (except the Attention line) in your letter. Also use the following final notations: cc, enc, P.S., reference initials, word processing code.
8. Conduct a brief survey of responses to block, indented, and modified block style. Which style do your classmates prefer? Which style do business people prefer?

Richard Ling manages a wholesale company that distributes food products to more than 300

restaurants and institutions. He tells of a pressing problem:

When I took over as manager, I noticed that my staff of six area supervisors spent too long composing letters. These men and women had not been trained as writers, but nevertheless were trying to respond on company letterhead to the dozens of requests, orders, inquiries, announcements, and invitations we receive each week from our clientele. What they produced, even after it had been edited by secretaries, was often downright embarrassing. They evidently didn't know how to write simple business letters.

I had a bright idea. "Make your contacts by phone," I told the group. "We don't really need to write letters." That was six months ago. Now, I'm sorry to say, I face a larger problem. My supervisors complain that they spend all day on the phone, often giving the same message several times. Some customers didn't get the message the first time, or confused it somehow. Others want to bicker or dicker. Still others simply want to chat about the weather. Meanwhile, my people aren't getting their work done.

Consider Richard Ling's dilemma. What place can routine business letters serve in a company? What are their advantages over a system that relies completely on telephone messages? How can supervisors be taught to write such letters?

Routine
and Informative Letters 10

LEARNING OBJECTIVES

To describe the importance of routine letters in business

To write effective requests, inquiries, and replies

To understand important differences between goodwill letters and sales letters

To write effective goodwill letters, announcements, condolence messages, congratulatory letters, thank-you letters, and cover letters

To understand the use and abuse of form and guide letters in business

To write useful form and guide letters

In your business career, you will write a wide variety of business letters, ranging from a simple inquiry or reply to a complicated claims or adjustment letter. In Chapter 9, we investigated principles and techniques that apply to all of these letters: appropriate format, letter parts, tone, and even conventions for folding letters and preparing envelopes.

The remaining chapters in Part Three treat the *differences* among the many types of business letters. In this chapter, we consider routine and informative letters—all those relatively simple messages that contribute to effective, efficient business life.

Here's an overview of the letters we will cover:

- Requests for information or service
- Routine inquiries
- Messages and replies
- Goodwill letters
- Announcements
- Condolence messages
- Congratulatory messages
- Thank-you messages
- Cover letters
- Form letters

THE GOALS OF THE BUSINESS LETTER

The great majority of letters that leave most offices are routine and informative in nature. These letters more than any others help or harm the image and reputation of a company. In learning to write such letters, therefore, we must first dispel the negative connotations of "routine." The word does not mean "boring" or "simplistic" or "unimportant." Routine business letters, instead, are *regular* and *customary* features of business life. As such, they have great importance. When they are absent, misinformation and misunderstanding can spread quickly through a business and among its customers.

Here is a quick mental drill to reinforce the concerns and connotations that *should* be on a writer's mind in approaching routine and informative correspondence. The drill asks you to call to mind the letters of a favorite business word: C L I E N T S. Then use each letter as a reminder of your goals in writing even the shortest business communication.

- C — Content should be clear, complete, and concise. Just what do you want to say? What facts and examples must be included? What can be left out?
- L — Letter formats matter. Will you write a note or a formal business letter? Will you include enclosures? Will copies be sent to others?
- I — *I* yields to *you* in good business letters. Concentrate on the interests of your reader.
- E — Easy reading makes good business. Use white space, short paragraphs, and a crisp, clean style to produce an inviting, readable letter.

> Old heads train new ones, old letters make convenient models, and old ways seem the safest ways. And so, many people continue to write in a style that would get a lot of laughs if it didn't do such damage.
>
> Tom Murawski, U.S. Air Force Academy. Reprinted with permission from *Simply Stated*, the monthly newsletter from The Document Design Center, American Institutes for Research.

The business day is hectic enough. Let your letter lighten, not heighten, the frustrations of the day.

N — The needs of your reader matter most. Even when your letter expresses your own needs, consider what your reader wants from you. How can your letter meet those needs?

T — The tone of your letter should be chosen with care. How do you wish to sound to the reader? Friendly? Firm? Respectful? Once you have decided on the tone appropriate to your letter, let all aspects of the letter cooperate to create that tone.

S — Sincere letters build trust. Show sincerity by showing interest in the details of your reader's needs, offering cooperation and assistance, and facing risks and shortcomings honestly and openly.

You can use this checklist to take notes in preparation for the writing of an actual business letter. In this way, you'll grasp the purpose, design, and organization of your letter *before* you begin to write. The planning process can take as little as a minute or two. Probably you will take some time to consider the composition of the letter anyway: these memory pegs ensure that you cover the topics crucial to the success of the business letter.

THE COST OF THE BUSINESS LETTER

Your ability to draft effective business letters *quickly* will matter in your career. Consider, for example, what it costs for a mid-level manager earning $60,000 per year to write a single letter. If the manager takes one month off for vacation each year and works a 40-hour week the rest of the year, he or she earns more than $30 per working hour. If a letter takes half an hour to be written and another half an hour for typing, proofing, revision, and mailing, the company—incredibly—has spent $30 just to get the letter on its way. This cost, of course, does not include all the peripheral expenses, such as typewriters, stationery, and so forth.

If only to earn their keep, business letters must work for a living

by speaking clearly.
by motivating action.
by creating intended images.
by building trust on the part of the reader.
by communicating goodwill.
by establishing written records.

Your ability to write effective business letters bodes well for a successful business career.

REQUESTS FOR INFORMATION OR SERVICE

These short letters help you reach out for helpful facts, advice, and service. Let's say, for example, that you saw an advertisement for a new photocopy machine. You want more information. Begin the body of your letter by asking for exactly what you want. Then, if necessary, provide any background details that you think are appropriate. Conclude with an expression of appreciation for your reader's willingness to provide what you request.

Notice in Figure 10-1 that the writer is *asking for what the reader is willing to provide*. He gets right to the point: he wants information. Specific facts and details are reserved for the heart of the letter. In the final paragraph, he does not hesitate to express his wishes: "Don't send a sales person to call." But, considering the reader's feelings and point of view, he goes on to assure the reader that he will write or call after reviewing the material requested. The content of the letter is concise and complete. The tone is brisk but not offensive.

Now let's consider a request for service. In Figure 10-2, notice that the writer concentrates on the *you* perspective as a way of reaching and motivating the reader, who may be less than willing to provide the service requested. Nancy Bridges knows that her vacuum system is under warranty and must be repaired by the installer. She also knows, however, that a friendly tone may motivate faster service on the part of Harold Reese. (She bases this judgment on her knowledge of Reese, her audience. With another reader, she might take a much sterner tone.) She provides facts Harold Reese will need to know to repair the system: what's wrong, when a repair person can enter the salon, and what arrangements can be made for after-hour servicing.

Your goal in writing requests for information or service is straightforward: you want your reader to know *what* you want, *when* you want it, and perhaps *why* you need it, and *how* and *where* it should be delivered.

ROUTINE INQUIRIES

Routine inquiries, which are inquiry letters frequently generated by your company and often received by the same readership over a period of time, have much the same goals as requests for information or service. If you are employed by a bank, you may need to write requests for depositor information or balances from other banks. If you work for a state or federal agency, you will probably write routine inquiries, often addressed to the same reader, requesting updates in information, personnel identification, or program descriptions.

Especially if you plan to write several routine inquiries to the same reader, do not make an effort to be original in the design of each succeeding

FIGURE 10-1

Request for Information

BRIGHT
EYES
PHOTOGRAPHY

3829 Lister Lane
New Haven, Indiana 32943

(293) 392-3942

May 7, 198_

Ms. Faye Cosner
Director of Marketing
Victoria Photocopy Systems
392 Langston Boulevard
Indianapolis, IN 38293

Dear Ms. Cosner:

Please send me product information and a price list for
your Victoria 9070 photocopier.

I'm particularly interested in the color capability of the
machine, as advertised in this month's issue of Photography
Today.

Thank you for your help. I don't wish to be contacted by a
salesperson, at this time. I will, however, get in touch
with you if I have further questions after reading the
material you send.

Sincerely,

James D. Blaston

James D. Blaston
Owner

JDB/ows

FIGURE 10-2

Request for Service

ADAM HAIR SALON

44 Wilson Road
Beverley Hills, CA 92849
(213) 302-3892

June 7, 198_

Mr. Harold Reese
Service Manager
Contractors Vacuum Systems
392 Frank Center Drive
Los Angeles, CA 90823

SUBJECT: Adjustment of vacuum system

Dear Mr. Reese:

You were right in your opinion last month that "we may have
to adjust the pressure control" on the vacuum system
installed here by Contractors Vacuum Systems on May 1, 198_.

When more than three hairdressers use the vacuum system at
once, the suction falls off substantially.

The system you installed has pleased us so far, and we trust
that you'll solve the suction problem promptly. We are open
8 A.M. to 5 P.M. Monday through Friday. I can also meet
your repair person here after hours if necessary. We'll
need the system repaired no later than June 12.

Thanks for your help.

Sincerely,

Nancy Bridges

Nancy Bridges
Manager

NB/col

inquiry. Your reader will appreciate the same look for the same kind of inquiry, allowing at-a-glance recognition of the kind of information you request. (Many companies use form letters to advantage for the same kind of inquiry.)

You can, however, vary each succeeding inquiry a bit by your statement of appreciation at the end of the letter. As your inquiries increase for a given reader, try to express your appreciation in stronger terms. Notice in Figure 10-3, for example, how the writer handles the fourth routine inquiry sent to one reader. This routine inquiry probably looks just like the other inquiries Ms. Velasquez has received from the Department of Social Services. She appreciates this sameness, however, because it lets her see at a glance what the document asks her to do. She doesn't have to read the letter in a close way, as she might have to if the writer had chosen an unexpected format for this inquiry. She also appreciates the concluding paragraph. It tells her that her efforts in responding promptly to the Department's requests have not gone unnoticed.

Consider the use of form letters for routine inquiries, but allow yourself the freedom to insert extra messages of appreciation as you ask more and more of particular readers.

ORDERS

It is impractical and expensive for most corporations to place orders by an original, composed business letter. Most often orders are handled by a printed order form, or a form or guide letter. While certainly less personal than a composed letter, these forms have the advantage of reminding the writer just what items of information must be included in most orders:

- Catalog information, including numbers and codes
- Quantity of items ordered
- Description of items (model, size, color, weight if applicable)
- Unit price and total price
- Identification of purchaser (your exact billing address)
- Shipping address
- Requested shipping method (UPS, Federal Express, and so forth)
- Payment method (COD, credit account, check, etc.)
- Requested delivery date
- Miscellaneous instructions (purchase order number, back order instructions, salesperson's name, and so forth)

For special orders or infrequent orders placed by small companies, an original, composed order letter may be called for. Include as much of the information above as necessary to make sure what you order is what you will get. You can also use this letter opportunity to establish or maintain goodwill by a sentence or two of appreciation for good service, fair prices, or other considerations, as shown in Figure 10-4.

FIGURE 10-3

Routine Inquiry

Maricopa County
State of Arizona
Department of Social Welfare

22 Federal Way   Phoenix, Arizona 60405   (493) 493-3920

February 9, 198_

Ms. Gloria Velasquez
Personnel Director
Fashion Fabrics, Inc.
40 State College St.
Phoenix, AZ 60405

SUBJECT: Wage verification, Mr. Henry M. Johnson

Dear Ms. Velasquez:

On the enclosed form, please provide a wage history for
your worker named above, S.S.#569-38-2053. This department
requires such wage information to process this applicant's
request for supplemental state medical insurance.

Please note that the form requests information on the
applicant's wages only during the past six months with your
company.

Thank you, Ms. Velasquez, for responding so promptly to
these requests. We do appreciate your cooperation.

Sincerely,

Glenda Jenson

Glenda Jenson
Social Worker
Processing Unit

GLJ:eir WP39523

FIGURE 10-4

Order Letter

Brent Sports World

91 Ocean Way
Bright's Beach, NC 39294
(303) 500-6011

August 4, 198_

Mr. Fred O'Neill
Orders Desk Supervisor
London Fishing Reels, Inc.
80 B Street
Pittsburgh, PA 48385

Dear Mr. O'Neill:

Please ship by U.P.S. fourteen (14) model #401 reels, as
advertised at $51.20 each in your 198_ Summer Wholesale
Catalog.

We understand from your catalog that orders in excess of
$500 receive a 10 percent discount and free shipping.
Thank you for applying those bonuses to this order.

As a longtime customer of yours, we appreciate the fast
service you always provide. If at all possible, we would
like to receive shipment of this order no later than August
10.

Sincerely,

Nancy Owens

Nancy Owens
Purchasing Agent

NOO/cor

MESSAGE/REPLY LETTERS

In situations in which fast communication takes precedence over attractive communication, message/reply letters are often sent to clients. The business writer must remember to ask *direct questions* in such letters. Without them, readers cannot easily determine what reply you need.

In Figure 10-5, the writer emphasizes the importance of the two questions he asks by using numbers and white space. The reader will probably find it easy, on the Reply portion of the letter, to jot down his responses to the questions.

Most message/reply letters are made up of colored, pressure-sensitive copies. The reader can write down his or her response, then tear off a copy to file. The original is returned to the sender. Western Union now markets Mailgrams with a message/reply format. The Mailgram received by the reader contains a mail-back envelope and space at the bottom for the reader's reply.

GOODWILL LETTERS

Increasingly each year, companies are finding spare time and extra funds to write letters that answer no specific inquiry, request, order, or complaint. These letters simply express goodwill—the intention of the company to act not only in an honest and fair way, but additionally with a friendly spirit.

Goodwill letters are distinct from promotional letters in that no effort is made to sell a specific product or service. Selling, of course, is going on in the goodwill letter—the selling of a reputation, a company, a set of associations.

Occasions for goodwill letters to clients can include a company anniversary, a contract anniversary, a relocation to a new facility, a holiday, or a special public event. Goodwill letters are also commonly sent to clients some time after a major purchase or business transaction. The letter can dispel the customer's uncomfortable feeling that "well, they've got my money—now they will forget me."

Goodness of any sort is a bit hard to introduce, and the first paragraph of the goodwill letter certainly poses a challenge to the business writer. When you want to step to the tune of goodwill, with which foot do you lead?

Try a brief statement of history, perhaps involving the company's long-time role in the community:

```
Since 1962, Bateman Sports Supply has sent its merchandise
along on some of the best hunting, fishing, camping, and
hiking trips in the Pacific Northwest.
```

Or mention a little known fact:

```
Bateman Sports Supply has hidden one secret well over the
years: our annual August closing for ''inventory'' has
actually been an excuse for one glorious week of fishing.
```

FIGURE 10-5

Message/Reply Letter

Message

March 5, 198_

Mr. Robert Jolson
3535 Washington Street
Washington, DC 57384

Dear Mr. Jolson:

We are ready to ship your order of oak picture frames.
Please respond by return mail to these questions:

    1. Do you want golden oak or dark oak frames?

    2. Do you want 11 or 17 large (18"x24") frames? The
       number on the order form is illegible.

Thank you for responding quickly. We're grateful for your
business.

Sincerely,

Jamie West

Jaime West
Order Clerk

Reply

Let the emphasis of the goodwill letter fall on what you want to do for others, not on how praiseworthy you have already been. Yesterday's goodness matters about as much as yesterday's bread.

> Bateman Sports Supply sees an opportunity to develop youth sports in Hunterville over the next few years. We've taken the first step by supporting the organization of a ten–team Little League, to begin play this summer. Boys and girls basketball teams are already on the drawing boards at the town Recreation Department, and Bateman Sports will do its share.

Finally, conclude with a "partnership" statement in which you welcome the reader into the act of sharing goodwill.

> These goals must involve the whole town, including those willing to coach, prepare the field, sew uniforms, provide sports supplies, and even bandage knees. Bateman Sports cares about the kids of Hunterville, and stands shoulder to shoulder with you to provide for their health, recreation, and enjoyment.

In Figure 10-6, the writer uses the occasion of the city's anniversary to thank and congratulate the citizenry.

This goodwill letter makes no effort to sell the services of Webber Property Management. (The letter *does*, however, make reference to "home" and "trust" and the members of the Webber staff.) Because the letter will be mailed to each home in Lakeview, the writer addresses it simply to "Those who live, work and play . . . ." If she had access to a mailing list of the citizens and word-processing equipment, it would have been possible (though expensive) to send an individually typed and personally addressed letter to each home. The writer keeps the text of the letter rather short, assuming that the reader will get the message and the effect of the letter quickly. More paragraphs of praise for Lakeview would not improve, and could detract from the effect of the goodwill letter.

A word should be added here about sincerity. Goodwill letters should never be merely manipulative in their ends—that kind of hypocrisy always shows through. The best goodwill letters say, in effect, "We do feel what we say we feel in this letter. We're not just pretending for the sake of advertising."

ANNOUNCEMENTS

The announcement can prove useful to professionals when they want to acquaint the public with a product, service, or event without a full-blown advertising campaign. A physician, for example, may want to let people know that he or she has changed office locations. A brief announcement is ap-

FIGURE 10-6

Goodwill Letter

WEBBER PROPERTY MANAGEMENT, INC.

91 Corvan Industrial Center   Lakeview, Washington 93823
(389) 490-2934

May 4, 198_

To: Those who live, work, and play
in the city of Lakeview, Washington

Dear Friends and Neighbors,

Today Lakeview celebrates its 100th birthday. We at Webber
Property Management want to take a moment to thank you

* for being part of a proud, progressive community.

* for sharing your friendship and trust with us over
the years.

* for lending your support to the charities, civic
organizations, schools, churches, and town projects
that have benefited us all.

As citizens of Lakeview, our partnership in working toward
common goals has made this city the "home" we wanted to
find. We've seen what we can do together. The years ahead
should prove both exciting and deeply satisfying.

Every member of the Webber staff sends warmest
congratulations to the City of Lakeview and its people on
this special day.

Sincerely,

Arlene Webber

Arlene B. Webber
President

ABW/eoc

propriate and does not reflect adversely on the doctor's professional reputation. Special company events, similarly, can be announced by means of this short business form.

Announcements should usually state their business in the first line of the letter body. Following lines can give necessary background, details, explanations, or qualifications.

You can suggest some feeling of pride or excitement in announcing the message. "The AVCO Tower Center will open at 10 A.M., Wednesday, Dec. 6, 1986" has less impact than "AVCO Financial Services proudly announces the opening of the AVCO Tower Center at 10 A.M., Wednesday, Dec. 6, 1986." Readers respond to emotional cues: if you reveal your feelings, readers will have an example of how they might want to feel.

In the announcement in Figure 10-7, for example, the writer expresses pleasure at the appointment of a new vice-president of operations for the company. Notice that the inside address and salutation have been omitted for the purposes of a general announcement. The writer states her own feelings about the appointment as a means of guiding the feelings of the reader. She leaves no doubt that Millicent Everly is welcome at Jackson Investment Trust. Supporting details, separated appropriately into paragraphs, follow the main announcement message. Notice that this same communication, if it were mailed to individuals (perhaps members of the board), could have been prefaced by a traditional inside address and salutation:

```
Mr. Ronald K. Smith
Member, Board of Directors
Jackson Investment Trust, Inc.
c/o Smith, Wilson and Smith
21 Western Blvd.
San Francisco, CA 93892

Dear Mr. Smith:
```

When you want to draw attention to a meeting, celebration, appointment, promotion, address change, or the like, consider using the announcement format. Readers appreciate the brevity, formality, and feeling in this message form.

THANK-YOU LETTERS

No one has measured whether we, as business people, are grateful as often as we should be. But browsing through the mail of any office will convince us that we do not *say* we are grateful often enough.

Thank-you letters can produce goodwill, cooperation, and trust on the part of the reader. For the writer, thank-you letters become a sensitizing habit—the practice of writing "thank-you" awakens the writer to the efforts other people have made on his or her behalf. In short, thank-you letters pay dividends all around.

FIGURE 10-7

Announcement

Jackson Investment Trust, Inc.

17 Wilshire Blvd.   Los Angeles, CA 92038   (839) 289-4834

March 14, 198_

As president and chief executive officer of Jackson Investment Trust, Inc., I take great personal satisfaction and pride in announcing the appointment of Millicent Everly as Vice-President of Operations.

Millicent Everly holds her M.B.A. in Financial Analysis from Stanford University. She brings twelve years of experience in financial management with three major financial institutions to her new position.

A welcoming reception for Vice-President Everly will take place in the board room (Suite 800, 9th floor) on Friday, March 21, 198_. Please join us.

Sincerely,

Cynthia Jackson

Cynthia Jackson
President

CJ/clr

Best of all, they are easy to write. Begin your message directly by expressing your thanks in words that are natural and sincere. Single out a specific example or detail in later lines for comment and praise. Conclude by reemphasizing your feelings of gratitude, perhaps offering cooperation or other benefits of some kind. (Avoid, however, the tit-for-tat "I owe you one" sentiment. It may make the reader feel that you are defining the limits of your gratitude.)

In Figure 10-8, the writer thanks the reader for providing valuable information. Notice how the second paragraph mentions specific matters for which the writer feels grateful. The writer avoids the common mistake of confusing gratitude with implied obligation: she does not say, in effect, "I'm grateful, so keep your favors coming." This note gives something back to a bank president who has given good advice. In its personal tone and concrete example, the letter conveys the sincerity and earnestness of the writer's feeling. Although the letter uses *I* often, the emphasis falls on what *you* (the bank president) have done.

Consider writing thank-you letters to employers and employees who have helped you, public and private agencies that have provided services or information, suppliers who have filled your orders promptly, and of course customers who have shown confidence in doing business with you. The few minutes you spend writing these simple letters are invested well.

CONDOLENCE LETTERS

These important messages convey sympathy. When misfortunes or calamities occur among your work force or clientele, you may be called upon to write a letter on behalf of the company to express not only your feelings but the combined feelings of others. Finding words at such a moment can be difficult. Even recommending a form for such a letter poses problems, since sincerity and naturalness of expression count far more than format on such occasions. The following advice, therefore, should be taken as one alternative among many for the writing of sincere condolence letters.

You may wish to begin with a direct statement of sympathy. Do not dwell on the event itself—the reader is all too aware of the circumstances. Instead, concentrate on positive memories and positive developments that may lie in the future.

Condolence messages seldom are more than a few short paragraphs. The bereaved reader appreciates your kindness in sending the message, but probably does not wish to read an extended letter at such a time of crisis.

In Figure 10-9, the writer expresses sympathy to the family of a coworker who has died suddenly. Notice the advantages of the direct approach, the positive emphasis, and the brief length. This short message tries to give a strengthening thought without overstepping its bounds into the realm of preaching. It may, of course, be handwritten rather than typed. For such short notes, note-sized paper may be used instead of standard typing paper.

FIGURE 10-8

Thank-You Letter

COMMONWEALTH LANDSCAPING, INC.

253 Bilford Way • Portland, Oregon 38203 • (493) 490-3902

December 20, 198_

Mr. Pablo Vincenti
President
National Bank of Portland
504 Fourth Street
Portland, OR 38203

Dear Mr. Vincenti:

I want to thank you for good advice, freely given, over the
two years that I have held accounts at your bank. As I
patted myself on the back yesterday for successful
investing and wise tax moves, I realized how many of those
decisions came as a direct result of your counsel.

In particular, I've been pleased with the IRA you brought
to my attention last year. My accountant showed me how
much it saved in taxes last year. You helped me get on my
feet as a business person, Mr. Vincenti, and I appreciate
it.

My best wishes for the coming new year.

Sincerely,

Rebecca J. Owens

Rebecca J. Owens
Owner

RJO/ped

FIGURE 10-9

Condolence Letter

**Milford
Petroleum
Products, Inc.**

55 Talbert Street
Wilsford, Pennsylvania 39843

(203) 403-9023

May 15, 198_

Peter and Susan Nelson
305 Richmond Avenue
Wilsford, PA 39842

Dear Peter and Susan,

All of us who knew and loved your father send our heartfelt
sympathy.

When my father died two years ago, it was Ken Nelson who
took me aside and said, "Remember the friendship." We
trust that in the difficult moments you will remember his
friendship and ours.

Call upon us if we can help in any way.

Sincerely,

Brenda Yesler

Brenda Yesler
Group Manager

BCY/aln

The keys to such messages are restraint and sincerity. Restrain yourself in the letter from pouring forth all of your own grief in consideration for the grief of your reader. Make every word sincere.

CONGRATULATORY LETTERS

Like thank-you letters, congratulatory letters express our best wishes for someone else. Business and personal life are filled with occasions and accomplishments: weddings, anniversaries, promotions, project completions, and so forth. You can build goodwill by marking such occasions with a sincere letter of congratulations.

In Figure 10-10, notice that the congratulatory message and its *cause* are placed early in the letter. Other comments and well-wishing, some of them humorous, perhaps, fill the rest of the letter. The conclusion often looks forward to other bright occasions. The congratulatory message in Figure 10-10 communicates the excitement felt by Virginia's friends at Best Medical Supply while also renewing friendships and building goodwill. While the letter was not intended primarily to open new business possibilities for Best Medical at Mercy General Hospital, the writer realizes that Virginia's continued friendship is both a personal and professional bonus. Note that the writer uses her first name followed by a comma rather than a colon. By such techniques, the writer makes the letter sound personal and friendly.

Watch the business news in your local paper or professional journal for items about people who deserve your congratulations. Take care not to attach sales riders to such messages. Neither you nor your reader wants to feel that the congratulations offered in the letter are motivated by selfish interests.

COVER LETTERS

One of the most common business letters, the cover letter, has only one job to do: to accompany another document. The cover letter usually refers to the document by name ("Feasibililty Study on Interstate Water Management") or, in the case of multiple documents, by type ("reports on water management"). The letter can also include any additional information you wish the reader to have ("Please note that these reports are now two years old and do not reflect recent legislation."). The letter commonly concludes with the writer's thanks and an offer to provide assistance if necessary.

The cover letter in Figure 10-11 accompanies a videotape of executive presentations and their review by a speech expert. This short letter introduces the contents of the package to the reader. In addition to providing some useful information (where to find comments on the videotape), the letter offers the writer's help and telephone numbers. The enclosure notation indicates the contents of the package.

FIGURE 10-10

Congratulatory Letter

Best Medical Supply, Inc.

11 Howell Street
Las Vegas, Nevada 49203
(893) 239-4903

April 28, 198_

Ms. Virginia Hernandez
433 Colwell Place
Las Vegas, NV 49203

Dear Virginia,

How happy we are at Best Medical Supply to congratulate you
on your appointment as Staff Supervisor at Mercy General
Hospital!

For those of us who have followed your career over the
years, this promotion and recognition come as no surprise.
Mercy General is fortunate to have your leadership and
commitment.

When you find yourself in our part of town, please stop by
to renew old acquaintances. Give us a call in advance, and
we'll set a bottle of champagne on ice so we can celebrate
your promotion in style!

Our best wishes, Virginia, for continued success.

Sincerely,

Michael V. Donovan

Michael V. Donovan
Manager

MVD/tow TF39023

FIGURE 10-11

Cover Letter

EXECUTIVE SEMINARS, INC.

398 Estley Drive   Newport, Rhode Island 38293   (483) 328-4893

May 7, 198_

Mr. Victor Wentz
Director, Human Resources
Western Technologies, Inc.
39854 E. Seventh Street
Seattle, WA 89384

SUBJECT: Review of executive presentations, with
          recommendations.

Dear Mr. Wentz:

The enclosed videotape contains the nine presentations
recorded on April 2, 198_, at your Everett facility.
Please note that my recommendations to each speaker appear
on the tape following the presentations themselves.

Thank you, Mr. Wentz, for the opportunity to be of service
to Western Technologies, Inc. Certainly call on me at my
office (number above) or my home (324/384-3920) if I can be
of help in any way.

Sincerely,

Vernon R. Kent

Vernon R. Kent
Director

VRK/wpi
Enc.: Videotape, "Western Technologies Presentations"

Not all cover letters are so uncomplicated in their construction. In a later chapter, we will discuss the development of a cover letter to accompany a very important package indeed—your résumé.

FORM LETTERS AND GUIDE LETTERS

In both form and guide letters, a standard text is reproduced for letters to a number of different readers. Prior to the advent of word processing, form letters could always be spotted in the day's mail by the unsightly gaps, blanks, and spaces filled in by hand or in type with information pertaining to the addressee.

Your account #50901 now shows an unpaid balance of $84 20 . If you feel this figure is not correct, please contact Jill Billings at 991-0421 .

Modern Form Letters

Word processing, including the use of high-speed printers, now makes it possible to send form letters that in every way look like hand-typed letters from your lawyer or company president. Particular information pertaining to the addressee appears woven into the form letter, with all margins and spacing perfectly adjusted.

These technological advances pose a challenge to both the writer and the reader. How can form letters be distinguished from individually composed letters written with only the addressee in mind?

If attractive printing no longer distinguishes individualized letters, the burden of distinguishing custom letters from form letters falls on style. Your custom letters should sound different from form letters in the way that your writing adjusts to the specific needs, interests, and capacities of the addressee.

In Figure 10-12, an individual's name has been inserted by electronic means into the standard text of this form letter.

Guide Letters

Companies pay for the time it takes their workers to compose business letters. Particularly in those business situations requiring the same letter text (billings, account information for new customers, and so forth), many companies choose not to write original letters each time such a letter must be sent. Instead, they settle upon a good model for the letter and place it in a guidebook for use by company writers. This process has several advantages:

1. A manager can give a customer's name to a secretary with the instruction to ''send letter 7.'' The manager does not have to write the letter.

FIGURE 10-12

Form Letter with Electronic Insertions

If number DC0112ML3, already registered in your name, is the grand prize winner

ARTHUR BELL
WILL BE PAID
ONE MILLION DOLLARS

Dear Arthur Bell,

You may have just won ONE MILLION DOLLARS in cash. SIX Personal Prize Claim Numbers have been registered exclusively in your name. **No one else has any of your numbers.**

And if DC0112ML3 is the grand prize number and you return it in time, we will be sending checks payable to Arthur Bell in your own Fullerton bank or any bank you choose. To be specific, you'll receive a new check for $40,000.00 every year for 25 years, and you'll collect ONE MILLION DOLLARS in all.

Or, you could choose the fabulous "MILLIONAIRE'S LIFETIME PLEASURE PASSPORT" that enables you to "join the jet set" and follow your fancy to the playgrounds of the rich and famous. Every year, **for the rest of your life,** you'll receive $10,000.00 worth of free air travel plus another $10,000.00 for hotels, dining and other land costs.

And you'll receive a virtually "bottomless wallet" that will be refilled with $20,000.00 CASH again and again every year, your whole life long.

Or you may be the winner of any of 5,031 prizes in the MILLION DOLLAR sweepstakes. You may win a new Mercedes-Benz 380 SL convertible or $50,000.00 cash.

2. The company can control what is said in legally or professionally sensitive areas. In many instances, guide letters *must* be used for certain business situations.
3. On average, the guide letter is better written than the letter that a busy manager might compose.

Guide letters also have disadvantages. Because writing involves hard work, many managers stretch their guide letters to cover situations that should be handled by individualized letters. Few customer complaints, for example, can be handled satisfactorily by a catch-all guide letter, though guides can certainly suggest good approaches to content and wording in such letters.

In Figure 10-13, the guide letter provides space for individualized information at several points (note the blanks). This guide letter lets a secretary quickly insert the name of the applicant into the appropriate places. A manager can tell the secretary which of the numbered items should be included in the letter—not all need appear.

Writing Form and Guide Letters

Because these letters can be put to so many different business uses, no single set of standards can guide the composition process. You can, however, refer to the sections within this text or other guides on the type of letter you wish to compose as a form or guide letter. A form sales letter, for example, should be designed along the lines suggested for the sales letter in Chapter 13.

Four general guidelines may help you avoid pitfalls in form and guide letters:

1. Remember that form and guide letters are used often, and therefore should be written, edited, and reviewed with extreme care.
2. Become aware of the company's policies controlling the use of form and guide letters you write. Who authorizes their use? Who will know when they are sent out? Can they be changed by others without permission?
3. Make sure to leave space for individualized information. Letters that appear to have come by the thousands off a printer and lack any individualized information are rarely read.
4. Establish a regular review period and process to assess the effectiveness of your form and guide letters. Are they appropriate for the changing needs of the company? Should they be rewritten? Part of your review, especially in the case of letters having to do with legal matters, should involve a lawyer. Changing legislation and legal interpretations can influence what you include and omit in form and guide letters.

Summary

1. Routine letters are important to the functioning of business life. Your routine letters play a key role in advancing your career.

FIGURE 10-13

Guide Letter

```
(date)

(inside address)

Dear        :

Thank you for your interest in establishing a wholesale
account at Myers Structural Metals, Inc.

We are eager to add                   to our list of
satisfied customers.  To process your application, however,
we must receive certified copies of the following business
documents:

        1. Your "d.b.a." certificate, showing all fictitious
           names under which your company now does business.
        2. A list of four business credit references,
           including addresses and telephone numbers.
        3. Your tax exemption certificate for retail selling.
        4. A list of all officers in your corporation, with
           addresses and telephone numbers.

We can process your application for credit within three
days after receiving the documents requested above.

Again, our thanks for your interest in an account.  We hope
to open an account bearing the name                   in the
near future.

Sincerely,



(name)
(title)

Enc.: "Credit Accounts at Myers Structural Metals, Inc."
```

2. The acronym C L I E N T S provides a handy checklist of items a writer should consider before beginning to write a letter, no matter how routine.
3. Business letters are expensive to produce, especially when the cost of the writer's time is calculated.
4. Requests for information or service should be direct and polite.
5. Routine inquiries should include a statement of appreciation, especially as the number of inquiries to the same reader mounts.
6. Message/reply letters must specify exactly what kind of response they wish the reader to provide.
7. Goodwill letters do not try to sell products or services in an explicit way.
8. Announcements, by their form and association with special occasions, can provide an effective communication channel in some business circumstances.
9. Thank-you letters are written too rarely in business. They serve important purposes in increasing motivation and building goodwill.
10. Condolence letters convey sympathy and should be written with sincerity and restraint.
11. Congratulatory letters can be brief, direct, friendly, and sometimes humorous, if appropriate.
12. Cover letters accompany other objects or documents and should contain information helpful to the reader.
13. Form and guide letters help business writers avoid the expense and effort of repeatedly redrafting standard letters. Form and guide letters must be used with discretion.

Questions for Discussion

1. Are routine and informative letters unimportant in business? Explain your answer.
2. What is a condolence message? What advice would you give to a business colleague who has to write such a letter?
3. What are three business situations in which an announcement would be an appropriate form to communicate a message?
4. Why, in your opinion, do business people so often fail to send thank-you letters? Why should they send such letters?
5. What are message/reply letters? How are they used? Why are they popular?
6. Is it wise to sell your product or service in a goodwill letter? Explain your answer.
7. What is a cover letter?
8. What are some of the uses and abuses of form and guide letters in business?
9. The text advises that requests be "direct." What does this mean? Give a brief example.

10. What kinds of information could be contained in a cover letter accompanying a catalog?
11. Discuss each of the points in the acronym C L I E N T S. Which points seem most important to you?
12. Which letter(s) treated in this chapter may well make use of humor? Give an example to illustrate your answer.

Exercises

1. Pretend that you need information from a church group regarding their beliefs or practices (perhaps for a term paper). Use the C L I E N T S pattern to prepare to write the letter. Write notes for yourself that sum up your thoughts for each catchword in the pattern. Then write the letter.
2. Write an inquiry to a professor at another university (the names and circumstances may be fictional). Assume, for this assignment, that you have received no response to your first inquiry at the time you write this letter.
3. Create a simple mock-up of a piece of message/reply stationery, or borrow a sheet of such stationery from a local business. Write the message portion of the letter, specifying what kind of response you want in the reply portion from your reader. Give the letter to a classmate, asking him or her to supply the reply portion. Evaluate how well your message worked by the reply it stimulated.
4. Write a goodwill letter to the community from some campus organization.
5. Write an announcement for an upcoming college event. Your letter should be addressed to college alumni.
6. Write a thank-you letter for assistance provided to you by a company (the circumstances may be fictional).
7. In the role of a manager, write a condolence letter to the relatives of one of your employees, now deceased.
8. Write a cover letter to accompany your college catalog. It is being mailed, let's say, to a sports star your college is trying to recruit.

Jim Reilly makes sales calls for a trade book

publisher. His story reveals the importance of
good yes letters in business:

*Frankly, I'm not much of a letter writer myself. But I had to teach my boss
a thing or two about effective letters. When I called on brand new accounts, they often seemed to have a chip on their shoulder—almost as if
they had been insulted by someone in the company. After a few sales calls,
I managed to win their trust and friendship. But I wondered why they
seemed so cold at the beginning.*

*Finally, the manager of Brenton Bookstore, one of my new accounts,
showed me the reason. In response to Brenton's application for a credit
account, my boss had mailed back an acceptance that said "Your account
number is 53042. Use this number on all orders and correspondence with
the company." That was it—not a single word of thanks or welcome. I had
to agree it was a cold greeting to a new customer.*

What opportunities did Jim's boss miss in welcoming new customers?
What do customers expect when they give a company their business?
What would you add to the account information above to produce a better
yes letter?

Conveying
Good News
and Goodwill   11

LEARNING OBJECTIVES

To describe the opportunity for sales and goodwill messages within *yes* letters

To write effective positive responses to orders, inquiries, requests, and invitations

To understand the place of conditions and qualifications in positive adjustment letters

To write positive adjustment letters that are clear and forceful and that build goodwill

To describe the importance of carefully chosen words in credit approvals

To write accurate and effective credit approvals

Successful business writers say "yes" as often as possible in their business letters. Can we fill your order? *Yes.* Can we answer your questions? *Yes.* Can we make an adjustment based on your claim? *Yes.*

When clients hear "yes," they value your company's participation in their own progress. You are letting them have their way, rather than standing in their way. We all like to have our way, and we like the people and companies who make yes possible. In fact, we translate our liking into action: we tell others about the company that helped us. We return to the company for future business.

"YES" LETTERS

"Yes" letters come in a wide variety of forms, but all rely upon a simple three-point plan:

1. *Deliver the yes message as soon as possible in the letter.* After all, you have good news you're eager to tell the reader. If at all possible, let the yes statement stand by itself without a clutter of conditions, comments, and qualifications in the same paragraph.

> **Not:** At the last meeting of the loan committee, your application no. 4705 for a construction loan in the amount of $70,000 was approved, provided that you acquire and maintain fire insurance in the amount of the loan on the construction project.
>
> **Instead:** We're pleased to approve your construction loan for $70,000.

Good news, when left to itself, establishes a moment of joy for the reader. Don't spoil that moment. Reserve all the specifics and additional information for a later paragraph.

2. *Remind the client, if necessary, what you are saying yes to.* Especially in contractual matters and questions of credit, it is wise to spell out the exact commitment you are and are not making by your yes response. Has the client, for example, asked for an extension of credit? After granting the request in the first paragraph, spell out in the second paragraph the precise details and conditions of your credit program.

> To protect your project and our investment, we will require that you acquire and maintain fire insurance for the amount of the loan.

3. *Sell the company's service or product.* A customer who has just heard you say yes to his or her request may be quite receptive to sales information. Here are five possible ways in which you can weave your sales message into the yes letter:

> Use language that your intended audience can understand. Using clear and simple language does not mean "talking down" to your audience, but it does mean avoiding unfamiliar jargon, technical terms, acronyms, legalese, long or convoluted sentences, and impersonal constructions.
> Reprinted with persmission from *Simply Stated,* the monthly newsletter from the Document Design Center, American Institutes for Research.

- Mention a related product or service your client might need.

> Our construction loan department offers an inexpensive voucher plan by which you can keep track of construction expenses and subcontracted work.

- Describe the future relationship you look forward to with the client.

> We look forward to a solid partnership with you in the development of the Seven Seas resort. Consider our participation, we ask, in future projects.

- Thank the client for past business and promise continued good service.

> Since 1972 you have been the kind of client we consider a company friend. We all will do our best to maintain our high level of service to you.

- Compliment the client on his or her current projects, and rehearse the company's capacity to assist.

> You deserve congratulations on seeing this project from initial design stage to this exciting time of construction. Keep in mind that Midwest Bank offers full-service banking to builders like yourself. We also offer loan bookkeeping, cash flow management, commercial checking, and computer payroll services.

- Mention current developments at the company and how they will affect the client.

> As you may have noticed, Midwest Bank is undergoing its own construction project with the building of three automated night tellers. If your checking needs occasionally require an after hours deposit or withdrawal, keep our automated tellers in mind. They will be ready to serve you by January 8.

POSITIVE RESPONSES TO ORDERS

Begin the *yes* letter to an order by stating exactly what you are saying yes to. You need not repeat the customer's entire order, of course, but do be sure to provide all the information the customer needs to understand what order has been approved. Go on in the next paragraph to explain any conditions, delays, product specifications, and shipping or billing information that the customer needs to know. Conclude with a statement of appreciation and, where appropriate, a sales message.

In Figure 11-1 notice how the writer seems pleased to say "yes" to the order. He says "yes" quickly in this letter, reserving details and the sales message for later paragraphs. Notice how the writer expresses feeling in words like "pleased," "enjoy," "thanks," and "best wishes." The writer wisely compliments the reader on her order and on the company's growing collection of art works.

Positive responses to orders can build goodwill and pave the way to frequent reorders. Even if you use a guide letter to suggest appropriate phrases, take the moment or two it requires to respond positively and persuasively to orders.

POSITIVE RESPONSES TO INQUIRIES

Like positive responses to orders, these short letters begin with the *yes* statement, then proceed to other paragraphs containing additional information and expressions of feeling. If the inquiry was complex in nature or if a considerable period of time has passed since receiving the inquiry, you may wish to preface your *yes* response with a brief restatement of the inquiry. You risk repeating information the reader already knows—but that risk is often preferable to the larger risk of saying yes to a forgotten inquiry.

In Figures 11-2a and 11-2b, two responses are exemplified, one with an explanation and one without. In the first, the writer repeats the essence of the inquiry before answering it. In the second, the writer simply answers the inquiry without repeating it. Notice how columns and white space are used effectively in the center of the letter.

POSITIVE RESPONSES TO REQUESTS AND INVITATIONS

These brief responses are too often treated in a routine way by business writers. The result can be missed opportunities at best and miscommunication at worst.

Notice how easily a response to a request can be misunderstood, particularly if a week or two has passed between receiving the request and writing the response.

```
Could Mr. Brady attend either the Democratic Committee
meeting on Thursday, May 4, or the Regional Caucus on
Friday, May 5?  If so, could Mr. Brady speak on one of three
topics?
        —Should the party endorse a primary candidate?
        —Should the party take a stand on tax reform?
        —Should the party favor import regulations?
```

FIGURE 11-1

Positive Response to an Order

Remington Galleries

Four Smith Place   Garden Shores, Florida 38923   (301) 302-4960

March 17, 198_

Belinda McNeil
Director, Human Resources
Tennebrach Petroleum, Inc.
3939 Industry Avenue
Miami, FL 30920

Dear Ms. McNeil:

On or before March 22, 198_, we will be pleased to ship
twenty-seven art posters from our series "Spring Morning"
to your Miami headquarters.

The posters will arrive by United Parcel, billed C.O.D.
Although we take extreme precautions against damage in the
packaging of our framed posters, you should check all
packages you receive with care. If you discover damage,
please notify us immediately, including the insurance
number marked on the damaged package.

We trust that you will find pleasure in seeing varieties of
"Spring Morning" in your corporate offices. When making
plans for decoration elsewhere in your facilities, please
consider the beautiful oil paintings and watercolors now
available in our fall catalog. These investment-quality
art pieces would be a handsome addition to your growing
collection of quality works.

Our sincere thanks and best wishes.

Cordially,

Morgan Fairmont

Morgan Fairmont
Sales Director

MF/eis

Enc.: The Remington Fall Catalog

FIGURE 11-2a

Positive Response to an Inquiry with an Explanation

REMINGTON ENTERTAINMENT, INC.

9789 Fifth Ave.
Chicago, IL 49693
(684) 709-4950

March 20, 198_

Calvin Murphy
30205 West Port Lane
Terminal Island, CA 92930

Dear Mr. Murphy:

In response to your inquiry regarding the true names of
actors and actresses under our management, we are happy to
provide the following information:

Stage name	Actual name
Trixie Rocklin	Patricia Rockinski
Troy Fields	Mortimer Schoel
Bronc Attlington	Bertram Attlington
Sissy Torrell	Sistine Torrellini

We're glad that you're interested in "our" stars and wish
you well with your continuing research, as described in your
letter.

Sincerely,

Harvey Remington

Harvey Remington
Owner/Agent

HR/tel

FIGURE 11-2b

Positive Response to an Inquiry Without an Explanation

REMINGTON ENTERTAINMENT, INC.

9789 Fifth Ave.
Chicago, IL 49693
(684) 709-4950

March 20, 198_

Calvin Murphy
30205 West Port Lane
Terminal Island, CA 92930

Dear Mr. Murphy:

We're happy to send along the true names of stars under our management:

Stage name	Actual name
Trixie Rocklin	Patricia Rockinski
Troy Fields	Mortimer Schoel
Bronc Attlington	Bertram Attlington
Sissy Torrell	Sistine Torrellini

We hope this information serves your needs. Best wishes with the research you described in your letter.

Sincerely,

Harvey Remington

Harvey Remington
Owner/Agent

HR/tel

Judge for yourself the effect of Brady's terse reply:

```
Dear Mr. Slather:

Yes, I believe I can attend.  I prefer your second topic,
though the third is also acceptable.

I look forward to meeting you.
```

Brady's brief yes answer left Slather less than enlightened. Will Brady attend one meeting or both? Will he choose the second or third topic? Slather, in fact, must hunt up his own copy of the invitation (if he retained a copy) to find out just what the second and third topics were.

Confusion of this sort can be avoided by including a brief summary of the request or invitation after the yes statement. In the positive response to an invitation in Figure 11-3, the writer reminds the reader about the nature of the invitation. The letter concludes with an appropriate expression of goodwill.

In some answers to requests and invitations, the yes response must be accompanied by qualifications and conditions. Let's say, for example, that this writer, Mr. Brady, wanted to include conditions having to do with his introduction at the convention. A paragraph can be inserted after the initial yes paragraph in the letter:

```
I am pleased to accept your kind invitation to the Friday
meeting of the caucus.

May I ask, however, that I be introduced to the audience in
my capacity as president of a construction company, not as a
board member of television station KYEX.  I wish to speak
freely about my political views without involving the
editorial and managerial positions taken by the station.
```

Here's another example, this time of a qualification on the part of the writer:

```
I am pleased to accept your kind invitation to the Friday
meeting of the caucus.

In fairness, however, I must remind you of my continuing
political support for Assemblywoman Linda Vollens, a
Republican.  In spite of my long-time Democratic ties, I
feel she is a superb legislator.  I mention this matter now
to prevent possible misunderstanding or embarrassment at the
caucus.
```

BUILDING GOODWILL

Particularly when responding to orders, business writers often miss an ideal opportunity for goodwill and sales reinforcement. Louisiana Carpet Supply, for example, places a first order for 400 boxes of "Tack–strip" carpet bonding from your company. Your options include the following:

FIGURE 11-3

Positive Response to an Invitation

■ **Brady**
■ **Construction**
■ **Inc.**

Trackson Park, No. 5
Beverley, Delaware 38674

(717) 899-1072

April 2, 198_

Mr. Ralph Slather, Director
Democratic Convention Committee
254 W. Third Street
New York, NY 10440

Dear Mr. Slather:

I am pleased to accept your kind invitation to the Friday
meeting of the caucus.

As you suggest, I'll speak for about forty minutes on tax
reform (one of the topics you offered).

I look forward to meeting you.

Sincerely,

James R. Brady
President, Brady Construction, Inc.

JRB/eg

- Ship the order and bill without comment.
- Ship the order and notify the client by carbon copy of the shipping order that the boxes are on their way.
- Ship the order and respond briefly in writing to a manager at Louisiana Carpet Supply, a new customer.

You cannot accompany each and every order with a special letter or note of response. But the occasion of any order marks an expression of trust in you by the customer, someone who believes that you can fulfill a need. As often as possible, you can respond to that expression of trust by a brief letter, such as the one in Figure 11-4. It not only says —"we're shipping the order"—but goes on to express appreciation and to "sell" the company.

Sometimes you will have to respond with a partial yes to an order that you were unable to fill completely. The letter in Figure 11-5, for example, emphasizes in the first paragraph what you were able to do and suggests later a timely solution for filling the rest of the order.

POSITIVE ADJUSTMENT LETTERS

In business, a client occasionally has bad luck with a product or service you provide. A microwave oven suddenly stops waving, a television becomes just a radio, or a waterbed turns into a fire hydrant. "Mother told me there would be days like this," you tell yourself.

The customer involved is making words, too, in the form of a claim letter addressed to you. Such a customer letter is often written in the heat of anger and disappointment, full of woeful descriptions of the product failure and the inconvenience and frustration *you* have caused. The letters often end with vague or not so vague threats about "further action" and "courts of law."

Prepare to write the positive adjustment letter by answering each of these questions to yourself. You need not answer yes to each question to justify the writing of a positive letter. You may decide to settle the issue by a positive response even if the customer is not right or cannot clearly prove fault on the part of the company. Your decision will be based on a complex set of factors, including your own judgment on a case-by-case basis and company policy.

1. Is the customer right?
2. Is the problem the company's fault?
3. Can I admit that fault?
4. Can I resolve the problem satisfactorily?

Begin your response by getting directly to the good news: "Yes, this company grants your claim." You need not repeat the details of the claim itself, except in a brief way to make clear the nature of the positive response. Especially if the details of the claim cause anger for the reader, avoid repeating what went wrong.

Let your yes statement be direct. It should satisfy the demand made against the company once and for all. Business letters cost money, and a half-yes merely invites further expensive correspondence, especially when lawyers become involved.

FIGURE 11-4

"Yes" Letter that Builds Goodwill

National Carpet Company Inc.

45 Express Way
Upland, Kentucky 59684
1-800-364-5865

February 12, 198_

Ms. Martha Cummings
Wholesale Manager
Louisiana Carpet Supply, Inc.
6783 Florence Street
Baton Rouge, LA 39534

Dear Ms. Cummings:

Your order of February 10 for 400 boxes of Tack-strip was
shipped to you on February 12 by Southeastern Trucking.
They promise delivery to your store no later than February
16.

Please note on the enclosed invoice that you qualified for a
10 percent discount because you agreed to pay C.O.D. for the
shipment.

A catalog of our most recent line is enclosed, with several
specials marked in red.

National Carpet Company, the volume leader in carpet
supplies, appreciates your business. We'll do everything we
can to ensure that our products and services keep you coming
back.

Sincerely,

Lennis Smythe

Lennis Smythe
Regional Manager
National Carpet Company, Inc.

LS/ow

Enclosure: National Catalog

FIGURE 11-5

Partial-"Yes" Letter

NUTONIC BUILDERS SUPPLY

22 W. Main Street   Missoula, Montana 39283   (382) 493-9302

April 9, 198_

Mr. Henry Morgich
Manager, Ace Homes, Inc.
495 Trent Street
Miami, Florida 39425

Dear Mr. Morgich:

Your April 5 order for 650 Tube-Chime Doorbell units
(#49592) was shipped that same day and should reach you by
April 10.

The remainder of your order, for 100 Choose-a-Tune Doorbell
units (#49852), will be shipped on April 15. This popular
item has been backlogged since the Christmas holidays.

Be assured that we will ship the Choose-a-Tune units by
express as soon as they are in stock, and in no case later
than April 15.

Thank you for choosing Nutonic Builders Supply for your
wholesale construction needs.

Sincerely,

Roberto Laiso

Roberto Laiso
Assistant Manager

RL/ce

In the letter in Figure 11-6, the writer makes reference to the claim itself only in the SUBJECT line. Thereafter, the claim is quickly granted in the yes paragraph that begins the letter. Necessary details are provided in the second paragraph. The writer tries to restore goodwill and customer confidence in the final paragraph.

Businesses do not make a regular practice, of course, of sending blanket yes letters in response to any and all claims against them. In a later chapter, we will discuss the "no" letter that must often be sent. But somewhere between these two answers is a middle ground: the positive adjustment letter that nevertheless takes time to educate the customer.

Let's say, for example, that Ms. Malloy's refrigerator is no longer under warranty when you receive her claim letter. Let's say, further, that your company decides to fix her refrigerator nonetheless. In your positive adjustment letter, you take time after the initial yes paragraph to educate Ms. Malloy, in a diplomatic way, about the realities of consumer purchases.

```
Although your refrigerator is no longer under warranty, we
will do our best to see that it is restored to good working
order.  At no expense to you, Garson Appliance Service in
your city will be glad to inspect your refrigerator and
resolve the problem to your satisfaction.

You may want to know, Ms. Malloy, that you have purchased
one of the most reliable refrigerators in the industry,
according to Consumer Reports.  We're confident that the
problem you are experiencing can be easily repaired.  At the
same time, we urge you to read warranty information
carefully for each appliance you buy.  In most cases,
repairs are the responsibility of the purchaser after
expiration of the warranty period.
```

Does such education do any good? Companies hope so. If the buying public begins to expect businesses and manufacturers to grant every claim, few companies can operate profitably. By including a brief paragraph of education for Ms. Malloy, Reston Appliances is making an effort to retain the meaning of important business concepts such as "warranty."

Finally, the positive adjustment letter provides a good opportunity to mend fences with disappointed customers. Obviously, a problem has led to the claim against the company. Your positive adjustment letter goes a long way toward repairing the feelings of disappointment and frustration. Buoyed by your yes response, in fact, the customer may be eager to learn of new products, services, sales, promotions, and so forth offered by your company. Include that information near the end of your positive adjustment letter.

CREDIT APPROVALS

Before writing a *yes* or *no* response to a credit application, consider some of the issues at stake. The applicant has revealed personal and business matters

FIGURE 11-6

Positive Adjustment Letter

RESTON
APPLIANCES, INC.

45 Harbor Street   Lowell, MA 49494   (317) 968-4857

April 6, 198_

Ms. Anna Malloy
4536 Oak Lane
Beaverton, MA 49524

SUBJECT: Your letter of April 3, 198_: refrigerator
malfunction

Dear Ms. Malloy:

According to our records, your refrigerator is still under
warranty. At no expense to you, Garson Appliance Service in
your city will be glad to inspect your refrigerator and
resolve the problem to your satisfaction.

Please make arrangements for their visit by calling 427-3842.

You may want to know, Ms. Malloy, that all Reston appliances--
including the revolutionary micropulse dishwashers--are on
sale beginning April 15. We've enclosed a sales catalog for
your review.

Thank you for giving us the opportunity to live up to our
reputation for quality and service in refrigeration products.

Sincerely,

Morgan O'Neill

Morgan O'Neill
Customer Relations

MO/wo

Enclosure: Sales Catalog

to you in confidence. You know, for example, how much the applicant makes and what debts he or she owes. Hopes have been aroused. The applicant looks forward to a positive answer from you. In some cases, his or her financial stability may depend upon your credit approval. In other cases, his or her dreams—a new car, perhaps a new home—depend upon you.

Your words, that is to say, must be chosen carefully and sensitively. In addition to dealing with the company's money in credit approvals, you are also dealing with people's problems, fears, hopes, and dreams.

Do not tease the reader, therefore, with ambiguous messages at the beginning of the credit approval letter. Write a succinct yes message that includes the precise terms of the credit granted. Like paper currency, a letter approving credit is virtually a form of money, at least for all transactions between your company and the customer whose credit you approve. Like a paper bill, the letter must bear exact notation of its "denomination" or limits to be of worth. The letter of credit approval, like other yes letters, concludes with a paragraph selling the company.

In the approval letter in Figure 11-7 notice the brisk yes beginning, the many details in the heart of the letter, and the restrained sales message in the final paragraph.

The writer delivers good news to the reader and, on the strength of that good news, proceeds to less easy reading: the precise terms of the credit arrangement. In a concluding paragraph, the writer tries to build goodwill and to express appreciation. A final sales message concludes the letter.

It is especially important to read over a credit approval letter before mailing. Some companies recommend that the writer put initials in the margin beside key amounts and provisions described in the letter. As Chapter 20 explores in detail, such letters together with the documents they summarize often become legally binding documents. An accidental misstatement—$100,000 instead of $10,000—can cause misunderstanding, mistrust, and even significant legal problems.

Summary

1. The occasions for yes letters are also occasions for building goodwill and communicating sales messages.
2. In making positive responses to orders, convey the yes message and any related details. Then provide a closing statement of appreciation, goodwill, and/or a sales message.
3. In making positive responses to inquiries, decide whether you need to repeat the substance of the inquiry in your reply.
4. Positive responses to requests and invitations should specify exactly what the writer is saying yes to.
5. In writing positive adjustment letters, the writer should announce the good news, explain any conditions or qualifications, and then express appreciation, goodwill, and/or a sales message.
6. Credit approvals must be precise in their statement of details and conditions.

FIGURE 11-7

Credit Approval Letter

Live____Wire____Lighting_____

597 Cactus Drive   Phoenix, Arizona 85734   (715) 394-7964

October 9, 198_

Mr. Robert Ortega
Best Home Products
4949 W. Thomas Road
Glendale, AZ 87584

Dear Mr. Ortega:

After reviewing your application, we are happy to approve
your request for a 90-day credit limit with us for $10,000.

Our credit agreement, enclosed for your approval and
signature, provides that wholesale orders may be charged to
your credit account for a period not to exceed 90 days.
Interest on the unpaid balance during that time will be 18
percent per year. We request that you do not exceed your
credit limit of $10,000. You will find additional terms and
conditions of this agreement, including billing and payment
procedures, in the "Credit Purchaser's Handbook" we have
enclosed for you.

We welcome you as a new customer and look forward to your
company's continued growth and success. We'll do our part
to provide you with the very best in fine lighting products.

Sincerely,

Cary Mellon

Cary Mellon
Credit Manager

CM/wu

Enc.: Credit agreement, "Credit Purchaser's Handbook"

Questions for Discussion

1. Why might you want to repeat the substance of an inquiry, request, or invitation in responding positively?
2. In general, should the yes message stand on its own or be attached to qualifications and conditions? Explain your answer.
3. How would you advise a writer to provide a partial yes response to a request or order?
4. What is the relation between the yes message and a sales message in a positive response letter?
5. In general, where should the good news of the yes message be placed in positive response letters? Why?
6. What considerations must be called to mind when writing credit approvals?
7. In what three ways can a sales message be woven smoothly into the yes letter?
8. What risk do you run when answering yes and not providing details explaining the context of your positive answer?
9. How can goodwill be increased through yes letters?
10. Why should the details of credit approval be stated precisely? Which details matter most of all?
11. Why must the yes letter sometimes be accompanied by conditions and qualifications? Give an example to illustrate your point.
12. What questions should be asked when preparing to write the positive adjustment letter?

Exercises

1. You're the manager of Frederick Trucking, Inc. Write a yes response to an inquiry from a local farmer who wants to ship produce to market. Include a sales message.
2. A professor writes to ask you, now a successful business person, to speak to a business class. Write back, accepting the invitation and repeating key details of the invitation.
3. The town mayor requests that your company hire unemployed teens. Respond with a partial yes to the request. Include a sales message and maintain goodwill.
4. A customer complains that your product has failed. Create the circumstances, then write a positive adjustment letter.
5. Approve the credit application of Ms. Frances Allison for a credit line of $5000 with your company. Include whatever conditions or qualifications you feel are necessary.
6. Write a positive response to a large order for your company's product.
7. Write a positive response to an invitation on the condition that some key detail of the invitation can be changed. Create the circumstances.
8. Write a partial yes response to an order for your company's product. Explain how the remainder of the order will be filled.

Barbara Fox has opened—and closed—four businesses in the past ten years. She's a bright, entrepreneurial manager. But something goes wrong:

It's hard to explain. My employees always seem to like me—some say I'm the best boss they've ever had. Customers, too, always praise me for going the extra mile to meet their needs. About the only people I don't get along with are the hardnosed types like my accountant. They fuss and fume over the most insignificant details. They put money ahead of people.

But I'll admit that I've had my share of bad luck in business over the past decade. My best friends tell me it's because I can't say "no." If an employee needs an extra week off, an advance on salary, or even a raise, I usually find myself saying "OK," even against my better judgment. I treat customers just as well, I guess. I can't remember when I didn't give in to a customer's complaint against my company.

I want business to be friendly, not antagonistic. I don't want to start any arguments, and I don't want enemies.

Consider Barbara Fox's approach to the business world. Why does she resist saying "no"? What does she think would happen if she did say "no"? What would, in fact, happen?

Conveying
Bad News and
Maintaining Goodwill 12

LEARNING OBJECTIVES

To analyze the difficulties involved in saying "no" in many business situations

To choose when to use buffers and explanations to convey negative responses

To write effective negative responses for orders, inquiries, requests, and invitations

To write negative adjustment letters that are clear, tactful, and productive in maintaining goodwill

To understand the sensitive human and legal issues involved in communications regarding credit

To write effective denials of credit

Just as surely as "yes" letters engender feelings of gratitude, appreciation, and friendliness in our readers, "no" letters can arouse anger, disappointment, and even hatred. No wonder we all find "no" letters hard to write.

In fact, we sometimes do everything in our power to keep a letter from really saying "no"—and end up confusing the reader.

A LESSON IN SAYING "NO"

Consider a case history in which the best of intentions led a business person into uncomfortable complications, all from an inability to say no—simply, politely, and firmly—with as much explanation as appropriate.

Rachel Yarmouth bought a used 1964 VW from Toppins VW. She developed a keen interest in the workings of the car and soon was performing minor maintenance and repair procedures herself.

When it came time for a transmission overhaul, Rachel did not flinch, but set about collecting shop manuals to guide her step-by-step in replacing gears and seals. She discovered, though, that she required a special tool—a gear puller—available only at the dealer.

She wrote a friendly letter to Henry "Hank" Foreni, service manager at Toppins VW. She reminded Foreni that she had bought her car at Toppins and asked to borrow a gear puller from the shop for a few days. Foreni wrote back the letter shown in Figure 12-1.

Foreni thought he had said "no" to Ms. Yarmouth in a friendly, effective way. She, however, read between the lines and found a message Foreni never intended: she could simply ask the mechanics to lend her the tool.

Much to Foreni's embarrassment, the next day found Ms. Yarmouth going from mechanic to mechanic in the garage, quoting Foreni rather freely to the effect that she might be able to borrow a gear puller from one of the mechanics.

None, of course, loaned out their tools. All felt some annoyance at Foreni for sending Ms. Yarmouth to them.

Ms. Yarmouth, not to be denied, called Foreni a few days later. She repeated her request for the tool. Foreni, caught short for words, told her he would have to get back to her. That afternoon, not wanting to talk with her by phone, he mailed this note:

```
    I spoke with the mechanics.  You see, the tool you want
to borrow costs about $95.  You can understand why they
don't lend out such expensive items.

    We do, however, value you as a customer and hope to
serve your auto needs.

                              Sincerely,

                              Hank

                              Henry Foreni
                              Service Manager
```

FIGURE 12-1

Letter Saying "No"

Toppins Volkswagon

385 Granite Lane
Boulder, Colorado 29583
385-3692

May 5, 198_

Ms. Rachel Yarmouth
395 Western Avenue Apt. 8
Boulder, Colorado 29583

Dear Ms. Yarmouth:

We're always happy to hear from customers, particularly
those who are finding their VWs to be an enjoyable hobby as
well as reliable transportation.

I certainly understand your need for a gear puller.
Unfortunately, all such tools at this dealership are
individually owned by the mechanics themselves. I don't
have the right, of course, to loan out their tools.

Best of luck with your project.

Sincerely,

Henry Foreni

Henry Foreni
Service Manager

HF/wy

Certainly, Foreni told himself, that's the end of it. Ms. Yarmouth read the letter twice—then set out for her bank. The next day she presented herself at Foreni's office with a cashier's check for $95.00—a bond, she said, to guarantee the safe return of the gear puller she planned to borrow.

Foreni, perspiring now, had to explain that mechanics just didn't lend out tools, *ever*. At last he managed to communicate what he should have written in his initial message: Toppins VW does not lend out tools. In other words, "no."

Ms. Yarmouth was left rather upset—not so much by the fact that she could not borrow the gear puller, but by the unnecessary and somewhat embarrassing rat-race she had been through.

For his part, Foreni—fearing Ms. Yarmouth's disappointment—had tried to soften the blow by pillowing elaborate excuses around "no." Naturally, Ms. Yarmouth took those excuses as rays of hope.

We save ourselves expensive losses and considerable embarrassment in business by learning to say "no" when we must. As in the case of Ms. Yarmouth, customers' feelings are hurt not so much by the "no" answer (which may be expected all along) but by the series of disappointments and deceptions caused by false hopes and dead ends. Had Ms. Yarmouth been told "no" with a truthful explanation from the beginning, she would have redirected her energies, perhaps toward buying the tool she wanted. Her anger at the end of the affair stemmed primarily from wasted hours and awkward confrontations.

SAYING "NO" IN A DIRECT AND CONSIDERATE MANNER

Recognize that many business inquiries, requests, and invitations are asking you a simple question: can you or can't you? These business men and women may not want to hear the reasons and justifications for your answer. "No" may be all they have time to hear before setting out in new directions. In short, don't presume to explain your negative answers on all occasions—your audience may not care about your explanation.

At times, of course, your correspondent may want to know why you've answered "no." A good test for such occasions is to put yourself in your reader's shoes. Would you appreciate an explanation of a negative response? If so, include such an explanation in your letter. This consideration on your part builds goodwill in the long run, even for customers to whom you say "no" in the short run.

Consider the examples of negative response letters in Figures 12-2 and 12-3. The first, while maintaining a friendly tone, does not justify the "no" answer. It mentions that the Office of Student Aid reviewed many excellent applications. By implication, the Office did not have enough money to serve all worthy applicants. But the letter does not spell out specifically why this applicant was denied. It would not have been helpful, the Office may have decided, to tell Francine Gillings that "your grades and test scores qualified you for aid, but your letters of recommendation, in our judgment, seemed some-

FIGURE 12-2

Negative Response Without an Explanation

Devlin University

Office of Student Aid   4 Callings Building   Kent, Utah 38923

May 7, 198_

Ms. Francine Gillings
4983 Wilton Place
Boise, Montana 48934

Dear Ms. Gillings:

This year the Office of Student Aid reviewed many excellent
applications, including yours, for scholarships and grant
assistance.

We regret that we are unable to offer you financial aid at
this time. You will find enclosed, however, a brochure
describing the many low-interest student loan programs now
available through local banks working in cooperation with
the Federal government and this university.

Best wishes for a successful academic year.

Sincerely,

Xavier R. Reyes

Xavier R. Reyes
Director, Student Aid

XRR/wor

Enclosure: "Low-Interest Student Loans"

FIGURE 12-3

Negative Response with an Explanation

PETERSON MICROSYSTEMS, INC.

12 Graves Road
Henderson, Ohio 38923
(423) 483-8934

January 3, 198_

Mr. Geoff Beams
7895 Trevor Lane
Henderson, Ohio 38923

Dear Mr. Beams:

Thank you for your thorough application for the position of
programmer at Peterson Microsystems and for the time you
spent in interviews. We certainly enjoyed meeting you.

We regret, however, that we cannot offer you the position you
seek at the present time. Our decision, made after long
deliberation, is based on two factors:

   1. All programmers here must often work with the UNIX
      operating system from the first day on the job. You
      have not had experience with UNIX.

   2. Our programmers must often work overtime on high
      priority projects. Your time commitments as a
      doctoral student, we feel, will make overtime
      impossible for you.

You must know, Mr. Beams, that we are interested in your
abilities and thank you for contacting Peterson Microsystems.
Please keep us in mind as an employer when the matters
discussed above no longer present obstacles to our mutual
association.

Sincerely,

Berta Kiely

Berta Kiely
Personnel Director

BK/ogi

> The more we practice writing, the faster the writing process becomes. We accustom ourselves to certain ways of expressing ideas—our own "style," we begin to call it.
>   Skilled business writing, like fine carpentry, can become a craft in which we take just pride. When we begin to enjoy building good memos, letters, and reports, we understand what Hemingway meant when he insisted that all good writing "is architecture, not interior decoration."

what hollow and restrained in their praise of you." In this case, the Office shields its decision-making process by not making available all the reasons that led to its negative decision.

By contrast, the letter in Figure 12-3 gives an explanation for the negative response. The writer wisely chooses to explain in detail why the reader's application for employment was turned down. Consider her reasons. First, the applicant has invested time and energy in making a thorough job application. The personnel director may feel that the applicant deserves more than a summary "no" response. Second, the company has a long-range interest in hiring the applicant at a later date—after his doctoral studies, perhaps, or when he has mastered UNIX. The explanation for the negative response lets the applicant know what he can do to change the "no" to a "yes."

In short, you must decide when circumstances require an explanation for your "no" response. As a general rule, provide an explanation for a negative response whenever it will help build goodwill or make possible future contacts. Do not provide an explanation if the reader clearly does not care for one, or if your explanation will unnecessarily complicate future contacts with the reader.

Let's consider one circumstance in which an explanation for the negative response led to unfortunate complications. An acquaintance from college days calls at your office and asks for a $1000 loan. For a number of personal reasons, you choose not to lend him the money. You mull over what to say.

I can't because I've only been at this job for a year and I haven't been able to save much.

You reject this response, since it invites him to come back with, "Great, I'll check back with you in about six months for the money."

I can't because I hardly know you. We weren't close, even in college.

But you reject this response, foreseeing his rejoinder, "I understand completely. Let me tell you about myself . . ." Face the fact that you don't want to lend the money. You don't have to explain "No." That statement is neither belligerent, unkind, nor offensive. It simply takes a stand that you will often have to take in business life.

As a manager, for example, you will face a steady stream of inquiries and requests regarding job reassignments, promotions, raises, and a host of other matters. You'll be asked to fire Charley, transfer Helen, fund the volleyball team, and sponsor a jog-a-thon. If you intend to support each of your "no" answers with a watertight web of explanations, you will find little time for any other activity in business.

Learn to use your right to say "no" simply, politely, and firmly.

THE IMPORTANCE OF THE BUFFER STATEMENT

A buffer is a positive or neutral statement—not a negative one—that serves as a middle ground, a starting place, for your negative response. Buffers allow the reader to feel comfortable with you before experiencing the discomfort of the "no" message. Here are four suggestions for creating effective buffers:

1. Choose a positive aspect of the subject at hand.

   We were frankly surprised when our small advertisement drew over 350 responses.

2. Praise the reader for personal or professional qualities.

   In your interviews, Mr. Johnson, we came to know a man with extensive managerial skill and good business instincts.

3. Concentrate on special needs.

   At Vector Direct Mail Sales, we have limited our new product acquisitions to cosmetics, electronic games, and jewelry.

4. Use time factors as explanations.

   Our production schedule demands that we settle upon a computer system that can be on-line no later than February 7, 1986.

In using such buffers, writers try to prepare the reader for a rational, not irrational, reception of the "no" response. Disappointment on the reader's part cannot be avoided entirely, of course. "No" means "no," in spite of buffers. But the writer's effort to provide a context and emotional buffer for the negative response often builds goodwill that transcends momentary disappointment.

NEGATIVE RESPONSES TO ORDERS

Businesses must often say "no" to orders. Sometimes the buyer's credit is not good, or the item ordered may be out of stock. At such times, use the model below in the letter saying "no" to the order.

- Begin with a positive buffer (perhaps a statement of appreciation for the order).
- Go on to a clear statement of what you can and cannot provide.
- Include any explanations or qualifications you feel will be helpful to the reader.

- Conclude with a statement of goodwill, appreciation, and/or a brief sales message.

In the example in Figure 12-4, Better Carpets regretfully must decline a huge carpet order. Notice how the writer leaves the door open for future business. He begins with a buffer of appreciation. The "no" message is explained in some detail. The reader understands *why* the small carpet company must decline the order. She may then be disposed to accept the compromise plan: a carpet order for twenty-two homes. The letter concludes with appreciation and an action suggestion ("meeting with you soon").

NEGATIVE RESPONSES TO INQUIRIES

As with orders, writers can say "no" to inquiries in a polite but firm way. Notice that the writer of the letter in Figure 12-5 chooses not to provide elaborate explanations for the "no" response. Perhaps he feels that his brief explanation ("security regulations") will satisfy the inquirer. He does provide a buffer emphasizing a positive aspect of the inquiry (the professor's interesting research). The "no" message follows, supported by the brief explanation ("security regulations"). The writer is able to offer an alternative in the form of a booklet. While it certainly does not meet the professor's need for Army data, it does provide a concrete expression of goodwill to close the letter.

NEGATIVE RESPONSES TO REQUESTS AND INVITATIONS

Busy professional people often have to choose what they can do from among the things they ought to do. They often find themselves saying "no" to worthwhile projects and causes.

Don Lyman had a successful import business. The price he paid, he felt, was high blood pressure and an on-again-off-again ulcer. Relief from job pressure came on the golf course every Wednesday. Don played with friends. He loved these moments: he realized they were good for him.

Don received a request from the local Rotary Club to lead a two-month seminar for high-school students interested in business careers. The seminar met for only one hour per week—but on Wednesdays. Don knew he should accept the invitation. He knew equally well that he didn't want to sacrifice golf. He wrote the "no" response that appears in Figure 12-6.

Has Don made up excuses? No, he has told the truth. Should he have offered more cogent excuses? No, he has the right to decline an invitation by the same token that the Rotary Club had a right to ask him. Were his friends at the Rotary Club outraged by his refusal? Of course not. Life moves on, especially business life, more quickly than we like to admit. The Rotary Club simply found a new seminar leader.

But how upset they would have been, with reason, if Don had flashed green, then red, then green, then red signals, only to not show up at the last minute.

FIGURE 12-4

Negative Response to an Order

BETTER CARPETS, INC.

59 Springfield Street   Sacramento, CA 89384   (893) 948-8993

March 19, 198_

Ms. Hanna Morley
Director, Interior Design
Western Homes, Inc.
273 Ghent Drive
Sacramento, CA 89384

Dear Ms. Morley:

Thank you for choosing Better Carpets as carpeting
subcontractor for the 385 homes in your Sierra Madre
subdivision.

Unfortunately, we must decline your order as it now stands.
Our decision, made reluctantly, is based on two
considerations:

> * As a relatively small carpet business, we have a
>   limited work force. A job as large as the Sierra Madre
>   would require their full energies for at least two full
>   months. We could not continue to serve the rest of our
>   customers during this period.
>
> * We would have to make substantial capital investment in
>   new equipment to accomplish the Sierra Madre job in the
>   time frame you specify. Such equipment would be idle
>   after the job was finished.

Please consider another plan. Better Carpets will carpet the
twenty-two model homes in the Sierra Madre tract at the
discount rate you requested for the 385 homes. We would be
pleased to work with you in selecting another competent
carpeting contractor for the larger job.

We appreciate the confidence you have shown in Better Carpets,
Ms. Morley, and look forward to meeting with you soon to
discuss our participation in the Sierra Madre project.

Sincerely,

Ronald C. Horton
President

RCH/iow

FIGURE 12-5

Negative Response to an Inquiry

United States Army

Ft. Ebson Station   Boulder, CO 38928   (389) 908-7834
Personnel Research Facility

April 12, 198_

Professor Andrew Higgins
Department of Biology
Northern State University
Wiley, CO   37923

SUBJECT: Your inquiry regarding stress testing

Dear Professor Higgins:

Thank you for your letter of April 6. We especially enjoyed
hearing of your research work and wish you well on its
successful outcome.

We cannot, however, provide the data you requested from Army
files because of national security regulations.

You may find of interest, however, a recent booklet
published for civilian researchers by the Army. I enclose
it for your review.

Sincerely,

Nathan Ramirez

Nathan Ramirez
Staff Sergeant
Medical Research Unit

NR/cox

Enclosure: "Universities and the Army: Partners for Peace"

FIGURE 12-6

Negative Response to a Request

Lyman Oriental Imports, Inc.

2358 Bureau Street
West Luxton, Connecticut 59394
(444) 492-6789

March 23, 198_

Mr. Jack Baily
President, Rotary Club
2554 Seventh Street
West Luxton, Connecticut 59394

Dear Jack,

Thank you for your invitation to lead a business seminar for
high-school students for the next two months.

Unfortunately, I've already made other commitments for those
dates.

With you, I recognize the importance of this worthwhile
project. Please let me know how I can support the present
seminar.

Sincerely,

Don

Don Lyman
Lyman Oriental Imports, Inc.

DL/cc

To deny a request or invitation, follow the model suggested for the "no" response to orders and inquiries:

- Begin with a buffer statement that says, in effect, "here's a positive thought we can share." Often, the buffer forestalls that age-old come-back from disappointed readers, "Oh, he probably didn't understand." You do understand, and must say no.
- Go on to the clear "no" response, followed with an explanation, if helpful. Perhaps alternatives can be suggested.
- Conclude with a positive message, perhaps a statement of appreciation, goodwill, and/or a sales message.

In the concluding paragraph you can express goodwill or well-wishing for the reader and the project or request at hand. Take care not to sound hypocritical. If, for example, you are the sole decision-maker on a project, it is less than candid to say "no" only to wish the project every success. When in good conscience you cannot wish the applicant or the project well, you can often conclude by simply thanking the parties involved for bringing the matter to you.

NEGATIVE ADJUSTMENT LETTERS

No business lasts long by granting every customer claim lodged against it. In learning to write "no" responses to claims, use the customer's own reasonable expectations as a framework or agenda for your letter. The customer expects

- to be heard (the positive "sharing" in the opening buffer statement tells the reader, "I heard you").
- to be answered decisively, not put off.
- to understand the grounds for your decision.
- to be treated with respect.

These reasonable expectations form a blueprint for "no" letters.

No single recipe can or should be *the* way to effective "no" responses to claim letters. Much depends upon consumer protection regulations and company policies applicable to the product or service you sell. Four general guidelines, however, can serve the writer well:

1. Assess the justice of the claim without bias. Make an honest effort to see the situation from the customer's point of view.
2. If the claim merits it, give what you are able to give, both in words and replacement merchandise or payment.
3. Take care not to use language that may cause you and your company future problems. Some of the simplest phrases can cause the most ticklish problems if a case is brought to court. In general, no sentence should suggest company responsibility or liability for a mishap, unless you have authorization for such statements.

4. No matter how angry and abusive the claim letter is, maintain a professional, even tone in your response. Do not yield to the temptation to arouse anger in your reader. Your goal should be to dispense goodwill, act fairly within your limitations, and put the problem to bed.

Observe how the blueprint can be used to deal with a messy, sticky customer claim.

In 1981, Maynard Manning bought a pressure cooker. He took it home to cook a beef stew for friends in his newly wallpapered kitchen. About twenty minutes after being put on the burner, the pan's top shot up with a roar of steam, carrying with it all the beef stew, atomized now to a fine, greasy spray. The wallpaper was ruined. Maynard checked the pressure cooker and discovered that the entire escape valve unit had blown off the lid of the pan. In his letter to the company, he asserted his claim:

> I demand that you replace not only my pressure cooker, but also reimburse me in the amount of $554, representing what it cost me to re-wallpaper my kitchen after your product failed in such a dangerous and destructive way.

The company, Presley Cookware, has a strict policy on customer claims. It will grant any claim involving replacement of a returned product; it will grant no claim for cash outlay; it will accept no liability under any circumstances. The customer relations representative operates under these guidelines. He knows, therefore, that he will say "no" to Mr. Manning's claim. The letter in Figure 12-7 follows his reasonable expectations.

Notice that the writer avoids telling Manning that he is wrong or has not followed directions with care. Such direct confrontation will lead only to anger and an end to communication. The writer takes a firm but not a hostile stand regarding the money demanded by the customer. Subtly, the writer never mentions the exact amount, allowing it to slip from attention.

A form of compromise is held out in the offer of a new pot, a slight but wise concession by the company. Many angry clients seek to save face more than recover money. Manning may well feel that a new pot, while far from his original demand, at least shows the company is willing to make amends.

Notice, too, that at no time does the writer admit fault on the part of the company. Such an admission of liability (fault assigned to someone) might be used against the company in a later lawsuit. In showing professional concern for the cause of the accident, the writer invites the customer to send in the damaged pressure cooker for examination.

Instead of expressing outright sympathy, the writer tries to move the focus to positive present and future events ("you weren't injured", "a new cooker," "absolutely no charge") rather than dwelling on the traumatic event causing Manning's claim letter. Expressing sorrow for each detail of the incident would only stir up bad memories for the reader. Therefore, the expression of sympathy is general and brief.

At times, you may choose to explain your decision *before* announcing your "no" response in a direct way. Consider this rearrangement of the body of the letter to Maynard Manning:

FIGURE 12-7

Negative Adjustment Letter

P R E S L E Y
C O O K W A R E

456 Yolda Boulevard   Baltimore, Maryland 50496
(888) 567-4859

December 5, 198_

Mr. Maynard Manning
4932 Seventh Street
Ft. Worth, Texas 50304

Dear Mr. Manning:

Thank you for your letter of December 2 in which you describe
a most unfortunate cooking incident. We are glad you weren't
injured.

While we are not able to pay the amount you suggest, we will
replace your Presley Cooker at absolutely no charge to you.
Please send your damaged cooker to us for replacement.

Our product engineers will inspect the returned cooker to
discover the cause of your accident. When you receive your
new cooker, may we remind you to read the accompanying
directions--particularly those involving temperature control--
before using the cooker. Steam cooking requires special
precautions.

You can count on receiving years of satisfying service from
your new cooker. Please contact us if we can be of help in
any way.

Sincerely,

Brad Wilcox

Brad Wilcox
Customer Relations

BW/wv

Decision

Explanation or
Interpretation

Thank you for your letter of December 2 in which you
describe a most unfortunate cooking incident. We are glad
you weren't injured.

Our product engineers will inspect your cooker to discover
the cause of your accident. Please return it (we will pay
postage) at your earliest convenience to the address above.
We will then replace your Presley Cooker at absolutely no
charge to you. When you receive your new cooker, be sure to
read the accompanying directions--particularly those
involving temperature control--before using the cooker.
Steam cooking requires special precautions.

You can count on years of reliable service from your new
cooker. Please call on us if we can be helpful in any way.

You must be the judge of whether to explain the grounds for your decision before or after the "no" response. The goal, in either case, is to *help the
reader understand and deal with your decision.*

CREDIT DENIALS

Many people continue to feel that their ability to qualify for credit reflects the
degree of their morality, reliability, and even intelligence. With such highly
charged stakes at hand, saying "no" to credit applications requires special
skill and care.

Applications for credit buying are typically reviewed by staff members
trained for such work. They forward their recommendations to the credit
manager, who makes a final decision on each case. As a business writer, you
may find yourself in such a managerial role. You no doubt will have to say
"no" to a large percentage of applicants for credit with your firm. How you
say "no" can make or break future business relations with these clients.

Before considering what to say to such applicants in a letter, consider
your assumptions about them. Is an inadequate credit record *today* absolute
proof of poor credit *forever?* No. Some of your best future clients may be
among the list of applicants receiving "no" letters today. Choose language
that will not alienate or offend these clients.

Will clients with an inadequate credit record cease to buy from your company on a cash basis as soon as they receive your "no" letter regarding
credit? No. The experience of major department stores such as Sears and
Penny's proves that if credit applicants are turned down in a polite way their
buying habits do not change. Choose words, therefore, that encourage rather
than discourage their patronage.

Finally, are the names on your list for "no" letters the dregs of society,
misfits, losers, and scoundrels? Emphatically no. By and large, these are ordinary citizens. The verdict of inadequate credit often comes from living too
short a time in one area, working too short a time on a new job, or recovering

financially from illness or divorce. No client on your "no" list deserves short, offensive treatment.

When you begin to write a "no" letter regarding credit, you may have the applicant's full credit history, including the details of outstanding loans, missed payments, and so forth. You will be guided by your company's policy regarding how much or how little explanation you should give in your letter of credit denial.

Figure 12-8 shows a typical letter denying credit from a company that, for legal reasons, does not choose to specify in exact detail why credit was denied. Notice that the reader *can* find out the reasons for denial, but must call a credit service to do so.

By contrast, the letter in Figure 12-9 tells the customer precisely why credit was denied. (It is not within the scope of this text to offer legal advice on which method is preferable. In all communications regarding credit, writers should have access to the advice of an attorney.)

Most "no" letters regarding credit have three sections, usually written as separate paragraphs.

Paragraph 1

Tell the client *how your company felt* when he or she made the effort to apply for credit. Mention the dates of application and amount of credit.

```
     Luxe Women's Wear appreciated your inquiry of May 2 and
your application regarding a credit line of $2500 at our
store.
```

Paragraph 2

Without undue stalling, *get to the heart of your action.* Say "no" politely and firmly.

```
     After careful review of your application, we are not
able to extend the credit you request at the present time.
```

If you wish to *qualify your action* in any way, add additional sentences.

```
You do qualify, however, for our Spring Shopper's Card,
allowing purchases up to $500.  Since we hope you'll become
a Spring Shopper at Luxe, I have taken the liberty of
enclosing a credit agreement for your signature.  Your card
will be mailed out the day we receive the signed agreement.
```

Paragraph 3

Conclude by thanking the client and/or by selling the merits of the company.

Thanks
```
     Luxe Women's Wear would like to express its gratitude
for your patronage.  We do hope to be able to act more
favorably on your credit application in the future.
```
Selling
```
     Luxe Women's Wear wants to invite you to its Priority
Sale, available only between 9 A.M. and 12 P.M. on May 10
```

FIGURE 12-8

Letter Denying Credit Without Explanation

Constant Attention Clothing, Inc.

33 Breeze Street   Carefree, AZ 98483   (894) 983-9843

July 19, 198_

Mr. William Connelly
5894 Sixth Avenue
Phoenix, AZ 89483

Dear Mr. Connelly:

We at Constant Attention Clothing were pleased to receive
your application on July 10 for a $3000 credit line.

At this time, we regret that we cannot approve your
application. If you wish more information on this action,
please contact TRW Information Services at 893/982-3893 to
review your credit history with a credit counselor. This
service is available without charge to you for sixty days
from the date of this letter.

Thank you, Mr. Connelly, for looking to Constant Attention
Clothing for the latest in affordable fashions. We will
continue to welcome your business and look forward to your
reapplication for credit at some time in the future.

Sincerely,

Victoria Y. Felton

Victoria Y. Felton
Manager, Credit Division

VYF/riw

FIGURE 12-9

Letter Denying Credit with Explanation

STUNNING KITCHENS, INC.

6869 Highway 9   Frontier, Nevada 89823   (893) 892-3849

May 7, 198_

Ms. Barbara Devon
3894 Western Walk Lane
Frontier, Nevada 89823

SUBJECT: Your credit application, April 25, 198_

Dear Ms. Devon:

We appreciated receiving your application for $5000 credit
with this company and have given your request careful
consideration.

Based on your salary and credit history, Ms. Devon, we are
unable to extend credit to you at this time. May we call your
attention to two items on your credit record that influenced
our decision:

* You are delinquent in payments to Harvest Furniture
  Co., Las Vegas, Nevada, in the amount of $585.

* Your extra income in the amount of $750 per month
  from real estate investments cannot be verified by
  public records.

If you have information on either of these items that does not
appear in your credit record, please contact us.

Thank you, Ms. Devon, for considering Stunning Kitchens, Inc.,
for the remodeling you contemplate. We'll be happy to serve
you as a cash customer or, assuming the matters above can be
cleared up, as a credit customer.

Our best wishes for your building project.

Sincerely,

Nancy O. Joplin

Nancy O. Joplin
Credit Manager

NOJ/poe

for special customers like you. Please bring the enclosed pass to be admitted to this outstanding sale.

Clients *can* take "no" for an answer, especially when you, the writer, don't surround the word with solemn, funereal overtones. Judge, for example, the effect of this heavy "no":

It is with regret that we must inform you that your application for credit has been denied.

The phrases "it is with regret" and "we must inform you" may seem appropriate for a death in the family, but certainly not for denial of credit.

When holding out hope for future credit, make sure that the hope you express is realistic. Asking a client to "reapply in a month or two" merely sets the stage for future disappointment if it is clear to you that the client has little chance of qualifying for credit at that time.

A credit manager for a Tucson jewelry store has a healthy approach to "no" credit letters.

I imagine that my client has just asked me if I carry baseballs in my jewelry store. "No," I say, "but I have other lovely things." In the same tone, when I have to deny credit I simply say, "No, but I welcome your business and I'll do my best to serve your needs."

That straightforward, respectful spirit goes a long way toward preventing the hurt pride and disappointment that can stem from letters denying credit.

Summary

1. Saying "no" does not have to offend the reader.
2. Negative responses to orders should provide explanations and, where possible, alternatives that build goodwill.
3. Negative responses to inquiries may or may not need accompanying explanations, as required by the circumstances.
4. Negative responses to requests and invitations should be truthful. Such statements often begin with a buffer statement.
5. Negative adjustment letters begin with a buffer statement, then provide a rationale for the negative decision. The decision itself may appear before or after the explanation. The letter concludes with a message intended to maintain goodwill.
6. Credit denials must be handled expertly and sensitively by business writers. These messages may or may not specify grounds for the denial, depending on the circumstances and company policy.

Questions for Discussion

1. What emotions are readers likely to feel when reading "no" letters that are too direct?
2. What is a buffer? How is it used in negative responses?
3. Must every "no" answer be explained thoroughly in business communications? Explain your answer.

4. Is it a good practice to write all negative responses without any explanation?
5. What are three types of buffers that may be used to begin "no" letters?
6. How can you say "no" to an invitation if you have no good excuse?
7. When you provide an explanation, should it appear before or after the "no" statement in a negative response letter? Discuss the pros and cons of each placement.
8. Why is denial of credit an emotionally difficult matter for many people? Describe ways in which writers can avoid angering the reader who receives a credit denial.
9. Describe your own feelings aroused by reading a "no" letter at some time in the past. How could those feelings have been influenced by different words in the letter?
10. In your opinion why do many "no" letters have an unfriendly and even hostile tone? Support your answer with reasons.
11. Moral considerations aside, why should explanations in "no" letters be truthful?
12. When is a buffer statement unneccessary in a "no" letter?

Exercises

1. Create a dialogue—like a comic strip—in which one character makes a request and the other says no. Write down what they actually say beneath your drawing of the characters. Write down what they are thinking above the characters.
2. Write a negative response to an order, while maintaining goodwill. Make up the circumstances.
3. A local political group has sent you a long questionnaire asking for your political and ethical judgments on a number of subjects. Write a negative response to the group, indicating that you will not answer the questions. Include only a brief explanation. Then rewrite the letter, including a lengthy explanation for your decision. On a sheet attached to this assignment, assess which of the two letters you prefer. Explain why.
4. Write a negative response to an invitation. Begin with a buffer. Offer alternatives to the reader.
5. In the role of a claims supervisor, write a negative adjustment letter to a customer who complains that your company's plant food killed his houseplants. Make an effort to maintain goodwill.
6. Write two negative responses to a request for your donated services as honorary chair of a local charity. In the first version of your letter, explain your reasons before stating the "no" message. In the second version, explain your reasons after the "no" message. On an attached sheet, explain which of the two letters you prefer and why.
7. Write a negative response to a credit application, explaining the grounds for your denial. Maintain goodwill.
8. Write a negative response to a credit application. Do not explain the specific grounds for your action; instead, refer the applicant to a local credit service for counseling. Maintain goodwill.

Fernando Avalos owns a cabinetry business in Placentia, California. He takes special pride in the

natural oak cabinets he builds—a trade taught to him by his father.

In good times, all the advertising I need is by word of mouth. Former customers tell their friends, who then come to me for cabinetry. But when the economy turns sour, my business dries up. I have to advertise. But there's my problem. As a small-business person, I obviously can't afford large ads in expensive architectural and decorating magazines. Besides, most of those magazines are national in scope. I just serve my immediate area. I don't like to run small classified ads in local newspapers. My shop has a story to tell, and I need to include pictures of our work.

Could a sales or promotional letter serve Mr. Avalos' purpose in reaching his immediate area? What advantages does such a letter have over magazine and newspaper advertising? How would you design such a letter if you were in Mr. Avalos' position?

Persuasive

Letters 13

LEARNING OBJECTIVES

To base persuasive arguments on the needs of your readers

To develop a persuasive argument for the sales letter using the S-A-L-E-S plan

To describe the advantages and disadvantages of sales by direct mail

To develop an effective direct mail sales letter

To use the A-C-T-I-O-N pattern to build effective claims letters

To evaluate factors that determine what kind of collection letter should be sent to overdue accounts

To write an effective series of collection letters

To some extent, all business letters are persuasive. All should consider the reader's point of view, then use persuasional strategies to communicate a message that will reach the reader effectively. But four letter types, more than any others, depend on persuasional techniques for their success:

- The sales or promotional letter—persuades readers to buy a product or service.
- The direct mail letter—a form of sales letter, persuades readers to shop for products and services by mail.
- The claims letter—persuades the reader, often a company employee in charge of customer service, to make requested adjustments because of a failure in a product or service.
- The collection letter—usually one in a series, persuades the reader to pay money he or she owes.

THE NATURE OF PERSUASION

But let's begin with what persuasive letters have in common: the need to persuade. How are readers persuaded?

You must demonstrate that the action you suggest (buying the product or service) serves the needs of the reader. Consider some of the needs the reader has:

The need for money	The need for health
The need for more free time	The need for comfort
The need for productivity	The need for entertainment
The need for importance	The need for security
The need for power	The need for knowledge
The need for attractiveness	The need for a desired skill
The need for friends	The need for reputation

These and other needs describe what *interests* the reader. If your product or service is to prove interesting as well, it must be linked in some way to a *need already felt by the reader*. In other words, persuasive letters make readers understand not merely that the product or service is good, but that it is good for them.

THE SALES AND PROMOTION LETTER

The terms "sales letter" and "promotional letter" mean the same thing in common business use: letters intended to sell a product or service. Occasionally you will find the term "promotional letter" reserved for selling *programs* and *product lines* rather than specific products and services. In common use, however, and in this text, the terms will be synonymous.

The work of creating an effective sales letter begins in the head, not on paper. The writer first decides to concentrate on "you," the reader, rather than "I." In the following example, notice how the focus of the sales concept changes:

> I—The new Chevette features a four-cylinder engine, revolutionary new suspension, and tinted windows.
>
> You—The new Chevette features a four-cylinder engine to save you money, a revolutionary new suspension to take the bumps away, and tinted windows for glare-free driving.

In the "you" example, the writer has used the reader's needs (for economy, comfort, and security) to sell the product. "The product is not just good," the writer seems to say to the reader. "It's good *for you.*"

Arousing the Needs of the Reader

But do readers always know what their needs are? Should the writer take time at the beginning of a sales letter to remind the reader of those needs?

It's an important question. On the one hand, sales letters that serve no felt need on the reader's part fail in their purpose. "It looks like a nice product," the reader says, "but I don't need it." On the other hand, a writer risks losing the reader's attention by beginning with several sentences describing what the reader needs—information the reader may already know.

That's where market research comes to the rescue. Either through professional research organizations or your own efforts, you must *assess your market* in order to know your readers. Are they aware of their need for your product? If so, begin your sales letter by showing how your product meets their need. Are they unaware that your product can help them? If so, begin by reminding them in a sentence or two of a problem they have been experiencing. Then let your product "come to the rescue" in the letter by providing an answer to that problem.

Product/Service First

In the letter in Figure 13-1, sent to experienced boaters, the writer assumes that the audience is well aware of the problems of corrosion involved with metal boat propellers. She moves immediately into information about the product at the beginning of the letter. The rest of the letter is used to demonstrate how the new product meets the needs of the reader—for a reliable item, a profitable item, and so forth.

FIGURE 13-1

Sales Letter with Product/Service First

Jensen Marine, Inc.

470 East Bay Drive
San Francisco, CA 89382
(893) 792-8932

May 30, 198_

Ms. Glenda Forbes
Manager
Pier Marine Supply
44 Dock Road
Oakland, CA 98392

Dear Ms. Forbes:

Jensen Marine proudly announces an all-plastic propeller.

First, consider the product:

    * Tested and approved by Nautical Labs.

    * Guaranteed for a <u>lifetime</u>.

    * Available in seven popular sizes for sports boating.

    * Can't corrode, chip, break, or dent.

Second, consider the price:

    * Less than half the wholesale price for comparable brass propellers.

    * Rings, pins, and fittings come with the propeller at no extra cost.

You can save money for your customers while still <u>making more profit per propeller yourself.</u>

Finally, consider the terms:

    * Jensen Marine will place an attractive stand-alone display rack of new plastic propellers in your store <u>on a consignment basis</u>, without cost to you.

    * Purchases of plastic propellers during the introductory period (ends July 15) will receive a 15% discount.

FIGURE 13-1

Sales Letter with Product/Service First (continued)

Jensen Marine, Inc.

470 East Bay Drive
San Francisco, CA 89382
(893) 792-8932

You've looked to Jensen Marine over the years for the technological advances that matter in boating. Thank-you for considering the new plastic propeller as a good business move--and a good move for boating.

Order information and forms are enclosed. Feel free to contact us (call collect) if we can be of help.

Sincerely,

Patricia Olloway

Patricia Olloway
Marketing Director

PO/wod
Enclosure: Order Information Packet

Here are two more examples of sales openers that assume the reader's awareness of a need related to the product or service offered for sale:

> You'll be glad to know that, at Crestline Commercial Brokers, all rental units are maintained by a property manager.

This opening would be appropriate for investors who know the problems of owner-maintained buildings. In the next example, the jeweler addresses a sales letter to experienced gem buyers:

> Francis Jewelry is proud to be the only wholesale jeweler in this city to offer a free Xray with each gem it sells.

The opening would be ineffective for an audience that was unaware of the need for an Xray to reveal characteristics and flaws in a gem.

Need First

For audiences that must be made aware of a need, begin the sales letter with a vivid description of the need your product or service fulfills. Let's say, for example, that you want to market a product called "Handi-File," an organizer for household and business receipts. A letter describing the need before announcing the product is shown in Figure 13-2. Notice that the writer *creates* the need for Handi-File by reminding the reader of important government regulations. A reader who otherwise might say "my filing is in reasonably good shape" could be led, by the first paragraph, to reconsider: "Files for the last three years? Maybe I should look into Handi-File." The writer lists the advantages of Handi-File *to the reader* and concludes with an action the reader can take (the phone call) to bring Handi-File to his place of business.

Developing the Sales Letter

Once you have analyzed the needs of the reader and determined how much or how little to assume, you can begin a step-by-step planning process for each part of the sales letter. One easy-to-remember pattern for the sales letter follows the letters *S-A-L-E-S:*

S—Spark the imagination and curiosity of the reader.
A—Announce the product or service.
L—List the advantages to the client.
E—Express appreciation and goodwill.
S—Specify exactly what the client should do—and when.

S — Spark the Imagination. The introductory sentence in the sales letter used to be called the "hook." No more. We no longer find opening one-liners clever, catchy, or persuasive. In a word, we find most "hooks" plain stupid.

FIGURE 13-2

Sales Letter with Need First

UNDERWOOD OFFICE SUPPLY

1948 W. Sixth Street   Spokane, WA 89283   (894) 493-8923

August 18, 198_

Mr. Thomas Barth
Manager
Comfort Retirement Home
385 Bedford Place
Spokane, WA 89283

Dear Mr. Barth:

As manager of Comfort Retirement Home, you probably are aware
that tax records must be retained for three years, as
required by Federal law.

Maintaining organized records suddenly gets easy with Handi-
File, a bookkeeper's dream come true.

Handi-File lets you

> * file documents by subject, author, and date
>   simultaneously.

> * call up just the file you want by using Dial-a-File.

> * preserve your files through fire and flood.

Frankly, we're excited about the product--and want you to see
what the excitement's about. The Handi-File display van will
visit your area on August 25-27.

Call 493-8923 for your personal appointment with a Handi-File
representative. The van will pull up to the curb in front of
Comfort Retirement Home. You can take as much or as little
time as you wish to see the Handi-Files on display inside.

You'll be glad you called for a visit from Handi-File, Mr.
Barth. Won't you do it today?

Sincerely,

Mildred T. Reynolds

Mildred T. Reynolds
Manager

MTR/oie
Enclosure: "Handi-File: The Filing Revolution"

```
Did you drive half your car to work this morning?
Is a killer hiding in your refrigerator?
Don't spend that coin—it may be your child's college
education.
```

We routinely throw such junk mail away without reading it through.

More sophisticated sales letters avoid junk mail tricks. Writers of these letters want to awaken the reader's attention and then guide it meaningfully to a consideration of a worthwhile product or service. Here are several ways to spark imagination and arouse curiosity without resorting to junk mail tricks.

1. Suggest in the first sentence that *you can do something unique* for the reader. Few of us can resist reading on to find out what that "something" is.

   ```
   Lesborn Tire Company offers you a new way of buying
   tires.
   ```

2. Drop an impressive name, if appropriate, and then associate the reader with that name.

   ```
   Astronaut Luke Seaborg, like you, knows the importance
   of regular eye examinations.
   ```

3. Mention local people, places, and events, if possible.

   ```
   Hinton, Iowa, had dirt streets when my grandfather built
   Higgins Drug Store—and his reputation—at the corner of
   Lake and Main.
   ```

4. Empathize—feel *with*—your reader.

   ```
   Cash emergencies occasionally catch us all off guard,
   especially as the holidays near.
   ```

In most sales letters, the imaginative beginning should not be more than a sentence or two long. A short, pointed opening provides an easy entry for the reader and helps to create the attractive "beginning, middle, and end" shape discussed in Chapter 3.

A — Announce the Product or Service. In this section of the letter, do your business in a frank, specific way. The reader has had his or her curiosity piqued in your opening sentences and now wants it satisfied. This portion should first advertise the product or service; only then can you afford to go on to such matters as the history of your company, the genesis of the product, or the expertise of your personnel.

```
At Lesborn Tire, just your signature, address, and
driver's license number let you drive away on a quality set
of Lesborn tires—with 24 to 36 months to pay.
```

```
Each November we celebrate Grandfather's Month at
Higgins Drug.  This November we offer a two-for-one sale on
all cosmetic items with large reductions on all other store
```

merchandise except pharmaceuticals. School supplies, for
example, have been marked down 40 percent.

Establish in this section of your sales letter an honest, assertive voice.
Speak up for what you have to offer, naming it in specific terms. Where space
permits, provide a persuasive example or two.

L — List Advantages or Opportunities.   Because the second paragraph of a
sales letter often turns out to be rather long, this section can profitably be
written along inset margins, with major points set off as a list.

> Floral Display, Inc., will take charge of the interior
> landscape of your office
> - by placing gorgeous tropical plants to advantage
>   throughout your workspace.
> - by maintaining these plants at the peak of condition
>   and beauty.
> - by helping you make inexpensive but stunning decorating
>   decisions using fresh, fragrant plants.

This section of the sales letter convinces readers that your advertised
claims in the second paragraph have practical applications to them. You have
a chance to demonstrate the wide variety of needs your product or service
can fulfill.

Like all sections of your sales letter, this one should avoid the pitfalls of
insincerity. Don't try to *sound* sincere—simply *be* sincere about what you say
your product or service can do.

E — Express Appreciation.   So far, your reader has faithfully followed your
train of thought through most of the sales letter. It is time to thank him or her
for considering your ideas, to praise the reader's company, or to express
goodwill. While compliments may seem to be unnecessary to you, they are
high interest items to readers. Compliments are like the first fish we ever
caught—big enough to keep, no matter how small. You want interest to be
high and dispositions to be rosy at this point in the letter because just around
the corner lie the final sentences that matter most: the call to specific action.
The following are typical examples of compliments and expressions of
goodwill.

> In its advertising and public offices, your firm is
> known throughout the industry for its continental flair.

> We admire the standard you have set for yourself and
> others.

> We appreciate your interest in living plants for lively
> people.

> We will be most pleased to visit your office for a free
> demonstration of the lush, tropical look live plants can
> bring to you.

S — Specify the Exact Action You Wish Your Reader to Take.   Finally, tell the reader in a clear, specific way what you want him or her to do—and when—to bring about the advantages described in the letter. Maintain the upbeat "yes" attitude. Be careful not to impose subtle and not-so-subtle threats: "Your life depends on your tires. Buy Safe-T tires now before. . . ."

Don't fall into the phony and stale cliches of a circus barker: "Right now, ladies and gentlemen, for only $35.95. . . ." Don't pretend that the end of the world is near: "Drop what you are doing *right now* and sprint down to Morgie's Market for our half-off sale on limes."

Instead, define an easy and appealing path of action for your reader. If the action is at all complicated, break it into separate steps.

>   Call Marci at 667–2451 to arrange for a free decorating
> analysis without obligation. If you prefer, mail the
> enclosed card to receive our color decorating catalog—with
> no strings or plants attached.

>   Present the enclosed coupon on or before May 10 at your
> local Safe–T Tire Store, 1325 South Olive Street. You'll
> receive $40 off your new set of four Safe–T tires.

Specific action statements often consist of an action verb (call, present, visit, and so forth), a specific address and telephone number, a specific time (now or on or before May 10), and one or more final advantages (free decorating analysis, color decorating catalog, $40 off).

Observe each of the ***S-A-L-E-S*** sections working together now in the complete sales letter shown in Figure 13-3.

DIRECT MAIL LETTERS

The broad range of letters that try to sell by means of the mail are called direct mail letters: subscription letters, luggage offers, insurance discounts, restaurant specials and so forth. Try to estimate the number of such letters you throw away each month. Many never get opened or are only half opened to satisfy the beginnings of curiosity ("Is there anything free inside?"). Now consider how often you respond to the sales pitches contained in direct mail. Do you actually send off a check after reading one letter out of five? One out of ten? One out of a hundred?

The direct mail sales letter presents formidable obstacles. Readers *usually* throw your message away without reading it. Postage rates, paper costs, and printing expenses continue to escalate. The public becomes increasingly resistant to direct mail techniques (like including a little pencil with a magazine subscription appeal).

Having faced the dark side of direct mail sales, we can go on to name its merits and extraordinary potential. Direct mail allows the consumer to shop in the privacy and comfort of the home. Direct mail involves relatively little business expense for you, the entrepreneur. You don't have to provide a

FIGURE 13-3

Complete Sales Letter

Floral Displays, Inc.

4982 W. Brooks, Suite 4   Toledo, Ohio 63587   (534) 678-9049

April 10, 198_

Mr. David Jenkins
District Manager
Coleberry Financial Services, Inc.
324 Wall Avenue
Toledo, Ohio   69587

Dear Mr. Jenkins:

Do you sometimes wish you could bring the park--trees,
flowers, shrubbery--back to the office with you after lunch?

Floral Displays, Inc., makes wishes come true. We rent out
and maintain gorgeous tropical plants for your office and
reception area. For less than $2 per day, we can surround
you in lush philodendron or hide you behind an elephant plant.

Plants make business more pleasant and more profitable.

    -- Clients appreciate your thoughtfulness and admire your
       taste in softening the bare edges of business life
       with lovely plants. Happy clients spend more, more
       often.

    -- Employee turnover (the great hidden expense for most
       businesses) is drastically reduced. Employees come to
       think of the office as an attractive, inviting place.

Take a moment right now to call Marci (678-9049) for a free
floral decoration analysis of your office. She will come at
your convenience, finish her work quickly, then dazzle you
with affordable decorating ideas. If you prefer, mail in the
enclosed card for our latest color catalog of decorating
ideas.

With best wishes,

Sandra T. Lansdon

Sandra T. Lansdon
Marketing Director

STL/bck
Enclosure: "Your Catalog Reservation" (return postcard)

S
A
L
E

S

showroom for your products. You literally can do business out of your garage so long as your "image" is maintained by the literature you send out. Direct mail marketers usually have few problems with returned merchandise. Even if the buyer is not entirely pleased with product, the practical task of rewrapping the merchandise and sending it (at the buyer's expense) back to the marketer becomes too troublesome for average purchasers. Stick the thing on the shelf and forget it, they seem to say.

There are techniques to get sales letters read once they arrive in the hands of potential customers, and these techniques are important weapons in the direct mail sales arsenal.

Envelopes

Writers of direct mail sales letters often forget the role played by the envelope. No matter how stimulating your sales appeal, readers will never see it if they do not first open the letter. In perusing the daily mail, most of us do not conscientiously open and read every piece of mail. We reach for personal letters, bills, and only then "anything that looks interesting."

In designing your strategy for direct mail, you must make a decision. Should your envelope look personalized? If not, how can it look interesting enough to gain the reader's attention. By "personalized," we mean an individually typed, high quality envelope (no address labels) that imitates the look of a letter that might arrive from your university or your lawyer. In past years, this approach proved too expensive for direct mail merchants because of typing costs. But with the advent of word-processing and high-speed letter quality printers, thousands of envelopes—all neatly addressed in carbon-ribbon type—can be turned out in a short time. Because the letter cannot be distinguished from important mail by the envelope alone, the recipient opens it. If the letter catches his or her attention and imagination in the first sentence, the direct mail merchant has won the first battle.

Alternately, we can choose to make the letter look especially interesting, even though label-addressed and enveloped in less expensive paper. *Time* magazine hit upon a technique to get letters opened when they included a tiny pencil, costing the company only a fraction of a cent, in each letter. Interestingly, the slight bulge in the envelope piqued the curiosity of readers. Once they opened it to find a pencil, they were primed to mark "yes" in the subscription coupon for *Time*.

Other direct mail merchants have made good use of an envelope window. Through the window they reveal not only the reader's name and address, but also the beginning of a highly stimulating message: "Congratulations! You have won. . . ." Of course, the reader cannot see what he or she has won until opening the letter.

Less successful techniques include the use of bright colors and dramatic graphics on the envelope itself. While these patterns do catch the eye, they do not necessarily motivate the recipient to open the letter. In one case, an envelope so perfectly framed a graphic of a country scene that readers hesitated to tear open the envelope and damage the picture.

No technique remains fresh for long. What worked for *Time* last year may not work next year. If you are involved in direct mail sales, try to come up with a fresh approach that would work on you when opening your own mail. Your chances of success using such a technique will be better than relying upon standard formulas.

Getting Attention

Once the reader has been tempted to actually open the envelope, the first sentence of the letter must catch and hold attention in a powerful way. Any of the techniques we have already reviewed for the first sentence of the "yes" sales letter may be used. In addition, consider the "give-away" opening. If you have enclosed a free sample of your product, mention it in the first sentence. If the reader can send for a free gift, say so in the first sentence. If wonderful prizes can be won in a contest, describe the competition right away. All of these techniques try to make the reader want something so much that he or she can't help but read on to find out how to get it.

A note of caution: be aware that a broad range of federal, state, and local laws now regulate the claims and business practices of direct mail merchants.

Addressing the Direct Sales Letter

From your mailing list, you may have first and last names for each of your readers. Or it may provide only street addresses, in which case the unattractive word "Occupant" is used, above the street address. Names and addresses were at first typed or handwritten at appropriate places within the shell of the direct mail letter. But now, by using a process called a "merging routine" on a word processor, the reader's name is merged not only in the inside address, but also in the salutation and, if you wish, at points throughout the text of the letter.

```
   . . .the prize.  All you have to do, Mr. Scott, is. . .
```

If you do not use name merging in your direct mail letters, you can imitate the look of a traditional business letter without actually having a name for the inside address and salutation (Figure 13-4).

Make a habit of saving letters that for one reason or another cause you to open the envelope and actually read the letter. Analyze those letters that work. Discover the techniques, cues, attractions, and temptations that worked on you, the reader. The practice of learning from your own experience will help you plan effectively to write direct mail sales letters for others.

CLAIMS LETTERS

A claims letter is a persuasive business letter in which you assert and support your demand for repayment, restitution, or replacement because of a failure

FIGURE 13-4

Direct Mail Letter Without Inside Address or Salutation

Remingford Cutlery

3355 Lakeview Drive   Orlando, Florida 89793   1-800-967-8978

May 15, 198_

We know
Lucky people
Like yourself,

Dear Neighbor,

Who have already received the finest set of kitchen knives
in the world--at incredible discount prices.

How much are you now paying for the best knives in your
kitchen? $15? $20? $25? Even these prices seem
reasonable for a top quality knife--one made from Belgian
stainless steel, triple-tempered to hold a razor edge.

But Remingford Cutlery has good news for you: The Heritage
Collection pictured below can be yours for <u>less</u> than you are
used to paying for a single high-quality knife. Included in
the Heritage Collection are

        * two paring knives,
        * one broad knife,
        * two fillet knives
        * one citrus fruit knife,
        * one heavy chopping knife,
        * two dicing knives.

Each of these gourmet-quality knives is fashioned in
Belgium by artisans for whom excellence is a tradition.
Each comes with a two-year unconditional money-back
guarantee.

The price? For the next ten days, you can purchase the
Heritage Collection at the pre-marketing price of $19.97.

Soon you'll see these fine knives in better department
stores at $39 and more. Act now! Check "YES" on the
enclosed postcard and drop it in the mail today.

With compliments to the chef,

Reginald H. Rosenbaum

Reginald H. Rosenbaum,
President
Remingford Cutlery

in a product or service. Along with the sales letter and proposal, the claims letter is one of the most powerful tools in a business writer's workshop.

Imagine, for example, that your company purchased a $4000 Model 61 photocopy machine. It was delivered with several bottles of photocopy toner, which you poured into the machine according to instructions.

The toner, you discover too late, was the wrong kind. It has gummed up the machine; no copies can be made at all. The salesman who sold you the machine says you should have noticed the error before pouring in the toner—the bottles were marked, ''For Model #41.'' He refuses to replace the machine or to pay for its repair. Meanwhile, your office work grinds to a halt for lack of a copy machine.

If you can imagine your own anger in such a situation, you know how difficult it can be to compose a steady, decisive, action-oriented letter in times of emotional stress. Without denying the validity of your feelings, set your course on *action*. The letters of the word (conveniently) remind you how to proceed in generating a demand letter that brings results.

Pre-writing | ***A — Assess the entire situation.***
Exactly what happened? Where do you place blame? Is there another side to the story? What would remedy the problem? When action must be taken? Who must take action?

Pre-writing | ***C — Consider your audience.***
Have you written to the person who has caused the problem or the person who can solve the problem?

Writing | ***T — Tell your side of the story in a clear, organized way.***
Avoid depicting those who made the mistake in derogatory terms such as ''idiots,'' or ''incompetents.''

Writing | ***I — Insist on specific, timely action.***
Don't leave the remedy to the imagination of your reader (as in the appeal to ''Do something!''). Spell out what you want done, and when.

Writing | ***O — Offer your cooperation.***
Assist in the effort to correct the situation.

Writing | ***N — Name specific actions to remedy the situation.***
Be specific, to the point of setting down dates and times of the day when you want to see something done. Name alternatives you plan to pursue, such as contacting higher levels of authority or turning the matter over to your lawyer.

Observe the ***A-C-T-I-O-N*** pattern in the claim letter shown in Figure 13-5. Notice how the writer first A—Assesses the situation by reviewing the facts and circumstances surrounding the photocopy incident. Next he C—Considers the audience. Addressing a letter to the obstinate sales representative probably will do little good, so our writer decides to send the letter to the manager of the photocopy store.

FIGURE 13-5

Claim Letter

Levi & Willard, Accountants, Inc.

3829 W. Fourth Street
New York, NY 10442
(801) 375-2943

March 15, 198_

Ms. Wendy Johnson, Manager
Target Photocopy Supply
3499 Lincoln Blvd.
New York, NY 19332

Dear Ms. Johnson:

On March 9, my firm purchased a model #61 photocopy machine
from your salesman, Mark Trebley. As your records will
show, we paid $4021 for the machine (invoice #29843). That
price included a six-month supply of toner, delivered to us
with the machine.

Tell

I personally poured the toner into the new machine in the
way that Mark Trebley showed me. Only when the machine
stopped making copies a few minutes later did we discover
that the wrong toner (for model #41) had been delivered to
us with our machine.

I phoned Mr. Trebley that same day. He claimed to be
"swamped" with customers and promised to phone back. After
my repeated efforts to reach him by phone, I called
personally at your store and confronted Mr. Trebley with the
error regarding the toner. He made these points:

    1.   Someone "in the storeroom" sent the wrong toner.

    2.   In his opinion, I was largely responsible for the
        problem since the toner bottles were labeled "For
        model #41."

    3.   The machine would need an extensive and expensive
        overhaul for which neither he nor your store would
        be responsible.

He and I have had no further contact.

Insist

I insist that you remedy the problem caused by your
personnel by replacing our photocopy machine with a free
"loaner" during the period of overhaul. To the detriment of
our accounting business, we have been without a copy machine
for almost a week. Therefore, please have the loaner sent
over no later than March 19.

Offer cooperation

We will not insist that the loaner be a new model #61. In
fact, we are willing to make do with any serviceable model
so long as it arrives by March 19.

FIGURE 13-5

Claim Letter (continued)

Name specifics

Levi & Willard, Accountants, Inc.

3829 W. Fourth Street
New York, NY 10442
(801) 375-2943

Please call me (375-2943) no later than 5 P.M. tomorrow. I
am confident that you are as anxious as we are to put this
problem to rest. If I have not received your call by noon
on Friday, March 17, I will reluctantly turn this entire
matter over to both my attorney and the Better Business
Bureau for action against you.

Sincerely,

Thomas Levi

Thomas Levi
Partner

c.c. Mr. Mark Trebley

TL/eb

Claims and adjustment letters, written well, can often resolve day-to-day business problems without the expensive and time-consuming involvement of lawyers, agencies, and regulatory commissions.

A final reminder on how to write successful claims letters comes from one who sees them fail everyday. Leland S. manages the consumer complaint division for a major auto company. He describes the kinds of letters that get little or no attention from his office:

Some people are so mad they can't make sense. From their letters, you cannot discover what went wrong, when it happened, or what they tried to do about it.

Others begin with elaborate threats regarding government agencies, lawyers, and even congressmen. We often withhold action on those letters. Any words we do send them can be used against us if the customer does go to court.

A few leave absolutely no possible solution open to us. A man in Florida, for example, had recurring problems with his cigarette lighter—and would settle, he said, for nothing less than a new replacement car. Of course we can't act when no reasonable course is left open to us.

Finally, there are letters we call "mazes." They wander about the topic, never really saying what the customer wants to complain about. Usually near the end of the maze, they invite us to call them so they can describe the problem in person. Scrambled letters get little or no response.

Learning from such experience, we can set ourselves to the task of writing demand letters that are *controlled, realistic,* and *organized.* That simple prescription proves easier said than done, though, when your temper is boiling regarding an injustice.

COLLECTION LETTERS

If the buying public were a pie cut into eight slices, two of those slices would represent people who regularly fail to make payments due on mortgages, consumer loans, and credit cards. Of those two slices, one slice simply has a variety of money management problems: unexpected expenses, illnesses, layoffs, poorly planned budgets, and so forth. They mean to pay, and will pay, but have had temporary upsets. The remaining slice (the hardcore debtors) often have resources upon which they can draw to pay their bills. They simply prefer to live on borrowed money from you instead of their own earned money.

When you first send a collection letter to someone, you may not know whether you are writing to an unintentional or an intentional debtor. Collection letters must be written in such a way that both groups are motivated to pay what they owe.

We can learn to write effective collection letters by considering a story from each of the two "slices" mentioned above—a slice of life, if you will.

The unintentionally delinquent debtor can be illustrated by James P. who is 39 and married with two children. He has missed one payment on his 1981 Ford pickup. He may miss the next payment, due in two days.

Well, I'm a carpenter and when we have rain like we've had lately, there's just no work. When there's no work, there's no money. I can't sell my truck because I need it for my livelihood. I've got a part-time job at the lumber company, but my wages there don't come near making the house payment, truck payment, and putting food on the table. Someone just has to wait for their money until times get better.

The intentionally delinquent debtor can be illustrated by Peggy Wilcox who is 26 and single. She works in the public relations sector of a large real estate development firm. She has many unpaid bills.

I look at it like this: you live life once, and nobody says that living has to be neat, you know what I mean? I admit that State Oil is dunning me for $206 I haven't paid on my gas card. Modern Ms. wants $96 for a crummy dress that practically fell apart after I charged it, and there were some other bills here and there.

But what do they all stack up to? I get different colored letters in my mail that I don't even open—I can tell a bill a mile away. They keep sending them and I keep throwing them away. My credit rating isn't A plus, but so what? I can always buy a car somewhere, even with poor credit. And I can get an apartment without a credit check. So they can keep sending their pink, yellow, and red letters. I'm probably never going to pay. I don't need to.

Certainly different collection letters are required for down-on-his-luck James and irresponsible Peggy. Unfortunately, you as a business manager will not know in advance whether you are dealing with a James or a Peggy.

The Appearance of Collection Letters

Before discussing techniques for writing the first collection letter, recognize that the delinquent debtor never even sees these carefully written words unless he or she chooses to open the envelope. Too often, well-designed collection letters go out in cheap pulp envelopes with a machine-addressed label pasted unevenly across the envelope face. The envelope shouts "junk mail" or "collection letter" and is promptly trashed.

Put your collection letter into a good quality, letter-sized envelope—the kind you would use for regular business communication. The address on the envelope, whether written by hand, typed, or printed by a word processor, should look like it could appear on an important letter.

In any collection letter, you as a business writer must make up your mind on five factors:

Assumed cause	Why has the debt not been paid?
Emotional stance	What tone will your letter use?

Specific action	What do you want the reader to do?
Time and place	When and where must the action occur?
Motivator	What motivational force inside the reader do you plan to address?

The Friendly Collection Letter

In the collection letter shown in Figure 13-6, the writer assumes that the debtor simply forgot to make the payment and needs a friendly reminder. While this assumption seldom reflects reality, business managers approach debtors in such a nonthreatening way for good reason. The first collection letter can bring more than a 50 percent response rate from delinquent debtors. Those who pay are relatively good customers who will provide future business if they are not chased away by brusque, surly collection language.

The emotional attitude of the letter, therefore, is friendly. Though the action statement names a specific amount to be paid, the time is stated generally ("now," "as soon as possible," "right away") and no specific place or person for payment is named. The writer tries to motivate the debtor based on his or her sense of responsibility.

In beginning the letter, the writer works for a sentence that makes its point, but in a somewhat friendly or even humorous way. An outright joke will not do, of course, because it negates the urgency to pay or backfires as sarcasm or satire. The letter is brief because clients will not read more. It relies upon the generation of goodwill and mutual respect to produce its end, the payment of the debt.

The Firm Collection Letter

If no response is received from the first collection letter, we can assume that a simple slip of memory is not to blame. Instead, we assume that some problem (illness, layoff, travel, and so forth) has interrupted the regular flow of payments. Our emotional attitude becomes firm with a hint of urgency. The specific action is spelled out in unmistakable terms, with a time and place named. We attempt to motivate the reader on the basis of a sense of fairness and business decency.

In the collection letter shown in Figure 13-7, notice that the product, a lawn chair costing $71.54, is not mentioned. If the letter reminded the debtor of the lawn chair, the seed of a defense might be planted in mind: "What about that chair? I never really found it comfortable. Do I really want to pay $71.54 for it now?"

Similarly, no statement appears offering to answer questions or adjust the payment schedule. A debtor who has questions or wishes to adjust a payment schedule will seek assistance; others will read the offer of assistance as a chance to talk their way out of the debt entirely.

The color of the second collection letter may be changed to distinguish it from the first collection letter for the reader. Perhaps with good purpose, many collection letters get a deeper and deeper shade of red as they proceed

FIGURE 13-6

Friendly Collection Letter

· WESTWINDS · PATIO · FURNITURE ·

5000 Brent Place   Ogden, Utah 39523   (707) 222-3434

August 6, 198_

Mr. William Forest
91 Cross Road
Ogden, Utah 39523

Dear Mr. Forest:

Did you forget us this month?

Your regular monthly payment of $71.54 has not arrived.
Please check your records to make sure that it was sent.

If not, consider this a friendly reminder to a client of
value.

Don't forget, by the way, to visit us during August for our
Clearance Sale on barbecue equipment.

Sincerely,

Boyd Richards

Boyd Richards
Assistant Manager

BR/we

FIGURE 13-7

Firm Collection Letter

· WESTWINDS · PATIO · FURNITURE ·

5000 Brent Place   Ogden, Utah 39523   (707) 222-3434

August 18, 198_

Mr. William Forest
91 Cross Road
Ogden, Utah 39523

Dear Mr. Forest:

Your account with us is seriously past due.

Please take a moment right now to write a check for $71.54
payable to Westwinds Patio Furniture. We have enclosed an
envelope for your payment.

You are no doubt eager to resolve this problem. So are we.

Sincerely,

Boyd Richards

Boyd Richards
Assistant Manager

BR/we

through the series, like the growing shades of apoplectic exasperation in a human face.

Quality envelopes, again, are crucial to the success of the letter. A signature should appear in ink, so that at least the illusion of personal attention is created.

At your discretion, a pre-addressed return envelope may be included as an additional prod to put a check in the mail. Some businesses even include a stamped envelope, reasoning that the money spent on postage is a good investment to reclaim a bad debt.

The Urgent Collection Letter

We now must assume that the debtor cannot or will not pay without strong motivation. Our emotional tone is now resolved, urgent, and straightforward. Name a specific time, place, and person to whom payment must be made. Attempt to motivate the customer by guilt, pride, and the beginnings of fear.

The urgent collection letter shown in Figure 13-8 includes a name for the debtor to contact. This creates the possibility that the debtor will call and arrange payments of some kind. Note, however, that two months payments are now due ($71.54 + $71.54 = $143.08), and it is unlikely that the debtor will write a large check when he could not or would not write a smaller one. The looming alternative is to turn the debt over to a collection agency which may retain as much as 50 percent of the debt if and when they collect it.

Bank of America has had some success in sending third collection letters (particularly on overdue VISA cards) by mailgram. These communiques look urgent among the other letters in the daily mail and do get opened. The recipient feels a seriousness of purpose on the part of the sender who uses a relatively expensive means of communication.

The Final Collection Letter

By now, the company has invested a considerable amount of time and expense in trying to rescue a bad debt. The last collection letter (before the collection agency begins its own series) assumes that the debtor will not pay and will make no effort to arrange partial payment. The letter in Figure 13-9 illustrates the characteristics of the final collection effort: its emotional stance is determined, tough, but not offensive. It names a last-ditch time, place, and person for payment. The principal motivator now is fear of legal action (not Mafia extinction!). The company no longer cares to consider future patronage from the debtor. It wants its money.

If this letter is not sent by mailgram, it can be given a semi-official look by sending it via certified mail, a somewhat less expensive technique. A registration number is pasted on the envelope by the post office at the time of certification. Hence, the letter arrives with considerably more impact than an ordinary letter.

Chapter 20 describes the narrow limits within which debts may be legally collected in the United States. Such legislation as the Equal Credit Opportun-

FIGURE 13-8

Urgent Collection Letter

· WESTWINDS · PATIO · FURNITURE ·

5000 Brent Place   Ogden, Utah 39523   (707) 222-3434

September 10, 198_

Mr. William Forest
91 Cross Road
Ogden, Utah 39523

Dear Mr. Forest:

Contact Mr. Valenzuela at 222-3434 immediately regarding
your delinquent account in the amount of $143.08.

You must act on this matter by 12 o'clock noon, Friday,
Sept. 18, to avoid action by our attorney. Bring your
payment to 5000 Brent Place, or mail it--today, please--in
the enclosed envelope.

With your attention to the debt of $143.08 today, we can
avoid future action.

Sincerely,

Boyd Richards

Boyd Richards
Assistant Manager

BR/we

FIGURE 13-9

Final Collection Letter

· WESTWINDS · PATIO · FURNITURE ·

5000 Brent Place   Ogden, Utah 39523   (707) 222-3434

September 20, 198_

Mr. William Forest
91 Cross Road
Ogden, Utah 39523

Dear Mr. Forest:

Seventy-two hours from the date of this mailing, your
delinquent account for $214.62 will be turned over to our
attorney, Ms. Lela Vincent, for collection by legal means.

You can still avoid legal proceedings against you by paying
your account in full no later than 12 o'clock noon, Friday,
Sept. 22, to Mr. Valenzuela at 5000 Brent Place (phone 222-
3434).

Your cooperation at this late date can benefit you in two
ways: you will avoid legal action against you, and you will
maintain your credit rating. Please act immediately.

Sincerely,

Boyd Richards

Boyd Richards
Assistant Manager

BR/we

ity Act (1974), the Fair Credit Billing Act (1974), and the Fair Debts Collections Practices Act (1978) have set forth strict guidelines for collection. The latter act specifies, for example, that a collector cannot call the debtor before 8 A.M. or after 9 P.M.; cannot make a series of calls in rapid succession; cannot threaten to make the debt public knowledge; and cannot continue to contact the debtor after receiving written notice from the debtor to stop.

Before using a collection series of your own devising, therefore, ask an attorney to review your words for possible violations of federal, state, or local codes. Historically, the collection of past-due money has been marred by violent gangland abuses. Modern laws, while seemingly antibusiness in their restrictive elements, are in fact an effort to protect debtors from harm at the hands of powerful merchants and lenders.

Summary

1. Effective persuasion is based on needs perceived by the reader.
2. Sales letters, like other forms of persuasion, emphasize the reader's interest—"you"—over the writer's interest—"I."
3. A writer must get to know his or her audience in order to write a successful sales letter. What do the readers need? How much do they already know? What information should be provided in the letter?
4. The *S-A-L-E-S* pattern provides one, but not the only, guideline for developing persuasive sales letters.
5. Direct mail letters should avoid stale attention-getting techniques typical of "junk mail." The opening lines of direct mail letters should be based on the needs and interests of the reader, freshly expressed.
6. A claims letter may be developed according to the *A-C-T-I-O-N* pattern. Writers use the claims letter to inform the reader of a problem and to call for action regarding it.
7. Effective collection letters depend on timing and persuasive language. The collection series communicates the growing concern and resolution of the writer.

Questions for Discussion

1. What is the "you" emphasis in sales writing? How does it differ from the "I" emphasis?
2. Discuss the assertion, "Persuasion is based on need." What implications does that statement have for writers of persuasional letters?
3. Discuss the *S-A-L-E-S* pattern. Why should steps be relatively short?
4. Some sales letters begin by reminding the reader of a need of some kind. Evaluate this approach to persuasional writing. When is such an approach appropriate? When is it inappropriate?
5. In what four ways can you spark the imagination of a reader in a sales letter without resorting to "junk mail" techniques?
6. What are direct mail sales letters? What challenges face those who write for this market?

7. What is a claims letter? How does the *A-C-T-I-O-N* pattern apply to the writing of such letters?
8. In what ways does anger undercut a writer's success in developing an effective claims letter?
9. Discuss the importance of timing and persuasive language in collection letters.
10. Describe the three stages in collection letters. How do they differ?
11. Why does the first collection letter avoid blunt language?
12. How do the assumptions of the writer change during the course of writing a series of collection letters?

Exercises

1. Write down three needs perceived by your reader. Call to mind a product or service that relates to those needs. Then develop a sales letter, based on the *S-A-L-E-S* pattern, that addresses those needs in a persuasive way.
2. Choose a sales letter you received recently. Find three common human needs that the letter proposes to satisfy. Note them in the margin of the letter. Then rewrite the letter based on three different human needs.
3. Choose a product or service. Write a sales letter to an audience knowledgeable about that product or service. Write a second version of the letter for an audience who might be expected to use the product or service, but who knows little about it.
4. Develop a direct mail letter for warm pajamas.
5. Write a claims letter based on the *A-C-T-I-O-N* pattern. Base your letter on some product or service in which you have been disappointed.
6. Write a series of three collection letters trying to motivate Walter Nesbitt to pay the $68 monthly payment he owes for a television set.
7. Contact a collection or credit agency in your city. Ask for information on its methods for collecting from overdue accounts. In written form, describe these methods and give your opinion of their effectiveness.
8. Use the letters you have at hand from exercise 6 or 7 above. For each, write down how you would respond to the letters if you were an intentional debtor. Then write down how you would respond to the letters if you were an unintentional debtor.

Successful
Business Speaking and
Listening

PART FOUR

Charles Worthington is a black entrepreneur and developer. He owns three construction companies and employs almost eighty people.

My complaint is not with my carpenters, masons, or electricians. I have my hardest times with my outside sales force—the people who make presentations to clients and bring in the business.

Technically, they're knowledgeable and up-to-date. But many of them simply don't have good presentation skills. They look amateurish and cast a poor light on the company. My worst cases are those sales people who have their presentations memorized down to the last word. They go on and on like a stuck record. The client quickly senses that the presentation is canned.

What would you recommend to Charles Worthington? What can he do for his sales people? What can they do for themselves?

Speaking and Listening Skills 14

LEARNING OBJECTIVES

To understand the importance of projection and articulation in business speaking

To develop personal ways to reduce stress related to speaking

To recognize the value of brevity in speaking

To practice strategies for meaningful gestures and eye contact

To establish and follow an organizational pattern in your speeches

To plan for effective visual aids

To grasp the importance of variety in pauses, volume, pitch, tone, and pace

To practice valuable listening techniques

Over the course of your career, you will speak hundreds of words for every one word you write. In dictation, phone conversations, one-to-one business conversations, meetings, and presentations, you will speak—for better or for worse—as your primary means to reach your own goals.

Because you want your spoken words to work well for you and for the company, you will have more than a casual interest in the Ten Do's and Don'ts of business speaking.

1. Do speak up. Don't mumble.
2. Do be brief. Don't belabor your points.
3. Do look at your listeners. Don't ignore others.
4. Do use natural gestures. Don't be stiff.
5. Do organize your points. Don't ramble.
6. Do maintain a comfortable pace. Don't rush or dawdle.
7. Do use visual aids when appropriate. Don't rely on words alone.
8. Do vary your volume, pitch, and tone. Don't drone.
9. Do use pauses effectively. Don't stop and start.
10. Do listen. Don't ignore others.

A fine checklist, wouldn't you agree? But so what? Does *knowing* such pointers lead automatically to *doing* them? Emphatically no. Like the Ten Commandments, the Ten Do's and Don'ts of business speaking are "should" statements, not "can" or "will do" statements.

Knowing what you should do does not by itself bring about the ability to do it. As a salesman in Denver put it, "I know what my bad speaking habits are, and I know I should change. But those habits are rooted someplace deep inside me. When I get up to speak, they just come out naturally, even when I know better. If I'm ever going to improve, my new speaking habits had better be rooted in that same place——really deep inside me."

True. The only speaking skills worth having are those that feel natural. When we're looking over the speaker's rostrum at an audience of business associates or customers, we have no time to recall checklists of do's and don'ts. We either have the necessary speaking skills "inside" or we don't have them at all.

The key question, then, for this chapter is how do effective speaking skills become a natural, almost unconscious habit in our business lives?

UNDERSTANDING WHY WE SPEAK THE WAY WE DO

We each cling to speaking habits for quite personal reasons. By becoming aware of some of those reasons—by laying them out on the table, so to speak, for examination—we can get to know our habits and understand why we cling to them. We can also choose to replace them with better skills.

Let's examine our speaking habits in each of the ten areas suggested by the Ten Do's and Don'ts.

Do Speak Up. Don't Mumble.

Why do business speakers so often mumble, their mouths full of marbles and their voices little more than whispers? They are responding to stress.

Notice an interesting phenomenon of stress: "I was so mad I *couldn't speak*!," "I was so frightened I *couldn't even scream*," "I was *speechless* with surprise," "I *can't tell* you how happy I am." Stress, whether negative or positive, acts upon the vocal apparatus in a direct way.

In the first stage of stress, a surge of adrenalin tightens the vocal cords and muscles, shutting down the natural tones and pitches of ordinary speech. The voice gets high, squeaky, breathless, and cracked.

We then make sure the second stage of stress takes over: the wave of embarrassment. We focus upon our inability to speak naturally and make every effort to hide our problem. We literally try to keep the words from leaving our lips (mumbling), and when they do we dribble them downward, not up and out to our audience. We're verbally hiding, like scared birds in the bush not really wanting to make a chirp.

Adjust Your Attitude. Recognize that you don't have to be perfect to be an effective speaker. In fact, if you did achieve absolute perfection in public speaking your flawlessness itself would be a major obstacle to human listeners. None of us warms up to perfection.

Learn to accept, therefore, your humanness as a speaker. Don't make demands upon yourself that no one else is making. You simply can't speak effectively while chastising yourself for little mistakes here and there.

This kind of self-acceptance is not an invitation to "what-the-hellism" or sloppiness. We learn to accept ourselves in order to come out of hiding, to shed our embarrassment and shyness.

You have heard friends say what terrible speakers they are! How their knees tremble, their voices waver, and their eyes dart nervously around the room.

Do you see where these speakers are spending their energy? Their focus is not on their message or their audience, but on themselves. They *care* about their trembling knees, their wavering voices, and their darting eyes. In other words they perpetuate their annoyances by concentrating on them.

Escape such self-destructive obsession by looking in a mirror and naming the faults you find so embarrassing. Then say good-bye to them:

"My knees tremble when I speak. But I don't care. I'm human.

"My voice wavers and my eyes dart around the room. But I don't care. I'm human."

No listeners ever ridiculed a speaker for a wavering voice—so long as the listeners sensed that the speaker cared about his or her *message*, not his or her stress symptoms.

Learning not to care about stress irritations pays an enormous dividend. "Stage two" of the stress experience simply doesn't happen anymore. We still feel the invigorating surge of adrenalin giving us extra energy, but we interpret that surge in a positive way. We talk right through the initial waver in our voice and tremble in our knees knowing that we have absolutely nothing to be embarrassed about. We're human, feeling human excitement, and talking to other humans who understand and sympathize with those feelings.

We're grateful, in fact, that we can talk to people who understand stress rather than to some kind of machine that expects perfection.

When we let "first stage" stress flow through our bodies without embarrassment, it subsides naturally after a moment or two, leaving us keyed up, alert, and full of energy. We've managed to turn the body's stress responses to our advantage as speakers.

Adjust Your Vocal Muscles. Now we can turn to the vocal muscles themselves. In that first clutch of excitement, what can a speaker do to avoid tight, breathless squeaks and cracks?

In privacy, before speaking, simply yawn—but not a polite, Boston yawn. Tip your head back and open your mouth wide into a big Georgia yawn. Wonderful physical mechanisms automatically take place when you yawn. You inhale deeply, then exhale thoroughly—a fine relaxer. Your mind associates yawning with peacefulness, rest, and sleep—so it turns from nervous fretting to a calm state. Your vocal muscles, tightened by adrenalin, stretch to their limits (feel your neck muscles, for example, when yawning). After stretching, the muscles return to a state of relaxation, not tension.

Now you are ready to speak up, not mumble. Choose members of your audience at the back of the room, and send your words out to them. Watch their faces as you speak to determine if they can hear you. Frowns, knit brows, and leaning forward or turning the head to one side indicate that they can't hear you well.

When you need to project your voice, don't try to talk louder. "Loud" speakers, like their electronic namesakes, grate on our nerves. Instead, project your voice by tightening your "belt muscles," those strong abdominal muscles lying under our stomachs and lungs. Raise your chin a bit higher to force your words up and out while tightening the belt muscles. Using this technique, public speakers in the days before amplified sound were able to speak to crowds of thousands in sports arenas and amphitheaters. The same technique will surely stand you in good stead for the conference and meeting rooms of today.

One important aspect of speaking up is articulation. The sounds of English words cannot be run together without distorting meaning. Sometimes this distortion can prove upsetting. The president of an Arizona chemical firm gave strict instructions by telephone to her salesperson:

"Whenyagetintatown, beshurtataknitrates." "Night rates" at the motel or "nitrates" with a glass of water? The boss didn't articulate her intentions.

Practice articulating, using the exercises at the end of this chapter. Don't worry if your initial efforts at clear articulation sound a bit different from ordinary conversation. Business speaking should be more distinct, more perceivable, than the fast, slurred language we use in everyday speech.

Do Be Brief. Don't Belabor Your Points.

People ramble on for two reasons: first, they want to postpone our opportunity to react to what they are saying until they are reasonably sure we will approve; second, they enjoy the spotlight of our attention and hate to give it up.

In the following ramble, the speaker simply wants to assert that he wants quiche for lunch, not salad.

"Let's see. I hear the salads are excellent here, but I had salad just yesterday, and you know how it is with salads—you can't eat them everyday, you know what I mean? There's the quiche, I suppose. . .but I don't really order quiche very often. Of course, this is spinach quiche, and I do like spinach quite a bit—if it is fresh, that is. I hate canned spinach. Salad or quiche, quiche or salad?"

These are the true crazy-makers of business life. They use words to postpone action. Only when we indicate our approval—"Have the quiche"—do they finally shut up. All the while they have subtly enjoyed their chance to hold the verbal stage.

Rambling speakers need to know that we hate their filibustering. They need to understand that the nods of approval and the "uh-hunhs" we give them during their long-winded performances are just efforts on our part to bring the drivel to an end.

Techniques for Controlling Rambling. We can undo a tendency to ramble on by examining our attitudes toward the approval—the ''strokes''—we get from others. When we were children, we may have learned to perform before Mom and Dad to get praise. We said the alphabet, played the piano, or sang a song as our parents watched.

Some business speakers have not escaped that child-parent model of performance. They take the stage while the rest of us sit in the audience, as it were.

Unfortunately, you and I are not willing to play Mom and Dad to our business colleagues. We get little joy out of enduring a long, rambling performance. Instead, we're anxious to participate, to respond. We want the speaker as soon as possible to give us a chance to speak. The model we want to establish is not child-to-parent but adult-to-adult.

Practice two techniques to make sure you are not guilty of rambling.

1. Ruthlessly pare your material to its essence. Notice how the text of this speech has been improved by trimming away unnecessary fat.

<u>*To date,*</u>
~~Up to the present point in time, the employees and the~~
<u>*has resisted take-over bids.*</u>
~~management of~~ Dartmoor Locks ~~have agreed between themselves~~

~~publicly and privately to maintain the present independence~~

~~of the company as an entity free from corporate entanglement~~

~~with foreign financial and industrial organizations seeking~~

~~to participate and even direct the interests and growth of~~

~~the company through the control and manipulation of its~~

~~financial resources.~~

2. Direct frequent questions to your listeners. Though they may not be called upon to actually answer the questions aloud, the listeners will form answers for themselves—and hence will have the feeling they are participating in your speech. Observe the questions in the following excerpt:

Question

Question

Our corporate headquarters fronts on the busiest thoroughfare in Atlanta. But what do those thousands of potential customers see as they look at our building? A gray, nondescript slab with an almost unnoticeable sign, ''Wendselly Air Purifiers.'' Could they enter our offices if they want-

ed to? Only if they discovered the side door, located on a one-way street with no parking. Before complaining about sinking profits at Wendselly, we have to ask a searching question: does our building itself invite the business we say we want?

Do Look at Your Listeners. Don't Ignore Others.

Our eyes, more than any other facial feature, reveal our responses to others: awe, approval, skepticism, confusion, ridicule, and rejection. Insecure speakers naturally fear ''reading'' the faces of the audience. If the speaker sees frowns or sneers, that evidence only amplifies self-doubt and unmanageable nervousness. Better, such speakers feel, not to look at all. So they stare down at supposed notes. When they do look up, they aim their view into the air above the heads of the audience, sometimes straight to the ceiling. One wag has called this habit the surest sign of the nervous speaker—looking to heaven for help.

If human faces put us off our track while speaking, we may be expecting far too much of those faces. Every individual in our audience has the right to raise eyebrows, wrinkle the forehead, squint the eyes, purse the mouth, shake the head in a variety of ways, and even look out the window while we are speaking.

By avoiding eye contact, we tell our audience that they should *not* exercise their rights: ''I'm uncomfortable looking at all of you. There's either something wrong with you or wrong with me.''

Listeners feel ill at ease, and show it on their faces, because you ask too much of them. You ask, in effect, that each face in the audience beam forth approval and respect for you. If not, you will simply hide your eyes.

Let your audience know by direct eye contact that they can feel comfortable looking any way they wish, even sideways and upside down, without making you anxious. You'll pay attention to their looks in an effort to make your message clear, but you won't use your emotions to hold their reactions hostage. They can simply ''be'' anyway they wish while listening to you.

Many expert debaters practice ''blinksmanship.'' They look eyeball-to-eyeball with one person in the audience until that person blinks or turns his or her eyes away. Then they shift their view to another person in another sector of the audience. In this way, they establish direct connection with individuals in the audience, not breaking that connection in a rude way by looking away at the wrong moment. Since blinks and eye-shifts occur every few seconds in an audience, the speaker never fears a ''stare-down'' with a listener.

The Question of Notes. Try to keep your eyes off notes or a manuscript and on your audience. The day of the formal oration alá Winston Churchill has passed. Even on the most formal occasions, audiences appreciate a warm, conversational flow in speeches. For most speaking situations, therefore, do not try to write down every word you plan to say. You'll end up reading your speech, or—just as bad—delivering it with that zombie-glaze across the eyes that says to all, ''I've mesmerized—I mean, memorized my whole speech.''

FIGURE 14-1

Speaker's Notecard

Opening Story

Major Points

Visual Aids

Personal Conclusion

> "The person with three hats..." –
> — Managers as <u>judges</u>
>   (promotional procedures)
> — "   as <u>organizers</u>
>   (job scheduling/formatting) – slides
> — "   as <u>friends</u>
>   (personal support, advice, encouragement)
> Express appreciation to present managers,
>   congratulations to new managers
> "When I began..."

If you wish an organizational safety net, create speaker's notes that you can place on the podium or table before you. Do not try to speak while holding a notecard in your hand. Your notes must work for you at a glance and hence must be tailored to your own needs. The card in Figure 14-1 shows one way to organize major points with reminders of supportive detail and examples.

Do Use Natural Gestures. Don't Be Stiff.

Speaking without using your hands is like hiking without shoes. It can be done. You can get where you're going. But you are overlooking an easy way to make the trip more comfortable, the speech more effective.

No one can choreograph gestures for a speaker ("now slam your fist down here, and raise your left arm half-way there . . ."). Gestures must come naturally, in close coordination with what we are saying and who we are. Notice, by the way, your own incredibly diverse repertoire of gestures used in everyday conversations with friends. You create emphasis, special meanings, levels of irony and sarcasm, and degrees of earnestness all with your hands and body.

The goal, then, is not to learn gestures, but to bring the natural gestures you already use into play in your business speaking.

FIGURE 14-2

Gestures Appropriately High and In View

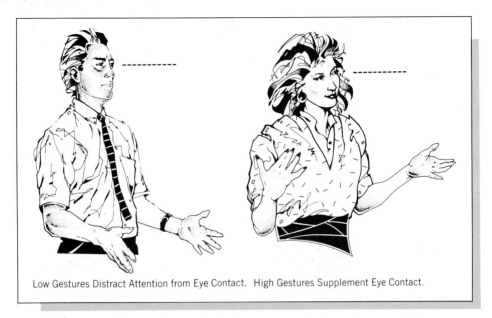

Low Gestures Distract Attention from Eye Contact. High Gestures Supplement Eye Contact.

Hands have an admirable way of doing just the right thing once you give them a chance. They can't gesture at all, of course, so long as you hold them rigidly at your sides or hold the edges of the podium in a death grip. Free your hands to do their thing by consciously placing them in a "take-off position."

- As you begin to speak, touch your fingertips together in front of you. It doesn't matter where or how your fingertips touch. Once they meet, let your hands move where they will. When you're tired of gesturing, let your hands rest comfortably at your sides or on the podium until you're ready to bring them to a new take-off position.
- Touch a button on your coat, shirt, or blouse just for a second. Your audience will never notice, but you will have placed one hand in another good take-off position for gesturing. At any time, the other hand can move to a button, then into action.
- Touch your cheek with the fingertips of one hand, then gesture. Most talented speakers keep their gestures relatively high on their upper bodies, so as not to distract attention from eye contact (Figure 14-2).

High gestures help the listener look *through* the gestures into the speaker's eyes. The audience is hardly aware of the gestures at all, and for that reason is all the more caught up in their effectiveness.

While no one has yet catalogued all the thousands of effective gestures we use to accompany speech, we can list gestures that don't work well.

The Pointer. Don't point at your audience over and over with one finger. Gesture instead with an open hand, making no one feel on the spot.

The Pumper. Don't raise and lower your arm in a repeated, energetic pumping motion. Any obsessively repetitive body movement distracts audience attention from what you have to say. Particularly taxing motions like "the pump" cause the audience to labor with you subliminally or at least empathize with the discomfort you must be feeling.

The Saint. Don't deliver an entire presentation with your hands folded solemnly in front of you. Like an interminable prayer, this posture becomes increasingly uncomfortable for an audience. They start to wonder if you ever plan to let your hands out of jail.

You can study quite masterful gesturing by turning to religious or political presentations on television. Turn the volume down, and observe the natural way in which body movement, facial gestures, and hand motions work together to contribute to meaning. While you may want to experiment with the gesturing techniques you see, don't try to copy another speaker's habits in any close way. Build upon gestures that you find natural and comfortable—the same ones you probably use to tell a professor why a paper is being turned in late.

Do Organize Your Points. Don't Ramble.

In Chapter 3, we treated twenty-two patterns for the organization of written materials. These same patterns can be used to advantage by the speaker, with one addition: the overview.

Unlike readers, audiences have no chance to glance back to your earlier words in an effort to clear up confusion. The pattern of your thought must be clear from the beginning. Speakers should make a practice, therefore, of setting forth a brief outline at the beginning of the presentation as shown in the two examples below.

> *We have to choose the type of building we want for our proposed Seattle branch. Consider three alternatives with me: 1. The downtown remodel/renovation office; 2. The industrial park office; 3. The suburban office. Each has advantages and disadvantages.*

Basing her speech on this overview, the speaker goes on to treat the advantages and disadvantages of each alternative.

> *We can plan most effectively by looking first at how we used to produce the K-14; then, at how we now produce it, using computer-aided design techniques; and, finally, at our production needs in the five years ahead.*

This speaker will work from past to present to future. At every point in the presentation, listeners will know where they are, where they have been, and where they are going.

Because attention spans even in highly intelligent and interested audiences rarely exceed thirty seconds at a stretch, speakers do well to provide

FIGURE 14-3

Typical Attention Curve for a Business Address

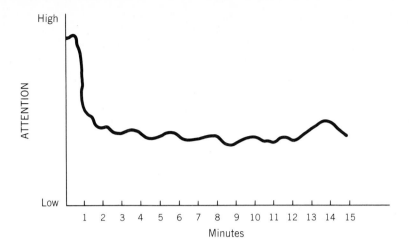

occasional reminders of where they are in the announced outline. A good reminder looks back to where the speaker has been, and forward to what lies ahead.

> *So much for the urban remodel/renovation office. We can now discuss the second alternative, the industrial park office.*

For longer presentations, the use of handouts or projected slides and transparencies can help both speaker and audience stay on the organizational path. The use of these techniques is treated extensively in Chapter 8.

Do Maintain a Comfortable Pace. Don't Rush or Dawdle.

Most business presentations proceed at a pace slightly slower than ordinary conversation. The listeners, after all, must have time to fully understand the words of the presentation.

Mentally establish a comfortable pace by saying (silently!) the Pledge of Allegiance (reprinted here for good measure).

> *I pledge allegiance to the flag of the United States of America, and to the republic for which it stands. One nation, under God, with liberty and justice for all.*

The familiar grammar school pace we used for that pledge serves well for most business speaking occasions. You can use the rhythms and pace of the pledge to set a tempo for yourself, much in the way a band leader counts off a measure (1, 2, 3, 4) before the band begins to play.

Do Use Visual Aids When Appropriate. Don't Rely on Words Alone.

Words, words, words, unrelieved by visual experiences, can quickly reach a point of diminishing returns. Figure 14-3 shows the typical attention span curve for a business address. Attention drops off rapidly after the audience

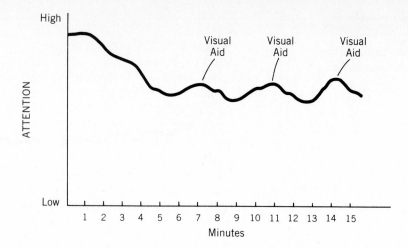

FIGURE 14-4

Attention Curve for a Business Address with Visual Aids

has heard about three minutes of the speaker's address. Attention perks up again from time to time, usually at moments when the speaker tells a diverting or colorful story of some kind. When the speaker indicates that the conclusion is in sight, attention rises somewhat. The audience hopes to catch a summary of the points it has missed.

Figure 14-4, by contrast, shows the attention curve when visual aids are used. The initial interest level is higher in expectation of enjoyable visual experiences to come. When those moments arrive, attention rises.

A Supplement to Words. Audiences love pictures, shapes, lines, and colors in addition to words. Whenever possible, accompany your presentation with something visual they can hold in mind not only as you speak but after the presentation as well. The range of possibilities for visual aids is attractively large:

Handouts
Slides
Overhead transparencies
Flipcharts
Blackboards
Felt-covered presentation charts
Physical models (architect models, scale models, etc.)
Movies
Maps
Television/videotape/videodisk
Computer monitors

Visual aids of these sorts make the audience feel that you have given special preparation to your speech. Just the presence of a slide projector in the meeting room brings a welcome air of anticipation in even the most sophisticated audience.

Do Vary Your Volume, Pitch, and Tone. Don't Drone.

Volume refers to how loud or soft you speak. *Pitch* is the relative highness or lowness of your voice, as measured against a musical scale. *Tone* is a catchall category for the many moods and textures of the voice: harsh, sarcastic, earnest, whimsical, pleading, solemn, giddy, and so forth.

When speakers fail to vary these key factors, the result is a relentless monotone that vaguely recalls a mosquito buzzing on a hot night or your neighbor's power saw running for an entire day.

No artificial prescription can help the droner. Matters of volume, pitch, and tone are tied so closely to what's being said to whom by which speaker that any general advice—"Emphasize the first word in each sentence"—is doomed to produce even a worse monstrosity than the drone itself.

Listening to Improve Speaking. Read the following short sentences aloud. Listen to your natural rises and falls in volume and pitch, as well as your choice of appropriate tone.

> *Mad: You have no right to use my name in that way.*
> *Sarcastic: Well, you didn't wreck the whole car.*
> *Innocent: I had no idea you already scheduled a meeting for that day.*
> *Earnest: I feel that I've served this company well, and deserve a raise as much as anyone else.*
> *Depressed: OK, we'll try it just one more time.*

If you heard no obvious changes in the volume, pitch, and tone of your voice, check your pulse to make sure you're alive. From their earliest years, human beings naturally create appropriate variations in speech. You do, too. Now that you've heard the kinds of adjustments you naturally make when you speak, use those abilities to your advantage in business speaking.

Tape record one of your business or classroom presentations to check your progress in varying volume, pitch, and tone. Listen with care. If you hear a drone, stop the tape at a particularly flat sentence or two. Say those sentences aloud, this time adding the variations in volume, pitch, and tone you may have omitted in the original presentation.

Do Use Pauses Effectively. Don't Stop and Start.

Just as new paragraph beginnings spell R-e-l-i-e-f for readers, so pauses in speaking mark the end of one listening task and the beginning of the next for the listener.

Probably the single greatest failing of business speakers today is their unwillingness to pause effectively. Fearing that a pause will be misinterpreted as temporary loss of direction, a sign of poor preparation, or a lack of "class," speakers rush along at a steady clip without a pause.

Pausing to Improve Speaking. As their listeners would love to tell them, such speakers are dead wrong about pauses. Listeners appreciate the chance to let important points sink in; the chance to let the senses relax for a moment; and the chance to mentally take a deep breath before plunging into concentration again on the next portion of the speech.

Pauses can be learned in a simple, painless, and wholly reliable way. Simply swallow. The typical swallow takes a little less than two seconds to accomplish—the perfect length of time, by fortunate coincidence, for the effective pause.

The swallow has the additional advantage of soothing the vocal chords, helping to promote a clear, pleasant voice quality. Best of all, the swallow is virtually unnoticed by your audience.

Where do pauses belong? Usually these brief breaks can prove effective

- before and after crucial points.
- at the end of each major section of the address.
- after especially significant or difficult names or terms.
- after an earnest comment.

Finally, let me make a personal observation. (Pause) I feel strongly that. . .

In gauging the length of your pauses, remember that you, the speaker, are energized by adrenalin, while your listeners operate under much less stressed conditions. A two-second pause may seem interminably long to you, but may be just right for your audience.

Pauses, like spices, can easily be overdone. Be careful not to fall into the habit of pausing after each thought. Your listeners will be left with the task of tying all your single, solemn sentences together into larger meanings.

Do Listen. Don't Ignore Others.

The word "communication" retains many of the meanings of its cousins, "communion" and "community"—in all cases, shared experience. Listeners do find ways to share with you what they are thinking while you are talking:

- They shake their heads, indicating approval or disapproval of your points.
- They reveal in their eyes and facial gestures such responses as acceptance, skepticism, resistance, and outright rejection.
- They use body language. Notice that some members of your audience sit comfortably, much as they would in a restaurant. Others slouch down in their chairs, seemingly weary with you; a few lean forward, their elbows on their knees; one or two rest chins-on-hands, eyes half open.
- They buzz, whisper, pass notes, and signal visually to others in the room.
- They break into your speech with questions.

These cues and clues upset many speakers, sending them to the hiding places of mumbling, loss of eye contact, absence of gestures, and so forth.

Answer the "Audience Question." After every business presentation, realize that your listeners were trying to tell you something and force yourself to answer one question, preferably in writing: What did I see, hear, or feel that let me know their response?

Here is one speaker's written response to this question.

The drumming fingers and swinging legs let me know that I should be more lively. Dull, weary eyes told me that some kind of visual aid was needed to spark interest. The frowns and forward leaning of some of the older employees suggested that perhaps they couldn't hear me, and that I should speak more distinctly and tighten my belt muscles for better projection. The quizzical looks of almost half the audience when I referred to "our notorious Canadian problems" indicated I should have explained what I meant right then and there. The appreciative nods from many listeners indicated support for my recommendations.

By answering the "audience question" in writing, you sensitize yourself to the needs of your listeners. You will soon find yourself answering those needs *while* you speak, instead of analyzing what you could have and should have done after the speech.

EFFECTIVE LISTENING

A Greek philosopher wrote, "The gods gave each of us one mouth and two ears. They should be used in that proportion."

We all have met a superb listener at least once in our lifetimes. When we are talking, they seem "all ears." Their changing facial expressions show how carefully they are following each of our words. They indicate by a nod or a slight vocal noise that they understand and sympathize with what we are telling them. When we pause, they ask questions that get right to the heart of the issue we've been trying to communicate.

We will all also admit that such listeners are rare. More commonly, we talk "at" people whose eyes wander around the room, whose faces appear inert no matter how arresting our news, and whose body motions indicate that they are staying around to hear us out only out of the thinnest thread of courtesy or obligation. We're not at all surprised when, after we've finished talking, such "listeners" respond, "I don't understand."

This treatment of listening is not about why others don't listen to us. Instead, we will focus on learning to listen to others. Like Ghandi and Tolstoy, who came to understand a simple life by leading one, we can understand how to attract listeners by learning to listen ourselves.

Clear Your Mind

Effective listening involves an initial risk, a leap of faith. You must be ready to grant that another human being might bring you something new, something you have not already guessed, something you might want to know. In other words, you cannot approach the act of listening with pre-defined notions of what a speaker *probably* will say or *is supposed to say* or *really wants to say*.

The poet Keats called this ability "negative capability." He refers to our capacity to say "no" to our need to make quick decisions. At the outset in conversation, we can learn to withhold judgment, to remain aware and alive to new possibilities.

Listen to the "Non-Words"

Much if not most of what we communicate to one another comes in the form of gestures, posture, expressions, and dress. You can tap into this valuable stream of information by simply looking at the speaker in a sustained way. Meet his or her eyes and hold them. Watch his or her face for signals of emphasis, misgiving, humor, and so forth. Be aware of what his or her body is doing. Are the hands flailing limply? What attitude do such gestures suggest? Is he or she pacing or fidgeting? What do these movements tell you?

Mentally Outline the Messages

Without becoming overly absorbed in your own mental work, try to find a structure—a path of meaning—in the many words flowing to you from the speaker. Often this path reveals itself simply by asking, in a silent way, the question *why?* as we listen. *Why* is the speaker telling me this story? *Why* is the speaker listing these facts? *Why* is the speaker disgusted by the boss's decision?

Such mental work on our part lets us hear the *deep* structure instead of merely the *surface* structure of the words coming at us. When we reply, we are prepared to get to the heart of the matter instead of wandering around its periphery.

Give the Speaker Signs

Communication fails when signals of interest and attention do not pass back and forth between speaker and listener. For this reason, perhaps, videotaped lectures have not swept human professors out of the classroom. No matter how famous the videotaped face and voice, the listeners know that they are observers, not participants, when the videotape begins to roll.

But how can you signal attention without interrupting the speaker? Simply nod your head, at an appropriate time, in a "yes" gesture. Try this technique on one of your professors. Notice for the rest of the lecture how often his or her eyes will return to you. You have sent a recognition signal and are rewarded—what luck!—with your professor's attention for the rest of the hour.

Let your voice indicate response and reaction to what the speaker is communicating. We have a curious and largely undocumented vocabulary of recognition sounds. Sometimes we puff air suddenly through our noses, as if beginning to laugh. At other times, we part our lips and let out the beginning sound of a word or a cough. We click our tongues against the roofs of our mouths. We use our hands to stroke our cheeks, rub our eyes, or scratch our heads. By such signals, we tell the speaker that we are being affected by their communication. We encourage them to continue.

Good listening pays dividends. First, we extend our own base of knowledge and insight by hearing others out. Second, we get the best from our speaker. Knowing that we are listening with care, the speaker summons his or her best efforts to make the words worth our attention. Finally, we build relationships. Friendship is impossible without sympathetic listening, and business friendships and relationships depend no less on its presence.

You may find the result of sympathetic, energetic listening quite powerful. Practice the preceding suggestions in your day-to-day relationships with friends, fellow students, and professors. Notice how much more important you make them feel by attentive, creative listening—and, in turn, how much more important they feel you are for your interest in them.

Summary

1. Effective business speakers project their voice and personality toward their audience.
2. Audiences appreciate brevity. Concise language involves less work for the listeners and brings a more powerful response to the words that are used.
3. Eye contact establishes a person-to-person bond between the speaker and the audience. This bond is necessary for successful communication.
4. Gestures should be natural, not forced, and coordinated with your points of emphasis in meaningful ways.

5. Audiences like the security of a perceptible structure in your speech. Organize your points for logical clarity and persuasive effect.
6. Speaking pace should be varied according to the ability of the audience to understand the speaker's message.
7. Visual aids can be powerful allies in the speaker's effort to communicate thoughts and feelings.
8. A varied tone, in keeping with the subject matter, helps maintain the interest and attention of the audience.
9. Effective pauses allow the audience to feel points of emphasis in the speech and to rest perceptual faculties for a moment before the speech moves on.
10. Active listening involves attention to both verbal and nonverbal clues to the speaker's message and intent.

Questions for Discussion

1. Of the Ten Do's and Don'ts of business speaking, which are the most applicable to you? Why?
2. Can deeply rooted bad speaking habits be overcome?
3. Why is it vitally important to accept your humanness as a speaker?
4. How can adjusting your vocal muscles just before delivering your speech help your presentation?
5. Is it possible to project your voice without talking loudly?
6. How do clear articulation in a speech and ordinary conversation differ?
7. What are two causes of a speaker's rambling?
8. What two techniques can help you to avoid rambling in a speech?
9. What are you indirectly inviting the audience to do when you avoid making eye contact with them? How would practicing "blinksmanship" help?
10. What kinds of gestures should speech givers avoid? Why?
11. What one basic addition to the twenty patterns for organization of written materials should the speaker make, and why?
12. Are visual aids a necessary part of good speech making?
13. How do good speakers use volume, pitch, and tone?
14. When are pauses most effective in speeches?
15. How can you use "negative capability" when listening to others?

Exercises

1. Practice projecting your voice without talking louder than normal.
2. Practice your articulation by reading aloud passages of complicated prose. Bring to class the most challenging text you can find and exchange it for examples brought in by your colleagues. (Make sure you give them a real tongue twister!) What about the passages is difficult? How must you adapt your ordinary speaking pace to articulate clearly these passages?

3. We've all encountered the "rambling speaker" at some time in our academic or business careers. Describe common reactions to the rambler. What feedback can you give the rambler to suggest that he or she get to the point?
4. For an upcoming speech, pare your material to avoid becoming a rambling speaker. Generate questions to ask your listeners. How will these questions elicit positive feedback and keep your message on track?
5. In preparing for an upcoming speech, create a speaker's note card following the example offered in Figure 14-1.
6. Watch an effective political leader, religious speaker, or game show host on television, and note what helpful body movements, facial expressions, and hand gestures contribute to his or her presentation. Practice similar techniques before a mirror in preparation for an upcoming speech.
7. Tape record your speech to check yourself for varying volume, pitch, and tone. Do you effectively avoid a monotonous speaking style?
8. Create an appropriate visual aid for an upcoming speech. After you have delivered the speech, be sure to ask your evaluators whether or not this visual aid seemed well suited for your needs.

Becky Tallison is a mid-level manager with a large title company in Washington. She supervises eight other title officers.

One of the pluses on my résumé when I was hired staight from college six years ago was my speech experience. In addition to my business courses, I had several courses in public speaking. I had even won a few trophies as a member of the college forensics team.

One of many surprises in my present position was how much I still had to learn about communication. For one thing, most of my important speaking does not occur in front of an audience at all. Instead, I'm talking on the phone or speaking one-to-one to other employees in my office. Usually I have no notes, no planned gestures, no visual aids—none of the speaking skills and techniques I had learned.

Now I'm training an assistant manager to work under me. I want him to learn good telephone and interpersonal skills. But where should he start? How do you teach someone to use the telephone effectively?

Evaluate your own telephone and interpersonal communication skills. Where did you learn to do what you do well? In what ways are you continuing to learn in these important areas?

Speaking One-to-One and in Meetings

15

LEARNING OBJECTIVES

To practice standard methods for dictation

To develop your skills in using the telephone for business purposes

To understand various communication channels used in person-to-person communicating

To participate in interviews with skill and insight

To recognize and use techniques for conducting and participating in meetings

We are known to one another, in business and in life generally, by the way we speak and listen. Think about the last person who spoke to you for more than a minute or two. Words and manner, no matter what the subject of the conversation, communicated so much to you.

You formed an opinion, for example, of the person's emotional state—angry, jovial, depressed, shy, and so forth. You made a tentative judgment about the person's intellectual powers—bright, insightful, slow-witted, or any of the stages in between. You assessed the speaker's attitude toward you—friendly, withdrawn, romantic, domineering, patronizing, and so forth. You decided whether the words you heard made sense or nonsense. In short, you listened.

The importance of speaking and listening cannot be overstated for success in business. This portion of the text will deal with the many forms of speaking and listening you will experience in the business world. Along the way, we will list—and try to alleviate—such barriers to effective speaking and listening as anxiety and self-centeredness.

This chapter begins with a discussion of the many forms of one-to-one speaking in business. We will then see how one-to-one speaking skills can also be used in groups, particularly in meetings.

Oral communication experiences in business can be arranged on an ascending ladder of difficulty and career importance, as shown in 15-1. Together, we can proceed up this ladder to discuss practical approaches and pitfalls for each common communication task.

DICTATION

As the lowest step on the ladder of oral skills, dictation provides a good training ground for some speaking skills. Your pace, volume, and enunciation matter here, if your transcriber is to convert your dictation successfully to a business letter, memo, or report. Because no audience is physically present when you dictate, you feel little or no anxiety.

Knowing Your Equipment

If you are dictating to a machine, know its operating procedures.

- How can you check the volume level of your dictation?
- How do you pause during dictation?
- How can you go back to review a portion already dictated?
- How can you revise a sentence or two without recording over (hence eliminating) other portions of your dictation?

The answers to these and other questions can be found in the user's guide accompanying your machine. Study this manual, and allow time for a practice session or two before beginning to dictate under pressure conditions.

FIGURE 15-1

Progressive Steps in Oral Business Communication

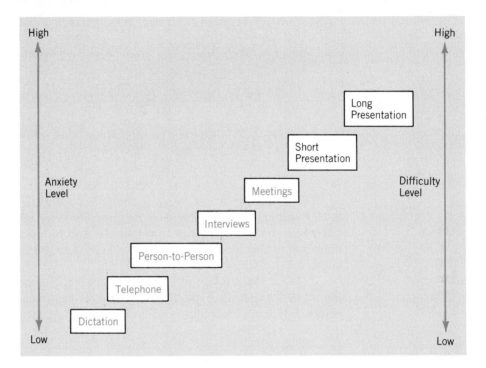

Your dictating equipment may have arms and legs, of course—in other words, a secretary. Get to know the habits and preferences of the man or woman who takes dictation from you. Adjust the speed of your words to suit the secretary. Settle upon signals to be used to indicate new paragraph beginnings, corrections, capitalization, special punctuation, and a long or unusual series of numbers.

Preparation

A business person's first dictating experience often ends in frustration. The machine or secretary works just fine, but the words won't seem to flow—or even budge, for that matter. Probably lack of preparation is to blame.

If you are initiating new correspondence, prepare for dictation by jotting down a brief outline of the major points you wish to cover. These notes are for your eyes only, and can be written in personal cue words only you understand. Keep your outline short. If you write too much, you may as well mail it. Dictation will prove redundant. Here is one outline for a letter to be dictated:

Some business writers keep a notebook—a "dictation book," they call it—for keeping track of their short outlines. Often an outline that works especially well in one sales letter, for example, can be used in later letters. The notebook is also a convenient place to keep a record of dates for items dictated.

If you are responding to correspondence, jot comments in the margins of the letters you receive (or a photocopy, if the original must be kept unmarked). Use your marginal notes to suggest material for dictation.

Dictating Procedure

When dictating by machine, respond to each of these items (and others that seem important to you):

1. *Who are you?* Identify yourself by name, division, and extension on the dictaphone.
2. *What is this?* Identify the kind of document you are dictating. "This is a business letter."
3. *Format and number of copies?* Specify what type style you wish to use, what kind of stationery the letter should be typed on, and how many copies are to be prepared. "Please use block style on company letterhead, two originals plus one copy to file."
4. *To whom?* Clearly and carefully give all information necessary for the inside address. Spell out all names, even usual last names like *Jordan* and *Smith* to prevent glaring errors (*Jorden* and *Smyth* may be the correct spellings). Indicate what salutation you wish to use. "Mr. Malcolm Jorden, 3589 Meredith Way, Cincinnati, OH 57847. Dear Mr. Jorden:"
5. *Message?* At an appropriate pace, dictate what you wish to say. Signal the beginnings of new paragraphs as instructed by your user's guide. Indicate punctuation to prevent unnecessary retyping. Conclude by giving the

complimentary closing you wish to use. Specify how your name should be typed in the signature block.

6. *Now what?* Specify what you want done with the letter you have dictated. When do you want to review it? Should it be routed to your office through company mail or hand-carried? Are any security precautions necessary for the information the letter contains? "Please hand-carry to my office as soon as possible."

7. *Special instructions?* Should the letter be accompanied with an oversized envelope to enclose documents you want to send along? Should the envelope be labeled Confidential or Personal? "Address and over-sized mailer, please."

8. *Thank your transcriber.* "Thanks!"

With practice, some executives are surprised to find that they can dictate as many as twenty short business letters and memos an hour by using dictation equipment and personnel.

The future holds even greater advances in efficiency. Led by Japanese companies, the computer industry is putting the last touches to voice-driven typewriters. A manager will be able to speak into a microphone and watch the letter being typed automatically. Internal spelling, grammar, and punctuation circuitry will censor and repair mistakes.

While this technology may seem a bit Buck Rogerish, the prototypes of voice-driven typewriters are already being field-tested and production models will probably soon be on the market.

THE TELEPHONE

One step up from dictation both in difficulty and in business significance is the verbal work you will do over the telephone.

Notice, first, how many advantages the telephone holds for business use. You can reach people inexpensively. You can break into a client's busy day without an appointment. You can argue or deliver bad news without the pain of seeing the client's face (or fist). You can get right to the point without the social preliminaries that we attach to in-person visits.

The phone also has its interesting limitations. Notice, for example, that you can't pause to think on the telephone. A pause of even a second or two produces the inquiry, "Are you still there?" All decisions made on the telephone are necessarily oral, and hence subject to later denial or re-interpretation.

As travel costs continue to escalate, though, and electronic communication replaces physical contact, we can expect the telephone to play a larger role in business life. We have already seen the advent of staffless businesses, in which a million-dollar-a-year firm acquires an 800 number and an answering service for orders from national ads. All other work is conducted literally out of the garage.

What do you sound like on the phone? You will never know until you record your end of several conversations over a period of days. Play back the tape and listen with a critical ear. Are you pushy? Monotone? Long-winded? Confused? Jot down those qualities that you wish to change. Then consider the guidelines summarized in the catch-phrase, **B-L-E-S-S** the Telephone.

B—Be likable. Because the person on the other end of the line cannot see your facial expressions, you must communicate tone of voice. We have all picked up the phone at times to hear a voice at the other end, apparently disgruntled, ''Jim?'' Such calls can come from even our best friends. They aren't disgruntled at all, but simply have an abrupt way of beginning phone conversations.

For business use, practice a smooth, friendly introduction to phone conversations. Greet the person you're calling, giving your own name as soon as possible.

''Hello, Mr. Wilkins? This is Sally Jenson at the *Daily News*.'' In Sally's case, she consciously tries to say the ''hello'' with a smile on her face and hence in her voice. Right from the beginning, the person she has called knows that this will be a friendly call, not another hassle in the business day.

L—Lead the conversation. Particularly if you made the phone call, be prepared to lead the conversation to important topics. In the case of important business calls, you may want to prepare a brief set of notes to which you can refer early in the conversation. Telephone conversation is much like dancing: it takes two, but one must establish the lead. Don't lose your listener by speaking too fast, or bore him or her by dawdling with your words. In most business conversations, you may want to maintain the lead until the listener comfortably enters in to respond. Do not imitate the unfortunate practice of some telephone solicitors who try to get a ''Yes'' response from their listener within the first ten seconds of conversation.

Not: ''Hello, Mrs. Brown? We're having a vacuum cleaner sale. You like sales, don't you?'' (pause for answer)

Reputable business men and women are careful not to ask their listener for commitments before all the pertinent facts have emerged in conversation.

E—Explain your key points. In the five to seven minutes of an effective phone conversation, provide explanation and examples of your key points. Ask the listener occasionally if he or she has questions. Ask if your information or proposal suits the needs of your listener. Try to get your listener to take over the lead, mentioning concerns that you can answer.

S—Sum up. Because telephone conversations are exclusively oral in nature, you should practice mid-conversation and end-of-conversation summary statements. These brief ''wrap-ups'' draw all the words passing back and forth to a point.

"Well, just to sum up: you're willing to back Tracy for the position if she can demonstrate some track record of financial management. Have I understood you correctly?"

The last question "Have I understood you?" gives the listener the chance to respond—and avoids the appearance that you have unilaterally decided upon the outcome of the conversation.

S—Say thanks. Appreciation rarely goes astray, and can hardly be overdone. If you are grateful to your listener, say so in specific terms. Try to avoid clichés and implied thanks.

Not: "Well, I guess you know how I feel. Bye."
Not: "I want to express my appreciation for your help. Goodbye."
Instead: "Thanks, John, for supporting Tracy. It means a great deal to me. I'll talk to you again in a few days. Goodbye."

For many businesses, the telephone is the primary artery for business new and old. With good reason, employees "BLESS" the telephone when it rings or when they pick it up to call a client, and some even tape a handy reminder of the *B-L-E-S-S* formula by their telephone.

Eight Hints for Speaking and Listening on the Telephone

1. *Don't shout or whisper.* The amplification equipment in the average telephone has a limited audio range. Extreme volumes will either not be carried at all or will be transmitted in distorted, harsh tones.

2. *Call back to correct a static-plagued connection.* Business calls are too important to "almost" make out what a client is saying. Instead, explain that you have a poor connection and will call back.

3. *Don't talk over the person you're speaking with.* If you can't seem to fit a word in edgewise, create pauses by approval statements.

"Precisely." (Your caller pauses to think about your approval; you take the opportunity to begin speaking.)

4. *Provide support cues.* Your client will find it unnerving to speak for an extended period into the void of silence. Provide reassurance by occasionally murmuring "yes," "right," "OK," and "uh-huh." These supportive cues encourage your client to tell you more, and to trust that your response will be favorable and accepting.

5. *Vary the tone of your voice.* The amplification equipment on telephones tends to make monotones of us all. Counteract this unfortunate tendency by speaking in a lively fashion.

6. *Keep telephone conversations short and to the point.* Clients often hesitate to get too deeply involved in subject matter over the telephone, espe-

cially because there is no written record of the conversation. Therefore, use telephone conversation to establish general understandings and to make arrangements for more definitive meetings in person. The advent of teleconferencing may drastically extend the usefulness of the telephone for decision-making use. When your listener's face is present on your screen and your face on his or hers, the likelihood is increased that final details of negotiations can be struck. After all, you're all "present" almost in the same way that you would be if you visited the client's office.

7. *Be aware of the effect background noise in your office may be having on your conversation.* While a typewriter may not interfere with your ability to hear your client (you have the receiver pressed to your ear), that same noise may make your words virtually lost on the other end of the connection. If you suspect that your client cannot hear you well, ask early in the conversation.

8. *Always set the telephone receiver down gently.* An abrupt crash, heard from your client's point of view, may be interpreted as a show of temper on your part. Even a friendly conversation can have a cloud drawn over it by the nagging question of why the receiver was banged down. "Did I say something wrong?"

Most telephone companies have business representatives who will be happy to provide telephone-effectiveness materials and seminars. Especially as telephone use grows in connection with televideo equipment and computers, successful business people will make good use of these free services.

PERSON-TO-PERSON SPEAKING

At least half of all the business words you speak will occur not in meetings or on the telephone but simply face-to-face with one or more business colleagues and clients. Many commonsense communication rules apply to such encounters, of course: speaking clearly, being brief, supporting points with examples, and so forth.

Learning to Listen

But the highest compliment that others can pay you—and one of your key *assets* as a business communicator—has to do not with your own speaking, but with your ability to make others feel comfortable speaking to you. We each know people who are good listeners. Consider what makes them so, summed up by the handy acronym *A-S-S-E-T-S.*

A—Attention. Signal to the person talking to you that you are giving him or her full attention. Visibly set down anything you hold in your hands. Establish good eye contact, and avoid abrupt body motions (indicating impatience) while listening.

Communication skills matter most of all during those precious few minutes when you are under direct review by your superiors, perhaps in an interview or conference. Fred Rentschler, president of Hunt-Wesson Foods, explains:

In a large corporation the exposure a young manager receives to those men and women who will affect his or her promotion may occur as seldom as five times a year and may be for no longer than a fifteen to thirty minute period. How succinctly one can define his or her objectives in the most candid and forthright manner will be the only impression that may or may not spell promotion.

S—Support. Support the speaker's efforts to communicate by giving frequent approval cues as mentioned above: "yes," "right," "true," and "I agree." Nod your head, smile, and gesture appropriately to let your speaker know that he or she is making sense to you.

S—Sympathize. Sympathize with the speaker's complaints or dilemmas. Refrain from offering solutions right away, or challenging the seriousness of the complaint. Let your speaker tell you what hurts.

E—Echo your speaker. As the famous psychologist Carl Rogers insisted, we can draw out someone else's deepest messages by simply saying back what we heard them say to us.

Statement: *If I don't get this promotion, Bev is going to be all over my case again about not standing up for my rights around here.*

Echo: *Your wife is concerned that you don't stand up for your rights. (spoken not as a question—which might seem to be prying—but instead as a simple statement, an echo.)*

Right. She can't understand that I . . . (speaker goes on to trust you more and more deeply).

T—Touch. In retail sales throughout the United States, the "touch revolution" is taken as more than a somewhat humorous business fad. Cadillac sales at a large Los Angeles dealership, for example, jumped almost 30 percent after a "touch-training" seminar. Salespeople were taught to politely and discreetly touch the arm or shoulder of the client—just a brief, warm pat or squeeze—at a key moment during the sales pitch. Clients, it turns out, have no special desire to be touched, but have an immense need to like the salesperson they deal with. The social touch, a somewhat risk-ridden matter, works wonders in establishing an "I-like-you-and-want-the-best-for-you" relationship with the client.

If touching sells Cadillacs, surely there is a proper place for the pat on the back, the handshake, and the squeeze of the arm in business. Watch for the use of the friendly touch by people you admire in your business life. Let their natural friendliness guide you in learning how to physically let people know you value their company.

S—Select the right environment. Person-to-person conversations that could lead to warmth and friendliness often misfire because neither party takes five seconds to say, "It's noisy out here. Let's go to a more quiet place." Show another person that you are concerned enough to find a suitable environment for a conversation.

A quiet place usually brings out the best in both parties. You can listen without distraction and the speaker can talk in a normal voice without shouting above machinery, traffic, and so forth.

Learning to Speak One-to-One

When it comes your turn to participate in the conversation, keep in mind the six qualities of a likable and persuasive conversationalist, as summed up in the following suggestions.

1. *Compliment your listener.* Find something in his or her accomplishments, attitudes, or goals to say a kind word about.

2. *Headline your own points.* Don't leave listeners in the dark about what you're trying to say. Begin by setting forth your main idea in a brief way. *I'm concerned about the methods for handling layoffs in the company.* (Your listener will now know the intent of further points you make.)

3. *Exemplify your points.* Don't ask your listeners to accept your point of view on faith alone. Point out supporting examples and details. *For example, our current personnel document makes no reference to length of employment when layoff decisions have to be made.*

4. *Enumerate your points for clarity.* *I favor a three-part plan. First, layoffs would occur strictly according to length of employment. Second, sectors of the company with low-profit or loss records would be subject to layoff first. Third, one executive earning over $45,000 would have to be laid off for every ten regular employees laid off.* (Your listener can keep track of your ideas.)

5. *Read your listener's face and eyes.* When a question or comment starts to appear, create a break in your own speaking and welcome the listener's contribution.

6. *Speak sincerely.* This advice goes far beyond rules for communication to include the whole realm of ethics. To be sincere means not to lie to your listener, even in small ways. To be sincere means to show emotions that are real, never faked for a manipulative purpose. To be sincere means to use the information you gather from trusted conversations in a trustworthy way.

INTERVIEWS

An initial job interview is usually not an effort by the company to accumulate more factual information about you. Instead, the company wants to see how you handle yourself, especially with words. Personnel directors commonly report "knowing" whether they will turn thumbs up or down on a candidate within five minutes of the beginning of the interview.

What can you do to succeed in those crucial first five minutes?

- Dress appropriately.
- Establish a friendly rapport by your natural smile and comfortable eye contact.
- Be ready to carry the conversation for a moment or two after the first question. Don't throw the ball back in the interviewer's court with curt yes/no answers. To prepare for interview openers, consider these typical questions.

Well, Barbara, tell us a little about yourself.

Why in the world did you decide to major in accounting?

Why would you like to work here?

You've probably considered a number of careers. Tell us about some of them.

I see you're about to graduate from Smith College. What can you tell us about your college?

By answering such interview openers in a comfortable, direct way, you establish your confidence to handle any question or comment that comes.

Don't be obsessed, by the way, with anyone's cautions against certain "no-no" words like "Well, . . . " or "you know." Concentrate on speaking clearly and personally. Interviewers do not count the number of times you use particular words.

If you purchase one of the many popular books on interviews, be careful not to form too established a mind-set regarding "the" typical interview. If you go into an interview expecting only typical questions, you may not do your best. Concentrate, in the following discussion, not on the questions but the questioners, their motives and assumptions.

The Campus Interview

Companies send representatives to your campus not to hire on the spot, but to accomplish three goals:

1. to give the company exposure among the graduating class.
2. to maintain mutually supportive relationships with the university and its faculty.
3. to develop "fishing lists" of bright, eager students who might later be asked for on-site interviews with the company.

In most cases, the representative interviewing you on campus will be, in fact, a rather low-echelon employee who doesn't mind "doing the colleges" for the company. You have every reason, therefore, to relax and do your best in a campus interview. You are not talking to the chairman of the board. Even if the representative stands agog at your abilities after the interview, he or she probably cannot offer you a position on the spot. Therefore, look at the campus representative as a human being, not a judge. Try to imagine his or her day, filled with interviews. Speak comfortably and sincerely—and thereby set yourself apart from the jittery masses, anxious to impress the interviewer at all costs.

The On-Site Interview

The "winners" of campus interviews receive invitations from the company for an on-site visit, and are asked to fill out an application for employment.

One or more personnel officers usually conduct the initial screening interview. Again, the first five minutes of the interview are all important. Be prepared to move quickly into a smooth, comfortable conversation, even if the first question is a stickler ("What did you think of our building as you drove up?") Try to avoid one-word answers.

At the on-site interview even more than the campus interview, expect to talk briefly about your specific field of training. Interviewers commonly get to this topic by asking one of the following questions:

- What aspect of your college studies seems particularly valuable to you?
- Did you have a special area of interest in college?
- What one class seemed of greatest practical value to you?
- What can you tell us about your academic preparation for this job?
- Well, what's going on in the Business School these days?

What if, in the process of answering a question, your tang gets tungled and you make an obvious mistake? Without making much ado over nothing, simply note your mistake and repair it:

> *When I studied macro-systems interacting spontaneously to factors, well, involving . . . I'm sorry, I want to say this more clearly: I studied the way major markets responded to international inflation.*

Your interviewer will be grateful for your clarification, and impressed that you could catch and repair a problem so gracefully.

Be prepared at both the campus and on-site interview to show interest in the affairs of the company. Your college business librarian can guide you to such publications as *Standard and Poor's* and *Valueline,* each summarizing the size, product or service line, and financial stability of the company.

Your questions and comments about the company are often invited by these kinds of questions:

- Do you have any questions for us?
- You've seen our operation today. Any questions?
- What's your opinion of our office arrangement here?
- What would you still like to know about the company?

A sheepish grin and a shy answer, "Well, nothing, really" will not score points for you when these questions are asked. Nor should you stall for time by such awkward ploys as, "Would you please repeat the question?" Prepare in advance some interesting questions for the company:

- Where is the company headed in the next five years?
- Is a new product line or service now under development?
- What are typical paths of advancement within the company?
- What are typical travel requirements for the position you seek?
- What subsidiaries does the company own?
- What training programs are available to new employees?

Do *not* broach sensitive or self-serving questions such as:

- Why has your stock lost nine points since May?
- How many sick days can I take per month? (This question may need to be asked, but phrase it tactfully.)
- How soon do I get a raise?

Conclude the interview by thanking the interviewer and, if appropriate, shake hands, including the hand of a woman interviewer if she offers it. Don't prolong this final moment, or make it awkward by last-minute parting shots: "By the way, I forgot to ask if . . ."

When you return home, write a thank-you letter to the interviewers, as described in Figure 18-8.

The Supervisory Interview

On the same day as your initial on-site interview or at a later time, you may be invited to interview with a division manager or supervisor. Expect this interview to be much less "slick" than the session conducted by the personnel officers. Long pauses may fall in conversation. The phone may ring, interrupting your discussion for a few minutes. The secretary may pop in from time to time with urgent business.

In all such disturbances, maintain easygoing good spirits, letting the supervisor know that you can cope with the ragged edges of real business activity.

Prepare to answer questions about your field:

- Have you done any work setting up annual reports?
- What accounting procedure would you use in this case?
- How would you structure a decision-making team for this kind of project?

When you don't know an answer, say so—but add that you could find out (name specific ways). No company wants to hire an employee who even during the interview tries to disguise an area of ignorance and fake competence.

Prepare specific questions for the supervisor:

- How do you handle a client's personal desires for a certain color or design in an ad?
- Do you use computer-aided graphics?

Practice does improve your interviewing skills. Many colleges provide mock-interview sessions, with constructive criticism. You can also set up informal interview practice sessions with fellow students. After fifteen minutes or so of questions, analyze the performance of the "applicant" according to the checklist shown in Figure 15-2, or one of your own design.

SPEAKING IN MEETINGS

If you want to see my company at its worst, listen in on our meetings, said one executive. Certain know-it-alls do all the talking; others won't speak at all. The person chairing the meeting loses track of the agenda—

FIGURE 15-2

Interview Checklist

☐ Were answers clear and direct?

☐ Was pace effective?

☐ Was volume appropriate?

☐ Was choice of words fitting?

☐ Were pronunciation and enunciation correct?

☐ Did applicant understand the questions?

☐ Did applicant make sense?

☐ Did applicant provide details and examples?

☐ Did applicant have a good grasp of subject area?

☐ Did applicant quickly become comfortable to be with?

☐ Did applicant try to relate to each member of the group?

☐ Did applicant demonstrate a sense of humor?

☐ Did applicant demonstrate maturity in handling difficult or sensitive questions?

☐ Did applicant make good eye contact?

☐ Did applicant use face, hand, and body language effectively?

☐ Did applicant avoid disruptive mannerisms?

☐ Did applicant appear well groomed and suitably dressed?

if there was an agenda to begin with. Inevitably, personality clashes take over until someone finally moves to adjourn. Mind you, these are good professional people on their own. But together in a meeting, oh my word!

Meetings can be no better than the sum effort of all participants. In our discussion, we will treat practical ways you can advance your interests and the company's interest while participating in and leading meetings.

Participating

Each meeting follows a somewhat predictable life cycle. After the chair brings up a topic for discussion, certain members—let's call them A, B, C, and D—speak up to have their say. After a period of such discussion, it becomes obvious that E, F, G, and H have not had a word to say. The chair tries to draw out their opinions, if possible. Then the burden of the discussion reverts back to the original speakers, A, B, C, and D for the remainder of the meeting.

Suggestion: Clearly, it is to your advantage to be one of the first people to contribute to a meeting. Like one of the first players to come to bat, you have a much better chance to influence the meeting not once but two or three times without appearing to dominate. Speaking up early also stimulates your adrenalin level, waking you up to the concerns before you. In all, you present yourself in a much better light by joining members A, B, C, and D rather than the silent contingent, E, F, G, and H.

Notice that when the silent ones do cough up a few words, their comments are often glib, marginal, and sometimes tinged with sarcasm. People who "contribute" to meetings in this fashion have the illusion that they are impressing others with their sophomoric wit and cynical intelligence.

Suggestion: When speaking in a meeting, make your point fully and sincerely, rather than taking potshots at the positions of others. In every meeting, some speakers are perceived as substantial, serious contributors while others are considered nit-pickers and back-biters who offer no constructive alternatives.

Like gunners priming for attack, some meeting participants spend their time either speaking or "loading up" for their next opportunity to speak. They seldom listen to the opinions of others.

Suggestion: Demonstrate in some visible way that you care what others have to say. Take notes, for example, as others speak, or keep a flowchart of the ideas as they develop in the meeting. Figure 15-3 is an example of a simple flowchart developed during a meeting on retirement policy. Use such notes to help provide continuity to the meeting by relating points made by other participants.

> *Jaime objected to management's proposal on the grounds that key managers will be unnecessarily ousted. I think Ted's comment supports that point: the health records of our managers who are now 65 to 70 are excellent. But what I'd like to know . . .*

Your fellow participants in the meeting will appreciate the way you organize the ideas of the meeting for the group.

Suggestion: When you speak and listen in a meeting, look at the faces in the room. What do they tell you? Can you recognize allies to your position? Can you tell who opposes your notions, or who is confused? Use the information you gather in this way to aim questions and comments at the right targets.

Unlike friendly conversations, meetings can be stultifyingly dull because the participants withhold support cues—even when they completely agree with the point of view being expressed.

Suggestion: Add persuasive power to your comments by occasionally giving a deserved compliment to another participant in the discussion. The

FIGURE 15-3

Simple Flowchart

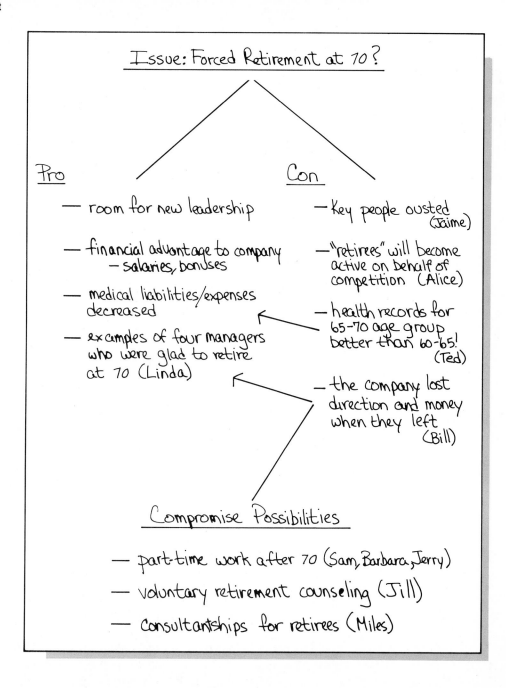

Issue: Forced Retirement at 70?

Pro

— room for new leadership

— financial advantage to company
— salaries, bonuses

— medical liabilities/expenses decreased

— examples of four managers who were glad to retire at 70 (Linda)

Con

— Key people ousted (Jaime)

— "retirees" will become active on behalf of competition (Alice)

— health records for 65-70 age group better than 60-65! (Ted)

— the company lost direction and money when they left (Bill)

Compromise Possibilities

— part-time work after 70 (Sam, Barbara, Jerry)

— voluntary retirement counseling (Jill)

— consultantships for retirees (Miles)

compliment need not be laid on with a trowel. A few sincere words will achieve a remarkable effect:

I think you hit the nail on the head, Samantha.

Michael is in a better position than any of us to speak to this issue.

I think Jerry put the facts in perspective for all of us.

When hurrying off to a business meeting, grab more than your briefcase and notes. Also take along those social skills you use to get along effectively with people in your everyday life. The meeting you're attending is a social occasion, after all, made up of people seeking feedback, praise, guidance, support, and attention.

Leading Meetings

One dubious reward for being a good participant in business meetings is that soon you find yourself tapped to lead meetings. Consider the following hints and guidelines for conducting effective meetings.

- *Provide notice of the meeting to all participants*. Include, if possible, an agenda—even a tentative one—so that participants can begin to gather their thoughts and notes for the meeting.
- *Take a minute or two at the beginning of the meeting for self-introductions—especially if you have fewer than twenty people attending.* This practice not only lets people meet one another by name, but also encourages free discussion. Simply by saying his or her name and company position, a participant has broken the ice. Speaking up later in discussion becomes easier.
- *State the purpose of the meeting clearly, but not in a dictatorial way.*

  This afternoon we'll discuss the sales commission structure now used in the company, and any other related matters that seem important to you.

You will be remembered with admiration by all meeting participants if you also state a time for adjournment.

  We'll adjourn promptly at 4:00 so that several of you can keep other appointments.

- *Avoid formal rules of order* (such as *Robert's Rules of Order* if possible). These artificial controls and safeguards may have a place in a large policy-making session, but they tend to discourage discussion in smaller meetings. Many participants fear "being out of order," or just do not know about parliamentary procedure. Rather than risk embarrassment, they fall silent.

Conduct the meeting, then, by commonsense methods: call on a variety of speakers, with fairness to each. Don't let one member of the group dominate discussion ("Let me stop you for a moment, Frank. Does anyone want to respond to the point Frank is making?") Assert control if discussion turns into a free-for-all. (''Just a minute, please. Please. Frances, you had the floor, and Bill after you.'')

• *Make good use of the blackboard or flipchart to keep major ideas, in order, before the attention of the group.*

• *Keep the meeting moving toward its goals by providing occasional brief summaries, followed by a question.*

> *So far, we seem to agree that Wilford Advertising has been too conservative in its representation of our line of clothing. I suppose the next logical question is whether Wilford can come up with more creative approaches. Any comments?*

• *Work toward consensus, not confrontation and early votes.* While a seven to five vote might decide matters in parliamentary procedure, a wise chair tries to prevent narrow majorities from dominating vocal and large minorities. Because the company usually has to move ahead with one voice, the meeting should proceed with discussion until compromises and understandings have been worked out that suit almost all members. When this meeting of minds is not possible, allow some outlet for minority opinion—a minority report, for example, or a later meeting to reconsider the issues.

• *Thank all participants for attending the meeting.* As soon as possible, distribute summary notes of the meeting, organized to highlight decisions made and actions recommended.

• *For your own growth as a chair, tape record several meetings with the group's permission.* Listen to the tapes. Do you speak too much in the meeting? Are your decisions fair to all members? Can you be heard? Do you keep the meeting on course by occasional brief summaries?

Chairing meetings places you in a visible position for judgment by upper management. Use this spotlight of responsibility to the best of your ability, without self-consciousness.

Summary

1. Efficient dictation depends upon knowing the equipment, preparing for dictation, and gaining practical knowledge of dictating procedures.
2. The use of the telephone for business can be enhanced by attention to the **B-L-E-S-S** formula: *B*e likable, *L*ead the conversation, *E*xplain your key points, *S*um up, and *S*ay thanks.
3. Successful person-to-person speaking depends as much upon how you listen as how you speak.
4. Campus, on-site, and supervisory interviews provide opportunities for you to demonstrate your abilities with words and ideas, especially in the areas of explanation and problem-solving.
5. Participating in and leading meetings requires careful attention to the purpose of the meeting, the attitudes of its members, and its moment-to-moment dynamics.

Questions for Discussion

1. Why are effective speaking and listening skills vital to good business communication?
2. Why is it important to be well prepared before giving dictation? How can you prepare?
3. What items should you respond to when dictating by machine?
4. What are some of the benefits and limitations of communicating by telephone?
5. Summarize the guidelines suggested by the catch-phrase, "*B-L-E-S-S* the telephone."
6. Is it necessary to jot down an outline of the points you expect to cover in a telephone conversation, or should telephoning—a verbal act—free you from the burden of writing ideas down?
7. Why is it a good idea to lead business conversation over the phone? Why is it useful to occasionally summarize the points you've covered in a phone conversation?
8. How can learning to be a good listener help your efforts as a business communicator?
9. What *A-S-S-E-T-S* do good listeners possess?
10. What should you do to succeed in the crucial first five minutes of an interview?
11. What are the main purposes of a campus interview? Why is it important to make a good initial impression at this interview?
12. Why is it to your advantage to participate in a meeting—to be one of the first people to contribute to the discussion?
13. What are some ways to ensure the participation and support of others at business meetings?
14. What responsibilities must meeting leaders accept? If you had to choose between leading a meeting and simply participating, following another's lead, which role would you prefer? Explain your choice.
15. Why is reaching consensus an important ingredient of a successful business meeting?

Exercises

1. Practice your speaking techniques by dictating an assignment onto tape. Play back the dictation. How does your voice sound? Are you able to transcribe the assignment successfully from your dictation?
2. Before the next phone call that you make, jot down an outline of the points you intend to cover and practice leading the conservation over the phone. How does the outline help you? How does your attitude toward the communication process change when you lead the conversation toward predetermined messages?
3. Recall a bad experience you've had carrying out a business conversation over the phone. If you could relive the experience, how would you prepare for it?

4. Recall a positive experience you've had carrying out a business conversation over the phone. Why was it successful?

5. Practice your listening skills by making a real effort to give your undivided attention to a speaker—either an acquaintance or a professor. Each time you feel tempted to let your attention wander, focus in on the speaker and try to think of a specific question you might ask about whatever he or she is saying. In casual conversation, go ahead and ask the question: get involved in the speaker's subject. In class, jot down the question and ask it at an appropriate time. Note the reactions to your questions. Did the speakers seem to appreciate your involvement?

6. "Gotcha!" The next time you are speaking to a friend or group, pay close attention to the various kinds of feedback that you get. How often does it seem to you that your listener really isn't paying much attention to what you have to say? Whenever you think your listener isn't listening, ask for his or her opinion about the point you just made. Note the reaction.

7. Carry out a mock interview session with a colleague. First act as interviewer, asking relevant questions of the applicant. Then change roles and play the part of the applicant. Compare notes with your colleague, and exchange constructive suggestions to improve interviewing skills.

8. (If feasible) report to work or school dressed in your oldest, most ragged clothes. Be comfortable and casual, if not downright seedy. How do people react to you? Record your findings.

   The next day, dress in your very finest clothes. Be attractive and professional. How do people's reactions to you change based on your physical appearance?

M ort Portfield, 55, is vice-president of western operations for a major chemical company. He came

up through the ranks as a bright, personable chemical engineer.

What I wouldn't give for my laboratory back! My present job satisfies all my financial aspirations and I like all aspects of my work except one—my obligation to give public speeches. Whether it's a five-minute introduction of a guest to the corporate headquarters or a luncheon address to the board of directors, I absolutely go through hell with speaker's nerves. I can't sleep the night before. I feel nauseated just before I begin to speak. I can hear my voice cracking and I sense the discomfort of my audience. They're probably worrying that something is wrong with me.

Well, there is! This thing with speaker's nerves is worse than a disease. I can't figure it out. I'm prepared when I speak. I certainly know my stuff after all these years. Why am I so frightened?

Without knowing Mort personally, we probably would have trouble answering his question specifically. But how would you answer it in a general way? What are speaker's nerves? How can they be controlled?

Oral

Presentations   16

LEARNING OBJECTIVES

To develop successful speeches of appreciation and introduction

To deal with speaker's nerves in a constructive way

To prepare appropriate luncheon and dinner addresses

To understand how business presentations are constructed and delivered

To develop effective longer presentations

Dictation, telephone work, person-to-person speaking, and participating in meetings unsually provide no cause for nervous anguish.

Not so when we reach the next step in our ascending order of speaking tasks, the short presentation, shown in Figure 16-1. Business men and women agonize over their two to twenty minutes (the usual limits of a short presentation) before an audience, even one made up of close business associates and friends.

We can condense their worries into one long moan: "I know I'm going to make a fool of myself. First of all, I'm a little overweight. When I get nervous, my upper lip shakes. My hands tremble. I get red in the face. I feel like I can't breathe. My heart starts knocking against my chest. I forget what I want to say. I don't just perspire or glow; I sweat. I hate, hate, hate to make speeches."

But make speeches you must if you intend to move into upper management positions in business. Don Keough, president of Coca-Cola, puts it well:

> As you move up through your career path, you're judged on your ability to articulate a point of view. Once you reach certain levels in an executive capacity . . . the ability to communicate perhaps a little better than others is a tremendous asset.

ANXIETY AND PUBLIC SPEAKING

Thomas Swanson, M.D., psychiatrist, poses the question—"What are the causes of anxiety or fear associated with public speaking?" and offers the following answer.

Anticipatory Anxiety

> *Basically, there is really only one process that causes fear of public speaking:* Anticipatory Anxiety. *This involves the process of saying "What if?" (What if I get nervous? What if I forget? What if the audience laughs at me? What if they think I'm stupid?) We learn to have anticipatory anxiety about speaking through previous bad experiences. We then live in dread that the previous negative experience will repeat itself. For most of us the anticipation is far worse than the actual anxiety we experience while doing the activity. One of man's greatest assets—the ability to think and plan—actually becomes a liability in this kind of situation.*

Dr. Swanson suggests the following techniques to self-treat or unlearn the fear or anxiety of public speaking.

1. Education. Simply learning methods of writing, speaking, and communicating will help to decrease anxiety. Knowing *what* to do helps. The principles in this book are an example.

2. Experience. For most of us the more we do something, the more relaxed and the less fearful we become. This is actually the most common way

FIGURE 16-1

Progressive Steps in Oral Business Communication

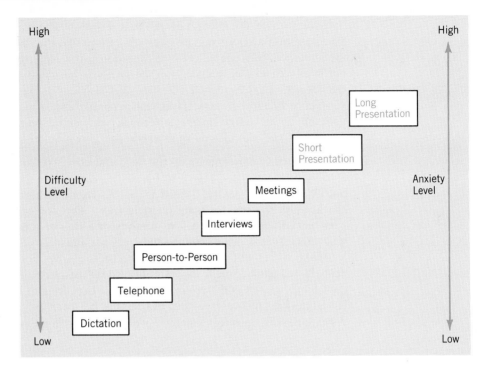

that people lose fear (we say *learn* to relax, or *desensitize*). An example is the anxiety that most of us experience during the first few days or weeks on a new job; we "hang in there"—keep going to work—and soon the anxiety diminishes.

3. *Think* differently about the situation. An important new concept in mental health is that successful people are able to change the way they think or believe about problems.

Two people in Anaheim, California, for example, reacted quite differently to their situations when they each lost their house and all belongings in a fire. In a TV interview hours after the fire, each was crying. The first said something like, "I can't stand it. I don't know what I'll do. It's the end. What's the point?"

The second said, "I'm upset. I don't like this. But I'm glad none of us was hurt. Oh, well. Life goes on." The subtle differences in the way people think make a great deal of difference in how they feel and cope with problems. Learning to talk to ourselves in more rational ways helps.

In the same way, we are talking to ourselves when we get in front of an audience. (If you are feeling *anything*, you are talking to yourself.) If you're anxious you're saying something like; "I *must* give a great talk and everyone *must* love it. If not, I'm a bad person in some way." (Notice how you're putting your whole self-esteem on the line simply by the way you think.) In contrast, the non-anxious person says something like the following: "I sure hope the audience likes the talk; but if they don't, it's okay. It's not what I prefer, but in any case, *I'm okay!*" In other words, your value, your worth, is not on the line.

There is another very important principle and consequence of talking to yourself in the latter manner: because your self-esteem is not on the line, you're relaxed. And if you're relaxed, you give a better talk!

4. Learn to concentrate on the here and now. We have to go back to what anxiety and worry is. They are the same. Anxiety is the process of focusing on the future and saying "What if . . . ?" By definition, the person focusing on the future is not focusing on right now. The person may be focusing on what *may* happen in just a few minutes or a day or a month, but not on the *now*. *Now* means this moment—this very second.

Take a moment right *now* to focus on the now. Focus on what you see, hear, taste, touch, smell. Pay attention to temperature, the feel of the book in your hand, noises in the environment, your breathing in and out, and so forth. It's important not to evaluate, but simply be aware of sensory experiences. When a person does this, anxiety, worry, or fear simply disappear.

THE APPRECIATION AND INTRODUCTION SPEECH

As a business leader, you will probably be called upon to "say a few words" about a company guest or colleague. In a short speech of appreciation, remember to do the following:

- Mention why the honored person deserves praise.
- Provide an effective example of the honored person's work or influence.
- Offer members of the audience the opportunity to participate in the appreciation (by applause, attending a party, or the like).

Before introducing a company guest or associate, determine from the person involved what educational attainments, work achievements, and positions of responsibility you can mention by way of introduction. In your introduction, be certain to suggest why the person is present with you (to look over the new office, to give a speech, for example). If your guest or associate will make a speech following your introduction, be careful not to steal the person's thunder, so to speak, by giving away a dramatic opening he or she plans to use.

Keep appreciations and introductions short, sincere, and warm. Except on quite formal occasions, such speeches rarely exceed five minutes in length.

Somewhere after the main course and before the dessert, you may have to stand before a speaker's podium to speak for twenty minutes or so to business associates or clients. These sorts of speaking occasions are not made in heaven. Waiters clink dishes as they clean off the tables; half the group lights up cigarettes for a relaxing after-meal attempt to choke the speaker. You have not enjoyed your meal, feeling butterflies starting to assemble within.

Make the best of these circumstances by pleasing your audience in three ways.

1. Choose an attention-getting opening. If you are reasonably sure that your first words will rivet the attention of the group, you can begin with confidence. Here are five tried and true openers (five more are treated later in relation to the longer presentation).

The Personal Story. Audiences respond to the intimacy and warmth of personal revelations so long as those reflections have a point.

> *When I was a child, my father and I had a favorite pond hidden in the midst of small hillocks in northern Pennsylvania. We never caught many fish there, but we talked a lot. We got to know each other. One day, driving to the pond, we rounded the last corner to find the pond, the little hills, the trees absolutely gone—hauled away, it turned out, by huge coal trucks. We got out of the car and walked a short way on the raw, torn, scraped earth. My father's only words were, "Remember this, Sarah. Remember."*

The speaker goes on to talk about the effects of technological change.

The Anecdote. Closely related to the personal story, the anecdote makes a point about an incident, but need not be personal in nature.

> *Americans have always enjoyed harpooning their political leaders. During Grover Cleveland's years in the White House, rumors flew regarding his extracurricular love relations. One cartoonist went so far as to depict a fatherless child on her mother's knee, imploring,*
> *"Ma, Ma, where's Pa?"*
> *The satiric answer followed—*
> *"In the White House, ha, ha, ha."*

The speaker proceeds to discuss why we hold political leaders in such low esteem.

Pointed Humor. A joke that has no point ("Where does a general keep his armies? In his sleevies.") has no place as the opener in a speech. Audiences expect you to relate a joke to your essential purpose.

> *The poet Wordsworth, for all his genius, never mastered the art of humility. In discussing Shakespeare one day, Wordsworth remarked to Charles*

Lamb that "anyone could write like Shakespeare if he had a mind to."
"Yes," replied Lamb quietly, "all he requires is the mind."

The speaker goes on to praise the quiet, inspired work of a company vice-president who is retiring.

The Unexpected Statement.

Audiences lean forward in mild shock when they hear a speaker say just the opposite of what they expect to hear.

I've been asked to talk about the wonders of the computer revolution. Well, it's all a matter of dirty sand and dirty water.

The speaker soon makes clear that she is speaking of the use of trace elements in silicon—dirty sand—and similar elements in simple cellular structures—dirty water—as the basis for computer technology.

The Local Fact or Site.

You can choose to open a speech by reminding your audience of a local fact or nearby site with special bearing upon your message.

Less than a mile from where we now sit, an Indian chief named Okanohok in 1837 signed over half of his tribe's 14,000 square miles of hunting territory for a government promise to supply the chief with 400 horses and 200 rifles.

The speaker goes on to disparage a takeover bid.

2. Once you have opened your speech and have earned the audience's attention, move immediately to your central topic. You can organize your thoughts by any of the patterns suggested in Chapter 3 or a pattern of your own. In a short speech, however, try to stress no more than three major points, or one point with three aspects.

Your speaking style should be energetic, direct, and conversational. Don't try to sound like Abraham Lincoln delivering the Gettysburg Address. Of course, Lincoln probably spoke in the common, unpretentious style that characterized his whole life. Be just that human and unguarded when you speak.

You may feel more secure with speaker's notes jotted on several cards. If so, do not let the cards interfere with your ability to look at your listeners and to gesture naturally. By setting the cards down on the rostrum at the beginning of your speech, you free your hands for communicating.

Especially when giving informal luncheon and dinner speeches, do not try to read from a manuscript. If you find that writing out every word of your speech helps you, spend time reading and re-reading the manuscript so that the speech can be delivered almost entirely by memory. When speaking the words you have memorized, try to make them sound natural and spontaneous.

Consider the use of visual aids in your speech. Each year we, as a culture, rely more on what we see and less on what we hear for important meanings. By using such aids as slides, transparencies, charts, and objects, you appeal to our appetite for visual meanings.

3. Close the short address by bringing your thoughts to a point in a memorable way. Each of the following closings provides that dramatic final moment (five more closings are treated later in the discussion of the longer presentation).

Words of Praise and Appreciation. You can close a short address by thanking your audience, praising all or some of its members for specific attributes or achievements, or expressing your appreciation in some other form.

It has been my job to discuss two negative influences on company revenues. Let me conclude by paying tribute, though, to 100 quite positive influences—those of you sitting before me.

The Call for Action. If you have tried to persuade your audience to take a particular course of action, close by calling for that action in specific terms.

Theories of management are just that—theories—until real people take the time and effort to make them work. Together we have discussed the importance of strong leadership in each of the company's divisions. In less than five minutes, each of you will return to your divisions and its people. Make the theory of effective management come to life by the words you say and actions you take this very afternoon.

The Summary Plus. Listeners appreciate a concluding summary, but also want to be left with something more, a "plus."

To sum up, we've seen three ways in which the San Moritz line of ski-wear can enhance profits at Leland Sports Supply.

1. The product line allows a healthy markup, with some advertising costs paid by the manufacturer.
2. Ski-wear will draw a new kind of customer into our store.
3. The introduction of ski-wear will give us a chance to test the market for other lines of sports clothing.

I leave you with one last bit of trivia—hardly worth mentioning, I suppose: the salesperson who sells the most San Moritz ski-wear this year gets an expenses-paid ski trip to San Moritz, Switzerland!

The Prediction. After marshaling facts and evidence for several minutes, you may conclude your speech by issuing a prediction or prophecy.

If we invest this year in CAD-CAM equipment, here's my prediction for the next few years. In 1985, we'll still lag behind the competition as we pay for our new equipment. In 1986, we'll draw even. By 1987, we'll lead the pack, and won't be overtaken for the foreseeable future.

The Return to the Beginning. If you began your speech in a rousing way, you may want to take your listener back to that moment for a wrap-up.

We began this afternoon with a question: Why diversify our product line when we're doing so well? You've seen evidence and heard argument to answer that question in two words. Why diversify? To survive.

A final note of caution: some luncheon and dinner speakers, overcome by the appreciative applause, feel called upon to say a few additional words, something of an encore. Resist this temptation. No matter how much the audience liked your speech, they are probably glad it has ended. Their perceptual work is over.

BUSINESS PRESENTATIONS

Like luncheon and dinner addresses, business presentations should grab attention right from the start. Probably your range of openings will be more restricted when making business presentations. You may not, for example, want to tell personal stories. Used with discretion, however, openers involving humor, anecdotes, and all the rest can work effectively even in a session that's "all business."

Because business presentations often ask for financial decisions instead of applause, your pattern of organization must be absolutely clear to your audience. Consider, therefore, handing out an attractive outline of your major points. The page can contain especially persuasive charts and tables or a list of terms new to the listener.

Conclude the business presentation with a call to action, using specific language:

Based on the evidence we have reviewed today, I recommend acquisition of Herder Printing by the company within the next 60 days. I will remain after the meeting to talk with those of you who wish to help draft a resolution to the Board of Directors regarding this most attractive acquisition.

THE LONG PRESENTATION

As you rise in business to positions of greater responsibility, you will find yourself addressing larger crowds for longer periods. A company-wide sales meeting, for example, may want you to speak for an hour. A local university invites you to deliver a forty-minute keynote address. A convention honors you by requesting a speech to its 700 members.

The stakes are high for you as a business leader and for the company's image.

After settling your nerves, turn your energies to the writing of a speech that has five distinct qualities:

Modern managers are virtually paralyzed without sound communication skills. U. J. LeGrange, vice-president and controller for Exxon Corporation, puts it bluntly:

I cannot overemphasize the importance of communication skills for effective business writing as well as effective presentations. Most of your formal education will be to sharpen your analytical skills. However, let me just remind you that the most carefully thought out analysis even with the appropriate conclusion is worthless if not communicated in an effective manner. Also, remember that much of what your supervisor will see and use to evaluate your performance will be your written and oral skills. Keep this in mind and take every opportunity to polish these skills as you go along. Your success will indeed ride on your ability to communicate.

- It grabs attention from the start.
- It takes the listener immediately into the main message of the speech.
- It divides in an easy, apparent way into natural steps or stages.
- It works upon the imagination by word pictures, examples, and actual visual aids.
- It concludes, not quits. The listener feels the end of a satisfying journey has been reached.

Opening the Long Presentation

Begin the longer presentation by choosing one of these common openers, one suggested for the shorter presentation, or one of your own devising.

The Striking Visual Aid. Some extremely effective longer presentations begin not with words but with pictures of some sort.

(The audience watches a brief 16mm film clip. In it, the camera moves down a crowded back street of New Delhi. Children in rags move toward the camera, their eyes and wretched physical features caught in momentary close-up as the camera moves along.)

When the speaker does begin the presentation, audience interest is high. Feelings have been aroused in a powerful way.

The Question. A direct question to the audience, followed by a pause for the question to sink in, can bring attention to a quick peak. The question also gets right to the heart of the speaker's message.

Aside from salaries, what can this company do to hold its best employees?

A long pause ensues while the audience considers the question.

The Quotation. Speakers can impart authority—and hence credibility before their audience—by beginning with a quotation from a recognized and admirable source.

> *John F. Kennedy could just as well have been talking about companies as countries when he said, "Ask not what your country can do for you. Ask what you can do for your country."*

The speaker goes on to discuss the importance of employee loyalty.

The Unusual Definition. Speeches should not begin with the grade-school opener, "*Webster's* dictionary defines my topic as follows . . ." Audiences have no particular interest in dictionary definitions. But you can grab attention, however, by altering common definitions in some way.

> *The word "profit" should be re-defined. It's no longer what a company earns after expenses. Rather, it's what the government lets a company keep.*

The Analogy. People find delight in making comparisons. If you suggest that pattern A is like pattern B in some way, the great majority of people will show some interest in discovering the points of similarity. Analogies are the speaker's way of drawing upon this quite human predilection.

An analogy is an extended comparison. The sudden sinking of the *Titanic,* for example, may be analogous to the sudden bankruptcy of a company hit by a crushing liability suit.

So long as analogies are not farfetched, audiences find them handy patterns for thinking about more complex matters.

> *The Pied Piper promised to charm the rats out of the village. And he kept his promise. But that same magic also had the power to steal away the children, each and every one.*

The speaker proceeds to compare the Pied Piper with an attractive government contract considered by the company. The contract brings relief from some problems, but may entail unexpected dilemmas later.

Developing the Long Presentation

After opening your longer presentation in an effective way, forecast your central concern and pattern of development. Audiences need a clear roadmap of where the speaker is headed, especially when the journey will be long.

Choose a pattern of development from Chapter 3 if you wish, or develop one of your own. Use the following checklist to guide your development of each stage in your argument:

1. Have you presented your point clearly?
2. Have you supported your point with interesting evidence, examples, and details?
3. Have you dealt with obvious objections to your point?

4. Have you shown the benefits of your point?
5. Have you summarized your point before moving on?

Like the short presentation, the long address usually has only one central concern, though often argued in three or more ways or stages. Speakers develop the long address not by casting their nets wider for more topics, but by digging deeper for substantial truths about a single topic.

Maintaining Interest in a Long Presentation

Even a highly gifted speaker must employ a variety of techniques to keep the interest of an audience during a speech lasting more than fifteen minutes. A tire industry leader put the problem in a humorous way: "In my business, the longer the 'spoke,' the greater the 'tire.'"

Consider using these interest-stimulators when delivering a long speech.

1. Use visual aids—slides, overhead projections, movie clips, or flip-charts—to spark interest. A hint: don't give away the interest value of your visual aid by using it too early or continuously throughout the speech. Often the presence of a slide projector in the room will give the audience patience to hear you out for several minutes. They know that you plan to show them pictures during the presentation; they're willing to wait for you.
2. Build to a climax in volume and emotion, then pause for dramatic effect.
3. Vary the content of your speech. If you are rehearsing facts and figures, follow with an entertaining story. If you are waxing philosophical for a time, follow with a down-to-earth, practical matter.
4. Move around. No law says that you have to remain behind a podium. High quality microphones now clip onto your clothing, allowing you to walk comfortably as you speak. Avoid pacing. Make a point, then take a few steps (a visual breather for your audience) and begin your next major point. When you want to strike a particularly intimate note with your audience, move toward them, as if speaking confidentially.
5. Build in "wake up" noises in the latter stages of your speech. Laughter always wakes up an audience. So does a distinct noise, like a clap of the hands. Such noises must relate to your content, of course, so as not to seem mere prods to renew attention.
6. Ask questions in your speech, then pause as if actually expecting answers. An audience that is thinking along with you, trying to answer your questions, cannot fall asleep on you.
7. Take risks by saying something a bit outrageous (but not offensive) in tone and content.

I've discussed the responsibilities of my position as chief executive officer of this company. I forgot to mention one reality of the job. I get lonesome. I need to see you all from time to time. I need to hear your ideas and to tell you mine.

8. Vary the kind and intensity of gestures you use. An audience tires quickly of any one movement repeated over and over. Consider beginning with rather modest gestures, becoming more and more communicative with your hands and body as your speech gains momentum.
9. Summarize the points you've made from time to time in the speech. A summary wakes up a sleepy listener, providing a chance to "catch up" and to make a new beginning in paying attention.
10. Tell your audience how much longer you plan to speak. When listeners know that the end is in sight, they perk up.

I see that I have less than five minutes remaining. Let me use that time to. . . .

The phrase, "In conclusion," serves the same function—"Wake up, listener! You only have one more chance to catch my message."

Concluding the Long Presentation

Conclude the longer presentation in any one of these ways or in one suggested for closing the short presentation.

The Visual Resolution. Especially if your presentation has begun with some stimulating or challenging visual display, conclude with a visual experience that somehow resolves the problems and issues posed in your speech.

For the past half hour we have seen the faces of starving children in India. Let me leave you, however, with a different vision (slide comes up). These, too, are children in India. Yes, they are well fed, well dressed, well groomed. That's their school in the background—the private school for the children of government officials. Until every child in India has a chance to look as healthy and happy as these children, we will not cease in our labors.

The Promise. As an alternative to calling the audience to action of some sort, the speaker can make a strong commitment in the form of a promise or pledge.

With your support, I promise a quick return to this company's historic policies of promotion within the ranks rather than hiring from outside for executive positions.

The Challenge. A shaving-lotion commercial used to show a sleepy male face being roundly slapped with aftershave. "Thanks, I needed that," was his familiar response. Speakers can try to verbally stun the audience at the end of the speech by means of a specific challenge, a bracing slap.

We cannot rely on political help to stop foreign incursions into our sector of the automobile market. Whether or not we survive—no, triumph—as a company depends on our combined creativity and hard work. To put it bluntly, your financial future and mine start this afternoon: are we willing to meet and beat the competition?

The Reflective Look Back. A speech full of challenges can gain persuasive power by looking back in its conclusion to how far we've come. You give the audience confidence that your proposed goals are attainable in the light of past accomplishments.

Yes, we face challenges in the 1980s and 1990s. But don't lose heart. Our challenges are tame compared to those of the day in 1939 when Mr. Millstead mortgaged his own home to meet company payroll; the day in 1952 when a fire burned the main factory to the ground; the days in 1974 when new environmental laws threatened to shut us down completely. We met the life-or-death challenges of those days. Surely we can meet the challenges we face now.

The Appeal to Emotion. Used appropriately, the appeal to emotion can send a crowd out of the room buzzing with excitement and zeal. Used awkwardly, emotional ploys can ruin an otherwise fine speech.

The key lies in the word, "appropriate." The emotions you project as a speaker and the emotions you ask for from your reader must be a natural outgrowth of the rest of the speech. You cannot, for example, lecture for forty minutes on technicalities of new tax laws and then suddenly plead for renewed, heartfelt dedication to the company and its goals.

The best emotional appeals occur after the speaker has made listeners feel important, strong, and sensitive to the needs of others. The audience can then afford to give the emotion asked by the speaker. An audience convinced of its weakness and vulnerability feels no strength to give emotion at all.

We've talked about relative risks and margins of safety in relation to the pharmaceuticals we produce. We've seen impressive statistics about the strides we've already made in preventing adverse drug reactions—only one user in a hundred, and so forth.

But stand with me by the hospital bed of that one patient experiencing an adverse drug reaction. Don't turn away from the suffering you see—the fright, the pain. That's the vision that keeps us working at our very highest level of commitment and skill. We want to remain the drug manufacturer that counts people, not numbers.

Following your extended presentation, the audience will probably applaud. It is customary to acknowledge their response by smiling and nodding in recognition. Remember not to yield to the temptation to add just a few extra remarks to such an appreciative audience.

Summary

1. Anxiety aroused by fear of public speaking can be reduced by focusing attention on the here and now.

2. Speeches of appreciation and introduction should be brief, sincere, and complimentary.
3. Luncheon and dinner addresses often involve an attention-getting opening, clearly defined points, and the judicious use of humor.
4. Business presentations are more formal than other short addresses and often make use of handouts and visual aids.
5. Longer presentations necessitate division into parts, frequent summations, and interest-keeping devices.

Questions for Discussion

1. What are the causes of anxiety or fear associated with public speaking?
2. There are some useful techniques for overcoming the fear of public speaking. What are they?
3. "It is vital to perform well when presenting a speech because in a very real way your listeners are judging your worth as a person rather than the credibility of your message." How would you attack or defend this attitude toward public speaking?
4. What are the features of the speech of appreciation or of introduction?
5. What are some common attention-getting openings for speeches?
6. What should you keep in mind when planning to use humor or jokes in your speech?
7. What speaking style is most effective for oral presentations?
8. What are the benefits and possible dangers of speaking from notes and manuscript?
9. If the audience seems well pleased with your speech, should you consider saying a few more words?
10. What are the five distinct qualities of an effective long speech?
11. Why do audiences appreciate a forecast of the main points you'll be covering in a longer presentation? Where should you place this "roadmap" in the speech?
12. What benefits and pitfalls do appeals to emotion in speeches suggest? What key should you keep in mind when appealing to your audience's emotions?
13. Is it a good idea to use visual aids continuously throughout an oral presentation? Explain your response.
14. What are "wake up noises"? How should they be used?
15. Why do direct questions help keep your audience's attention focused on your presentation?

Exercises

1. Attend a public speech given by a professional speaker. (Your college or university should sponsor many such appearances.) Note the particular strengths and weaknesses of this speaker. Report your observations to the class.

2. Interview your colleagues who have also given speeches and experienced common anxieties associated with public speaking. Share your own experiences with them. As a group, determine some effective ways to overcome anxiety. One good way is to identify friendly faces in the audience to whom you address your speech. For your next class speech, talk directly to some familiar group members and see if your confidence grows. Be sure to thank your colleagues for their help.

3. For an upcoming speech, devise an appropriate effective opening. Try out a variety of possibilities before deciding on your final choice.

4. If you have written out a manuscript of your upcoming speech, practice it using a tape recorder. First, read the speech into the recorder. Next, deliver the speech referring to your manuscript only when necessary. Play back the two versions, comparing your style of voice in each. Which delivery sounded more persuasive, and why?

5. To develop confidence in speaking without notes, practice giving impromptu speeches. Informally in a discussion group, develop and exchange possible topics for speeches with your colleagues. Each group member should then speak "off the cuff" for about five minutes on the topic of his or her choice. Based on the group's feedback, determine the effectiveness of your speaking skills.

6. One way to overcome the fear of public speaking is to focus on the here and now, resisting the temptation to ask yourself, "What if my listeners don't like my speech?" Practice focusing on the present moment by describing in detail your sensory perceptions. Right *now*, what do you see? hear? smell? taste? feel?

7. Write a short speech of appreciation thanking your company executives for awarding you $100 in recognition of your perfect attendance record. The speech will be delivered at an informal luncheon in your honor.

8. Your company, Datatron Systems, Inc., has decided to install a new medical insurance program. Although the fees to employees are reasonable—$35 a month for complete coverage of individual employees and their immediate families—the program will not cover their visits to private physicians. Instead they must see doctors at a medical network. Many employees have expressed their dissatisfaction with the proposed plan, arguing that they will be treated like objects on an assembly line, never seeing the same doctor twice. You have been assigned the task of convincing them to accept the proposal. Prepare a speech to be delivered at the next union meeting a week from today.

Communicating About Employment

PART FIVE

Barbara Quigley will graduate from a small but

prestigious business school next month. She hasn't worried about finding a job.

I'm a firm believer in specialization—don't do something someone else can do better. Take job searching, for example. I know nothing about it. None of my courses prepared me for it in any way.

Therefore, I'm leaving the job search to people who are trained in such things. Luckily, there's an agency downtown called Contacts Unlimited that can prepare my résumé, have it professionally printed, and arrange job interviews for me. I'm not sure what their fee is yet, but I'm sure it's worth every cent. Just having my résumé prepared by someone else is a load off my mind. I didn't really know what to include or not include.

What do you foresee in Barbara's immediate future—a job or disappointment? Can job seekers opt out of the process of preparing résumés, letters, and applications? Can such work be left to "capable professionals"?

The

Job Search

17

LEARNING OBJECTIVES

To evaluate the services of commercial employment agencies

To develop a personal strategy for the job search

To locate and create job leads

To use public and college job location services

In questioning more than a score of chief executive officers of major corporations about their own writing attitudes and experiences, we asked "Do you recall a particular writing task that changed the course of your career?"

A few recalled particular letters, reports, and proposals that had marked career turning points. But most, interestingly, named forms of career writing:

> *I spent a whole day composing a bright, direct letter to accompany my résumé. That letter, along with good luck, started me on my way.*
>
> *The time and effort I spent on my résumé probably made the single largest contribution to my initial career opportunities.*
>
> *Believe it or not, the most important piece of writing I did at the beginning of my career was two paragraphs long: the brief essay I had to write as part of my job application. I took time to do it right and received praise—and a job—from those who interviewed me.*

Not all of us "do it right" when it comes to career writing. The task of writing a good application and résumé probably comes just at the most hectic and exhilarating period of our lives—the spring of graduation and the summer of job-hunting. Though we have written hundreds of pages during our college careers, we often run out of time and words for the written documents that, more than any other, start us on our way to success.

ALL THAT FREE ADVICE

Sometimes we take one of the shortcuts to application and résumé writing, paying our $45 or so for a perfunctory half-hour conference with a "résumé specialist," who promises to turn out a dynamite document revealing us in the best light possible.

The résumé we receive may be attractive, but it may also contain substantive errors and misstatements. We find ourselves muttering, "I graduated in 1983, not 1982—and my major was Accounting, not Accounts. That summer job at McDonald's should really not be called 'food management engineering' on my résumé." In other words, we may find ourselves—after considerable expense—stuck with a document that will cause us embarrassment and moments of explanation during interviews.

The avalanche of chatty articles in popular magazines, all titled approximately, "Make a Splash with Your Résumé" also provide questionable guidance at times.

Some recommend artsy-craftsy graphics, some extol the importance of an "action photograph." Some belittle traditional headings like "Education" and "Work Experience" as old hat, while others urge experimentation with colored papers and inks.

Before sending off a mauve résumé, however, take a moment to check the qualifications of the authors of such "filler" articles. Again and again, we meet the same sort of author: a free-lance writer involved in sending out his or her own résumé.

Where can you find sound, proven advice to guide the writing of some of the most important words you'll ever put on paper? One good place is the Association of Business Communication's study titled, "A Survey of the Chief Personnel Officers in the 500 Largest Corporations in the United States to Determine Their Preference in Job Application Letters and Personal Résumés." The information and advice found in this chapter are largely based on the wealth of data contained in that landmark study. For good measure, twenty personnel directors of large and small corporations in several states were personally interviewed.

Their answers, contained in the career writing advice and examples of this chapter, may surprise you. Professionals, it turns out, consider a lot of the splashy suggestions of popular writers to be just plain belly flops.

FINDING THE JOB

Our training, interests, and abilities determine the general field of our job search. But in this high-tech age, in which jobs and job descriptions change almost monthly, few of us can know with any precision exactly what job we seek. The very process of job hunting may help us to decide on a career. A finance major, of course, rarely strays into a career as a surgeon. But finance majors often do find themselves in a wide variety of creative, lucrative positions that simply can't be predicted. One successful job seeker put it this

FIGURE 17-1

Record Card for Job Search

Position _____ Date _____
Company _____
Address _____
_____
Phone _____
Contact name _____
Action taken _____ (date)
Response received _____ (date)
_____
Notes:

way: "I looked at the same little section in the Help Wanted ads every week. There were never more than two, maybe three ads for the position I sought. But holding those pounds and pounds of Help Wanted pages made me think, I qualify for more of these thousands of jobs than just the two or three I've been looking at. I just needed to broaden my horizons."

Locating and Creating Job Leads

Establish a system of record keeping for your job search. You can, for example, keep a file of 3 x 5 cards modeled after the card shown in Figure 17-1. Such a file will help to prevent duplication of effort and embarrassing mistakes. You may, at any one time, have as many as fifty résumés circulating in the professional world. A file keeps your many fishing lines from becoming tangled.

Once you have set up a system, consider various job sources.

Tips and Introductions from Friends

Personal referrals continue to work magic for job seekers. Managers who have no time at all for interviewing find a few minutes to see you, all because "Frank" or "Sue" called to say how bright you were. The brief interview later turns into a job offer. But how does one find the Franks and Sues, who in turn know the managers and supervisors and vice-presidents? One way is to let every one of your friends and acquaintances know that you are looking for a job. Speak freely about the broad range of your interests. Ask friends and acquaintances to let you know if they hear of an opening, or of a pending resignation or retirement, in your field.

Some job seekers have personal business cards printed up for this purpose. While friends may have your phone number and address, the large number of casual acquaintances in your life may not. If they have your card, they can let you know when a job possibility arises.

Career Opportunities with Former Employers

Review career opportunities in companies for whom you have worked part-time or during the summer. While your temporary employment may have placed you at the service end of a corporation's business—serving food, inventorying materials, shipping orders—you should not overlook the upper level career possibilities there. Enough of the Horatio Alger myth still survives in American business for companies to find pride in bringing someone along from the bottom of the ladder. Your experience even in the most mundane company responsibility may give you an important step up over the competition when it comes time for selecting management trainees. The company knows you, and you know the company's operation in a practical way.

Visit Personnel Offices

A stop at a company's personnel office to inquire about job openings and to pick up application packets may prove productive. Personnel officers do not mind seeing you as an uninvited visitor so long as you do not press them for what they cannot provide: instant evaluations of your chances for a job, definitive lists of what positions are available in the company, or a willingness to interview you.

Your purpose in visiting the personnel office of a company is simply to express your interest in any openings they have, and to pick up any materials they routinely give away to interested job seekers. This process, of course, could be accomplished by mail, with less effort on your part. But that's just the point: by visiting for just a moment or two in person, you show more effort than the average job seeker. Secretaries in the office and perhaps the personnel director see your face, shake your hand. Later, when your résumé arrives for review, they nod "Oh, I remember . . .''

While visiting the personnel office, find out (and jot down the exact spelling) of the personnel director's name, or any other company official with whom you plan to correspond. Record these names in your file. Mail addressed to a named person usually gets opened and read by that person. Mail addressed to a title or office (Personnel Director or Personnel Office) usually is opened and read by a secretary.

Your presence on the spot, so to speak, has an additional advantage. Many job seekers have literally walked into a job on their first visit to a personnel office. These happy coincidences happen often enough to warrant your personal visit to companies within driving range of your home. The crucial key, again, is not to ask for too much.

College Placement Services

Make use of your college's placement services. Participate in any workshops in interviewing skills, résumé preparation, and application procedures they may offer.

Companies seeking new employees in your area work closely with the campus placement office. They often send representatives to your campus to interview prospective employees. Sign up for such interviews.

Find out if your college department maintains a file of help-wanted notices from business and industry. Departments such as Marketing, Finance, Accounting, and Management frequently receive invitations from local companies to send graduates for interviews. These notices sometimes are posted for students to see, but too often are simply filed.

The College Placement Annual

This volume every year lists more than 1,000 employers who are seeking entry level employees. For many of these companies, the *Annual* contains specific job descriptions, salary ranges, and information on company projects and policies. Your library or college placement office will have the latest edition; if not, the *Annual* can be purchased at major bookstores in the early spring of each year.

Newspaper, Journal, and Magazine Help Wanted Ads

These advertisements can be read by anyone but require a bit of business savvy to be fully understood. The most common ads are *company advertisements* in which the name and address of the company are clearly stated, sometimes accompanied by a contact name (''Ms. Barker'') for those interested in making application.

Company Ad

> LANGSFORD MEDICAL CO., INC., an industry leader in hospital and doctor supply, seeks an Inventory Analyst. Experience in computer inventory systems required, with medical knowledge helpful. Salary commensurate with experience. Top benefits, potential advancement. Apply to Box 4563, Willowborough, New Hampshire 39574

Also common are *agency ads* placed by private employment agencies that receive percentages of the salaries of employees they ''place.'' Agency ads typically describe positions in more glowing terms than company ads: ''Outstanding opportunity . . . unlimited potential . . . truly exceptional benefits package.'' Respond to agency ads with your eyes wide open.

Agency Ad

> READY TO TAKE CHARGE?
> Great opportunity for motivated person with sales background to head up regional commission sales group. Salary plus bonus incentives. Some travel. Call Gil Branch, 592-3942. Equal Opportunity Employer.

Job seekers also encounter *blind ads,* some placed by the country's most prestigious corporations and some placed by fly-by-night scoundrels. A typical blind ad does not specify a company, a location, or an agency.

Blind Ad #1

> National company seeks reliable management trainees for expansion territory in Sun Belt. Knowledge of mass marketing techniques essential, college degree optional depending on experience. Send resume to Drawer 92, *Los Angeles Times.*

Companies run blind ads for a number of reasons. Often they don't want their present employees to know that supervisory staff is being hired from the "outside." The company may not want its competitors to know about expansion plans or regional campaigns. Perhaps the company is protecting its public image by disguising the fact that it needs qualified personnel immediately. Hospitals, for example, often run blind ads when they seek nurses, administrators, and support personnel.

A blind ad can be used to snare unwary job seekers. What realities do you suppose lie behind blind ad #2?

Blind Ad #2

> Don't read on unless you're determined to make at least $60,000 this year, and twice that amount next year. We're seeking men and women who fit in socially, who present themselves well, who like to set and meet their own goals. We provide full training. Write to Box 523, *New York Times,* for an appointment with Mr. Blackley.

Upon investigation, a job seeker would discover (after investment of time and energy) that the ad was placed by Mr. Blackley himself, who—virtually out of a briefcase—runs a business called "Psychonetics." He meets you in the lounge of the Sheraton hotel (since he lacks an office) and proceeds with his pitch. For $2500, he'll let you in on the ground floor of the greatest thing since sliced bread. "Psychonetics" teaches professional people to unleash their hidden psychic strengths, thereby mastering those around them. Your job? To offer "Psychonetics" franchises to others, on a commission basis. Mr. Blackley estimates that you could easily make $60,000 your first year.

Beware of blind ads. If you respond to them, judge your first contact (whether a letter or phone call) with the advertiser with care. At the first sign of psychonetic falderall in any of its thousands of guises, set your course back to your primary goal: finding a satisfying career.

Job-Seeker Ads

Some job seekers place ads on their own in such business publications as *Wall Street Journal, Business Week,* and large urban newspapers. While these ads are usually quite expensive, they occasionally bring worthwhile responses. Look over such ads in business newspapers and trade journals. Before advertising yourself, you may want to call one of the advertisers to ask if the results justified the investment.

Public Agency Ads

Public agencies (usually listed under *employment* in the white or yellow pages of your phone directory) provide free job listings. These often pertain to temporary or day-labor positions. No stone, however, should go unturned, especially if you can determine by a single phone call if any public agency listings seem attractive to you.

Summary

1. The time and energy spent on career writing in its various forms can be crucial in obtaining jobs and promotions.
2. Commercial employment agencies should be evaluated with care before one's career search is given over to them.
3. Friends, former employers, newspapers, college placement services, directories and other sources all can produce job leads.
4. Blind advertisements for jobs should be scrutinized with special care. While many such ads are legitimate, others are only disguised forms of promotion.

Questions for Discussion

1. In what ways can good writing skills aid job seekers?
2. Who is "the résumé specialist"?
3. Where can you find sound, proven advice to guide your career writing?
4. How do professionals commonly view the splashy suggestions given by job-search specialists?
5. How might the very process of job hunting help you to decide on a career?
6. What are the benefits of keeping a job-search file?
7. In what ways can a personal referral help your efforts to gain employment?
8. What advantage is there in applying for a job with a company for whom you have worked part-time?
9. Is it a good practice to pay brief visits to company personnel offices when pursuing leads for jobs?
10. What information should you be sure to gather on your visit to a personnel office? Why?

11. How can college placement services help your job search?
12. What is *The College Placement Annual?*
13. Are all "help wanted" ads useful resources for the serious job seeker?
14. Why might a company run a "blind ad"?
15. How should you respond to a blind ad?

Exercises

1. Start a job-search file by listing companies or businesses with whom you would like to gain employment. Gather the relevant information on these companies, following the guidelines offered elsewhere in this chapter. How many prospective employers have you located? Which seem most appealing?

2. Write a letter asking an employer or professor for a letter of recommendation. Consider your tone and persuasive strategy when making the request. Remember, the way in which you ask for a recommendation might affect the recommendation itself.

3. Write a contact letter to the personnel director at a company with whom you have worked part-time, requesting information about possible full-time employment at a later date. Place the director's response in your job-search file.

4. Visit the personnel offices of a company for whom you would like to work. Assume that you are not under great pressure to find a job at present, so you should be able to greet the office staff without feeling that you must walk out with a job. Simply introduce yourself and leave a résumé for consideration. Make sure that you write down the personnel director's name for inclusion in your job-search file. Later, record the experience and repeat this procedure at several attractive companies. Compare visits.

5. Visit the college placement service office at your college or university. If the office keeps placement files, start one. Record your impressions and place any relevant information you gather in your job-search file.

6. Familiarize yourself with *The College Placement Annual,* available at your college career development center or library. What are the strengths and weaknesses of this annual?

7. Leaf through the "help wanted" ads of the Sunday edition of a major newspaper in your area. Which ads seem like good leads? Which make you skeptical? Why?

8. Interview a friend or family member who holds an attractive job. Find out how difficult the job was to acquire. How long did your subject search for the job? How many applications did he or she send out? How many interviews did he or she carry out?

Answers to A Quick Quiz for the Job Candidate: **1.** False. **2.** False. **3.** False. **4.** True. **5.** True. **6.** False. **7.** False.

Roberta York is personnel director for an aerospace company. She reviews advertised

positions and participates in initial screening for many positions.

My husband says that I should write a book on résumés. I've told him so many stories over the years about unusual résumés that have crossed my desk.

If I were to write such a book, which I probably never will, the first chapter would be titled "Expectations." I think that job seekers really expect me to take ten or fifteen minutes to read a résumé. The first step in their education on the résumé would be to face the fact that big decisions—whether to interview them, for example—are often made within ten or fifteen seconds of reading.

Chapter Two would be called "Save My Eyes." I've seen (and permanently filed) hundreds of résumés that have the "more is good" philosophy. Every square centimeter of the page is crammed with words, words, words. A reviewer literally can't see the forest for the trees.

Do Roberta's comments surprise you? Do you think she is atypical or less than conscientious as a person involved in the hiring process? How can your documents be designed to succeed within the limited time span that Roberta mentions?

Writing

About Employment

18

LEARNING OBJECTIVES

To write an effective application letter

To develop a clear, attractive and complete résumé

To write thank-you letters for interviews

To write letters of job acceptance, refusal, and postponement

To write effective letters of recommendation

It is no accident that so many aspects of the job search and application process involve writing. What better way to assess the language skills of a prospective applicant than to ask him or her to generate letters of application, résumés, application essays, and other forms of written communication? Those whose skills are deficient will reveal their weaknesses by their writing or, more often, will seek other work, requiring fewer word skills.

But let's not concentrate on those who drop out. What about you? Are you able to sell yourself as a valuable addition to a company's work force? Are you able to find just the right words to describe yourself and your potential in an application letter and résumé? Of course you can.

THE APPLICATION LETTER

The personnel directors of *Fortune* 500 companies (referred to in the ABCA study earlier) indicated strong preference for an initial contact in writing from the job seeker. That preference makes sense. Without your résumé before them, what can company representatives say to you? Any encouragement or commitments they do make prior to seeing your written application may have to be taken back, once your record lies open.

Begin the application process, therefore, not with a telephone call but with an application letter accompanied by a résumé.

By convention, letters of application are attached by paperclip to the résumé. This time, convention serves a useful function. Often your letter of application will be removed from your résumé before the latter document is sent through the company for review. If the letter had been stapled to the résumé, there is a good chance that—rip—your résumé will go forth to decision-makers missing its upper-right corner. The paper clip holds your application package together on the personnel director's desk, yet allows easy separation for other readers or for photocopying.

Letters of application, like other business letters, are typed on 8 1/2 by 11″ white or off-white bond paper. Beware of trendy pastel shades of stationery. When your materials are photocopied by the company, such stationery does not reproduce in legible form.

The Invited Application Letter

An *invited* application letter (one in response to a company advertisement) opens by making reference to the position described in the ad and where the ad was seen. See the letter in Figure 18-1, for example.

Note that the letter of application typically has three parts:

1. Clear response to a clear invitation. The invitation is mentioned in case the company has several job openings advertised in various places.
2. Reference to the attached résumé, with a highlight or two pointed out in a polite way.
3. Appeal for an interview, with contact address and phone number.

FIGURE 18-1

Invited Letter of Application

```
                                    4857 Birch Road, Apt. 3
                                    Glenview, IL  59684
                                    August 9, 198_

        Ms. Gloria Hrief
        Personnel Director
        Benway Manufacturing, Inc.
        400 Railway Center Dr.
        Glenview, IL  59684

        Dear Ms. Hrief:

            As a June graduate in Accounting from Illinois State
        University, I am delighted to answer your advertisement
        (Register, August 8) for an entry level accountant in your
        farm equipment division.

            You may be interested not only in my accounting
        preparation and experience, as described in the enclosed
        resume, but also in my summer employment driving Benway
        tractors on my uncle's farm.

            If my application merits an interview for this position
        or another in your company, please write or call (397-3948).
        I look forward to meeting you.

                                    Sincerely,

                                    Robert Collins

                                    Robert Collins
```

FIGURE 18-2

Uninvited Letter of Application

247 Levitt Street
Walston, Alabama 66644
June 2, 198_

Mr. Herbert Reid
Manager, Software Systems
ATC Autonetics
577 First Street
Walston, Alabama 66644

Dear Mr. Reid:

   From reading Byte magazine, I've noticed rapid
expansion during the last few months in ATC software
products. If your need for state-of-the-art software
specialists is also expanding, I hope my enclosed resume
will interest you.

   While I have worked extensively in systems using
FORTRAN 77, COBOL, and various forms of BASIC, my Senior
project was done in LISP--a language I find full of
potential for ATC's most interesting work in artificial
intelligence.

   If an interview is possible, I will be pleased to come
to your office when you wish. In any case, I hope we will
find occasion to compare notes on the hi-tech advances that
interest us both.

                                   Sincerely,

                                   Brenda Noel

                                   Brenda Noel

                                   Telephone: 397-6784

> Does the business world care about the level of your writing skills?
> Listen to Paul Dillingham, vice-president of the Coca-Cola Company:
>
> *In today's complex society, the ability to communicate effectively is essential. I am appalled at the number of graduates coming out of our universities in recent years who cannot compose a simple, readable letter. I recently saw an application for employment by a college graduate who neglected to answer a number of important questions on the form. Surely he will have difficulty finding a job.*

Application letters, according to personnel directors, should be short and to the point. The reader is eager to get on to the résumé where your story will be told in close detail.

The Uninvited Application Letter

An *uninvited* letter of application requires a more creative opening. You are writing, after all, to a company official who has not indicated to you that a job is even open. You begin, therefore, by breaking the ice, as shown in the letter in Figure 18-2.

The uninvited application letter moves immediately to the "you" perspective—something in the first sentence that interests or involves the reader. True, you are graduating soon. True, you are seeking a job. True, you may do good work. But none of these statements is particularly interesting to the reader who has not even asked you to knock on his or her door.

The following are some ways of beginning with the "you" perspective:

- Mention a common name, perhaps a professor at your university who may have put you in contact with the reader.
- Mention common professional interests or products.
- Mention developments in the company that you have observed, either from your reading or from your experience with company products or services.
- Express appreciation for the moment or two of the reader's time necessary to consider your qualifications.

The letter of application can demonstrate to the reader that you are a polite, literate, and persuasive person. The letter should not try to outdo or redo the résumé itself by rehearsing a number of work experiences or accomplishments. Select one or two of your most impressive or interesting achievements, and weave them smoothly into the course of the application letter so as not to appear to brag.

In the final paragraph of the uninvited letter of application, consider leaving the door open for something less than a job interview. If a company has no openings at the moment, the manager may still wish to make your acquaintance with an eye toward future openings. Make it clear that you would be happy to visit with him or her even though there may be no openings at present.

THE RÉSUMÉ

As treated here, the mailed résumé always is accompanied by a letter of application. Handbooks on business writing do occasionally mention a catchall one-page "application résumé" that supposedly makes the writing of a letter unnecessary. But personnel managers make clear that they look for a traditional résumé accompanied by an application letter. They feel that briefer combinations of the two traditional documents end up slighting the applicant's record by omitting information for the sake of space. The most important guidelines for the job application process can be summed up in the Ten Rules of the Résumé:

1. Always accompany a mailed résumé with a letter of application.

2. Keep the résumé to one page if possible, two if necessary, and three never.

Decision-makers, including personnel administrators, supervisors, and managers, will give your résumé perhaps 15 to 20 seconds of their time before deciding—with finality—whether you're worth a second, more intensive look at a later time. Résumés, therefore, must make their point quickly, preferably all in one glance at one page.

3. Type flawlessly.

Résumés have no room for misspellings, erasures, or grammar or punctuation errors. Personnel directors concur that little mistakes on such a crucial personal document are probably the tip of the iceberg, suggesting the kind of mistakes a potential employee will make on company projects. Once you have written your résumé, your mistakes may be almost invisible to you. Ask a friend or professor to proofread your work before distributing it to employers.

4. Practice "at-a-glance" appeal.

Résumés, like business letters, strive for a "look" in the first few seconds of perception by the reader. Notice in the before and after illustrations shown in Figure 18-3 how a balanced, well-designed résumé invites the reader's attention and approval.

FIGURE 18-3

Contrasts in Résumé Appeal

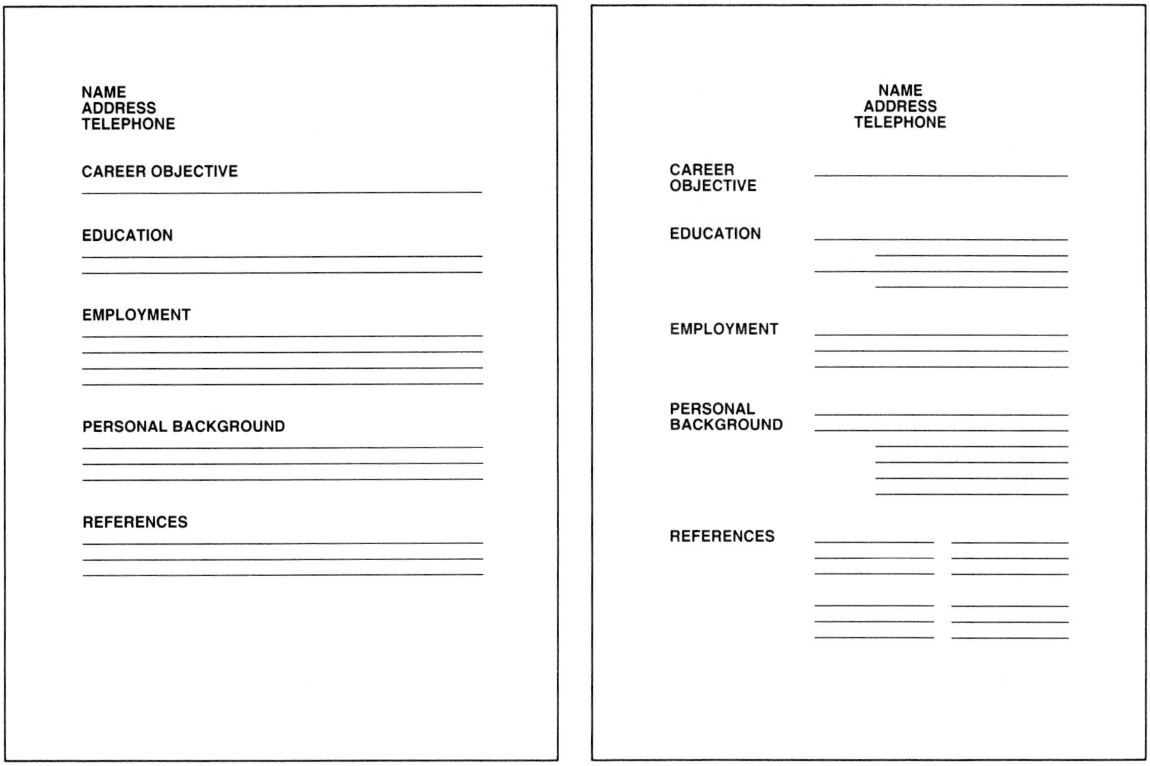

Cramped, hard to read

At-a-glance readability

Here are some techniques used to create résumés with at-a-glance appeal:

- Make headings parallel in meaning also parallel on the page.
- Surround important headings with white space.
- Allow the eye to read by installments (separate sections of print), not in large dense blocks.
- Use capitals with discretion for special emphasis.
- Use lines and conservative graphic symbols (bullets, asterisks, dashes) to unify and organize the résumé.

5. Don't seem bizarre.

Weigh carefully the relative merits of extreme creativity—the sort that produces a highly unusual résumé that stands apart from traditional forms.

By a substantial majority, personnel directors favor a crisp, well-designed traditional résumé over a flamboyant, albeit creative résumé.

This advice, of course, must be applied with discretion. Some professions, such as graphic design, photography, interior decoration, and so forth, may well expect résumés to give some hint of the applicant's creative flair. Financial and managerial businesses, by contrast, often prefer job applicants to demonstrate their ability to *fit in* (the traditional approach to the résumé) before showing their ability to *stand out* (the creative résumé). Right or wrong, such businesses probably fear hiring a "kook." The creative résumé that may look bright, refreshing and avant-garde to you in your college environment may not work well crossing a busy personnel manager's desk at 4:30 on a particularly hectic Thursday afternoon.

6. Use judgment in deciding whether to include your picture on your résumé.

In general, personnel directors do not favor pictures on résumés. Pictures, of course, cannot be required of applicants because of protections provided in Affirmative Action laws. When applicants voluntarily include pictures, many personnel directors urge these guidelines:

- Have a print shop offset or photocopy the picture onto the paper of your résumé itself. Do not try to tape, staple, or paper-clip a photo to the résumé. Such pictures inevitably become separated from their résumé. Standard size for résumé pictures is 2 x 3 (passport size).
- Place your picture in a subordinate place on the résumé page so that it does not become the focus of attention.

The great majority of résumés do not make use of pictures. To determine whether your picture adds to the persuasiveness of your résumé, show a version of the résumé with and without a picture to several friends, business men and women, and your professors. Then follow your own judgment.

7. Emphasize four crucial elements: *name and address, career objective, education,* and *employment experience.*

Other elements may be included, but these four stand out bold and clear within the first few seconds of reading.

8. Choose the form of the résumé that fits you best.

Your choices come down to two: the chronological résumé and the functional résumé. As explained in the following pages, the chronological résumé (see Figure 18-4) organizes your experience according to years. If you have quite a bit of education but not a great deal of work experience, the chronological résumé allows you to highlight your academic work.

The functional résumé (see Figure 18-5) suits those who have proven their abilities through years of professional activity. It groups work experiences under two to four (seldom more) major abilities you have demonstrated over the years.

9. Personalize the résumé if possible.

Companies are no more fond of receiving a standard-issue résumé from you than friends like to receive a mimeographed letter. Especially if the company plans to invest many thousands of dollars in your salary and training, it has a right to expect you to adjust the facts and assertions on one sheet of paper, your résumé, to suit the needs of the job you seek.

This process of adjustment, of course, is easier said than done. Writing one good résumé may take several days from start to finish—and the thought of writing a separate résumé for each job lead seems wearying.

There is a technique, however, for personalizing your résumés without the burden of restructuring and retyping. Step-by-step, it works like this:

1. Prepare your résumé on a carbon ribbon typewriter. Type in all those categories of information that will not change from application to application. These categories may include Education, Personal Background, References, and so forth. Leave other categories such as Career Objective and Work Experience partially or completely blank.
2. Have your résumé, including the omitted portions, offset printed (about 10 cents per copy) or photocopied on good quality paper, using a high resolution copy machine.
3. When it comes time to apply for a given position, roll the printed résumé into the *same* carbon ribbon typewriter you used to create it in the first place. Carefully line up your margins and type line with the print on the résumé. Now you are ready to add a description of your career objective personalized to the business opportunity at hand. You will be surprised to see that the portion you type is virtually indistinguishable from the letters printed by an offset or a high quality copy machine. If you wish, you can make copies of your "filled-in" version of the résumé to send out.

General, abstract version

```
CAREER OBJECTIVE:
Restaurant management, with eventual progress into corporate
responsibilities
```

Personalized version

```
CAREER OBJECTIVE:
Begin as a management trainee in Auntie's Kitchen chain, and
progress with experience to Franchise Representative
```

Businesses, like people, love to see their own names and interests in print. Satisfy that need by personalizing your résumé in any way possible.

You may consider mentioning the company name or personnel director's name in a closing sentence of goodwill and availability, as illustrated in Figure 18-4. You may also want to custom tailor your employment experiences to suit the needs of each employer from whom you seek work.

---

10. Create your résumé like an artist, not a photographer.

Your résumé should select those qualities that represent you at your highest potential—what you plan to be—instead of trying to state all the details of the what you have been. An oil painting may be said to be true to life even though it does not record all the imperfections recorded in a Polaroid picture. So your résumé should create a true version of you, but need not catalog every twist and turn of your life.

Consider leaving out such extraneous matters as these:

- A brief job that has little to do with your application
- Personal facts that don't concern your employer
- Insignificant responsibilities listed under particular jobs
- College affiliations, memberships, societies, and sports teams that go beyond making the point that you are a social, likable, and active person

We can now examine the two most useful résumés in close detail.

The Chronological Résumé

Place your name, usually in capital letters, at the top of the résumé, followed by your mailing address and telephone number. Note that your name is usually centered for eye-catching emphasis (Figure 18-4).

A special note about your telephone: if you are regularly away from your phone during business hours and have no answering machine or service, identify two numbers at the top of the résumé—your home number and a message number where the employer can be sure to reach someone during business hours. Probably thousands of job offers are lost each year because employers (who hate to write letters) have no luck reaching job applicants by telephone.

Stating Your Career Objective. In a prominent heading, type CAREER OBJECTIVE or CAREER GOAL. If you want to state more than one goal, type this head in the plural.

Applicants often agonize over this brief statement of objective. They hesitate to state too grand a goal (company president) for fear of being laughed at; they hesitate to state too limited a goal (grocery checker) for fear of seeming without ambition.

Resolve this problem by stating a two-part objective:

CAREER OBJECTIVE:
Beginning as a salesperson, I want to progress with
experience to supervisory work on a regional level.

```
CAREER OBJECTIVE:
In the short term, client portfolio analysis, evaluation,
and recommendation; in the long term, management of a
pension fund trust
```

By such "short-term, long-term" statements, you have the best of both worlds. You indicate to your reader that you are realistic about entry level positions, but that you also have aspirations in mind for more lofty goals.

The career objective of the résumé can easily be personalized on each résumé you send out.

```
CAREER OBJECTIVE:
To begin in Henderson and Schmidt's Accounting division;
with experience and further education, to supervise tax
analysis and planning for major corporate clients
```

```
CAREER OBJECTIVE:
To learn Northwest Bank's operations in the management
training program; later, to work in a supervisory capacity
in Northwest Bank's real estate loan sector
```

If you cannot obtain specific information about the titles and hierarchies of job positions within a company, write more general objectives.

```
CAREER OBJECTIVE:
To work in cash flow management and economic analysis, with
growing managerial responsiblity
```

Describing Your Education. Begin by listing your most recent degree, then other degrees and significant periods of academic work.

```
B.A. in Economics, University of Pennsylvania, 1983
A.A., Windsor College, 1980
Certificates of Participation in two National Science
   Foundation Summer Seminars:
   "Solar Energy Alternatives," University of California
      at Davis, 1981
   "Geothermal Resources and Their Applications," Harvard
      University, 1982
```

You may choose to group information pertaining to one degree beneath that degree before moving on.

```
B.A. in Economics, University of Pennsylvania, 1983
   Senior thesis: "A Comparative Analysis of Coin— vs.
   Ticket—System Mass Transit Programs"
```

Be careful, though, that the information you list does not interfere with your résumé's "at-a-glance" appeal. Your busy reader will not want to wade through pages of documentation, no matter how impressive.

If you are sending out your résumé before receiving a degree, do not list the degree as a *fait accompli*. Instead, consider ways of gaining the force of the degree on your résumé without bending the truth.

```
Candidate for B.A. in Finance, University of Texas.  Degree
    expected  June, 1987.
```
(or)
```
I have completed all but 12 units required for the B.A. in
    Business Administration, University of Southern
    California.  Degree expected June, 1987.
```

In general, do not list high school or academy diplomas on your résumé.

Sometimes you may wish to elaborate upon your educational experience, perhaps to compensate for limited work experience. In that case, create meaningful subcategories for "EDUCATION."

```
Degrees
Pertinent Coursework
Awards and Scholarships
Publications
Future Educational Plans
```

In listing pertinent courses, do not try to repeat the entire transcript of your college work. List six to ten particularly relevant courses by title (and professor, if his or her prominence will help your cause).

```
Pertinent Courses

Advanced Macroeconomic Analysis
Principles of Economic Policy
Economics of Public Finance
Econometrics
Models and Economic Forecasts
Benefit-cost Analysis
Advanced Business Writing
    Cumulative G.P.A 3.46 on 4-point scale
```
(or)
```
    G.P.A. in Major, 3.8 or 4-point scale, while working 20
    hours per week to pay for college expenses
```

While few employers hire on the basis of college grades alone, you should not hesitate to put down a good G.P.A. on your résumé. The brief explanation that you worked while achieving your good grades also impresses some employers.

Listing Awards and Scholarships. You need not list awards and scholarships in chronological order. Place those items first that will be most meaningful and impressive to your reader. If you won a scholarship to college at the end of your high-school years, list the scholarship by name and date.

Awards and Scholarships

Outstanding First-year Student, School of Business, 1981
Chevron Scholarship, 1982-83
Dean's List, 1980-1984
Rotary Club Tuition Award, 1979

Listing Publications. Be sure to list any writing you have done for college newspapers, newsletters, or student society publications. Employers will value these listings as a sign that you write well—no matter what the prestige level of the publication in which your writing appeared.

Publications

"Summer Internships in Business," Management Society
    Newsletter (Lawlor College), February, 1983
"A Business Major Looks at Career Opportunites," Lawlor
    College Clarion, May 6, 1983

Before concluding their college careers, students are well advised to take the initiative in submitting articles to campus and trade publications. Several hundred such journals and magazines are listed in *Writer's Market* each year. As established business writers know, many fine articles have grown out of well-written college term papers and case studies.

Mentioning Future Educational Plans. While this category remains optional on your résumé, you should consider its advantages. Your employer has every reason to be even more interested in your future than in your past (the traditional emphasis of the résumé). If you plan to acquire a new business skill, master another language, or work toward advanced degrees, why not say so?

Future Education Plans

I have begun taking graduate courses toward my M.B.A. at
Occidental College.

Describing Your Employment History. Begin by listing your most recent work experience, then previous jobs. When your job had a title (Night Manager), use it. If your job had no title, feel free to name the job within the bounds of truth (a recreation job might be titled "Swimming Instructor," but not "Nautical Locomotion Consultant").

EMPLOYMENT (also called employment experience, work
  experience, employment background, or experience)

1983 Accounting Intern, Bliss and Wethers, Accountants,
      Boulder, Colorado (Jan.-May, part-time)
1982 Night Manager, Cleaver Restaurant
1981 Assembly Line Supervisor, Jay-Ray Cosmetics
1980 Assembly Line Worker, Jay-Ray Cosmetics

If your employment has been steady year by year, emphasize that fact by placing the date first, as illustrated in Figure 18-4. If, on the other hand, you have had long employment gaps, give the dates less emphasis by placing them after the job listing.

```
EMPLOYMENT

        Accounting Intern, Bliss and Wethers, Accountants,
            Boulder, Colorado. Jan.-May, 1983 (part-time)
        Night Manager, Cleaver Restaurant, 1982
```

You do not have to account for each and every month of your employed life on such a list. Employers, too, want to get to the heart of the matter: what *significant* experiences have you had?

If you have had virtually no paid work experience at all, list volunteer experiences related to business concerns. Perhaps you have helped to manage the financial affairs of a club at school or a church organization.

Under no circumstances should you simply skip the EMPLOYMENT section of your résumé. Employers will look for this category, even if it has only one work item listed under it.

Job titles alone often fail to give a clear picture of your employment background. You can use the subcategory, "Responsibilities," to list significant aspects of the job.

```
EMPLOYMENT

Accounting Intern, Bliss and Wethers, Accountants, Boulder,
    Colorado. Jan.-May, 1983 (part-time)

    Responsibilities: worked under the supervision
        of a senior accountant in preparing
        evaluations and audits; particularly
        enjoyed participating in the writing of
        financial analyses

Night Manager, Cleaver Restaurant, 1982

    Responsibilities: supervised staff of nine;
        managed cash and ordering of provisions;
        participated in hiring interviews
```

In listing your responsibilities (not "duties"), choose active verbs: supervised, oversaw, managed, headed, assisted, helped, and so forth. To give your job a spark of life, occasionally tell how you *felt* about what you did.

```
    enjoyed meeting clients
(or)
    liked preparing press releases
```

Take care not to overstate the titles or responsibilities of past positions. Remember that you are writing for a street-wise business audience not prone to gullibility. They don't expect you to have the corporate background of a CEO.

Once you have listed your name and address, career objective, education, and employment, the essential business of your résumé is concluded. You now have a chance to reveal yourself a bit more fully as a person, using the optional section called *personal background* or *personal data*.

Providing Personal Background. Don't feel awkward mentioning aspects of your life that seem to have little to do with business. Your employer needs to know if you are going to fit in as a working partner. Your brief details in *personal background* can reassure the employer that you can cope successfully with a world of people, not just machines. You must judge each of the following items, however, by whether they help or hurt your job search.

1. Age—Will your chances of employment be better if your employer knows how old you are?
2. Marriage and Children—Does the job you seek require a "family" man or woman? Will your employer make assumptions about your stability or job loyalty based on your family status?
3. Health—Will an employer appreciate your assurance that your health is "excellent"?
4. Hobbies and Physical Activities—Can you suggest your vigor and wide-ranging interests by a short list of your recreational activities and hobbies? Some students make sure to list one strenuous sport (jogging, swimming, hiking, racquetball) as a way of suggesting good health.
5. Community Involvement—Many employers, for reasons including a concern for company image, rate candidates highly who share their time and talents in the community.
6. Where You Were Raised—In some parts of the country, you can be considered "one of us" if you were raised in the state or region where your prospective employer is based. Mention where you were raised only if you are sure it will help your efforts.

If space allows, consider writing out your personal information in *full sentences*. In a résumé otherwise composed of short, staccato phrases, the practice of writing out personal comments and facts can add a touch of sincerity and warmth to the page.

Listing References. You can simply suggest that "References will be furnished upon request." Better, though, to take the time to list three or four references in the way shown below:

```
Dr. Alfred Williams
Chief of Internal Medicine
Central Union Hospital
Topeka, Kansas 70589
(385) 482-6859
```

Note that the reference is identified by name, position, address, and telephone number.

FIGURE 18-4

Chronological Résumé

```
                              MELBA FORRESTER
7614 Traverse Drive
Hartford, Connecticut 10287
Home: (312)397-2784  Message: 395-6784

CAREER OBJECTIVE        I want to join McCoy/Adams Advertising
                        as an entry level accounts
                        representative; with experience and
                        training, I want to progress to a
                        supervisory role in creative projects.

ACADEMIC PREPARATION    Degrees

                        B.A. in Marketing, with honors,
                        University of Washington, 1983

                        Pertinent Coursework

                        Professional Selling
                        Marketing Management
                        International Marketing
                        Quantitative Market Analysis
                        Advertising Management

                              G.P.A. 3.8 on 4-point scale

                        Awards and Scholarships

                        Laketon Art Scholarship, 1982
                        Peabody Prize, Washington State Art
                        Show, 1981

                        Publications

                        "Ads That Sell," Advertising Society
                        News, University of Washington, May,
                        1982

                        Future Educational Plans

                        I am now enrolled in an M.B.A. program
                        at the University of Washington.

EMPLOYMENT      1983    Field representative, Rent-a-Treasure
                        Art, Inc., Hartford, Connecticut (part-
                        time)

                            Responsibilities:  call on upscale
                            corporate clients; rent, deliver,
                            hang art in their offices;
                            especially enjoyed providing
                            decorating advice
```

FIGURE 18-4

Chronological Résumé (continued)

```
                    1982    Store clerk, Computer Village,
                            Hartford

                                Responsibilities:  Demonstrate
                                product and close sales on home
                                computers

                    1981    Designer, painter of super-graphics,
                            Weston Playhouse, Hartford (summer)

                                Responsibilities:  designed and
                                painted eight wall-sized panels

     PERSONAL BACKGROUND      I enjoy hiking, classical music, and
                             ethnic cooking.  I take my membership
                             seriously in the National Marketing
                             Society, and in the Sisterhood, a
                             civic organization that provides
                             guidance for runaways.

     REFERENCES              Furnished upon request.

         I deeply appreciate your consideration of my
     application.  I will be happy to visit McCoy/Adams
     Advertising to meet with you in person.
```

It is wise (and polite) to ask—not inform—your references if you intend to include their names on your résumé. You thereby provide time for them to call your qualities and accomplishments to mind well before the phone rings. By asking references in advance for permission to include their names, you also give them a chance to politely decline your request.

Finally, you can choose to include the still uncommon but quite persuasive *complimentary close* for the résumé. Your signature is optional.

```
Thank you for considering me for a position at Beckman
Instruments. I will be happy to provide any additional
information you wish and to visit your offices for an
interview at your convenience.
```

This gracious concluding note allows you to mention the company name again (the "you" perspective) and to plant a key word in your reader's mind: "interview."

The Functional Résumé

Unlike the chronological résumé, which tends to emphasize your education and potential, the functional résumé emphasizes what you've proven you can *do*.

The functional résumé, too, opens with your name (usually capitalized), and address, and telephone number positioned in an eye-catching way. The *career objective* and *education* portions are handled in the same way as in the chronological résumé.

But in writing the *employment* section of the résumé, prepare for major changes. Instead of listing your jobs one by one in chronological order, decide what *major abilities* you have developed and proven in those positions. Let those abilities, stated as brief phrases, serve as categories under which you can place individual job experiences.

As illustrated in Figure 18-5, you need not keep such job experiences in chronological order. Put your most impressive jobs first, your least impressive jobs last within a category. Let the emphasis fall on the job title and description of responsibility, rather than upon the dates you held the job (though dates should always be specified).

Finally, in the *personal background* and optional complimentary closing of the functional résumé, follow the suggestions made for these sections in our discussion of the chronological résumé.

Many employers favor the functional résumé, especially for experienced applicants, because the document gets right to the key issue: what can this applicant do? Note that those abilities, when stated in the *demonstrated abilities* or *major strengths* section, can be cast as nouns—"Supervision," "Planning"—or as verb phrases—"Supervise employees effectively," "Plan for task completion," or "Organize shipping procedures."

Once you have written your résumé, you can begin planning how to prepare multiple copies for distribution to prospective employers.

FIGURE 18-5

Functional Résumé

```
                       CLIFFORD OWENS
                      9215 Branch Drive
                    Los Gatos, CA.  90432
             Home: (515) 767-4857  Message: 386-4968


                       CAREER OBJECTIVE

To join the Business Publications group at Metropolitan;
after experience as a writer, to work into an editorial
position.

                         EDUCATION

M.A. in English, Southern Methodist University, 1983
B.A. in Finance, Lester College, 1980
A.A. Sage Community College, Bridgeton, Texas, 1974

                   DEMONSTRATED ABILITIES

Ability to write well

Instructor, Business Writing, Southern Methodist
University, 1982, 1983.  Taught business memo, letter,
proposal, and report writing.

Member, American Business Communication Association.

Ability to edit publications

     Assistant editor, Neighbors (Texas Life), 1979, 1980

     Editor, News and Views (campus Newspaper), Lester
     College, 1974

Knowledge of the insurance business

     Office manager, Allstate Insurance, Bridgeton, Texas,
     1976-1977.  Supervised six sales people.  Served as
     area manager for the sales region.

     Insurance sales representative, Allstate Insurance,
     Bridgeton, Texas, 1973-1975.  Sold auto, life, and fire
     policies; handled client claims.

                     PERSONAL BACKGROUND

I've always considered myself a "people person," and most of
my hobbies and activities are socially related: bowling,
camping, and barber-shop quartet singing.  I'm married, with
two teenage children.  My health is excellent.

References will be furnished upon request.

Thank you for reviewing my application for a position with
Metropolitan.  I will be happy to meet with you personally.
```

The Personalized Résumé

If you are applying to only a half dozen or so employers, you may simply want to type personalized résumés for each application. For a larger number of applications, consider having your résumé (with portions to be personalized left blank) duplicated by offset printing or high quality photocopy. Do not ditto or mimeograph résumés. You can specify the weight and quality of paper you wish the printer to use. White twenty-pound rag bond assures a crisp, durable résumé that will not yellow or wrinkle easily. If you choose to print a photo onto your résumé, let your printer offer advice on obtaining the best reproduction possible.

Getting the Résumé to the Prospective Employer

Attach your application letter to your résumé with a paper clip. Whether you deliver your résumé and application letter in person or by mail, include both in an envelope addressed to a *person* (not an office or a company). A telephone call can usually provide the name and specific address of the appropriate person.

Delivery by Hand. Personnel offices are glad to receive your application materials during business hours. If you have not made an appointment, never "drop in" to a manager's office for the purpose of delivering your résumé. If you want your résumé to find its way to the manager's hands, mail it to him or her. Be careful, however, not to go over the head of the personnel director and established application procedures.

Once you've delivered your résumé, don't wait expectantly for someone to read it in your presence. Probably a secretary or the personnel manager will simply thank you and perhaps offer to call if a position develops. Demonstrate your own professionalism by accepting this answer in a friendly, polite way.

Mailing the Résumé. Fold your résumé and application letter together, not separately, so they open as one package for the reader. Type the envelope as neatly as you have typed the résumé itself. Except under time emergencies, do not mail your résumé by Special Delivery. You may accidentally create a reception for your résumé of disappointment and mild ridicule.

FOLLOWING UP ON THE APPLICATION

When a Response Doesn't Come

There is no precise number of days or weeks after which you should inquire after an unanswered application. Use your own judgment, being careful not to appear rude or impatient. Companies often appreciate your polite inquiries as a sign that you're actively interested in the job.

The follow-up letter is a traditional business letter in which you

- Politely remind your reader *when* you mailed your résumé. Mention any correspondence you have received from the company since that date.
- Repeat your willingness to be considered for a position (name it). Ask your reader to let you know if your application is still being actively reviewed.
- Conclude by expressing appreciation to your reader for his or her efforts on your behalf.

The letter in Figure 18-6 is an example.

When the Response Does Come

The moment your first response comes from your first career application may live with you forever. You rip open the envelope to discover one of three words: *yes*, we'll interview you; *no*, but good luck; or, *maybe* we can find a position for you.

If the answer to your job search is "Yes, we'll interview you," write a letter of response by return mail. If the employer's letter directs, also notify the company by telephone.

Accepting an Invitation to Interview. Write a brief business letter to the person who invited you to visit the company for an interview. Repeat the time and date of the interview, and indicate your pleasure at the invitation. Offer to bring additional application materials (letters of recommendation, transcripts, college projects, and so forth) with you.

Conclude by thanking your company hosts for the opportunity to pursue your application. Express your eagerness to visit with them. Figure 18-7 shows an example of an acceptance letter.

Responding to "No." If the answer you receive is "no, but good luck," take a moment to write the kind of letter no manager forgets: the "thank-you-and-I'm-still-interested" letter. Express your appreciation for their attention to your application, and (if you wish) mention briefly that you felt understandable disappointment at their decision. Express your willingness to be considered for future openings. Ask that your application be kept in an active file. Conclude with thanks and your suggestion that your paths may cross again soon.

WRITING OCCASIONED BY THE INTERVIEW

When you arrive (a little early) for a job interview, you may be surprised to find more crucial writing tasks awaiting you. Many job applications now ask the applicant to fill in more than the blanks. He or she must also write a short essay on a topic of the company's choosing. A sample of the candidate's writing can reveal much. A large real estate development firm in Florida, for example, asks interviewees for management positions to write a brief response to this question:

FIGURE 18-6

Follow-up Letter

```
                                          14 Briarcliff Street
                                          Lincoln, Nebraska  80848
                                          April 13, 198_



        Ms. Beverly Browne
        Personnel Director
        Kraco Medical Wholesale, Inc.
        125 Seventh Street
        Omaha, Nebraska  80422

        Dear Ms. Browne:

             You may recall receiving my application, mailed March
        20, for a position as a proposal writer at Kraco.

             May I ask a favor?  Please check to see if my
        application is under review.  If so, I'll certainly wait
        with patience.  If not, perhaps you could inform me of
        current openings at Kraco for which I might qualify.

             I appreciate your help.  Thank you!


                                          Sincerely,

                                          Lillian Morgan

                                          Lillian Morgan

                                          Telephone:  395-3875
```

FIGURE 18-7

Letter Accepting an Invitation to Interview

6142 Souther Lane
Raleigh, North Carolina 67042
March 1, 198_

Mr. Frederick Range
Personnel Director
Forbes Financial Services
8802 Clime Street
Raleigh, North Carolina 64011

Dear Mr. Range:

I'm pleased to accept your invitation for an interview
on March 9, 198_, at 8:30 A.M. If you wish, I can bring
with me any additional information or documents you would
like to see in support of my application.

Thank you for this opportunity to discuss with you my
qualifications for a position at Forbes.

I look forward to meeting you.

Sincerely,

Bradley Morris

Bradley Morris

Leaders often must make unpopular decisions. Discuss your own way of handling the social pressure occasioned by an unpopular decision you make.

These kinds of questions sometimes appear in your mailbox as part of an application form to be completed and mailed back to the company prior to your interview. In that case, you have time to plan your response, to work out a rough draft, and to revise your answer until it pleases you.

But employers also use such questions to test your writing abilities (and thinking abilities) in those nervous fifteen or twenty minutes prior to the beginning of the interview when you are under pressure.

Meet this on-the-spot writing challenge by reading the question over at least three times. Each time you should find yourself grasping the *content* and *intent* of the question more firmly.

Question: Leaders must make unpopular decisions. Discuss your own way of handling the social pressure occasioned by an unpopular decision you make.

First Reading Does this question require me to list and explain several unpopular decisions made by leaders in the past? No.

Second Reading Does the question require me to describe an unpopular decision I once made as a leader? No.

Third Reading Does the question require me to suggest how I handle social pressure arising out of an unpopular decision I've made? Yes.

Once you have located the heart of your question, briefly plan a format, using as few as three major parts, for your response. Here are two patterns that might suit the question above.

Alternative One
- The easy way out of social pressure for a leader
- The more difficult way out of social pressure for a leader
- Why the more difficult way proves more successful

Alternative Two
- The effect of social pressure in the short run
- The effect of social pressure in the long run
- How leaders direct attention from the short run to the long run

These patterns are not usually written down at all or at best are simply jotted onto scratch paper as a working outline for the answer. A word of caution: never feel that your two or three minutes spent in such planning are wasted time that should have been spent in "actually writing" the essay. Though your pen is not moving during the planning process, you are directly involved in the process of writing. Your short outline will help prevent writer's block, and provide an organizational framework for your response.

When you find yourself faced with an essay question before an interview, practice the routine described below:

- Read the question three times, looking for its central concerns.
- Plan a three-part (or more) framework for your response.
- Write in a free, conversational style.

AFTER THE INTERVIEW

The Letter of Thanks

After the interview, be sure to write a brief letter of thanks. If a company has devoted two hours and three interviewers to the interview, the cost of the time alone may exceed $200 to the company. Even if the interview did not go well for you, demonstrate your gratitude for the company's interest and expense by writing your thanks.

As illustrated in Figure 18-8, begin by thanking the interviewers by name, if possible, and focusing on one or two particular aspects of the interview for special comment. Then express your eagerness to work for the company and your willingness to supply further information. Conclude in a complimentary way, mentioning the company name if possible.

Now the w-a-i-t-i-n-g begins. During this difficult time, be sure that you can be reached by telephone. As personal judgment dictates, decide when the waiting has become excessive, and then write a polite letter of inquiry.

The Letter of Acceptance

If the answer to your job search is "yes," and you decide to accept an offer, write a brief letter of acceptance, as shown in Figure 18-9, covering each of these key points and others that seem important to you:

- Accept the job offer, repeating exactly what you are accepting. This practice helps to prevent misunderstandings on both sides.
- Describe the arrangements you have agreed upon for the position.
- Thank your new employer (by name) for acting favorably on your application. Express your eagerness to begin work, and to face new challenges.

The Letter of Postponement

You may find yourself faced with two or more job offers at once—or holding one job in expectation of another. In either case, you can often postpone offers for a short time while you make up your mind.

Do not feel traitorous in requesting an extension of time from a company you seemed so eager to join. Businesses understand that good candidates have many options. Usually, these businesses are willing to cooperate with you.

As illustrated in Figure 18-10, touch each of these key elements in your letter of postponement.

FIGURE 18-8

Thank-You Letter for an Interview

```
                                    112 Smithson Street
                                    Las Vegas, Nevada  35082
                                    December 20, 198_




        Mr. Richard Hall
        Personnel Director
        Tri-State Mills, Inc.
        204 Cactus Way
        Las Vegas, Nevada  35082

        Dear Mr. Hall:

            I enjoyed meeting you, Ms. Watkins, and Mr. Valenzuela
        last Thursday afternoon.  You made me feel quite comfortable
        (not a common interview experience)!  I was especially
        interested in our discussion of Japanese "just-in-time"
        scheduling procedures, and their possible application at
        Tri-State Mills.

            I'm more eager than ever to join you at Tri-State and
        certainly will be pleased to supply any additional
        information you require to support my application.

            Again, my thanks for a stimulating afternoon.


                                    Sincerely,

                                    Rose Ramirez

                                    Rose Ramirez
```

FIGURE 18-9

Letter of Acceptance

41 Wilmore Place
Boston, MA 02108
January 4, 198_

Mr. James Kennedy
Director, Advanced Design
Microtech, Inc.
28 Linden Street
Waltham, MA 02611

Dear Mr. Kennedy:

I am most pleased to accept the position you offer in
your letter of Jan. 1: System Engineer Step 3, with an
annual salary of $36,500.

As you know, I have arranged to leave my present
position on Jan. 20. I will be able to report to my new job
at Microtech on Jan. 21. Prior to that time, I will be
happy to begin the process of filling out employee documents
and security clearances. In addition, I would like to pick
up your division training manual to acquaint myself with
Microtech policies and procedures.

You must know how happy I am to be joining Microtech.
Please communicate my thanks to Mr. Langley, Ms. Crawford,
and Mr. Thomas, who showed me every consideration during the
application and interview process. I especially appreciated
your help, and look forward to working as your colleague.

Sincerely,

Duncan Phillips

Duncan Phillips

- Express appreciation at receiving the job offer, the substance of which you repeat back in the letter.
- Request an extension of time for a specific period while you make your decision.
- Communicate gratitude for favorable action on your application.

The Letter of Refusal

At times, you will have to decline a job offer. Do so in a way that burns no bridges; you may seek a position with the company again in the future.

As suggested in Figure 18-11, include each of these key elements in the letter of refusal:

- Politely decline the job offer. You need not mention its specific details. You can decide whether or not to explain your decision. Don't sound more sorry than, in fact, you are.
- Communicate thanks for the company's interest, Express goodwill for their people and projects.

The Letter of Resignation

How quickly time passes. You have been on the job for several years, and the time has come to resign. Many important points must be covered in this, your final communication with your employer. Include the following:

- Express your intention to resign. Give the effective date.
- Reflect upon significant projects and people during your career with the company.
- Decide whether to reveal the new position you are accepting.
- Offer to help provide a smooth transition, if possible, for your successor.
- Express thanks for the professional and personal associations you have enjoyed in your old job.

Tact is especially important in a resignation letter, even when the circumstances of your resignation are less than rosy. Many of the resignation letters turned in result not in resignation at all, but job promotions and raises. A company hates to lose good employees to the competition.

Realize that your letter of resignation may be read as a challenge by upper management—a challenge to offer you new projects and financial rewards to keep you with the company. A tactful resignation letter, therefore, rouses no anger in the reader. Notice in Figure 18-12 that the letter subtly suggests how valuable the resigning employee has been to the firm.

The Letter of Recommendation

You not only leave a letter behind when you leave—the letter of resignation—but you take letters with you to your new employer—letters of recommendation.

FIGURE 18-10

Letter of Postponement

960 Lake Way
Tacoma, WA 40211
April 9, 198_

Ms. Willa Frank
Personnel Director
AKF Industries, Inc.
9210 Cranston Street
Tacoma, WA 40211

Dear Ms. Frank:

I was deeply pleased to receive your letter of April 7, in which you offer me the position of Assistant Inventories and Supplies Accountant at AKF, with an annual salary of $33,000.

May I consider your offer open until April 20? I will send my written response to you no later than that date.

Accept my thanks for your favorable action on my application and for your kindness during the extended interview process. I do hope the time extension I have requested will be acceptable to you.

Sincerely,

Lisa Tomlinson

Lisa Tomlinson

FIGURE 18-11

Letter of Refusal

214 Riverdale Drive
Banning, CA 92004
February 9, 198_

Mr. Travis Freeman
President
Freeman Furniture Wholesale, Inc.
20 Bleyer Road
Beaumont, CA 92084

Dear Mr. Freeman:

    Thank you for your letter of February 7, in which you extend a job offer as Marketing Director at Freeman Furniture. While I deeply appreciate the opportunity, I am not able to accept because of other professional commitments made in the last few days.

    For your interest in my application and your personal kindness during my interview, I thank you. Best wishes for a prosperous future.

Sincerely,

Kenneth Williams

Kenneth Williams

FIGURE 18-12

Letter of Resignation

1140 Seally Drive
Wichita, Kansas 35011
August 8, 198_

Ms. Catherine Browne
Director
Trend Design
84 South Street
Wichita, Kansas 35011

Dear Ms. Browne:

After seven satisfying and productive years with Trend
Design, I am resigning to take over the directorship of
another company. I wish to make my last day Sept. 2, if
that date is acceptable to you.

This decision was difficult, especially as I considered
how much the talented people at Trend, including yourself,
have meant to my professional development and personal
pleasure during the past several years. Together, we have
certainly had our share of winning projects.

We can discuss the date of my departure, if you need my
help in training a replacement.

Be assured that you have my best wishes for continued
success.

Sincerely,

John Bradshaw

John Bradshaw

When you are asked to *write* a letter of recommendation, tell the requester frankly whether or not you can write a favorable letter. If not, the requester then has the chance to ask someone else.

In writing the letter, you have considerable freedom to treat any aspect of your personal and professional relation with the person you are recommending. In general, do not "guess" about job requirements in the new position for which you are recommending the person. Rather, focus on the past and the present facts of your relationship.

The following points may suggest topics to include in a letter of recommendation:

How long and in what capacity have you known the person?

What can you say about the person's character and personality? Does he or she work well with others? Is he or she responsible? Creative?

If possible, describe one or more specific occasions on which the person excelled. What did he or she do? How did it turn out?

How does the person stack up against others you have observed in similar roles?

What success can you predict for the person? Summarize the factors that make your prediction more than a wild guess.

Conclude with a particularly warm compliment to the person. Offer to elaborate upon your recommendation by letter or phone. Provide your name, title, address, and phone number.

Recognize that 90 percent or more of all letters of recommendation are generally supportive of the person recommended. The key in a good letter of recommendation, then, is not simply to write favorable things, but to provide enough detail in the letter so that the reader can form his or her own high opinion of the person recommended.

Summary

1. The application letter, necessary each time you mail a résumé, should be brief, tied to your résumé by references to highlights, and appropriately personalized.
2. The résumé is best developed by the job-seeker himself or herself in preparation for interviews.
3. Chronological résumés often suit recent graduates better than functional résumés, which are more appropriate for those with more work experience.
4. Special letters or phone messages are called for in response to an invitation for an interview or a job offer.
5. The thank-you letter after an interview can be an important aid in securing a job.
6. Letters of postponement, refusal, and resignation all involve discretion, honesty, and brevity.
7. Letters of recommendation should be descriptive, complimentary, and sincere.

Questions for Discussion

1. Should you begin the application process with a letter of application accompanied by a résumé, or a phone call? Justify your choice.
2. Identify the typical parts of a letter of application.
3. What strategies should you use in an uninvited letter of application?
4. What are the Ten Rules of the Résumé?
5. What is meant by the phrase "at-a-glance appeal"? How can you promote at-a-glance appeal when organizing your résumé?
6. What four crucial elements should always appear on the résumé?
7. How do the chronological résumé and the functional résumé differ? Which pattern would you follow when writing a résumé? Explain.
8. Is it important to personalize your résumé? How can you do so?
9. What are the features of the follow-up letter? When should you write one?
10. What information should be in a letter accepting an invitation to interview?
11. Why might you write a "thank-you-but-I'm-still-interested" letter after being rejected for a job opening?
12. What kinds of writing can you expect to do at an interview?
13. If you are required to write an essay at your interview, what routine can you follow?
14. What are the features of the letter of acceptance?

Exercises

1. Write a letter of application in response to a job opening described in a newspaper advertisement.
2. Write an uninvited letter of application to a company with whom you would like to gain employment. How will your strategy change in comparison to the strategy you used when writing the invited letter of application for exercise one?
3. Create a personal résumé. Experiment with several different versions until you arrive at the one that best suits your needs. Show the different versions to friends and family members, seeking their opinions as well. Be sure to keep copies of the final résumé in your job search file.
4. As an experiment with form, rewrite your functional résumé in chronological form, or your chronological résumé in functional form.
5. Write a follow-up letter to the invited application letter you composed for exercise one.
6. Write a follow-up letter to the uninvited application letter you composed for exercise two. How will you handle your strategy differently when following up on an uninvited application?
7. Write a letter accepting an invitation to interview for the position you applied for in either exercise one or two. What necessary information will you include?
8. Write a letter of acceptance to the employers you interviewed with for exercise seven.

Other Applications of Business Communication

How's your imagination? Picture the case of Harry Porter, a business time traveler from the 1980s

who invented a way by which he could zip forward to the year 2020. Harry wanted to look in on the state of

business communication at that future date.

Here's his report:

I'm amazed on two scores: how much things have changed and how much they have remained the same. The length of business documents has changed—most are much shorter than we used to write in the 1980s. Few are on paper. Electronic mail and electronic filing are used everywhere. Screens for reading documents are much larger and more visually comfortable than our old monitors. Each has a photocopy function allowing the user to print out whatever appears on the screen. Headings and Subject lines appear much more prominently than on documents in the 1980s. Here in the future everyone is in a hurry, with little time to sort out the subject of a document. Communication has to happen fast or it doesn't happen at all.

At the same time many things have remained the same. Business leaders still place a premium on employees who can think clearly and logically, express themselves concisely, and interpret information with insight. Those are old skills we thought were important even back in the 1980s.

Based on Harry's report from the future, how might you best prepare yourself for communicating in the decades ahead?

Innovations
in Business
Communication   19

To understand the impact of the electronic communication revolution upon business communicators

To grasp the importance and influence of word processing, electronic mail, data bases, and other computer technologies

To prepare effectively for teleconference experiences

To adjust to new communication technologies by following six techniques for writing and speaking

"There's no other reason to automate than to improve your bottom line," says Bonnie Canning, senior vice-president, Micronet. And to do so, the electronic office arrives just in the nick of time. More than half of the nation's workers are now white-collar employees—almost 50 million strong, and growing at a rate 20 percent faster than the labor force as a whole. The total cost of office operations for these workers in 1980, according to Booz, Allen, & Hamilton, management consultants, was $800 billion, with an additional $600 billion for payroll and fringe benefits for the white-collar labor force. Without cost-saving electronic innovations, office costs could soar to an incredible $1.5 trillion by 1990.

Put more specifically, businesses in the 1970s found themselves spending 40 to 50 percent of total expenses just for office costs—up from the 20 to 30 percent range of just a decade before. By the beginning of the 1980s, the white collar was choking the efforts of American business to compete profitably.

To the rescue—the electronic office. Led by incredible technological breakthroughs in silicon chip manufacture, fiber optics, and magnetic storage media, the Information Age has swept upon the office not as a fad but a welcome fact of life. Gil Davidson, administrative services manager at American Cyanamid Corporation, makes the point in a concrete way: "As a direct result of our upgraded word-processing equipment, we expect to save about $1 million annually through increased productivity." Andrew Turner, assistant office chief at the Ohio Environmental Protection Agency in Columbus echoes, "With today's word-processing technology, we have eliminated our backlog, and the work force has pride in what they produce."

That work force includes the boss, by the way. Frank Petro, vice-president of Arthur D. Little, Inc., points out that "the real benefit from office automation will be in making executives and professionals more productive." The payroll for these people, Petro points out, is now running more than $600 billion, double the amount spent by business on its clerical workers.

SAVING MONEY, TIME, AND EFFORT

To glimpse how the innovative office machines now coming to market will revolutionize business communication and practice, we can transport ourselves a mere three or four years into the future—ten or twenty would be almost unimaginable—to look in on Frieda Future, a successful mid-level manager at Commercial Interiors, Inc., a nationwide firm that furnishes large commercial offices.

The time is 8 A.M. Frieda, we're surprised to find, is not at her urban office in downtown Chicago. Instead, she is still at home in suburban River Forest. In fact, she drives in to work only on Fridays. The other four days she "telecommutes"—that is, works at home in full communication with office staff (many at their homes) and clients. Frieda avoids the crush of rush-hour traffic and enjoys the creature comforts of her home. She calculates that she saves 20 percent of her income she would otherwise have to

FIGURE 19-1

Office of the Future

spend on commuting expenses, restaurant meals, and an extensive (and expensive) business wardrobe. Her four-year-old son, Bobby, can pop into her home office from time to time without seriously disrupting the day.

Thanks to such telecommuting, Frieda's company has been able to reduce its expensive downtown office space by two-thirds in the last few years. Executives and managers no longer have personal offices, but instead are provided with managerial suites on their day "in." Frieda, for example, will have an office waiting for her on Friday—the same office used by Frank Guilliam on his day at the office, Thursday.

Commercial Interiors knows how happy its executives are with the telecommuting arrangement. In fact, the company uses the plan as a powerful and inexpensive means to build employee loyalty. The back-breaking expense of replacing key people every year or two has been reduced by almost 80 percent. Frieda keeps her job because she loves it.

The Work Station

The most prominent feature of Frieda's home office is the work station ("my playpen," she jokes). This combination desk/computer console looks no more forbidding to operate than a microwave oven. Work stations like Xerox's 8010 Star, for example, are designed for ease of operation. Users can begin to operate the work station in minutes and be fully proficient in a matter of hours, according to David E. Liddle, a vice-president at Xerox. Manufacturers of work stations learned early that managers and executives cannot be expected to learn complicated programming and operating procedures in the course of a hectic business day. Like Frieda's, work stations have to be simple to use.

Frieda is comfortable at her work station. She lounges comfortably in an overstuffed parlor chair. Even if she wishes to type, Frieda can set the light keyboard in her lap (as in the case of IBM's popular Personal Computer).

But Frieda types very little these days. Led by Japanese companies, the manufacturers of work stations have made the keyboard obsolescent by voice recognition devices. Frieda simply speaks to the work station in English, not code words, and the component devices follow her direction.

The Work Day

A large checkerboard of video displays ("flat" projection devices) almost fills up an entire wall of Frieda's home office. On this "electronic greaseboard" she will, screen by screen, display and deal with the various printed, verbal, and graphic messages sent her way during the day.

To begin, Frieda calls onto one square her agenda—"list of things to do"—for Monday. Commercial Interiors over the weekend has called in a few additions to the list, Frieda notes. By means of her computerized telephone, similar to the ETS-100 computer phone, the company has called in three agenda items that were received by the work station and stored in memory, and now are ready for display along with Frieda's own items for attention.

Sending Electronic Letters

The first item on Frieda's "to-do" list is a letter. She speaks it into her computer, which then transmits it in a flash to the recipient's electronic mailbox in California. In Frieda's own electronic mail system, a "message waiting" catalog shows mail that has arrived. She can call up letters on any of her screens, ask the work station to read the letter aloud, or print out "hard copy" on the laser printer.

Receiving Electronic Letters

Frieda can place each item of her daily mail on a separate screen before her in order to scan for items of importance. "Cancel screens 1, 3, 5, and 8," she says to the computer. That's the electronic equivalent of throwing junk mail away.

Electronic Filing. "Save screens 2, 4, 6, and 7," she commands. The computer automatically files those messages according to key words ("descriptors") placed at the beginning of each message by the message sender. For convenience, the messages are stored on disks that remain by Frieda's side in her work station. For security, however, each message is "backed up" on central computer storage via telephone line links between Frieda's home and the main office.

Computer Security. Because Frieda's files contain information of a sensitive and proprietary nature, her work station maintains an elaborate safeguard against business espionage. Each message filed or transmitted is "encrypted" with a mathematical key.

Data Bases

The next item on Frieda's agenda is a proposal she is writing for Midwest Financial Associates. Frieda displays several of the proposal pages on the screens before her. "I want to know union rates for wallpaper hanging," she says to the computer. In a matter of seconds, the computer selects the appropriate data base for that information, isolates the requested information, and displays it in bar graph form on the electronic greaseboard. Frieda likes the visual representation of information and, at the press of a key, incorporates it as part of page 7 of her proposal.

More than 2400 data bases are now available to businesses, including the mammoth Dialog system maintained by Lockheed Corporation and the ERIC data base sponsored by the Department of Health, Education, and Welfare.

The Computer Telephone

During this period of work, Frieda has not been immune to that bane of executives—the telephone. In fact, in the last half hour, Frieda has received six important phone calls, each answered by her computerized telephone in her voice with a promise to phone back within twenty minutes. A display screen shows Frieda the number of the party calling and, if the party wishes, a name or company identification. Frieda now looks at the list of names and numbers on the screen. "Dan Henderson," she tells the work station.

Even though the call is long distance for Frieda, the expense is not great. Her computer phone monitors the least expensive and most available trunk lines. If a bad connection develops, the computer automatically switches the call to a better line without breaking the connection.

Not all of Frieda's associates have such carte blanche with the telephone. Commercial Interiors maintains a computer review of productivity vs. expense on the telephone. Frieda spends about $300 per month in phone expenses, but produces $150,000 or more in business for the company each year. By contrast, some of Frieda's colleagues were spending $500 or more per month on the telephone without a matching amount of business. The company's computer telephone system ended that wasteful use of the phone, and distributed telephone privileges according to productivity.

When a less than successful employee dials a long distance number, the company computer asks for a clearance number (available only through management). If no clearance number is forthcoming, the call will not be completed on a company phone. In this way, Commercial Interiors has managed to stop telephone abuse, which in many corporations has been estimated at more than $100 per employee per month spent in nonbusiness telephoning.

Frieda's computer telephone has many other advanced features. When a party calls and reaches her busy line, she hears a pleasant tone to let her know that a call is waiting. The party's number and name are displayed for her on the screen, to help her determine whether to take the call right away or continue her present conversation. Her work station is equipped with Videophone, allowing her to see the person to whom she is speaking. Many times, Frieda says, the look in a person's eyes or a nod of the head conveys valuable business information.

Frieda's phone has a "camp on" feature, which automatically dials back a busy number as soon as the line is free. With ease she can set up conferences with several separate phones, with the video on each phone used for presenting graphs and charts to the group.

But Frieda's favorite use of the phone comes when she consults with a client. These business conversations cost the client money, much like a conversation with a lawyer. Frieda says to her work station, "Let's call Mervin Fields, number on file." When Frieda reaches Fields, the computer flashes a message as she talks: "Please record the topic of this conversation." Frieda types in a few brief words of reminder as she continues talking with the client. She might, for example, type in "Solar glass possibilities."

When the conversation is concluded, the computer automatically records the time, length, date, and topic of the conversation, as well as the parties involved. At the end of the month, the computer prints out automatic billings for these consultations. Frieda estimates that she earns an extra $30,000 per year for the company by recording each and every one of these easy-to-overlook consultations.

The Teleconference

Frieda now prepares for an important conference in London in less than an hour. Using the graphics programs in her work station, she creates a series of charts showing how proper interior design can work together with the image-making efforts of advertisers to create a common company theme. As she completes work on each colorful chart, she stores it electronically in a file for use in the conference. Because she will have to give a brief address to the group, she also puts speaking notes onto one of the screens on her electronic greaseboard.

Then Frieda sits back to wait for London to come to her. No longer do business people bother to transport their physical bodies hither and yon for a face-to-face conference. That experience can be had electronically, without sacrificing personal warmth. Business people can come to know one another by teleconference just as television viewers feel they "know" television stars.

At 10 A.M. the work station alerts Frieda to get ready to appear "on camera." A video camera in her home office turns on at the same time that cameras send the images of the group in London to her. A major portion of her large electronic greaseboard now becomes almost a cinema screen, and she feels in the presence of the London group as they all talk together. Frieda's presentation goes quite well, especially when she uses her charts (drawing them from computer memory to appear by means of the computer on the video board in London). Two of the conference participants have questions about one aspect of a particular bar graph. She is able to change the graph immediately for clarification.

American businesses spent an incredible $18 billion in travel expenses in 1982. Much of that money went not for productive face-to-face business encounters, but for canceled and delayed air flights, cabs stalled in traffic, mixed-up hotel reservations, and all the other executive nightmares of business trips. Although Frieda does travel in connection with her work, she manages to avoid needless travel. Through such savings, the company has reduced its travel budget more than 50 percent.

Teleconferencing gained immense popularity from the early 1980s. At that time, Picker Corporation, an RCA subsidiary, gathered 450 salespeople and managers together not at one location but at thirty Holiday Inns around the country. All participants were linked by teleconference audio and visual equipment. Corporate communications director Frank P. Bean spoke of the conference in glowing terms: sales soared after the conference, and "whereas a similar, conventional-type sales conference in 1972 cost us around $500,000, this one came in at under $100,000." TRW's information services group also staged a teleconference, linking thirty-three locations and 1,800 clients and prospects gathered at Holiday Inns.

So successful have these "televents" been that Holiday Inns now has 128 sites in 40 states equipped with satellite earth stations for conference use.

Learning to Use and Educating the Computer

Frieda found it easy to learn to use the work station and other peripheral devices because of "real time education chips." These high memory marvels are no bigger than a bottle cap, but contain a whole semester's course in the operation of the machine at hand.

Real time education allows the manager to begin using a sophisticated machine even before he or she has mastered the skills required. In the process of using the machine, the manager learns what to do and not to do. A voice—yes, a patient voice—speaks up when problems occur. The learner can't go wrong because the real time education chip coaches and advises at every stage. In the early 1980s these instruction chips appeared first in simple form on automobiles—"you have left your keys in the ignition." With the advent of high memory chips, much more sophisticated education could take place.

Frieda not only learns from her work station, she also teaches it. Occasionally the "spell guard" function in her computer runs across a word in Frieda's dictation that is not in the computer's dictionary. The computer asks, "What does 'guava' mean?" Frieda answers that a guava is a tropic fruit and goes on to describe it a bit. The computer stores that information under "guava" in its memory and never has to ask again.

Frieda's current educational endeavor involves her computer's capacities for artificial intelligence. She would like to be able to ask her computer such questions as "what theme might be most appropriate for corporation X's executive offices?"

The computer needs help in knowing how to handle these broad, evaluative questions. It asks Frieda a series of questions in an effort to learn. She provides answers and guidance. With their mutual effort, the computer eventually becomes more than a data gatherer, preserver, organizer, and locater. By means of artificial intelligence programming, the computer can assist Frieda even in her creative choices. The computer can offer ideas, and rational supporting arguments to back them up. Frieda may choose to reject the computer's ideas, of course, as she might reject the ideas of a friend or colleague. When Frieda does choose a different path than that suggested by the computer, she explains her choice to the computer so that next time the computer will be a bit more intelligent.

Portable Computers

When she does leave her work station to travel to the urban office, she takes along a briefcase computer and portable telephone. While on the train, subway, or freeway, she can communicate with her work station or central office. Her work station continues to work for her while she is away. Phone calls are answered and forwarded efficiently. Frieda can order correspondence sent from her work station automatically. Using the video equipment at her urban office, she can review mail received electronically at her home.

Frieda enjoys her relationship with the computer and feels none of the anxieties so often associated with using it. "If an interior decorator can get along with a work station," she says, "anyone can."

CHALLENGES OF THE COMPUTER REVOLUTION

The electronic servants of Frieda's work experience are not science fiction: all, in fact, exist in prototype or are commercially available at this moment. But so what? How will these and other technological marvels affect us as business communicators?

More Words

Look, first, for a dramatic increase in the number of words you are expected to "process" (read, write, revise, and file) each day. Word processors make it easier and faster to *produce* words. New copy machines make it easier and faster to *reproduce* words. Electronic mail allows senders to distribute messages to thousands of recipients at the press of a key. In addition, more words will come back to haunt us from microfilm and microfiche storage. Every business communicator must make preparation, as described in the final pages of this chapter, for dealing with a business world awash with words.

> Although writers are responding differently to different aspects of the word processor, most seem to agree that the gains lie in speed and efficiency, freeing up the creative process by making the physical process of producing copy easier.
>
> Reprinted with permission from *Simply Stated,* the monthly newsletter from the Document Design Center, American Institutes for Research.

More Information

Thanks to the more than 2400 data bases now available to business, every modem-equipped microcomputer becomes a gateway to vast stores of information. But are we prepared to *use* this information? A grammar school teacher in California put the problem in clear outline: "With our new computer and modem, my students can access reams of information on even the smallest topics. One youngster ordered up 210 pages on the goldfish for a school report. He brought the pounds of fanfold paper up to my desk. 'Now what?' he asked."

Business communicators, too, may well ask "Now what?" if they have not been trained to analyze, organize, and limit the data they draw from powerful data bases. "Data isn't information," points out Victor Walling, senior strategic planner at SRI International. "You need to have information assembled in a way that will help you make decisions. The communication experts of the future will be good not only at gathering information, but at interpreting it with intelligence."

More Ready-Made Messages and Documents

As more and more business documents are committed to storage by means of word processing, the temptation will inevitably grow to reuse old language rather than to generate new language. Writing is, after all, hard work. Calling up an old document to insert new names and numbers is much easier. In many cases (such as the collection letter or order response), such efficiency may have a place. But the danger exists that more complex business communications will also be cut out of old dough. Writers must guard against this inevitable drift toward standard, stereotyped, pre-formed language. Especially in a computer age, the authentic, persuasive human voice—whether in writing or speaking—remains the single most potent communicator.

More Words, Information, and Stereotypes

Business communicators can practice six techniques to survive and thrive in an age of high-tech communication advances.

Early Messaging. To cope with the ever growing problem of more words in business, make every effort to catch the reader's eye *early* with your main message. Busy executives may give your correspondence or documents a mere glance; you will want to make sure that glance counts and draws them further into reading your words. Specifically, use the first paragraph of memos, letters, proposals, and reports to *say something* important about your topic.

Concise Style. Each year short reports are getting even shorter in business, but few would claim that less communication is taking place. You *can* communicate your full message in fewer words. Follow the techniques discussed in Chapter 3, including reliance on active verbs, concrete diction, logical organization, and clear transitions.

Format Considerations. Documents must not only be readable but must, at a second's glance, *appear* readable. Use white space, headings, and the other techniques described in Chapter 9 to create a favorable mindset on the part of your reader. Even before reading begins, he or she should say, in effect, "This document looks organized, clear, and professional."

Appropriate Personality. Although business documents should never have the deeply personal tone of diaries, they can borrow techniques from friendly letters to achieve a warm, human tone. These techniques include well-wishing, disclosure of feelings as well as thoughts, and the many other topics discussed in Chapter 10.

Efficient Writing. Writer's block is a luxury business communicators can't afford now, and certainly will not have time for in the future. Practice the techniques for generating and organizing ideas discussed in Chapter 3 so that, given a writing task, you can begin work in an efficient and effective way.

Natural Writing. The days of pretentious guff in business communication— "the facilitation of the extraneous factors, thus ameliorating . . ."—are fading. Modern, busy executives have no time to wonder what words mean. Following the techniques discussed in Chapters 3 and 14, write and speak naturally, in the voice that is "you."

Summary

1. The movement toward electronic offices is driven by the need to save time, money, and human energy.
2. Several new communication devices promise business writers and speakers more convenience, flexibility, and security.
3. The computer telephone will be more useful for business purposes than the traditional telephone because it keeps track of calls, handles calls more efficiently, and is more portable.
4. The teleconference helps businesses save money on travel by sending electronic images instead of physically transporting bodies.
5. The crush of more and more words upon business men and women is best relieved by general use of a more concise business style.
6. The availability of more data does not guarantee a more meaningful operation unless there is intelligent interpretation.

7. Even though word processing makes the use of ready-made documents easier than ever before, effective communicators use them only when original communications are unnecessary.

Questions for Discussion

1. How has the Information Age helped cut office costs?
2. What will the work station of the future look like? What services will it offer?
3. What are data bases?
4. What features do computer telephones offer? How can companies prevent the misuse of computer telephones?
5. What advantages does teleconferencing offer cost-conscious executives?
6. What is real time education? What particular benefits does it offer first time computer users?
7. How will new technological advances affect business communicators' ability to gather and interpret information?
8. What place will the authentic, persuasive human voice play in the impersonal computer age?
9. How can "early messaging" help business communicators to cope with more words?
10. What are six techniques for surviving in an age of high-tech advances?

Exercises

1. Jump into your time machine and project yourself into the world of the future. Describe a typical day in your life as a student.
2. Inspect the computer telephones on display in your local telephone outlet store. What new technological breakthroughs in telecommunications have occurred even since the publication of this textbook?
3. Practice using a computer. Your college or university will most likely provide word-processing centers for students. Record your experiences. If you already have computer knowledge, summarize how this knowledge has affected your communication skills.
4. Find out what computer system is used by the company you applied to in the exercises for Chapter 16. Research that system. What are its capabilities and limitations? (Demonstrating familiarity with the system should distinguish you when you really apply for a position in the company.)
5. Practice early messaging. Write a message in which you lead up to your main point after some preliminary remarks. Now rewrite the message, placing your main point early in the message. Compare the two versions.
6. Practice including appropriate personality in your writing. Write a business message as impersonally as you can. Then rewrite the message providing the missing personal touch. Show both versions to a friend. Which was preferred?
7. Write a pretentious business message. Go to a thesaurus if necessary to find "windbag" synonyms that will contrast with the clean, concise, natural words you'll use to humanize the memo.

Cheryl Harmon, owner of Westmont Office Supplies, is fuming. She has just had to pay $25,000 to

her least favorite client—a man who used to owe her $1028.

I can't believe it! I thought his court case against me for libel was just a stalling technique to keep from paying his debts. When the judge found me guilty you could have knocked me over with a feather.

It all began when his account for office supplies became overdue. I tried everything I could think of to collect from him. Finally I decided to write a letter to his business partner telling exactly what I thought about the free-loading louse. I'll admit the letter wasn't tactful, but who wouldn't be mad after months of non-payment?

Well, it turns out his business partner broke off their business dealings in part because of angry accusations in my letter. I received the court summons for libel shortly thereafter. Now I'm out $25,000 plus the $1028 I tried to collect.

Do you understand why the court found Cheryl Harmon guilty? How could she have dealt with the outstanding debt in a better way? Should she have contacted an attorney for advice in bill collecting?

Business

Communication

and the Law

20

Since the signing of the Magna Carta, business law in all Western nations has placed substantial weight on the *giving of one's word*, in oral or written form. Instead of shedding blood or piling up stones, we finalize business transactions and understandings in three ways.

Words of commitment: we will, we agree to, we promise
Acts of commitment: the use of signatures and seals
Documents of commitment: deeds, notes, letters, and contracts

Therefore, business people must take their words seriously not only as vehicles for communication but also as significant legal instruments. In a memo, letter, or proposal, your words influence the affairs of others. Sometimes that influence proves negative: you must deny a promotion, file a claim, demand payment, or turn down a proposal. How do people respond? Often they fight you, sometimes in court. They cite your words as evidence against you.

If, for example, you berate a competitor as a thief or liar in the presence of others, your words can return to haunt you as evidence in a slander suit. At other times, your words may arouse expectations in others. Clients may trust your evaluation of a home for sale as "$20,000 under market price." Buyers may rely on a piece of paper warrantying the serviceability of a washing machine. When these expectations are dashed, people return to your words as evidence that they have been misled.

These scenarios of blame, anger, and disappointment are not intended to make business life out to be a vale of strife and suffering. Not every client wants to sue, and the great majority of your words—even those written in haste and poor judgment—will not face legal review or challenge.

But some will. Unfortunately, not everyone wins in the real world of business. When your company wins a major contract, several other companies have lost the competition. When you as a salesperson capture 50 percent of your sales territory, other salesmen and saleswomen are falling behind and, perhaps, facing termination.

Enter litigation. People and companies fight for financial survival with every means at their disposal, including legal suit. If your success acts detrimentally upon their survival, they will review the means by which you achieved your success. If they find (or think they find) questionable business practices, they may well seek legal redress. Primary evidence in such suits, of course, will be your words, as found in memos, letters, advertisements, contracts, reports, and so forth.

LEGAL VULNERABILITY

The purpose of this chapter is not to offer specific legal advice for such moments, but instead to suggest areas of legal vulnerability for the business communicator. These areas of legal hazard are like shoals in navigable waters: the goal is not to give up sailing, but to learn to avoid the shoals through knowledge, judgment, and alertness.

The stakes are high. Misspoken and miswritten communications each year cost people their careers and companies their profits. Court-awarded damages stemming from ill-chosen words easily run to more than $1 million per day in American courts.

To become more aware of areas of legal vulnerability, we can assess the major laws pertinent to six key areas of interest for every business communicator:

1. You and Your Employer
2. You and Your Files
3. You and Your Customer
4. You and Your Employees
5. You and the Government
6. You and Your Product or Service

In each of these areas, business communicators should weigh the legal implications of their words with care.

You and Your Employer

As an employee, the chances are good that you function as a legal agent for the company. No, your contract does not include such "agency" as a part of your job description. Your status as an agent for the company is implied by your employment. "Agency" means, simply, that the company is responsible for your work-related actions and words. Your words, especially on paper, are as binding for the company as if they had been penned by the chairman of the board.

When writing on company letterhead or when identifying yourself by job title, you probably cannot escape your role as agent even if you use such disclaimers as "speaking unofficially" or "off the record." Nor can the company escape responsibility by claiming that your words did not reflect the will of the management or board of directors. Your employment itself marks the company's implicit obligation to supervise your activities and pronouncements. Figure 20-1 presents a number of situations that have legal implications which could easily occur while doing business. See if you can spot areas of legal hazard by mentally working through this quiz. Specific answers to each question appear at the end of the chapter.

For the sake of the company as well as their careers, business communicators must exercise judgment, discretion, and a high degree of legal awareness when writing memos, letters, proposals, and reports involving any of the following:

- Personnel hiring and firing
- Claims
- Warranties, commitments, assurances
- Contracts
- Labor negotiations
- Tax planning

FIGURE 20-1

Have You Broken the Law?

1. A customer owes you $97. You suspect that your letters are reaching his address, but that he is simply not opening them. To make sure that he at least reads your words, you type NOTICE OF LAWSUIT on the front of the envelope. Inside, the letter explains firmly but politely that you want to avoid legal action, and therefore demand payment.

Have you broken the law?

2. Frank Vincenti, star football quarterback, buys a car from your dealership. You send out a catchy promotional letter to 1000 prospective clients proudly urging them to "buy where Frank Vincenti buys."

Have you broken the law?

3. You sell a stereo system on credit, and mail the usual bill for the Oct. 1 payment. You receive no payment for several weeks. Finally, on Nov. 15, a letter arrives from the customer. You open the letter to find not a check but a series of questions about the bill: how you determined the amount due, when the grace period expires, how much interest you are charging, and so forth. Not having time to deal with the matter, you put the letter aside until a few days before Christmas.

Have you broken the law?

4. A young couple applies for credit at your store. You order a credit report. It shows several small delinquencies and many late payments. You reluctantly must write to the young couple that you cannot grant credit based on their credit record. You offer the observation that they "should learn to pay their bills on time if they expect merchants to give them credit."

Have you broken the law?

5. You've dealt with two investors, Mort and Alonzo, who live together. Mort has been extremely fair with you in all business dealings; Alonzo, however, has seemed shifty and deceitful. Yesterday, he managed to swindle you out of $3000. You write a scorching letter, accusing him of "dishonest dealing, hypocrisy, and fraud." Rather than wait for mail delivery, you seal the letter in an unmarked white envelope and drop it off in their mailbox. You secretly hope that Mort will read the letter before Alonzo, thereby learning what a cheat his partner is. Perhaps Mort can even help persuade Alonzo to right his wrong.

Have you broken the law?

6. You're new in town. To get acquainted, you mail out 2500 plastic credit cards to upscale buyers for use in your store.

Have you broken the law?

7. You publish *Sports Legends,* a series of books on the Olympics. As an introduction, you mail the first volume in the series to 5,000 people, instructing them to return payment for $8.95, or simply to return the book. You are shocked when most of the 5,000 people keep the book and don't pay. You turn their names over to a collection agency.

Have you broken the law?

8. You can't seem to reach Alf Charleson, who owes you $185 on a furniture purchase. You call his employer to explain why you're looking for Alf and to solicit help.

Have you broken the law?

9. After three months, Alf owes you $470. You hate to turn the account over for collection. Instead, you call Alf's cousin to explain the urgency of the debt and to get help finding Alf.

Have you broken the law?

FIGURE 20-1

Have You Broken the Law? (continued)

10. You finally obtain Alf's address and telephone number. You call him about the debt at 7:45 A.M, just before he leaves for work.

Have you broken the law?

11. You receive a short letter from Alf instructing you not to continue calling him about the debt. You shake your head at his nerve, and continue to call.

Have you broken the law?

12. You turn down a good job applicant with the explanation that, although she is more qualified than other candidates, you had to abide by Affirmative Action guidelines in hiring a minority applicant.

Have you broken the law?

13. In your company, you have gathered names and addresses of 600 customers who have borrowed at least $5000 during the last three years. A friend who is starting up his own finance company offers $1500 for the names. You comply.

Have you broken the law?

14. In designing a package label, you advertise your product as "the best yet least expensive wood glue on the market today." In fact, several glues of equal quality sell for less.

Have you broken the law?

15. You interview an excellent candidate for a position in your company, but must write to her that the job requires a younger woman.

Have you broken the law?

16. John Rakes, handicapped by a withered arm, tries to convince you in his job interview that he can work effectively in the Graphics division. Though you admire John's spunk, you must write back that his handicap simply makes him unsuitable for the job.

Have you broken the law?

17. You're looking for a sales manager free to travel, and you think you've found your person. In the interview, you politely ask the young man if he and his wife plan to start a family soon.

Have you broken the law?

18. One of your employees has his wages garnisheed by a local merchant for not paying an overdue bill for a stereo. You do business in a small town, and it does your image no good to tolerate the presence of such people in your company. You fire the employee.

Have you broken the law?

19. You hate to turn down credit applications. Rather than state the refusal of credit in the cold, impersonal words of a letter, you make a practice of calling applicants in person. You thank them for their applications, and ask them to reapply when their credit records have improved.

Have you broken the law?

20. You're presenting an office seminar on the importance of accurate spelling in business communications. In a college workbook, you find an excellent worksheet on spelling. You photocopy thirty copies for use by the office staff.

Have you broken the law?

- Pricing policies
- Interstate trade
- Formal charges, complaints
- Legal questions
- Affirmative Action, Equal Opportunity matters
- Reference letters
- Sales letters representing products and services
- Any topic over which tempers run high

This long cautionary list is not intended to discourage managers from writing entirely, but to remind them to exercise care in the words they choose. Often you may decide to seek legal counsel before "publishing" your words (in the legal sense, to make them known to another party).

Few companies, however, can afford to place a lawyer at the side of each of their business communicators. Therefore, more and more companies provide their writers with "guide letters" to suggest legally approved wording for problematic letters. In the case of a termination guide letter, for example, the legal staff of a company takes time to weigh the legal ramifications of each word in the letter before recommending its use. In Figure 20-2a, notice how the guide letter prevents potential legal entanglements when compared to an original letter on the same topic, Figure 20-2b. Guide letters, though seemingly a restriction on the writer's freedom, can prevent disastrous legal complications.

When employers do not provide guide letters for legally hazardous areas of communication, the burden falls upon the business writer to check out the legal risks involved in his or her words. Company documents cannot be rendered harmless, by the way, simply by typing "Personal" or "Confidential" on the envelope or letter. These words have no standing in court, and in no way shield your words from legal review.

In business dealings for your employer, remember that oral agreements are vastly more difficult to enforce than written agreements. When transacting business, therefore, insist on a written and signed statement describing the terms of the agreement at hand. If the other party is unwilling to give written commitment, you have reason to beware of deception and dishonesty.

In Communispond's survey of 200 executives, managers expressed an almost unanimous desire that business communications be brief. In the light of the legalities of business language, concise business communications have less chance of straying into legally hazardous territory. In Figure 20-3a, notice how the longer version of the "no" letter sets the company up for future legal trouble when compared to the shorter letter in Figure 20-3b.

Many companies sponsor regular legal seminars, in which lawyers discuss current danger areas with business writers. A number of excellent books and articles also deal with the legal aspects of business communications.

You and Your Files

When your company faces suit in court, attorneys for the plaintiff (the party pressing charges) will make an effort to gather supporting evidence and docu-

FIGURE 20-2a

Guide Letter Suggested by Legal Staff

LIBRON CHEMICALS

400 Parkway Drive
Newark, NJ
700-400-1011

April 9, 198_

Mr. Raymond Duncan
Libron Chemicals
West Trenton Branch
241 Auburn Street
Trenton, NJ 29487

Dear Mr. Duncan:

I must inform you that your employment with Libron Chemicals
will be terminated, effective May 10, 198_.

This action has been taken in compliance with company
personnel policies and applicable state, Federal, and union
regulations. Copies of these policy documents may be
obtained at the company personnel office.

If you have questions regarding this action, please contact
Marion Hart at 385-2953.

Sincerely,

Davis Wilborn

Davis Wilborn
Vice-President

DW/em

FIGURE 20-2b

Original Letter Flawed by Potential Legal Snares

LIBRON CHEMICALS

400 Parkway Drive
Newark, NJ
700-400-1011

April 9, 198_

Mr. Raymond Duncan
Libron Chemicals
West Trenton Branch
241 Auburn Street
Trenton, NJ 29487

Dear Mr. Duncan:

This company has been under pressure from state and Federal
regulatory agencies to hire more minorities. Unfortunately,
you must be terminated, effective May 10, 198_, to make room
for these new employees.

In general, your work record here has been superb. You did
take more sick days than we expected, though you never
exceeded the number provided in your contract of
employment. Your large family made it somewhat difficult to
send you on extended travel assignments.

For all these reasons, we have reluctantly chosen you as the
employee in your work unit to be terminated. Good luck in
seeking a career elsewhere.

Sincerely,

Davis Wilborn

Davis Wilborn
Vice-President

DW/em

FIGURE 20-3a

Long Letters Can Stray into Illegal Areas

Seabreeze Financial Group

1000 Harbor Way
Baltimore, Maryland 30402
(717) 666-0990

May 2, 198_

Ms. Susan Todd
5 Fletcher Road
Baltimore, Maryland 30402

Dear Ms. Todd:

We can offer no encouragement in your job search because of
your age, 57. We've found that the company's time and money
simply are not well spent providing training for people who
will soon retire.

Just in case a temporary position becomes available, we will
keep your file active for a period of nine months. If an
opening develops for which you are suited, we will notify
you.

Sincerely,

Reginald Blanchard

Reginald Blanchard
Manager

RB/ss

FIGURE 20-3b

Short Letters Avoid Illegal Areas

Seabreeze Financial Group

1000 Harbor Way
Baltimore, Maryland 30402
(717) 666-0990

May 2, 198_

Ms. Susan Todd
5 Fletcher Road
Baltimore, Maryland 30402

Dear Ms. Todd:

We appreciate your interest in employment at Seabreeze
Financial Group.

Although we cannot offer you a position at the present time,
we wish to keep your application in our active file for nine
months. If a suitable opening occurs, be assured that we
will notify you.

Sincerely,

Reginald Blanchard

Reginald Blanchard
Manager

RB/ss

---

mentation, both by subpoena and deposition (legal mechanisms to draw pertinent information into the open). Your files may contain letters, notes, memos, and other communications which, though written in good faith, can be turned against you and your company.

A supervising manager at a large accounting firm, for example, hired a young man who happened to follow a colorful variation of Zen Buddhism. On company stationery, the manager wrote the following words in a note to her boss, a partner in the firm:

```
. . . his occasional facial decoration (the dots of colored
ink and bits of glitter) will alienate some of our more
traditional clients.
```

A copy of the memo was filed, incorrectly, in the young man's personnel file. When, two years later, the company tried to fire him for a variety of inadequacies, the man accused the firm of religious discrimination. The company officials denied that the man's religious customs or dress ever influenced their decision. But the man's lawyers, as you can imagine, were ecstatic to discover, waiting in his personnel file, a memo apparently corroborating the discrimination charge.

Be careful, therefore, not only about what you write, but what you save. Many companies have ''purge'' policies, requiring managers to shred business documents more than three years old (the time expiration for most tax matters). Other companies establish and enforce strict photocopy rules. Some documents absolutely may not be photocopied and hence are marked ''For Eyes Only'' or ''Do Not Copy.'' These documents frequently contain details of future product planning, marketing strategies, or personnel decisions. Almost all companies take precautions in disposing of documents. Trash bins are hunting grounds for a variety of interested parties: activists, seeking to build a case against a company; industrial spies, looking for product details; and even government agents, trying to establish tax or regulatory violations.

You and Your Customer

Not only good business practice but also the law dictate that you communicate with the customer in a truthful, timely, and unambiguous way.

Warranties and Guarantees. The Consumer Product Warranty Act and Federal Trade Commission Improvement Act of 1975 specifically prohibit companies from using difficult, ambiguous language to hide information or contingencies that a customer needs to know. In the following garble, can you spot the hidden disclaimer in favor of the company?

```
. . . furthermore, the party of the first part does warrant
said product for a period of time not to exceed ninety days,
during which time said party shall repair or replace a
product proven defective by independent examination, if the
```

```
putative defect proves, in said party's judgment, not to
stem from user-induced causes.
```

In other words, the company will decide whether or not you abused your widgit. If so, the company will not repair or replace it.

In plain English (and legal English since the 1975 legislation), this warranty speaks clearly:

```
Acme Industries will stand behind this product for 90 days
from the date of purchase.  If the product fails to perform
properly during this time, return it to Acme Industries.  We
will promptly repair or replace the product, at our option,
and return it to you without charge.
```

Credit. Since the passage of the Fair Credit Billing Act of 1974, managers have had to exercise extreme care in how they determine credit worthiness and what they put into writing once they make their determination.

As we would expect, prejudices against color, race, religion, and national origin are strictly prohibited by the legislation. But managers must also avoid the consideration of a credit applicant's age (hence, future years of high earning potential) or marital status. Nor may they inquire about future plans for a family. Managers may not ask a married woman to obtain the signature of her husband on the application, if it is her desire to establish credit in her own name.

Credit refusals, according to the law, must be written to the applicant. Here managers do well to state the refusal without detailed explanations and evaluations. Compare the two letters of refusal shown in Figures 20-4a and b.

Collections. In 1978, the Fair Debt Collection Practices Act placed strict limits on collection procedures.

- When you can contact someone who owes you money
- How many times you may call
- To whom you may write (not employers or relatives)
- What you may say
  No false impressions (a collection letter marked "Tax Information")
  No threats (". . . or you'll regret it.")
  No slanderous language
- What you must provide
  Timely responses
  Accurate records
  Understandable documents

Because collection practices have such a marred history, legislation is strict—with potent financial and criminal penalties for violators. Any business writer drawing up collection letters should read the pertinent legislation and also seek legal review for letters before they are mailed out.

You and Your Fellow Employees

As a manager, you will communicate often with and about your employees. In many cases, what you say and how you say it are prescribed in federal and state legislation.

Privacy. Inevitably as an employer, you will hold in your possession employee documents containing personal information—age, marital status, health history, employment performance records, reference letters, and security clearances. Since the passage in 1974 of the Federal Privacy Act and subsequent state legislation, strict regulations guide how you can use this information and to whom you may show it.

Most companies develop personnel policy documents to set forth, both for managers and employees, the ground rules by which confidential information is to be handled. If your company has such policies, follow them. If not, exercise caution when revealing to a third party any fact, opinion, or assumption based on confidential knowledge. When in doubt, seek legal advice. Many managers make a practice of asking the employee in question to grant signed permission before revealing confidential information.

Equal Opportunity and Affirmative Action. A massive body of law now surrounds the landmark Civil Rights Act of 1964 and the Equal Employment Opportunity Act of 1972. Managers are constrained by law not to consider race, religion, age, sex, land of birth, or physical impairments in making hiring and firing decisions. None of these items, therefore, should appear even by innuendo in any business document relating to employment.

Probably the most visible result of these laws has been the establishment of Affirmative Action programs in companies large and small. Contrary to the oversimplifications we sometimes hear, Affirmative Action programs do not "hire minorities at all costs." Instead, these programs try to evaluate the hiring and firing policies of the company. Have certain groups been omitted from consideration or treated unequally once hired? If so, why? The result of this evaluation leads many companies

> to advertise job openings more widely,
> to adjust pay and position inequities within the company, and
> to plan for the inclusion of slighted groups.

These goals may seem hopelessly idealistic. But Federal and state legislation has put teeth into Affirmative Action reforms by making the awarding of government contracts contingent upon solid progress in bringing minority groups into the company.

The Handicapped. The Vocational Rehabilitation Act of 1973 started a flood of legislation protecting the handicapped individual against discrimination in the workplace. Private and public foundations have made extensive use of radio

FIGURE 20-4a

Effective Refusal

Gasco Appliance Company

6021 West Belmont Avenue
Fresno, California 94440

January 20, 198_

Mr. Calvin Stockly
222 Wembley Lane
Fresno, CA 96854

Dear Mr. Stockly:

We appreciate your interest in a Gasco credit card. We are
unable to grant credit at this time, but would welcome
reapplication at a future date.

Details of your credit history may be reviewed by calling
Lambert Credit Reporting Service, 209-493-5847.

Again, thank you for your application. We look forward to
your continued business and do hope to give a more favorable
answer regarding credit in the future.

Sincerely,

Rhonda Leaver
Credit Manager

RL/ot

FIGURE 20-4b

Wordy Refusal

Gasco Appliance Company

6021 West Belmont Avenue
Fresno, California 94440

January 22, 198_

Mr. Calvin Stockly
222 Wembley Lane
Fresno, CA 96854

Dear Mr. Stockly:

We must deny your request for credit for the following reasons:

1. You haven't paid $92 owed to Fresno Furniture since 4/4/8_.

2. You have a record as a "late payer" with People's Loan and Thrift. Often your payments are as much as three weeks overdue.

3. In 1978, action was taken against you in small claims court for the collection of $752. The claim was resolved, but still stands as a bad mark against your credit worthiness.

You understand, I'm sure, why our action cannot be more favorable.

Sincerely,

Rhonda Leaver

Rhonda Leaver
Credit Manager

RL/ot

and television time to remind employers how valuable—in dollar and cents terms—the handicapped can be as employees. Some federal grant and tax programs now provide incentives for employers who hire and train the handicapped. The question is now, Can he or she do the job? and no longer, Do I want to hire a handicapped person?

Labor Relations. In all matters related to communication with workers, managers should be guided by the Labor-Management Relations Act as interpreted in the many publications of the National Labor Relations Board. Communications during periods of unionization and strikes are particularly subject to close regulation. Managers, for example, cannot threaten or bribe employees in matters related to labor movements and negotiations. Even subtle suggestions ("You won't ever regret voting 'no'. . . ") are strictly prohibited. Before making public statements on labor matters, managers do well to seek legal advice.

Recommendations. Prior to 1974 and the Family Educational Rights and Privacy Act, managers wrote letters of recommendation on the assumption that they would never be seen by the person being evaluated. Too often, falsehoods and half-truths contained in such "carte blanche" letters went uncorrected. Sometimes these negative comments dogged the steps of an employee for years, a secret and unexpungable ledger in his or her employment file.

Legislation now permits virtually all students and many employees to review their own letters of recommendation, unless they have signed a waiver to that right. Therefore, managers writing reference letters must choose words that in no way can be interpreted as libelous (defamation in writing). While no absolute measurement can be taken, letters of recommendation have taken a definite turn away from negative comments since 1974. Some say this development has been less than helpful to employers seeking accurate recommendations. Others welcome the new emphasis on what a prospective employee *can* do rather than what he or she *can't* do. Many managers who feel they must include negative judgments in a letter of recommendation simply decline the request to write a letter.

You and the Government

Over your business career, you will send hundreds of pages of written commitments to governmental agencies. These pages will include tax documents, regulatory forms, incorporation papers, and a host of other filings. In drawing up these documents, you should take into account the special challenges posed for the business writer by the Freedom of Information Act of 1966.

Businesses routinely send product, process, and service descriptions to governmental agencies. Under "sunshine" legislation, these documents are available for public view—including the close inspection of competitors eager to discover trade secrets, formulas, assembly details, and so forth. The business writer faces the challenge of satisfying government requirements for information without divulging valuable company secrets

A second set of strict government laws involves the use of the mails. The purpose of the dozens of laws pertaining to the mails is to eliminate fraud in its various guises.

The following opening of a come-on letter, for example, defrauds the public by deceitfully and cruelly offering what it cannot deliver:

```
Dear Health-Conscious Reader,
     Has cancer touched your family?  If so, rush $39.50 for
a six month supply of Vaccitabs—the only tablet guaranteed
to drive cancer out of a diseased body and away from a
healthy body . . .
```

Legislators have felt that this kind of communication lures the most vulnerable members of society. When the pills turn out to be mere flour and sugar, the buyer has little recourse. For all practical purposes, he or she cannot sue for $39.50, especially if the company is out of state. Hence, legislation makes it illegal to promote fraud by means of the mail.

While you undoubtedly have no intention of hawking false cures by mail, you may plan to use the post for direct sales or prospect letters. Obtain and read postal regulations pertaining to such sales. If you are unsure whether your words match your product in a fair way, seek legal advice.

You and Your Product or Service

With the passage of the Fair Packaging and Labeling Act of 1966 came new standards particularly for the words that accompany products and services on labels, packages, and instructions. Claims made in these forms may express the manufacturer's enthusiasm for the product ("New! Incredible!"). Labels cannot deceive the consumer by falsehoods, exaggerations, misleading comparisons, and inaccurate specifications. Lined leather gloves, for example, may be advertised to be "as warm as toast," but not as having "rabbit fur lining" when, in fact, synthetic material was used.

To abide by such laws and the wider demands of integrity, managers must often exert a restraining influence on the enthusiasms of ad writers and marketing specialists. What may seem innocent and mild overstatement regarding a product can too easily mushroom into actionable deception in court.

Equal care must be taken not to infringe copyright laws. When a document is published, it bears a copyright designation identifying the person or company owning rights to the work. Extended passages from the copyrighted document cannot be reproduced for commercial purposes by others. Your professor, for example, cannot legally mimeograph thirty copies of a good grammar worksheet he or she finds in a copyrighted workbook.

When you need to borrow sections of a copyrighted work, write to the publisher or holder of the copyright for permission to use the passages.

YOUR WORDS AND THEIR LEGAL CONSEQUENCES

While in business communication classes, you will doubtless experiment with a variety of expressive techniques—stern letters, effusive advertisements, personal memos, and so forth. When you begin your career, however, you must realize that words have legal consequences for you and your company. This fact should not stand as a stoplight to powers of expression, but should flash "caution" on those occasions when you enter the hazard zones of business writing.

Summary

1. Your employer may be held liable for words you write on company stationery or as agent for the company.
2. Communications involving employment are constrained by many laws and regulations. Business communicators should know these legal provisions before writing employment-related documents.
3. The language of warranties and guarantees must meet legal guidelines.
4. Communications involving credit and collection are especially vulnerable to litigation. They should be reviewed by an attorney familiar with business law.
5. Language used in letters or documents to federal, state, or city agencies must be evaluated with care for potential legal hazards.

Questions for Discussion

1. Why is it important for business communicators to take their words seriously as legal instruments?
2. Daily, how much money do American courts award in damages stemming from ill-chosen words? What does this figure suggest to you about the legal ramifications of your business communications?
3. Is it possible to escape your role as a legal agent of your company when working on company time?

4. What general topics or writing assignments in particular pose legal jeopardies for the business writer?
5. What is a "guide letter"?
6. In what way does brevity avoid legally hazardous territory?
7. Why should you be especially cautious when writing memos which will be stored in company files?
8. What guidelines did the Consumer Product Warranty Act and Federal Trade Commission Improvement Act of 1975 establish for business communicators?
9. How does the Fair Credit Billing Act of 1974 affect managers' decisions about their customers' credit worthiness?
10. What limitations does the Fair Debt Collection Practices Act of 1978 place on writers of collection letters?
11. Why is it important for employers to keep their employees' personal files private?
12. What effects have Affirmative Action programs had on businesses' hiring and firing policies?
13. What should employers keep in mind when writing letters of recommendation?
14. What is "sunshine" legislation, and how does it affect the business writer?
15. What guidelines are set forth in the Fair Packaging and Labeling Act of 1966?

Exercises

1. Research slander and libel cases in your college's or university's law library. Bring a case to class and share it with your colleages. How could litigation have been avoided?
2. Ted Benson, a lathe operator with CDC, Inc., has applied for a newly opened management position with the company. He seems qualified to do the job. The only spots on his work record are a few late arrivals to work and an unwillingness to work overtime. He also has no college degree. The real problem, however, is his personality. The two managers with whom he'd be working closely, Sandra Samuelson and Don Starman, have told you that he's an "obnoxious twit." You are assigned to write a letter to Ted turning down his application for advancement in the company. Consider the legal ramifications of the message.
3. Carla Bonoff has applied for credit with your wholesale supply company. However, a quick check with TRW reveals that Ms. Bonoff never pays her bills on time, and is delinquent on several accounts. You think it would be unwise to take a chance. Write a letter turning down her application for credit.
4. When Henry Collier worked as plant manager for RanTech Corporation, he contacted your architectural firm, asking you to design a new employee lounge to be added to the company's main building near the cafeteria. Three weeks later when you called to set up an appointment to present

the plans to Mr. Collier, you discovered that he had left RanTech for greener pastures. The Vice-President of Operations currently fulfilling Collier's old duties said he knows nothing about the plans, and denied that RanTech owed you any money for your work, since Collier had not gone through the proper channels before contracting you. You argue that Collier was acting as a legal agent for RanTech when he hired you. Write a letter to Ran Tech asking for your payment.

5. Joel Kincaid has been a valuable employee with your company for over two years. Recently you were saddened to discover that he had contracted AIDS. While the disease has certainly affected his usually cheerful personality, his work seems to be up to par. However, his fellow employees don't want to work near him. They fear that they might contract the disease, and have written a petition to you asking that Joel be fired. The company has a responsibility to all its employees, and in this case, the needs of the many outweigh the needs of the few, they argue. Consult with the company physician and make a decision. Then write one letter to Joel and another addressed to the petitioners, presenting your decision. What are your legal responsibilities in this situation?

6. Elizabeth Pope is seriously delinquent on her student loan payments. She owes eight months worth of payments and contact letters have produced no results. It's time for a stronger collection letter. Write one, but consider your legal responsibilities under the Fair Debt Collection Practices Act of 1978.

7. In today's mail you received a letter from Peter Bagdasarian, a recent job applicant to your company. Apparently Peter has a friend at DataTron; the friend told him that a black woman had been hired instead of him because of the company's Affirmative Action policy. Bagdasarian's tone in the letter was angry. He feels qualified for the job and is threatening to bring reverse discrimination charges against DataTron. Write him a letter before he takes this unnecessary and troublesome action.

8. Leo Musgrove was recently let go from DataTron because of his abuse of sick leave time. Oddly enough, he has asked you, his department manager, to write a letter of recommendation for him. You explain that it would be difficult to recommend him for the exact reason that he was let go. He says that he must have a letter, even if you have to "tell the truth." His work for the company was adequate—he just wasn't around to do it often enough. Additionally, you like Leo, so you want to help him out. Write a letter of recommendation, but be honest to your reader as well as helpful to Leo.

Answers to Figure 20-1, Legal Quiz, *"Have You Broken the Law?"*

Each of these questions should probably be answered "yes," though the court would no doubt consider individual circumstances in reaching its decision. These answers sum up the thrust of legislation on each of the topics treated in the quiz questions.

1. In collection letters, you may not purposely deceive the debtor by your words on the letter or on the envelope.
2. If you use Frank Vincenti's name without permission, you may be guilty of violating his right to privacy.
3. By law, you must respond to inquiries about credit billing within 30 days.
4. You may be guilty of violating fair credit laws and libel laws by drawing unwarranted conclusions from credit information.
5. By sending your message to Alonzo in such a way that Mort might reasonably be expected to open and read the letter, you may be guilty of libel.
6. Credit cards, by law, may not be mailed to recipients who do not request them.
7. An unrequested item received through the mail may be considered a gift. In trying to collect, you may be breaking the law.
8. You may not reveal the details of a debt to the debtor's employer.
9. You may not reveal the details of a debt to the debtor's friends or relatives.
10. You may not contact the debtor by telephone except between the hours of 8 A.M. and 9 P.M.
11. Upon receiving written and signed notice from the debtor instructing you not to contact him or her by phone, you must desist. You are allowed legal means of contact only, as strictly prescribed by law.
12. You may be guilty of reverse discrimination in turning down a candidate solely on the grounds that he or she is not a minority.
13. You may be violating the right to privacy of the individuals named on your list. The friend opening the finance company may be violating the law as well by accepting and using the names.
14. If you knowingly claim qualities for your product in clear contradiction to the facts and intend to deceive the public by such claims, you may be guilty of misrepresentation and fraud.
15. By law, you cannot discriminate in employment on the basis of age.
16. By law, you cannot discriminate in employment against handicapped people who may reasonably be expected to perform effectively.
17. In interviewing candidates for employment, you may not inquire into future family planning.
18. You may not fire an employee for one garnishment of his or her wages.
19. All credit refusals must be in written, not oral, form.
20. Copyrighted workbooks may not be photocopied, even for nonprofit and educational use, without permission from the copyright holder.

Large and small businesses face an expensive problem with managers sent abroad for extended

duty: they don't stay very long. Listen to Brett Alman, a wholesale food executive recently returned—six

months early—from an assignment in Japan:

I stayed in Japan a total of five and one-half months of my one year assignment. I couldn't take it anymore. The first month, of course, was quite exciting. My family and I saw the usual tourist sights and enjoyed the shopping and food of Japan.

We were treated politely, even with deference, by my Japanese fellow workers. But gradually we came to feel more and more alone. The language was incredibly hard to learn, and my job duties left no time for formal tutoring. My wife and kids really had no one they could communicate with as friends. We felt as if a party were going on while we stood outside and stared in through a window.

I thought I would be more prepared for an international assignment. I realize now that preparing for business abroad involves far more than looking at slides and postcards of famous sites.

Have you ever traveled for an extended period in a foreign country without knowing the language? Can you understand Brett Alman's feelings? What could he and his family have done to prepare more adequately for a foreign business experience?

International

Business

Communication 21

Sun's up. You shut off your Belgian alarm clock, shower, splash on some French cologne, pull on a Peruvian sweater to match your English jeans (made in Hong Kong) and Italian boots, glance at your quartz watch assembled in Mexico, hop into your Japanese car with genuine Levi seat covers and a custom German radio. You're the All-American kid.

As consumers, we are all deeply involved in international trade every day. But few of us feel comfortable dealing with other cultures. Little in our national history has prepared us to understand foreign customs.

Our great-grandfathers didn't trade abroad because they made steel and pushed it around with steam. Getting goods to market in this huge land was task enough. Our grandfathers didn't trade abroad because they made motors that ran on oil and electricity. This country bought up motors as fast as they were produced, then saw to it that each citizen had a steady supply of gas and electricity to run them.

Our fathers began to trade abroad because they could ship plastics and chemicals at a profit in huge cargo ships. It was still easier, though, to buy and sell American.

We trade abroad because we sell information that the world needs. At the speed of light we can transmit our "goods" via communication satellite to virtually any spot on earth. By picking up a telephone in Spokane, we can close a transaction in Paris. By pressing a computer key in Yonkers, we can send charts and reports spilling out of high-speed printers in Australia. By turning on our cable TV, we can monitor transactions live on the Japanese stock exchange. Surely for us as for Milton's Adam and Eve in *Paradise Lost,* "the world stood before them, fresh and new."

But we are still trying to grow beyond the insularity and provincialism of our ancestors. Relatively few of us have lived abroad for more than a quick vacation. Even fewer speak a foreign language, in spite of high school and college language classes. It is no wonder that when we venture into international business we come across not so much as the "Ugly American" as the "Ignorant American."

This chapter cannot provide a Michelin guide to business customs in each of the hundreds of nations in the world. But we can make some progress toward the following:

- understanding the importance of cultural differences
- learning to recognize key areas of human interaction
- determining where to go for advice regarding business customs abroad
- isolating those aspects of language that matter most for clear communication in international business
- looking into international trade relations that lie ahead for us all

CULTURAL DIFFERENCES MATTER

Consider five international business nightmares, all based on cultural facts (though the names have been changed).

In 1982, Carl Travis journeyed from St. Paul, Minnesota, to do business with Som Sharma at his huge clothing factory outside Puwahla, India. Carl wanted to propose a joint venture involving Sharma's money and factory and his own American marketing contacts. Carl's proposal presented "extraordinary opportunities" for success by means of Indian import clothing shops in the United States.

As Carl presented his proposal, the taciturn Sharma shook his head from side-to-side. I'm not doing well, Carl told himself, and redoubled his persuasive efforts. Sharma shook his head back and forth more earnestly. After almost forty-five minutes, Carl snapped his briefcase shut in consternation and stood up to leave. He apparently hadn't gotten to first base with his proposal.

Later at his hotel, Carl learned an expensive lesson from the Indian concierge: Indians in many regions of the country express approval by shaking the head back and forth, the same gesture that Americans use for disapproval.

Margaret Owens sat looking out at the Tokyo skyline from a managerial suite rented for the purpose of interviews. She wanted to find half a dozen enthusiastic Japanese representatives to market a line of pharmaceuticals in Japan. After ten interviews had been completed, Margaret was dumbfounded. Not one applicant spoke up in a direct, forceful manner, in spite of his or her stellar academic record and recommendations. Not one met her eye-to-eye for very long. None seemed comfortable speaking openly and frankly about accomplishments and aspirations.

Margaret reported her discouraging interview results to the Vice-President of Oriental Markets for the drug company—only to endure the most embarrassing lecture of her life. To speak up, she learned from the vice-president, can be taken as impertinence, especially if one emphasizes personal accomplishments. To meet the eyes in some business situations is, in many Oriental cultures, an indication of disrespect or even hostility.

Local mining magnates in Kajari, Pakistan, accepted Fred Revin's invitation to a business dinner at a local restaurant. Fred was pleased to begin the meal with nonbusiness small talk. But after fifteen minutes of pleasantries, he wondered when the conversation would turn to business. He hesitated to broach business topics directly for fear of offending custom. The evening wore on in small talk, to Fred's immense frustration.

In fact, the Pakistani miners were wondering why Fred invited them to dinner. While several minutes of chat are ordained by Pakistani custom, the host—Revin—has the obligation to shift matters to business topics thereafter. Everyone was waiting for Fred to make his move.

Jean Simonds was pleased to accept an invitation for dinner at the home of Klaus and Sonya Griegl, Belgian camera manufacturers. On her way to dinner, Jean spotted some lovely white chrysanthemums at a flower shop. She bought the flowers as a gift for her host.

To her dismay, the flowers brought a stiffly gracious response from her hosts, who set them aside quickly. White chrysanthemums, she learned later, are only presented to mark mourning in Belgium.

In Venezuela, oil broker Cal Farnswell could not help but compliment Venezuelan manager Maria Ortiz on her gorgeous, flowing black hair. Obviously pleased, she received the compliment with a glowing smile. Cal then inquired if her hair was difficult to care for. The smile dropped. The ignorant American had trampled on an important Latin American custom: avoid questions about the personal lives of acquaintances.

Each of these business people initially reacted with shock: "Well, how was I supposed to know?" So that you will not find yourself asking the same question, don't attempt to interact in a new culture before becoming aware of your own assumptions and blind spots. The following are eleven sensitivity areas of cultures around the world.

1. How do men relate to women, and women to men? Though you may not agree on the fairness of relations between the sexes in other cultures, simply knowing their ground rules helps you avoid disastrous social and business pitfalls.

2. How does the culture indicate respect? Consider the roles of silence, direct questions, seating arrangements (remember the infamous seating struggles at the Vietnamese peace talks?), eye contact, gestures, gifts, compliments, and invitations.

3. How does the culture view human time and space? Does an appointment at 7 P.M. mean "7 sharp" or "sevenish" or, as in some Latin countries, around 8? Is one business day, once passed, gone forever (the American notion of linear time) or does the same circumstance repeat itself over and over (the Eastern cyclical view of time)? What of space? Should you stand a bit closer to Frenchmen than you are used to standing to Americans?

4. What are strict taboos in the culture? Is alcohol, for example, accepted, winked at, or absolutely unthinkable? Is your host's off-color joke an invitation for uproarious laughter or a subtle test of your own mores?

5. How are business commitments made in the culture? By oral approval? By a handshake? By signing of documents? Sometimes American business people take oral assurances as evidence that the deal is "a sure thing." When they discover that their hosts are merely being pleasant and agreeable, they often feel cheated and "led on." Try to establish in advance the words and actions in the culture that will let you know your deal is moving forward to commitment.

6. What nonverbal cues are used in the culture to pass information to you, or to pass private understandings between members of the culture? How should you interpret the "V" sign in England? (Sometimes an obscene gesture.) How are you to understand an apology delivered with a big smile in Japan? (Utter sincerity, not a charade.) What does the eye pull mean in Italy

and Spain? (Careful, I'm on to you.) Why does your host in India grimace when, in crossing your legs, you point your soles toward him or her? (An insult.)

7. What words can you learn to indicate your interest in another culture? The whole matter of language and translation bears looking into before entering upon business relations in another culture. Should you supply your own translator? Will he or she be trusted? What should you conclude if your host insists on providing his or her own translator for you?

8. How should one dress for business and social occasions in the host country? Before "going native" in dress, consider the risks of losing your identity as a foreign visitor and hence your immunity to some forms of criticism. In our own country, no one expects the visitor wearing Tibetan ceremonial gowns to cope well with cabs, train schedules, and all the other hassles of urban life. We bend to help. But the same visitor in typical American street clothes may be treated with irritation and impatience. Similarly, your clear identification as an American abroad can bring a modicum of helpfulness from the host country.

9. How do your foreign hosts reason? This rather large question can be dealt with in practical, not philosophical, ways. Do your hosts favor direct propositions supported by evidence? Do they wish to consider your reputation, your family roots, your personal success, your age, your sex, your educational attainments? Do they want to hear your arguments or merely to share your friendship? Is a business relation to be based on rational analysis or trust?

10. What aspects of the host country's religious or political life must be understood for effective business relations? Are certain times of the day set aside for worship, not work? Is work automatically canceled on some holidays, or is it optional? Must certain work groups be separated due to political differences? Are some job tasks disliked for religious or political reasons?

11. What prejudices against you as an American must you overcome in the culture? Do your hosts automatically assume that you throw money around in a careless and tasteless way? Do they assume that your appetites for food, booze, and sex are out of control? Do they look upon you as a steam-roller, a modern Roman who believes that might makes right? In all these matters, you may have to exert your imagination and energies to show yourself as you are, not as you are thought to be.

WHERE TO GO FOR ANSWERS

These important questions rarely go unanswered for long. You do find out, often painfully, what your host country feels, thinks, believes, and values. But the goal for the astute international business man or woman is not to find out the hard way through personal blunders and faux pas. There are ways to begin to learn about your foreign hosts before you leave home.

Visit the Country's Embassy or Consulate

Most trade-seeking nations maintain experienced ambassadors and consuls with extended staffs in major U.S. cities, particularly New York, Washington, and Los Angeles. You can make an appointment with the commercial secretary at the embassy to learn how to approach businesses—and often whom to approach—when you visit the foreign country. If you cannot visit in person, write a letter describing your business interests. Solicit the help of the embassy in making your venture mutually profitable.

Enroll in Cultural Training

Many schools, clubs, and organizations provide cultural awareness training. The following groups will provide you with information about their services and general advice about cultural preparation.

Overseas Briefing Associates
201 East 36th St.
New York, NY 10016

The Business Council for International Understanding
The American University
Washington, DC 20016

The Intercultural Communications Network
1860 19th St., N.W.
Washington, DC 20009

These organizations can acquaint you with such universal business conventions abroad as *name cards*. Similar in size and format to business cards used in this country, name cards contain not only your name, title, and company in English, but also on the reverse side the same information translated into the language of your host country. Especially important in such a translation is the statement of your title. Corporate "president," for example, in English does not signify the same thing in Japan. There, a "president" is an honored, retired, and relatively powerless former leader of industry. Probably your title as "president" would be rendered "senior director" to communicate your status clearly in your host country.

Such name cards are given and taken freely in your business dealings. You may easily dispense a hundred such cards in your first week in a foreign country and take in twice that number. Many countries publish name card collection books, complete with hierarchical interior divisions so you can store your collected name cards in a pecking order of sorts. Without such cards of your own, you may have difficulty establishing your credentials in business contacts that come your way through the day.

Ask People Who Have Been There

Except for personal experience itself, no learning is so potent—or trusted—as the testimony of someone similar in background to your own. Find out if

FIGURE 21-1

anyone in your company or another company has visited the country in question. Find time to listen to stories of his or her experiences. You may even find the inevitable slides helpful (see Figure 21-1).

Ask questions and seek guidance from secondary resources such as the country's national airline serving your city (Swiss Air, British Airways, and so forth). At such places, you probably will meet someone ''here'' who knows someone ''over there''—and that someone can prove invaluable to you as an initial cultural contact.

American banks that do business abroad and foreign banks in this country can often prove helpful to you. Also, draw upon the considerable resources of the United States Chamber of Commerce. It publishes a number of booklets on trade relations. Each foreign country seeking trade will probably also have a chamber of commerce anxious to serve you. In most cases, you can reach this office by writing to the Office or Ministry of International Trade in the capital city of the country that interests you.

Study the Language

Above all, begin *language training* in the tongue of the culture you intend to visit. Every American knows how helpless a foreign visitor can be in this country without a few words of English.

If you lack an elementary knowledge of your host country's language, you will feel increasingly isolated from the social life of the country the longer you stay. Work associates will chat amiably among themselves, leaving you dependent upon a translator or virtually isolated from the friendly banter of the day. Don't be concerned that your mastery of the language is incomplete. Your hosts will take it as a compliment that you are trying to learn their language at all and will help you at every turn.

CATEGORIES OF CULTURAL DIFFERENCE

The following table lists central ways in which cultures can differ. In reading the table, compare your own culture in each category to another culture with which you are familiar.

1. GREETINGS—appropriate or inappropriate gestures (such as handshake or touching), verbal greetings (what to say); how close together persons stand when greeting or conversing, conversation topics, etc.
   a. meeting a person the first time:
   b. everyday acquaintances:
   c. close friends:
   d. elderly people:
   e. women:
   f. youth:
   g. children:
   h. leaders in the culture:
   i. to show special respect:
   j. from a distance:
   k. use of family name or first name:
   l. use of titles (such as Mr. or Dr.):
   m. compliments with greetings (what to compliment, how to give and receive compliments, and when):

2. VISITING a family at home—what should and should not be done in the following situations.
   a. greeting:
   b. entering the house:
   c. gifts and flowers (what is appropriate; when and how to give, receive and open gifts):
   d. compliments on possessions, decor, or to family members:
   e. proper conduct (in the living room, parlor, or guest welcoming area):
   f. conversation (what topics are best and when people usually talk):
   g. table manners (seating arrangements, when a guest should begin to eat, excusing oneself from the table, etc.):
   h. utensils and how to use them:
   i. conversation at the dinner table:
   j. compliments on the food:
   k. saying farewell and leaving:
   l. parties and social events (What should be remembered by a guest to best interact with the host and other guests? What is expected of the guest?):
   m. words to avoid:

3. TALKS, SPEECHES AND PUBLIC ADDRESSES to groups of people.
   a. subjects or topics which these people are especially fond of or those which should not be referred to:
   b. gestures which help or hurt communication:
   c. the way the speaker stands or sits in front of the group:
   d. hints on using an interpreter:

4. MEETINGS—punctuality, best ways to begin and end the meeting, seating arrangement, eye contact, and using an interpreter.
   a. large formal meetings:
   b. small group sessions (about 3–15 people):
   c. private interview with an individual:

5. GESTURES—those which help to carry a message and those which should be avoided.
   a. with hands:
   b. head:
   c. eye and eye contact, eyebrows, face (Is it customary to look a person directly in the eyes when speaking? What would be the reaction to this by a person in this culture?):
   d. legs (such as crossing the legs when sitting down):
   e. feet (moving things with them, pointing them at people, gesturing with them, putting them on one's desk, etc.):
   f. posture (standing and sitting down, hands on hips, etc.):
   g. touching (another person, male and female, etc.):
   h. shoulders:
   i. arms (such as folding them or putting them around another's shoulders):
   j. smiling and laughing customs (When is a smile appropriate or inappropriate? In what situations does a smile mean something other than happiness and good will?):
   k. yawning:
   l. calling someone to you with your hands (palm facing up or down, etc.):
   m. handing, passing, or giving things to another person:

6. PERSONAL APPEARANCE.
   a. clothing:
   b. eye glasses and sun glasses:
   c. hats:
   d. other:

7. GENERAL ATTITUDES of (1) adults, a. male b. female: (2) teenagers, a. male b. female, about:
   a. nature and man's role in it:

b. society, groups, and the individual, self:

c. wealth, clothes, possessions:

d. work, success, failure, and fate:

e. government, politics, taxes, police welfare assistance:

f. personality traits that are considered good or bad in a person:

g. role of men and women:

h. sexual promiscuity, abortion:

i. time, punctuality:

j. youth, teenagers:

k. elderly people:

l. physically or mentally handicapped:

m. business and economic progress:

n. war and the military:

o. crime and violence:

p. majority groups, races and minority groups (special likes, dislikes, or problems):

q. other nations and their people (special likes, dislikes, or problems):

r. longevity, retirement and death:

s. political systems (socialism, communism, imperialism, democracy, etc.):

t. humor:

u. promises, agreements, and trust:

v. community participation:

w. revenge, retributions, repayment of wrongs received:

x. animals, pets:

y. showing emotions:

z. gambling, drinking alcoholic beverages, drugs:

aa. giving and receiving criticism:

bb. making decisions in business, among peers:

cc. education:

dd. what possessions or achievements indicate status (for men and women, adult and youth):

8. LANGUAGE—dialects, use of English, etc.

9. RELIGION—general attitudes toward religion, predominant beliefs.

10. SPECIAL HOLIDAYS—specific dates and how these holidays are celebrated.

11. THE FAMILY.

a. average size of family:

b. attitudes about the family and its role in society:

c. teenagers' role in the family:

d. role of the elderly in the family:

e. authority, obedience, roles of father, mother, and children (making decisions in the family):

f. system of family inheritance:

g. milestone experiences in life for a male:

h. milestone experiences in life for a female:

i. special activities which are used to show that a person has become an adult (or otherwise changed social status):

j. who in the family works (father, mother, children):

k. average daily schedule and activities for fathers, mothers, children:

12. DATING AND MARRIAGE CUSTOMS.

a. from what age does dating begin? How important is dating? Why?:

b. is dating in larger groups or individual couples?:

c. common dating activities:

d. chaperones:

e. acceptable and unacceptable dating behavior:

f. engagement customs:

g. attitude about marriage:

h. age at which most men marry:

i. age at which most women marry:

j. how much influence the family has in deciding about marriages:

k. prerequisites to marriage (such as completion of education or financial independence):

l. desirability of children (birth control):

m. attitude about divorce:

n. attitude toward displaying affection in public (such as between husband and wife or parents and children):

13. SOCIAL AND ECONOMIC LEVELS— including size of different general classes, average income and what it provides for the family, general housing conditions and possessions (such as refrigerator, range, toaster, cars, radios, telephones, televisions, etc.).

14. DISTRIBUTION OF GROUP—rural or urban, what cities or areas, group population for areas concerned and what ratio group population is to total population in these areas.

15. WORK.

a. the economy of the group (What are the main occupations of the people, industries, and important products?):

b. individual work schedules (hours per day, days per week):

c. age at which people begin working:

d. choosing a job:

16. DIET.

a. average diet, size of meals when they are eaten:

b. special foods which are usually given to guests:

c. Is mealtime important for some other reason than just nutrition?

17. RECREATION, SPORTS, ARTS, MUSIC, LEISURE TIME.

a. family cultural and physical recreation and sports activities (including vacations):

b. individual recreation, games, sports of children, youth, adults, and elderly:

c. distinctive arts of the culture which a visitor should know about:

18. HISTORY AND GOVERNMENT.

a. history of the group, including facts and events considered most important by the people and why:

b. heroes, leaders of the group and why they are esteemed:

c. group goverment systems, differences from regular local government:

19. EDUCATION.

a. education in the group:

b. any private education systems within the group:

20. TRANSPORTATION AND COMMUNICATION SYSTEMS—their use and significance to the group.

a. bicycles:

b. individual cars and road system:

c. buses:

d. taxis:

e. other:

f. mass communication (such as TV, radio, newspapers, magazines):

g. individual interpersonal communication (such as telephones, postal service):

h. any special or unusual methods of trade, exchange, communication, or transportation:

21. HEALTH, SANITATION, MEDICAL FACILITIES—including general attitude about disease.

22. LAND AND CLIMATE—including geographical effects on the history of the group, problems posed today by the geography or climate where these people are located.

23. "UNIVERSAL" SIGNALS OR NON-VERBAL CUES a newcomer should know that indicate approval or disapproval, acceptance or rejection in this society.

This list is a partial summary of some aspects of culture which can unite people who share the same basic attitudes, backgrounds, and lifestyles. Since these characteristics can vary widely between cultures they can be a source of misunderstanding and miscommunication.

Source: ''Categories of Cultural Difference,'' Language Research Center, Brigham Young University, 1976. Reprinted by permission.

EXAMINE YOUR OWN LANGUAGE AND CULTURAL HABITS

While you investigate your host country's customs and language, remember to examine your own ways of speaking and writing.

Avoid Slang and Colloquialisms

Learn to pare slang and colloquialisms from the words you use for international business. Robert Bell, Magnetic Resonance Specialist for General Electric, comments:

> *When I travel to business meetings abroad, I have to remember that my ordinary mode of friendly conversation contains many idioms (such as "right on the money") that foreign colleagues will find strange and uninterpretable. I remind myself to speak "plain vanilla" English around those who don't know the language well.*

One American manager wrote the following sentence to a foreign businessman with limited English skills. "By the way, I've shipped the computer order we discussed last week."

The American manager was shocked to receive a telex from his foreign client: "What is 'the way' you refer to? Urgent to know." The English language is rich in such innocent colloquialisms. But for the sake of clear business dealings abroad, the business communicator must be aware of words and phrases subject to misunderstanding.

Slow Down Your Speech

Adjust the pace of your speaking to match the rate of comprehension of your foreign host. You will often do business with men and women abroad who have, through hard work, acquired more than a bit of English. If you rush ahead at the same speaking pace you would use with a native speaker, you unintentionally dash these people's efforts to communicate with you. Before leaving for an international trip, practice slowing down your speech without sounding patronizing. Look directly at the person to whom you are speaking, so that he or she can see the words as they form on your lips and notice your facial and hand gestures.

Some Americans adopt a quizzical frown in speaking to foreign persons; the look is not intended as a negative scowl, but instead as a visual way of asking, "Are you following me?" Be careful not to use the frown in this way. It will regularly be misinterpreted as condemnation or impatience. If you want to check for comprehension, raise your eyebrows and give an inquiring smile. That visual gesture will produce either a nod of comprehension from your foreign friend, or an indication that he or she has not understood.

To test the powers of facial gestures in such situations, notice your own inability to remember foreign words and phrases when looking into the stern, unsmiling face of a German policeman or French butcher. When we see indications of disapproval, our powers of language freeze up. When we see smiles of approval, we can think of quite a few words and phrases. We surprise ourselves in demonstrating what the Germans call "Sprachgefühl"—a natural way with words.

Check for Comprehension

Learn to check often (in polite ways) to see if your listener is comprehending. In a telephone conversation, for example, pause to ask "Am I being clear?" or "Do you understand?" or simply "O.K.?" In face-to-face conversations, do not mistake a courteous smile on your listener's face as a sign of complete comprehension. Particularly in Oriental cultures, your listener will give you a smile simply as a polite gesture. Oriental listeners may even nod and say "yes" repeatedly, all in an effort to show respect to you. All the while, they may almost entirely misunderstand what you are saying. Good barometers of such misunderstanding are the eyes. Watch to see if your listener's eyes respond to your words. If you notice a glazed, lost look, back up and begin again in a simpler fashion.

Marshall McLuhan has captured our common destiny in his description of "spaceship earth." "There are no passengers on spaceship earth," he wrote. "We are all crew." As the ability to know—and to know almost instantaneously—transforms lives and cultures around the planet, no business person can hide in a regional or national niche and expect to avoid the influence of the Information Revolution. While a hardware store owner in Wichita may not sell hammers to Red China, he or she will want to be the first to know when hammers imported from Poland are sold 20 percent cheaper than the American variety. Larger corporations will have no reason to limit their marketing horizons to national borders, especially as jet travel and communication devices make the world what McLuhan calls a "global village."

As business corridors open to new markets, we will often stub our verbal toes in efforts to communicate. In the words of John Naisbitt, author of the best-selling book, *Megatrends,*

> *We are living in the "time of the parenthesis," the time between eras (between the Industrial Era and the Information Era). The time of the parenthesis is a great and yeasty time . . . a time of great change and uncertainty (and we must make uncertainty our friend) . . . and a time of great opportunity. In stable eras everything has a name and everything knows its place . . . and we can leverage very little. But in the time of the parenthesis we have extraordinary leverage and influence . . . individually . . . professionally . . . and institutionally . . . if we can get a clear sense, a clear conception, a clear vision of the road ahead. My God, what a fantastic time to be alive!*

Summary

1. Business men and women who plan to do business abroad must recognize the importance of cultural differences.
2. This chapter suggests eleven key areas in which cultures can be evaluated.
3. Several agencies offer cultural awareness materials and training for business people headed abroad.
4. Because language is the most important link between people, business men and women should examine their own use of English in relation to the language needs of their foreign listeners.
5. At all levels, business is becoming internationalized. Business trips to and communications with other cultures will be a reality for more and more business people in the years ahead.

Questions for Discussion

1. What are the eleven sensitivity areas of world cultures?
2. How could the use of human time and space affect your business transactions in a foreign country?

3. What are some steps you may take in order to acquaint yourself with your foreign host before leaving the States?
4. What are name cards? How are they used?
5. Should you ever rely on a colleague's personal experience in a foreign country you plan to visit?
6. What is probably the most significant way you can prepare ahead for your visit to a foreign country?
7. Why is it important to speak "plain vanilla" English in business meetings abroad?
8. When speaking English with a non-native speaker, what habits should you avoid?
9. How can visual gestures aid your communication with a foreign businessman who does not speak your language well?
10. How can you check your listener's comprehension over the phone?
11. In a face-to-face conversation, what are good barometers of lack of comprehension?
12. Explain Marshall McLuhan's statement, "There are no passengers on spaceship earth . . . . We are all crew."
13. What is the "time of the parenthesis"? What are its advantages?

Exercises

1. Pick a country that you would like to visit on business some day. Write a letter to the embassy or consulate of that country, requesting as much information as is available on travel and business opportunities there. Keep this information in your files for future use.
2. Research attitudes on the relationship between men and women in the country of interest to you. How might the relations between sexes in this country affect your communication with your host?
3. Extend an invitation to a potential business associate in a foreign country. Convey the proper respect for his or her culture.
4. Continue your research on the foreign country of your choice, and identify strict taboos which you'll want to be aware of. What particular taboos might you have violated, had you not taken time to investigate the cultural differences between your country and the foreign country?
5. How should you dress to make the best impression possible in the foreign country which interests you?
6. Identify the religious and political ideologies you would most likely encounter in the country you are researching. How do these ideologies resemble or differ from your own? How will you avoid possible difficulties in these areas?
7. "Yankee go home." If you are an American citizen, how might you be regarded in the country of interest to you? Investigate current perceptions about America held in that country. If these perceptions are negative, how do you plan to present yourself positively?
8. Compile a list of colloquialisms or slang which might be misinterpreted by a foreign business person with limited English skills.

Cases

The writing and speaking assignments in these cases may be used with any chapter in the text. Each case, however, bears a Part number (in brackets) to indicate the particular Part of the text emphasized in the case at hand.

Raytex Computers, Inc. [1]

While pursuing a business degree two years ago, you met two classmates who would change your life: Bob Simmons and Kathy Leavitt. After graduation, the three of you pooled your resources, slim though they were, to form Raytex Computers, Inc. In your first six months you were able to produce the prototype of the Raytex Companion, a lap-sized computer that fit neatly into a briefcase and included a small built-in printer capable of printing neat business letters.

On the strength of that prototype, Raytex attracted a sizable venture capital loan and began production.

Now, three years later, the company has reached a plateau of sorts. Certainly Raytex has been successful in its region of the country. But you want to market your product nationally before a competitor beats you to the opportunity.

That kind of growth will require more investment capital, more employees, a larger plant, more sophisticated marketing and advertising strategies, and a host of other changes.

As directors of the Raytex corporation, the three of you have become used to production planning: how many silicon chips to order, how many assembly line workers to hire, and so forth. But your expansion plans call for a new kind of planning—the planning of crucial business communications with banks, advertising agencies, lawyers, accountants, and others. "Once," Bob Simmons jokes, "my years were all spent with a soldering iron in my hand. Now all you'll let me touch is a pen."

Consider the new challenges that face Bob, Kathy, and you as you make the transition from managers of technology (production line management) to managers of communication (information and persuasion management).

Individual Writing Activities

1. In your role as a director of Raytex, list the major communication activities, both written and oral, that you will face during your national expansion campaign. For example, you will have to make presentations to financial institutions to seek new capital.
2. Write a personal letter to Bob, thanking him for his leadership in the technological sector of the company. Explain to him why he must now get used to using a pen more than a soldering iron as a manager.
3. Write a personal letter to Kathy, thanking her for heading up the difficult area of personnel management at Raytex. Suggest the kinds of changes you foresee in her responsibilities as Raytex begins to penetrate national markets.

Group Writing Activities

1. Meeting in groups of three (representing the three directors of Raytex), draw up a job description for a business communicator to assist the directors. Specify the kind of background you require as well as the typical tasks in which the communicator will be involved day to day.

2. Again meeting in groups of three as directors, decide how you can train your managers in communication skills to prepare them for your national expansion campaign. Devise a plan for such training; specify what will be taught, by whom, and when. Set aside an appropriate amount of money to cover the expense of this training effort.

Individual Speaking Activities

1. Tell a group of assembled Raytex managers why the company has decided to "go national" at this time. Point out the distinct advantages of being the first company to market a lap-sized computer on a national scale.
2. Describe the meteoric growth of Raytex, speaking informally as if addressing a local Rotary Club meeting. Focus upon the key ingredients that made for your company's success. Use information contained on the fact sheet accompanying this case.

Group Speaking Activities

1. Participate in a brainstorming session involving other Raytex directors and managers. Try to come up with an orderly and effective plan for national expansion. Present your decisions to a larger group.
2. Participate in a closed-door directors' meeting with Bob and Kathy (in other words, a group of three). Decide through discussion on a fair division of responsibility regarding the major tasks involved in national expansion. Who will speak to the bankers? Who will handle advertising? Who will oversee hiring? Consider these and other topics, then give an oral summary of your decisions to a larger group.

FACT SHEET Raytex Computers, Inc.

Gross Sales
1982	$362,000
1983	$824,000
1984	$1,903,000
1985	$3,852,000

Product Line	Units Sold				Projected
	1982	1983	1984	1985	1986
Raytex Personal Computer	202	409	1082	3277	6279
Raytex Dot Matrix Printer	54	201	804	1203	3079
Raytex Color Monitor	21	54	302	812	1502
Raytex Lap Computer (in production)					2300
Employees	14	28	97	143	166
Earnings per share	− .06	− .02	.21	.54	.85

MINI-CASE 1A The Cleveland Business Seminar

Writing Activity

As Director of Extended Education at Cleveland Business College, you are preparing a two-day seminar in communication skills for business managers and sales people. List eight topics you want to cover in the two-day class. In a sentence or two, briefly explain why each topic is important for the group.

Speaking Activity

Speak informally to a group of managers and sales people (who, by the way, may look remarkably like your classmates.) Try to persuade them to enroll in the seminar on communication skills.

MINI-CASE 1B Career Day at Old Central High

Writing Activity

As a graduate several years ago of Central High, you have been invited back as keynote speaker for Career Day. After all, you have certainly distinguished yourself in business since your days at Central. In speaking with the Career Day planning committee, you are dismayed to learn that every department in the school has a Careers presentation except the English department. The chair of the English department explains that "there really aren't any jobs for English majors except teaching."

In preparation for your keynote address, write down a list of the skills learned in English and speech classes--skills that later prove crucial to business success.

Speaking Activity

Tell a group of people about your own business success. Focus upon the important role communication skills played in your career advances.

MINI-CASE 1C The Perfectionist

Writing Activity

As branch manager of Kenneson Financial Management, you set strict standards for all communications that leave the office. You don't tolerate capitalization errors, for example, or sentence fragments.

The secretaries have generally agreed that you are "just impossible" and even "absurd" in your expectations. They have begun sighing loudly and rolling their eyes when you insist that a letter or report be retyped to remove errors.

To guide the secretaries, write down at least ten errors, with one example of each, that you want to banish from writing in the office.

Speaking Activity

Speak informally to a group of your employees about the importance of the "little things" in written business communications. In drawing together your thoughts, consider such matters as the effect of writing errors upon the company image.

Can't Get Started [1]

You are understandably excited about your first day as Unit Supervisor in the communications division of Cosmopolitan Insurance Company. You will direct the writing efforts of seven employees, working on such projects as brochures, advertisements, form letters, and reports.

The previous supervisor was dismissed, you learned, for not providing "direction and leadership" for the unit's writers. You resolve, therefore, to be a hands-on supervisor from your very first day.

Your first day begins at 8 o'clock with the customary introductions and well-wishing. You are somewhat surprised by 9 o'clock to see that none of the writers has yet begun to work. You ask several if they have projects to work on. "Oh, yes," they reply, "we all have plenty to do."

By 10 o'clock, you are dumbfounded to see almost every writer still nursing a morning cup of coffee, talking at the water cooler, or flipping through the newspaper. You promptly call a meeting to get to the heart of the problem.

One writer seems to speak for the rest. "Well, you don't start writing the way you start your car. It's an art, and sometimes it takes several hours to get motivated. Most of us experience Writer's Block until about 11 o'clock every morning."

Individual Writing Activities

1. Write a step-by-step guide for overcoming Writer's Block.
2. In a polite but firm memo to the writers in your unit, set forth your expectations of their activity beginning at 8 A.M. every morning.
3. Write up an account of your first day for your journal.

Group Writing Activities

1. After discussing Writer's Block in groups of three or more, each participant writes down his or her own method of overcoming moments of stagnation and frustration in writing.
2. In the role of writers within the unit, meet in small groups to generate a written reply to the new supervisor's outrageous suggestion that actual writing be undertaken before 11 A.M. each day.

Individual Speaking Activities

1. Deliver an informal pep talk to your writers on overcoming Writer's Block in an efficient way.
2. Tell how you manage to break through the blocks and dead ends that so often accompany the writing process.

Group Speaking Activities

1. Meeting together as a unit, discuss the supervisor's suggestion that the morning be spent more productively each day. Assign roles within your group. One person

can play the supervisor, another a militant advocate of the writer's freedom to hours of unstructured thinking, another a lazy writer who simply hates to begin work before 11 A.M. each day, and so forth. Your meeting may not produce agreement, but at least the new supervisor will have a clear idea of the issues involved.

2. One of the perpetual problems in the unit is deciding just how long a given writing assignment should take. Meet as a group, again including the supervisor, to devise some guidelines for estimating the amount of time needed for a given writing project. You may want to develop time estimates for each of these projects:

> a one-page sales letter
> a two-page form letter
> a half-page advertisement (text)
> a four-page brochure
> a six-page report

Lies, Lies, Lies [2]

Like the competing colas, your company's product—Dreamboat cream-filled cupcakes—has its fierce competitors. While you don't mind a fair fight for market dominance, you do despise the cheating, lying advertisements appearing on nation-wide television during the last two weeks: "An independent survey revealed that children from Oregon to Vermont are switching from Dreamboat cupcakes to Super Spongies. Why? Probably because Dreamboat cupcakes contain absolutely no dairy products: no milk, no cream, no butter. Growing kids need good nutrition. Join the thousands who would rather have a Spongie."

Individual Writing Activities

1. Prepare an advertising counterattack by listing those claims you can refute, those claims you can explain away, and those claims you must admit. Develop your own set of claims against Spongies. For additional background information, use the fact sheet accompanying this case.

2. Pay particular attention to Spongies' "independent survey." In a one- or two-page memo, demonstrate (by making up whatever evidence you require) that the Spongies company is using statistics in a deceptive way.

3. In a page or two, compare the ingredients of Dreamboat cupcakes with Spongies. Argue that Dreamboats have superior nutritional value.

Group Writing Activities

1. Meet with at least three other company members to write the text of a television ad to counteract the effect of the Spongie advertising.

2. Meet with several other company members to plan for a new product in the Dreamboat line. Write a one- or two-page description of the new product.

Individual Speaking Activities

1. Deliver a short presentation on Dreamboat cupcakes to your stockholders' meeting. They need to be reassured that the popular Spongie ads are not correct, and can be counteracted.
2. Speak briefly and informally to your advertising group on the importance of absolute truthfulness in the treatment of statistics.

Group Speaking Activities

1. Meet with other company members to devise a strategy to counteract the Spongie advertisements.
2. Hold a news conference at which you and other company members answer questions about the impact of the Spongie ads on the Dreamboat line of pastries. Have some of your classmates play the parts of newspaper and television reporters.
3. Play the role of President of Dreamboat Corporation on the telephone with another class member playing the part of the President of Spongie Corporation. State your charges frankly and try to work toward a solution.

MINI-CASE 3A Hothead

You are *the* Carlson in Carlson Commercial Properties, Inc., a successful industrial and commercial real estate brokerage. Your best sales person, Trini, has immense vitality and an equally ferocious temper.

Writing Activity

Choose one of Trini's particularly angry memos to a fellow employee (you, of course, will have to write this memo). By rewriting the memo in a more professional form, demonstrate ways in which strong messages can be communicated clearly without resorting to passion and hysteria.

Speaking Activity

In a discussion group of three or more members, let one classmate play the role of Trini. Discuss the place of anger in business writing and speaking. The group members should subtly offer Trini alternatives to verbal explosions. Trini, on the other hand, may be able to offer the group helpful insights into frank, spontaneous communication.

MINI-CASE 3B A Word or Two of Advice

As a mid-level manager at Hudson Holding Company, you are simultaneously pleased and scared when the president of the company asks you for a few words of advice on his (or her) speaking style. You've heard the president speak before, and the experience was not overwhelming.

Writing Activity

In an extended memo to the president, suggest at least three common sense principles for public speaking. In each case, tell why the principle at hand is important.

Speaking Activity

With a classmate playing the role of the president, conduct an informal interview in which you ask the president to describe particular areas of insecurity or discomfort in public speaking. Go on, then, to discuss possible solutions.

MINI-CASE 3C Single Sentence Sarah

At Varithon Environmental Research, one of your best research scientists writes all of her reports in single sentences.

Writing Activity

Make up at least ten such single sentences, choosing a topic such as smog, water pollution, toxic waste sites, and so forth. Then, by rewriting the sentences in paragraph form, show how the task of reading the report becomes easier and more enjoyable.

Speaking Activity

In a group of three or more members, discuss the value of paragraphs in business writing. Prepare for the discussion by gathering examples of short and long paragraphs in various kinds of business writing, including advertising. Try to decide as a group when to choose single sentences, short paragraphs, or long paragraphs in business writing.

Chips [2]

It has all happened so fast. Eighteen months ago you were baking chocolate chip cookies out of your home for a local delicatessen. Now you run The Chips Corporation, a complex business, supplying the greater New York City area with cookies from your secret recipes. You employ eight bakers, a fleet of delivery trucks, and several managers, supervisors and accountants to keep the whole operation running smoothly.

Smoothly? You smile ruefully, looking at the pile of "communications" piled on your desk (see the fact sheet accompanying this case). In this rapid growth period, no one took time to organize the kinds of communications useful to managers in the business. As a result, everyone jotted notes on whatever paper was available. Even important business letters sometimes went out in handwritten form.

Individual Writing Activities

1. You resolve to end the paper chaos. Choose at least eight forms of business communication. By describing the uses, stationery, routing and filing requirements for each form, you will be establishing a systematic network for written communication in your company.
2. Write a memo to your office staff, directing that all in-house memos follow a prescribed form. Specify that form.

Group Writing Activities

1. Meet together in groups of three or more to decide upon a color code for in-house stationery. Write up a brief information sheet guiding other employees in the use of the color code.
2. Meet together in groups of three or more to chart the flow of written communications within the company. Who writes to whom? Create a list of suggestions to streamline communication.

Individual Speaking Activities

1. Prepare for your appearance on a network talkshow by drawing up speaking notes for a three minute monologue on your company's rise to success. Deliver the monologue, into a tape recorder if possible.
2. Your bakers need an occasional pep talk. Develop a short, informal speech emphasizing their importance to the company. Suggest future rewards and opportunities.

Group Speaking Activities

1. Meet with your key managers. Discuss how your company can keep and even extend its share of the market.

2. Sit down with a group of chocolate chip cookie afficionados. Discuss with them the merits and shortcomings of your cookies.

FACT SHEET Chips

Three examples of communications from Chips Corporation prior to efforts to overhaul business writing within the company.

Letter to a supplier:

20# flour by June 2 – no later!

Bill COD

Owner,
Bill Lengol

Letter to an overdue account:

Mr. Ledderer, my records show that you bought several dozen trays of our product over the past three months for sale in your two delicatessens. Have you made payment for these? Did I send you a receipt of any kind? We're trying to straighten out your account, and it appears that you owe us. Please respond.

Letter to a bank president

Dear Sir/Madame;

For some time, as you may be aware, we have been in your neighborhood in the cookie business in New York. And now we are seeking expansion financing, you see we need a new production oven which will cost more than we are able to raise from our own invested funds and therefore are turning to the excellent reputation of your bank for helping small businesses such as us in these matters. Thank you.

Sincerely,

Bill Lengol

Insert Tab A in Slot B [2]

You have worked at Drayco Toys, Inc., long enough to see tastes come full circle. Parents used to buy model kits and toys they assembled themselves for Johnny and Jill. Then, with fast foods came fast toys—ready to use right off the shelf. Now the pendulum has swung back. You think parents are ripe for your great idea: a kit out of which a parent can build any number of toys for the kids.

Individual Writing Activities

1. Write a memo to your immediate supervisor, asking for time to develop the proposal described above.
2. Write a memo to four fellow employees, asking them to participate in the development of the proposal.

Group Writing Activities

1. Divide the task of writing a proposal into several segments, one for each member in the proposal writing team. Discuss the development of the proposal, then write a rough draft. Use the information contained in the fact sheet accompanying this case.
2. Play the role of a proposal evaluation team. You have been asked to look over the rough draft developed in activity # 1 above. Read the rough draft, discuss it, then make constructive suggestions for its improvement.
3. On the basis of the evaluation group's suggestions, write a final draft of the proposal. Each member may write a section of the proposal, with one or more members acting as editor for the document as a whole.

Individual Speaking Activities

1. As originator of the idea, prepare and deliver a brief summary of your proposal to an assembled group of managers. Answer their questions after your presentation.
2. Address a group of parents. In a short impromptu presentation, try to make your idea sound attractive.

Group Speaking Activities

1. Choose two class members to play ''devil's advocate'' in speaking against your idea. Defend the proposal as well as you can.
2. Meet with the proposal writing team. Discuss alternative ways in which the proposal could be developed.

MINI-CASE 5A Just to Be Sure

Not all supervisors at Colwell Engineering have master keys to the drafting building. You have a key, and therefore also bear responsibility for its use or misuse. This

> **FACT SHEET Drayco Toys**
>
> Contents of the DRAYCO Make-It-Yourself Toy Kit (proposed)
>
>   1. 30 pieces of interlocking tubing
>   2. 40 miniature girders (aluminum)
>   3. 20 fasteners
>   4. 3 electric circuits with switches
>   5. 1 battery pack
>   6. 7 electric modules for circuits (item #4)
>   7. 1 AC/DC miniature motor with drive train
>   8. 4 sets of wheels (various sizes)
>   9. 4 small cans of spray paint, metallic colors
> 10. 3 light bulbs with sockets
> 11. 8 pulleys (various sizes)
> 12. 3 lengths of cable
> 13. 1 set of reduction gears, for motor (item #7)
> 14. 12 exterior panels
> 15. 1 sign-making kit for miniature signs/labels
> 16. 1 instruction manual including 200 toy ideas that can be constructed from the kit

afternoon Ted Bryant asks to borrow your key in order to work late. "Don't worry," he promises, "I'll lock up when I leave."

Writing Activity

Write a memo-to-file, recording the fact that you lent the key to Ted.

Speaking Activity

Try to convince your superiors to give keys to all supervisors so that the awkward practice of lending out keys can stop. Discuss the pros and cons of your idea with them.

MINI-CASE 5B Moving Day

You own and manage Cardiel Carpeting, and never at a better moment: you have the opportunity to carpet an entire industrial park, a job that may last as long as a year. Unfortunately, the industrial park lies 45 miles from your present location.

Writing Activity

Write a short report, estimating the number of employees required to complete the work at the industrial park and the travel arrangements necessary to transport them there.

Speaking Activity

Address your employees, explaining to them the opportunity the company seeks. Suggest how their commuting or relocation will be rewarded suitably.

MINI-CASE 5C The Great Outdoors

Arbor Aerospace owns a gymnasium, a soccer field, an Olympic-sized swimming pool, a tract of forest land, and a fleet of sailboats, all for the recreational use of employees. As Director of Personnel Services, you have been asked to make employees aware of these facilities.

Writing Activity

Write an information sheet for posting on bulletin boards throughout the company. Organize the sheet so that, at a glance, an employee can tell what activity is available where, when, and for whom.

Speaking Activity

Gather together a group of three or more employees. Brainstorm about the kind of recreational facilities the company should try to provide in the future.

MINI-CASE 5D Winding Down

You head up Manufacturing Assembly #7, a series of stamping machines requiring a crew of nine. You are aware that, since you took over the job, your unit has produced slightly less and less each month.

Writing Activity

In a short report to management, describe the gradual slowing in production and explain its causes. Make positive suggestions for remedying the situation.

Speaking Activity

Conduct an impromptu noon-time meeting with your crew. Speak your mind about the slowdown, and solicit their opinions and feelings. Work toward a constructive spirit in the meeting.

For All the Right Reasons [3]

For the past four years, you have built up your retail antique business, The King's Head, on a rural highway outside Sacramento, California. Yesterday you received word from a real estate agent that a large furniture store had gone bankrupt downtown. The store lease was available to you at an advantageous price (see the fact sheet accompanying this case). To move or not to move, that is the question.

Individual Writing Activities

1. Write a letter to the broker, requesting full details on the property available, including terms of the lease.
2. Make a list of all the reasons you want to move, then all the reasons you don't want to move. Make a second list of all the reasons your customers may want you to move, and all the reasons they may not want you to move.
3. Assume for this activity that you do decide to move. Write a letter of goodwill to your present customers. Inform them of your move, emphasizing ways in which their interests will be better served (the "you" perspective).
4. Assume for this activity that you do decide not to move. Write a letter to the broker informing him or her of your decision.

Group Writing Activities

1. Together with six other merchants along your stretch of highway, you form the Highway 9 Business Group, a chamber of commerce of sorts to promote trade along Highway 9. Meet with at least three other business leaders (your classmates) to draw up a promotional letter for mailing to 5,000 area homes.
2. The Highway 9 Business Group needs a form letter inviting other businesses in the area to join the association. Together with at least three other people, draft the form letter. Focus upon what the association can do for the merchant.

Individual Speaking Activities

1. At its first bi-monthly meeting, the Chair of the Highway 9 Business Group calls upon you to say a few words about why you decided not to sell out and move into the city. Speak to the group for three to five minutes on that topic.
2. A local service club invites you to speak briefly on antiques. Choose some aspect of that broad topic, and deliver a five to seven minute presentation.

Group Speaking Activities

1. A merchant new to the Highway 9 Business Group sits at a conference table with at least three members of the group, including you. The new merchant asks all of you to discuss the future of the Highway 9 area, as you foresee it. Participate in the discussion. The student playing the role of the new merchant can help to

generate discussion by asking a series of lively questions. (For example, ''What's going to happen to the swamp behind the antique store?'')

2. The Highway 9 Group decides to interview the new merchant for membership. First decide upon the procedure and questions for the interview, then lead the questioning. Decide at last upon the new merchant's application.

Visit for a Day, Stay for a Lifetime [3]

Together with two partners, you have developed Pebble Brook Shores, a 1,000 unit lakeside village of condominiums (see the fact sheet accompanying this case). Your buyers, you project, will come primarily from the neighboring community of Tremont (population 110,000).

Unfortunately, Tremont's citizens are served by only one newspaper, the *Triton*. The editor of the paper has stood staunchly against the development of Pebble Brook Shores, and now refuses your advertising.

You must find some other way to advertise your development in Tremont.

Individual Writing Activities

1. Write a promotional letter, with blanks left for the addressee's name to be filled in by word processing.
2. Write a goodwill letter to the Tremont Chamber of Commerce. Represent your development as a healthful addition to the community.
3. Write a letter to your attorney. Rehearse the details of the *Triton's* refusal to accept your advertising. Ask for legal counsel in enforcing your right to advertise.
4. Write a letter of thanks to the first family to buy a lakeside condominium.
5. Respond positively or negatively, as you wish, to a claims letter from a purchaser of a condominium. The purchaser alleges that a malfunctioning dishwasher is your responsibility during its first year of operation.

Group Writing Activities

1. Meet with your partners. Write the text for a full page newspaper advertisement on the Pebble Brook Shores development.
2. Meet with a group of bankers. Write a brief, accurate statement of the financing that they are willing to make available to approved buyers of your condominiums.
3. Meet with your lawyers. Draft a direct letter to the *Triton*, insisting upon your right to place an advertisement.

Individual Speaking Activities

1. Briefly address the Chamber of Commerce. Describe the kind of community you have tried to create at Pebble Brook Shores.
2. In a brief presentation, report to your partners on sales at Pebble Brook Shores during the first six months.

Group Speaking Activities

1. Meet with at least three residents of the condominium development. Listen to what they like and dislike about Pebble Brook Shores. Offer your opinions, projections, assurances, and explanations.
2. Meet with the maintenance staff at Pebble Brook Shores. Explain forcefully that they have not been doing a good job, and that residents have been complaining. Listen to any explanations they offer, then work toward a constructive solution.

MASTER CASE 8

Convening the Convention [3]

In exactly seven months, two days, four hours and ten minutes, retailers of cotton products from throughout North America will descend upon your city for the 19th Annual Cotton Products Convention, sponsored by your employer, the United Cotton Products Association. As executive assistant to the president of the Association, you bear full responsibility for organizing the convention and preparing for the guests.

Individual Writing Activities

1. Using the fact sheet accompanying this case, write a letter of inquiry to the Starflight Hotel. Ask a number of specific questions about their convention facilities. Describe your needs.
2. Write a letter of invitation to Senator Rosa Freeman of Georgia. Invite her to deliver the keynote address. Describe the purpose of the conference, its constituency, and the honorarium and travel funds you can make available to the Senator.
3. Write a letter of request to the mayor of your city. Ask for public services (such as police and paramedic service) that you will require during the convention. Demonstrate, if possible, that the convention is in the interest of the mayor's city.
4. By means of a business letter, place an order for three thousand name tags. Specify the kind of name tag, its advertised price, any pertinent code numbers, and the requested date of delivery. Add any other information necessary for the purchase of the name tags.
5. By means of a business letter, reserve the convention facilities of the Starflight Hotel. Abide by any request the hotel has made for a deposit. Specify the arrangements you expect from the hotel during the convention.
6. Write a letter of refusal to a cotton goods wholesaler who wishes to set up a booth in the main hotel lobby during the convention.
7. Write a letter of refusal to Army General Willard "Pap" Reynolds, retired, who has offered to speak to the convention without charge.
8. Write a letter answering the inquiry of a retailer in New Jersey who wants to know why the convention charges have been raised this year from $35 to $65.

Group Writing Activities

1. Together with a group of Association staffers, write a single page welcoming retailers to the convention. The page will appear inside the front cover of the convention program.

FACT SHEET Cotton Products

Membership profile: United Cotton Products Association

Total membership: 5320

Regional distribution:

Northeast	1032
South	3021
Midwest	503
Other	754

Average age: 54

Average income: $28,400 per year

Occupations represented: retail cotton products merchants, wholesalers, farmers, brokers, researchers, advertisers, marketers, production specialists, government relations experts

Sexual distribution of membership: 73 percent male, 27 percent female

Annual membership dues: $100

---

2. Playing the role of retailers attending the convention, write the text of a petition calling for the resignation of the Association president. Make up whatever circumstances you wish.

Individual Speaking Activities

1. Prepare and deliver a short presentation to the City Council. Describe the convention, its impact upon the city, and its positive effects upon tourism and shopping.
2. Prepare and deliver a short introduction, perhaps three to five minutes in length, to introduce Senator Freeman as the keynote speaker.

Group Speaking Activities

1. Meet with other Association staffers to decide how to handle the expected union groups that will demonstrate outside the convention center.
2. Act as moderator of a panel at the convention. Your topic is "Reasonable and Unreasonable Restraints upon Cotton Advertising."

MASTER CASE 9
Food, Glorious Food [3, 4]

For less than two weeks you have tried to catch on to your new job as Director of Customer Relations for Quantity Foods, Inc. All kinds of duties come your way during the work day: impromptu plant tours for the Girl Scouts, visiting dignitaries from Nepal, consumer activists on the road from Des Moines, and so forth. Mail, too, has been coming in over the transom. You resolve to answer as many of the letters as possible today.

Individual Writing Activities

1. Write an adjustment letter to Porthfield C. Kaye, who found your chicken soup a bit too salty (and returned the half-used can wrapped in aluminum foil).
2. Write an adjustment letter to Ms. Brenda Donnelly, who paid 74 cents a can for your cranberry sauce only to discover "an even larger can of cranberry sauce made by Pacific Foods, selling for only 69 cents." She demands a refund of 74 cents.
3. Write an adjustment letter to Herbert Lillian, stock manager of Lincoln Super Market. An order of 600 boxes of powdered sugar arrived in damaged condition; 250 of the boxes were too damaged to be sold.
4. In the role of a grocery customer, write a claims letter to the Customer Relations department. In a can of Quantity Foods' kidney beans, you found a bean-sized stone. Unfortunately, you found it the hard way by biting down and cracking a $750 crown on a tooth. Decide in your claim letter what you want to ask for.

5. In the role of a retailer doing business with Quantity, write a claim letter regarding the under-shipment of some 40 cases of canned vegetables. You ordered 260 cases, and you only received 220 cases.

Group Writing Activities

1. Working with other members of the Customer Relations staff at Quantity Foods, draft a one- or two-page document stating the company's policies with regard to customer claims. Be as specific as possible, and try to cover the most predictable cases that will arise.
2. Again working with the Customer Relations staff, draft a one- or two-page document that can be sent to the customer explaining Quantity Foods' attitudes toward its products, its expressed and implied warranties, and its customer service policies.

Individual Speaking Activities

1. Prepare and deliver a short presentation of two or three of Quantity Foods' newest or most unusual products. Address a group of interested consumers.
2. Explain the steps Quantity Foods takes to ensure freshness. Address your remarks to a group of nutritionists. Take time to answer their questions after your short speech.
3. Propose the elimination of a certain line (of your choice) from the Quantity Foods family. Address an assembled group of company executives. Speak on the basis of complaints received in your department.

Group Speaking Activities

1. Participate in a "future-think" session with other company members. Brainstorm and speculate on what particular foods will be the hot sales items in the coming five years.
2. Lead a panel of two or three other company members in interviewing a candidate for "Radio Chef," a popular program sponsored by your company. The old chef ate his way to an early death, and you're looking for a personable man or woman to replace him.

MASTER CASE 10

You're Sitting on My Profit [3, 4]

You manage the collections department at Gold Coast Furniture Mart, a huge wholesaler and retailer of mid-priced residential and commercial furnishings. While you have several sets of form letters available on word processing and mail merge, you still take time to write some letters yourself to larger accounts. You also supervise the writing of letters by others in your group.

Individual Writing Activities

1. Write a first collection letter to Mr. and Mrs. Gunther Armstrong, who purchased a $2300 living room set last year. The Gunthers have made their agreed-upon monthly payment of $79.69 regularly for the past eleven months. The current payment, however, is now 20 days past due.
2. Write a final collection letter to Betterbuy Waterbeds, Inc., who purchased $6700 worth of office furnishings from you six months ago. You have received only one monthly payment, in the amount of $187.50. No one from Betterbuy has responded to your past letters.
3. Write a second collection letter to National Mattress Supply. Their account, payable monthly in installments of $368, is now 40 days past due. The manager of the company phoned ten days ago to say that "a check is in the mail." No check has arrived so far.
4. Write a first collection letter to the Urban Recovery Center for Homeless Teenagers. The Center purchased six inexpensive mattresses and bed frames from you five months ago. The monthly payment is $38.20. All payments except the last have been made on time.
5. Write a first collection letter to the president of the city's chamber of commerce, Ms. Wanda Frank. Ms. Frank purchased an expensive burled walnut dining set, and agreed to make monthly payments of $102. She put 20 percent down on the set two months ago, and has not sent any payments to date. At last month's chamber meeting, she mentioned to you how much she was enjoying her new table.

Group Writing Activities

1. Together with a group of your collection letter writers, draft a series of four all-purpose collection letters, to be used in series as an account becomes increasingly delinquent.
2. Working with senior managers and sales people in the company, develop written profiles of four common types of customers at your furniture store.
3. Together with the sales manager, draft a statement for customers. Explain in the statement what kind of credit is available at your store, and how a customer can qualify. Explain the penalties and consequences of failure to pay.

Individual Speaking Activities

1. Prepare and deliver a short speech (five to seven minutes) for the local Rotary Club. Speak on the topic, "Why Some People Just Don't Pay Their Bills."
2. Prepare and deliver a short speech at a regional meeting of the Account Adjusters Association. Speak on "Powerful Motivators in Debt Collection."

Group Speaking Activities

1. Meet with other staff members in your group to discuss the use of innovative language in bringing about payment of overdue accounts.
2. Together with a vice-president in your company, interview a representative of Caldwell Auto Marts, a company that wants to furnish its seven dealerships with your products—purchased on credit, of course. Let a classmate play the part of the Caldwell representative. Supply him or her with some credit data for use in the interview.

MINI-CASE 10A A Part of the Family

Writing Activity

Write a sales letter for use in direct mail advertising. Try to attract subscribers to a new venture, a magazine called *Pets on Parade*.

Speaking Activity

Prepare and deliver a five to seven minute presentation for the Dog Lovers Club. Speak to them about the magazine, including the features you plan to include.

MINI-CASE 10B If You Have Time, Your Honor

Writing Activity

Your college Marketing Club is interested in the legal implications of labels and advertising. A local authority on the subject is the Honorable Rhoda Morley, judge of Superior Court. While you realize how busy she is, you nonetheless trust your powers of persuasion in writing a letter inviting the judge to speak to your Club. Write such a letter.

Speaking Activity

Prepare and deliver a three to four minute introduction of the judge. Address your remarks to the Marketing Club.

MINI-CASE 10C Slow-Pays and No-Pays

You open a pharmacy in a relatively small town of 40,000. In an effort to win friends and customers, your advertising offers liberal credit arrangements. When several of the town's most prominent citizens apply, you are faced with a dilemma: how do you tell two of the City Council members and a prominent lawyer that they simply don't qualify for credit due to past unpaid bills?

Writing Activity

Write a letter refusing credit to one or more of the people described above.

Speaking Activity

A local service club invites you to a weekly luncheon. There you are asked to introduce yourself, and say a few words about your pharmacy. Oblige the group for three or four minutes.

MINI-CASE 10D Rotten Apples

You open a collection agency in a city known for its heavy volume of commerce, both retail and wholesale. During your first three months of operation, you acquire many accounts—but all of them turn out to be hard-core debts that no one else has been able to collect.

Writing Activity

Write two or three letters to be used in such cases. The success of the letters may well determine the success of your business.

Speaking Activity

Congratulations! Your letters worked when no one else's would, and you collected a fine profit for your effort. The regional association of collection agencies wants you to speak to its next meeting on the formula you used for generating such powerful letters for hard-core debtors. In a five to seven minute speech, describe your magic.

MINI-CASE 1OE Meet the New Boss

Writing Activity

As Personnel Director for a multi-state bank, you have the duty to inform branch managers of a new set of officers in the corporation. Write a letter introducing the new executives. Describe the responsibilities of each.

Speaking Activity

Meet with the new officers of the bank. Discuss with them new opportunities and challenges that the bank will face in the coming two or three years. You might consider, for example, new residential or commercial developments in your part of the country.

MASTER CASE 11

Take Me, I'm Yours [5]

It's April. In less than two months you will graduate with a B.A. in Finance. Uncle Albert and Aunt Rose told you employers would be beating a path to your door as you neared graduation. Well, the path could use a bit more beating. You have no leads at all.

But wait—is that an employment ad on the finance department bulletin board?

"National company seeks entry-level financial managers with strong academic preparation in cash flow analysis and institutional lending practices. Salary commensurate with proven abilities and preparation. Fringe package outstanding. Send résumé to Alfred T. Ross, Seattle *Express,* Drawer 965A, Seattle, Washington 93772."

That's you they're asking for!

Individual Writing Activities

1. Prepare a letter of application to accompany your résumé.
2. Prepare a résumé (chronological or functional, as you wish.)

3. Write to Mr. Ross, inquiring about the nature of the company and the job advertised.
4. Write a brief note to a former employer or an instructor. Ask for a letter of recommendation. Mention the kind of position you seek, and suggest some areas of focus for the letter.
5. Assume that you learn which company Mr. Ross represents. Write a letter of inquiry to the company, asking for the kind of information you think you will need in preparing for a possible interview.

Group Writing Activities

1. Together with three or four of your fellow graduating classmates, draw up a two or three page informal report addressed to underclassmen. Point out the experiences and activities in college that seem to make a difference when it comes time to look for a good job. In other words, play big brother or sister to a business major who still has several semesters left. Offer advice and recommendation.
2. Too many of your classmates have chased blind ads in the employment section only to come up disappointed. Join with them in writing an open letter to a newspaper. Suggest in your letter the kinds of substantive evidence a newspaper should require from the advertiser before allowing a blind ad to run.

Individual Speaking Activities

1. In preparation for a possible interview, speak for two or three minutes about the most valuable work-related experience you have had. How can that experience contribute to your success in the job for which you are applying?
2. Present your résumé as if it were a short oral presentation. Introduce, then sell yourself.

Group Speaking Activities

1. In a group of three or four, exchange résumés. Offer advice and constructive criticism.
2. Practice ''round-robin interviewing'' with a group of your classmates. One person asks an interview-type question of someone else in the group. After giving an answer, it becomes that person's turn to ask an interview question of someone else in the group.

MASTER CASE 12

Oh My Gosh, They Want to Interview Me [5]

You receive a letter from CTW International praising your qualifications as expressed in your letter and résumé. The manager who wrote the letter invites you for an on-site interview on Friday, May 20, at 9 A.M.

Individual Writing Activities

1. Write a letter accepting the job interview. Make up a name for the manager.
2. Assume that the interview went well. Write a letter of thanks to those who interviewed you.
3. Time passes so slowly when you're waiting for some action on the part of the prospective employer. Write a polite letter of inquiry in an effort to learn where the company is in its decision-making process regarding your application.
4. When it rains, it really rains. On the same day that you receive a job offer from CTW International, you also receive an offer from FinanceWest. You need time to decide. Write a polite letter to each company, asking for a period of time (you decide how long to ask for) to respond to their offers.
5. Write a letter of acceptance for one of the two job offers named in activity #4 above.
6. Write a "no thanks" letter to the employer whose offer you did not accept.

Group Writing Activities

1. Discuss possible approaches to the following essay topic from an M.B.A. application: "Why do you seek an advanced degree in business?" After discussion, put your best ideas into a short essay answer of about a page or so.
2. Discuss the most difficult moments (experienced or imagined) in interviews. Create a list of important do's and don'ts for interviewing.

Individual Speaking Activities

1. In a short presentation of three to five minutes, describe the range and depth of your academic preparation for your chosen career. For what aspects of the job did college prepare you well? In what areas will you require further preparation?
2. Interviews often conclude with the invitation, "Do you have any questions for us?" Draw together several meaningful questions that might serve well at such a moment. Speak them to a classmate to test their usefulness.

Group Speaking Activities

1. Together with several of your classmates, interview a "candidate" for a hypothetical position. After the interview, let the candidate listen in on your evaluative discussion.
2. Divide your résumé into its several parts, giving each part to a different classmate. Sit back with the rest of the audience to listen as your chosen group of classmates presents your résumé aloud, trying to make you sound as admirable as possible. Listen for areas of strength and weakness in your résumé.

MINI-CASE 12A Back Home Again

Writing Activity

You're fortunate to be applying for a career position with a company for whom you have already worked during the summers. Write an application letter reminding them of your previous experience with the company.

Speaking Activity

Speak for three or four minutes on the advantages you will have over a newly hired employee who has never worked for the company before. Imagine that your audience is an interview panel at the company.

MINI-CASE 12B My Life and Times
Writing Activity

Your work experience has been limited to a couple of fast-food summer jobs; you have not had extensive work experience in accounting, your major. Create a chronological résumé that emphasizes your academic preparation and de-emphasizes your work experience.

Speaking Activity

Speaking as you might to an interview panel, discuss your academic preparation, naming favorite courses, methods, instructors, and texts.

MINI-CASE 12C But I Can Do the Job!
Writing Activity

Your college work has been spread over three universities and two decades. But here you are, at an eager age of 36, ready to graduate. Write a functional résumé that emphasizes the positions of considerable responsibility you have held. Use the functional résumé to de-emphasize your rather spotty academic career.

Speaking Activity

Draw together a three or four minute presentation on the work experiences you have found most valuable. Present your short speech to a group of classmates. Ask for evaluation and constructive criticism.

MINI-CASE 12D Maybe I Will, Maybe I Won't
Writing Activity

After sending out two dozen résumés, you are pleased to be invited to no less than seven on-site interviews. Three of these turn into job offers, all at once. Write a letter to each employer, asking for a week to make your decision and reply.

Speaking Activity

Invent hypothetical job offers, then make up a brief two or three minute "sales" presentation for each position. Give the two presentations to classmates. Let them tell you which sounded most attractive. Use this technique later when you must decide between two difficult choices.

MINI-CASE 12E Take This Job and Shelf It

Writing Activity

Invent circumstances that would lead you to resign from a job. Write a letter of resignation, deciding which of the circumstances to mention in the letter.

Speaking Activity

Using one or more classmates as an executive audience, go in to these "bosses" and resign, making whatever explanation you feel is appropriate under the circumstances you invent.

MINI-CASE 12F I Didn't Bring My Typewriter

Writing Activity

You were pleased to be invited to the offices of Schmidt, Leonard, and Coy for an on-site interview. You did not expect, however, to be handed a pre-interview application asking for short essay answers. Write an answer to this application question: "What kind of morals are appropriate in business?"

Speaking Activity

A common interview question involves your ability to work well with others, especially with a supervisor. Try to answer this question aloud in a cogent way: "No one likes to be bossed. How do you prefer to work—alone or with others?" Speak your answer to a few classmates, and learn from their helpful responses.

MINI-CASE 12G She's Too Good for Words

Writing Activity

You have admired the work of Fran Credens for two or three years. You're pleased, therefore, when she asks you for a letter of recommendation. Write the letter, making up whatever circumstances you wish.

Speaking Activity

Using a telephone if possible, give a verbal recommendation of Fran. Speak clearly, allowing a classmate hypothetically on "the other end" to ask occasional questions and make comments.

MASTER CASE 13
Trucks to Remember [5]

As Creative Director for Right Now Advertising, Inc., you have taken personal charge of finding an advertising theme for Cross-country Trucking, one of your larger accounts. The president of the trucking firm wants an image the public can remember easily. That image has to reflect friendliness, reliability, and a certain degree of charm.

Individual Writing Activities

1. Write a memo to your advertising staff. Call a meeting to discuss the Cross-country account and other matters. Include a brief agenda in your memo.
2. Write a business letter to the president of Cross-country Trucking. Assure the president that your firm is working hard on the matter of an advertising theme, and that you will have results no later than (you specify a time).
3. You have a bright idea for a slogan befitting the trucking company. Write up the idea in the form of a short proposal.
4. The president of your company wants to know how work is proceeding with the Cross-country account. Write a short report summarizing the steps you have taken and any results you have achieved.
5. In developing your advertising campaign, you need some hard facts about the trucking industry. Write a letter of inquiry to the American Trucking Association.
6. The American Trucking Association proves helpful beyond your expectations, all without charge. Write a thank-you letter to the director of the Association.
7. You have come up with a logo for Cross-country Trucking. Before proposing it to the trucking company, you have to make sure another company is not now using the logo. Write a letter to your lawyer, asking that a search be undertaken to check out the availability of the logo.

Group Writing Activities

1. After a particularly productive brainstorming session, you and your creative colleagues are ready to write a rough outline to use to develop a short presentation of your chosen theme for the Cross-country account. Write the outline, noting places where visual aids can be used effectively.
2. You have one minute on national television for a Cross-country advertisement. Work with your creative colleagues to write the text for the commercial. Describe the scenario of action and scenery that takes place along with your words.

Individual Speaking Activities

1. Prepare a short presentation on your chosen advertising concept for Cross-country Trucking. Deliver the presentation to a group of executives in your advertising company. Ask their advice, then rework the presentation accordingly.
2. Deliver the presentation of the Cross-country advertising concept to a group of Cross-country executives. Use visual aids to make your points in a memorable way.
3. Develop and read the text of a one-minute television or radio commercial for Cross-country Trucking. Ask a group of listeners to give you feedback on the content and delivery of the message.
4. Prepare and deliver a short speech of five to seven minutes on the methods you used to come up with the advertising package for Cross-country Trucking. Your speech will be given to the American Trucking Association at their annual convention, and probably will produce a flood of new business for your firm.

Group Speaking Activities

1. Brainstorm with at least three other members of your company about a workable and exciting advertising concept for Cross-country Trucking. It will be your

responsibility to summarize ideas and points of view for the group at the end of the brainstorming session.

2. Assume that you have developed an advertising package for Cross-country Trucking. Assign one portion of the package to each member in your group. Together, you will present the entire package to Cross-country management. Use visual aids appropriately.

3. Three representatives of your advertising company meet with three representatives of Cross-country Trucking. Each side gives ideas, reactions, preferences, and possibilities. At the end of the session, try to reach consensus on the areas of agreement and disagreement in the group.

Take Me Away From All This [3, 4]

You manage Shangri-la Tours, a rapidly expanding chain of travel agencies specializing in exotic tours to out-of-the-way places. Business is great—so great, in fact, that you can't continue to manage your own travel agency while supervising the other branches as well. You need to hire someone to manage the home office. He or she must have all the expected background for such a position, but must also possess a flair—a magnetism that makes middle-class customers want to leave the safe world behind and venture (profitably for you) to steaming jungles and windy peaks. In other words, you're looking for a special person indeed.

Individual Writing Activities

1. Write a letter to an executive employment agency. Describe the kind of manager you seek, and the terms of employment.
2. Write advertising copy for a two-page brochure on one of your exotic vacations.
3. Write a letter to all other branch supervisors, letting them know that applications are being taken for the job described above.
4. Write a short report for the directors of your corporation. Describe the specific ways in which you plan to restructure management of the various branch offices once you have hired a replacment for your own position as an office manager. Argue that the changes you propose will benefit the company.

Group Writing Activities

1. Meet with at least three of your branch supervisors. Brainstorm about several new exotic vacation possibilities. Write down a list of tasks for each member of the group so that your ideas become reality.
2. Ask each of your branch supervisors to write one or two pages profiling the kind of person you should hire for home office manager. Work together as a group to combine the various profiles into one written description of Mr. or Ms. Right.

Individual Speaking Activities

1. Address a group of senior citizens (your classmates will do). Try to interest them in "the vacation of their wildest dreams."
2. Prepare and deliver a short presentation addressed to the directors of your corporation. Argue for the need to replace you as home office manager to free up your valuable time.
3. Pretend that you are the special person Shangri-la Tours seeks for home office manager. Speak about your unique qualifications and background, as if in an interview situation.
4. Using a dictaphone or tape recorder, dictate a letter to Shangri-la Tours. Indicate your interest in the position of office manager, and suggest the range and depth of your qualifications.

Group Speaking Activities

1. With one person playing the role of job applicant, assemble a group of three or four company representatives to interview the candidate.
2. In a group made up primarily of past travel clients, lead a discussion of the values of exotic, risk-filled vacations.
3. Working with a company group of three or four members, divide the typical exotic vacation into stages. Assign one stage to each member of your group. Together, make a short presentation that endeavors to "sell" the vacation to a local travel club.

MINI-CASE 14A Kudos

Writing Activity

Your company, Sanders Fasteners, Inc., was mentioned favorably in an article in *Modern Management*. Write a letter thanking the author of the article.

Speaking Activity

You will be interviewed on the radio show, "Down to Business." The interviewer has asked you to prepare a two or three minute presentation answering the lead-in question, "Just what does Sanders Fasteners do?" Prepare and deliver your answer.

MINI-CASE 14B What a Mess!

Writing Activity

Your new building on 47th Street seems to be coming along nicely. The foundation has been poured, and structural work is now beginning. Your immediate business neighbors don't agree. You receive a letter signed by several area businesses. They complain that your construction site is an eyesore and an impediment to their trade. Write a letter responding to their complaints.

Speaking Activity

Your letter did not succeed in settling matters. The merchants in the vicinity of your new building want to meet with you in person. Prepare an introductory statement of two to three minutes in length. Deliver it, as if to the complaining neighbors.

MINI-CASE 14C Do You Have a Minute?

Writing Activity

You work under a tyrannous supervisor. As much as you hate to go to the company vice-president with problems, you decide that you must take action. Write a memo to the vice-president asking for a private meeting and suggesting the content you wish to discuss.

Speaking Activity

In the role of the company vice-president, discuss the problem brought to you by the employee above (another classmate).

MINI-CASE 14D Loose Lips Sink Ships

Writing Activity

You own and manage a remarkably successful corporation that markets a line of household pesticides for critters ranging from fleas to roaches to mice. You must hire a Director of Public Relations—a particularly sensitive position, since your toxic products are constantly under scrutiny by consumer groups and governmental agencies.

Write a job description for the kind of person you seek to hire for this crucial position.

Speaking Activities

Assume that you have located a talented applicant for the position (played by a classmate). Test his or her powers to cope with the press and government inquiries by firing a series of tough questions at the candidate. Afterwards, discuss what you liked and disliked about the answers.

MINI-CASE 14E The Car That Whirrs

Writing Activity

Your company makes an electric car for around-town driving. While success has been slow in coming, your third-quarter profits show a surge in sales. Write a promotional letter for wide public distribution. Let the world know that things are looking up for electric transportation.

Speaking Activity

Gather a group of three or four company executives. Discuss your rise in sales during the third quarter. Decide what caused the sudden jump, and how to keep it going.

MINI-CASE 14F New from Sunshine

Writing Activity

Sunshine Products markets small household appliances. Write the copy for a full page magazine advertisement for your revolutionary new instant ice-maker.

Speaking Activity

Using visual aids where needed, present the new instant ice-maker (or another product of your own choice) to a group of interested consumers.

MINI-CASE 14G In the Spotlight

Writing Activity

The American Small Business Owners Association has asked you to address its national convention. Write a letter of acceptance, specifying the topic on which you will speak and any arrangements you will require for the address.

Speaking Activity

Develop and deliver a ten-minute formal address on a topic of your choice. Present your speech as if speaking to a convention such as that mentioned above.

MASTER CASE 15

Business as Usual [6]

You are a mid-level supervisor in a large management advisory service named after its founders, Millits & Brody. The company has many things in its favor: a strong, loyal staff; a bright, well-located building; and a solid reputation. But with each passing day you see more clearly that your company is falling behind the competition. Your office equipment is hopelessly antiquated. Not a single word processor can be found in the office. All work, even repetitive forms, must be hand typed.

Writing Activities

1. Write a short report addressed to company management. Point out specific ways in which the company suffers by clinging to an office technology of the past.
2. Write a letter to a local office equipment supplier (you may invent the name and address). Invite the supplier to demonstrate the latest generation of office equipment. Describe your company's particular needs.

Speaking Activities

1. In an oral proposal, present your case for the initial introduction of two word processing stations in the office. Use visual aids where appropriate. Address your remarks to an assembled group of company executives.
2. Play the role of an office equipment consultant. In a presentation of five to seven minutes, select two or three kinds of modern office machines that could drastically speed up and enhance the work at Millits & Brody.

Words, Words, Words [6]

As a farsighted business leader, you saw the light early in the electronic revolution of the office. At considerable expense, you installed word processing stations, electronic mail connections, high speed printers, and all the rest of the modern marvels available for the office.

While communication within the company has certainly improved, you now find yourself drowning in an embarrassment of riches: you and most of your managers have too many words to deal with each day. Memos, letters, proposals, and reports fly out of the machines at a flash only to pile up on desks throughout the office.

Writing Activities

1. Write an extended memo to your managers. Suggest practical steps they can take to deal with the new flood of words.
2. Write an information sheet for your employees. The purpose of the sheet is to guide their writing efforts. Suggest practical ways they can do their part to halt the glut of words, words, words. Advise them how to write more effectively, not simply to write less.

Speaking Activities

1. You have a reputation for getting through your daily reading matter in record time. A group of executives in the company invites you to speak to them for five to seven minutes about techniques you use to read quickly, to organize, and to remember.
2. A group of secretaries expresses anxiety that new machines will mean a new office staff. Address the group and speak candidly about your estimate of the impact of new electronic office machines upon the present office staff.

MINI-CASE 16A Special on Lamb Chops

Writing Activity

You own and manage a wholesale meat supply house, and do most of your business with restaurants. Using a word processor if possible, write a promotional letter advertising a special on lamb chops during the month of June. Structure the letter in such a way that you can use the same text to advertise a different cut of meat to different restaurants by means of the word processor. Type two versions of the letter, each to a different restaurant.

If you do not have access to a word processor, type a form letter that will accomplish the same purpose as the letter described above. Type as least two versions of the letter, each to a different restaurant.

Speaking Activity

Some of your sales promotions are made by telephone. Prepare and deliver a two to three minute telephone presentation of one of your upcoming specials.

MINI-CASE 16B Fast but Ugly

Your company has invested heavily in electronic mail, and now sends all in-house messages by that means. A good portion of mail sent out of the company also goes by electronic mail, with sometimes unfortunate results. Though they are fast, electronic messages arrive with none of the style of traditional, bond-stationery letters (with attractive placement of the text under an impressive letterhead). Electronic mail usually arrives looking little better than a telegram. The message is difficult to read and seems . . . well, so plain and unexciting.

Writing Activity

Write an information sheet for your company's business writers. Show them how electronic mail can be made more distinctive and readable, if not pretty.

Speaking Activity

Conduct a brief experiment. Place a neatly typed business letter on letterhead stationery in a person's hands for no more than five seconds. Then take the letter away and ask the person a short series of questions of your devising: did the letter seem important? did the letter seem respectful? did the letter reflect effort on the part of the author? and so forth.

Then take exactly the same text printed out as it would appear had it arrived by electronic mail. Ask the same series of questions. Compare results and draw together conclusions for class discussion.

MASTER CASE 17
But That's What You Said [3, 6]

For the past ten years, you have directed a corporation calling itself "Automagic Specialties." With offices now in six states, you can usually live up to your claim of finding rare and exotic automobiles for upscale clients. Much of your promotional work is done through the mails. Your employees—auto brokers, as they like to be called—send out letters advertising the specific characteristics of the cars they have available.

Writing Activities

1. Write a guide letter to suggest wording for these promotional letters mailed out by your employees.
2. Write a list of "no-no's" for your employees. Describe by example the kind of representations they should not make about the cars they advertise. In each case, explain why.

Speaking Activities

1. One of your more expensive cars will go up for auction soon. The auctioneer asks you to prepare a two or three minute promotional presentation on the car, to be delivered at the auction. Prepare and deliver the short speech.
2. A dissatisfied customer, Cal Vinegard, writes to tell you that his expensive Cord purchased from your company has turned out to be a lemon. He expects you to refund his money, or face legal suit. Place a telephone call to Cal in an effort to reach a mutually acceptable resolution to the problem. A classmate can play the role of Cal, with the telephone arrangements simulated.

MASTER CASE 18

Have We Got a Deal for You [3, 4, 6]

At Diversified Investment Group, your active staff makes oral and written representations regarding a wide variety of investment vehicles, ranging from soy bean futures to gold speculation to blue chip stocks.

Writing Activities

1. Draft a general, commonsense guide to business ethics for your employees to read and follow.
2. To demonstrate the difference between enthusiastic salesmanship and misleading deception, write side-by-side descriptions of an investment possibility of your choice. One description should be straight-forward and honest; the other description should illustrate how words can be used to distort facts and deceive readers.

Speaking Activities

1. You yourself were "burned" by a sharp con artist. In a presentation of five to seven minutes, tell how you were deceived and describe the reparations you want. Present your case as if speaking to the judge in a civil suit.
2. The local Rotary Club has invited you to speak for a few minutes on the most spectacularly successful investments you have ever heard of. Oblige them for five to seven minutes. Use visual aids to illustrate your points.

MINI-GASE 18A Agent for the Company
Writing Activity

At Sondervan Publishing Company, you are responsible for training six to eight new book sales people each year. Write a one page summary of the concept of "agency," illustrating by example what they should and should not do, say, and write in the name of the company.

Speaking Activity

A writers' group asks you to speak on the kind of books Sondervan Publishing wishes to acquire in the coming year or two. Prepare and deliver a five to seven minute presentation on the topic.

MINI-CASE 18B Lurking in the Files
Writing Activity

No one has taken time to clean out the files at Fobrichi Fabrics since 1945. Create a list of business documents that can be located and destroyed. Specify how you want the documents destroyed.

Speaking Activity

Some employees, tired of going through old files, ask you to explain why it is necessary to purge files occasionally. Gather your thoughts, then speak for three to four minutes on the subject.

MINI-CASE 18C Absolutely Guaranteed
Writing Activity

Find a product warranty that strikes you as being particularly obscure and obtuse. Rewrite the warranty in clear, effective English.

Speaking Activity

A customer claims not to understand the terms of a particular warranty. Find a product warranty, then lead the customer (a classmate) through its terms, explaining the implications of the language at hand.

MINI-CASE 18D Would We Hire You?
Writing Activity

You manage the huge suburban fast-food restaurant called Burger-buzz, which each year employs more than two hundred people in various capacities. Write one or two pages summarizing the hiring procedures and policies of the restaurant. Be specific about what matters are and are not considered in hiring.

Speaking Activity

A local high school invites you to speak on Career Day. After your presentation, a student asks, "What are my real chances of advancing in the company if I do a good job serving burgers?" Answer that question frankly, illustrating your point with examples.

MINI-CASE 18E I Found It in the Classified Section

Writing Activity

You direct the classified advertising division of a large urban newspaper. Recent court rulings have suggested that you may be held partially responsible for any fraudulent ads that appear in your newspaper if you did not exercise reasonable care in soliciting and reviewing the advertisements and advertisers. Write a "watch-out" list for your classified ad staff. Specify the kind of ads that should be checked out carefully before running them in the paper.

Speaking Activity

Your church group asks you to speak for a few minutes on the ethics of advertising. What can and cannot be claimed for a product or service? Prepare and deliver a five to seven minute speech on the topic.

MASTER CASE 19

Mirror, Mirror [5, 6]

You work as a manager for Associated Chemical Products, a multi-national corporation with a wide product line ranging from chemicals for the production of plastics to pharmaceuticals. Your particular responsibility lies in the area of personnel management. You hire and sometimes participate in the firing of administrative personnel for your foreign operations. You claim, in fact, to know more people in more foreign countries than the Secretary of State.

Writing Activities

1. Write a guide for use by your company's foreign visitors when they visit the United States. Of course you cannot write a complete history or geography text. Instead, try to indicate some of the subtle customs or cultural habits of our people. Foreign visitors might be interested in knowing, for example, what the "thumbs up" sign means in this country. Choose fifteen or twenty such cultural items for your guide.
2. Write a letter in English to a foreign company executive about to visit the home office for the first time. Present in your letter an agenda of events for the day of his or her visit, adding any additional information the visitor may find helpful.

Speaking Activities

1. Your college alma mater has a foreign exchange club. As a person knowledgeable about foreign travel and business, you agree to speak for seven to ten minutes on

the topic, "What to do and say when you don't know what to do or say in a foreign culture."

2. Your boss pooh-poohs the idea of a short training seminar for employees going abroad to work. In a presentation of five to seven minutes, argue that the seminar is important. Address your remarks to a group of company executives, including the boss so opposed to the seminar.

Get Ready, Get Set, Get Educated [6]

As Marketing Director for Teletronics Video Systems, you oversee a new sales effort on the part of the company: sending twenty bright, personable sales people abroad to establish the Teletronics image and product line in foreign countries. Each company representative will have specialized training for the country of his or her destination. But before they go off to such seminars, you gather the group together for a general presentation on cultural differences.

Writing Activities

1. Write an agenda for the presentation, pinpointing your major points in a memorable way. The agenda will be kept by participants as a summary of the presentation.
2. Your immediate supervisor, a vice-president in the company, has asked you to write a "worst case scenario" for the kinds of things that might go wrong when twenty Teletronics sales people go abroad. Consider various aspects of cultural differences, then write a short report to the vice-president on the topic.

Speaking Activities

1. Address the assembled sales people on the topic, "Keeping Your Eyes and Ears Open to New Experiences and Surroundings."
2. Join with two or three other company members in interviewing candidates for foreign service. Devise an insightful list of interview questions that will let you determine which candidates are most likely to succeed abroad.

MINI-CASE 20A Do I Curtsy?

Writing Activity

The foreign president of Okiba Electric Motors, Tokyo, has written to you, the executive assistant to the president of MacAdam Engines, to request advice. Precisely how does one greet an American corporate head? Does one sit or stand? The questions go on and on.

Write (in English) a letter explaining usual corporate protocol to the foreign visitor. Be reassuring and supportive.

Speaking Activity

Your company president phones to ask how a Japanese corporate president expects to be treated. Speak for three or four minutes on the basis of your knowledge, your research, or your common sense.

MINI-CASE 20B Dear Ambassador

Writing Activity

You felt chills of excitement when you received notice that you would spend the summer in France on company business. Only later did you realize that you knew virtually nothing about the ways in which the French conduct business.

Write a letter to the French Embassy requesting any publications or information pertaining to business practices in France. Ask any questions that seem appropriate or necessary.

Speaking Activity

Interview a foreign student at your college or a business person. Take notes on interesting cultural differences, then share your findings with classmates.

Supplemental Cases

These supplemental cases offer additional opportunities for writing and speaking occasions growing out of real-life situations, and may be used with any chapter in the text.

Burnout

You were pleased last year to be hired directly out of college for a mid-level management position at Auto World Wholesale, a major supplier of auto parts and accessories to retail auto stores. The position has challenged your business training, ingenuity, and—at times—your patience. For one thing, you've had to supervise four sales people, all at least fifteen years older than you and all with several years' experience with the company. They have never shown discomfort or jealousy over your position. But that's just it: they never seem to feel much of anything toward their jobs.

Your compensation from the company is based partially on salary and partially on earnings achieved by your sales group. You're thinking about getting married soon, perhaps even buying a house. You need a high level of performance from your group to meet your own earning goals this year.

But Bill, Susan, Hank, and Richard seem to have other ideas—or worse, no ideas at all. Over the years they have each developed steady customers and now do little more than make their regular rounds. Hank even jokes about it, calling himself "the milkman." Their earning records are undistinguished—slightly below average for the company as a whole. They are all dependable, of course, and never miss a day of work. Their sales per month are predictable almost down to the dollar. They seem satisfied with rather meager paychecks—"just enough to buy gas for my fishing boat," as Bill often remarks with a yawn.

WRITING

Memo A

Write a memo report addressed to upper management. Describe your plan for motivating your employees during the upcoming quarter.

Memo B

Write a memo addressed to all four of your employees. Summarize for them the highlights of your motivational ideas for the upcoming quarter. Try to use encouraging language.

Letter A

Write a business letter to an old college friend who now holds a position similar to yours in another industry. Describe in frank terms your problems with your employees. Ask advice on how to motivate achievement.

Letter B

Write a promotional letter to be sent to potential clients by your four sales people. Create whatever "special sales" information you require for purposes of the letter.

Report

Write a two-page report for the Vice-President of Sales. Summarize the problem of stagnation in your group, citing figures to substantiate your point (you may invent the figures). Go on to describe your plans to turn the situation around. Ask for any action you wish the vice-president to take regarding the situation.

SPEAKING

Meeting

Ask classmates to play the roles of your four employees. Call them together for a meeting. In advance, establish an agenda emphasizing your plans for setting new records as a sales unit. Try to bring about a change of attitude in your employees during the meeting.

Interview

Interview each of your four employees. Try to understand the causes behind their lackadaisical attitudes. Use the interview to let them know your attitudes toward the company, your own goals, and your expectations of them.

Speech

Prepare a brief presentation to be delivered to upper management in the company. Summarize the successes and failures of your work unit. Make projections for what the group can accomplish in the coming quarters under your leadership. For the sake of credibility, explain how you will bring about change in employees known in the company for their slow-paced approach to sales and career.

Computer Security

For the past three years you have managed the Texas production facility of Barkley Aerosystems. Your primary product line features a wide range of high-pressure hoses and connections for hydraulic systems in commercial and military aircraft.

Over the past three months you've received sporadic reports from your computer division that odd—and often expensive—mistakes were cropping up in key programs. Six milling machines, for example, were down for three days while programmers poured over thousands of lines of CAD/CAM (computer assisted design/manufacture) code, looking for mysterious errors.

Once found, the errors proved even more mysterious. Key numbers in the code had been changed with seeming abandon. Phrases such as "gotcha" and "hi there" appeared among lines of "garbage"—worthless code—that managed nevertheless to bring important aspects of your operation to a standstill.

You've had two of your best programmers looking at the problem in their spare time (which, unfortunately, has been only a few hours). But today you must take more forceful action. Payroll has been delayed for more than 200 employees because of another maddening incidence of vandalism in important computer codes.

You assess the seriousness of the situation. If the press finds out about your "ghost in the computer," you'll have a lot of explaining to do to security-conscious military agencies. Only a few people are supposed to have access to the computer code. You certainly don't want to challenge their integrity—in fact, you need their help to find the culprit. You speculate that an outside "hacker" may be gaining access to your computer by telephone connection.

Whoever or whatever is the cause, you resolve to put a halt to it as soon as possible. You give the matter of computer vandalism top priority.

WRITING

Memo

Write a memo to employees in the computer division. Tell them how concerned you are about the situation and its implications. Ask for any information or help they can offer.

Letter

Write a letter to Kelly Boyce, Ph.D., a computer consultant. Describe, in nontechnical language, the problems you are experiencing. Invite Dr. Boyce to your office to discuss the possibility of a consultantship. Specify what you want done in general terms, reminding Dr. Boyce of the confidential nature of your letter.

Report

Write a short report for upper management on the computer vandalism problem. Let them know how and when the problem first occurred and what has happened since. Describe your plan of attack on the problem. Ask for any additional authorization or funding you will need to carry out your plan.

SPEAKING

Speech

Prepare a short informative speech to be delivered to company employees. Describe the facts known to you and discuss the seriousness of the situation. Let employees know in a specific way what they can do to resolve the problem.

Interview

Interview two of your longtime employees in the computer division about the problem. Draw up your own agenda of questions for the interview, being sure to include questions about new employees, after-hours workers, and the possibility of an outside "hacker."

Computer Slowdown

Bing Brothers Toy Company, Inc., is a happy place—or at least it *had* been a happy place prior to the switch-over five years ago to computerized inventory, shipping, and accounts control. As manager, you've seen the company grow from 34 employees in 1972 to more than 150 today. Most of them work hard and find real satisfaction in their jobs.

Then there are the computer people. You can't figure it out. They get paid more per hour than anyone else in the factory, yet all you hear from them are complaints beginning with "how do you expect us . . . " and "we can't possibly . . . "

There have been days when you felt like cleaning house in the computer division and starting over with fresh, enthusiastic employees down there. But programmers and systems analysts are hard to find and expensive. Besides, you personally do not know much about computers. You hesitate to try to start over.

But today something has to be done. The Christmas invoices, according to the computer division, won't be ready for another week—that's $302,000 in billings! When you phoned Griff Hanford, director of the computer section, to insist that the invoices go out sooner, he said something under his breath about "running these computers yourself."

WRITING

Memo A

Write a memo to file regarding the problem with Christmas invoices. Give a detailed account of how much the delay cost the company in lost interest and impaired cash flow. Mention names when appropriate.

Memo B

Write a memo to the computer division. Set forth your expectations for performance from that work unit. Make an effort to clarify any misunderstandings from the past. Try to establish a productive, positive, but no-nonsense working relationship with the unit. Refrain from personal attacks.

Letter A

Write a letter to the National Association of Manufacturers, Member Inquiries Desk, 19280 W. 98th Street, Seattle, Washington 60387. Try to find out if your industry has time/work standards for computerized invoicing procedures. Do others in your business experience more or fewer problems than you do? Can your Association offer you advice or references for help?

Letter B

Write a letter to Industraining, Inc., a firm specializing in business- and industry-related seminars. Find out if they offer an intensive, on-site "introduction to computers'' course—something you and other non-computer-literate managers could take to give you a better grasp of the problem you're facing in the computer section.

Short Report

Write a short report to the board of directors of your company. Describe how the atmosphere within the company has changed since many vital company functions have been given over to the computer division. Give an appropriately detailed description of the problems you encounter with that work group, along with an analysis of the reasons for the problems. Describe to the board how you intend to lead the company to more harmonious and productive working relationships.

SPEAKING

Speech

Prepare a short speech to give to employees in the computer division. While your tone need not be argumentative or harsh, make sure that they understand the seriousness of your message. You want to make them a cooperative, progressive part of the company—not stubborn prima donnas hiding behind complicated machines.

Interview

Conduct an interview with an employee or employees from the computer division. Try to get to the heart of the problem you face with that group. What is really causing the slow-down? Who is responsible? What can be done? Be sure that you make clear to the employees being interviewed that their remarks will not be used against them or in an indiscreet way.

Interview

Interview someone new to head up your computer division. Describe the problems there in a frank way. Ask how the job applicant would go about resolving the situation.

U.S. West Airlines

Progress is not without its air pockets and bumps. You are vice-president in charge of advertising for a new and aggressive airline serving twelve cities in Washington, Oregon, Nevada, and California. You've been in business now for nine months, and the red ink expected in the first few months has already started to turn black. You face a tough decision, however, involving your advertising.

An early television commercial for the company shows passengers receiving free cocktails, newspapers, and magazines—a gimmick to draw attention and business away from the major carriers. Unfortunately, the company cannot sustain the high cost of these giveaways and still remain competitive in the deregulated world of airline fares. Two weeks ago your company president called a halt to the giveaway.

The commercial, however, continues to be broadcast. For one thing, it is the only slick piece of television advertising the company has been able to afford so far. In addition, you got a good price on the commercial by giving healthy residuals to actors and actresses appearing in the advertising spot. Some of these people would be cut out of the picture if the extended "free services" scenes were taken from the commercial. Such a violation of their contracts could only be prevented by cash payments—large ones—to compensate the actors and actresses involved. Right now the company must avoid any more strain on its cash flow.

As vice-president of advertising, you have to recommend a course of action.

WRITING

Memo

Write a memo to all company employees who have direct contact with the public. Instruct them in specific terms on how to handle passenger complaints about not receiving advertised giveaways. Reveal to them the approach you're taking to resolve the awkward situation.

Letter A

Write a letter to the Better Business Bureau, responding to their charges of false advertising. Outline for them the steps the company is taking to bring advertising into conformity with actual services offered.

Letter B

Write a letter to Aman Litzo, manager of the small film company that produced your "free services" commercial. Describe the changes that must be made in the commercial if it is to be used in the future. Ask for advice on how these changes can best be made without involving inordinate expense due to renegotiation of actor/actress contracts.

Press Release

Write a clear, accurate, balanced statement regarding your advertising problem for distribution to the press. Concentrate on what the company plans to do in the immediate future to make sure that no passenger is hoodwinked. Respond to charges that the company deliberately put forth advertised special services it never actually intended to deliver to the public.

SPEAKING

Speech

Deliver a speech to your board of directors. Describe the problems company employees have encountered when dealing with passengers who expect free services that are no longer offered. Discuss the complications involved in changing the television advertisement. Set forth your recommended course of action, and ask for their support.

Meeting

Invite several company employees to a "brainstorming" session in which you try to uncover any unexplored alternatives related to your advertising problem. Can passengers be given something in place of the advertised giveaways? Can a clever phrase be used to turn the advertising disaster into an opportunity?

Qualitron Telescopes

Not bad, you tell yourself. Only two years out of college, and you direct the quality control unit for a prestigious manufacturer of hobby telescopes. The pay was already good and, with each six-month performance review, getting better all the time.

The memo you received today, however, might cause problems. Ms. Elaine Morgan, production manager, wrote the memo to let you know about certain complaints. It seems that the company's complaint desk over a period of a few weeks has received six customer complaints about flawed lenses and damaged parts, all supposedly approved as satisfactory by Inspector No. 17. Morgan wants to know who Inspector No. 17 is and what you are doing to supervise his or her obviously sloppy inspection work.

You worry about her request. Inspector No. 17, you know, does not exist. Since taking over your supervisory role, you've joked with your eight inspectors about the numbering system. "Just put on an inspection sticker," you told them. "We don't keep track of numbers. That's just advertising for the customer."

Morgan and others above you will certainly disagree. They set up the inspector numbering system as a quality control check on employees. They will be less than pleased to discover that you have not been abiding by company procedures. More difficult yet, what is she to tell the complaint desk about Inspector No. 17? And what is the complaint desk to tell the customers who have complained?

WRITING

Memo A

Write a memo responding to Morgan's request for information. Consider your words with care, knowing that they may have a far-reaching impact upon your job future and that of employees working under you.

Memo B

Write a memo to the complaint desk. Discuss how they might answer the six customers who have complained about the work of Inspector No. 17.

Letter A

Write a form letter for the complaint desk to be used in the case of the six customers who complained about Inspector No. 17. Make some provision in the letter for adjustment of the problems experienced by the customers because of the poor inspection work of your unit.

Letter B

Write a confidential query letter to a competing firm. Discover if any opportunities are open in its organization for someone with your skills.

Report

Write a short report for Morgan, production manager, in which you discuss how the inspection problem came about, your role in it, and your plans as a supervisor to improve the work of your unit.

SPEAKING

Speech

Prepare a brief talk for the employees who work under you in the inspection unit. In preparing the speech, decide how you want to handle the difficulties you've gotten into. In your talk, discuss how procedures in your work unit are going to be different. Give your employees some guidance on how they should respond to inquiries about past inspection procedures, especially those involving inspection stickers from Inspector No. 17.

College Spirit

You established Strider Shoe Company next door to the university for a reason. First, you liked dealing with the college community and saw a real market there for quality sports shoes and dress shoes. Second, you graduated from the university and had fond memories of the place. You attend most of the sports events and many cultural events at the university.

But a store owner has to pay the bill. Your problem is not selling shoes—your trade is strong, and each year grows stronger. The problem involves donations. Because of your location, every campus organization seeking merchant contributions comes to you first. You've said "yes" to everything from $100 for a handicapped children's camp to $600 for your store name on volleyball T-shirts. While you want to do your part to help worthwhile causes, your accountant warns you that you're contributing far too much for the good of the business.

What can you say or do?

WRITING

Letter A

Write an effective "no" letter to the Alpha Gamma Society at the University. They had stopped by your store to request a donation of $500 toward resurfacing the track. Thousands of pairs of your shoes, they pointed out, had run around that track over the years.

Letter B

Write a letter to the university's student newspaper, for publication in the "Letters" column. Explain in an upbeat fashion what student organizations can and can't expect from Strider Shoe Company as far as donations are concerned. Discuss the problems a university merchant faces in trying to say "yes" to every request he or she receives.

Proposal

Write a short proposal to the University Business Leaders Association, a gathering of area business owners. Suggest some means by which businesses can group together to support student undertakings. Point out any advantages or disadvantages you see in such a plan.

SPEAKING

Speech

You're the guest speaker at the University Business School forum, a regular lunch-hour get-together at which local business people speak to aspiring business students. Prepare a short speech in which you discuss the opportunities and problems involved in merchant donations. You may want to solicit student opinion on how a merchant can say "no" without losing valued student customers.

Interview

Interview a public relations major who wants to work for you part-time. He or she claims to have insight into how you can handle the problem of excessive contributions without alienating students. Discuss the complexities of your problem with the job applicant during the interview.

No Parking Zone

In Business School, you majored in the Entrepreneur Program. Not six weeks after graduation, you put your training to use by purchasing the first truck for your small shipping company. Now you own five trucks, and business is exploding. With your profits, you've been able to make a down payment on a comfortable home. Though the house itself is far from spectacular, you were attracted by the large lot and parking area.

Your trucks rumble into town now at all hours of the day and night. Usually they park in leased space you have acquired downtown. Occasionally, however, the leased space is filled with other equipment. At such times, you've told your drivers, simply park in the long driveway at the house. There's plenty of room.

The neighborhood association disagrees—vehemently. You've received a letter of complaint signed by twelve members of the association. They dislike the sight and noise of a truck on their residential streets. They mention danger to children and pets. They're concerned about exhaust odors.

You don't want to be a bad neighbor, but neither do you want to be pushed around. Your drivers are extremely careful—more so than your neighbors. You think your neighbors should be more grateful for the goods that trucks help to provide and less concerned with how trucks look in a residential area.

WRITING

Memo

Write a memo to Bert Trabeck, your dispatcher. Give him specific instructions on what to tell drivers about parking at the house.

Letter

Respond to the concerns of the neighborhood association by writing a cogent letter. Deal with their complaints and also express your point of view. If you wish, suggest a workable compromise.

SPEAKING

Meeting

In a group of six to eight, simulate a meeting of the neighborhood association, with the truck owner in attendance (assign one class member to this role). As discussion grows heated, take careful note of ways by which some speakers communicate ideas and points of view without angering their listeners.

After the meeting, break out of your roles to discuss what you observed: how some speakers take and hold the floor, how points of view are expressed and challenged, how anger and humor affect understanding, and how the many can "gang up" on the one.

Speech

In the role of the truck owner, prepare a short, well-reasoned speech for presentation to the neighborhood association. Respond to their concerns directly and raise issues of your own. If you desire, conclude by suggesting a compromise suitable to all parties.

Prestige Limousine Service

Together with Rosemary Fenton, a college friend, you have decided to take the plunge: the two of you are going into business for yourselves. Specifically, you are now the proud owner—thanks to a bank loan—of a limousine, the first of what you hope will soon be a fleet. You've called your fledgling business "Prestige Limousine Service." An advertising agency helped you prepare ad copy for the Yellow Pages and area newspapers.

But funds are running a bit low. You want to do everything you can at this point to get the business going without investing any more of your money. Therefore, you and Fenton decide to take a two-pronged approach. On the internal level, you plan to write your own promotional and collection letters. You want these standard items to be in place by the time you open for business. On the external level, you plan to become better acquainted in the community by becoming more involved in local activities.

WRITING

Memo A

Write a memo to Fenton offering to take on the task of drafting the promotional and collection letters for the business. Include in the memo suggestions for how she can contribute to the writing projects.

Memo B

Write a memo to file to record the fact that you donated a two-way radio to the business for use in the limousine and that you will be reimbursed for the cost of the radio out of the first profits from the business. The memo should be initialed by both owners.

Letter A

Write a letter of Franklin Insurance Agency, to the attention of agent Martha Czeli. Describe your idea of making the limousine available on a "U-Drive" basis to clients. Inquire what insurance coverage she would recommend for such a plan.

Letter B

Write a letter to Marlene Victors, attorney-at-law. Describe the nature of your business. Seek her assistance in forming a corporation to replace the partnership you now have with Fenton. Be sure to request information on the costs involved in incorporating.

Report

Pretend that Prestige Limousine Service has now been in business for six months. Draw up a short report that summarizes the major developments of the past six months. Conclude with recommendations for the next six months and, if you wish, for a longer term.

Proposal

Several wealthy clients have shown interest in investing in your company. Write a short proposal for presentation to them. Show what you plan to do with their invested funds and what they can reasonably expect to gain.

Collection Letters

Write first-stage, second-stage, and third-stage collection letters of the sort that could be put into memory in the word processor for use at a later date. Establish a tone in keeping with your business.

SPEAKING

Speech

Prepare a short speech that you could use to introduce your new business to a business or civic organization such as the Rotary Club. Be sure to communicate the essential facts about your business enterprises in a lively way. Answer questions from the audience after your speech.

Meeting

With classmates playing the roles of Fenton, a banker, and an advertising agent, sit down for a planning meeting. It is your job to establish and carry through a brief agenda of discussion items. You might, for example, want to discuss the nature of expansion plans once the business is going well. You and Fenton will probably want to ask the advertising agent what he or she thinks of your promotional letter.

Interview

It takes a special personality to drive a limousine. Ask three classmates to "apply" for the job. Interview each in turn, perhaps with another classmate playing the part of Fenton as a co-interviewer. Make your decision after the interviews have been completed. Then discuss with the class the standards you used in interviewing and why you made the choice you did.

All in the Family

You can't deny that Uncle Frank has offered you a fine opportunity in his invitation to join Beston Home Construction, Inc. Yet you have some doubts about joining a company headed by a relative. Will other employees take you seriously? Will you be given "special" treatment because of your relationship to Uncle Frank, the company president? Will you ever feel that you have earned your own way?

You resolve to apply for the job, but through the front door, not the back. You want to be hired for what you are, not whom you know.

WRITING

Résumé

Write a résumé for a position with Beston Home. Attach a cover letter that does not focus primarily upon your relationship with Uncle Frank.

Letter A

Write a business letter to Uncle Frank to thank him for the opportunity he has offered you at Beston Home. Although your tone may be somewhat more personal than that in a traditional business letter, keep the letter businesslike in form and purpose. Communicate to Uncle Frank your strong desire to earn your own way, beginning with the job application process.

Letter B

Pretend that you have decided not to seek employment with Beston Home. Write a business letter to Uncle Frank to tell him of your decision and some of the reasons underlying it. Express appreciation for the confidence he showed in you by his offer.

Letter C

You face a dilemma. On the one hand, you have an offer from Uncle Frank to join Beston Home. On the other hand, Imperial Finance has approached you with an offer to join them as a construction loan officer. Write a letter to each company, asking for a reasonable period of time (you should specify how many days) to respond to their offers.

SPEAKING

Interview

Ask several classmates to play the roles of Beston executives, including the role of Uncle Frank. They will interview you for a position with Beston Home. (You should decide with them in advance which position you seek—for example, inventory supervisor, accounts receivable clerk, shipping supervisor, sales representative, milling foreman, and so forth.)

Presentation

Make a short presentation to an assembled group of Beston Home executives, again including Uncle Frank. Point out pertinent facts about your background, education, experience, skills, and aspirations. Emphasize what you can do for Beston Home.

Art for Money's Sake

It had seemed like a lark during the first few months. In place of a summer job, you had tried to have fun and make a little money by selling highly imaginative pieces of "art." All you had done, in fact, was collect shiny and interesting old automotive parts from a local junkyard. Mounted on a background of black velvet and framed in chrome picture frames, these parts took on a certain charm as art pieces. At least they stimulated conversation.

You could not have predicted how popular your pieces would become. The largest newspaper in your city ran a half-page spread on the "daring creativity" and "functional beauty" of your pieces. Since the article appeared, you've been interviewed by radio and television hosts, magazine writers, and even a graduate student doing a dissertation on modern art.

At the same time the value of your pieces has skyrocketed. A mounted hubcap you entitled "Moon Child" brought $1800 in a gallery last week. Suddenly you find yourself in a lucrative business—one that requires management and organization.

WRITING

Catalog

You have been asked by a prominent art gallery to write a paragraph to accompany each of six pieces going on display next week. Call to mind six creative pieces, then create an explanatory paragraph to accompany each one.

Memo

Write a memo to your newly hired business manager. Describe two or three ideas you have for diversifying beyond the limits of auto parts in art. Ask for his or her opinion of your ideas.

Letter A

Write a letter to the city newspaper thanking the editors for the special coverage given to you in recent issues. Describe to them how much your career has been affected by their interest. Mention current and future plans, along with any other topics you feel might be appropriate.

Letter B

Write a letter to the editor of an art magazine. A recent article there called you an "art opportunist" and "conscienceless profiteer." Your auto pieces, the article said, were "crude fakery" with absolutely no artistic significance. Defend yourself in a persuasive, not belligerent, way.

Letter of Application

On the basis of your recent successes, you decide to apply to the National Art Institute, a prominent art school, to seek more training and perhaps an academic degree in art. Write a letter of application that summarizes your career in art and future goals.

Promotional Letter

You want to interest more galleries in your art pieces. Write a letter promoting your work. Include specific details on the commission you are willing to pay on sales. Discuss any other business matter you feel is appropriate in the promotional letter.

Collection Letter

You know that Eastside Gallery has sold three of your pieces in the last sixty days. The total sales price was substantial: $4700. By contract with the gallery, you should have received 60 percent of that amount by now. You have received nothing. Write a collection letter in which you insist on prompt payment.

SPEAKING

Speech

Present a short speech to a civic organization like the Soroptimists or the Art Auxiliary. Describe how you got started and what you were trying to do. Comment on your sudden fame and its effect on you and your work. Give some idea of where you are going in the future. If you wish, answer questions from your audience after your speech.

Media Interview

Ask a classmate to play the role of radio or television host. Answer his or her questions about your art career. If possible, tape-record or videotape your interview for later review and analysis.

Interview

With profits soaring, you recognize that you must hire a business manager. Interview three classmates for this position. Describe in detail what you will require. After the interviews have been concluded, choose which applicant you wish to hire. Explain the reasons for your choice. Ask each applicant what he or she liked or disliked about the interview process.

More Than Numbers

You are now in your second year at one of the "Big Eight" accounting firms. You like your job and your colleagues. You've been praised for your work so far and feel certain that you will be promoted quickly in the company.

Margaret Fong, a partner in the firm, called you in last week to thank you for your role in establishing an employee suggestion box for the company. She urged you to seek out other areas in which the day-to-day operations of the company could be improved.

You take her invitation as the ideal opportunity to do something about a real problem you see in the company. Although your colleagues add, subtract, multiply, and divide with impeccable skill, many of them write very poorly. As a result, the end product seen by the client—an end product made up primarily of words—often reflects poorly upon the company.

WRITING

Memo

Write a memo to Margaret Fong, keeping her up-to-date on your investigation into company writing habits. What have you done so far? What are you doing now? What are you planning to do? How can she help?

Letter

Write a letter to the dean of your university's business school. Describe to him or her the writing problems your company faces. Ask advice on what to do. Does the business school have faculty members who are willing to lead on-site workshops in writing? Can the dean recommend self-study texts or effective correspondence study in business writing?

Report

The partners in the firm are impressed by your discoveries regarding the writing problems in the company. Margaret Fong authorizes you to prepare a short report of your findings, with recommendations for the improvement of writing. Write the report, remembering to demonstrate the writing skills you are recommending to others.

SPEAKING

Presentation

Make a presentation as if to a gathering of firm executives. Describe the problem of poor writing in the company, and explain what you think are its causes. Recommend some course of action (you may exercise your judgment and creativity here) to resolve the problem.

Interview

The firm's partners have authorized you to interview three company employees about their attitudes toward writing. Do so, trying to discover actual problems and possible solutions. You may choose to interview the three employees one at a time or together. Your classmates, of course, will play the roles involved in this case. The writing problems they describe, however, can be quite real.

Meeting

Your inquiry into company writing habits has now been concluded. Attend a meeting called to discuss the matter. Make a brief presentation of your findings, then join in discussion. Try to guide the group to accept your concluding recommendations.

The Bald Truth

For almost a year you have served as assistant editor for a nationwide household magazine, *Welcome Home*. You like the variety entailed in your job. Each day brings different tasks, ranging from proofing articles to lunching with advertising clients to seeking new article topics.

Take today's job, for example. You have to investigate the facts behind ad copy sent in by Jensen Pharmaceutical Enterprises, Inc. The firm is a relatively new advertiser in your magazine and so far has advertised mainly vitamins. But this month's ad copy is a real hair-raiser: "Amazing Discovery! Synthetic Protein Formula Cures Baldness!" The ad copy included "before" and "after" pictures showing a man with and without a healthy crop of hair.

Your managing editor (bald, by the way) worries about the reputation of the magazine when such ads are run. If the ad proves utterly false, the magazine loses face and credibility with its readers. Your job, the editor says, is to check out Jensen Pharmaceutical's claim before the ad is run.

WRITING

Memo

Write a memo to your editor. Respond to his or her wish that you check out the Jensen baldness claim. Describe how you plan to go about your investigation. Set a time-line for reaching a conclusion. Ask for any advice or guidance you will require.

Letter

Write a letter to Jensen Pharmaceutical Enterprises. Explain the delay in running their ad. Request substantiation of their claims. Be careful not to impugn the integrity of a client who has already run several ads in your magazine.

Report

Write a short report to the managing editor. Summarize the results of your investigation of the Jensen claim to cure baldness. Make a recommendation regarding running the ad.

Proposal

Your work on the Jensen Pharmaceutical Enterprises case has suggested to you a set of guidelines to apply to virtually all ads received by the magazine. Write up your ideas in the form of a short proposal addressed to the managing editor and editor-in-chief. What should advertisers be able to prove about their claims? How active should the magazine become in seeking out the truth behind advertised claims? Should the magazine warn readers that advertised products in the magazine are not approved or tested by the magazine? Consider these and other questions in drawing up your own list of guidelines for the proposal.

SPEAKING

Telephone

Use a tape recorder to record both sides of a "conversation" between you as assistant editor and a classmate as an executive at Jensen Pharmaceutical Enterprises. If unplugged telephones are available, hold the phone to your ear as you talk. Tell the executive about your editor's concerns, and describe the kind of assurance you want before running the ad.

Meeting

You have been invited to an on-site meeting at Jensen Pharmaceutical Enterprises to discuss the truth behind the "cure-for-baldness" claim. Your classmates will play the roles of Jensen executives, scientists, and technicians. Make a brief presentation in which you describe what your editor wants before running the advertisement. Answer questions and respond to concerns raised by the group.

Interview

Jensen Pharmaceutical has arranged interviews with three clients who (they say) have grown hair as a direct result of using Jensen products. Your classmates will play the roles of these individuals. Interview them one at a time or all together. Try to assess the worth of Jensen's claims. After the interviews, join in a discussion with classmates concerning the effectiveness of your interview techniques.

Soft Sales of Software

No one had to tell you, as a marketing major, about the "hot" sales possibilities in software. You were especially excited, therefore, about joining the nation's largest software distributor, SOFTWORLD, as assistant director of marketing.

The company represents and promotes more than 4000 individual software titles for a wide range of personal, home, and business microcomputer applications. Profits are soaring at SOFTWORLD, thanks in part to your aggressive advertising policies.

You have a growing concern, however, for the company's image as it grows larger and richer. SOFTWORLD is no longer the "wonder child" of the industry, plunging boldly ahead through thick and thin. You now have name recognition and growing respect. The question is how to build upon that respect so that SOFTWORLD becomes synonymous with quality and integrity.

Unfortunately, much of your reputation depends not on what SOFTWORLD is or does but on how well the software it sells really works. That software, of course, is developed by other companies and merely distributed through SOFTWORLD. A disgruntled user, however, can't help but blame SOFTWORLD when a given piece of software proves to be defective or misadvertised.

WRITING

Memo

Write a memo to the director of your customer assistance department. Explain your concern for the company image in relation to product failure. Request the names of three customers you might contact to investigate the problem. Describe briefly one or two of your ideas for protecting both the customer and the reputation of the company.

Letter

Write to a customer who has had an unsatisfactory experience with a SOFTWORLD product. Explain the purpose of your investigation. Make arrangements to meet with the customer for an interview. You may want to arrange for some kind of compensation for the customer's time. Include a brief list of questions you will want to discuss in the interview. Conclude with an appropriate expression of appreciation on the part of the company.

Report

Write a short report on the relation between product breakdown and company image for the Steering Committee at SOFTWORLD. Summarize the results of your investigation into customer attitudes and experiences. Discuss what has been tried and what can yet be tried to maintain and improve company image. Conclude with specific recommendations. (What warranty, for example, could the company provide with each piece of software it distributes?)

Proposal

SOFTWORLD alone cannot underwrite the quality of the thousands of pieces of software it sells. Write a proposal to the manufacturers of such software. Propose a quality guarantee of some sort on the part of the manufacturer to indemnify the distributor against claims made by customers. Could the manufacturer, for example, agree to replace software found to be unsatisfactory or issue a refund? You do not have to specify a particular manufacturer's name on the proposal. Instead, write the copy for a general proposal that could be sent, with individual names entered via word processing, to many manufacturers.

SPEAKING

Speech

Deliver a short speech to a group of executives at SOFTWORLD. Describe what you see as the growing problem of software breakdowns as they reflect upon the company. What can be done? How can company policies protect both the customer and the company's reputation? Consider these and other questions in preparing your speech and recommendations.

Interview

Based on letters recieved by your customer assistance desk at SOFTWORLD, you select three customers who have had unsatisfactory experiences with software distributed by SOFTWORLD. Each agrees to meet with you to discuss the problem. Interview the customers alone or together. Find out what went wrong in the products they purchased from SOFTWORLD. Try to discover to what extent they hold SOFTWORLD, the distributor, responsible for the problem. After the interviews have been concluded, discuss your interviewing methods with classmates.

Getting Your Act Together

When you moved to Coltonville, population 30,000, you thought you were moving to a cultural wasteland. But you've been surprised. It turns out that Coltonville has its own amateur theater group. You're now an active member looking forward to the spring production of *South Pacific*. In preparation for casting tryouts, you've been warbling in the shower a bit: "Some enchanted evening . . . "

The theater group faces a few organizational problems, in your view. All members pay a yearly membership fee of $25 to help support the work of the group. In addition, local businesses often donate money and supplies during the year. All of these funds are affectionately known as the "kitty," a loose treasury maintained by the officers of the organization.

You certainly are not concerned that any of the officers are profiting at the expense of the theater group. But as a business person yourself, you feel that the theater group would be better served by some essential financial organization and planning. The "kitty" should be placed in an interest-bearing bank account, for example. The group should apply for nonprofit tax status so that donations could be tax deductible. These are just a few of your ideas for structuring the finances of the group more adequately. You're sure that merchants in the area would be even more willing to make donations if the theater group presented a more organized approach to money matters.

At the same time you know that such reform will be resisted by many members, some of them founders of the group. "This isn't New York City," Harry Mills will say, "and we don't have to run this group like a business. It's fun we're interested in, not profit."

WRITING

Letter

Write a letter to Edith Allen, the president of the theater group. In a diplomatic way, suggest the merits of a structured approach to the group's finances. Include whatever other comments or topics seem appropriate and helpful to you.

Promotional Letter

Assume that your reforms have been successful and that a structured financial management system is now in place in the theater group. You have even received nonprofit tax status. Write a promotional letter to area merchants in which you ask for support, highlighting the fact that their contributions can now be deducted from taxes.

Report

The theater group is sufficiently impressed with your point of view to ask you to draw up a short report of the current financial state of the group, with recommendations for improvement. Write the short report, keeping in mind the communication needs of your audience: clarify points with substantiating detail.

Proposal

Based on your report, the executive committee of the theater group wants to employ a financial professional to set up and maintain the accounts and financial affairs of the theater group. They ask you to write a short proposal suggesting what kind of professional they should retain and how he or she might be located. They also want you to suggest approximately how much money the group can expect to pay for such services. Write the proposal, including a job description for the individual you want to employ.

SPEAKING

Speech

Make a brief presentation to the officers and members of the theater group, perhaps at their monthly meeting. Describe the problem of unstructured finances as you see it. Point out the disadvantages of such chaos without placing blame. Propose specific steps the group can take to place its finances on a more sound footing. Try in your presentation to counter arguments of the sort that Harry Mills is sure to make. If you wish, answer questions from the group after your presentation.

Interview

If available, choose a classmate with some accounting experience to play the role of an accountant brought in to discuss new financial planning for the theater group. Interview the accountant, seeking specific advice on how the day-to-day business of the group can be structured more effectively and safely. After the interview, discuss the strong and weak points of the interview with your classmates.

Meeting

Present your ideas to the theater group in the give-and-take of open discussion at a meeting. Assume that the topic of annual contributions is being discussed at the meeting. Ask several classmates to begin the discussion of how merchants can be coaxed into contributing. Insert your proposal for structured financing into the free flow of discussion. After the meeting, discuss the advantages and disadvantages of trying to make your point in discussion form rather than presentation form.

Seeing Is Believing

You're still in college, and you think you've hit upon a gold mine. The idea is simple. Home and business security services commonly affix stickers to windows of buildings and automobiles to indicate that the property or item is protected by the firm at hand. For example, Ace Alarm and Security, Inc., attaches its triangular "ACE PROTECT-ED" stickers to each window of a house it wires with a burglar alarm.

Your idea is to sell the effect of protection without the expense of the real McCoy. In other words, you want to market protection stickers for cars, houses, and businesses that will tend to discourage thieves without costing more than a few dollars to the purchasers of the stickers.

The stickers, of course, have to look professional to create the intended effect. There's the problem. A run of 5000 plasticized, gummed stickers in two colors will cost you $1200 in start-up costs. In addition, you figure that you need another $2000 for the many start-up items required by a new business.

WRITING

Memo

One of your most assertive and successful sales people is on the verge of getting you into serious trouble. He "forgets" to make clear that the stickers he sells are entirely bogus in the security services they purport to represent. Several clients have called your office for claims forms on which to report losses. Write a memo to this sales person, with a copy to file. Include whatever admonition you feel is appropriate. Be specific about your suggestions for improvement.

Inquiry Letter

Write a letter to an attorney whose name you have found in the Yellow Pages. Describe your idea for selling stickers and inquire if such representation is legal. It is true, of course, that the stickers claim something that just isn't so: no company, in fact, provides security protection for the building or vehicle to which the stickers are attached. But is a falsehood really a falsehood when its purpose is to discourage thieves? You want to be sure of your legal grounds before putting money into the project. Be sure in the letter to make provision for paying the attorney for his or her time in answering your letter. You may also want to be careful not to give the attorney a "blank check" to do as much research as he or she wants to at your expense.

Report

Through two acquintances of a friend, you are able to raise the initial capital to start your business. Your investors require, however, that you summarize in a report for them the status of the business after six months. That period is now approaching. Develop the report, looking at past accomplishments, present projects and problems, and future goals.

SPEAKING

Speech

Prepare a short presentation of your idea and needs for venture capitalists. Be specific about what they will give to you and what you will give to them.

Interview

Ask three classmates to play the roles of established security-service executives. Visit each of them individually to seek information about stickers. Recognize that they may not be willing to divulge hard-won business information, nor may they like your idea of "fake" security stickers.

Meeting

Assume that your business is off and rolling and that you have gathered together several college students willing to sell your stickers on a commission basis. Conduct an initial sales-training meeting with your sales personnel. Discuss how they should and should not represent your product. Be specific about the commission structure you offer. Include other matters of interest on an agenda you create and carry out.

General Hospital

As a hospital administrator, you expect to deal with many unexpected problems. You don't expect to be a dormitory counselor.

The problem, frankly, is the behavior of the nurses and orderlies, both male and female, while on duty at the hospital. Most of these men and women are in their twenties, and all seem bent on having an uproariously good time while working.

The hospital, in your view, certainly doesn't have to be a solemn place—and dare not seem like a morgue. But a perpetual series of giggles, whoops, and general horse-play in the halls goes far beyond the hospital's motto, "A Happy, Healthy Place." You resolve to salvage the hospital's image before the board of hospital examiners begins receiving patient complaints.

WRITING

Memo

Write a general memo to all staff. Describe the problem of uproarious behavior during working hours, being as specific as possible about its effect on patients and the public. Specify new operating procedures regarding decorum, describing what sanctions may be taken against violators. Conclude with an effective plea for cooperation.

Letter A

Write to Gareth Johning, Director of the Human Factors Institute, a training organization active in the health field. Describe the personnel problem you are facing. Give your opinion about what can be done about it. Ask his advice as well. Invite a representative of HFI to call upon you at the hospital. Perhaps you can involve HFI in a series of seminars for nurses and orderlies—seminars that will teach them the difference between *happy* and *crazy*.

Letter B

Write a letter responding to the complaint of Clarence O'Neill, released from the hospital after a long recuperation from a heart attack. O'Neill complains that his recovery was hindered by the general level of laughter and noise generated by the nurses and orderlies in the rooms and halls. "Often I was awakened by screams of laughter at 2 A.M.," O'Neill writes. "They certainly have a right to be gleeful, but not at the expense of my health."

Report

A member of the hospital board of directors—not a particularly supportive personality—has caught wind of your effort "to put long faces on all the nurses," as he puts it. He asks you to report to the board in writing about your current efforts to bring decorum to the hospital halls. Write this short report, describing the problem as you see it. Discuss the steps you are taking to resolve the problem without casting gloom over the hospital.

SPEAKING

Speech

Make a presentation to a gathering of hospital nurses and orderlies. Impress upon them the importance of professional decorum while on duty. Suggest the seriousness of your purpose by spelling out what the hospital administration plans to do to put "teeth" in your requirements for professional behavior.

Interview

Ask several classmates to play the roles of nurses and orderlies involved in the horseplay mentioned above. Interview them individually, then as a group, to determine what causes and perpetuates the party spirit in the halls of the hospital. Use the interview, in addition, to reinforce the new policies on decorum that you recommend.

Mountains and Molehills

Why, you ask yourself, do Mondays always have to be such crazy days? You've managed L'Envy, an upscale interior decoration service, for almost a year now. It has been everything you wanted in a management opportunity. Company growth has been surprisingly rapid, and you've come in contact with some of the most creative, successful people in your region. Then there is Monday.

This morning, as always, Nesbitt Duplication Service brought by supplies for your photocopy machine. The delivery person set down the supply boxes next to the customer service desk in your showroom. No one apparently noticed that one bottle of toner was leaking through the box, onto the polished hardwood floors, and over and underneath the scalloped wool carpeting. The leak wasn't noticed until Bert, the supply room clerk, came to move the boxes to the back room. By that time several feet of hardwood flooring had been stripped bare by the corrosive liquid. Worse, more than three feet of the scalloped wool carpeting had been soaked and permanently discolored by the fluid.

WRITING

Memo

Write a memo to Bert in the supply room. Since he knows what arrives where in the office, involve him in the process of developing better receiving procedures. Describe ideas you have for such procedures.

Letter A

Write a claim letter to Nesbitt Duplicating Services. Describe the extent of the problem cause by the leaking bottle. Insist on specific action by Nesbitt to repair the damage caused by the leak.

Letter B

In the role of a Nesbitt executive, write a response letter in which you deny responsibility for the incident. The leak, you claim, was apparently not present when the boxes were unloaded from the truck and brought into your building. Only after sitting on your showroom floor for a period of time, you claim, was the leak discovered. It could have happened because of carelessness on the part of your staff. Nesbitt will pay nothing.

Letter C

Again in your role as manager of L'Envy, reply to the denial sent to you by the Nesbitt executive. Reinforce your demand for action by suggesting what steps you plan to take if Nesbitt does not act. If you feel it appropriate, make a bid for acceptable compromise and cooperation.

SPEAKING

Telephone Conversation

Use classroom telephones to tape-record the following conversation. Call the manager of Nesbitt Duplicating Services to describe the problem caused by the leaking bottle. Estimate the damage caused by the fluid. Insist upon action of your choice. In deciding what action to require of Nesbitt Duplicating Service, recall that the scalloped wool carpeting is permanently discolored. The style and color are no longer available.

Appendixes

A Guide to Grammar, Mechanics, and Usage

This concise guide will limit its scope to practical problems faced by college and career business writers. For a more complete grammar of the English language, refer to one of the comprehensive handbooks available, such as the *Handbook of Current English,* published by Scott, Foresman and Company, or other handbooks available in your school's Business Communications library.

SENTENCES MUST BE COMPLETE

English sentences are composed of a subject (a noun or pronoun) and a predicate (containing a verb).

> (noun)　　+　(verb)
> *Western Electric　explored fiber optics.*
> (subject)　　+　　　(predicate)

Nouns name people (Clark Kent), places (Cincinnati), things (boxes), ideas (freedom), and activities (thinking).

Verbs describe action (pushes, sends, reaches) and states of being (is, are, was, were).

Commands ("Go for coffee.") are complete sentences, though they seem to be missing a subject. The subject *you* is implied:

> *(You)　　Go for coffee.*
> (implied　　(predicate)
> subject)

When a group of words lacks either a subject or a predicate, the result is a writing error called a sentence fragment.

> *Fragment:* And walked aimlessly for hours. (no subject)
> *Fragment:* Waking from a bad dream. (no predicate)
> *Fragment:* The man who left his briefcase in the car. (no predicate)

While advertising and magazine writers use sentence fragments freely, more traditional business prose does not allow the sentence fragment.

Quick-Test*

Directions: Mark S for complete sentences and F for sentence fragments.

1. Seeing you there by the bridge.
2. The way he looked at the supervisor before quitting.
3. Often holding his paycheck before my face.
4. From where I sat in the third row.
5. Which explains his affection for working long hours.

*Students should write answers to the Quick-Tests on a separate sheet of paper.

For Further Practice: Correct each of the sentence fragments you identified above.

SENTENCES MUST BE DISTINCT

When two sentences run together as one, the result is a writing error called the **run-on** sentence.

> *Error: Sandra gave creative energy to the company she sparked the imaginations of others by using her own.*

When a writer unsuccessfully tries to repair a run-on sentence by using only a comma, the result is a writing error called the **comma splice.**

> *Error: Sandra gave creative energy to the company, she sparked the imaginations of others by using her own.*

Run-on sentences and comma splices can easily be repaired in any one of six ways.

1. Separate the two sentences with a period.
   Error: The mills needed raw materials the workers needed jobs.
   Correct: The mills needed raw materials. The workers needed jobs.

2. Join the two sentences with a semicolon.
   The mills needed raw materials; the workers needed jobs.

3. Join the two sentences with a comma and a conjunction.
   The mills needed raw materials, and the workers needed jobs.

4. Join the two sentences with a semicolon and a conjunctive adverb followed by a comma.
   The mills needed raw materials; however, the workers needed jobs.

   Common conjunctive adverbs

accordingly	besides	hence	likewise	otherwise
also	consequently	however	moreover	still
anyhow	finally	indeed	nevertheless	then
anyway	furthermore	instead	next	therefore

5. Join the two sentences with a subordinating conjunction.
   The workers needed jobs because the mills needed raw materials.

   Common subordinating conjunctions
   Time: before, after, since, until, till, when, whenever, while, as
   Place: where, wherever
   Manner: as if, like
   Reason: because, since, as, so, that
   Contrast: though, although, even though
   Condition: if, unless, whether (or not)

6. Join the two sentences together with a relative pronoun.

   Error: Bernard Clay is an engineer, he banished the slide rule from our offices.
   Correct: Bernard Clay is the engineer who banished the slide rule from our offices.

Common relative pronouns

Who	Whose
Whom	That
Which	

Quick-Test

Directions: Mark R for run-on sentences, CS for comma splices, and OK for correct sentences.

1. The slander suit was dropped on Friday, it caused too much notoriety for the plaintiff.
2. Management trainees felt the pressure of competition the seminar leaders had let them know that only four would be hired.
3. No job offers absolute bliss I think my job offers more satisfaction than most.
4. Reaching high overhead for a piece of wire, Mac showed me the new wiring pattern for the fuselage.
5. We don't attend many of the office parties, we don't even drink.

For Further Practice: Correct each of the flawed sentences you have identified above.

SENTENCES MUST BE ORDERLY

Like machines, sentences must have their parts in the right places to work properly.

> *Error:* Sarah placed both hands on the podium rising to speak.
> > (The podium is not rising to speak!)
> *Correct:* Rising to speak, Sarah placed both hands on the podium.
> Sarah, rising to speak, placed both hands on the podium.

Words like "rising to speak" add extra meaning to (or "modify") the subject of the sentence, Sarah. Always keep such modifiers close to the word they modify to prevent distorted and silly meanings.

> *Error:* He left his car behind smoking a cigar.
> *Correct:* Smoking a cigar, he left his car behind.

Quick-Test

Directions: Write MM beside any sentence containing a misplaced modifier. Write OK beside any sentence in which the modifiers appear close to the word they modify.

1. Francine missed the child veering suddenly to the left.
2. Caught on a light fishing line, the huge trout struggled angrily for freedom.
3. By moving to the country, John said good-bye to the company in the South where his father was manager.
4. Putting his lecture aside, the topic of political radicalism caught the attention of the professor.
5. The security guard advised Wilson to put the mementoes in the steel vault that he treasured.

For Further Practice: Rewrite the flawed sentences you have identified above. Place modifiers in their proper positions.

SUBJECT/VERB AGREEMENT

By acquired habit as speakers of English, we usually choose verbs that agree with the subjects in our sentences.

> *Factories sometimes cost* (not *costs*) *too much in the suburbs.*

Sometimes, however, we trip up by attaching a singular subject to a plural verb or vice versa.

> *Each of the workers leaves* (not *leave*) *at 5 P.M.*
> (singular)   (singular)

Other easily mistaken singular subjects are either/or—

> *Either Jill or Mary answers our needs.*

—everyone—

> *Everyone of them knows the head supervisor.*

—and subjects separated by or:

> *The computer or the teletype causes* (not *cause*) *static on the telephone.*

Some plural nouns have singular meanings.

> *Economics is difficult but enlightening.*
> (singular)

Other plural nouns include *aesthetics, checkers, mathematics, mumps, physics, politics,* and *statistics* (when referred to as a field of study).

Collective nouns can take singular or plural verbs, depending on whether they refer to a group as a unit or as a collection of individuals.

> *The team was organized by Henderly.* (a group)
> *The team play their hearts out every game.* (individuals)

Quick-Test

Directions: Choose the verb that agrees with the subject.

1. Every position (entail, entails) risks as well as opportunities.
2. Either money or ambition (drive, drives) our top sales people.
3. A report or a proposal (need, needs) to be written soon.
4. Politics (lead, leads) to hot tempers at the club.
5. Each member in the three societies (attend, attends) at least six meetings per year.

PRONOUN CHOICE

Pronouns in a sentence must agree with the noun to which they refer.

> *Every one of the packages lost its wrapper.*
> (not *their*)

1. Use a plural pronoun to refer to two nouns joined by *and.*
   Wilson and Anderson gave their resignation speeches together.

Use a singular pronoun to refer to subjects preceded by *each* or *every*.

Each manager and each supervisor gave his or her approval to the project.

2. Use a singular pronoun to refer to nouns separated by *either/or* or *neither/nor.*
   Either the door or the hallway needs its annual coat of paint.

3. Use a singular or a plural pronoun to agree with collective nouns such as committee, crew, group, majority, number, and team, depending on whether it refers to a group as one unit or as a collection of independent individuals.
   The crew wins another of its many races.
   The crew are ready to receive their ribbons.

4. Use a singular pronoun to refer to *everyone.*
   Everyone has a right to express his or her own opinion.

5. Use a singular or plural pronoun to refer to *some* or *most,* depending on whether *some* or *most* refers to singular or plural nouns.
   Some of the sport has lost its excitement.
   Some of the sports have lost their excitement.

6. Use *I, we, you, he, she, it,* and *they* as subjects.
   He, she, and I went to the personnel office.

7. Use *me, us, you, him, her, it,* and *them* as direct objects, indirect objects, and objects of prepositions.
   The job affected him and her in positive ways.
   Send Tom and me the bill.
   Send the bill to Tom and me.

8. Use *who* as a subject.
   Who tells the boss what to do?
   I want to meet the person who tells the boss what to do.

9. Use *whom* as an object.
   Give the package to whom you wish.

Quick-Test

Directions: Choose the correct word in each sentence.

1. The study of statistics is popular for (its, their) usefulness.
2. Either your son or your husband lost (his, their) place in line.
3. The group left (its, their) seats.
4. Everyone from those companies understands (their, his or her) job.
5. Some of the cooking has lost (its, their) flavor.
6. Most managers budget (his or her, their) time effectively.
7. Give the bonus to the salesperson (who, whom) turns in the most orders.
8. The attaché case belongs to Bob, (who, whom) I sent to San Diego.
9. If the question were up to you and (I, me), we could settle it quickly.
10. No one except John and (me, I) knows the combination to the safe.

SEMICOLONS

1. Use semicolons to separate closely related main clauses.

Creative business managers know how to delegate authority; they give their employees a sense of importance by involving them in significant ways.

2. Use semicolons to separate items in complex lists.
The assembly line faced a variety of problems: workers who, left to themselves, wasted time; machinery that dated from the Eisenhower years; and rushed schedules that brought perpetual panic.

Quick-Test

Directions: Punctuate the following sentences correctly with semicolons. Some sentences may not require punctuation.

1. Few researchers knew the library better than Jane she virtually lived there during waking hours.
2. Bradford guessed that the company faced financial problems however, he never suspected bankruptcy was imminent.
3. Two years seemed too little time to produce a new generation of automobiles no matter what the president said.
4. Seven employees threatened to quit the rest decided to stay on and fight for their rights.
5. Richard saw the bright side of urban life: specialty shops close to the factory for easy marketing apartments within biking distance of the job and, an interesting variety of neighbors.

COLONS

1. Use colons to signal the introduction of an example, an explanation, a quotation, or a list. Colons should always follow complete sentences.

   Error: The ingredients of the concrete: Portland cement, lime, sand, pea gravel, and water.
   Correct: The ingredients of the concrete were the following: Portland cement, lime, sand, pea gravel, and water.

2. Use colons in time designations and after greetings in formal letters.
   The workday begins promptly at 8:00 A.M.
   Dear Ms. McCoy:

Quick-Test

Directions: Punctuate the following sentences correctly with colons.

1. The safety deposit box contained gems diamonds, rubies, and sapphires.
2. Please pick up your time card by 11 00.
3. His letter began in a formal way ''Dear Mr. Wells We appreciate your interest in our organization.''
4. He had all the qualities of a talented executive but one sociability.
5. Bring three things to the meeting your notes, your questions, and your patience.

APOSTROPHES

1. Use apostrophes to mark missing letters in contractions.
   isn't   they've   she's

2. Use apostrophes to form some plurals.
   Ph.D.'s   C.O.D.'s

3. Use apostrophes to indicate possession.
   Singular: business's   boss's   manager's   woman's
   Plural: businesses'   bosses'   managers'   women's

   a. It's = it is *It's important to me.*
      Its = belongs to it *The table is missing its leg.*

   b. Personal pronouns (hers, theirs, ours) do not take apostrophes.
      The job is hers if she wants it.

   c. The impersonal pronoun *one* uses an apostrophe.
      One's work can also be one's recreation.

Quick-Test

Directions: Punctuate the following sentences correctly with apostrophes.

1. Its almost a year since the childrens toys division merged with Franks group.
2. Womens opportunities in the workplace have widened in the last decade.
3. Our companys marketing office doesnt require Ph.D.s to figure out marketing strategies.
4. Ones career often depends upon circumstances that arent entirely predictable.
5. The childrens profits are theirs to keep.

QUOTATION MARKS

1. Use quotation marks to separate others' words from your own.
   He called out, "Please step forward if you wish to bid."

2. Use quotation marks to set off titles of short poems, short stories, songs, chapters, essays, or articles.
   "How to Write a Résumé"   "The Lake Isle of Innisfree"

3. Use quotation marks to indicate irony.
   His "university degree" was in fact a diploma purchased for $300.

Quick-Test

Directions: Punctuate the following sentences correctly with quotation marks.

1. The personnel director said, Please follow me to the interview.
2. Franci's article, Finding a Management Position, caught the attention of the entire office.
3. The facts you refer to are just rumor.
4. Do you have questions for us? the interviewer asked.
5. No, replied the applicant, but I may think of some later.

ITALICS

1. Use italics (or underlining) to mark the titles of books, plays, movies, newspapers, and magazines.

The *Wall Street Journal* reviewed the financial aspects of *Star Wars*.

2. Use italics to identify foreign words and phrases.
   The visitor used the German word for work, *arbeiten*.

3. Use italics to give special emphasis.
   We asked the supervisor not only *how* to do the job, but *why* it should be done at all.

4. Use italics to set off words that you wish to call attention to as words.
   Tell the technical writers they use *is* too often.

Quick-Test

Directions: Mark the following sentences correctly with italics (by underlining).

1. Read how to invest in silver in Changing Times magazine.
2. He forgot to notice that all important word if in the letter of promotion.
3. The words Mon cher let Priscilla know her client felt pleased by the outcome of the real estate deal.
4. The Los Angeles Times ran an article on speculation in gold futures.
5. Try to close the negotiations without any if's, and's, or but's.

PARENTHESES

1. Use parentheses to enclose explanation or details.
   The 507 press (a fabrication press for plywood) saved the company $82,000 in one year.

2. Use parentheses to enclose publisher information in a footnote.
   John Renley, *Common Stock Investment Strategies,* (New York: Williams Press, 1983).

Quick-Test

Directions: Punctuate the following sentences correctly using parentheses.

1. We sat beside the Controller head financial officer of the corporation at the board meeting.
2. The essential materials of an automobile steel, rubber, plastic, and glass can be stockpiled in unlimited quantities.
3. Be sure to read a study of Vencer Productions in *Four Success Stories* Benchmark Publishing: Miami, 1980.
4. A power mitre box a tool used for cutting precise corners is a necessity for a professional carpenter.
5. We saw only one edition of *Corporation Records* Crownstead Publishing Toledo, Ohio, 1982.

DASHES

1. Use dashes to separate a series from the rest of the sentence.
   The essential materials of the automobile—steel, rubber, plastic, and glass—can be stockpiled in almost unlimited quantities.

2. Use dashes to mark off an afterthought.
Her resignation came only after repeated attempts to get the raise she wanted— and deserved, for that matter.

3. Use dashes to separate a parenthetical comment.
Ledger books—the kind used for professional bookkeeping—were being sold at half price.

Quick-Test

Directions: Punctuate the following sentences correctly using dashes.

1. The partners in the firm Benson, Smith, and Troy met for more than three hours with the new supervisor.
2. She couldn't understand why her employees accepted the pay reductions so rationally unless, of course, they preferred low-paying jobs to no jobs at all.
3. The basic elements of sales success confidence, sociability, integrity formed the curriculum of the sales seminar.
4. At his retirement party, we presented Jack with a gift he didn't expect his very own gavel.
5. Exotic fruits mangoes, papaya, and breadfruit filled the basket.

HYPHENS

1. Use hyphens to mark divisions within hyphenated words.
editor-in-chief   twenty-one   (but one hundred and five)

2. Use hyphens to divide words into syllables when division is necessary at a line-end.
*cor-   corpo-   corpora-
poration   ration   tion*

Quick-Test

Directions: Punctuate the following sentences correctly using hyphens.

1. We watched the old man of war sail into port on the twenty second day of January.
2. Five hundred and three sales people gathered in Denver.
3. He defended the water cooled engine.
4. My father in law thought I was only twenty one.
5. The word *establishment* should be divided into syllables in this way: (rewrite the word, dividing it properly with hyphens).

CAPITALIZATION

1. Use a capital letter to begin sentences, direct quotations, and most lines of poetry.
*Let your employees feel that they matter.
He asked, "Why did you call?"*

2. Capitalize the names and initials of persons, places, and geographical areas.
   Henry Higgins   Hinton, Iowa   the South

3. Capitalize the names of organizations and their members.
   Rotary Club   Rotarians

4. Capitalize the names of ships, planes, and spacecraft.
   Voyager II   the Queen Elizabeth

5. Capitalize the names of ethnic groups, races, nationalities, religions, and languages.
   Jewish   Romanian   Native American   English

6. Capitalize the names of days, months, holidays, and historical periods and events.
   Friday   October   the Roaring Twenties   Memorial Day

7. Capitalize the first word and all other major words in titles of books, plays, poems, musical compositions, films, and works of art.
   "Some Enchanted Evening"   The Sound and the Fury
   Star Wars

Quick-Test

Directions: Capitalize the following sentences correctly by writing in the correct capital above the incorrect letter.

1. a secretary asked me, "why do you stay so late every evening?"
2. when i traveled through the south i found few chicanos.
3. after reading to kill a mockingbird last december, i began paging through several other american novels.
4. she sang the star spangled banner on july 4.
5. hurricane albert hit the west and south with particular fury.

USAGE

1. Choose the correct principal parts of verbs
   We choose one verb form for the present, one for the past, and one for the past participle (signaled by has, have, had, was, were, has been, have been, had been).

Present	Past	Past Participle
arise	arose	arisen
bear	bore	borne
begin	began	begun
blow	blew	blown
break	broke	broken
burst	burst	burst
buy	bought	bought
catch	caught	caught
choose	chose	chosen
come	came	come

Present	Past	Past Participle
creep	crept	crept
drag	dragged	dragged
draw	drew	drawn
drown	drowned	drowned
drink	drank	drunk
drive	drove	driven
eat	ate	eaten
fall	fell	fallen
fling	flung	flung
fly	flew	flown
freeze	froze	frozen
get	got	got, gotten
give	gave	given
go	went	gone
grow	grew	grown
hide	hid	hidden
know	knew	known
lay	laid	laid
lead	led	led
lie	lay	lain
prove	proved	proved, proven
raise	raised	raised
read	read	read
ride	rode	ridden
rise	rose	risen
run	ran	run
see	saw	seen
shake	shook	shaken
sing	sang	sung
sit	sat	sat
slide	slid	slidden, slid
speak	spoke	spoken
swear	swore	sworn
swim	swam	swum
swing	swung	swung
take	took	taken
tear	tore	torn
tell	told	told
wear	wore	worn
write	wrote	written

2. Choose the word you intend

a lot a great amount of (slang)
allot to portion out

advice a recommendation
advise to inform, suggest

accept to take, receive
except to leave out

affect to influence
effect the outcome, result
effect to bring about

lose to give up
loose unattached, unsecured

proceed to go ahead
precede to appear before

stationary still, unmoving
stationery writing paper

3. Spell correctly by checking your dictionary often.

Common Misspelled Words in Business

absence	especially	notable	separate
accidentally	exaggerate	noticeable	sergeant
accommodate	excellence	occurred	severely
accumulate	existence	occurrence	sieve
advice	experience	omitted	similar
advise	familiar	optimistic	sophomore
a lot	February	parallel	stationary
allot	foreign	paralyze	stationery
amateur	forty	pastime	studying
analyze	fourth	performance	subtle
appearance	generally	personal	successful
arctic	government	personnel	surprise
arguing	grammar	physical	tendency
argument	height	possession	than
arithmetic	heiress	precede	then
athletic	homemade	preferred	their, there, they're
attendance	humorous	prejudice	thorough
beginning	hygiene	principal	through
beneficial	immediately	principle	to, too, two
benefited	incredible	privilege	tragedy
break	independence	probably	tries
Britain	interesting	proceed	trouble
bureau	irresistible	professor	truly
business	its, it's	pronunciation	typically
choose	laid	prophecy	usually
chose	lead	prophesy	unbelievable
committee	led	qualm	utterance
conscience	lightning	quarrel	vaccinate
conscious	loneliness	quiet	vain
definitely	loose	quite	vein
desperate	lose	quizzes	villain
dictionary	losing	receive	weather
disappearance	marriage	receiving	weird
disastrous	mathematics	referee	wholly
dissatisfied	maybe	reference	writing
effect	miniature	referred	
eligible	miracle	restaurant	
embarrass	mysterious	rhythm	
eminent	necessary	sacrilegious	
environment	neurotic	schedule	
equipped	ninety	seize	

Format of Letters, Reports, and Proposals

FIGURE A-1

**Standard Business
Letter Layout, Block
Style**

At least
double space

Double space

Double space

Double space

Double space

At least
double space

At least
quadruple space

At least
double space

Single space

At least
double space

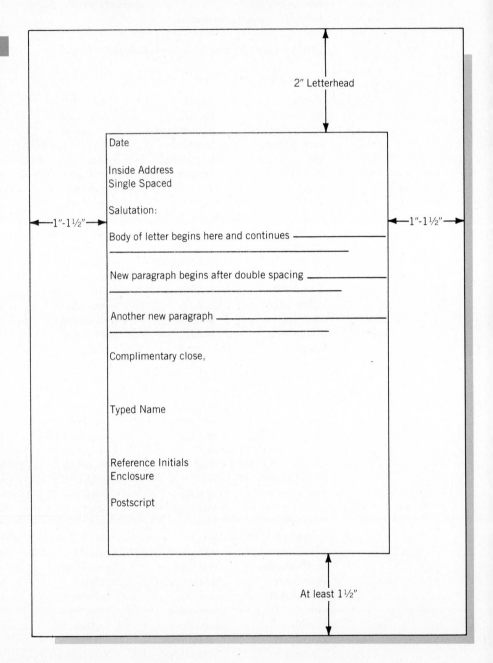

2″ Letterhead

1″-1½″

Date

Inside Address
Single Spaced

Salutation:

Body of letter begins here and continues

New paragraph begins after double spacing

Another new paragraph

Complimentary close,

Typed Name

Reference Initials
Enclosure

Postscript

1″-1½″

At least 1½″

Standard Business Letter Layout, Modified Block Style

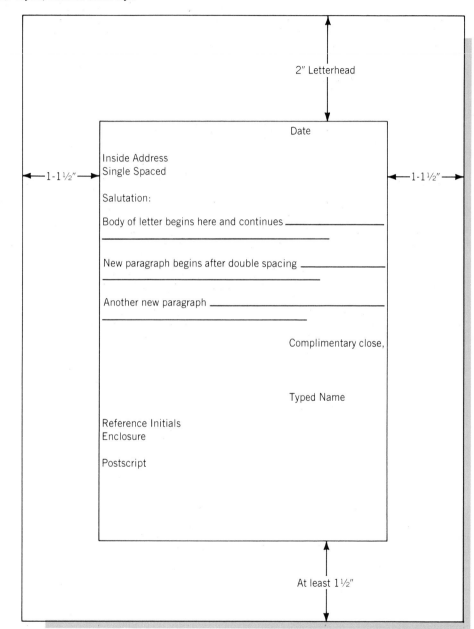

Standard Business Letter Layout, Indented Style

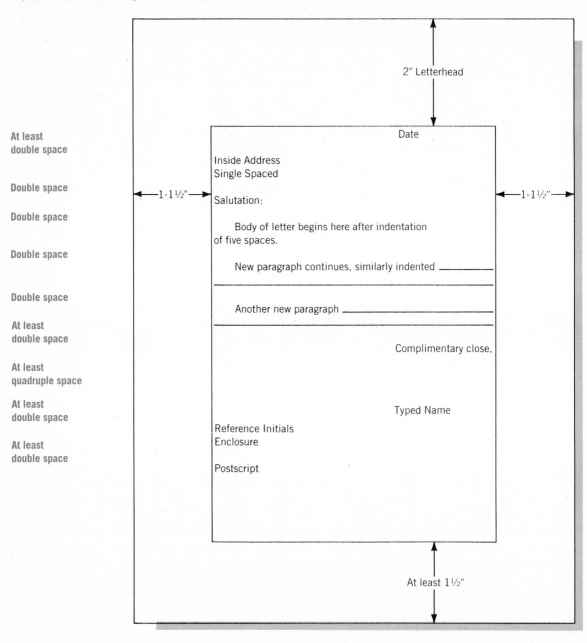

At least
double space

Double space

Double space

Double space

Double space

At least
double space

At least
quadruple space

At least
double space

At least
double space

2″ Letterhead

Date

Inside Address
Single Spaced

Salutation:

    Body of letter begins here after indentation
of five spaces.

    New paragraph continues, similarly indented

    Another new paragraph

Complimentary close,

Typed Name

Reference Initials
Enclosure

Postscript

1-1½″

1-1½″

At least 1½″

Envelope Layout for Standard and Note-Sized Envelopes

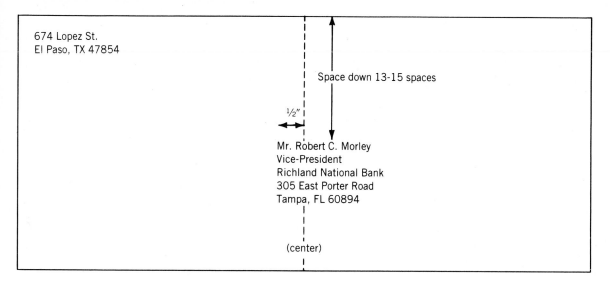

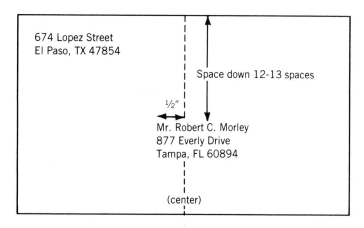

Title Page Layout for Report or Proposal

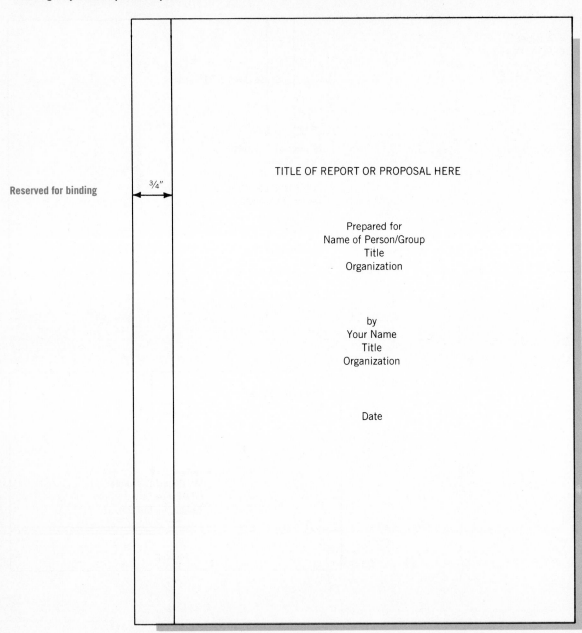

Reserved for binding

¾″

TITLE OF REPORT OR PROPOSAL HERE

Prepared for
Name of Person/Group
Title
Organization

by
Your Name
Title
Organization

Date

Table of Contents Layout for Proposal or Report

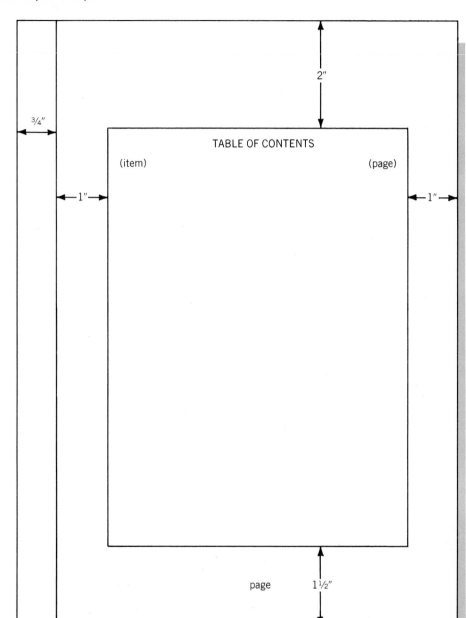

First Page Layout of the Body of a Proposal or Report

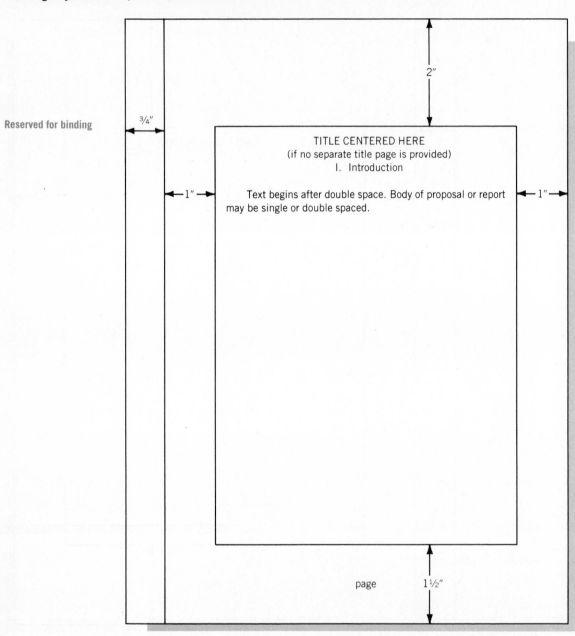

Reserved for binding

¾"

2"

1"

1"

TITLE CENTERED HERE
(if no separate title page is provided)
I. Introduction

Text begins after double space. Body of proposal or report may be single or double spaced.

page   1½"

Typical Text Page Layout for Proposal or Report

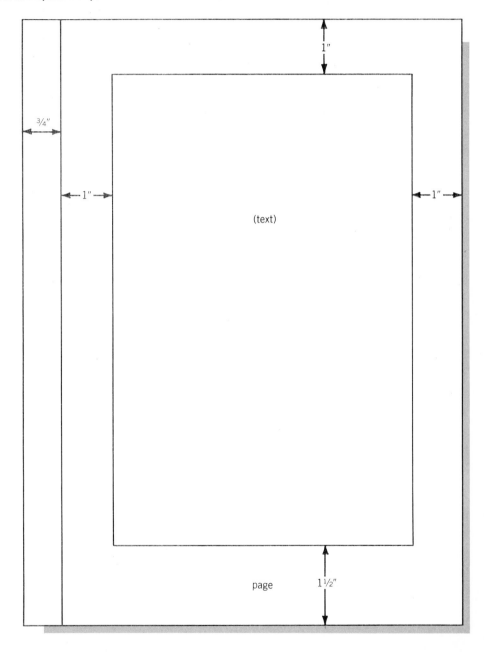

Reserved for binding

3/4"

1"

1"

1"

(text)

page   1 1/2"

Bibliography Layout for Proposal or Report

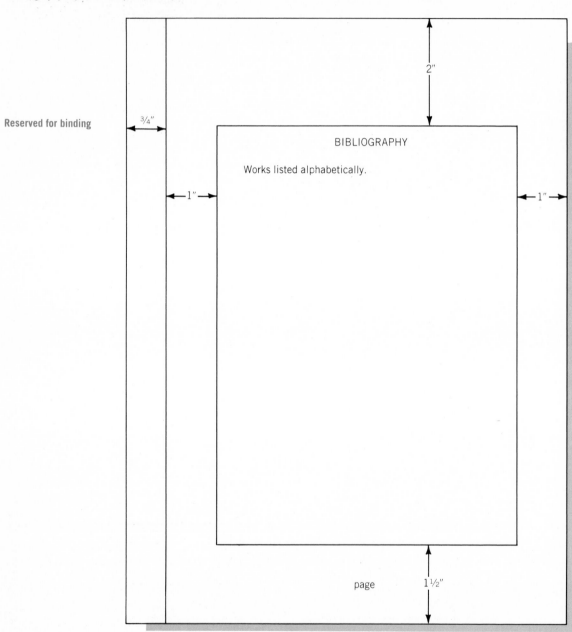

**Order of Pages in a
Short Proposal**

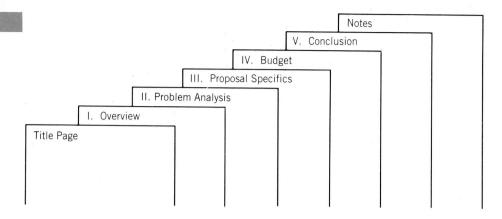

**Order of Pages in a
Long Proposal**

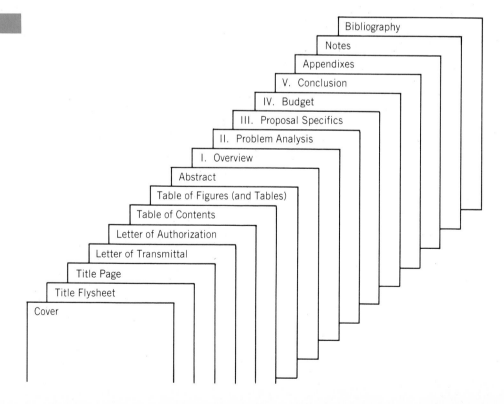

**Order of Pages in a
Short Report**

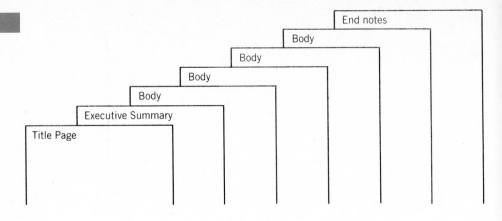

**Order of Pages in a
Long (Formal) Report**

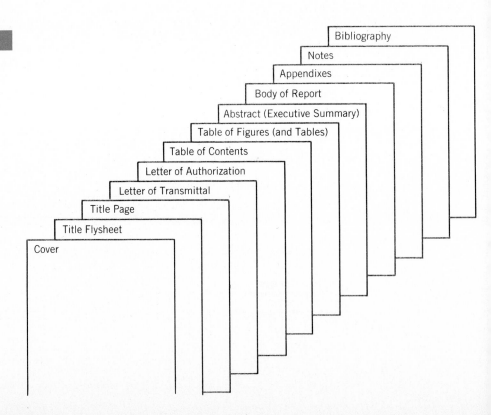

A Guide to Documentation

FOOTNOTES

Common features in longer forms of business writing, footnotes serve two related purposes: 1. to supply the reader with additional information you don't want to include in your main text, and 2. to identify the source of facts, ideas, or quotations contained in your text. Footnotes commonly appear at the bottom of the referenced page or at the end of a proposal or report, listed in order of appearance.

The reference number of a footnote appears as a number typed slightly above the line of text, like this.[22] Whenever possible, the superscripted number should appear at the end of the sentence. In the case of a footnoted quotation, the reference number is placed outside the final quotation mark.

When listing footnotes at the bottom of each referenced page, indent five spaces before the superscripted number:

[16]Regina Tolleson and Virginia Welstead, "Founding a Business by and for Women," *Modern Career,* March 1985, p. 121.

When footnotes appear at the end of a document, list them in order of appearance on a page titled, FOOTNOTES or simply NOTES. Again, indent the first line of each footnote five spaces, and *single space* all lines within a single reference. Provide at least double spacing between footnotes.

The conventions of footnoting differ somewhat from style manual to style manual. Once you have chosen a particular guide to follow (such as the following guide), follow its prescriptions exactly.

First References

A Book by One Author

[1]Dorothy Westmont, *Theories of Executive Management,* 2nd ed. (New York: Smith Tews, 1986), p. 342.

A Book by Two or More Authors

[2]Frank Dessings and Virginia Collings, *Advertising in America, 1970-1980,* 3 vols. (Boston: Benton, 1986), 3: 221.

[3]Sumi Fukado and Osha Sotori, *Time Management Studies in Japanese Corporations,* trans. Herbert Victor (New York: Wilcox, 1985), p. 32.

A Magazine Article

[4]Barbara Fremont, "Asking Government for Help," *Business Week,* June 6, 1986, p. 42.

[5]"Glamour Stocks in the Eighties," *Wall Street Summary,* Aug. 1, 1985, p. 132.

A Journal Article

⁶Calvin Osterley, "Economic Models for Silver Futures," *Review of Economic Theory* 11 (1985): 22–25.

A Newspaper Article

⁷"Interviewers List Priorities," *New York Times,* 16 April 1985, Sec. C, p. 22.

A Conference Paper

⁸Sandra Bowden, "The Psychology of Successful Collection," *Proceedings of the National Business Conference,* ed. G. B. Crown (San Francisco: Fountain, 1986), p. 258.

A Report, Pamphlet, or Booklet

⁹Omaha Better Business Bureau, *Starting a Small Business* (Omaha, Nebraska: Business Press, 1985), p. 55.

Personal Correspondence

¹⁰Henry Smith, Smith Corporation, August 11, 1985, letter to author.

An Interview

¹¹Interview with Katherine Omar, President, Omar Industries, Seattle, Washington, June 5, 1985.

An Informational Footnote

¹²While the figures quoted here appear to substantiate my argument, I am aware that other interpretations are both possible and popular.

Later References to a Source Already Cited

When the previously cited work has an author, cite the author's last name and the page reference:

¹³Bowden, p. 55.

¹⁴Dessings and Collings, p. 97.

If you have cited more than one work by one author or set of authors, use a shortened version of the title in your subsequent footnote:

¹⁵Dovesmith, "Buyer's Guide," p. 413.

Note that any work mentioned in this shortened form must first have been introduced in the footnotes by full citation.

BIBLIOGRAPHY

A bibliography differs from a list of footnotes in two ways. First, the bibliography or-ers works alphabetically, not in order of appearance in the text. Second, the bibliography lists not only works quoted but also works consulted (and therefore of potential use to someone seeking additional information on your topic). The bibliography is often placed as the last page in a report or proposal.

Bibliographic references are listed in alphabetical order on one or more pages in a report section titled BIBLIOGRAPHY. Lines within an individual bibliographic reference are usually double-spaced, with triple-spacing (or more) provided between references. As illustrated below, "hanging" lines are used with all lines but the first in an entry indented five spaces.

Like the rules for footnotes, the conventions for bibliographic references vary slightly from style manual to style manual. Once you have chosen your guide, however, follow its rules carefully.

A Book with One Author

Graham, C. K. *Reaching for Profits*. New York: Financial Press, 1985.

A Book with Two or More Authors

Gunther, Katherine, and C. O. Serthy. *The Practical Approach to Corporate Tax*

Planning. New York: Williams and Ferman, 1986.

A Magazine Article

Henderson, Roy. "Managing the Managers." *Executive Monthly,* January 1985,

pp. 177–89.

A Journal Article

Forbes, W. C. "An Analysis of Employee Attitudes in Four-Day-Week

Environments." *Business Trends* 15 (1986), pp. 23–44.

A Conference Paper

Trent, Gunther. "Four Ways to Beat Burn-out." In *Publications of the National*

Personnel Association, ed. C. Wentley, pp. 354–67. Los Angeles: NPA

Press, 1985.

A Newspaper Article

Jemson, Barbara. "Profit-sharing Plans Win Approval." *Los Angeles Times,* 13

May 1985, Sec. E., p. 12.

A Report, Pamphlet, or Booklet

Labor Relations Board. *Policies of the Labor Relations Board with Regard to*

Racial and Religious Prejudice. Washington, D.C.: Labor Council, 1986.

Personal Correspondence

Foster, R. N. Foster Products, Inc., August 3, 1985. Letter to author.

An Interview

Wellingham, Arnold, Chairman of the Board, Welham Associates. Portland,

Oregon: January 14, 1986.

ACKNOWLEDGMENTS

All photographs and illustrations not credited are the property of Scott, Foresman and Company.

Positions of photographs are shown in abbreviated form as follows: top (t), bottom (b), center (c), left (l), right (r).

Photographs taken expressly for Scott, Foresman are the property of Scott, Foresman and Company:

John Weinstein for Scott, Foresman and Company, x (bl), xii (bl), xv (bl), xvii (bl), xviii (b), xix (b), xxiv, 1, 98, 99, 210, 211, 342, 343, 402, 403, 448, 449.

x (tl), Four by Five
x (tc), Comstock
x (bc), Four by Five
x (r), Four by Five

xi (l), Four by Five
xi (tc), Comstock
xi (bc), Four by Five
xi (r), Comstock

xii (tl), Courtesy CPT Corporation
xii (tc), Courtesy Burroughs Corporation
xii (tr), Courtesy Hewlett-Packard

xv (tr), Comstock

xvii (tl), Comstock
xvii (tr), Courtesy Burroughs Corporation

xviii (t), Lincoln Russell/Stock Boston

xix (t), Dan McCoy/Rainbow

xxi, Courtesy CPT Corporation

xxii, Courtesy Steelcase, Inc.

2, NASA
9, Fig. 1-1, Courtesy Apple Computer, Inc.
11, Fig. 1-2, Cameramann International
16, Courtesy CPT Corporation, Minneapolis, MN.
48, Courtesy Steelcase, Inc.
76, Courtesy Apple Computer, Inc.
100, Courtesy Steelcase, Inc.
124, Courtesy Hewlett-Packard
172, Courtesy CPT Corporation, Minneapolis, MN.

186, Courtesy Burroughs Corporation
191, Fig. 8-1, Architects: Perkins & Will, Courtesy Hedrich-Blessing

Credits for Color Insert between pages 192– 193:

6 (t), Christopher Morrow/Stock Boston
6 (b), Courtesy Hewlett-Packard
7 (t), Courtesy Geographic Systems, Inc., Andover, MA.
7 (b), Cameramann International
8, Gregg Mancuso/Stock Boston

198, Fig. 8-12, Clarence A. Moberg
206, Fig. 8-21, Gorham Kindem
207, Fig. 8-23, Gorham Kindem
212, U.S. Postal Service
246, Stacy Pick/Stock Boston
274, Tom Grill/Comstock
292, Tom Grill/Comstock

314, Dick Durrance II/Woodfin Camp & Assoc.
344, Courtesy Burroughs Corporation
364, Comstock
414, Lincoln Russell/Stock Boston

450, Courtesy PicTel Corporation, Peabody, MA.
453, Fig. 19-1, Dan McCoy/Rainbow
462, Dan McCoy/Rainbow
484, Robert Azzi/Woodfin Camp & Assoc.
491, Fig. 21-1, Cameramann International

Index

G

Generalizations, 129
Gestures, in oral presentations, 352–54, 398
    in speaking, 352–54
Goodwill
    building, 282, 284
    conveying bad news and maintaining, 294–312
    letters, 256, 258, 259
Grammar, 34
    checking for errors in, 73
Grapevine communications, 37
Graphics software, 9–10
Grouped bar graph, as visual aid, 194, 195
Guarantees, 473–74
Guide letters, 268, 270, 271, 468, 469
    for placing orders, 253
Guide words, beginning sentences with, 90

H

Handouts, as visual aid, 202, 203
Handwriting, importance of good, in short memos, 112
Help wanted ads, 410–11
Hemingway, Ernest, 7
Hidden significance pattern of organization, 61
Hub and spokes communication pattern, 39
Human Use of Human Beings, The (Weiner), 26

I

Idea circle, 55–56
Ideas, organization of, 58–65
Indented style, 223, 225
Informational/instructional writing
    sample, 180, 184
    steps in, 178–79
    types of, 177–78
    writing instructions, 181–83
Information retrieval techniques, 59
In-house communication principles, 103
    brevity, 109
    exercising judgment in, 103–4
    filing, 107
    identifying standard procedures for, 105–6
    initiating, 107
    presentation, 108–9
    routing, 106–7
    sending whole message, 108–10
    using positive language, 104–5

Inquiries
    negative responses to, 301, 303, 304
    positive response letters, 278, 280, 281
Inside address, in business letter, 234–35
Instructions. *See* informational/instructional writing
International Communications Network, 490
International correspondence
    avoiding slang and colloquialisms in, 494–95
    checking for comprehension, 495
    and cultural differences, 42–43, 486–94
    future of, 496
    slowing down speech rate, 495
Interviews, 375–76
    campus, 376
    checklist for, 379
    on-site, 376–78
    supervisory, 378
Introduction speech, 390
Introduction to Rhetorical Communication, (McCroskey), 28
Invention
    classic questions, 56–58
    finding ideas, 54–55
    idea circle, 55–56
Invitations
    negative responses to, 301, 304–5
    positive responses to, 278, 282, 283
Is construction, 83
I version, 216

J

Job search, 406. *See also* Interviews
    career opportunities with former employers, 409
    college placement services, 410
    help wanted ads, 410–11
    job-seeker ads, 412
    public agency ads, 412
    résumé writing, 406–7, 420–24
    tips and introductions from friends, 408–9
    visiting personnel offices, 409–10
Job-seeker ads, 412
Judgment, exercising of, in in-house communication, 103–4
Jung, Carl, 29

K

Keats, John, 360
Korsybski, 18

Noise, effect of, on communication, 24–25
"No" letters, 294–300
    buffer statement in, 300
    for denying credit, 308–12
    for making adjustments, 305–8
    for responding to orders, 300–301, 302
    for responding to requests and invitations, 301,
      303, 304, 305
Non sequitur, 129
Nonverbal communication barriers, 45
Notes
    in long report, 176
    in speaking, 351–52
Noun clusters, avoiding, 84–85

O

Office automation, 452–53
    computerized telephone, 455–56
    computers in, 457–60
    data bases, 455
    sending and receiving electronic letters, 454–55
    teleconference, 456–57
    work day, 454
    work stations, 453–54
One-to-one communications, 366
    diction, 366–69
    interviews, 375–78
    listening, 372–74
    in meetings, 378–83
    speaking, 374–75
    telephone, 369–72
On-site interviews, 376–78
Opinion pattern of organization, 63
Oral presentations, 388. *See also* One-to-one
  communications; Speaking skills
    anecdotes in, 391
    anxiety and, 388–90
    appreciation speech, 390
    business, 394–99
    call for action in, 393
    humor in, 391–92
    introduction speech, 390
    local facts or sites, in, 392–93
    luncheon/dinner addresses, 391–94
    personal stories in, 391
    predictions, 393
    summary plus, 393
    unexpected statements in, 392
    visual aids for, 202–8, 355–56, 395, 397

    words of praise/appreciation in, 393
    wrapping up, 394
Orders
    negative responses to, 300–301, 302
    positive responses to, 277–78, 279
Organization, use of, in speaking, 354–55
Organizational barriers to communication, 44–45
Organizational chart, as visual aid, 200
Organizational communication patterns, 36
    structured communication, 36, 38–40
    unstructured communication, 36–38
Osgood, C. E., 24, 25
Outlines, 64–65
Overclaim, 66
Overseas Briefing Associates, 490

P

Pagination, in long report, 174, 176
Paragraph
    checking for unity and coherence, 94–95
    effective development of, 91–94
      enumeration, 92–94
      exposition, 91–92
      question, 94
"Partnership" statement, in goodwill letters, 258
Passive voice, elimination of, 82–83
PATS (please act on timely specifics) statement,
  117–19
Pauses, use of, in speaking, 357–58
Perceptive filter, 30
Perceptual barriers to communication, 43–44
Personalization, of résumés, 423–24, 434
Personal stories, in oral presentations, 391
Perspective pattern of organization, 61
Persuasive letters, 316. *See also* Sales letters
    accessing needs of reader in, 317
    nature of persuasion in, 316
    need first, 320, 321
    product/service first, 317, 318–19, 320
Petro, Frank, 452
Photographs
    in résumés, 422
    as visual aid, 191
Physical barriers to communication, 42
Physical objects, as visual aid, 207
Pictograms, as visual aid, 197
Pie chart, as visual aid, 196, 197
Pitch, varying of, in speaking, 357
Policy writing, 178
Positive language

V

Vagueness, avoiding, 81–82
Value pattern of organization, 64
Variety pattern of organization, 62
Video teleconferences, 12
Visual aids
    for business writing, 191–202
    checklist for using, 189
    deceptive practices in using, 190–91
    for oral presentations, 202–8, 355–56, 395, 397
    reasons for using, 188
Vocational Rehabilitation Act (1973), 475
Voice, 78
    business, 79
    emotional, 78, 79
    encyclopedia, 78, 79
Voice chip, 34
Voice-driven typewriters, 369
Volume, varying of, in speaking, 357

W

Walling, Victor, 459
Warranties, 473–74
Weaver, Warren, 20, 24, 26
White space, effective use of, 117, 182–83
    effective use of, in longer memos, 117
Whorf, Benjamin, 18, 21–22
Wiener, Norbert, 26
Wordiness
    avoidance of, in short memos, 112–13
    elimination of, 86–87

Word processing, 8–10
    use of merging routine in, for direct mail letters, 327
Words. *See also* Wordiness
    correct use of, 86
    creation of reality with, 21–22
    effects of, 24–25
    elimination of unnecessary, 71
    perception of, 22–24
Words and Things (Brown), 23
Work stations, 453–54
Writer's block, 50, 81
Writing
    diction in, 5
    length, 5
    for the future, 5–6
    tone in, 5

Y

"Yes" letters, 276–77
    building goodwill with, 282, 284
    for credit approvals, 287, 289
    for making adjustments, 284, 287, 288
    for responding to inquiries, 278, 280, 281
    for responding to orders, 277–78, 279
    for responding to requests and invitations, 278, 283
You approach
    in sales letters, 316–17
    in business writing, 216, 219